# THE LONDON
# BLUE
# PLAQUE
# GUIDE

### 3RD EDITION

First published in 1999
This edition first published in 2009

The History Press
The Mill, Brimscombe Port
Stroud, Gloucestershire, GL5 2QG
www.thehistorypress.co.uk

© Nick Rennison, 1999, 2003, 2009

The right of Nick Rennison to be identified as the Author
of this work has been asserted in accordance with the
Copyrights, Designs and Patents Act 1988.

British Library Cataloguing in Publication Data.
A catalogue record for this book is available from the British Library.

ISBN 978 0 7524 5050 6

Typesetting and origination by The History Press
Printed in Great Britain

# THE LONDON
# BLUE
# PLAQUE
# GUIDE

## 3RD EDITION

NICK RENNISON

The History Press

# CONTENTS

Acknowledgements                                      VII

Introduction                                          IX

Maps                                                  XIII

Map Index                                             XXI


A to Z of Names                                       I


Bibliography                                          277

Alphabetical List of Names by Profession              278

Alphabetical List of Names by Postal Code             285

# ACKNOWLEDGEMENTS

I would like to thank the following friends and family members who, over the years, helped me to complete the three editions of this book by showing me quotes and anecdotes about Blue Plaque subjects or by pointing me in the direction of useful books: my late father, Philip Rennison, my mother Eileen Rennison, Hugh Pemberton, Susan Osborne, Andy Taylor, Andrew Holgate, Gordon Kerr, Richard Shephard, Paul Skinner, Andy Walker and Eve Gorton. While I was compiling the first edition of the guide in the late 1990s, Gillian Dawson of Westminster City Council, Geoff Noble of English Heritage and Ruth Barriskill of the Guildhall Library all helped to make my job easier. The first two editions of the book both benefited from the editorial input of Rupert Harding and Clare Bishop of Sutton Publishing. This third edition, published by The History Press, could not have been produced without Jo de Vries, its Editorial Director, whose interest in the project and enthusiasm for it encouraged me to update a book which I first wrote more than a decade ago.

The author and publisher are grateful for permission to reproduce pictures:

from the English Heritage Photographic Library: pp. 100, 182

from *Illustrated London News*: pp. 11, 12, 13, 37, 51, 64, 70, 72, 78, 82, 96, 100, 104, 114, 124, 144, 151, 161, 166, 180, 186, 192, 196, 197, 214, 266, 270

by courtesy of the National Portrait Gallery, London: pp. 79, 83, 97, 109, 133, 172, 188, 193, 215, 217, 219, 223, 245, 255, 259

# INTRODUCTION

The idea of placing commemorative plaques on the houses of the great and the good was first mooted in 1863 by William Ewart. Ewart was a Liberal MP whose most significant achievement was the passing of the Public Libraries Act of 1850, which he had introduced as a private member's bill the previous year. In putting forward the idea of commemorative plaques he wrote that 'the places which had been the residences of the ornaments of their history could not but be precious to all thinking Englishmen'. (Ewart himself now has his own Blue Plaque in Eaton Place, erected 100 years after he first proposed the idea.) Sir Henry Cole, the first director of what we now know as the Victoria and Albert Museum, was one of those who most vigorously championed Ewart's proposal. Ewart's original intention had been that the government would fund a plaque scheme, but the administration of the day declined to do so. The Royal Society of Arts (RSA) stepped into the breach and in 1864 formed a committee to oversee the choosing and erection of the first plaques. The committee was enthusiastic about the idea that the plaques might give pleasure to 'travellers up and down in omnibuses etc', and that they 'might sometimes prove an agreeable and instructive mode of beguiling a somewhat dull and not very rapid progress through the streets' but, as committees do, it took time to turn its words into actions. It was not until 1867 that the first plaque was erected under the auspices of the RSA. This was placed on 24 Holles Street, once the home of Lord Byron and now, sadly, demolished.

The erection of plaques under the RSA was a slow and stately process. By 1901, when the scheme was taken over by the London County Council (LCC), thirty-six plaques had been put up in thirty-four years. Many of these have now disappeared, the victims of development, demolition and wartime bombs. The oldest plaques still in place are those to Napoleon III in King Street and to the poet John Dryden in Gerrard Street – both date from 1875. Under the LCC the speed with which plaques were erected quickened slightly; they were in charge of the scheme for 64 years and put up more than 250 plaques in that period. When, in 1965, the LCC metamorphosed into the Greater London Council (GLC), the new organisation took responsibility for the plaques. Under the GLC the geographical and cultural range of the plaques both expanded. Plaques were erected in outlying London boroughs that had not been under the jurisdiction of the LCC, and there was a more populist choice of people deemed worthy of commemoration. (Somebody at the GLC seemed to have a particular fondness for old music-hall stars. At least half a dozen were given their own plaques in the GLC years.) In 1985, with the abolition of the GLC, a new home had to be found for the Blue Plaque scheme (as it was now popularly known) and the Local Government Act of that year gave the responsibility to English Heritage.

What criteria are used to select the recipients of a Blue Plaque? Any scheme which, in the same year (2000), can commemorate the last Viceroy of India, Lord Mountbatten, and the comic actor Will Hay, star of the classic 1930s film *Oh, Mr Porter*, obviously has pleasingly wide-ranging terms of reference. When the official scheme began under the RSA, there were few hard and fast guidelines but, under the LCC and GLC, rules developed, and English Heritage now publish a set of principles for the choosing of those honoured by Blue Plaques. The people chosen must be 'regarded as eminent by a majority of members of their own profession or calling'. They must have 'made some important positive contribution to human welfare or happiness'. They must 'deserve national recognition' and they must 'have had such exceptional and outstanding personalities that the well-informed passer-by immediately recognises their names'. Perhaps the last condition, difficult enough to define, is sometimes honoured in the breach rather than the observance. Would even a very well-informed passer-by immediately recognise the name of Augustus Siebe, the inventor of the closed diving helmet, whose plaque in Denmark Street was recently unveiled? Or Robert Polhill Bevan, the Camden Town painter, whose plaque was unveiled in 1999? Maybe not, but who would begrudge them their plaques? Part of the delight in coming across London plaques is the stimulus it often gives to discovering more about the city's past inhabitants. The principle of selection on which English Heritage has been most insistent is the one of time. Without exception, people will not be considered until they have been dead for twenty years or until the centenary of their birth, whichever date comes first. Inside these guidelines, and a few others, English Heritage works hard to come up with new people to commemorate; at present, between ten and twenty new plaques are unveiled each year. English Heritage has also shown itself eager to democratise the process of choice. If you know of a building and individual that you believe worthy of a plaque, you are free to contact English Heritage with the suggestion.

The success of the official London Blue Plaque scheme means that it has been widely copied both in the capital and in other parts of the country. English Heritage itself has, in the last few years, sponsored an expansion of the Blue Plaque scheme into other English cities. Liverpool already has English Heritage plaques to more than a dozen of its famous residents, including the poet Wilfred Owen, the Beatle John Lennon, the toy manufacturer Frank Hornby and Sir Ronald Ross, the man who discovered the role of the mosquito in the transmission of malaria (Ross also has a London plaque in Cavendish Square). At the end of 2002 the first English Heritage plaques in Birmingham were erected on houses where the brothers Cadbury, chocolate manufacturers and philanthropists, once lived. Plaques were also installed in Southampton and Portsmouth but, for a number of reasons, the plaque schemes in cities outside London proved unworkable and they are currently suspended.

In London there are a host of 'unofficial' plaques too – in other words those not put up under the auspices of the RSA, the LCC, the GLC or English Heritage. Many Greater London boroughs have their own schemes. Islington has been home to some remarkable people over the years and the borough council has erected plaques to such luminaries as the Labour politician Fenner Brockway (put up while the long-lived Brockway was still alive), the composer Benjamin Britten and the painter Walter Sickert. The Borough of Bromley has plaques to (among others) Sir Thomas Crapper, the aptly named sanitary engineer, the illustrator Charles Keeping, the folk songwriter and playwright Ewan McColl, Sir Malcolm Campbell, one-time holder of the world land and water speed records, and the naval architect Sir Victor Shepheard, who designed the royal yacht *Britannia*. Lewisham, similarly, has plaques to some of its former residents, including Sir George Grove, founding editor of the famous music dictionary, Ernest Dowson, the decadent poet of the 1890s who was born in the borough, the aeronautical engineer Sir Barnes Wallis (inventor of the 'bouncing bomb') and the German theologian Dietrich Bonhoeffer, who was pastor of a church in Forest Hill for two years in the 1930s before returning to Germany where, in 1945, he died at the hands of the Nazis. Hendon Corporation has also erected plaques to some interesting people, including the Edwardian cricketer Gilbert Jessop, the sixteenth-century cartographer John Morden and the ballerina Anna Pavlova.

Many non-governmental societies and groups have also sponsored the erection of plaques within London. Since 1995 Comic Heritage, which is part of the Heritage Foundation, has been unveiling its own Blue Plaques to late-lamented comic talents, including Eric Morecambe, Hattie Jacques, Tony Hancock, Sid James and Harry H. Corbett. In 1997, as part of the celebrations for the centenary of the first movie, the British Film Institute sponsored a number of plaques to commemorate individuals who made a significant contribution to film history. These included Birt Acres, who made the first British moving picture in Barnet in 1895, Cecil Hepworth, a pioneering director and producer, and the legendary comedian Bob Hope, who was born in a house in Eltham, SE9. The Heath and Old Hampstead Society has been behind the erection of a number of plaques to well-known Hampstead residents, including the cellist Jacqueline du Pré and the photographer and designer Cecil Beaton.

Some groups and organisations have sponsored one-off plaques. The Greek poet Constantine Cavafy lived in England for seven years as a child and adolescent because the family business was there and, in 1974, the London Hellenic Society was instrumental in placing a plaque on the house in Queensborough Terrace where the Cavafys lived in the mid-1870s. The Brazilian statesman and lawyer Ruy Barbosa lived in Holland Park Gardens in the 1890s, and the Anglo-Brazilian Society has marked his stay with a plaque on No. 17. A few plaques have outlived their sponsors. On a building in Haymarket, once the Carlton Hotel, there is a plaque to Ho Chi Minh, the Vietnamese Communist leader, who worked in the kitchens there for a brief period just before the First World War. It was placed there by an organisation, no longer extant, called the Britain Vietnam Association.

Finally there are those plaques – and there are many – that have been erected privately by those individuals who simply want to record a distinguished previous resident in their house and, perhaps, to add extra distinction to the property. The people thus honoured range from the very well known to the unequivocally obscure. There are several private plaques to Dickens who, in his early career, flitted from address to address. Matthew Arnold has an LCC plaque in Chester Square and a recently erected private one in Harrow-on-the-Hill. There are also plaques to less renowned but none the less interesting people, including the American poet Hilda Doolittle (Mecklenburgh Square), Lady Byron (who ironically still has an existing plaque while her husband does not), the record producer Joe Meek (Holloway Road), the *Punch* illustrator Linley Sambourne (his house at 18 Stafford Terrace, W1, is also preserved as a museum and monument to upper-middle-class Victorian taste) and the physician James Parkinson, who was the first to describe the disease that bears his name (Hoxton Square).

Primarily this is a guide to the individuals who have been honoured by a plaque sponsored by the official Blue Plaque scheme. There are now close to 800 official plaques, most to individuals but a few to historic buildings or events and all the ones in place as of the end of January 2009 are included in this guide. Visitors to Central London will come across plaques belonging to two other schemes. There are those erected by the Corporation of the City of London. Most of these referred to buildings which once stood on a site but some refer to individuals and I have included those that do. Westminster City Council has a scheme of Green Plaques, nearly all of which refer to individuals and I have included all these in this guide. Where an individual has an official plaque and others erected privately, I have, for the sake of completeness, included the private ones as well. Many private individuals and organisation have sponsored "unofficial" Blue Plaques and for reasons of space I have not been able to include these. All the plaques that are not part of the official English Heritage scheme have been marked as such in the text.

# MAPS AND
# MAP INDEX

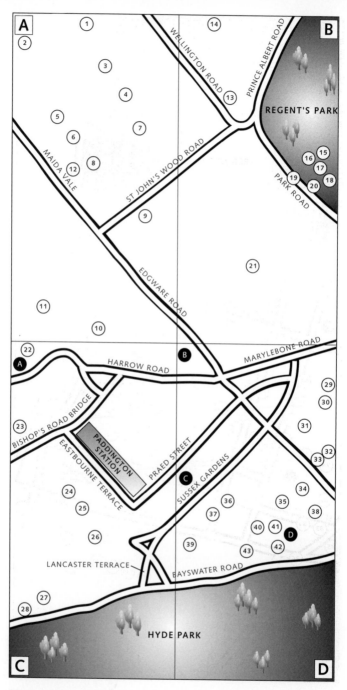

**Map 1;** index pp. XXI–XXII

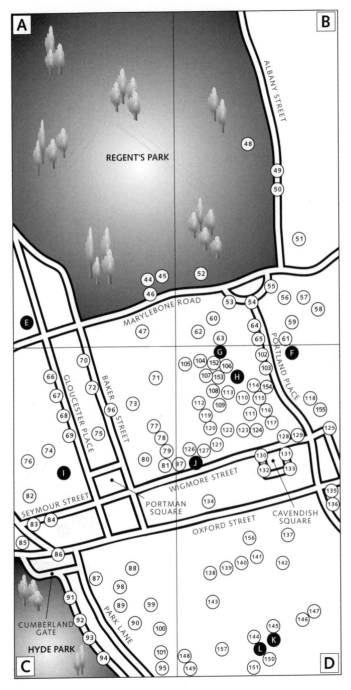

**Map 2;** index pp. xxii–xxiv

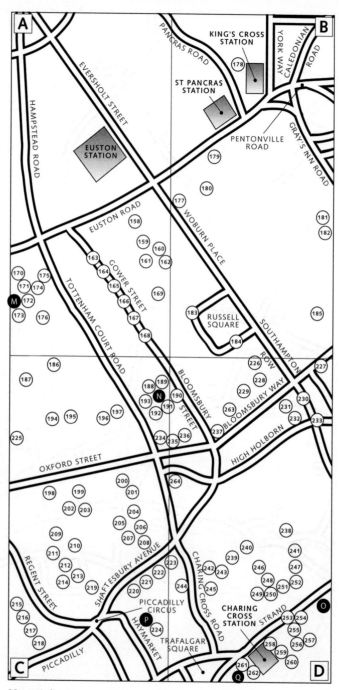

**Map 3;** index pp. XXIV–XXVI

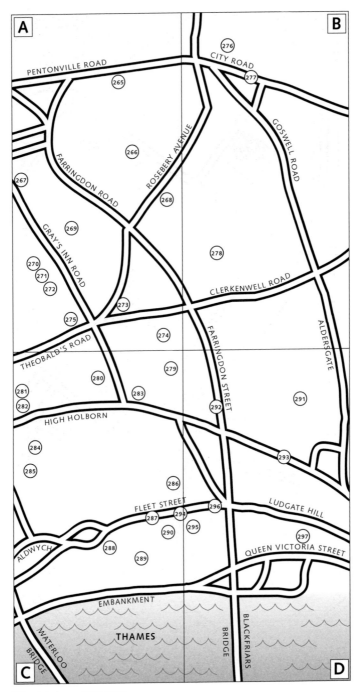

**Map 4;** index pp. XXVI–XXVII

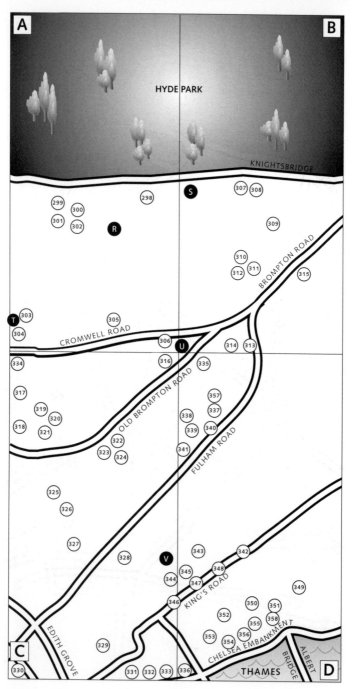

**Map 5;** index pp. xxvii–xxviii

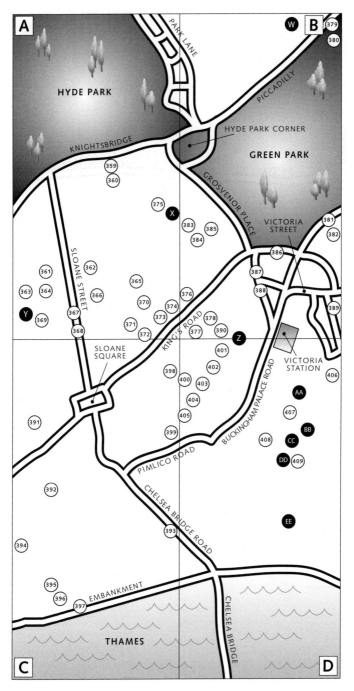

**Map 6;** index pp. XXVIII–XXIX

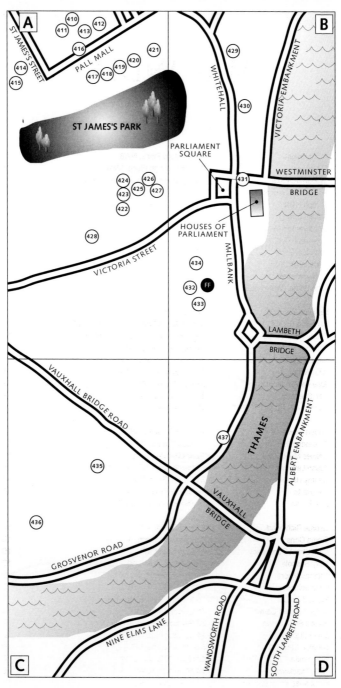

**Map 7;** index pp. xxix–xxx

# MAP INDEX

## Map 1

| | | | |
|---|---|---|---|
| 1. | Laura Knight | 16 Langford Place, NW8 | 1A |
| 2. | T.H. Huxley | 38 Marlborough Place, NW8 | 1A |
| 3. | Sir Edward Elgar | Abbey Studios, Abbey Road, NW6 | 1A |
| 4. | Sir Thomas Beecham | 31 Grove End Road, NW8 | 1A |
| 5. | Joseph Hertz | 103 Hamilton Terrace, NW8 | 1A |
| 6. | William Strang | 20 Hamilton Terrace, NW8 | 1A |
| 7. | Sir Lawrence Alma-Tadema | 4 Grove End Road, NW8 | 1A |
| 8. | Sir Joseph Bazalgette | 17 Hamilton Terrace, NW8 | 1A |
| 9. | Emily Davies | 17 Cunningham Place, NW8 | 1A |
| 10. | Lokamanya Tilak | 10 Howley Place, W2 | 1A |
| 11. | John Masefield | 30 Maida Avenue, W2 | 1A |
| 12. | John William Waterhouse | 10 Hall Road, NW8 | 1A |
| | | | |
| 13. | Madame Tussaud | 24 Wellington Road, NW8 | 1B |
| 14. | Benjamin Britten | 45a St John's Wood High Street, NW8 | 1B |
| 15. | Beatty & Cochrane | Hanover Lodge, Outer Circle, NW1 | 1B |
| 16. | Anthony Salvin | 11 Hanover Terrace, NW1 | 1B |
| 17. | Ralph Vaughan Williams | 10 Hanover Terrace, NW1 | 1B |
| 18. | H.G. Wells | 13 Hanover Terrace, NW1 | 1B |
| 19. | Jose de San Martin | 23 Park Road, NW1 | 1B |
| 20. | E.H. Shepard | 10 Kent Terrace, NW1 | 1B |
| 21. | Haydon & Rossi | 116 Lisson Grove, NW1 | 1B |
| | | | |
| 22. | Robert Browning | Warwick Crescent, W2 | 1C |
| 23. | Alexander Herzen | 1 Orsett Terrace, W2 | 1C |
| 24. | Charles Manby | 60 Westbourne Terrace, W2 | 1C |
| 25. | Susan Lawrence | 44 Westbourne Terrace, W2 | 1C |
| 26. | Tommy Handley | 34 Craven Road, W2 | 1C |
| 27. | Bret Harte | 74 Lancaster Gate, W2 | 1C |
| 28. | J.M. Barrie | 100 Bayswater Road, W2 | 1C |
| | | | |
| 29. | George Richmond | 20 York Street, W1 | 1D |
| 30. | Emma Cons | 136 Seymour Place, W1 | 1D |
| 31. | Cato Street Conspiracy | 1a Cato Street, W1 | 1D |
| 32. | Mary Seacole | 157 George Street, W1 | 1D |
| 33. | Thomas Moore | 85 George Street, W1 | 1D |
| 34. | Olive Schreiner | 16 Portsea Place, W2 | 1D |
| 35. | Richard Tauber | Park West, Kendal Street, W2 | 1D |
| 36. | Violet Bonham-Carter | 43 Gloucester Square, W2 | 1D |
| 37. | Robert Stephenson | 35 Gloucester Square, W2 | 1D |
| 38. | Marie Taglioni | 14 Connaught Square, W2 | 1D |
| 39. | Winston Churchill | 3 Sussex Square, W2 | 1D |
| 40. | W.H. Smith | 12 Hyde Park Street, W2 | 1D |
| 41. | W.M. Thackeray | 18 Albion Street, W2 | 1D |
| 42. | Sir Charles Vyner Brooke | 13 Albion Street, W2 | 1D |
| 43. | Sir Giles Gilbert Scott | Chester House, Clarendon Place, W2 | 1D |

| A. | Margery Allingham | 1 Westbourne Terrace Road | 1C |
| B. | Henry Sylvester Williams | 38 Church Street, W2 | 1D |
| C. | Hertha Ayrton | 41 Norfolk Square, W2 | 1D |
| D. | Dame Lucie Rie | 18 Albion Mews, W2 | 1D |

# Map 2

| 44. | Ernest Jones | 19 York Terrace East, NW1 | 2A |
| 45. | Sir Charles Wyndham | 20 York Terrace East, NW1 | 2A |
| 46. | Francis Turner Palgrave | 5 York Gate, Regent's Park, NW1 | 2A |
| 47. | Charles Eamer Kempe | 37 Nottingham Place, W1 | 2A |
| | | | |
| 48. | Charles Cockerell | 13 Chester Terrace, NW1 | 2B |
| 49. | Constant Lambert | 197 Albany Street, NW1 | 2B |
| 50. | Henry Mayhew | 55 Albany Street, NW1 | 2B |
| 51. | Fabian Society | White House, Osnaburgh Street, NW1 | 2B |
| 52. | F.D. Maurice | 2 Upper Harley Street, NW1 | 2B |
| 53. | Lord Lister | 12 Park Crescent, W1 | 2B |
| 54. | Marie Tempest | 24 Park Crescent, W1 | 2B |
| 55. | Sir Charles Wheatstone | 19 Park Crescent, W1 | 2B |
| 56. | James Boswell | 122 Great Portland Street, W1 | 2B |
| 57. | John Flaxman | 7 Greenwell Street, W1 | 2B |
| 58. | Samuel Morse | 141 Cleveland Street, W1 | 2B |
| 59. | David Hughes | 4 Great Portland Street, W1 | 2B |
| 60. | Dr Grantley Dick-Read | 25 Harley Street, W1 | 2B |
| 61. | Dante Gabriel Rossetti | 110 Hallam Street, W1 | 2B |
| 62. | Sir Arthur Conan Doyle | 2 Upper Wimpole Street, W1 | 2B |
| 63. | Sir Arthur Wing Pinero | 115a Harley Street, W1 | 2B |
| 64. | United States Embassy | 98 Portland Place, W1 | 2B |
| 65. | Frances Hodgson Burnett | 63 Portland Place, W1 | 2B |
| | | | |
| 66. | Wilkie Collins | 65 Gloucester Place, W1 | 2C |
| 67. | John Robert Godley | 48 Gloucester Place, W1 | 2C |
| 68. | Sir Gerald Kelly | 117 Gloucester Place, W1 | 2C |
| 69. | Tony Ray-Jones | 102 Gloucester Place, W1 | 2C |
| 70. | William Pitt the Younger | 120 Baker Street, W1 | 2C |
| 71. | Octavia Hill | 2 Garbutt Place, W1 | 2C |
| 72. | Charles Babbage | Dorset Street, W1 | 2C |
| 73. | Sir Francis Beaufort | 51 Manchester Street, W1 | 2C |
| 74. | Anthony Trollope | 39 Montagu Square, W1 | 2C |
| 75. | Michael Faraday | 48 Blandford Street, W1 | 2C |
| 76. | Mustapha Pasha Reschid | 1 Bryanston Square, W1 | 2C |
| 77. | George Grossmith Junior | 3 Spanish Place, W1 | 2C |
| 78. | Frederick Marryat | 3 Spanish Place, W1 | 2C |
| 79. | Alfred Milner | 14 Manchester Square, W1 | 2C |
| 80. | Sir Julius Benedict | 2 Manchester Square, W1 | 2C |
| 81. | John Hughlings Jackson | 3 Manchester Square, W1 | 2C |
| 82. | Elizabeth Garrett Anderson | 20 Upper Berkeley Street, W1 | 2C |
| 83. | Michael Balfe | 12 Seymour Street, W1 | 2C |
| 84. | Edward Lear | 30 Seymour Street, W1 | 2C |
| 85. | Randolph Churchill | 2 Connaught Place, W2 | 2C |
| 86. | Tyburn Tree | Marble Arch Traffic Island, W2 | 2C |
| 87. | P.G. Wodehouse | 17 Dunraven Street, W1 | 2C |
| 88. | Sir Thomas Sopwith | 46 Green Street, W1 | 2C |

| 89. | Leo Bonn | 22 Upper Brook Street, W1 | 2C |
|---|---|---|---|
| 90. | Sir Robert Peel | 16 Upper Grosvenor Street, W1 | 2C |
| 91. | Anna Neagle | 63–64 Park Lane, W1 | 2C |
| 92. | Sir Moses Montefiore | 99 Park Lane, W1 | 2C |
| 93. | Keith Clifford Hall | 140 Park Lane, W1 | 2C |
| 94. | Benjamin Disraeli | 93 Park Lane, W1 | 2C |
| 95. | Lord Ashfield | 43 South Street, W1 | 2C |
| 96. | Viscardo Y Guzman | 185 Baker Street, W1 | 2C |
| 97. | Simon Bolivar | 4 Duke Street, W1 | 2C |
| 98. | George Seferis | 51 Upper Brook Street, W1 | 2C |
| 99. | Sir Frederick Handley Page | 18 Grosvenor Square, W1 | 2C |
| 100. | Sir Alexander Korda | 21/22 Grosvenor Street, W1 | 2C |
| 101. | Charles X | 72 South Audley Street, W1 | 2C |
| | | | |
| 102. | Thomas Gage | 41 Portland Place, W1 | 2D |
| 103. | Earl Roberts | 47 Portland Place, W1 | 2D |
| 104. | Sir John Milsom Rees | 18 Upper Wimpole Street, W1 | 2D |
| 105. | Sir Arthur Conan Doyle | 2 Upper Wimpole Street, W1 | 2D |
| 106. | W. E. Gladstone | 73 Harley Street, W1 | 2D |
| 107. | Sir Evelyn Baring | 36 Wimpole Street, W1 | 2D |
| 108. | Elizabeth Barrett Browning | 50 Wimpole Street, W1 | 2D |
| 109. | Henry Hallam | 67 Wimpole Street, W1 | 2D |
| 110. | Sir Charles Lyell | 73 Harley Street, W1 | 2D |
| 111. | Florence Nightingale | 90 Harley Street, W1 | 2D |
| 112. | Victor Weisz | Welbeck Mansions, New Cavendish St, W1 | 2D |
| 113. | Alfred Waterhouse | 61 New Cavendish Street, W1 | 2D |
| 114. | Sir Edwin Lutyens | 13 Mansfield Street, W1 | 2D |
| 115. | John Loughborough Pearson | 13 Mansfield Street, W1 | 2D |
| 116. | Sir Robert Mayer | 2 Mansfield Street, W1 | 2D |
| 117. | Charles Stanhope | 20 Mansfield Street, W1 | 2D |
| 118. | Edmond Malone | 40 Langham Street, W1 | 2D |
| 119. | Sir Patrick Manson | 50 Welbeck Street, W1 | 2D |
| 120. | Thomas Young | 48 Welbeck Street, W1 | 2D |
| 121. | Thomas Woolner | 29 Welbeck Street, W1 | 2D |
| 122. | Hector Berlioz | 58 Queen Anne Street, W1 | 2D |
| 123. | Sir George Still | 28 Queen Anne Street, W1 | 2D |
| 124. | J.M.W. Turner | 23 Queen Anne Street, W1 | 2D |
| 125. | Joseph Nollekens | 44 Mortimer Street, W1 | 2D |
| 126. | Edward Gibbon | 7 Bentinck Street, W1 | 2D |
| 127. | Sir James Mackenzie | 17 Bentinck Street, W1 | 2D |
| 128. | Sir Joseph Clover | 3 Cavendish Place, W1 | 2D |
| 129. | George Edmund Street | 14 Cavendish Place, W1 | 2D |
| 130. | Herbert Asquith | 20 Cavendish Square, W1 | 2D |
| 131. | Quintin Hogg | 5 Cavendish Square, W1 | 2D |
| 132. | Sir Jonathan Hutchinson | 15 Cavendish Square, W1 | 2D |
| 133. | Sir Ronald Ross | 18 Cavendish Square, W1 | 2D |
| 134. | Martin Van Buren | 7 Stratford Place, W1 | 2D |
| 135. | Washington Irving | 8 Argyll Street, W1 | 2D |
| 136. | William Roy | 10 Argyll Street, W1 | 2D |
| 137. | Prince Talleyrand | 21 Hanoveer Square, W1 | 2D |
| 138. | Colen Campbell | 76 Brook Street, W1 | 2D |
| 139. | George Frederic Handel | 25 Brook Street, W1 | 2D |
| 140. | Jimi Hendrix | 23 Brook Street, W1 | 2D |
| 141. | Sir Jeffry Wyatville | 39 Brook Street, W1 | 2D |
| 142. | Horatio Nelson | 147 New Bond Street, W1 | 2D |
| 143. | Ann Oldfield | 60 Grosvenor Street, W1 | 2D |
| 144. | George Canning | 50 Berkeley Square, W1 | 2D |

| 145. | Robert Clive | 45 Berkeley Square, W1 | 2D |
|---|---|---|---|
| 146. | Lord Brougham | 5 Grafton Street, W1 | 2D |
| 147. | Sir Henry Irving | 15a Grafton Street, W1 | 2D |
| 148. | John Gilbert Winant | 7 Aldford Street, W1 | 2D |
| 149. | Florence Nightingale | 10 South Street, W1 | 2D |
| 150. | Lady Dorothy Nevill | 45 Charles Street, W1 | 2D |
| 151. | Lord Rosebery | 20 Charles Street, W1 | 2D |
| 152. | Ethel Fenwick | Upper Wimpole Street, W1 | 2D |
| 153. | Sir Frederick Treves | 6 Wimpole Street, W1 | 2D |
| 154. | London Auxiliary Ambulance Service | Weymouth Mews, W1 | 2D |
| 155. | Olaudah Equiano | 73 Riding House Street, W1 | 2D |
| 156. | Ernest Bevin | 34 South Moulton Street, W1 | 2D |
| 157. | Terence Donovan | 30 Bourdon Street, W1 | 2D |
| | | | |
| E. | Sir Laurence Gomme | 24 Dorset Square, Marylebone, NW1 | 2A |
| F. | Edward R. Murrow | Weymouth House, 84–94 Hallam Street, W1 | 2D |
| G. | Sir Stewart Duke-Elder | 63 Harley Street, W1 | 2D |
| H. | George Frederick Bodley | 109 Harley Street W1 | 2D |
| I. | Sake Dean Mahomed | 102 George Street | 2C |
| J. | James Smithson | 9 Bentinck Street, W1 | 2D |
| K. | William Petty | 9 Fitzmaurice Place, W1 | 2D |
| L. | Harry Gordon Selfridge | 9 Fitzmaurice Place, W1 | 2D |

# Map 3

| 158. | Hugh Price Hughes | 8 Taviton Street, WC1 | 3A |
|---|---|---|---|
| 159. | John Maynard Keynes | 46 Gordon Square, WC1 | 3A |
| 160. | Robert Travers Herford | Dr Williams' Library, Gordon Square, WC1 | 3A |
| 161. | Lytton Strachey | 51 Gordon Square, WC1 | 3A |
| 162. | Virginia Woolf | 50 Gordon Square, WC1 | 3A |
| 163. | George Dance the Younger | 91 Gower Street, WC1 | 3A |
| 164. | Charles Darwin | Biological Science Building, Gower St, WC1 | 3A |
| 165. | Dame Millicent Fawcett | 2 Gower Street, WC1 | 3A |
| 166. | Lady Ottoline Morrell | 10 Gower Street, WC1 | 3A |
| 167. | Pre-Raphaelite Brotherhood | 7 Gower Street, WC1 | 3A |
| 168. | James Robinson | 14 Gower Street, WC1 | 3A |
| 169. | Christina Rossetti | 30 Torrington Square, WC1 | 3A |
| 170. | Sir Charles Eastlake | 7 Fitzroy Square, W1 | 3A |
| 171. | August von Hofmann | 9 Fitzroy Square, W1 | 3A |
| 172. | George Bernard Shaw | 29 Fitzroy Square, W1 | 3A |
| 173. | Virginia Woolf | 29 Fitzroy Square, W1 | 3A |
| 174. | Andres Bello | 58 Grafton Way, W1 | 3A |
| 175. | Francisco de Miranda | 58 Grafton Way, W1 | 3A |
| 176. | Matthew Flinders | 56 Fitzroy Street, W1 | 3A |
| | | | |
| 177. | W.B. Yeats | 5 Woburn Walk, WC1 | 3B |
| 178. | Sir Nigel Gresley | West Offices, King's Cross Station, N1 | 3B |
| 179. | Paul Nash | Queen Alexandra Mansions, Bidborough St, WC2 | 3B |
| 180. | Sir Rowland Hill | Cartwight Gardens, WC1 | 3B |
| 181. | Sir Syed Ahmed Khan | 21 Mecklenburgh Square, WC1 | 3B |
| 182. | R.H. Tawney | 21 Mecklenburgh Square, WC1 | 3B |
| 183. | T.S. Eliot | 24 Russell Square, WC1 | 3B |
| 184. | Sir Samuel Romilly | 21 Russell Square, WC1 | 3B |
| 185. | John Howard | 23 Great Ormond Street, WC1 | 3B |

| | | | |
|---|---|---|---|
| 186. | Sir Robert Smirke | 81 Charlotte Street, W1 | 3C |
| 187. | Henry Fuseli | 37 Foley Street, W1 | 3C |
| 188. | William Butterfield | 42 Bedford Square, W1 | 3C |
| 189. | Henry Cavendish | 11 Bedford Square, W1 | 3C |
| 190. | Lord Eldon | 6 Bedford Square, W1 | 3C |
| 191. | Thomas Hodgkin | 35 Bedford Square, W1 | 3C |
| 192. | Anthony Hope | 41 Bedford Square, W1 | 3C |
| 193. | Ram Mohun Roy | 49 Bedford Square, W1 | 3C |
| 194. | Samuel Taylor Coleridge | 71 Berners Street, W1 | 3C |
| 195. | Thomas Stothard | 28 Newman Street, W1 | 3C |
| 196. | Charles Laughton | 15 Percy Street, W1 | 3C |
| 197. | Coventry Patmore | 14 Percy Street, W1 | 3C |
| 198. | Percy Bysshe Shelley | 15 Poland Street, W1 | 3C |
| 199. | Willy Clarkson | 41–43 Wardour Street, W1 | 3C |
| 200. | Sir Joseph Banks | 32 Soho Square, W1 | 3C |
| 201. | Arthur Onslow | 20 Soho Square, W1 | 3C |
| 202. | Jessie Matthews | 22 Berwick Street, W1 | 3C |
| 203. | Thomas Sheraton | 163 Wardour Street, W1 | 3C |
| 204. | John Logie Baird | 22 Frith Street, W1 | 3C |
| 205. | Karl Marx | 28 Dean Street, W1 | 3C |
| 206. | William Hazlitt | 6 Frith Street, W1 | 3C |
| 207. | Dr Joseph Rogers | 33 Dean Street, W1 | 3C |
| 208. | Wolfgang Amadeus Mozart | 20 Frith Street, W1 | 3C |
| 209. | Charles Bridgeman | 54 Broadwick Street, W1 | 3C |
| 210. | John Polidori | 38 Great Pulteney Street, W1 | 3C |
| 211. | Canaletto | 41 Beak Street, W1 | 3C |
| 212. | John Hunter | 31 Golden Square, W1 | 3C |
| 213. | Sir Morell Mackenzie | 32 Golden Square, W1 | 3C |
| 214. | Portuguese Embassy | 23–24 Golden Square, W1 | 3C |
| 215. | George Basevi | 17 Savile Row, W1 | 3C |
| 216. | Richard Bright | 11 Savile Row, W1 | 3C |
| 217. | George Grote | 12 Savile Row, W1 | 3C |
| 218. | Richard Brinsley Sheridan | 14 Savile Row, W1 | 3C |
| 219. | William Hunter | Lyric Theatre, Great Windmill Street, W1 | 3C |
| 220. | Edmund Burke | 37 Gerrard Street, W1 | 3C |
| 221. | John Dryden | 43 Gerrard Street, W1 | 3C |
| 222. | Paul de Lamerie | 40 Gerrard Street, W1 | 3C |
| 223. | Turk's Head Tavern | 9 Gerrard Street, W1 | 3C |
| 224. | Sir Mortimer Wheeler | 27 Whitcomb Street, WC2 | 3C |
| 225. | H.H. Munro | 97 Mortimer Street, W1 | 3C |
| | | | |
| 226. | Sir Hans Sloane | 4 Bloomsbury Place, WC1 | 3D |
| 227. | Benjamin Disraeli | 22 Theobalds Road, WC1 | 3D |
| 228. | Lord Chesterfield | 45 Bloomsbury Square, WC1 | 3D |
| 229. | Robert Willan | 10 Bloomsbury Square, WC1 | 3D |
| 230. | W.R. Lethaby | Central School of Arts and Crafts, Southampton Row, WC1 | 3D |
| 231. | Sir John Barbirolli | Southampton Row, WC1 | 3D |
| 232. | Cardinal Newman | 17 Southampton Place, WC1 | 3D |
| 233. | Thomas Earnshaw | 119 High Holborn, WC1 | 3D |
| 234. | Randolph Caldecott | 46 Great Russell Street, WC1 | 3D |
| 235. | George Du Maurier | 91 Great Russell Street, WC1 | 3D |
| 236. | Augustus Charles Pugin | 106 Great Russell Street, WC1 | 3D |
| 237. | Thomas Henry Wyatt | 77 Great Russell Street, WC1 | 3D |
| 238. | Henry and John Fielding and others | Bow Street, WC2 | 3D |
| 239. | John Logie Baird | 132–35 Long Acre, WC1 | 3D |
| 240. | Denis Johnson | 69–76 Long Acre, WC1 | 3D |

| 241. | Dr Johnson and Boswell | 8 Russell Street, WC2 | 3D |
| 242. | Ken Colyer | 11–12 Great Newport Street, WC2 | 3D |
| 243. | Sir Joshua Reynolds | 5 Great Newport Street, WC2 | 3D |
| 244. | Sidney Webb | 44 Cranbourn Street, WC2 | 3D |
| 245. | Thomas Chippendale | 61 St Martin's Lane, WC2 | 3D |
| 246. | Thomas Arne | 31 King Street, WC2 | 3D |
| 247. | Thomas De Quincey | 36 Tavistock Street, WC2 | 3D |
| 248. | Jane Austen | 10 Henrietta Street, WC2 | 3D |
| 249. | William Terriss | Adelphi Theatre, Maiden Lane, WC2 | 3D |
| 250. | J.M.W. Turner | 21 Maiden Lane, WC2 | 3D |
| 251. | Voltaire | 10 Maiden Lane, WC2 | 3D |
| 252. | David Garrick | 27 Southampton Street, WC2 | 3D |
| 253. | The Savoy Theatre | The Strand, WC2 | 3D |
| 254. | Sir Richard Arkwright | 8 Adam Street, WC2 | 3D |
| 255. | Thomas Rowlandson | 16 John Adam Street, WC2 | 3D |
| 256. | Robert Adam | 1–3 Robert Street, WC2 | 3D |
| 257. | The Adelphi | Adelphi Terrace, WC2 | 3D |
| 258. | Rudyard Kipling | 43 Villiers Street, WC2 | 3D |
| 259. | Samuel Pepys | 12 Buckingham Street, WC2 | 3D |
| 260. | Clarkson Stanfield | 14 Buckingham Street, WC2 | 3D |
| 261. | Benjamin Franklin | 36 Craven Street, WC2 | 3D |
| 262. | Heinrich Heine | 32 Craven Street, WC2 | 3D |
| 263. | Bertrand Russell | Bury Place, WC1 | 3D |
| 264. | Augustus Siebe | 5 Denmark Street, WC2 | 3D |
| | | | |
| M. | Robert Salisbury | 21 Fitzroy Square, W1 | 3A |
| N. | Sir Harry Ricardo | 13 Bedford Square, WC1 | 3C |
| O. | William Lilly | Strand Underground Station | 3D |
| P. | Tom Cribb | 36 Panton Street, SW1 | 3C |
| Q. | Herman Melville | 25 Craven Street, WC2 | 3D |

# Map 4

| 265. | Edward Irving | 4 Claremont Square, N1 | 4A |
| 266. | George Cruikshank | 69–71 Amwell Street, EC1 | 4A |
| 267. | Thomas Carlyle | 33 Ampton Street, WC1 | 4A |
| 268. | Joseph Grimaldi | 56 Exmouth Market, EC1 | 4A |
| 269. | W.R. Lethaby | 20 Calthorpe Street, WC1 | 4A |
| 270. | Vera Brittain & Winifred Holtby | 58 Doughty Street, WC1 | 4A |
| 271. | Charles Dickens | 48 Doughty Street, WC1 | 4A |
| 272. | Sydney Smith | 14 Doughty Street, WC1 | 4A |
| 273. | Giuseppe Mazzini | 10 Laystall Street, EC1 | 4A |
| 274. | Giuseppe Mazzini | 5 Hatton Garden, EC1 | 4A |
| 275. | Dorothy L. Sayers | 24 Great James Street, WC1 | 4A |
| | | | |
| 276. | Charles Lamb | 64 Duncan Terrace, N1 | 4B |
| 277. | John Wesley | 47 City Road, EC1 | 4B |
| 278. | John Groom | 8 Sekforde Street, EC1 | 4B |
| | | | |
| 279. | Sir Hiram Maxim | 57d Hatton Garden, EC1 | 4C |
| 280. | Sir Samuel Romilly | 6 Gray's Inn Square, WC1 | 4C |
| 281. | Dante Gabriel Rossetti | 17 Red Lion Square, WC1 | 4C |
| 282. | John Harrison | Summit House, Red Lion Square, WC1 | 4C |
| 283. | Thomas Chatterton | 39 Brooke Street, EC1 | 4C |

| 284. | Spencer Perceval | 59–60 Lincoln's Inn Fields, WC2 | 4C |
|------|------------------|----------------------------------|----|
| 285. | William Marsden | 65 Lincoln's Inn Fields, WC2 | 4C |
| 286. | Samuel Johnson | 17 Gough Square, EC4 | 4C |
| 287. | Samuel Johnson | Johnson's Court, Fleet Street, EC4 | 4C |
| 288. | | Essex Street, WC2 | 4C |
| 289. | Charles Lamb | 2 Crown Office Row, Temple, EC4 | 4C |
| 290. | William Hazlitt | 6 Bouverie Street, EC4 | 4C |
| | | | |
| 291. | Charles Wesley | 13 Little Britain, EC1 | 4D |
| 292. | Labour party | Caroone House, Farringdon Street, EC4 | 4D |
| 293. | Guglielmo Marconi | British Telecom Building, Newgate St, | 4D |
| 294. | Thomas Tompion | 69 Fleet Street, EC4 | 4D |
| 295. | Samuel Pepys | Salisbury Court, EC4 | 4D |
| 296. | Edgar Wallace | Corner of Ludgate Circus, EC4 | 4D |
| 297. | Thomas Linacre | Knightrider Street, EC4 | 4D |

# Map 5

| 298. | Sir Malcolm Sargent | Albert Hall Mansions, Kensington Gore | 5A |
|------|---------------------|----------------------------------------|----|
| 299. | Sir Robert Baden-Powell | 9 Hyde Park Gate, SW1 | 5A |
| 300. | Enid Bagnold | 29 Hyde Park Gate, SW1 | 5A |
| 301. | Sir Leslie Stephen | 22 Hyde Park Gate, SW1 | 5A |
| 302. | Winston Churchill | 28 Hyde Park Gate, SW1 | 5A |
| 303. | Dame Ivy Compton-Burnett | Braemar Mansions, Cornwall Gardens | 5A |
| 304. | Charles Booth | 6 Grenville Place, SW7 | 5A |
| 305. | Sir Charles James Freake | 21 Cromwell Road, SW7 | 5A |
| 306. | Sir John Lavery | 5 Cromwell Place, SW7 | 5A |
| | | | |
| 307. | Sir Francis Galton | 42 Rutland Gate, SW7 | 5B |
| 308. | Lord Lugard | 51 Rutland Gate, SW7 | 5B |
| 309. | Bruce Bairnsfather | 1 Sterling Street, SW7 | 5B |
| 310. | E.F. Benson | 25 Brompton Square, SW3 | 5B |
| 311. | Stéphane Mallarmé | 6 Brompton Square, SW3 | 5B |
| 312. | Francis Place | 21 Brompton Square, SW3 | 5B |
| 313. | Jenny Lind | 189 Brompton Road, SW7 | 5B |
| 314. | George Godwin | 24 Alexander Square, SW3 | 5B |
| 315. | Sir Benjamin Thompson | 168 Brompton Road, SW3 | 5B |
| | | | |
| 316. | Sir John Millais | 7 Cromwell Place, SW7 | 5C |
| 317. | Sir William Gilbert | 39 Harrington Gardens, SW7 | 5C |
| 318. | Sir Edwin Arnold | 31 Bolton Gardens, SW5 | 5C |
| 319. | Viscount Allenby | 24 Wetherby Gardens, SW5 | 5C |
| 320. | George Borrow | 22 Hereford Square, SW7 | 5C |
| 321. | Sir Herbert Beerbohm Tree | 31 Rosary Gardens, SW7 | 5C |
| 322. | James Froude | 5 Onslow Gardens, SW7 | 5C |
| 323. | Andrew Bonar Law | 24 Onslow Gardens, SW7 | 5C |
| 324. | W.E.H. Lecky | 38 Onslow Gardens, SW7 | 5C |
| 325. | Rosalind Franklin | Donovan Court, Draycott Gardens | 5C |
| 326. | Mervyn Peake | 1 Drayton Gardens, SW10 | 5C |
| 327. | Frank Dobson | 14 Harley Gardens, SW10 | 5C |
| 328. | Sir Stafford Cripps | 32 Elm Park Gardens, SW10 | 5C |
| 329. | George Meredith | 7 Hobury Street, SW10 | 5C |
| 330. | John Ireland | 14 Gunter Grove, SW10 | 5C |
| 331. | Hilaire Belloc | 104 Cheyne Walk, SW10 | 5C |

| 332. | Isambard Kingdom Brunel | 98 Cheyne Walk, SW10 | 5C |
| 333. | Mrs. Gaskell | 93 Cheyne Walk, SW10 | 5C |
| 334. | Alfred Hitchcock | 153 Cromwell Road, SW5 | 5C |
| | | | |
| 335. | Sir Henry Cole | 33 Thurloe Square, SW7 | 5D |
| 336. | Sylvia Pankhurst | 120 Cheyne Walk, SW10 | 5D |
| 337. | Sir Nigel Playfair | 26 Pelham Crescent, SW7 | 5D |
| 338. | Robert Fitzroy | 38 Onslow Square, SW7 | 5D |
| 339. | W.M. Thackeray | 36 Onslow Square, SW7 | 5D |
| 340. | Béla Bartók | 7 Sydney Place, SW7 | 5D |
| 341. | Joseph Hansom | 27 Sumner Place, SW7 | 5D |
| 342. | Percy Grainger | 31 King's Road, SW3 | 5D |
| 343. | Dame Sybil Thorndike | 6 Carlyle Square, SW3 | 5D |
| 344. | Augustus John | 28 Mallord Street, SW3 | 5D |
| 345. | A.A. Milne | 13 Mallord Street, SW3 | 5D |
| 346. | Princess Astafieva | 152 King's Road, SW3 | 5D |
| 347. | Sir Carol Reed | 213 King's Road, SW3 | 5D |
| 348. | Ellen Terry | 215 King's Road, SW3 | 5D |
| 349. | George Gissing | 33 Oakley Gardens, SW3 | 5D |
| 350. | Leigh Hunt | 22 Upper Cheyne Row, SW3 | 5D |
| 351. | Captain Scott | 56 Oakley Street, SW3 | 5D |
| 352. | William De Morgan | 127 Old Church Street, SW3 | 5D |
| 353. | Sir Alexander Fleming | 20a Danvers Street, SW3 | 5D |
| 354. | George Eliot | 4 Cheyne Walk, SW3 | 5D |
| 355. | Rossetti & Swinburne | 16 Cheyne Walk, SW3 | 5D |
| 356. | J.M.W. Turner | 129 Cheyne Walk, SW3 | 5D |
| 357. | François Guizot | 21 Pelham Crescent, SW7 | 5D |
| 358. | Lady Jane Francesca Wilde | 87 Oakley Street, SW3 | |
| | | | |
| R. | Dennis Gabor | 79 Queen's Gate, SW7 | 5A |
| S. | Junius and John P. Morgan | 14 Princes Gate, SW1 | 5B |
| T. | Sir Terence Rattigan | 100 Cornwall Gardens, SW7 | 5A |
| U. | Dr Margery Blackie | 18 Thurloe Street, SW7 | 5B |
| V. | Joyce Grenfell | 34 Elm Park Gardens, SW10 | 5C |

# Map 6

| 359. | George Bentham | 25 Wilton Place, SW1 | 6A |
| 360. | Lillie Langtry | 8 Wilton Place, SW1 | 6A |
| 361. | Jane Austen | 23 Hans Place, SW1 | 6A |
| 362. | Dorothy Jordan | 30 Cadogan Place, SW1 | 6A |
| 363. | Sir George Alexander | 57 Pont Street, SW1 | 6A |
| 364. | Lillie Langtry | 21 Pont Street, SW1 | 6A |
| 365. | Lord John Russell | 37 Chesham Place, SW1 | 6A |
| 366. | William Wilberforce | 44 Cadogan Place, SW1 | 6A |
| 367. | Sir Charles Dilke | 76 Sloane Street, SW1 | 6A |
| 368. | Sir Herbert Beerbohm Tree | 76 Sloane Street, SW1 | 6A |
| 369. | Arnold Bennett | 75 Cadogan Square, SW1 | 6A |
| 370. | Thomas Cubitt | 3 Lyall Street, SW1 | 6A |
| 371. | Lord Avebury | 29 Eaton Place, SW1 | 6A |
| 372. | Frederic Chopin | 99 Eaton Place, SW1 | 6A |
| 373. | Stanley Baldwin | 93 Eaton Square, SW1 | 6A |
| 374. | Neville Chamberlain | 37 Eaton Square, SW1 | 6A |
| 375. | Mountbatten | 2 Wilton Crescent, SW1 | 6A |

| | | | |
|---|---|---|---|
| 376. | Lord Halifax | 86 Eaton Square, SW1 | 6B |
| 377. | Prince Metternich | 44 Eaton Square, SW1 | 6B |
| 378. | George Peabody | 80 Eaton Square, SW1 | 6B |
| 379. | Sir Henry Pelham | Rear of 22 Arlington Street, SW1 | 6B |
| 380. | Sir Robert Wapole | 5 Arlington Street, SW1 | 6B |
| 381. | Wilfrid Scawen-Blunt | 15 Buckingham Gate, SW1 | 6B |
| 382. | Sir Leslie Hore-Belisha | 16 Stafford Place, SW1 | 6B |
| 383. | Walter Bagehot | 12 Upper Belgrave Street, SW1 | 6B |
| 384. | Lord Tennyson | 9 Upper Belgrave Street, SW1 | 6B |
| 385. | Henry Gray | 8 Wilton Street, SW1 | 6B |
| 386. | Sir Henry Campbell-Bannerman | 6 Grosvenor Place, SW1 | 6B |
| 387. | F.E. Smith | 32 Grosvenor Gardens, SW1 | 6B |
| 388. | Henry Pitt-Rivers | 4 Grosvenor Gardens, SW1 | 6B |
| 389. | Cardinal Manning | 22 Carlisle Place, SW1 | 6B |
| 390. | Matthew Arnold | 2 Chester Square, SW1 | 6B |
| | | | |
| 391. | Admiral Jellicoe | 25 Draycott Place, SW3 | 6C |
| 392. | Bram Stoker | 18 St Leonard's Terrace, SW3 | 6C |
| 393. | Jerome. K. Jerome | Chelsea Gardens, Chelsea Bridge Road | 6C |
| 394. | Mark Twain | 23 Tedworth Square, SW3 | 6C |
| 395. | Oscar Wilde | 34 Tite Street, SW3 | 6C |
| 396. | Peter Warlock | 30 Tite Street, SW3 | 6C |
| 397. | Lord Ripon | 9 Chelsea Embankment, SW3 | 6C |
| 398. | William Ewart | 16 Eaton Place, SW1 | 6C |
| 399. | Vita Sackville-West | 182 Ebury Street, SW1 | 6C |
| | | | |
| 400. | Lord Kelvin | 15 Eaton Place, SW1 | 6D |
| 401. | Dame Edith Evans | 109 Ebury Street, SW1 | 6D |
| 402. | Ian Fleming | 22 Ebury Street, SW1 | 6D |
| 403. | George Moore | 121 Ebury Street, SW1 | 6D |
| 404. | Wolfgang Amadeus Mozart | 180 Ebury Street, SW1 | 6D |
| 405. | Harold Nicolson | 182 Ebury Street, SW1 | 6D |
| 406. | Joseph Conrad | 17 Gillingham Street, SW1 | 6D |
| 407. | Winston Churchill | 34 Eccleston Square, SW1 | 6D |
| 408. | Laura Ashley | 83 Cambridge Street, SW1 | 6D |
| 409. | Aubrey Beardsley | 114 Cambridge Street, SW1 | 6D |
| | | | |
| W. | Bert Ambrose | The May Fair Hotel, Stratton Street, W1 | 6B |
| X. | F.M. Viscount Gort | 34 Belgrave Square, SW1 | 6A |
| Y. | Count Edward Raczynski | 8 Lennox Gardens, SW1 | 6A |
| Z. | Mary Shelley | 24 Chester Square, SW1 | 6B |
| AA. | Sir Michael Costa | Wilton Court, 59 Eccleston Square | 6D |
| BB. | Arthur Haygarth | 88 Warwick Way, SW1 | 6D |
| CC. | Swami Vivekanada | 63 St George's Drive, SW1 | 6D |
| DD. | Jomo Kenyatta | 95 Cambridge Street, SW1 | 6D |
| EE. | Douglas Macmillan | 15 Ranelagh Road, SW1 | 6D |

# Map 7

| | | | |
|---|---|---|---|
| 410. | Nancy Astor | 4 St James's Square, SW1 | 7A |
| 411. | Lord Derby | 10 St James's Square, SW1 | 7A |
| 412. | W.E.Gladstone | 10 St James's Square, SW1 | 7A |
| 413. | William Pitt the Elder | 10 St James's Square, SW1 | 7A |
| 414. | Francis Chichester | 9 St James's Place, SW1 | 7A |

| | | | |
|---|---|---|---|
| 415. | William Huskisson | 28 St James's Place, SW1 | 7A |
| 416. | Thomas Gainsborough | 82 Pall Mall, SW1 | 7A |
| 417. | General De Gaulle | 4 Carlton Gardens, SW1 | 7A |
| 418. | Lord Kitchener | 2 Carlton Gardens, SW1 | 7A |
| 419. | Lord Palmerston | 4 Carlton Gardens, SW1 | 7A |
| 420. | Lord Curzon | 1 Carlton House Terrace, SW1 | 7A |
| 421. | W.E. Gladstone | 11 Carlton House Terrace, SW1 | 7A |
| 422. | Admiral John Fisher | 16 Queen Anne's Gate, SW1 | 7A |
| 423. | Sir Edward Grey | 3 Queen Anne's Gate, SW1 | 7A |
| 424. | Lord Haldane | 28 Queen Anne's Gate, SW1 | 7A |
| 425. | Lord Palmerston | 20 Queen Anne's Gate, SW1 | 7A |
| 426. | William Smith | 16 Queen Anne's Gate, SW1 | 7A |
| 427. | Charles Townley | 14 Queen Anne's Gate, SW1 | 7A |
| 428. | Winston Churchill | Caxton Hall, Caxton Street, SW1 | 7A |
| | | | |
| 429. | Scotland Yard | | 7B |
| 430. | H.M. Stanley | 2 Richmond Terrace, SW1 | 7B |
| 431. | John Peake Knight | 12 Bridge Street, SW1 | 7B |
| 432. | Sir Michael Balcon | 57a Tufton Street, SW1 | 7B |
| 433. | Eleanor Rathbone | Tufton Court, Tufton Street, SW1 | 7B |
| 434. | Siegfried Sassoon | 54 Tufton Street, SW1 | 7B |
| | | | |
| 435. | Major Walter Wingfield | 33 St George's Square, SW1 | 7C |
| 436. | Douglas MacMillan | 15 Ranelagh Road, SW1 | 7C |
| | | | |
| 437. | Millbank Prison | Millbank, SW1 | 7D |
| | | | |
| FF. | W.T. Stead | 5 Smith Square | 7B |

# A TO Z
# OF NAMES

## ABRAHAMS, HAROLD (1899–1978) *Olympic athlete, lived here*

HODFORD LODGE, 2 HODFORD ROAD, NW11

Anyone who has seen the Oscar-winning 1981 film *Chariots of Fire* knows something of the achievements of Harold Abrahams. Played in the film by Ben Cross, Abrahams was the gold medal winner in the 100 metres at the 1924 Olympics in Paris, unexpectedly beating the American Charley Paddock, then regarded as 'the world's fastest human'. As the film makes clear, Abrahams's victory was controversial because he had employed Sam Mussabini, a professional trainer, to coach him and, in those days of strict amateurism, it was considered hardly gentlemanly to do so. Presumably Mussabini's advice was usually more wide-ranging than that contained in the note he is said to have left with Abrahams on the day of the race. 'Only think of two things,' it read, 'the report of the pistol and the tape. When you hear the one, just run like hell until you break the other.' A year after his triumph in Paris, Abrahams broke his leg during training for the long jump, another event in which he excelled, and was forced to give up competitive athletics. Once retired, he became a lawyer (he had studied law at Cambridge) but he continued his involvement in sport. He was athletics correspondent for the *Sunday Times* for many years and was also a regular broadcaster on the BBC. He was elected President of the Amateur Athletics Association in 1976, two years before he died.

## ADAM, ROBERT (1728–1792) *architect;* THOMAS HOOD (1799–1845), *poet;* JOHN GALSWORTHY (1867–1933), *novelist and playwright;* SIR JAMES BARRIE (1860–1937); *and other eminent artists and writers, lived here*

1–3 ROBERT STREET, WC2

Robert Adam was the son of a distinguished Scottish architect and, together with his younger brother James, created some of the most original British architecture of the second half of the eighteenth century. From 1761 to 1769 Robert was Architect of the King's Works, a position in which James succeeded him. Robert Street, named after the elder Adam brother, was part of a larger and more ambitious project to transform an area between the Strand and the Thames. Nos 1–3 Robert Street are original Adam buildings in which the brothers themselves lived from 1778 to 1785. Thomas Hood, the writer of elaborately punning verse and of *The Song of the Shirt*, lived there in 1828–30. Barrie, author of *Peter Pan*, was a long-term resident who had a flat there from 1911 until his death. Galsworthy, one of Britain's few Nobel laureates for literature, lived there briefly during the last two years of the First World War.

## ADAMS, HENRY See under entry for UNITED STATES EMBASSY

## ADAMS-ACTON, JOHN (1831–1910) *sculptor, lived here*

14 LANGFORD PLACE, NW8   **WESTMINSTER**

John Adams-Acton was one of the most prominent portrait sculptors of his day, particularly known for his busts of Gladstone who sat for him many times and became a personal friend. He was also the only Protestant sculptor ever to be allowed to take sittings from Pope Leo XIII. Although a Protestant, Adams-Acton's connections with the Catholic Church were strong and one of his finest works was the effigy of Cardinal Manning to be seen in Westminster Cathedral. Sadly, Adams-Acton, on leaving the cathedral on one occasion, was hit by a passing vehicle and never fully recovered from his injuries, dying two years later.

## ADELPHI TERRACE *This building stands on the site of Adelphi Terrace built by the brothers Adam in 1768–1774. Famous residents in the Terrace include* TOPHAM AND LADY DIANA

BEAUCLERK, DAVID GARRICK, RICHARD D'OYLY CARTE, THOMAS HARDY *and* GEORGE BERNARD SHAW. *The* LONDON SCHOOL OF ECONOMICS *and the* SAVAGE CLUB *also had their premises here.*

## ADELPHI, WC2

One of the greatest acts of architectural vandalism in London this century was the destruction of the Adelphi, an imposing development of terraced houses on the site of what had once been Durham House, which had been built by the four Adam brothers in the early 1770s. At the time the Adams took on the site it was a slum area but they transformed it into a series of elegant Georgian town houses. They were demolished in 1936. Topham Beauclerk, a descendant of Charles II and Nell Gwyn, was a good friend of Dr Johnson, who was devastated by his early death. Beauclerk's wife Diana was a daughter of the Duke of Marlborough and a talented amateur artist. David Garrick lived here in the 1770s and his widow, who survived him by more than forty years, continued to do so until her own death in 1822. The impresario Richard D'Oyly Carte lived here through the years of his triumphs in producing the Gilbert and Sullivan operas and, in the 1860s, Thomas Hardy studied in an architectural practice that had its offices here. George Bernard Shaw moved in with his wife, Charlotte Payne-Townshend, after their marriage in 1898. He was closely connected with the development of the London School of Economics which was situated in the Adelphi from 1896 to 1902. The Savage Club, named after the reprobate eighteenth-century poet Richard Savage, had premises there from 1888 to 1907.

## ALDRIDGE, IRA (1807–1867) *Shakespearian actor, 'The African Roscius', lived here*

### 5 HAMLET ROAD, UPPER NORWOOD, SE19

The greatest black actor of the nineteenth century was born in New York, the son of a preacher. He came to London as a young man in order to further his career on stage. In 1825, aged only eighteen and billed as a 'Man of Colour', he appeared in the lead role in a play entitled *A Slave's Revenge* at the Royal Coburg Theatre and, over the next few decades, he performed in towns and cities all around Britain. Othello was, unsurprisingly, a favourite role but he also took on many other parts usually associated with white actors. Throughout his career Aldridge was obliged to struggle against the unthinking, often ludicrous racism of the day. One newspaper told its readers, in all seriousness, that it was quite impossible for him to pronounce English properly 'owing to the shape of his lips'. Yet less prejudiced reporters in Aldridge's audiences were in no doubt that they were in the presence of a great actor. One writer noted that the evenings he saw Aldridge play Shakespeare 'were undoubtedly the best I have ever spent in the theatre'. Much of the African Roscius's later career was spent touring Europe and he died in the city of Łódź in what is today Poland. He is buried in the Evangelical Cemetery there.

## ALEXANDER, SIR GEORGE (1858–1918) *actor-manager, lived here*

### 57 PONT STREET, SW1

One of the great actor-managers of his day, Alexander ran the St James's Theatre in King Street, Piccadilly, from 1891 until his death. The 1890s were his period of greatest artistic and commercial success. He appeared in the dual role of Rudolf Rassendyll and the King in *The Prisoner of Zenda* and was the first to stage several of Oscar Wilde's plays, including *The Importance of Being Earnest*, in which he appeared as John Worthing. Less successful was his staging of Henry James's play *Guy Domville*. On the first night, when Alexander came to the line, 'I am the last of the Domvilles', a voice from the gallery called back, 'Well, at any rate, that's a comfort to know'.

## ALLENBY, FIELD MARSHAL EDMUND HENRY HYNMAN, VISCOUNT, (1861–1936) *lived here 1928–1936*
### 24 WETHERBY GARDENS, SW5

One of the last great cavalry commanders and a scholarly soldier, who could quote Plato and Homer in the original Greek, Allenby was educated at Sandhurst and, as a young man, saw much service in South Africa, both before and during the Boer War. At the start of the First World War he was in command of the cavalry division which formed part of the British Expeditionary Force sent to France and, the following year, was given charge of the Third Army. Allenby remained on the Western Front until 1917, taking command of the Allied troops at the battle of Arras, but the Front was scarcely an arena in which to display cavalry skills. This chance came when Allenby was transferred to Palestine where, aided and abetted by the guerrilla forces under Lawrence of Arabia, his army swept the Turks aside and took first Jerusalem and then Damascus. After the war Allenby was high commissioner in Egypt for a number of years. He lived in Wetherby Gardens after he had retired from the Army and from public life.

## ALLINGHAM, MARGERY (1904–1966) *writer of crime fiction and creator of Albert Campion lived here 1916–1926*
### 1 WESTBOURNE TERRACE ROAD   **WESTMINSTER**

Margery Allingham was one of the great writers of the Golden Age of English detective fiction and her most famous creation, the affable and gentlemanly Albert Campion, is one of the most engaging of all the amateur detectives the period produced. Allingham came from a family of writers and her first stories were published when she was still in her teens. Campion made his debut in a book published in 1929 and went on to appear in nearly twenty others. Aided sometimes by his wife, the beautiful Lady Amanda, sometimes by the Scotland Yard inspector, Stanislaus Oates, and sometimes by his manservant, the weirdly named Magersfontein Lugg, he solved his mysteries with charm and panache. He is an almost peripheral figure, however, in what many would claim as Allingham's finest novel, *The Tiger in the Smoke*, in which a ruthless killer named Jack Havoc is loose in the fog-enshrouded streets of a London that is now long gone. Margery Allingham once described the essential ingredients of a crime novel as 'a Killing, a Mystery, an Enquiry and a Conclusion with an element of satisfaction in it'. For more than forty years her own novels made stylish use of these four essentials.

## ALMA-TADEMA, SIR LAWRENCE (1836–1912) *painter, lived here 1886–1912*
### 44 GROVE END ROAD, ST JOHN'S WOOD, NW8

Alma-Tadema, one of the most successful painters of Victorian England, was born in the small town of Dronryp in the Netherlands. Trained as an artist at the Antwerp Academy, he moved to London in 1870 and became a naturalised British citizen three years later. Alma-Tadema specialised in meticulously painted reconstructions of life in the ancient world, particularly Ancient Rome, and these proved enormously appealing to his Victorian patrons and buyers. He was one of the most highly paid artists of his time and was awarded a knighthood in 1899 and the Order of Merit in 1905. As one critic remarked, Alma-Tadema's scenes of everyday life in the Roman world appear to be peopled by 'Victorians in togas' and his reputation suffered when Victorian art went out of fashion. More recently his work has been reassessed and his energy and technical skill acknowledged. His house in St John's Wood was once the property of another successful artist of foreign extraction, James Tissot.

## AMBROSE, BERT (c.1896–1971) *dance band leader, lived and played here, 1927–1940*
THE MAY FAIR HOTEL, STRATTON STREET, W1

Born in the East End of London, the son of a Jewish wool merchant, Benjamin Baruch Ambrose began playing the violin as a child. He was taken to America by his aunt when he was in his teens and it was in the States that he launched his professional career as a musician. His American experience stood him in good stead when he returned to London and he was working as a highly paid band leader when he was still a very young man. As Bert Ambrose, or often just Ambrose, he was one of the stars of British popular music in the 1920s and 1930s and his band enjoyed major success on radio, in the recording studio and live on stage in nightclubs and West End hotels. The May Fair Hotel in Stratton Street now carries a Blue Plaque which celebrates Ambrose's years as maestro in residence there. His name will always be linked with those of two legendary female singers. 'The Forces' Sweetheart', Vera Lynn, sang with his band in the late 1930s and, twenty years later, he discovered and managed the teenage Kathy Kirby. It was backstage at the recording of a TV appearance by Kirby that Ambrose collapsed and died in 1971.

## *In this house* SUSANNA ANNESLEY, *mother of* JOHN WESLEY, *was born 20 January 1669*
7 SPITALYARD, BISHOPSGATE, EC2   **CITY OF LONDON**

Susanna Annesley, the daughter of a well-known Nonconformist, married Samuel Wesley in 1690 and together they had seventeen children, among them John and Charles, the founders of Methodism. She died in 1742 and was buried in Bunhill Fields. John preached a funeral sermon by his mother's grave and later wrote of the service, 'It was one of the most solemn assemblies I ever saw or ever expect to see on this side of eternity.'

## ARDIZZONE, EDWARD (1900–1979) *artist and illustrator, lived here 1920–1972*
130 ELGIN AVENUE, W9

Ardizzone's father, who was French, worked in the Far East for a telegraph company and Edward was born in Haiphong in what is now Vietnam. He was brought to England as a young boy and raised in Suffolk by his maternal grandparents. After leaving school, he joined his father's firm as a clerk in London but the urge to draw and paint was ever present and, at the age of twenty-seven, he horrified his family by giving up his secure job to work as a full-time artist. They need not have worried. Within a short while he had had his first one-man show in London and won his first commission as an illustrator. He began to write and illustrate his own books for children in the 1930s – the first was *Little Tim and the Brave Sea Captain* in 1936 – and continued to do so for the rest of his life. Over the years, he also produced illustrations for books by many other writers, from *Stig of the Dump* by Clive King to the Barsetshire novels of Anthony Trollope. An official war artist during the Second World War (when he accompanied the British Expeditionary Force to France and, in London, was briefly arrested as a spy while sketching during the Blitz), Ardizzone was one of the most original and distinctive illustrators of the twentieth century.

## ARKWRIGHT, SIR RICHARD (1732–1792) *industrialist and inventor, lived here*
8 ADAM STREET, WC2

Born into a poor family in Preston, Arkwright first showed his entrepreneurial talents when he moved from a job as a barber to become a dealer in discarded human hair, collecting material for the creation of wigs. He also showed his inventiveness by devising a method of his own for dyeing the hair. However, he is best remembered for his innovations in the cotton industry which he entered about 1767, joining forces with another inventor, John Kay, to produce the spinning-frame, which created cotton thread of a strength not hitherto possible from a machine. In 1771 he set up a factory in Derbyshire that used water power to drive his machines and the profits from this went to open further mills. Arkwright's success was resented both by business rivals and those who were put out of work by his frames. In 1779 a mob burned down one of his mills in Chorley but it was fighting against the tide of history. Arkwright was knighted in 1786 and, by the time he died, was a very wealthy man indeed.

......................................................................................................................

## ARNE, THOMAS (1710–1778) *composer, lived here*
31 KING STREET, COVENT GARDEN, WC2

Arne was the son of an upholsterer and coffin-maker but the family was a musical one. His father was an amateur enthusiast who was a friend of Handel, and his sister and brother were both singers who performed in his operas and masques. Arne became one of the leading lights of eighteenth-century musical and theatrical life and worked extensively with Garrick at the Drury Lane theatre. His settings of Shakespearean songs such as 'Where the Bee Sucks' and 'Blow, Blow, thou Winter Wind' continue to be performed but he is best remembered for 'Rule Britannia', which was first heard in his 1740 masque *Alfred*.

......................................................................................................................

## ARNOLD, SIR EDWIN (1832–1904) *poet and journalist, lived and died here*
31 BOLTON GARDENS, SW5

Arnold, who spent time in India as a young man, was a student of Eastern languages and religions and is best known for *The Light of Asia*, first published in 1879. This poem in blank verse, which looks at the life and teachings of the Buddha through the medium of an imagined follower, was enormously popular with its original Victorian audience. Arnold was also a journalist who joined the staff of the *Daily Telegraph* in 1861 and was made editor in 1873. In this latter capacity he was responsible for committing the paper to half the expense of Stanley's second expedition into the interior of Africa to complete exploration begun by Livingstone.

......................................................................................................................

## ARNOLD, MATTHEW (1822–1888) *poet and critic, lived here*
2 CHESTER SQUARE, SW1

## MATTHEW ARNOLD (1822–1888) *lived here 1868–1873*
BYRON HOUSE, CLONMEL CLOSE, BYRON HILL ROAD, HARROW-ON-THE-HILL.
**PRIVATE**

The son of the great reforming headmaster of Rugby, Thomas Arnold, Matthew Arnold was born in the heart of the Victorian intellectual élite. He was educated at Rugby and at Oxford where he won the Newdigate Prize for a poem on Cromwell. He spent his career as an inspector of schools and wrote and lectured widely on educational and social issues. *Culture and Anarchy*, a collection of essays published in 1869, was a blistering attack on Victorian culture and on the English as a nation dominated by an 'inveterate inaccessibility to ideas'. He introduced the word 'philistine' into the language in its sense of one who is indifferent or hostile to culture and enlightenment. As a poet he embodied Victorian doubts and insecurities in poems such as 'Dover Beach'. He lived in Chester Square for ten years from the late 1850s.

## ASHFIELD, ALBERT HENRY STANLEY, LORD (1874–1948) *first Chairman of London Transport, lived here*

43 SOUTH STREET, MAYFAIR, W1

Albert Stanley, later to become Lord Ashfield, was born in Derbyshire but emigrated with his family to America as a child and it was in Detroit and New Jersey that he proved a dynamic manager of tramway and street-car companies. Brought back to his native country to join the Underground Group, Ashfield was managing director between 1910 and 1919 and chairman and managing director from 1919 to 1933. When Labour came to power in 1929 Herbert Morrison became Transport Minister and looked to bring transport under public control. As a businessman Ashfield wished to rationalise the Underground system and integrate it with other transport systems within the capital. The views of socialist and businessman coincided and the outcome, after some years of negotiation and diplomacy, was the London Passenger Transport Board, of which Ashfield was the first chairman from 1933 until the year before his death.

## ASHLEY, LAURA (1925–1985) *dress designer, began her clothing businesses here with her husband Bernard 1954–1956*

83 CAMBRIDGE STREET, SW1   **WESTMINSTER**

Laura Mountney married Bernard Ashley in 1953 and it was in their flat in Cambridge Street, Pimlico, that she first began to design and hand-print textiles and fabrics. Soon major London stores, like Heals and Liberty, were buying her designs. By the early sixties she was designing dresses, blouses and other clothes and in 1967 the Ashleys opened their first shop in Kensington. Over the years Laura Ashley became synonymous with a certain sort of style and, by the mid-eighties, there were more than 200 shops selling, and eleven factories manufacturing, her clothes, fabrics and wallpapers. Sadly, in 1985, the woman whose talents as a designer had created this business, fell down the stairs in her house and she died the following week.

## ASQUITH, HERBERT HENRY, 1ST EARL OF OXFORD *and* ASQUITH (1852–1928) *statesman, lived here*

20 CAVENDISH SQUARE, W1

## HERBERT HENRY ASQUITH, 1ST EARL OF OXFORD AND ASQUITH

27 MARESFIELD GARDENS, NW3   **HAMPSTEAD PLAQUE FUND**

Born in Yorkshire and educated at Balliol College, Asquith was elected to Parliament in 1886 and his abilities were soon recognised. He was Home Secretary in Gladstone's last administration, Chancellor of the Exchequer between 1905 and 1908 and succeeded Campbell-Bannerman as Prime Minister in 1908. Asquith's time in office was a period of both achievement and crisis. The Liberal administration was one of the great reforming governments of the century, establishing old age pensions, national insurance and other social measures that prefigured the welfare state. Yet the years before the First World War were those in which suffragettes chained themselves to railings in pursuit of the vote, the Ulster Volunteers promised violent opposition to Asquith's proposals for Irish Home Rule and the House of Lords had to be threatened with a vast new influx of members before it would agree to controversial taxation measures in Lloyd George's budget. Asquith continued as Prime Minister when war came but was ousted in 1916. Briefly leader of a much-diminished Liberal party in the 1920s, he retired to the House of Lords in 1925.

## ASTAFIEVA, PRINCESS SERAPHINE (1876–1934) *ballet dancer, lived and taught here*
### 152 KING'S ROAD, SW3

Although Princess Astafieva danced with Diaghilev's legendary Ballet Russes, it is as a hugely influential ballet teacher that she is best remembered. She arrived in England in 1910, retired from the stage three years later and began to work as a teacher. Her house in the King's Road, known as The Pheasantry, was the site of her dance studio from the last years of the First World War until her death, and many of the best-known figures in British ballet, including Margot Fonteyn, Anton Dolin and Alicia Markova, were taught there.

## ASTOR, NANCY (1879–1964) *first woman to sit in Parliament, lived here*
### 4 ST JAMES'S SQUARE, SW1

Born in America, Nancy Astor became the first woman to sit in the British Houses of Parliament in 1919 when she took over the Plymouth Sutton seat of her husband who had moved into the Lords on inheriting his father's viscountcy. She remained in the Commons as a Conservative MP for the next twenty-five years. Outspoken on social issues, particularly those affecting women and the family, she was also a firm believer in the evils of the demon alcohol and an advocate of temperance reform. As a member, in the thirties, of the pro-appeasement Cliveden set, she was not one of Churchill's greatest admirers. When a fellow Tory MP, bemoaning Churchill's lack of consistency, tact and party loyalty, said to her, 'We just don't know what to make of him', she is said to have replied, 'How about a nice rug?'

## ATTLEE, RICHARD CLEMENT (1883–1976) *Prime Minister, lived here*
### 17 MONKHAMS AVENUE, WOODFORD GREEN

## RICHARD CLEMENT ATTLEE (1883–1976)
### HEYWOOD COURT, LONDON ROAD, STANMORE    **HARROW HERITAGE TRUST**

His political opponent, Churchill, is alleged to have described Attlee as 'a modest little man with much to be modest about'. Yet it could be argued that Attlee was one of the greatest Prime Ministers this century and that the Labour government that he led from 1945 to 1951 was one of the most far-reaching in its achievements. From a conventional upper middle class background, Attlee became a convert to socialism as a young man and was elected to Parliament in 1922. After the rift in the Labour Party caused by Ramsay MacDonald, Attlee found himself successively deputy leader under George Lansbury and, on Lansbury's resignation in 1935, leader of a much depleted parliamentary party. He was Deputy Prime Minister in Churchill's war-time coalition and then led a revitalised Labour party to its landslide victory in 1945. After the Tory resurgence in the 1951 election Attlee stayed on as leader of the opposition for four years and then retired with an earldom.

## AUBREY HOUSE *stands on the site of Kensington Wells, an early 18th century spa. Former residents include* SIR EDWARD LLOYD; RICHARD, 1ST EARL GROSVENOR; LADY MARY COKE, *diarist;* PETER AND CLEMENTIA TAYLOR, *philanthropists;* WILLIAM CLEVERLY ALEXANDER, *art lover.*
### AUBREY HOUSE, AUBREY WALK, W8

Built in the eighteenth century on the site of an earlier property, Aubrey House is one of the largest private houses in Kensington and has a Blue Plaque on one of its walls that commemorates six previous residents who attained a degree of renown. Sir Edward Lloyd, the man who transformed the original property into the building we see today, was a minor politician at the time of Pitt the Elder. Richard Grosvenor, 1st Earl of Grosvenor, who took on the lease of the property from Lloyd in the 1760s, was also a politician and famed in his day as a breeder of thoroughbred racehorses. Lady Mary Coke, who lived in the house from the late 1760s to the late 1780s, was the daughter of the Duke of Argyll and an eccentric aristocrat in an age of eccentric aristocrats. The writer Horace Walpole was a friend who dedicated his famous Gothic novel T*he Castle of Otranto* to her but even he described her as 'violent, absurd and mad'. Her diaries and letters, published after her death, paint an idiosyncratic and revealing picture of eighteenth-century upper-class life. Peter Taylor was a radical MP for more than twenty years in the second half of the nineteenth century and, together with his wife Clementia, he was a leading campaigner for women's suffrage. He was one of a small number of MPs to support John Stuart Mill's attempts in the 1860s to extend to women the same political and voting rights that were granted to men. In the years that they lived at Aubrey House they made it a centre of middle-class radicalism in London and major European political figures, such as Mazzini were regular visitors there. William Cleverly Alexander was a wealthy banker and art collector who was an early patron of the flamboyant American painter James McNeill Whistler. Whistler was employed to create designs for several rooms in Aubrey House, although sadly none survive.

## AUROBINDO, SRI (1872–1950) *Indian spiritual leader lived here 1884–1887*
### 49 ST STEPHEN'S AVENUE, W12

'If a religion is not universal, it cannot be eternal,' Sri Aurobindo once wrote. 'A narrow religion, a sectarian religion, an exclusive religion can live only for a limited time and a limited purpose.' Aurobindo dedicated much of his life to the propagation of the kind of universal religion in which he believed. He was born into an Anglophile Indian family in Calcutta and he received an intensive Western-style education which culminated in study at King's College, Cambridge. Returning to India, he moved away from the westernising beliefs of his family and became an ardent advocate of Indian nationalism. Indeed, for a time, he was seen as one of the leaders of the nascent movement for India's independence and was imprisoned by the British in consequence. On his release he went into exile in Pondicherry, then still ruled by the French, and there he was converted from belief in political power to belief in spiritual power. He devoted the rest of his life to the development of his philosophy, gradually gaining admirers and disciples around the world. Sri Aurobindo and his brothers lived at the address in St Stephen's Avenue in Shepherd's Bush, under the care of a Mrs Drewett, when they were pupils at St Paul's School in nearby Hammersmith.

## AUSTEN, JANE (1775–1817) *novelist, stayed here 1813–1814*
### 10 HENRIETTA STREET, WC2   **WESTMINSTER**

## JANE AUSTEN *novelist, stayed with her brother Henry in a house on this site 1814–1815*
### 23 HANS PLACE, SW1   **PRIVATE**

'Three or four families in a country village is the very thing to work on', Jane Austen wrote in a letter to one of her relatives and, in novels like *Pride and Prejudice*, *Sense and Sensibility* and *Emma*, she followed her own advice to great effect. Born in a Hampshire village where her father was rector, she spent most of her life in the midst of her family there, at Bath and at Chawton, another village in the county. Although she had several suitors she never married. She died of Addison's disease in Winchester at the age of forty-one. She visited London on a number of occasions, staying with her brother Henry in Henrietta Street and, later, Hans Place. Although she had initial difficulties in getting her novels published (and *Northanger Abbey* and *Persuasion* were both published only after her death), Jane Austen had distinguished fans during her lifetime, including the Prince Regent. The Prince's Librarian wrote to her suggesting that she might like to compose 'an historical romance, illustrative of the history of the august house of Coburg'. Wisely, she chose not to do so.

## AVEBURY, BARON: SIR JOHN LUBBOCK (1834–1913) *scientist, born here*
29 EATON PLACE, SW1

Both scientist and politician, Sir John Lubbock had a long career as one of the great and good of Victorian England. The son of a well-known banker and astronomer, he joined the family banking firm straight from school at Eton but, encouraged by Darwin, a friend of his father, he pursued his interest in natural history. He wrote a number of books (*Prehistoric Times, The Origin of Civilization*) on early man and became an expert on the social organisation of bees and ants. It is to Lubbock the politician that we owe the Bank Holiday. Entering Parliament as MP for Maidstone in 1870 he drew up the bill which became the Bank Holidays Act the following year. In a parliamentary career that lasted thirty years he was also responsible for several other pioneering acts of social reform, including the Ancient Monuments Act of 1882 and the Shop Hours Act of 1889.

## AYER, PROFESSOR SIR ALFRED (1910–1989) *philosopher, lived here 1980–1989*
51 YORK STREET, W1   **WESTMINSTER**

Ayer was born in London and educated at Eton and Oxford. From 1946 to 1959 he was Professor of Philosophy at University College, London, and then returned to Oxford as Wykeham Professor of Logic, remaining there until his retirement in 1977. Ayer made his name in his twenties when he published *Language, Truth and Logic*, the first book to introduce the ideas of logical positivism into English. This forceful and tightly argued work caused much controversy with its assertions that moral and religious affirmations were, when placed under stringent analysis, literally meaningless. Ayer remained a convinced atheist throughout his life but caused a stir in his later years when he published an account of his own 'near-death experience', in which he made some concessions towards religious feelings and a religious interpretation of life.

## AYRTON, HERTHA (1854–1923) *physicist, lived here 1903–1923*
41 NORFOLK SQUARE, W2

Hertha Ayrton was one of the leading female scientists of her day. Born Phoebe Marks, the daughter of a Jewish clockmaker and his wife, she adopted the name 'Hertha' in her teens after reading a poem of that title by Algernon Swinburne. (Swinburne himself took the name from Germanic mythology.) She was an early student at Girton College, Cambridge, where she studied mathematics, and then went on to study electrical engineering in London with the well-known physicist William Edward Ayrton. She married him in 1885. Husband and wife worked together until his death in 1908. Hertha Ayrton was a trailblazer for women scientists in many ways. In 1899, she became the first female member of the Institute of Electrical Engineers. She was also the first woman ever to read out a scientific paper of her own to a meeting of the Royal Society and the first to win the Hughes Medal, awarded by the Society for 'an original discovery in the physical sciences, particularly electricity and magnetism or their applications'. Despite this, the Society, refused to elect her as a member. 'We are of the opinion that married women are not eligible as Fellows of the Royal Society,' the Council decreed when her name was put forward. The house in Norfolk Square was both Ayrton's home and her laboratory.

## BABBAGE, CHARLES (1791–1871) *mathematician and pioneer of the modern computer, lived in a house on this site 1829–1871*
1A DORSET STREET, W1   **WESTMINSTER**

CHARLES BABBAGE, *mathematician, astronomer and computer pioneer was born near this site*
CORNER OF LARCOM STREET AND WALWORTH ROAD, SE17,
**SOUTHWARK COUNCIL**

Babbage was one of the greatest British mathematicians of the nineteenth century and a man far ahead of his time. From 1823, when he became Lucasian Professor of Mathematics at Cambridge, he spent nearly fifty years working, intermittently, on a calculating machine and anticipated many of the developments in electronic computers this century. He lived and worked in Dorset Street for many years and died there in 1871. In poetry, as in mathematics, Babbage was a stickler for accuracy. When he read Tennyson's lines, 'Every minute dies a man/Every minute one is born', he was troubled enough to write to the poet and suggest that, 'in the next edition of your excellent poem the erroneous calculation . . . should be corrected as follows: Every minute dies a man/And one and a sixteenth is born.' In subsequent editions Tennyson left the lines as they were.

......................................................................................................

BADEN-POWELL, ROBERT (1857–1941)
*Chief Scout of the World, lived here*
9 HYDE PARK GATE, SW7

Baden-Powell lived at Hyde Park Gate with his family from soon after his father's death in 1860 until the time he joined the Army in 1876. He was an unexceptional member of the officer classes, serving in India, Afghanistan and Matabeleland, before he won fame as the defender of Mafeking against the Boers in 1899–1900. The siege was lifted by Lord Roberts after more than 200 days and Baden-Powell found himself the darling of a jingoistic nation. His first Scout camp was held on Brownsea Island in Poole Harbour in 1907 and the following year the Boy Scout movement was formally instituted, with Baden-Powell formulating the famous motto that a Scout should always 'be prepared'. A Scout, Baden-Powell also maintained, should be one who 'smiles and whistles under all circumstances'. The Scout movement developed with remarkable speed and by the 1920s huge jamborees of Scouts from around the world were being held. The rest of Baden-Powell's life was devoted to the movement.

......................................................................................................

BAGEHOT, WALTER (1826–1877) *writer, banker and economist, lived here*
12 UPPER BELGRAVE STREET, SW1

In one of his works Bagehot declared, 'business is much more amusing than pleasure' and many of his writings reflect his consuming interest in the ways people organise their societies both politically and economically. Educated at University College, London, Bagehot was called to the Bar but decided instead to enter the bank owned by his father. He was soon a regular contributor to a number of magazines and in 1860 he became the editor of *The Economist*, whose founder, James Wilson, was, conveniently, his father-in-law. He continued as editor until his death in 1877. Bagehot's most famous work and the only one still read today is *The English Constitution*, an erudite account of the workings of government which rapidly became a classic after publication in 1867.

## BAGNOLD, ENID (1889–1981) *novelist and playwright, lived here*

29 HYDE PARK GATE, SW7

Although she produced a number of novels, plays and autobiographical works, Enid Bagnold is one of those writers fated to be remembered by one book only. In her case it is *National Velvet*, first published in 1935, which tells the story of a young girl who wins a horse in a raffle and eventually rides it to victory in the Grand National. The film version of 1944 was one of the first successes for the teenage Elizabeth Taylor. Enid Bagnold had spent much of her childhood in the West Indies and, during the First World War, she served as a nurse and ambulance driver. After the war she moved in a world where many of the leading social, political and cultural figures mingled and she drew upon that world in her fiction. Her 1931 novel, *The Loved and Envied*, has a central character clearly based on the flamboyant socialite Diana Cooper. Enid Bagnold was still publishing when she was in her eighties but never repeated the success of *National Velvet*.

## BAILLIE, JOANNA *poet and dramatist, born 1762, died 1851, lived in this house for nearly fifty years*

BOLTON HOUSE, WINDMILL HILL, NW3

Born in Lanarkshire to a family which claimed descent from the great Scottish hero Sir William Wallace, Joanna Baillie may be almost forgotten today but, in her day, she was one of the best-known women writers. She published a collection of poetry in 1790 that was admired by no less a figure than Burns, but her greatest success was in drama. As an early biographer put it, 'It was whilst imprisoned by the heat of a summer afternoon, and seated by her mother's side engaged in needlework, that the thought of essaying dramatic composition burst upon her.' Her series of *Plays on the Passions*, written in blank verse, were intended to be read rather than performed, but one had a successful run in Drury Lane and later plays were similarly acclaimed on stage. She and her sister lived in Bolton House for half a century, having moved to London after the death of their father.

## BAIRD, JOHN LOGIE (1888–1946) *first demonstrated television in this house in 1926*

22 FRITH STREET, W1

## JOHN LOGIE BAIRD *television pioneer, lived here*

3 CRESCENT WOOD ROAD, SYDENHAM, SE26

*From this site* JOHN LOGIE BAIRD *broadcast the first television programme in Great Britain on 30 September 1929*

132–135 LONG ACRE, WC2 **ROYAL TELEVISION SOCIETY**

Born in Scotland and trained as an electrical engineer at Glasgow University, Baird only turned to work on the transmission of visual images after the failure of a number of business ventures, including the selling of marmalade and Australian honey. It was in Hastings, where he had settled, that he began his research in the early twenties. He moved to London in 1924 and rented an attic at 22 Frith Street to serve as a laboratory. It was there that some members of the Royal Institution had the privilege to form the first television audience. The system eventually adopted by the BBC in 1936 was not that of Baird, which proved a great disappointment to him and to the fortunes of the Baird Television Development Company, but he continued to experiment and succeeded in producing both 3-D and colour images before his death in 1946.

---

## BAIRNSFATHER, BRUCE (1888–1959) *cartoonist, lived here*
1 STERLING STREET, MONTPELLIER SQUARE, SW7

Born in India, the son of a soldier, Bairnsfather served in France during the First World War and there began contributing humorous black and white sketches of life at the Front to magazines back home. His most lasting invention, who appeared in the volumes of *Fragments from France* which Bairnsfather published during the war and after, was 'Old Bill', a lugubrious but stoical private soldier, struggling to keep going amidst the chaos of the trenches. Bairnsfather's single most famous cartoon showed 'Old Bill' crouched in a shell-hole, remarking to his fellow-shelterer there, 'Well, if you knows of a better 'ole, go to it.' Old Bill and his two companions, Bert and Alf, became so popular that there was even a play, *The Better 'Ole*, written by Bairnsfather and a fellow officer, to bring their exploits to the West End. After the war Bairnsfather started his own weekly comic paper but, although he continued to work throughout the twenties and thirties, and was an official war-cartoonist to the US Army in the Second World War, the years when his talents had coincided with history were undoubtedly those of the Western Front.

---

## BALCON, SIR MICHAEL (1896–1977) *film producer, worked here, 1938–1956*
EALING FILM STUDIOS, EALING GREEN, W5

## BALCON, SIR MICHAEL (1896–1977) *film-maker, lived here 1927–1939*
57A TUFTON STREET, SW1 **WESTMINSTER**

Born in Birmingham, Michael Balcon began his career in films as a regional distributor and became one of the most important figures in the British industry. In 1923 the first film he produced, *Woman to Woman*, had as its art director a young man called Alfred Hitchcock. Balcon gave Hitchcock his first chance to direct and was behind the production of his most famous British films, including *The Thirty Nine Steps*. Balcon also founded Gainsborough Pictures in 1928 and was chief of production at Ealing Studios when the famous Ealing comedies (*Kind Hearts and Coronets, Passport to Pimlico, The Ladykillers* and others) were made there. Knighted in 1948, Balcon's last major contribution to British films was to act as executive producer of *Tom Jones* in 1963. He lived in Tufton Street from 1927 until 1939.

---

## BALDWIN, STANLEY (1867–1947) *Earl Baldwin of Bewdley, Prime Minister, lived here*
93 EATON SQUARE, SW1

Three times Prime Minister (in 1923–4, 1925–9 and 1935–7), Baldwin was also the leading Tory in Ramsay MacDonald's National Government in 1931–5 and thus one of the dominant figures in British politics for most of the twenties and thirties. His periods in office included two major national crises, the General Strike and the furore over Edward VIII's abdication, both of which he handled with great political skill. However, modern historians have criticised both his foreign policy, which began the disastrous trend towards appeasement of the fascist dictators, and his economic policy, which did little to

relieve the hardships of depression. It was Baldwin who, in a by-election speech in 1931, famously accused the press barons of the time of exercising 'power without responsibility, the prerogative of the harlot throughout the ages.' When the Tory grandee, the Duke of Devonshire, heard of this speech, he is said to have remarked, 'That's done it. He's lost us the tarts' vote now.' Baldwin retired from politics in 1937 and was rewarded with an earldom.

........................................................................................................................

## BALFE, MICHAEL WILLIAM (1808–70) *musical composer, lived here*
12 SEYMOUR STREET, W1

Born in Dublin, Balfe was a child prodigy who made his debut as a violinist in his ninth year and played in orchestras in London and Rome while still a teenager. Balfe was also gifted as a singer and he appeared in a Paris production of *The Barber of Seville* in 1827 at the instigation of Rossini himself, under whom Balfe had studied. He wrote music from an early age and it is as a composer of operas and operettas that he is best remembered. Most of his career was spent in England where, in 1846, he was appointed conductor of the London Italian Opera. His operatic works such as *The Bohemian Girl*, *The Rose of Castile* and *Falstaff* are rarely performed today but two of his melodies, 'I Dreamt I Dwelt in Marble Halls' (an aria from *The Bohemian Girl*) and 'The Harp That Once Through Tara's Halls', remain familiar.

........................................................................................................................

## BALLANTYNE, R.M. (1825–1894) *author of books for boys, lived here*
DUNEAVES, MOUNT PARK ROAD

Ballantyne's own life was often as adventurous as that of the heroes of his best-selling fiction. He worked for the Hudson's Bay Company in the wilds of Canada when he was a young man and, even after he became a successful author, his insistence on extensive research meant that he travelled widely and worked, briefly, at a variety of occupations, including firefighter, miner and lighthouse-keeper. His best-known work is *The Coral Island*, in which three youths show astonishing resourcefulness when shipwrecked on a desert island and prove more than a match for such dangers as sharks and cannibals. In a sequel, *The Gorilla Hunters*, the protagonists endanger a number of species with their enthusiasm for indiscriminate slaughter of the African wildlife they encounter. Very much of the period in which they were written, Ballantyne's tales of manly Victorian heroes none the less remained popular well into this century.

........................................................................................................................

## BANKS, SIR JOSEPH (1743–1820) *President of the Royal Society; and* ROBERT BROWN (1773–1858) *and* DAVID DON (1800–1841), *botanists, lived in a house on this site.* THE LINNEAN SOCIETY *met here 1820–1857*

32 SOHO SQUARE, W1

Sir Joseph Banks sailed with Captain Cook on his first expedition between 1768 and 1771 and, on his return, became a pillar of the scientific establishment. He was elected President of the Royal Society in 1778 and held the position for more than forty years. Robert Brown, born in Montrose, also sailed as a naturalist on an expedition to the southern hemisphere, accompanying Flinders on his voyage to Australia between 1801 and 1804 and returning to England with close to four thousand plant specimens. He was Librarian to the Linnean Society, a botanist respected throughout Europe and, from 1827, Botanical Keeper at the British Museum. David Don, also a Scotsman, was the son of the Curator of the Botanic Gardens in Edinburgh and came to London with a letter of introduction to Brown. He became his secretary and succeeded him as Librarian to the Linnean Society. He died in the house in Soho Square. The house belonged to the Linnean Society which had been founded in 1788 to promote the study of all branches of natural history. Sir Joseph Banks was one of its first honorary members.

## BARING, EVELYN, 1ST EARL OF CROMER (1841–1917) *colonial administrator, lived and died here*

### 36 WIMPOLE STREET, W1

To describe Evelyn Baring as a colonial administrator is to risk underestimating the extent of his power in Egypt in the 24 years he was Consul-General there. For long periods he was, in effect, governing the country, although the Egyptian kings, under Ottoman sovereignty, were nominally in charge. Baring, a member of the banking family, had spent time in India as Finance Minister when he was sent to Egypt in 1883. The following year, General Gordon's posting to the Sudan and his death at the hands of the Mahdi's followers destabilised the whole region but Baring continued his plans to put the country on what he saw as a sound financial footing. In the late 1890s, under Kitchener, British troops restored Sudan to Egyptian rule. Baring retired from Egypt in 1907 and the country was formally established as a British protectorate in 1914.

## BARLOW, WILLIAM HENRY (1812–1902) *engineer, lived and died here*
### 'HIGHCOMBE', 145 CHARLTON ROAD, SE7

Everyone has heard of Isambard Kingdom Brunel. Few people, other than railway buffs, have heard of the other engineers who helped to create the Victorian rail network. William Henry Barlow was one of these unsung heroes of the pioneering days of the railways. He worked especially on the Midlands lines and was also responsible for laying out the southern part of the London and Bedford line including St Pancras Station. By the 1870s Barlow was an acknowledged expert on the problems and difficulties of railway engineering and when, in 1879, a train plunged off the Tay Bridge into the river below, killing 100 people, he was invited to sit on the enquiry into the disaster. He was also given the job of designing the new bridge across the Tay.

## BARNARDO, DR THOMAS JOHN (1845–1905) *began his work for children in a building on this site in 1866*

### 58 SOLENT HOUSE, BEN JONSON ROAD, E1

## DR JOHN BARNARDO, *founder of Barnardo Homes*
### 30 COBORN STREET, EC3 **BOW HERITAGE**

Born in Dublin, Barnardo was working as a clerk in the offices of a wine merchant when he underwent a religious conversion and became persuaded of the evils of drink. Leaving the wine merchant, he began preaching in the Dublin slums and then travelled to London, intending to train as a doctor and become a medical missionary in China. Instead he found his life's work in London. Appalled by the numbers and the condition of the homeless children in the East End, Barnardo, while still a student, rented a run-down building on a site now covered by part of a housing development and began his mission to ease the lives of these children. The first of what became many Barnardo's Homes was opened in Stepney in 1870. The charity that Barnardo founded, and to which he devoted his life, is still in existence.

## BARNETT, DAME HENRIETTA (1851–1936) *founder of Hampstead Garden Suburb; and* CANON SAMUEL BARNETT (1844–1913) *social reformer, lived here*

HEATH END HOUSE, SPANIARDS ROAD, HAMPSTEAD. NW3

Samuel Barnett's interest in London's poor was first aroused when he went to a Whitechapel parish in the 1870s. He went on to found Toynbee Hall, as a place where the privileged undergraduates of the universities could mix with the workers of the East End, to the mutual benefit of both classes. His wife Henrietta, who assisted him in this venture and other social and educational projects among the poor, hoped that Hampstead Garden Suburb would also enable the classes to mix comfortably in pleasant, semi-rural surroundings. She purchased land on the old Wyldes Farm between Hampstead and Golders Green and, in 1907, the suburb was begun under the direction of the designers of Letchworth Garden City. Well-known architects were invited to design individual houses including Sir Edwin Lutyens, who didn't always see eye to eye with the suburb's patroness. She is, he wrote, 'a nice woman but proud of being a philistine – has no idea beyond a window box full of geraniums, calceolarias and lobelias over which you can see a goose on the green.'

## BARRIE, SIR JAMES (1860–1937) *novelist and dramatist, lived here*
100 BAYSWATER ROAD. W2

Barrie was born in the Scottish village of Kirriemuir and he first became known as a writer for a series of novels set in 'Thrums', a thinly fictionalised version of his birthplace. He began to write for the theatre in the 1890s and his greatest success was, of course, *Peter Pan*, which was written while Barrie was living in Bayswater Road. His house was just across from Kensington Gardens where Barrie much loved walking and where he met the Llewellyn-Davies family on whom the Darlings in the play (and Peter Pan himself) are largely based. Barrie much admired the verve, spirit and wit of the young Llewellyn-Davies boys. He records that, when he admonished one of them for eating too much ice-cream, saying, 'You'll be sick tomorrow morning if you eat that,' the boy instantly, and with great aplomb, replied, 'I shall be sick tonight.' Barrie wrote plays both before and after *Peter Pan*, and some are occasionally revived, but his fame rests on the story of Never-Never Land. That he once remarked, 'Some of my plays peter out, and some pan out,' is probably an apocryphal story.

See also under entry for ROBERT ADAM

## BARRY, SIR CHARLES (1795–1860) *architect, lived and died here*
THE ELMS. CLAPHAM COMMON NORTH SIDE. SW4

Barry was the great master of the Italianate Revival in English architecture, the movement which used the forms of Italian Renaissance architecture in secular nineteenth-century buildings. Barry travelled in Italy as a young man and his work on the Travellers' Club in Pall Mall, and the Reform Club next door, shows the influence of the buildings he admired during his travels. Ironically, the building for which Barry is most famous is a prime example not of the Italianate Revival but of Victorian Gothic. When a competition was announced in 1835 for a new Houses of Parliament (the old buildings had been destroyed by fire the previous year) Barry would have preferred to submit designs for an Italianate building. However, the competition rules stipulated that the building could only be in a Gothic or Elizabethan style. Assisted by Augustus Pugin, the fanatical enthusiast for all things Gothic, Barry drew up the designs for what is now one of the great national symbols and a magnet for London's tourists.

## BARTÓK, BÉLA (1881–1945) *Hungarian composer, stayed here when performing in London*
7 SYDNEY PLACE, SW7

Born in Nagyszentmiklos in Hungary, Bartók was an infant prodigy on the piano, appearing for the first time in a public concert when only ten. He went on to study at Budapest Conservatory, where he was appointed Professor of the Piano in 1907, and the years before the First World War saw the start of his interest in the folk music of Eastern Europe. The rhythms and forms he found in these folk songs were to be adapted and incorporated into his own increasingly experimental and original compositions. Bartók's works include six string quartets, three piano concertos and the opera *Duke Bluebeard's Castle*. The difficulty of his work and the demands it made on the ear meant it did not easily gain a wide audience and Bartók continued to appear as a concert pianist throughout the twenties and thirties, including several visits to London. Driven into exile in America by the Nazi occupation of Hungary, Bartók died there in 1945.

## BASEVI, GEORGE (1794–1845) *architect, lived here*
17 SAVILE ROW, W1

The building for which Basevi is most famous is probably the Fitzwilliam Museum in Cambridge but he also had a major impact on the architecture of London in the late Regency and early Victorian periods. A cousin of Disraeli, Basevi studied under Sir John Soane, the architect of the Bank of England, and had soon established himself as an architect in demand. When Lord Grosvenor and the builder and entrepreneur Thomas Cubitt were planning to develop the land that came to be known as Belgravia it was to Basevi that they turned. Basevi also designed clubs in St James's, churches and country homes, often in the classical revival style which he also employed for the Fitzwilliam Museum. In 1845 Basevi was inspecting the bell-tower of Ely Cathedral, when he slipped and fell to his death.

## BATEMAN, H.M. (1887–1970) *cartoonist, lived here*
40 NIGHTINGALE LANE, SW12

One of this century's most prolific and distinctive cartoonists, Bateman is best known for his 'The Man Who . . .' series in which people react in horror to the social solecisms perpetrated by an innocent offender. The titles of the cartoons ('The Man Who Lit His Cigar Before the Royal Toast', 'The Man Who Threw A Snowball at St Moritz' etc.) show how dependent Bateman's humour was on a rigid code of manners that has been long outdated but, in the twenties and thirties, his work was immensely popular. Born in New South Wales, Bateman came to Britain with his family when he was a small child and grew up in suburban London. After studying for several years with an expatriate Dutch painter who had a studio in Earls Court, Bateman began to sell his cartoons to *Punch* and other periodicals and was soon launched on his career as a humorous illustrator that was to culminate in 'The Man Who . . .' series. By the 1940s Bateman's work seemed old-fashioned and he retired to the country to paint for his own pleasure and to write. He lived on until 1970, dying on the Maltese island of Gozo, which had been his home for several years.

## BAX, SIR ARNOLD (1883–1953) *composer, was born here*
13 PENDENNIS ROAD, STREATHAM, SW16

Bax was a prolific composer who worked in a variety of forms from symphony (he wrote seven between 1921 and 1939), to songs, to brief piano pieces. Although born a Londoner, Bax, as an artist, was attracted strongly to all things Irish and to all things Celtic. He wrote poetry and short stories set in Ireland under the name of Dermot O'Byrne and set poems by Yeats, Padraic Colum and other writers of the Irish literary revival to music. One of his best-known pieces, the tone poem *Tintagel*, also reflects his identification with the Celtic world. Bax was knighted in 1937, made Master of the King's Musick in 1942 and died in 1953 in Cork. It was Bax who originated the often-quoted advice that 'you should make a point of trying every experience once, except incest and folk-dancing', ascribing the words, in his autobiography, to a 'sympathetic Scot of my acquaintance'.

## BAYES, GILBERT (1872–1953) *sculptor, lived here 1931–1953*
### 4 GREVILLE PLACE, NW6

Room III in the Victoria & Albert Museum has another, more descriptive name. It is called 'The Gilbert Bayes Sculpture Gallery'. Of those who visit it, probably only a small percentage have heard of the man after whom it was named but Gilbert Bayes was once one of Britain's best-known and most admired sculptors. The son of a painter and etcher, Bayes studied at the Royal Academy Schools in the late 1890s and won a travelling scholarship which enabled him to spend time in both Paris and Rome. Returning to London, he set up his own sculptural studio which rapidly attracted a wide range of commissions. Bayes had a long-lasting association with the ceramics manufacturer Doulton and one of his finest works is a sculptural frieze entitled 'Pottery Through the Ages', which once adorned Doulton's London headquarters and is now in the V&A. Other works include a relief outside Lord's cricket ground and – perhaps his most familiar piece – the figure entitled 'Queen of Time', which supports the clock on the Oxford Street façade of Selfridges.

## BAYLIS, LILIAN (1874–1937) *manager of the Old Vic and Sadler's Wells theatres, lived and died here*
### 27 STOCKWELL PARK ROAD, SW9

Lilian Baylis's parents were both singers who emigrated to South Africa in 1890 and she first earned her living as a music teacher in Johannesburg. Returning to England in 1898 she joined her aunt, Emma Cons, in running the Old Vic, which was then a temperance music hall known as the Royal Victoria Hall and Coffee Tavern. When Emma Cons died in 1912, Lilian Baylis took sole charge of the Old Vic and turned it into one of the great theatres in London. Between 1914 and 1923 she oversaw new productions of all of Shakespeare's plays. She also supervised the rebuilding of Sadler's Wells theatre which opened in 1931 as a centre for the performance of opera and ballet. Lilian Baylis was famously committed to her work and expected all who joined her to be similarly dedicated. Sybil Thorndike, working at the Old Vic during the First World War, excused her late arrival at a performance by describing the Zeppelin raid that had held her up. 'Raid,' Lilian Baylis snapped, 'What's a raid when my curtain's up?'

## BAZALGETTE, SIR JOSEPH WILLIAM (1819–1891) *civil engineer, lived here*
### 17 HAMILTON TERRACE, ST JOHN'S WOOD, NW8

One of the greatest feats of Victorian engineering runs beneath the streets of London and it was the work of Sir Joseph Bazalgette. Bazalgette, the son of a Royal Navy Commander of French extraction, was appointed Chief Engineer to the Metropolitan Board of Works in 1855 and immediately set about the construction of a vast new drainage system for the capital. Finally completed in 1875, Bazalgette's network consisted of nearly 1,300 miles of sewers criss-crossing the city, 82 miles of which were main intercepting sewers. They remain at the core of today's system. Bazalgette also designed several of the bridges across the Thames, including Battersea Bridge and Hammersmith Bridge, and the construction of the Victoria and Chelsea Embankments was also part of his grand scheme of improvement for the city. Some of this work was undertaken at the same time as the expansion of the Underground system and Bazalgette had the frustration of building part of his new road by the Thames only to see it dug up a few years later so that railway track could be laid.

BEARD, JOHN (*c.*1717–1791) *singer and* WILLIAM EWART (1798–1869) *promoter of public libraries, lived here*

HAMPTON BRANCH LIBRARY, ROSE HILL, HAMPTON

John Beard was one of the leading figures in the eighteenth-century London theatre. Renowned particularly for his gifts as a singer, performing at Drury Lane, Covent Garden and in the pleasure gardens of Ranelagh and Vauxhall, Beard was also an actor and a theatre manager. In 1761 he took over the management of the Covent Garden theatre from his father-in-law, the celebrated pantomime artist John Rich. His six years there were not without their troubles. In 1763 the audience, enraged by the management's refusal to allow the customary half-price entry after a certain point in tthe evening's entertainment, nearly destroyed the theatre in a riot. Beard retired to Hampton and is buried in the churchyard there. He shares his plaque with the reforming MP and campaigner for public libraries, William Ewart.

BEARDSLEY, AUBREY (1872–1898) *artist, lived here*
114 CAMBRIDGE STREET, SW1

Beardsley's life and career, cut short by tuberculosis, may have been brief, but his output of work was prodigious and it was soon clear that he was one of the cultural figures who defined the 1890s. As early as 1896 Max Beerbohm was claiming that he belonged to 'the Beardsley period'. Beardsley first came to notice in 1893 with illustrations for an edition of Malory's *Morte D'Arthur* and he became a *succès de scandale* the following year as art editor of the infamous *Yellow Book* and illustrator of Oscar Wilde's play *Salome*. Both Beardsley and his work were often fiercely criticised on moral grounds. When one journalist described him as 'sexless and unclean', Beardsley wrote to his editor in reply, 'As to my uncleanliness, I do the best for it in my morning bath, and if he has really any doubts as to my sex, he may come and see me take it.' Beardsley died at Mentone in 1898, aged only twenty-five and a convert to Roman Catholicism.

BEAUCLERK, TOPHAM AND LADY DIANA
See under entry for ADELPHI TERRACE

BEAUFORT, SIR FRANCIS (1774–1857) *admiral and hydrographer, lived here*
51 MANCHESTER STREET, W1

Born in Ireland, the son of a clergyman, Beaufort joined the Navy in 1787. He saw much action during the Napoleonic wars and in one skirmish he received no less than nineteen wounds – three sword cuts and sixteen musket shots. Somehow surviving this determined effort to finish his career permanently, Beaufort began to show his particular gift for surveying. Between 1810 and 1812 he was in command of a mission to combine the surveying of the south coast of Turkey with the suppression of piracy in the area. This was brought to an abrupt end when some of the pirates, objecting to being suppressed, attacked Beaufort's ship and he was again seriously wounded. Beaufort was appointed hydrographer in 1829, a post he held until two years before his death. To this period of his life belongs his most lasting memorial, the Beaufort scale of wind force.

## BECKET, ST THOMAS A  *born in a house near this site*
86 CHEAPSIDE, EC2  **CITY OF LONDON**

Becket was the son of a wealthy merchant of Norman origins and entered the household of the Archbishop of Canterbury in his early twenties. Showing exceptional abilities, he came to the notice of Henry II who appointed him Chancellor in 1155. Until he became Archbishop of Canterbury himself seven years later, Becket had seemed a notably worldly man but, in his new role as the highest churchman in the land, he adopted a new asceticism and, to the fury of his king, began to meddle in the exceptionally complicated dynastic politics of the time. Tradition claims that Henry's unfortunate rhetorical question – 'Will no man rid me of this turbulent priest?' – sent four knights hastening to Canterbury to dispose of Becket. He was killed in the cathedral in a murder that shocked the Christian world, drove Henry to ever more elaborate acts of contrition and resulted in 1173 in the canonisation of Becket.

## BEECHAM, SIR THOMAS, CH (1879–1961) *conductor and impresario, lived here*
31 GROVE END ROAD, ST JOHN'S WOOD, NW8

The son of a millionaire who had made his money from Beecham's Pills, Sir Thomas Beecham began his career as a conductor at the Wigmore Hall in 1906. Over the next fifty years he became the most famous of British conductors, founder of both the London Philharmonic and the Royal Philharmonic Orchestras and the man largely responsible for popularising the music of such composers as Richard Strauss, Sibelius and Stravinsky in Britain. Sir Thomas also won a reputation as a wit, given to impromptu (and often uncomplimentary) pronouncements on music and musicians. Certainly he seems to have had a low opinion of the musical sophistication of his audiences. He once remarked, 'There are two golden rules for an orchestra: start together and finish together. The public doesn't give a damn what goes on in between.'

## BEERBOHM, SIR MAX (1872–1956) *artist and writer, born here*
57 PALACE GARDENS TERRACE, W8

'The Incomparable Max' was essayist, novelist, caricaturist, wit and parodist. He appeared on the London literary scene in the 1890s as a *wunderkind*, who ostentatiously called his very first volume of essays *The Works of Max Beerbohm*, and wrote, ironically, that at school he had been 'a modest good-humoured boy. It is Oxford that has made me insufferable.' He wrote for *The Yellow Book* and was associated with leading figures of the time such as Oscar Wilde and Aubrey Beardsley. Yet, whereas so many of the other cultural icons of the *fin-de-siècle* suffered from drink, disgrace or early death, Max Beerbohm marched confidently into the new century and ended his life in 1956 as a Grand Old Man of letters. He succeeded George Bernard Shaw as drama critic of *The Saturday Review* and held the position until 1910 when he married the American actress Florence Kahn and retired to a villa in Rapallo, Italy. There he wrote the fantastical and whimsical novel about Oxford undergraduate life, *Zuleika Dobson*, which remains his best-known work. Apart from the war years, Beerbohm spent the rest of his life in Rapallo.

## BELLO, ANDRES (1781–1865) *poet, jurist, philologist and Venezuelan patriot, lived here in 1810*

58 GRAFTON WAY, W1

Born in Caracas, Bello was the most remarkably wide-ranging Latin American intellectual of his day. As well as being the first important Venezuelan poet, he was also essayist, journalist and historian. A close friend of 'the Liberator' Simon Bolivar, he involved himself in his country's struggle for independence and was an influential voice among those canvassing for support from British politicians and governments. He spent the years from 1810 to 1829 in London. Returning to Venezuela, he continued his career as a polymathic writer and was the first Rector of the University in Caracas.

## BELLOC, HILAIRE (1870–1953) *poet, essayist and historian, lived here 1900–1905*

104 CHEYNE WALK, SW10

Born in France, of half-French parentage, Belloc was one of the most prolific and versatile writers of his time, producing dozens of volumes of poetry, fiction, travel-writing and fiercely opinionated essays. He collaborated so frequently with G.K. Chesterton, and their views were seen as so similar, that Bernard Shaw humorously imagined them as one composite creature, 'Chesterbelloc'. More rudely the poet T. Sturge Moore called them 'two buttocks of one bum'. Today Belloc is best remembered for his light verse, collected in such volumes as *Cautionary Tales* and *A Bad Child's Book of Beasts*. These introduced children (and adults) to, among many others, Lord Lundy who 'from his earliest years/Was far too freely moved to tears' and Matilda who 'told such dreadful lies/It made one gasp and stretch one's eyes.' During his time in Cheyne Walk Belloc was contemplating a political career and he was elected MP for Salford in 1906. He left party politics a few years later, disenchanted with the fudge and compromise required for success.

## BENEDICT, SIR JULIUS (1804–1885) *musical composer, lived and died here*

2 MANCHESTER SQUARE, W1

Like composers such as Handel and J.C. Bach in the previous century, Julius Benedict was born on the Continent but achieved his greatest success in Britain. He became a naturalised citizen and was knighted in 1871. As a teenager in Germany he had shown great promise and was introduced to Beethoven before studying for a period under Weber. Benedict's earliest operas were produced in Italian in the late 1820s and early 1830s and, after arriving in London in 1836, he embarked on a long career as both conductor and composer of operatic works. His most successful opera, based on a melodrama by Dion Boucicault, was *The Lily of Killarney*, perhaps a curious choice of subject for a native of Stuttgart. Benedict also wrote two symphonies, a piano concerto and many shorter works.

## BENES, DR EDWARD (1884–1948) *President of Czechoslovakia, lived here*

26 GWENDOLEN AVENUE, PUTNEY, SW15

Escaping an impoverished upbringing through education, Benes became a lecturer at Prague University and a close associate of T.G. Masaryk, the father of the independent Czech nation. Exiled from his country by the First World War, Benes helped Masaryk establish the Czecho-Slovak National Council in Paris and, when the nation first came into being after the war, he was made Foreign Minister of Czechoslovakia in 1918. He held this position for most of the twenties and thirties and eventually replaced the 85-year-old Masaryk as President in 1935. Nazi expansionism made a refugee out of Benes again and he had seven years of exile in Britain. The first two years were spent at the house of his nephew in Putney. In 1940 he was recognised as the head of the Czechoslovakian government in exile and moved to the embassy in Grosvenor Square. After the war Benes returned to his country as President but resigned after the Communists took control in 1948.

## BEN-GURION, DAVID (1886–1973) *first Prime Minister of Israel, lived here*
75 WARRINGTON CRESCENT, MAIDA VALE, W9

Born in Plonsk in what is today Poland, David Ben-Gurion hebraicised his original name of David Green and was, from an early age, a committed Zionist. Moving to settle in Palestine in 1906 he wrote back to his father, 'settling the land – that is the only real Zionism; everything else is only self-deception, empty verbiage and merely a pastime.' At a period when Zionist labour movements were of central importance to the cause, Ben-Gurion was Secretary-General of the General Federation of Labour, played a key role in the formation of Mapai, a political amalgamation of the major Labour groups, and, from 1935 to 1948, was Chairman of the Jewish Agency Executive, the settlement arm of the Zionist movement. When the state of Israel was created in 1948, the politically experienced Ben-Gurion was the clear choice for prime minister. He served two terms in the office, from 1948 to 1953 and from 1955 to 1963.

## BENNETT, ARNOLD (1867–1931) *novelist, lived here*
75 CADOGAN SQUARE, SW1

Bennett was born in Hanley in the heart of the Potteries, the setting for much of his best fiction, and moved to London in 1888. During the 1890s he gradually established a reputation as a writer and in 1902 *Anna of the Five Towns* became his first major critical success. Other novels set in the Potteries followed (*The Old Wives' Tale*, *Clayhanger*) but Bennett himself had become a metropolitan figure who lived in London and Paris for the rest of his life. In later years he was invited by Beaverbrook to write a regular column for *The Evening Standard*, through which he became the most powerful and influential book reviewer of the time. Bennett died of typhoid, allegedly contracted in France, when he had drunk a glass of suspiciously murky water in order to demonstrate the perfect safety of the nation's water supply.

## BENNETT, SIR WILLIAM STERNDALE (1816–1875) *composer, lived here*
38 QUEENSBOROUGH TERRACE, W2

Born in Sheffield, Sterndale Bennett was a musical prodigy who entered the Royal Academy of Music as a ten-year-old and, as a teenager, wrote a piano concerto that won praise from the likes of Mendelssohn and Robert Schumann. Indeed, Schumann later dedicated one of his own collections of piano pieces to Sterndale Bennett. In the 1830s music continued to pour out of Bennett, including several more concertos and symphonies, but by the 1840s his inspiration seemed to have failed him and he turned to conducting, playing (he was a brilliant pianist) and teaching. He became Professor of Music at Cambridge and later principal of the academy he had attended as a precocious ten-year-old. Only in the last decade and a half of his life did he begin to compose again when he produced cantatas and a further symphony.

## BENSON, E.F. (1867–1940) *writer, lived here*
25 BROMPTON SQUARE, SW1

The son of an archbishop of Canterbury, Benson had two brothers who also became writers. A.C. Benson was a writer of biography and memoir who also produced the words for 'Land of Hope and Glory'. R.H. Benson wrote many novels and, a convert to Roman Catholicism, apologetics for his new faith. Edward Frederic Benson was as prolific a writer as his brothers and, like theirs, his work was largely forgotten until a sequence of light, comic novels was rediscovered and dramatisations of them televised. His 'Mapp and Lucia' series, which began with the publication of *Queen Lucia* in 1920, found a new audience. Benson never married and never had a close relationship with anyone of either sex. Even his brother Arthur, not a notably passionate man himself, found him a strangely passive person. He had, Arthur said, 'never lived his life at all; only stayed with it and lunched with it.'

## BENTHAM, GEORGE (1800–1884) *botanist, lived here*
25 WILTON PLACE, BELGRAVIA, SW1

The nephew of the philosopher Jeremy Bentham, George Bentham was a precociously gifted child who was able to read Latin, French, German and Russian before he was 10 and had even taken the opportunity offered by his family's stay in Sweden to study the language of that country. He was eventually able to read botanical works in fourteen different European languages. A logician who wrote *Outlines of a New System of Logic* as a young man, Bentham then devoted his intellectual energies for more than fifty years to the study of botany. While living at Wilton Place he travelled daily to Kew to examine and describe scientifically the thousands of plant specimens from around the world which were sent there. The result was the monumental *Genera Plantarum*, which he compiled with Sir Joseph Hooker and which was published over a twenty-year period. Bentham also wrote a *Handbook of the British Flora* for a less specialised readership.

## BENTLEY, JOHN FRANCIS (1839–1902) *architect, lived here*
43 OLD TOWN, CLAPHAM, SW4

Bentley was a Roman Catholic and his finest work as an architect is Westminster Cathedral, which he was commissioned to design in 1894. The foundation stone of the new Catholic cathedral was laid the following year. Bentley was born in Doncaster and was, at first, apprenticed to a firm of mechanical engineers. However his exceptional gifts as a draughtsman were soon recognised and he was invited to join the offices of an ecclesiastical architect. Throughout his career Bentley worked almost exclusively on church architecture. As well as the cathedral he produced major churches in Watford and Bayswater and, after Westminster Cathedral had been started, he was invited to New York to advise on the construction of a new cathedral in Brooklyn. In addition to his architectural design Bentley took an interest in other applied arts including stained glass and metal-work.

## BERESFORD, JACK (1899–1977) *Olympic rowing champion lived here 1903–1940*
19 GROVE PARK GARDENS, W4

Jack Beresford was one of the great Olympians of his era. Like Sir Steven Redgrave, he won medals in rowing events at five consecutive Olympics, although the older champion could manage only three golds and two silvers, whereas Redgrave won five straight golds. None the less, Beresford was the dominant personality in his sport for most of the 1920s and 1930s. In the notorious 1936 Olympics held in Berlin, often known as Hitler's Olympics, he was chosen to carry the flag for the British team in the opening ceremony. The son of Julius Beresford, who had himself won a silver medal in the rowing events at the 1912 Olympics, he fought and was wounded in France in the last year of the First World War. After the war, he joined his father's furniture-making firm. He took his first medal at the games of 1920, where he came second to John B. Kelly (later the father of Hollywood star and future princess Grace Kelly) in one of the most exciting single scull races of all time. Beresford went on to compete in the next four Olympics and would almost certainly have taken part in the 1940 Games had they not been cancelled because of the Second World War.

---

## BERLIOZ, HECTOR (1803–1869) *composer, stayed here in 1851*
### 58 QUEEN ANNE STREET, W1

The greatest of French romantic composers, Berlioz was much inspired by English literature. The overpowering impact of Shakespeare on his imagination was enhanced by the equally overpowering impact made on him by the actress Harriet Smithson, whom he first saw as Ophelia in an 1827 performance of *Hamlet*. Some years later the two married but, offstage, the magic was not quite the same for Berlioz and the marriage was not a happy one. Shakespeare remained a permanent influence, however, and *Roméo et Juliette* and *Béatrice et Bénédict* are among a number of Berlioz's works that have a direct Shakespearean source. Berlioz visited England several times and his stay in 1851 was as the French judge of musical instruments at the Great Exhibition. It was not a job he found congenial. 'It splits your head,' he wrote, 'to hear these hundreds of wretched machines, each more out of tune than the next.'

---

## BERNAL, JOHN DESMOND (1901–1971) *crystallographer, lived and died here*
### 44 ALBERT STREET, NW1

Known as 'Sage' by his peers because of his extraordinarily wide-ranging knowledge and interests. Bernal was born in Ireland to an American mother and a father who could trace his family back through the generations to Sephardic Jews living in Spain. Educated at the Catholic school of Stonyhurst and then Cambridge, Bernal was a brilliant mathematician and physicist but his most original work was in biology. He established X-ray crystallography as an important tool for biological study and opened up a field of research that proved to be of major significance to later biologists. During the war, Bernal's well-known communism might have stood in the way of his employment by the government, but one minister was so impressed by his intellect that he said he wanted him 'even if he was as red as the flames of hell'. Some of his ideas were more fanciful than others – he worked for a while on a project to create artificial icebergs for use as aircraft carriers – but his work on the impact of bomb damage and on the Mulberry harbours used for the D-Day landings was of major importance to the war effort. Although he left the Communist Party in 1934, Bernal remained a committed Marxist throughout his life, firmly believing that it was the creed that offered a truly 'scientific' analysis of society and its future.

---

## BESANT, ANNIE (1847–1933) *social reformer, lived here in 1874*
### 39 COLBY ROAD, SE19

In her long life Annie Besant was the fervent advocate of many causes. She became the sister-in-law of the writer Walter Besant but left her clergyman husband, who treated her brutally, to join Charles Bradlaugh in his campaigns against religion and for birth control. She was tried with Bradlaugh for the publication of a pamphlet which, the prosecution claimed, was indecently specific in its description of contraceptive methods. Converted to Socialism, Annie Besant, whom George Bernard Shaw described as 'the greatest orator in England', spoke out on behalf of the Bryant and May match-girls when they went on strike in 1888 and helped them organise for victory. Soon afterwards her innate mysticism surfaced and, led by a voice that advised her to 'Take courage for the light is near', she found her next cause in Theosophy, the strange variant of Eastern religion devised by Madame Blavatsky. Driven by her new faith Annie Besant moved to India, where she spent much of the rest of her life, and became an enthusiastic supporter of Indian nationalism.

## BESANT, SIR WALTER (1836–1901) *novelist and antiquary, lived and died here*
FROGNAL END, FROGNAL GARDENS, NW3

Besant was one of those prodigiously energetic Victorians whose achievements were many and various. Primarily he was a writer. In the 1870s he collaborated with James Rice on a number of novels, including the quaintly titled *Ready Money Mortiboy*, a bestselling story of an unrepentant prodigal son. Rice died young in 1882 but Besant went on to write novels on his own that highlighted his concern for social justice and the plight of the East End poor. One of these, *All Sorts and Conditions of Men*, contained the seeds of the idea for the People's Palace, a centre for social, educational and recreational facilities, which was opened in the Mile End Road in 1887. In 1884 Besant founded the Society of Authors, which continues to fight for the rights and interests of authors. He also wrote historical biographies and, in the 1890s, began an enormous survey of London's history, volumes of which continued to be published after his death.

## BESTALL, ALFRED (1892–1986) *illustrator of Rupert Bear, lived here 1936–1966*
58 CRANES PARK, SURBITON, KT5

Alfred Bestall did not create Rupert Bear, who was the brainchild of the artist Mary Tourtel, but he took over responsibility for illustrating the strip in the *Daily Express* in 1935. He continued to write and draw the stories for the next thirty years and to provide occasional illustrations for Rupert annuals for much longer. It was Alfred Bestall who expanded the scope of Rupert's adventures in Nutwood and made them a national institution. The son of a Methodist missionary, he was born in Mandalay in Burma, far from the typically British landscapes he drew so often for the Rupert strips. Sent back to Britain for his schooling, he went on to study art in Birmingham and London before a burgeoning career as an illustrator was interrupted by service in the First World War. From the 1920s onwards, Bestall illustrated books for both children and adults, and his cartoons and drawings appeared in magazines such as *Punch* and *The Tatler* but it is his Rupert Bear strips that will always be remembered. Most of these were drawn while Bestall was living in the suburban house in Surbiton which now carries his Blue Plaque. He retired to north Wales, an area of Britain he had long loved and died in a nursing home there at the age of ninety-three.

## BETJEMAN, SIR JOHN (1906–1984) *poet, lived here 1908–1917*
31 HIGHGATE WEST HILL, HIGHGATE, N6

## BETJEMAN, SIR JOHN (1906–1984) *Poet Laureate, lived here*
43 CLOTH FAIR, EC1  **PRIVATE**

'Too many people in the modern world view poetry as a luxury, not a necessity like petrol,' John Betjeman said not long after being appointed Poet Laureate in 1972, 'But to me it's the oil of life.' Throughout Betjeman's life, he was as committed to his vocation as a poet as many more solemn and serious writers, but he also became famous and much-loved for his sense of fun and his love of architecture, railways and the unsung delights of the London suburbs. Born in north London into a family of Dutch origin, he studied at Oxford but left without a degree. He worked on *The Architectural Review* in the 1930s and began publishing volumes of his poetry in the same decade. For the rest of his life, he earned his living from his journalism and his verse.

He once gave his occupation in *Who's Who* as 'poet and hack'. In his later years, both before and after his appointment as Poet Laureate, he gained wider fame through his campaigns to preserve threatened historic buildings and through his appearances on TV. A statue of John Betjeman was unveiled at St Pancras Station when it was re-opened in 2007 to commemorate his role in saving it from closure forty years earlier. The previous year the plaque placed on his childhood home in Highgate had been but one of the ways in which the centenary of his birth was marked.

........................................................................................................................

## BEVAN, ROBERT POLHILL (1865–1925) *Camden Town Group painter, lived here 1900–1925*

### 14 ADAMSON ROAD, NW3

Bevan moved to Adamson Road with his Polish wife Stanislawa in 1900, and lived there for the rest of his life. Born in Hove, Bevan travelled extensively as a young man and painted in places as diverse as North Africa and Brittany, where he knew and worked with Paul Gauguin. He married Stanislawa in Warsaw in 1897. Once settled in London, Bevan became a familiar figure in the capital's artistic circles. He was a member of the group of painters known as the Fitzroy Street Group and was a founder, with other artists such as Walter Sickert and Spencer Gore, of the Camden Town Group, which held three joint exhibitions in 1911 and 1912. Although he is best known for his scenes of London street life, Bevan also painted many landscapes during frequent stays in Devon and Cornwall. He continued to visit Poland regularly – on one occasion he was even arrested by Tsarist police as an alleged spy – and retained his links with the French art world. In 1921 he and his friend and fellow artist Charles Ginner organised an exhibition called *Peintres Modernes Anglais* at the well-known Galerie Druet in Paris. In 1925 Bevan was taken ill while staying in Devon and died in St Thomas's Hospital, London, a few weeks later.

........................................................................................................................

## BEVIN, ERNEST (1881–1951) *Trade Union leader and statesman, lived here in Flat No. 8, 1931–1951*

### 34 SOUTH MOULTON STREET, W1

One of the architects of the twentieth-century British trade unionism and a leading figure in both Churchill's War Cabinet and Attlee's Labour government of 1945–1951, Ernest Bevin was born in Somerset and began hi union career in Bristol. When, in the early 1920s, more than thirty smaller unions combined to form the giant Transport and General Workers Union, Bevin was elected as its general secretary, a post he held for nearly twenty years. When Churchill invited him to join the War Cabinet as Minister of Labour in 1940, Bevin was not even a member of parliament (although he had stood unsuccessfully in several elections from as early as 1918) but a month later he won a by-election in Wandsworth and entered the Commons. He became one of the most important members of the War Cabinet and, after Labour's landslide victory in 1945, he was appointed Foreign Secretary. In the difficult post-war years he was instrumental in the creation of NATO and cementing relations between America and Europe but, by the early 1950s, poor health caught up with him. He resigned from the Attlee government in March 1951 and died a month later. Bevin was renowned as a pugnacious and robust political fighter. When told that a cabinet colleague with whom he was at loggerheads was 'his own worst enemy', Bevin was swift to respond – 'Not while I'm alive, he ain't'.

........................................................................................................................

## BLACKIE, DR MARGERY (1898–1981) *homeopathic physician, lived and worked here 1929–1980*

### 18 THURLOE STREET, SW7

Homeopathy has often been a controversial branch of medicine, with many doctors and scientists denying its efficacy, but it had no greater or more able champion in the twentieth century than Dr Margery Blackie. Dr Blackie qualified as a doctor at the Royal Free Hospital's School of Medicine for Women in 1923 and joined the staff of the London Homeopathic Hospital in Great Ormond Street the following year. With another homeopath, she went on to establish a private practice in Kensington, first at Drayton Gardens and then in Thurloe Street. The building in Thurloe Street was both Dr Blackie's home and her consulting rooms for more than half a century. The high point of her career and the culmination of a lifetime spent caring for the sick came in 1969 when she received an appointment as an official Physician to the Queen. She was the first woman to receive the honour. She was already in her seventies when she was given the royal appointment but she continued to see private patients for another decade until she herself became too ill to work. Her chief legacy is the Blackie Foundation Trust, established after her death 'to promote research and awareness of homeopathy and its benefits'.

......................................................................................................................

## BLAKE, WILLIAM
See under entry for JOHN LINNELL

......................................................................................................................

## BLIGH, WILLIAM (1754–1817) *Commander of the 'Bounty', lived here*
100 LAMBETH ROAD, SE1

## WILLIAM BLIGH (1754–1817) *who transplanted breadfruit from Tahiti to the West Indies, lived in a house on this site 1785–90*
REARDON STREET, E1   **HISTORY OF WAPPING TRUST**

Bligh is remembered as the captain whose ship was seized in what has become the most famous mutiny in British naval history. The *Bounty* was sent to Tahiti to transport breadfruit plants to the West Indies but a six-month stay amidst the varied pleasures of the Pacific island left Bligh's men unenthusiastic about the rigours of the return journey. On 28 April 1789 they mutinied, led by Fletcher Christian, the ship's second-in-command. Set adrift by the mutineers in a 23-foot-long open boat, given few provisions and no chart, Bligh, together with eighteen men who had remained loyal to him, sailed more than three and a half thousand miles to the Dutch colonies in the East Indies. Bligh may not have been the sadist of popular imagination but he must have, undoubtedly, been a poor manager of men. Later in his career, as Governor of New South Wales, he was again the target of mutinous subordinates who had him arrested. He is buried at St Mary-at-Lambeth, now the Museum of Garden History.

......................................................................................................................

## BLISS, SIR ARTHUR (1891–1975) *composer, lived here 1929–1939*
EAST HEATH LODGE, 1 EAST HEATH ROAD, NW3

Bliss was one of the most versatile English composers of this century who used a variety of media to express his musical ideas. As well as concertos for piano and cello, chamber music and cantatas, he wrote ballets (*Checkmate* and *Miracle in the Gorbals*), film scores, most famously for the 1936 film of H.G. Wells's *Things to Come*, and music for radio and television. One of his most striking works is the choral symphony *Morning Heroes*, written in 1930 as a tribute to the men who died in the First World War, a war in which Bliss himself served. After that war he rapidly gained his reputation as an innovative composer and was invited to spend considerable periods of time working in the US. He was in the States when the Second World War broke out and did not return to Britain until 1941 when he took a job at the BBC. He became Director of Music there the following year. Knighted in 1950, Bliss succeeded Bax as Master of the Queen's Musick three years later.

*In a house on this site lived* ROBERT BLOOMFIELD (1766–1823) *poet*
KENT HOUSE, TELEGRAPH STREET, EC2   **CITY OF LONDON**

Born in Suffolk, Bloomfield worked as a farm labourer before moving to London in an effort to make his living as a shoemaker and to write. *The Farmer's Boy*, written while he was living in the poet's traditional residence, a garret, caught a vogue for verse about rustic life. Published in 1800, with illustrations by the wood engraver Bewick, it was a huge success. Although Charles Lamb, writing to a friend, claimed, 'I have just opened him but he makes me sick', Bloomfield found many more sympathetic readers and the book was translated into several European languages. He was unable to repeat the success of *The Farmer's Boy* with his other work and he died, half-blind and wretchedly poor, in a Bedfordshire village.

BLUMLEIN, ALAN DOWER (1903–1942) *electronics engineer and inventor, lived here*
37 THE RIDINGS, W5

Although his name is not well known, Alan Dower Blumlein made a very significant contribution to Britain's war effort in the first years of the Second World War. This electronics engineer was responsible for the 'in-flight' radar system used by Bomber Command which guided the aircraft to their targets. In 1942 he was testing improvements to the system when the Halifax bomber in which he was a passenger crashed and Blumlein and his colleagues were killed.

BLYTON, ENID (1897–1968) *children's writer, lived here 1920–1924*
207 HOOK ROAD, CHESSINGTON

ENID BLYTON, *children's author*
83, SHORTLANDS ROAD, BROMLEY   **BOROUGH OF BROMLEY**

BLYTON, ENID (1897–1968) *popular writer of over 700 books for children*
354 LORDSHIP LANE, SE22   **SOUTHWARK COUNCIL**

Despite the reservations and criticisms often expressed about her books by parents and librarians, Enid Blyton remains, over forty years after her death, one of the most popular of all writers among children themselves. Born in London, Enid Blyton went to school in Beckenham where, like the heroines of her future school fiction, she was head girl and captain of games. She trained as a teacher and was working in Hook Road as a nursery governess when she wrote her first book, *Child Whispers*. This was the start of a phenomenal career in which she wrote more than 700 books, had worldwide sales of 200 million in her lifetime and created characters such as Noddy, the Secret Seven and the Famous Five who have been loved by generations of children. She once described how these characters came to her. 'I shut my eyes for a few minutes,' she wrote in a letter, 'with my portable typewriter on my knee – I make my mind a blank and wait – and then, as clearly as I would see real children, my characters stand before me in my mind's eye. I see them in detail – hair, eyes, feet, clothes, expression – and I always know their Christian names but never their surnames. (I get those out of a telephone directory afterwards!)'

BODLEY, GEORGE FREDERICK (1827–1907) *Gothic architect, lived here 1862–1873*
109 HARLEY STREET, W1

In the second half of the nineteenth century, the Gothic Revival style dominated church architecture in Britain and George Frederick Bodley was one of its leading exponents.

He trained under Sir George Gilbert Scott (architect of St Pancras Station) and it was while articled to Scott that he first adopted the principles which led to his becoming the leading ecclesiastical architect of the late Victorian era. Bodley's churches can be found all over Britain, from Liverpool to Brighton, and also very much further afield – he designed a cathedral built in Hobart, Tasmania – but some of his finest buildings are in London. St Michael's in Camden Town and Holy Trinity, South Kensington are two surviving examples of Bodley's London churches. Bodley was not only an architect but also a published poet and a designer of everything from wallpapers to church furnishings. He was a friend to many of the second generation of Pre-Raphaelites and William Morris and Edward Burne-Jones received a number of their earliest commissions for stained glass through him.

## BOLIVAR, SIMON (1783–1830) *liberator of Latin America, lodged here in 1810*
4 DUKE STREET, W1

'The art of winning', Simon Bolivar once said, 'is learned in defeat' and, in the course of the turbulent ups and down of his astonishing career, he had plenty of occasions to reflect on the truth of his maxim. Known as 'El Libertador', Bolivar played the leading role in liberating six present-day South American republics from Spain's colonial rule and, at different times in his life, was an all-powerful dictator and a fugitive from the Spanish authorities. Born into a family of Venezuelan aristocrats, he travelled to Spain in his teens and there met the woman who became his wife. She died after only a year of marriage and Bolivar, although only twenty years old when widowed, never married again. The bereaved Bolivar returned to Europe several times and it was on one of these trips, carried out to seek diplomatic support for the idea of Venezuelan independence, that he lodged briefly in Duke Street. Back in South America, he began his career as a general commanding the troops fighting for independence and, over the next few years, he experienced both remarkable victories and disastrous defeats. The early 1820s saw Bolivar's greatest achievements as first Venezuela, then Ecuador and Peru were liberated by his armies. In 1825 the Congress of Upper Peru created a new republic named Bolivia in his honour. Two years later all that he had created was under threat as internecine fighting between rival generals tore the new republics apart. Bolivar survived a major assassination attempt in 1828 but died two years later, worn out by tuberculosis and by the stresses of the factional warfare that independence had brought.

## BOMBERG, DAVID (1890–1957) *painter, lived and worked here 1928–1934*
10 FORDWYCH ROAD, NW2

'I look upon nature while I live in a steel city,' Bomberg wrote in the catalogue for his first one-man show and there is a tension between the aggressively modern and the pastoral in all his work. Born in Birmingham, Bomberg studied at the Slade and then travelled to Paris where he met the leading avant-garde artists including Picasso and Modigliani. His greatest success as a painter came just before the First World War when he was associated with Wyndham Lewis's Vorticist Movement and, during the war, when he was an effective, if unconventional, war artist. In the twenties and thirties Bomberg travelled widely, in Palestine and Spain, Morocco and Russia, and his work often reflects these travels.

## BONAR LAW, ANDREW (1858–1923) *Prime Minister, lived here*
24 ONSLOW GARDENS, SW7

After Andrew Bonar Law had died and been buried in Westminster Abbey, Asquith said of him, 'It is fitting that we should have buried the Unknown Prime Minister by the side of the Unknown Soldier.' Bonar Law served only seven months as Prime Minister, retiring because of ill health in May 1923 and dying in October of the same year. He had been born in Canada but moved to Glasgow to complete his education and became a leading figure in the industrial life of that city. He became MP for one of the Glasgow constituencies in 1900 and, when Balfour resigned as leader of the Tories in 1911, Bonar Law, even though he had never sat in a Cabinet, was the compromise candidate for new leader. He served in coalition governments throughout most of the First World War, including a period as Chancellor of the Exchequer under Lloyd George, the man he later succeeded for his brief time as Prime Minister.

---

## BONHAM-CARTER, LADY VIOLET, BARONESS ASQUITH OF YARNBURY
(1887–1969) *politician and writer, lived here*

43 GLOUCESTER SQUARE, W2

The daughter of the Liberal Prime Minister, Violet Asquith married the scientist and civil servant Sir Maurice Bonham-Carter in 1915. Throughout her life she was a prominent figure in the Liberal party (she was the President of the Liberal party Organization at the end of the Second World War) and a member of the cultural great and good. During the war years she was a governor of the BBC. She wrote a number of books of memoirs, including a personal study of Winston Churchill, and was created a life peeress in 1964. Her last reported words before she died were the splendidly enigmatic 'I feel amphibious.'

---

## BONN, LEO (1850–1929) *founded the Royal National Institute for Deaf People here*
9 June 1911

22 UPPER BROOK STREET, W1   **WESTMINSTER**

In 1911 Leo Bonn, a wealthy banker, was experiencing severe problems with his hearing and received lessons in lip reading. He began to gain new insights into the difficulties against which the deaf battled and was particularly moved by a visit he paid to a school for deaf children in Stoke. Bonn persuaded the school's owner to join with him to create an organisation intended to promote the interests of the deaf, and the inaugural meeting of the National Bureau for the Deaf was held in the dining room of Bonn's house in Upper Brook Street on 9 June 1911. The new organisation, with Bonn as its President until 1914, grew and was renamed the Royal National Institute for the Deaf in 1924. Leo Bonn died five years later.

---

## BOOTH, CHARLES (1840–1916) *pioneer in social research, lived here*
6 GRENVILLE PLACE, SW7

A wealthy shipowner from Liverpool, Booth moved to London in his thirties and soon began what was to be his life's work, the vast *Life and Labour of the People of London* which appeared in seventeen volumes between 1891 and 1902. 'As there is a darkest Africa, is there not also a darkest England?' Booth asked, with a rhetorical flourish, and his work was intended to shine the light of statistical science on this darkness. Dividing London into eight social classes, four above the poverty line and four below, Booth set out to analyse the structure of society as precisely as he could, based on on-the-spot investigations and case studies. One of the results of his work was a series of street maps, still fascinating today, which use different colours to denote different classes living in close proximity in the Victorian metropolis.

---

## BOROUGH, STEPHEN AND WILLIAM
See under entry for SIR HUGH WILLOUGHBY

## BORROW, GEORGE (1803–1881) *author, lived here*
### 22, HEREFORD SQUARE, SW7

One of the more extraordinary personalities of the nineteenth century, George Borrow was writer, linguist, boxer, horseman, prodigious traveller and unrestrained romantic. Born in Norfolk, he was briefly articled to a solicitor before travelling and studying in England, France, Germany, Russia and the East. For five years in the 1830s he distributed Bibles for the British and Foreign Bible Society in the war zone that was Spain at the time. Throughout his travels Borrow claimed particular affinity with the Romany peoples and his best-known books, *Lavengro* and *The Romany Rye*, tell of his adventures among them. He lived in London throughout the 1860s but retired to East Anglia on the death of his wife in 1872. Borrow could not always readily distinguish fact from fiction and he may well have exaggerated both his linguistic attainments and his insider's knowledge of the gypsies. However, his books retain a picaresque charm and liveliness.

## BOSWELL, JAMES (1740–1795) *biographer, lived and died in a house on this site*
### 122 GREAT PORTLAND STREET, W1

In his great biography of Dr Johnson, Boswell himself remarks, 'I own, Sir, the spirits I have in London make me do everything with more readiness and vigour.' Although he was born in Scotland and obliged to spend a good deal of time in Edinburgh, where he unenthusiastically practised the law, Boswell loved the drama and excitement of London, which he visited as often as he could. When he first met Dr Johnson in 1763, at Davies's bookshop in Covent Garden, Boswell was lodging in Downing Street and taking full advantage of the opportunities London offered – drinking, womanising, sightseeing, playgoing and then drinking some more. Over the next twenty years Boswell, in his sojourns in the capital, recorded his conversations with Johnson and the final result was *The Life of Dr Johnson*, first published in 1791. By that time Boswell had deserted the Scottish law circuit and moved permanently to London, where he lived at a house in Great Portland Street, increasingly suffering from depression and the consequences of years of heavy drinking.

See also under entry for DR SAMUEL JOHNSON

## BOULT, SIR ADRIAN, CH (1889–1983) *conductor, lived at Flat No. 78 1966–1977*
### MARLBOROUGH MANSIONS, CANNON HILL, NW6

Adrian Boult studied at Christ Church, Oxford, and in Leipzig with the celebrated Hungarian conductor Arthur Nikisch, before making his debut at Covent Garden in 1914. His debut as an orchestral conductor came four years later. He was still conducting regularly when he was in his nineties. In that lifetime in front of an orchestra he was a particular champion of English music and gave the first performances of a number of works by Vaughan Williams. He was the first conductor of the BBC Symphony Orchestra when it was formed in 1930. In the twenty years before his reluctant departure from the orchestra he shaped much of the BBC's musical policy and gave the orchestra a worldwide reputation. He moved on to the London Philharmonic Orchestra where he was principal conductor from 1950 to 1957 and President from 1965.

## BOW STREET *was formed about 1637. It has been the residence of many notable men, among whom were:* HENRY FIELDING (1707–1754), *novelist;* SIR JOHN FIELDING (*d.* 1780), *magistrate;* GRINLING GIBBONS (1648–1721), *wood carver;* CHARLES MACKLIN (1697?–1797), *actor;* JOHN RADCLIFFE (1650–1714), *physician;* CHARLES

SACKVILLE, EARL OF DORSET (1638-1706), *poet; and* WILLIAM WYCHERLEY (1640?-1716), *dramatist.*

19-20 BOW STREET, WC2

Built in the shape of a bow, Bow Street was described at the end of the seventeenth century as 'well inhabited and resorted unto by gentry for lodgings.' Henry Fielding was a magistrate as well as a novelist and, with his half-brother Sir John Fielding, was responsible for the formation of a group of thief-takers who became known as the Bow Street Runners. Grinling Gibbons's work can be seen in St Paul's and in many of the great houses of England, from Chatsworth to Burghley. Charles Macklin was an Irishman who became one of the most celebrated of eighteenth-century actors, particularly impressive in his portrayal of Shylock. He survived a murder trial for killing a fellow actor in a quarrel and was still performing in his nineties. Radcliffe was a Yorkshireman who was the most respected physician of his day, attending the royal family on many occasions. He left bequests that helped establish the Radcliffe Library in Oxford. Sackville was a notoriously dissipated nobleman and favourite of Charles II, who was a patron of poets and himself wrote satirical and lyrical verse. Wycherley, one of the best-known Restoration dramatists, wrote the comedies *The Country Wife* and *The Plain Dealer.*

---

BRADLAUGH, CHARLES (1833-1891) *advocate of free thought, lived here 1870-1877*

29 TURNER STREET, E1

Bradlaugh, a journalist and freethinker, was at the centre of two of the more notable controversies of Victorian England. In 1876, in company with Mrs Besant (later the leader of the Theosophist Movement), he was put on trial for publishing a banned pamphlet called *The Fruits of Philosophy*, which advocated birth control. A heavy prison sentence, later quashed on appeal, was handed out to him. In 1880 Bradlaugh was returned as Radical MP for Northampton and was invited to take the standard oath on entering the House of Commons. A fervent atheist, Bradlaugh refused and was promptly escorted from the premises. Over the next several years Bradlaugh made many attempts to take his seat amidst unparliamentary scenes of uproar and he was led forcibly from the house on a number of occasions. The ridiculous stand-off between Bradlaugh and parliamentary tradition only came to an end when a new Speaker was appointed in 1886 who allowed the rebel merely to affirm his allegiance to the House rather than take an oath upon it.

---

BRAILSFORD, HENRY NOEL (1873-1958) *writer, champion of equality and free humanity, lived here*

37 BELSIZE PARK GARDENS, NW3

Throughout his life as a writer, journalist and political activist, Brailsford was motivated by a belief in the power of socialism and international cooperation to improve the world. He was teaching philosophy at Glasgow University when, in 1897, he travelled to join the Greek Foreign Legion in the war against Turkey. This experience of warfare, which he described in a book called *The Broom of the War God*, affected him profoundly. He joined the Independent Labour party in 1907 and was an influential and respected voice of the Left for the rest of his life, editing Labour publications and providing leader columns for newspapers such as the *Manchester Guardian* and the *Daily Herald*. As a historian he published widely but was an acknowledged expert on the radical movements of the English Civil War. His book *The Levellers and the English Revolution* remains of value.

## BRAIN, DENNIS (1921–1957) *horn-player, lived here*
### 37 FROGNAL, HAMPSTEAD, NW3

Dennis Brain's career was one of great promise dazzlingly fulfilled and then tragically cut short. He came from a family of horn-players. His father was professor of the instrument at the Royal Academy of Music and principal horn in the BBC Symphony Orchestra for many years. His uncle played for Sir Henry Wood and later moved to America as principal horn in the Los Angeles Philharmonic. Dennis Brain was prodigiously gifted and Benjamin Britten wrote his *Serenade for Tenor, Horn and Strings* especially for him and Peter Pears when Brain was still only in his early twenties. Other contemporary composers, including Hindemith and Malcolm Arnold, wrote pieces for him and he was already acclaimed as the finest horn-player in Europe when he was killed in a car crash in Hertfordshire, aged only thirty-six.

## BRANGWYN, SIR FRANK (1867–1956) *artist, lived here*
### TEMPLE LODGE, 51 QUEEN CAROLINE STREET, W6

Brangwyn was a versatile artist who became a well-known figure in the art world of the 1890s and early 1900s and then, in the course of a long life, rather faded from view. Only recently has the variety and vigour of his work been rediscovered. Born in Bruges, the son of an architect and craftsman, Brangwyn moved back to London with his family in 1875 and, while still in his teens, was working for William Morris's company and submitting paintings to the Royal Academy summer exhibition. He went on to become a skilled practitioner in many media. He was a fine illustrator and draughtsman, a painter in oils who used colour and light to great effect, a watercolourist and etcher. Perhaps his most notable works were the large-scale murals he created for such places as Skinners' Hall and the House of Lords. Brangwyn was elected an RA in 1919 and was knighted in 1941, by which time he had become a rather unjustly neglected figure in the art world.

## BRIDGE, FRANK (1879–1941) *composer and musician, lived here*
### 4 BEDFORD GARDENS, W8

Bridge was born in Brighton and entered the Royal College of Music in 1896 to study violin and piano, later winning a scholarship to pursue further studies in composition under Sir Charles Stanford. After graduating in 1903 Bridge spent the next twenty years dividing his energies between a successful career as a viola-player in such groups as the English String Quartet, regular appearances as a conductor with a number of orchestras and his own work as a composer. Many of Bridge's most lastingly popular music, works such as the suite *The Sea* and his string sextet, belong to this period when he was juggling three different musical careers. In 1922 he met millionaire patron of the arts Elizabeth Sprague Coolidge and, with her financial assistance, Bridge was able to retire to the quiet of a Sussex village and devote himself more exclusively to composing. During these years a young Benjamin Britten studied composition with him before going to the Royal College of Music. Bridge died in 1941 in the midst of work on a large-scale piece for string orchestra, which remained unfinished.

## BRIDGEMAN, CHARLES *landscape gardener, lived here 1723–1738*
### 54 BROADWICK STREET, SOHO, W1

Bridgeman became Royal Gardener in 1728, in succession to Henry Wise. With Wise, Bridgeman had earlier done much to lay out areas of Kensington Gardens and he was also responsible for work at country houses such as Marble Hill House in Twickenham. Perhaps his most distinctive and influential work was carried out with the Earl of

Burlington and the architect William Kent at the Earl's palladian villa in Chiswick. They combined to produce a garden that moved away from the formal design popular at the time and towards a greater freedom and integration with nature that was to become characteristic of English gardens later in the century.

## BRIGHT, RICHARD (1789–1858) *physician, lived here*
11 SAVILE ROW, W1

Perhaps the greatest accolade a doctor can gain is to have a disease named after him. Richard Bright, after studying medicine in Edinburgh and on the Continent, and arriving at Guy's Hospital in 1820 as assistant physician, was made a full physician there four years later. In 1827 he published his researches into dropsy, a term then bestowed on almost any ailment characterised by a build up of fluid in the tissues. Bright linked a number of cases to kidney disease – 'the indication of disease to be deduced from an albuminous condition of the urine.' His diagnostic apparatus, an iron spoon and a candle, were simplicity itself. 'If albumen be present,' he wrote, 'you perceive before it reaches the boiling point that it becomes opaque . . .'. Bright's Disease entered the medical dictionary. Curiously two of Bright's colleagues at Guy's were Thomas Addison and Thomas Hodgkin, both of whom also lent their names to diseases.

## BRITTAIN, VERA (1893–1970) *and* HOLTBY, WINIFRED (1898–1935) *writers and reformers, lived here*

58 DOUGHTY STREET, WC1

## VERA BRITTAIN, (1893–1970) *author, lived here 1923–1927*
117 WYMERING MANSIONS **WESTMINSTER**

Vera Brittain's book *Testament of Friendship* is the record of the exceptionally close friendship between herself and fellow writer and feminist Winifred Holtby, which was cut short by Holtby's early death. They met at Oxford, to which they had both returned after the traumas of nursing the wounded in the First World War, and shared the house in Doughty Street when they arrived in London to make careers as writers and radical thinkers. Holtby is now best known for her posthumously published novel *South Riding*, the portrait of a Yorkshire community and one strong female character in it. Vera Brittain is remembered for *Testament of Youth*, a deeply moving account of her own early struggles to gain the education so often denied to women at the time and of the appalling toll the Great War took of the men of her generation. She was the mother of the politician Shirley Williams.

## BRITTEN, BENJAMIN, OM (1913–1976) *composer, lived here 1931–1933*
173 CROMWELL ROAD, SW5

## BRITTEN, BENJAMIN (1913–1976) *composer and* PETER PEARS, *singer (1910–1986) lived and worked here 1943–1946*

45 ST JOHN'S WOOD HIGH STREET, NW8 **WESTMINSTER**

## BENJAMIN BRITTEN, *composer*
8 HALLIFORD STREET, N1 **ISLINGTON BOROUGH COUNCIL**

Born in Lowestoft, Britten won a scholarship to the Royal College of Music and was already a prolific composer as a student. In the thirties he wrote much incidental music for films and, through his work for the GPO film unit, met W.H. Auden. Britten set works by Auden and the poet provided the text for Britten's first opera *Paul Bunyan*, later withdrawn by the composer and not performed again until the seventies. Britten spent the first years of the Second World War in America but he returned to Britain in 1942 and the following year he and his partner Peter Pears moved to St John's Wood. Britten wrote *Peter Grimes* while living there and it was an immediate success when it was first performed in 1945. Further operas, *Billy Budd* (with a libretto by Eric Crozier and E.M. Forster) and *Gloriana*, for the coronation of Elizabeth II, confirmed Britten's reputation as the most important English composer of his day. Together with Peter Pears, whom he had met as a student at the Royal College, and Eric Crozier, Britten founded the Aldeburgh Festival in 1948 and many of his later works were premiered there.

......................................................................................................

## BROOKE, SIR CHARLES VYNER (1874–1963) *last Rajah of Sarawak, lived here*

### 13 ALBION STREET, W2

The White Rajahs of Sarawak were a phenomenon of nineteenth-century imperialism that lasted until the middle of the twentieth century. In 1838 James Brooke set sail for Sarawak, a province of Borneo, and found the area in a state of turmoil. Putting his armed ship at the service of the Sultan, Brooke helped to crush a rebellion and was rewarded by being appointed Rajah of Sarawak. He held the post until his death in 1868 when it was handed on to his nephew Charles. The new Rajah ruled the province for nearly fifty years, expanding his territory and imposing his mark as an administrator and politician. In 1917 he was succeeded by Charles Vyner Brooke, his son and the third White Rajah of Sarawak. In 1941 Vyner Brooke established the first representative government for Sarawak but Japanese invasion meant it was short-lived. After the war, Sarawak, with the blessing of Vyner Brooke, became a British colony but timing was again bad. Colonialism was in inevitable decline and Sarawak became part of Malaysia.

......................................................................................................

## BROWN, FORD MADOX (1821–1893) *painter, lived here*

### 56 FORTRESS ROAD, KENTISH TOWN, NW5

Born in Calais, Brown studied and worked on the Continent before settling in London after the death of his first wife in 1846. He soon came to know the young artists of the Pre-Raphaelite Brotherhood and, although never officially a member of the group, he was in sympathy with their artistic aims. Dante Gabriel Rossetti worked briefly in Brown's studio and Brown became a partner in the arts and crafts firm William Morris established. Two of his most famous paintings reflect his involvement with the PRB. *The Last of England*, an emigrant couple gazing mournfully out of the picture frame, was inspired by the departure to Australia of the Pre-Raphaelite sculptor Thomas Woolner. *Work*, painted while he was at Fortress Road, is a painstakingly detailed street scene in Hampstead. In later life he produced a series of frescos depicting local and social history for Manchester Town Hall.

......................................................................................................

## BROWNE, HABLOT KNIGHT, ALIAS 'PHIZ' (1815–1882) *illustrator of Dickens's novels, lived here 1874–1880*

### 239 LADBROKE GROVE, W10

Hablot Knight Browne's fame as the illustrator of ten of Dickens's novels rests on the tragedy of another artist. Robert Seymour illustrated the first two installments of *Pickwick Papers* but, suffering badly from depression, he committed suicide before the third installment was due to appear. The young Browne, who had recently worked with Dickens on a short pamphlet, was drafted in to replace him. Taking the pseudonym of 'Phiz' to echo Dickens's then *nom de plume* of 'Boz', Browne went on to illustrate nearly all of the novelist's major works for the next twenty-three years. Dickens ended the relationship in 1859, having sent a number of letters to his publisher complaining about Browne's dilatoriness in providing sketches for *A Tale of Two Cities*. 'Dickens probably thinks a new hand would give his old puppets a fresh look,' Browne commented to a friend, 'Confound all authors and publishers, I say!' Browne illustrated the works of many other Victorian writers, including Harrison Ainsworth, Charles Lever and Anthony Trollope. In 1867 he was partially paralysed by a stroke but he continued to work intermittently until his death. Browne's son, Gordon, was also a prolific illustrator whose work was still appearing in books and magazines in the 1920s.

......................................................

## BROWNING, ELIZABETH BARRETT (1806–1861) *poet, lived here*
99 GLOUCESTER PLACE, W1

## ELIZABETH BARRETT BROWNING (1806–1861) *poet, lived in a house on this site 1838–1846*

50 WIMPOLE STREET, W1

The story of Elizabeth Barrett, her tyrannical father and her elopement with fellow-poet Robert Browning is better known than any of the poetry she wrote. Yet she was a much admired writer in her day who published poetry from her teens and was seriously considered as a candidate for Poet Laureate when Wordsworth died in 1850. Born in Durham, she grew up on family estates near Malvern and in 1821 suffered the riding accident which was to make her an invalid for much of her life. As years passed further illnesses and bereavements, including the death by drowning of a much-loved brother, confined her even more to the sick-room, although she continued to publish and make a literary name for herself. One of her admirers was Robert Browning who wrote to her about her work. 'I do, as I say, love these books with all my heart – and I love you too.' Meetings in Wimpole Street confirmed their mutual love and, in order to avoid the opposition to her marriage of her increasingly possessive father, the couple married secretly and departed for Italy. It was in Italy that Elizabeth Barrett Browning gave birth to a son and also wrote her two best-known works, *Sonnets from the Portuguese* and the novel in verse, *Aurora Leigh*. She died in Florence and is buried in the Protestant cemetery there.

......................................................

## BROWNING, ROBERT (1812–1889) *poet, lived in Warwick Crescent 1862–1887*
17 WARWICK CRESCENT, W2   **WESTMINSTER**

## ROBERT BROWNING (1812–1889)
179 SOUTHAMPTON WAY, SE5   **PRIVATE**

## ROBERT BROWNING (1812–1889)
29 DE VERE GARDENS, W8   **PRIVATE**

When Robert Browning eloped with Elizabeth Barrett and they went to live in Italy, she was much the better-known poet of the two. Although Browning had been publishing his work since the 1830s, and had gained the favourable attention of the ageing Wordsworth, it was not until the publication of *Men and Women* in 1855 that he reached a wider public. After his wife's death in 1861 he returned to London with his son and they made their home in Warwick Crescent. The publication of *Dramatis Personae* in 1864 increased his reputation and *The Ring and the Book*, a massive narrative poem in blank verse, gave him a fame with nineteenth-century poetry readers second only to that of Tennyson. Browning said that he had found the story of a seventeenth-century Italian murder in a 'square old yellow book' he picked up at a bookstall in Florence. Browning continued to return frequently to Italy and it was on a trip to Venice that he died in 1889.

## BRUMMELL, BEAU (1778–1840) *leader of fashion, lived here*

4, CHESTERFIELD STREET, MAYFAIR, W1

Born the grandson of a gentleman's gentleman, Beau Brummell none the less progressed through Eton and Oxford to become arbiter of fashion to Regency England and presiding genius of White's Club in St James's Street. His friendship with the Prince Regent enabled him to impose his own exquisite views on dress and deportment on the high society of the time but his eventual quarrel with the Prince led to his downfall. When he then met the Regent in the company of fellow dandy Lord Alvanley and the Prince ostentatiously ignored him, Brummell's response ('Alvanley, who's your fat friend?') ensured that he was unlikely to return swiftly to royal favour. Debts drove him abroad in 1816 and after more than twenty increasingly desperate years Brummell died, poor and insane, at an asylum in Caen.

## BRUNEL, SIR MARC ISAMBARD (1769–1849) *and* BRUNEL, ISAMBARD KINGDOM (1806–1859) *civil engineers, lived here*

98 CHEYNE WALK, SW10

The elder Brunel was a Frenchman, born in Rouen, who had escaped revolutionary France to a career in America, where he was chief engineer for New York City. He returned to Europe in 1799 and settled in England. He and his wife moved to Cheyne Walk in 1808, two years after the birth of their son Isambard, and stayed there until 1825, by which time Isambard was helping his father in his attempt to construct a tunnel under the Thames. The Thames Tunnel suffered many setbacks and it was not until 1842 that it was finally completed. By this time the younger Brunel had moved on to some of the engineering projects for which he is most famous. He had planned the Clifton Suspension Bridge, although it was not completed until the 1860s; the *Great Western*, the first steamship built to cross the Atlantic, was launched in 1838; and Brunel had taken up the post of Engineer of the proposed Great Western Railway. His dedication to work for the railway was immense. He travelled throughout the West of England in a long, black carriage, dubbed the 'Flying Hearse', in which he worked, ate and slept. The strain was often great and he once wrote to a friend, 'If I ever go mad, I shall have the ghost of the opening of the railway walking before me . . . a little swarm of devils in the shape of uncut timber, half-finished station houses, sinking embankments, broken screws, absent guard plates, unfinished drawings and sketches. . .'. The railway was completed in 1851 and Brunel went on to build the *Great Eastern*, then the largest vessel ever built, in the 1850s, but years of overwork had exhausted him and he died of a stroke in 1859.

## BURGOYNE, GENERAL JOHN (1722–1792) *lived and died here*

10 HERTFORD STREET, W1

Few generals have written highly successful Drury Lane comedies. Few dramatists have been called upon to command British forces overseas. Burgoyne, known to his contemporaries as 'Gentleman Johnny', was both general and playwright. His most successful play, *The Heiress*, was staged in 1786 and contrasts the well-bred Gayvilles with the pretentious and social-climbing *nouveau riche* Alscrips. Nine years before this literary triumph Burgoyne had the misfortune to be the general in command of British troops at Saratoga when they were surrounded by the American armies under General Gates and forced to surrender. This, the first major success of the American forces, marked the failure of a crucial aspect of British strategy in their war against the colonies and persuaded the French to recognise the nascent American republic.

## BURKE, EDMUND (1729–1797) *author and statesman, lived here*
### 37 GERRARD STREET, W1

According to Dr Johnson, 'If a man were to go by chance at the same time with Burke under a shed, to shun a shower, he would say – "this is an extraordinary man".' Born in Dublin, the son of a barrister, Burke came to London to read for the Bar himself but was drawn into the literary and political worlds of the eighteenth-century capital. He was one of the original members of the famous Club founded by Johnson and Sir Joshua Reynolds and, after entering the Commons in the 1760s, he became one of the most powerful parliamentary orators of the time. He opposed government policy in the American colonies and later led the attacks on Warren Hastings and his conduct in India. In 1790, Burke published his most famous work, *Reflections on the Revolution in France*, in which he argued forcefully (and prophetically) that revolutionary principles were dangerous abstractions that would lead to violence if put into practice. The book was published during the time he was living in Gerrard Street. Although hailed as a political philosopher and the father of conservatism, Burke himself at no time held any political office higher than that of Paymaster to the Forces.

## BURNE-JONES, SIR EDWARD (1833–1898) *artist, lived here 1865–1867*
### 41 KENSINGTON SQUARE, W8

## SIR EDWARD BURNE-JONES, (1833–1898)
### SAMUEL RICHARDSON HOUSE, NORTH END CRESCENT, W14
**BOROUGH OF HAMMERSMITH AND FULHAM**

Born in Birmingham as plain Edward Jones, Burne-Jones made his name a double-barrelled one in order to distinguish himself from all the other Joneses in the world. At Oxford he formed his lifelong friendship with William Morris and, through his work as founder of, and contributor to, *The Oxford and Cambridge Magazine*, came to the notice of Rossetti. Moving to London in 1856, Burne-Jones became a partner in the applied arts company founded by Morris and its chief designer of stained glass. As a painter Burne-Jones was the leading figure in the second generation of Pre-Raphaelites whose works, filled with medieval knights and ethereal maidens, make Rossetti's assessment of him as an undergraduate seem appropriate. 'Ned Jones,' Rossetti wrote to a friend, 'is one of the nicest young fellows in – *Dreamland*.'

See also under entry for D.G. ROSSETTI

## BURNETT, FRANCES HODGSON (1849–1924) *writer, lived here*
### 63 PORTLAND PLACE, W1

The author of a children's classic, *The Secret Garden*, Frances Hodgson Burnett was also the creator of Little Lord Fauntleroy, the impossibly angelic young hero with the long curls who appeared in a novel of the same name in 1886. Born in Manchester, she emigrated with her family to America when she was sixteen and published her first novel in 1877. *Little Lord Fauntleroy* was a major bestseller and she became an increasingly popular and wealthy author. She lived in Portland Place between 1893 and 1898, the year in which her marriage to Dr Moses Burnett ended in divorce. A further marriage to a much younger man also ended in divorce and Frances Hodgson Burnett became an increasingly eccentric figure, nicknamed 'Frilly' in her declining years because of her devotion to elaborate clothes and wigs.

## BURNEY, FANNY (MADAME D'ARBLAY) (1752–1840) *authoress, lived here*
### 11 BOLTON STREET. W1

The daughter of the musicologist Charles Burney, Fanny Burney was a quiet and unnoticed member of her father's artistic circle before the publication of her first novel *Evelina* propelled her into the limelight. She became a favourite of the ageing Dr Johnson and, although the book had been published anonymously, her fame soon spread. In 1786 Fanny Burney was appointed to a position at court but her diaries make clear how much she hated this. She succeeded in retiring on health grounds in 1791 and two years later married a French refugee officer, General D'Arblay. She lived with D'Arblay in Paris from 1802 to 1812 and, after his death in 1818, divided her time between London and Bath. Through much of this period she was writing. She wrote many plays but only one was ever produced. She wrote diaries which were published after her death. She wrote further novels of quiet social comedy in which innocent heroines were introduced to the sophistications of social life. As one critic has written, 'To read Miss Burney is rather like having a mouse's view of the world of cats: the cats are very terrifying, but the mouse's sense of the ridiculous could not be keener.'

## BURNS, JOHN (1858–1943) *statesman, lived here*
### 110 NORTH SIDE. CLAPHAM COMMON. SW4

When John Burns became President of the Local Government Board in the Liberal government of 1905, he became the first working-class man to sit in the Cabinet. Born in Vauxhall, Burns had worked, as a boy, in a candle factory but was trained as an engineer. For a brief period he worked in West Africa but most of his time was spent in London where he rapidly gained a reputation as an active trade unionist and a powerfully eloquent public speaker. In the 1880s he was arrested and tried a number of times for alleged offences against public order and he was one of the leaders of the 1889 dock strike. Burns entered parliament in 1892 as an Independent MP for Battersea. After joining the Liberal government he continued in office until 1914. At the outbreak of war, Burns, a pacifist, resigned from his post as President of the Board of Trade and, in 1918, retired altogether from public life.

## BUSS, FRANCES MARY (1827–1894) *pioneer of education for women was headmistress here 1879–1984*
### CAMDEN SCHOOL FOR GIRLS. SANDALL ROAD. NW5

'Miss Buss and Miss Beale / Cupid's darts do not feel / How different from us / Miss Beale and Miss Buss.' So runs the anonymous piece of doggerel, supposedly the work of a schoolgirl from the late nineteenth century. The Miss Beale from the poem was Dorothea Beale, the headmistress of Cheltenham Ladies College from 1858 to 1906. The Miss Buss was Frances Mary Buss, who opened the North London Collegiate School for Girls in 1850 when she was only twenty-three years old. The first person to call herself a 'headmistress', Buss became a central figure in the struggle to improve education for women in the nineteenth century. She campaigned for a woman's right to a university education and admission to Oxford and Cambridge, and was also an early advocate of women's suffrage.

## BUTLER, JOSEPHINE (1828–1906) *champion of women's rights, lived here 1890–1893*
### 8 NORTH VIEW. WIMBLEDON COMMON. SW19

Josephine Butler was born into a wealthy but radical family (her father was a cousin of Lord Grey, prime minister at the time of the 1832 Reform Act) and married the educationalist George Butler in 1852. Personal tragedy was to be the trigger for her involvement in the social reforms for which she is remembered. In 1863 her young daughter died in an accident witnessed by Butler, so, trying to assuage her grief, she plunged herself into charitable work and campaigns for women's rights. She was a leading figure in the movements to extend women's educational opportunities but became a controversial figure in Victorian Britain because of her advocation that prostitutes had rights. 'Men,' she once wrote, 'have imposed on women a stricter rule in morality than they have imposed on themselves or are willing themselves to obey.' The focus for her campaigning became the Contagious Diseases Act, a blatantly discriminatory piece of legislation that targeted and scapegoated those women who were often forced into prostitution and an existence rife with disease. In the mid-1880s, after the repeal of the act, Butler joined forces with the rambunctious journalist W.T. Stead to highlight the trade in young teenage girls who were then sold into a life of prostitution. The result was a parliamentary act of 1885 that raised the age of consent from thirteen to sixteen years of age.

---

## BUTT, DAME CLARA (1873–1937) *singer, lived here 1901–1929*
### 7 HARLEY ROAD, NW3

Clara Butt possessed a strong contralto voice which matched her formidable figure. Standing more than 6 feet in height, she had an imposing presence on the concert stage. She was born in Southwick and went to London in 1890 on a Royal College of Music scholarship, making her professional debut two years later. In her career she became particularly identified with rousingly patriotic tunes like 'Land of Hope and Glory' and Elgar wrote his work *Sea Pictures* specifically for her voice. During the First World War she performed special concerts for charities such as the Red Cross and she was made a Dame of the British Empire in 1920.

---

## BUTTERFIELD, WILLIAM (1814–1900) *architect, lived here*
### 42 BEDFORD SQUARE, WC1

One of the high priests of Victorian Gothic, Butterfield was a devout Anglican of evangelical tendencies who dedicated his life to renewing and re-invigorating church architecture. St Alban's in Holborn and St Augustine's in Queen's Gate are both Butterfield's work but his masterpiece is All Saints, Margaret Street, just north of Oxford Circus. In its lavish decoration and its use of contemporary materials and techniques to reproduce medieval effects, it is one of the more extraordinary examples of Victorian church architecture in the capital. John Betjeman wrote of it, 'For the smallness and confined nature of the site the effect of space, richness, mystery and size is amazing.'

---

## BUXTON, SIR THOMAS FOWELL (1786–1845) *anti-slavery campaigner, lived and worked here*
### THE DIRECTORS' HOUSE, OLD TRUMAN BREWERY, 91 BRICK LANE, E1

Brother-in-law of the prison reformer Elizabeth Fry, Sir Thomas Fowell Buxton himself campaigned to better the lot of those incarcerated in Britain's dangerous and unsanitary jails, but he is best remembered for his involvement in the anti-slavery movement. When William Wilberforce was obliged, through ill-health, to step down from leadership of the anti-slavery campaigns in the House of Commons, it was Buxton who replaced him. 'One of the ill effects of cruelty,' he once said, 'is that it makes the bystanders cruel.' He was determined that the parliamentarians of his day should not stand by while the cruelties of slavery persisted and he worked ceaselessly to persuade them that they needed to take action. His efforts and those of his fellow campaigners were finally rewarded by the passing of the Slavery Abolition Act of 1833. Buxton's later years were spent in further campaigning to ensure that the ban on slavery within the British Empire was properly enforced. Before he entered Parliament as the MP for Weymouth in 1818, Buxton had been a partner in the Brick Lane brewery of Truman, Hanbury & Buxton and it is on one of the old brewery buildings that the Blue Plaque has been placed.

## CALDECOTT, RANDOLPH (1846–1886) *artist and book illustrator, lived here*
46 GREAT RUSSELL STREET, WC2

Caldecott was born in Chester, the son of an accountant, and his family, initially, dissuaded him from a career in art. For some years he worked in banking and it was not until he was in his mid-twenties that he arrived in London with a portfolio of work to show publishers. His first success was with illustrations for an edition of a Christmas work by Washington Irving and he soon established himself as a gifted illustrator of such works as Cowper's *John Gilpin* and Goldsmith's *Elegy on a Mad Dog*, combining innovative use of text and picture with a nostalgic evocation of a rural past. He also illustrated many books specifically aimed at children. He suffered from ill health for much of his life and died in Florida, where he had gone to escape the rigours of an English winter. The Caldecott Medal is awarded in America each year to the artist of the best children's picture book.

## CAMPBELL, COLEN (1676–1729) *architect and author of 'Vitruvius Britannicus', lived and died here*
76 BROOK STREET, W1

Born in Scotland, Campbell became the leading exponent of Palladianism, the movement to employ the ideas of the sixteenth-century Italian architect Andrea Palladio in an English, eighteenth-century context. Campbell's masterpiece no longer survives. Wanstead House in Essex was built for the 1st Earl Tylney between 1715 and 1720 and one contemporary wrote admiringly of it that it was 'one of the noblest houses, not only in England, but also in Europe.' In the early nineteenth century the heiress of Wanstead married a nephew of the Duke of Wellington who squandered his wife's inheritance with such thoroughness that the house had to be pulled down and sold for building stone. Other work by Campbell does survive, including part of Burlington House and the house he built for himself in Brook Street. *Vitruvius Britannicus*, which Campbell published between 1717 and 1725, is explained by its lengthy subtitle – 'the British Architect; containing the plans, elevations and sections of the regular Buildings, both publick and private, in Great Britain, with a variety of New Designs.'

## CAMPBELL-BANNERMAN, SIR HENRY (1836–1908) *Prime Minister, lived here*
6 GROSVENOR PLACE, SW1

Henry Campbell, born in Glasgow, was obliged to extend his name in 1871 in order to inherit a fortune from a maternal uncle who had insisted that his name of Bannerman live on in that of his heir. Campbell-Bannerman did so but he did not like his new name, writing years later to a friend, ' I see you are already tired, as I have long been, of writing my horrid long name. I am always best pleased to to be called Campbell *tout court* . . . An alternative is C.B.' Once described by a contemporary as 'a jolly, lazy sort of man with a good dose of sense', Campbell-Bannerman, who had entered Parliament in 1868 as MP for Stirling Burghs, was a compromise candidate for leader of the Liberal party in the late 1890s. Perhaps to his own surprise as well as that of others he proved a reasonably effective choice and, as Prime Minister from 1906–8, led one of the great reforming administrations of the century. He was the last Prime Minister to die while in office.

## CANAL, ANTONIO (CANALETTO) (1697–1768) *Venetian painter, lived here*
41 BEAK STREET, W1

The Venetian painter Canaletto was, of course, best known for his panoramic views of his native city. He began painting these in his early twenties, after starting his career as a designer of theatrical scenery, and by the 1740s many of his patrons were English aristocrats on the

Grand Tour. In 1746, armed with letters of introduction, he arrived in England and lodged in Beak Street, then known as Silver Street. He stayed for nine years, producing views of London, particularly the Thames, and committing to canvas the country houses of the nobility. At first he was extremely successful but rumours were later circulated, probably by rival artists, that the man in Silver Street was not who he said he was, that he was not the real Canaletto but a second-rate imitator passing himself off as the great man. These rumours must have contributed to Canaletto's decision in 1755 to return to Venice, where he lived and painted until his death.

## CANNING, GEORGE (1770–1827) *statesman, lived here*
50 BERKELEY SQUARE, W1

Canning, who was Prime Minister for only 100 days before dying of pneumonia, is a rarity among those who have held that office for two reasons. He was one of the few Prime Ministers to have fought a duel and one of even fewer who published a volume of collected verse in his lifetime. His poetry appeared in 1823. His duel was fought on Putney Heath in 1809. Canning was, at the time, Foreign Secretary and his opponent, Lord Castlereagh, was War Minister and believed that Canning had been insufficiently supportive of his policy. Pistols at dawn seemed the only suitable response. In the ensuing confrontation Canning was wounded slightly in the leg. Both ministers then resigned, but returned to politics shortly afterwards. Canning became Foreign Secretary once more in 1822, ironically replacing Castlereagh who had committed suicide, and remained in this office until presented with his brief opportunity to hold the highest position in government.

## CARLILE, WILSON (1847–1942) *founder of the Church Army, lived here*
34 SHEFFIELD TERRACE, W8

Wilson Carlile began his working life in the family's silk business but a slump in the early 1870s brought disaster to the silk trade and he was obliged to look for his vocation elsewhere. He was already moving towards the belief that it might be a religious one and he acted as organist during many of the revivalist meetings in England of the American evangelists Moody and Sankey. In 1881 he was ordained as a priest but he soon grew concerned about the gap between the church and the working classes and the following year he resigned from a curacy in Kensington to found the Church Army, organised on similar lines to Booth's Salvation Army, which had been created four years earlier. Carlile was involved with the administration of his Army, and with the social work it undertook, for the rest of his long life. In 1905 he was appointed an honorary Prebendary of St Paul's Cathedral in recognition of his work with the Church Army.

## CARLYLE, THOMAS (1795–1881) *essayist and historian, lived here*
33 AMPTON STREET, WC1
24 CHEYNE ROW, SW3   **CARLYLE SOCIETY**

Carlyle, who wrote like a Biblical prophet reincarnated as a man of letters, was one of the great sages of Victorian England and his influence on intellectual life in the nineteenth century can scarcely be underestimated. Born in Ecclefechan in Dumfriesshire, Carlyle worked in Scotland as a schoolteacher, private tutor and translator from German. He paid his first visit to London in 1824, and finally settled there in 1834, the same year his extraordinary philosophical fantasy *Sartor Resartus* was published in book form. For the rest of his life Carlyle lived at Cheyne Row, working on a sequence of historical, literary and philosophical books, which are little read today but were eagerly devoured by his contemporaries. *The French Revolution* was published in 1837 (even though part of Carlyle's manuscript had been accidentally destroyed by a maid at John Stuart Mill's house), to be followed by *Past and Present* in 1841 and *Latter Day Pamphlets* in 1850. Carlyle spent many years of his life researching and writing a vast *History of Frederick the Great*, which was finally published between 1858 and 1865. Carlyle was married to Jane Welsh, a woman as remarkable in many ways as he was, but the marriage was not a happy one. 'It was very good of God to let Carlyle and Mrs. Carlyle marry one another,' Samuel Butler is reputed to have remarked, 'and so make only two people miserable instead of four.'

........................................................

## CARTER, HOWARD (1874–1939) *Egyptologist and discoverer of the tomb of Tutenkhamun, lived here*

19 COLLINGHAM GARDENS, SW5

When he made the archaeological discovery of the century Howard Carter was already an experienced excavator of the Egyptian past. He went to the country first as a youthful draughtsman on an expedition led by Flinders Petrie, of University College, London, and, by the time he was invited, in 1907, to conduct digs under the patronage of the amateur Egyptologist Lord Carnarvon, he was an old hand. Carter's excavations of the royal tombs at Thebes, conducted over many seasons, yielded many discoveries but culminated in the spectacular find of the nearly intact burial of Tutenkhamun. Carter himself described the moment when he peered through a hole in a sealed door and saw the treasures for the first time. 'As my eyes grew accustomed to the light, details of the room within emerged slowly from the mist, strange animals, statues and gold – everywhere the glint of gold.'

........................................................

## CASLON, WILLIAM (1692–1766) *The foundry established by William Caslon, typefounder stood on this site 1737–1909*

21-23 CHISWELL STREET, EC1

Born in Worcestershire, Caslon served his apprenticeship to an ornamental engraver of gunlocks and barrels and, when he first moved to London in 1716, he established himself in the same, highly specialised business with a workshop in the Minories. However, he soon began also to cut type for printers and one of the printers for whom he worked became his benefactor when he set him up in what became the first of Caslon's three foundries. By the time he moved to Chiswell Street, Caslon was acknowledged as the creator of a series of particularly elegant typefaces which, although the foundry has gone, are still in use today. Caslon died at Bethnal Green, where he had a house outside the bustle of the city as it then was.

........................................................

## CASTLEREAGH, VISCOUNT (1769–1822) *statesman, lived and died here*

LORING HALL, WATER LANE, NORTH CRAY

In Shelley's poem of 1819, 'The Mask of Anarchy', the poet writes: 'I met Murder on the way-/ He had a mask like Castlereagh.' Castlereagh was hated by Shelley and other radicals because he was a prominent figure in the reactionary government of Lord Liverpool, although, as Foreign Secretary, he was less responsible for repressive measures like the Peterloo Massacre than many of its other members. From an Irish family, Castlereagh had helped Pitt carry through the union of English and Irish parliaments in 1800 and was War Minister twice between 1805 and 1809. He was Foreign Secretary during the last two years of the fight against Napoleon and represented Britain at the Congress of Vienna, which followed French defeat. Always subject to melancholy and depression, Castlereagh, driven to distraction by overwork, cut his throat with a pen-knife at his country house in North Cray.

........................................................

## CATO STREET CONSPIRACY *discovered here, 23 February 1820*

1A CATO STREET, W1

In 1820 a group of radical republicans, led by veteran agitator Arthur Thistlewood, planned to assassinate the Cabinet as its members sat down to dinner in Lord Harrowby's house in Grosvenor Square. Thistlewood hoped this would be a prelude to a nationwide rising. The authorities knew of the plot in advance, and it was doomed to failure. On 23 February the conspirators were captured in the loft of a stable in Cato Street after a brief fracas during which Thistlewood fatally wounded one of the Bow Street Runners sent to apprehend them. Thistlewood and four of his men were found guilty of high treason and were hung at Newgate on 1 May 1820. All died bravely although Thistlewood, aggravated by one of his comrades' boisterous singing of 'Death or Liberty' on the scaffold, is alleged to have said, 'Be quiet, Ings; we can die without all this noise.'

........................................................................................................................................................

## CAVELL, EDITH (1865–1915) *pioneer of modern nursing in Belgium and heroine of the Great War, trained and worked here 1896–1901*

LONDON HOSPITAL, WHITECHAPEL, E1

## EDITH CAVELL (1865–1915)
ST LEONARD'S HOSPITAL, KINGSLAND ROAD, N1, **BOROUGH OF HACKNEY**

Born in a small village in Norfolk, where her father was vicar, Edith Cavell studied and travelled on the Continent before undertaking her training as a nurse at the London Hospital. After a period as superintendent of the Highgate infirmary she went, in 1906, to Belgium to become matron of the Ecole Belge d'Infirmières Diplomées, later to be renamed the Ecole Edith Cavell. On the outbreak of war and the German invasion of Belgium she chose to remain at her post and, in 1915, she was arrested and charged with helping refugees to escape. Despite diplomatic attempts to save her she was found guilty and, on 12 October of that year, she faced a firing squad. After the war her body was returned to England and, following a service in Westminster Abbey, was buried in Norwich Cathedral. Sir George Frampton's statue of Edith Cavell, dressed in her nurse's uniform, stands in St Martin's Place, looking out towards Trafalgar Square.

........................................................................................................................................................

## CAVENDISH, HONORABLE HENRY *natural philosopher, lived here, born 1731, died 1810*
11 BEDFORD SQUARE, WC1 · ERECTED PRIVATELY BY THE DUKE OF BEDFORD *c.* 1903, ADOPTED BY THE GLC IN 1983

Cavendish, the grandson of the Duke of Devonshire, was a notoriously reclusive man. Sir Joseph Banks said of him that, 'He probably uttered fewer words in the course of his life than any man who ever lived to four score years, not at all excepting the monks of La Trappe.' He ordered his dinner by leaving notes on a table for servants to find and his female staff were told they would be instantly dismissed were he ever to catch sight of them. He was also a gifted experimental scientist who was the first to 'discover' hydrogen and to prove that water was the result of the combination of two gases. Much of his work he left unpublished at his death. His papers were studied and edited by James Clerk Maxwell in the 1870s; he found that the silent and solitary Cavendish had anticipated a number of later theories but had not felt the need to divulge them to anyone else.

........................................................................................................................................................

## CAYLEY, SIR GEORGE (1773–1857) *scientist and pioneer of aviation, lived here*
20 HERTFORD STREET, W1

Long before the Wright brothers made their first flight, an inventive Yorkshire squire was experimenting with a variety of aerial contraptions. Sir George Cayley, whose London home was in Hertford Street, came from a family that had been lords of the manor in the North Yorkshire village of Brompton for many centuries and it was near the ancestral home, Brompton Hall, that he conducted his experiments. As early as 1804 Cayley had constructed his first model glider but it was not until he was an old man that he succeeded in building a machine that could travel any distance with a man on board. Unable (or unwilling) to pilot the machines himself, Cayley was in the habit of ordering his servants airborne. In 1853 his coachman was at the rudimentary controls of a glider that travelled 50 yards in the air before plummeting groundwards. The coachman emerged from the wreckage and promptly gave notice, arguing (quite reasonably) that he had been hired to drive, not to fly.

## CECIL, VISCOUNT, OF CHELWOOD (1864–1958) *creator of the League of Nations, lived here*

16 SOUTH EATON PLACE, SW1

The son of the Conservative Prime Minister, the Marquess of Salisbury, Robert Cecil was educated at Eton and Oxford and entered Parliament in 1903, the year after his father had retired from public life. He was a junior member of the coalition government during the First World War and, as a minister in the Foreign Office, was chiefly instrumental in drawing up the document that eventually became the covenant of the League of Nations. Cecil was one of the politicians most committed to the ideals of the League and served as President of the League of Nations Union for more than twenty years. After the coming of the Second World War destroyed the hopes on which the League had been founded, he became an equally ardent advocate of the United Nations, declaring, 'the League is dead. Long live the UN', and becoming an honorary life President of the United Nations Association. He was awarded the Nobel Peace Prize in 1937.

## CETSHWAYO (*c.*1832–1884) *King of the Zulus, stayed here, in 1882*

18 MELBURY ROAD, W14

Cetshwayo was the Zulu king whose warriors inflicted one of the most crushing and unexpected defeats on British troops in imperial history. In 1879, the Zulu impis annihilated an invading force of British soldiers and their African allies at the Battle of Isandhlwana. In response, the British government poured men and resources into South Africa, columns of soldiers marched on Cetshwayo's capital at Ulundi, his armies were slaughtered and, eventually, he was captured and deposed. In 1882, the defeated king was allowed to travel to London, where he met the Prime Minister, and to journey to Osborne House on the Isle of Wight, where he had an audience with Queen Victoria. During his summer-long stay in Britain, he lived at Melbury Road off Kensington High Street and became, briefly, the talk of the town. Music-hall songs celebrated his visit and his supposed potential to flutter female hearts. 'White young dandies, get away, O!/You are now 'neath beauty's ban/ Clear the field for Cetewayo/ He alone the ladies' man.' Photographs taken on the visit of the twenty-stone plus ex-monarch, uncomfortably squeezed into frock coat and trousers, suggest that he was actually a rather unlikely ladies' man. After his visit to London, Cetshwayo went back to Zululand where he was reinstated as ruler but only over a much-reduced territory. He died less than two years after his return to his kingdom.

## CHADWICK, SIR EDWIN (1801–1890) *public health reformer, lived here*

5 MONTAGUE ROAD, RICHMOND

One of the great battles in nineteenth-century London was that waged against the ill health and disease that resulted from rudimentary sanitation, and one of the leading figures in this battle was Edwin Chadwick. As a young man Chadwick worked as a lawyer and journalist and in 1832 was appointed to the Poor Law Commission. He became a tireless investigator of poverty and deprivation. His work as a Poor Law reformer and administrator was extended by his three-volume *Survey into the Sanitary Condition of the Labouring Classes in Great Britain* which eventually led to the passing of a series of public health acts in the late 1840s. For the rest of his life Chadwick, who was finally knighted in the year before his death, continued to campaign for public health measures. His singlemindedness is revealed by his reply when asked by Napoleon III what he thought of Paris. 'Sire,' Chadwick said, 'they say that Augustus found Rome a city of brick and left it a city of marble. If your majesty, finding Paris stinking, will leave it sweet, you will more than rival the first emperor of Rome.'

---

## CHAIN, SIR ERNST (1906–1979) *biochemist and developer of penicillin, lived here*
9 NORTH VIEW, WIMBLEDON COMMON, SW19

The son of a Russian chemist and industrialist, Ernst Chain was born and educated in Berlin. When Hitler came to power, Chain, as a half-Russian Jew, whose political sympathies were with the left, realised that his career and possibly his life were at risk and he moved to Britain. In 1935, he took up a post as lecturer in pathology at Oxford and began work with the Australian scientist Howard Florey on the investigation of the natural antibacterial agents produced by some micro-organisms. The two men were soon led to the published work of Sir Alexander Fleming. Fleming had discovered and described penicillin a decade earlier but it was left to Florey and Chain to develop it as a curative medicine for infectious diseases. For his work on penicillin, Chain shared the 1945 Nobel Prize for Medicine with Florey and Fleming. After the war, unimpressed by the prospects for research in his field in Britain, he moved to Italy, where he was given charge of a research centre in microbiology. He did not return permanently to the UK for thirteen years until he was appointed professor of biochemistry at Imperial College where he remained until his retirement.

---

## CHAMBERLAIN, JOSEPH (1836–1914) *statesman, lived here*
188 CAMBERWELL GROVE, SE5

## JOSEPH CHAMBERLAIN (1836–1914) *statesman, lived here*
25 HIGHBURY PLACE, N5

During a speech in 1885, Joseph Chamberlain told his audience, 'I care little for party . . . except to promote the objects which I publicly avowed when I first entered Parliament.' He lived up to his words, for he has the distinction of being the one man who split both major parties during his political career. Chamberlain first came to notice in Birmingham, where he was mayor from 1873 to 1876 and created a model for city administrations throughout the country. Elected to Parliament he was soon a leading member of Gladstone's Liberal government but, in 1886, unable to stomach the idea of home rule for Ireland, he resigned and led his supporters into the Tory Party. Nearly twenty years later, opposed to the idea of Free Trade to which the party was committed, he resigned from the Tories. The party split asunder and the Liberals won a landslide victory in the 1906 elections. Two of Chamberlain's sons, Austen and Neville, followed him into politics.

---

## CHAMBERLAIN, NEVILLE (1869–1940) *Prime Minister, lived here 1923–1935*
37 EATON SQUARE, SW1

Famously (or infamously) Neville Chamberlain, the son of the Victorian and Edwardian politician Joseph Chamberlain, was the Prime Minister who was of the opinion that a policy of appeasement towards Hitler and Nazi Germany was the correct one to pursue. When Germany annexed the Sudetenland in 1938, Chamberlain (who had succeeded Baldwin as PM the previous year) said in a radio broadcast, 'How horrible, fantastic, incredible, it is that we should be digging trenches and trying on gas-masks here because of a quarrel in a far-away country between people of whom we know nothing.' Three days later he returned from Munich, waving a piece of paper and claiming that he had achieved, in his discussions with Hitler, 'peace in our time'. Disillusionment soon set in. Even Chamberlain could not ignore the Nazis' further territorial aggression and it was to honour his commitment to Poland that Britain declared war on Germany in 1939. Chamberlain, under mounting criticism, resigned as PM in May 1940, to be replaced by Churchill, but continued to serve in the Cabinet, leaving it only five weeks before his death from cancer in November of that year.

## CHAMBERS, DOROTHEA LAMBERT (1878–1960) *lawn tennis champion, lived here 1887–1907*

### 7 NORTH COMMON ROAD, W5

Dorothea Lambert Chambers was the first superstar of women's tennis. Under her maiden name (Douglass) and then her married name of Chambers, she was women's singles champion at Wimbledon seven times between 1903 and 1914. Her most convincing victory was in 1911 when she defeated Dora Boothby 6–0, 6–0 in the final. It was to be another seventy-seven years before Steffi Graf became only the second woman to triumph in a Grand Slam singles final without losing a game. Chambers continued to play tennis at the highest level until she was well into her forties. In 1919, when Wimbledon resumed after the First World War, she was involved in an epic contest with the much younger Frenchwoman, Suzanne Lenglen. Lenglen won but only after a gruelling struggle, which left both women too exhausted to be presented, as originally planned, to King George V and Queen Mary who had watched the match from the royal box.

## CHAPMAN, HERBERT (1878–1934) *football manager, lived and died here*

### 6 HASLEMERE AVENUE, HENDON, NW4

If asked to name Britain's greatest ever football manager, some might choose Alex Ferguson. Some might choose Matt Busby or Bill Shankly, or Alf Ramsey. Those with a greater sense of history would probably go for Herbert Chapman. In the 1920s, Chapman created not one, but two great sides. Like many successful managers, he had not had a distinguished playing career himself but, first at Huddersfield and then at Arsenal, he built teams that carried all before them. He arrived at Huddersfield Town in 1921, winning the FA Cup in his first full season in charge and going on to take the League title in 1924. His side defended the title the following year and Chapman then chose to head south for the capital, answering an advertisement Arsenal had placed for manager which had included the proviso that, 'Gentlemen whose sole ability to build up a good side depends on the payment of heavy and exorbitant transfer fees need not apply.' At Highbury, he succeeded in avoiding exorbitant transfer fees but still moulded a team that won the FA Cup in 1930 and the League title in 1931 and 1933. Chapman was not around to see Arsenal win further League titles in 1934 and 1935. He died of pneumonia in January 1934 but it was the team he had created which triumphed both times.

## CHARLES X (1757–1836) *last Bourbon King of France, lived here 1805–1814*

### 72 SOUTH AUDLEY STREET, W1

Born into the splendid privilege of the French *ancien régime,* Charles, as Comte D'Artois and brother to the king, Louis XVI, was one of those most resistant to the forces of change that swept through his country in the years before the French Revolution. Known as a fierce advocate of royal absolutism, he fled France only weeks after the storming of the Bastille in July 1789, and became a leader of the French *émigré* royalists. He spent many of his years of exile in London, living at the house in South Audley Street, but returned to France following the defeat of Napoleon and the accession of his elder brother as Louis XVIII. Charles had learned little, if anything, from his experience of exile and appeared to believe that he could return the country to how it was when he was a young man. When he succeeded his brother as king in 1824, he and a succession of reactionary ministers, most notably the Prince de Polignac, tried to turn back the clock of French history. In 1830, when the Chamber of Deputies denounced Polignac's ministry, Charles responded by dissolving it, restricting suffrage and imposing censorship of the press. The result was the July Revolution. Charles abdicated in favour of his grandson but the French had had enough of the dynasty, and the throne was offered to the Duc d'Orléans, who became King Louis-Philippe. Charles, older but no wiser, returned to London, once again in exile. He died six years later in a small town called Goritz, then part of the Austrian Empire, now part of Slovenia.

*In a house on this site* THOMAS CHATTERTON *died 24 August 1770*
39 BROOKE STREET, EC1 **CITY OF LONDON**

As a boy growing up in Bristol, Thomas Chatterton haunted the medieval church of St Mary Redcliffe. Fascinated by the dusty documents and relics from earlier centuries still to be seen there, Chatterton wrote his own pseudo-archaic verse and invented an author for them in the wholly imaginary fifteenth-century monk, Thomas Rowley. Chatterton moved to London in April 1770 to try and earn a living as a writer but success did not come quickly and Chatterton, depressed, took arsenic in his garret room in Brooke Street. He was seventeen years old. Later romantic poets were powerfully affected by Chatterton's story. Wordsworth called him 'the marvellous boy . . . that perished in his pride' and Keats dedicated *Endymion* to his memory.

CHELSEA CHINA *was manufactured in a house at the north end of Lawrence Street 1745–1784.* TOBIAS SMOLLETT (1721–1771), *novelist, also lived in part of the house from 1750 to 1762*

16 LAWRENCE STREET, SW3

For nearly forty years Chelsea China was made in a factory in Lawrence Street, which centred on a house that had previously been the residence of the Duchess of Monmouth. Collectors and experts on this porcelain divide production into a number of different periods, of which the Red Anchor period in the early 1750s is generally considered to be the most successful artistically. The factory was, in its last days, owned by the same man who ran the Derby porcelain works and when the Chelsea factory closed in 1784, all the moulds and firing ovens were moved to Derby. The story that Dr Johnson once tried his hand at making porcelain in the Chelsea works is almost certainly apocryphal.

TOBIAS SMOLLETT was born in Dumbarton and, after brief attendance at Glasgow University and a spell in the Navy, settled in London to earn his living as a surgeon and as a writer. His first novel, *The Adventures of Roderick Random*, appeared in 1748. He went on to publish several further novels, to translate Cervantes and to make his forceful presence felt in both journalism and the theatre. His health was poor and, after leaving Monmouth House, he travelled much in Europe looking for a climate that would improve it. He was a notably ill-tempered traveller, hugely unimpressed by nearly everything foreign, as his book *Travels Through France and Italy* bears witness. He died in Italy in 1771.

CHESTERFIELD, PHILIP, 4TH EARL OF (1694–1773) *statesman and author, lived in this house*

RANGERS HOUSE, CHESTERFIELD WALK, SE10

A statesman and diplomat, Chesterfield was also a leading figure in the literary world of Augustan London and was a friend of writers like Pope and Gay. In the year after his death his widow published his letters to his illegitimate son Philip Stanhope. These had been designed to instruct the gauche young man in the politer arts of high society. Much admired at the time, they are probably little read today, although some years ago they were, surprisingly, revealed to be among the favourite works of the romantic novelist Catherine Cookson. Chesterfield may be best remembered today as the man whose patronage was so loftily dismissed by Samuel Johnson. 'The notice which you have been pleased to take of my labours, had it been early, had been kind; but it has been delayed till I am indifferent and cannot enjoy it, till I am solitary and cannot impart it, till I am known and do not want it …'

## CHESTERTON, GILBERT KEITH (1874–1936) *poet, novelist and critic, lived here*
11 WARWICK GARDENS, W14

## GILBERT KEITH CHESTERTON *was born here 29 May 1874*
32 SHEFFIELD TERRACE, W8   **PRIVATE**

Chesterton was educated at St Paul's and at the Slade School of Art and his illustrations decorate his own early work and books by friends such as Hilaire Belloc. However, he soon became known as a prolific journalist, able to turn his gift for wit and paradox on a wide array of literary, social, political and religious issues. His first novel was *The Napoleon of Notting Hill*, a fantasy set in a future London, and he wrote several others but he is best known for his Father Brown stories, in which an unassuming Roman Catholic priest solves apparently insoluble mysteries through logic and his knowledge of the human heart. Chesterton himself became a Roman Catholic in 1922. Chesterton was renowned for his vast bulk and for his absent-mindedness. In the middle of one lecture tour he is alleged to have telegraphed to his wife, 'Am in Market Harborough. Where ought I to be?'

## CHEVALIER, ALBERT (1861–1923) *music hall comedian, was born here*
17 ST ANN'S VILLAS, W11

Chevalier's father was a French teacher at Kensington Grammar School. His mother was Welsh and he was given the names Albert Onesiure Britannicus Gwathveoyd Louis. Unsurprisingly, when he chose a career in show business, he decided to use only the first of these. After appearing in burlesque and melodrama for a number of years he launched himself as a music hall performer and became one of the most popular stars of the day. Despite his cosmopolitan and lower middle-class background his image was that of the archetypal Cockney coster. He 'Knocked 'em in the Old Kent Road', sang of 'The Narsty Way 'E Sez It' and declared that 'It Gets Me Talked Abaht.' However, by far his most famous song was 'My Old Dutch', with its affectingly sentimental confession that 'There ain't a lady livin' in the land/As I'd swop for my dear old Dutch.'

## CHICHESTER, SIR FRANCIS (1901–1972) *single-handed circumnavigator of the world 1966–1967, pioneer aviator, sailor and author, lived here 1944–1972*
9 ST JAMES'S PLACE, SW1   **WESTMINSTER**

Best remembered for his pioneering solo voyage around the world in 1966 and 1967, Chichester was not only a yachtsman but also an outstanding airman and a specialist in long-distance flights. Born in Barnstaple, he emigrated to New Zealand in 1919 and amassed a fortune there as a land agent, returning to Britain in 1929. In 1930, soon after he had taken up flying, he became only the second man to fly solo from Australia to England and made several other record-breaking flights in the 1930s. Only after the Second World War, in which he had worked as an air navigation instructor, did he take up sailing and he was in his mid-sixties when he made his epic voyage around the world in Gypsy Moth IV. In 1967, soon after sailing into Plymouth Harbour at the end of his round the world trip, Francis Chichester was knighted by the Queen, using the same sword that Elizabeth I had used to knight Francis Drake.

CHIPPENDALE, THOMAS *The workshop of Thomas Chippendale and his son, cabinet makers, stood near this site 1753–1813*

61 ST MARTIN'S LANE, WC2

In the first half of the eighteenth century nearly all the finest furniture that adorned the houses of the wealthy came from France and the Continent. One of the first English furniture makers to produce high quality pieces was Thomas Chippendale, who opened his workshop in St Martin's Lane in 1753 and, in the following year, published his book, *The Gentleman and Cabinet Maker's Director*. This, the first catalogue of its kind, contained his own drawings and designs for his elegant neo-classical furniture and was intended as a sales tool to persuade patrons to buy his pieces. However, it also had a widespread influence on other craftsmen and Chippendale's style filtered down to dozens of less gifted imitators. Chippendale died in 1779 and was buried in St Martin-in-the-Fields but his son continued the business until 1813.

CHISHOLM, CAROLINE (1808–1877) *philanthropist, 'The Emigrants' Friend', lived here*

32 CHARLTON PLACE, N1

Caroline Chisholm was born the daughter of a farmer in Northamptonshire but she gained her title 'The Emigrants' Friend' for her work on behalf of poor, especially female, arrivals in Australia, a country where she is better remembered than she is in Britain. Her portrait was, for many years, on the Australian five dollar note. She arrived in Sydney, together with her husband, in 1838 and, appalled by the sight of destitute emigrants on the streets, set about what became a long campaign to find work and accommodation for them. Her Female Immigrants' Home opened in 1841. The Chisholms returned to London in 1846 and established an organisation that loaned money to would-be emigrants, to be repaid when they were settled in the colony. Although she did go back to Australia for a period in the 1850s and 1860s, Caroline Chisholm spent much of her later life in comparative obscurity in Liverpool and London.

CHOPIN, FREDERIC *From this house in 1848 Frederic Chopin (1810–1849) went to the Guildhall to give his last public performance*

4 ST JAMES'S PLACE, SW1

FREDERIC CHOPIN, *Polish composer and pianist*
99 EATON PLACE, SW1   **PRIVATE**

Born in Poland, where his French father had settled, Chopin, like so many other musical geniuses, showed his gifts at an early age, playing for the first time in public when he was eight and publishing his first works seven years later. It was in Paris that he found his greatest fame and it was there that he met the writer George Sand in 1836, with whom he conducted a turbulent relationship. Most of Chopin's works – nocturnes, polonaises, mazurkas – are for piano and he was renowned in his lifetime as much for his virtuoso performances of them as for their composition. When he arrived in London in 1848, fleeing from the revolution in France, Chopin, who was consumptive, was already an ill man but he was obliged to look for pupils to teach and concerts to play. He went north on a concert tour of cities, including Manchester, Edinburgh and Glasgow, and returned, drained, to give the performance in aid of Polish refugees which is commemorated by the plaque. A week after the recital, on 23 November 1848, Chopin returned to Paris where he died the following year.

CHRISTIE, DAME AGATHA (1890–1976) *detective novelist and playwright, lived here 1934–1941*

58 SHEFFIELD TERRACE, W8

## AGATHA CHRISTIE

CHRISTIE COTTAGE,
CRESSWELL PLACE, SW10  **PRIVATE**

The most popular writer in the history of crime fiction, Agatha Christie is famous as the creator of two legendary detectives, the Belgian super-sleuth Hercule Poirot and Miss Marple, the elderly spinster of St Mary Mead. Born Agatha Miller, she came from a prosperous family living in Devon and was educated at home, never attending school or university. In 1914 she married Archie Christie. During the First World War he became a fighter pilot and she entered the nursing profession. It was during the war years that she began to write and her first novel, *The Mysterious Affair at Styles* (also the first Poirot novel), was published in 1920. She went on to write more than eighty crime novels, including such famous works as *Murder on the Orient Express*, *The Murder of Roger Ackroyd* and *Death on the Nile*. She experienced a crisis in her private life during the mid-1920s. Her husband, in love with another woman, asked her for a divorce. Already disturbed by the death of her mother, Christie suffered some kind of breakdown. She disappeared for nearly three weeks, while family, police and press searched for her. She was eventually found in a Harrogate hotel; where she had been living under an assumed name. She was remarried in 1930 to the archaeologist Max Mallowan and it certainly seemed a happy match. As she once jokingly wrote, 'An archaeologist is the best husband any woman can have. The older she gets, the more he is interested in her', and she accompanied him on a number of archaeological digs in Mesopotamia and the Middle East. Agatha Christie died in 1976 by which time hundreds of millions of her books had been sold worldwide.

........................................................................................................................

## CHURCHILL, LORD RANDOLPH (1849–1895) *statesman, lived here 1883–92*

2 CONNAUGHT PLACE, W2

Randolph Churchill was born into the heart of the English aristocracy, the son of the 7th Duke of Marlborough, and entered Parliament as a Tory in his mid-twenties. He was soon seen by some as the great hope for the future of the party, although to many others he was an irritating gadfly, as likely to embarrass his own leadership as the opposition. However he gathered about him a small group of supporters known as 'the Fourth Party' and when Lord Salisbury took office as Prime Minister in 1885, Churchill was too powerful a figure to exclude from his Cabinet. He was made Secretary of State for India and, the following year, Chancellor, although, since he once said of decimal points, 'I never could make out what those damned dots meant,' his grasp of economics may have been rudimentary. This was the high point of Churchill's career. Disagreeing with colleagues, he resigned after only a few months and never held office again. The last years of his life were blighted by ill health and mental difficulties almost certainly brought on by syphilis, and he died while still only in his mid-forties.

........................................................................................................................

## CHURCHILL, SIR WINSTON, KG (1874–1965) *Prime Minister, lived and died here*

28 HYDE PARK GATE, KENSINGTON GORE, SW7

# SIR WINSTON CHURCHILL, KG (1874–1965) *spoke here at the former Caxton Hall 1937–42*

CAXTON HALL, CAXTON STREET SW1
**WESTMINSTER**

# SIR WINSTON CHURCHILL, KG *lived here 1909–1913*

34 ECCLESTON SQUARE, SW1  **PRIVATE**

The son of Randolph Churchill and the American heiress Jennie Jerome, Winston Churchill served as a soldier in the Sudan and as a war correspondent in the Boer War before entering Parliament in 1900 as a Conservative. Four years later he crossed the floor to join the Liberals, not the last time he would change parties, and he was Home Secretary and then First Lord of the Admiralty in Asquith's government between 1910 and 1915. In 1924 he rejoined the Conservative party and was Chancellor of the Exchequer for five years under Stanley Baldwin. In the early thirties he was in the political wilderness, unlikely to serve in the National Government of Ramsay MacDonald, whom he had made the butt of one of the most memorable of all parliamentary metaphors. As a child, Churchill said, he had visited Barnum's Circus with his parents. 'The exhibit on the programme I most desired to see was the one described as the Boneless Wonder. My parents judged that the spectacle would be too revolting and demoralising for my youthful eyes, and I have waited fifty years to see the Boneless Wonder sitting on the Treasury bench.' As the thirties wore on Churchill was increasingly a voice calling in the political wilderness but man was matched with historical moment in 1940 when he returned to power to lead the wartime coalition government. Churchill's strength as a leader in war was his absolute concentration on the destruction of Hitler. 'If Hitler invaded Hell,' he once said, 'I would at least make a favourable reference to the Devil.' After the war he had to suffer the bitter pill of defeat in the 1945 election. When his wife told him that it was, perhaps, a blessing in disguise, he could only reply that, 'At the moment it seems quite effectively disguised.' Churchill returned again as Prime Minister between 1951 and 1955 and when he died in 1965, his end seemed to mark the passing of a particular era in British history.

---

## CLARKSON, WILLY (1861–1934) *theatrical wigmaker, lived here*
41–43 WARDOUR STREET, W1

Willy Clarkson was the most famous theatrical wig-maker and costumier of the early part of the twentieth century. He had joined his father's wig-making firm in his teens and gradually built up its theatrical side until he was supplying wigs and costumes to most of the West End theatres. When he moved into newly built premises in Wardour Street in 1905 the foundation stones were laid by two theatrical legends who had made use of Clarkson's services – Sarah Bernhardt and Sir Henry Irving. Clarkson's wigs were sometimes used for less innocent purposes than the stage. When, in 1910, Dr Crippen, having murdered his wife, fled the country with his mistress, they both travelled disguised in Clarkson wigs.

---

## CLAYTON, REVEREND P.T.B. 'TUBBY' (1885–1972) *founder of Toc H, lived here*
43 TRINITY SQUARE, EC3

Toc H was a response to the horrors of trench warfare in the First World War. The original Toc H was a house in Poperinghe, Belgium, the main forward base on the road to Ypres. Bought by Neville Talbot, senior chaplain in the British Army's 6th Division and named Talbot House in memory of his brother, the club became a haven for all ranks, and was universally known by its initials TH, or Toc H in the language of the signallers of the time. Philip Clayton, nicknamed 'Tubby', was the chaplain put in charge of the house and it was his influence that made Toc H so loved an institution during the war and an organisation that exists to this day. Clayton's eccentric appearance but loveable personality was described by a close colleague. 'He was the living embodiment of Chesterton's Father Brown. Clothing was always a trial – buttons would persist in coming off, breeches would gape at the knee, shirt cuffs would wear out.'

........................................................................................................................................

## CLEARY, FRED (1905–1984) *tireless in his wish to increase open space in the city*
CLEARY GARDEN, HUGGIN HILL, QUEEN VICTORIA STREET, EC4
**CITY OF LONDON**

........................................................................................................................................

## CLEMENTI, MUZIO (1752–1832) *composer, lived here*
128 KENSINGTON CHURCH STREET, W8

Like his contemporary Mozart, Clementi was a musical prodigy. Indeed in 1781 the Austrian Emperor Josef II arranged for the two pianists and composers to conduct a kind of musical duel. Neither of them emerged conclusively victorious from the encounter. Clementi had been born in Rome, the son of a silversmith. He was performing as a church organist at the age of nine and, in 1766, came to the attention of the wealthy English politician and businessman Peter Beckford, who adopted him and brought him to England. Clementi was to spend most of the rest of his life in England, gaining money and renown as composer, conductor, virtuoso and, latterly, piano manufacturer. He published many pieces for piano, of which the best known are the *Gradus ad Parnassum* of 1817, training pieces for generations of keyboard students. Clementi died in Evesham, Worcestershire, where he had lived for many years.

........................................................................................................................................

## CLIVE OF INDIA, LORD (1725–1774) *soldier and administrator, lived here*
45 BERKELEY SQUARE, W1

Born in Shropshire, Clive joined the East India Company in 1743 and first made his mark as a military commander, instrumental in successes against French rivals on the sub-continent. He returned to England in 1753 a wealthy man but extravagance forced him to travel back to India two years later in search of a new fortune. His second fortune was built on his victory at the battle at Plassey in 1757 and on his period as Governor of Bengal from 1764 to 1767. Impeached by Parliament on charges of corruption, he was finally acquitted but the allegations took their toll and it seems highly likely that Clive committed suicide in November 1774 at his house in Berkeley Square. It seems also highly likely that many of the charges against him were substantively true. Opportunities for corruption in India at the time were immense. Indeed Clive himself acknowledged this during the proceedings against him when he cried out, 'By God, Mr Chairman, at this moment I stand astonished at my own moderation.'

........................................................................................................................................

## CLOVER, DR JOSEPH (1825–1882) *pioneer anaesthetist, lived in a house on this site*
3 CAVENDISH PLACE, W1   **WESTMINSTER**

During the nineteenth century anaesthetics was a science in its infancy. One of those who contributed most to its growth was Joseph Clover. Born in Norfolk, Clover trained at University College, London, and practised as a surgeon before specialising in anaesthetics in the 1850s. He was soon the leading figure in the field in London, attending well-known people like Florence Nightingale and Sir Robert Peel and devising new means of administering ether and chloroform, the most commonly used anaesthetics of the day. Clover died in 1882 and is remembered in a lecture named after him which is given every two years at the Royal College of Surgeons.

## COBDEN, RICHARD (1804–1865) *statesman, died here*

23 SUFFOLK STREET, SW1

One of the most successful political campaigns of the nineteenth century was that in favour of free trade in general and against the restrictions of the Corn Laws in particular. Richard Cobden, a calico printer who had settled in Manchester, was, together with John Bright, the leader of this crusade for free trade. The Anti-Corn Law League was founded in 1838 and Cobden and Bright campaigned ceaselessly, both inside and outside Parliament, for the repeal of the restrictive legislation. Prime Minister Sir Robert Peel, originally in favour of the Corn Laws, was persuaded by the Anti-Corn Law League and by the sufferings of the Irish during the potato famine, that change was needed and the laws were finally repealed in 1846. Cobden continued in parliament as an advocate of international free trade and peaceful co-operation between nations, denouncing the Crimean War and vocally supporting the North in the American Civil War. Cobden neglected his own finances in pursuit of what he saw as the greater good but his popularity as a public figure meant that subscriptions in 1845 and 1860 raised £80,000 and £40,000 on his behalf.

## COBDEN-SANDERSON, THOMAS JAMES (1840–1922) *founded the Doves Bindery and Doves Press in this house, and later lived and died here*

15 UPPER MALL, W6

Cobden-Sanderson was a barrister who, through friendship with William Morris, became a leader in the movement to revive the art of typography. He moved to Hammersmith in 1893, establishing the Doves Bindery, and seven years later he founded the Doves Press. In producing a number of exquisitely crafted volumes (including what became known as the Doves Bible), the Press carried the tradition of William Morris and the Kelmscott Press into the twentieth century. Sadly, financial difficulties forced the Press to close in 1916 whereupon a disillusioned Cobden-Sanderson threw his type into the Thames.

## COBHAM, SIR ALAN (1894–1973) *aviator, was born here*

78 DENMAN ROAD, SE15

In the 1920s and 1930s aviators, from the American Charles Lindbergh to the Yorkshirewoman Amy Johnson, were national heroes and international celebrities. One of the greatest of them all was Alan Cobham. Cobham had been a member of the Royal Flying Corps, the predecessor of the RAF, during the First World War but he first became famous after the war when he joined the de Havilland company as a test pilot and began a series of long-haul flights around the world. In 1921, he toured Europe, flying 5,000 miles and visiting 17 cities in three weeks. He flew several gruelling flights around Africa, including one from London to the Cape of Good Hope and back, and, in 1926, the year he was knighted, he piloted a plane from England to Australia. 'A man is never too old to fly,' Sir Alan Cobham once said, 'I will never give up flying until I am too old to crawl into my machine.' He was as good as his word and continued to take to the air himself throughout his later career as an enthusiastic advocate of air travel for all and as the founder of an aeronautical company still in existence today.

## COCHRANE, THOMAS, EARL OF DUNDONALD (1775–1860) *and later* DAVID, EARL BEATTY (1871–1936) *admirals, lived here*

HANOVER LODGE, OUTER CIRCLE, REGENT'S PARK, NW1

One of the most extraordinary men ever to serve in the Royal Navy, Thomas Cochrane first came to notice as a brilliantly daring captain in the Napoleonic Wars, who led a spectacular fireship attack on the French fleet in 1809. He became a Radical MP, attacking naval corruption, but was himself convicted of fraud in 1814, stripped of the knighthood he had been given and imprisoned. Breaking out of jail, he made a surprise reappearance in Parliament and had to be forcibly removed. After his official release from prison he offered his services to the navies of Chile and Peru in their struggles against Spanish imperialism, and was soon successful in making the nascent republics rulers of their own waters. Returning to England, after further adventures in Brazil and Greece, he was exonerated, his honours restored and reinstated in the Navy in 1832. He retained his belligerence into old age, pressing for a command in the Crimean War and displaying profound disappointment when the government decided an octogenarian officer was not required.

DAVID BEATTY, although he gained a reputation as a bold and daring strategist, had an altogether more conventional career than Cochrane. After service in the Sudan and the Boxer Rebellion he was singled out for promotion and, by the outbreak of the First World War, was in command of the Battlecruiser Squadron. Early in the war he had successes in the Heligoland Bight, sinking three German cruisers, and in a naval encounter on the Dogger Bank, and was one of the major players in the inconclusive Battle of Jutland in 1916. During the battle Beatty, watching British cruisers sinking beneath the waves, allegedly turned to a subordinate and remarked, 'Chatfield, there seems to be something wrong with our bloody ships today.' In that same year he replaced Jellicoe as commander of the Grand Fleet and, after the war, spent eight years as First Sea Lord.

......................................................................................................................

## COCKERELL, C.R. (1788–1863) *architect and antiquary, lived and died here*
### 13 CHESTER TERRACE, NW1

Cockerell, one of the most successful of nineteenth-century British architects, began his career in the offices of his father and then worked with the architect of the British Museum, Robert Smirke, before starting his own practice in 1817. Two years later he was appointed surveyor of St Paul's Cathedral, the first of a number of public positions which culminated forty years later in the presidency of the Royal Institute of British Architects. He also became architect to the Bank of England and was, for nearly twenty years, Professor of architecture at the Royal Academy. Although Cockerell built extensively in London (the imposing Sun Life Offices in Threadneedle Street, demolished in 1970, were his), his most famous and impressive design was for the Taylor Institution in Oxford, built in the 1840s.

......................................................................................................................

## COLE, SIR HENRY (1808–1882) *campaigner and educator, first Director of the Victoria and Albert Museum, lived here*

### 33 THURLOE SQUARE, SW7

SIR HENRY COLE *lived here 1879–1880. He originated the custom of sending Christmas cards and was largely responsible for the foundation of the Kensington Museum. He was also a great postal reformer.*

### 3 ELM ROW, NW3   HAMPSTEAD PLAQUE FUND

South Kensington owes much of its importance as a centre of culture and learning to Henry Cole. Born in Bath, Cole was Chairman of the Society of Arts at the time the Great Exhibition was first mooted and, when a committee was formed to further the idea, it was Cole who became one of its most energetic and forceful members. After the Exhibition had ended and South Kensington was proposed as a site for a museum to continue the work of educating the public that it had begun, Cole was again in the forefront of those campaigning for the museum. The Albert Hall was also very much Cole's idea and, in 1876, he helped found the National

Training School for Music which was to evolve into the Royal College of Music. As well as his work as a committee man Cole was an art critic and journalist and, under the pseudonym of Felix Summerley, wrote a series of illustrated children's books.

......................................................................................................................

## COLERIDGE, SAMUEL TAYLOR (1772–1834) *poet and philosopher, lived here*
7 ADDISON BRIDGE PLACE, W14

## SAMUEL TAYLOR COLERIDGE, *English poet and critic. Lived here in Highgate Village for nineteen years and in this house from 1825 until his death in 1834.*
3 THE GROVE, N6   **ST PANCRAS BOROUGH COUNCIL**

The son of a Devon clergyman, Coleridge showed precocious talent as a schoolboy and, as an undergraduate, the instability that was to overshadow his life. He disappeared from Cambridge for several months and enlisted in the dragoons under the unlikely pseudonym of Silas Tomkyn Comberbache. It was also at Cambridge that he first took opium, which was later to dominate his life. He met Wordsworth in 1797 and, the following year, they published *Lyrical Ballads*, which included what is probably Coleridge's best-known poem 'The Rime of the Ancient Mariner'. The next two decades were a time of escalating personal and creative difficulty for Coleridge, as his addiction to opium grew, his marriage was ruined by an obsessive love for Wordsworth's sister-in-law and he was estranged from many friends. In 1810 when he moved into Addison Bridge Place, staying with the lawyer John Morgan and his family, his life was in tatters. He followed the Morgans to Berners Street and tried unsuccessfully to give up opium. It was only when he moved to Highgate as a guest of Dr Gillman that Coleridge was able to bring his life under some control. He stayed with the Gillmans for the rest of his life, metamorphosing into a semi-legendary figure to the younger generation of writers.

......................................................................................................................

## COLERIDGE-TAYLOR, SAMUEL (1875–1912) *composer of the 'Song of Hiawatha' lived here*
30 DAGNALL PARK, SOUTH NORWOOD, SE25

Coleridge-Taylor's father, a doctor, was from Sierra Leone and his mother from England and he entered the Royal Academy of Music in 1890 as a violin student. He later studied composition there under the tutelage of Charles Stanford. His most famous works remain the three cantatas based on Longfellow's poem *Hiawatha* but he wrote prolifically in his short life and other works include a concert overture inspired by the life of the Caribbean revolutionary Toussaint L'Ouverture and a violin concerto. In his lifetime his work was much in demand both in Britain and in the USA, a country that Coleridge-Taylor three times toured as a conductor.

......................................................................................................................

## COLLINS, WILLIAM WILKIE (1824–1889) *novelist, lived here*
65 GLOUCESTER PLACE, W1

The son of a well-known landscape painter, Wilkie Collins owed his unusual Christian name to his father's admiration for the Scottish artist Sir David Wilkie. His first literary endeavour was a life of his father and, encouraged by his friend Dickens, he went on to write two of the greatest examples of what was known as 'sensation fiction', the novels *The Woman in White* (1860) and *The Moonstone* (1868). After publication of the latter, Collins's work was rarely as popular as it once had been and an epigram by Swinburne suggests one of the reasons why. 'What brought good Wilkie's genius near perdition?', Swinburne wrote, 'Some devil whispered – "Wilkie, have a mission"'. Much of Wilkie Collins's later fiction is marred by his determination to move away from mystery and suspense, at which he excelled, to fiction with a social purpose, at which he did not. His personal life had also become extraordinarily complicated and by the 1870s he was supporting two mistresses and a laudanum addiction. Collins died in 1889 and a last novel, *Blind Love*, was completed by Walter Besant.

## COLLINS MUSIC HALL *was here from 1862–1958*

10-11 ISLINGTON GREEN, N1

What was to become one of the most famous of London's music halls was opened by the comic singer Sam Collins in 1862 in the Lansdowne Arms pub. Originally called the Lansdowne Music Hall, it ran into immediate difficulties with the licensing authorities and had to close. Re-opened in November 1863, it was now known as Collins Music Hall but Sam Collins died only two years later. His widow took it over and it became one of the leading halls on the circuit. All the stars of music hall and variety from Marie Lloyd and Little Tich to Gracie Fields and Tommy Trinder played at Collins at some stage in their careers. Its nickname, 'the Chapel on the Green', allegedly referred to the propriety of the entertainments it staged, which other halls couldn't always match. It was destroyed in a fire and the site is now occupied by a Waterstone's bookshop.

## COLYER, KEN (1928–1988) *In the basement of this building was Studio 51 Ken Colyer played New Orleans Jazz here 1950–1973*

11-12 GREAT NEWPORT STREET, WC2 **WESTMINSTER**

One of the leading figures in the British movement of the forties and fifties to revive the sounds of New Orleans jazz, Ken Colyer was born in Great Yarmouth and was first introduced to the music that would shape his life when he was still at school. Joining the Merchant Navy as a young man, Colyer jumped ship as soon as he reached New Orleans and went to sit in with some of the legendary jazzmen in the city. Discovered by the authorities, he was deported as an illegal immigrant. Back in the UK, his reputation enhanced by his escapade, he worked with other musicians of the time such as Chris Barber and then, in 1954, formed his own band, which played and toured for the next thirty years.

## COMPTON-BURNETT, DAME IVY (1884–1969) *novelist, lived here 1934–1969*

5 BRAEMAR MANSIONS, CORNWALL GARDENS, SW7

In Ivy Compton-Burnett's fiction, highly stylised and carefully constructed dialogue masks but cannot hide the stories of petty domestic tyrannies, familial cruelties and small-scale struggles for power that lurk beneath the surface of the upper middle-class lives she describes. Much of the impetus for this unforgiving fiction must have come from her own family circumstances. Her father married twice and she was the eldest of seven children from the second marriage. The first marriage had produced five children. Two of her brothers died young. Her two youngest sisters jointly committed suicide. From this emotional confusion and turmoil her books eventually appeared, her first characteristic novel being *Pastors and Masters* in 1925. Another eighteen followed including *Daughters and Sons, Men and Wives* and *Parents and Children*. During some of the years at Braemar Mansions she shared her life with the writer and antique collector Margaret Jourdain, who died in 1951.

## CONAN DOYLE, SIR ARTHUR (1859–1930) *creator of Sherlock Holmes, lived here 1891–1894*

12 TENNISON ROAD, SOUTH NORWOOD, SE25

## SIR ARTHUR CONAN DOYLE, (1859–1930) *writer, worked and wrote his stories here in 1891*

2 UPPER WIMPOLE STREET, W1 **WESTMINSTER**

Conan Doyle came from a family of artists and illustrators – his uncle worked for *Punch* and his grandfather was a political caricaturist – but he trained originally as a doctor. He began writing in the 1880s and Sherlock Holmes made his first appearance in *A Study in Scarlet* in

1887. As more stories appeared the character gained enormous popularity. The description on the plaque at Tennison Road would probably annoy Conan Doyle. He was a prolific writer of historical romances, wrote the Professor Challenger stories and a massive history of the Flanders campaign in the First World War. He campaigned fiercely against miscarriages of justice and was long interested in spiritualism. He resented the fact that he was known chiefly for the creation of Holmes and attempted to kill him off by sending him and Professor Moriarty plunging over the Reichenbach Falls. The public would have none of it, however, and Conan Doyle was obliged to bring the great detective back in more novels and stories.

## CONRAD, JOSEPH (1857–1924) *novelist, lived here*
### 17 GILLINGHAM STREET, SW1

Few English novelists have created their fiction from the raw material of a life as adventurous as that of Joseph Conrad. He was born Konrad Korzeniowski to Polish parents living in what is now the Ukraine. His father, a writer and translator, was also involved in revolutionary plots against the Tsar and was sent into an exile which claimed the life of his wife, Conrad's mother. Conrad's father himself died four years later and the eleven-year-old was entrusted to the care of an uncle. In 1876 Conrad began a twenty-year career as a seaman, during which he ran guns for Spanish revolutionaries, sailed on wool clippers to Australia and came to know the ports and cities of the Far East intimately. He had begun service on British ships in 1878 and, in 1886, probably in order to gain his master's certificate from the Board of Trade, he became a naturalised British subject. Retiring from the sea in the 1890s Conrad wrote his first novel *Almayer's Folly* in 1895. He married and, exchanging his adventurous life for the sedentary life of a writer in Ashford, Kent, went on to produce those books (*Lord Jim*, *Nostromo* and *Heart of Darkness* among them) which have given him a lasting status in English literature.

## CONS, EMMA (1837–1912) *philanthropist and founder of the Old Vic, lived here*
### 136 SEYMOUR PLACE, W1

Emma Cons was a woman of great energy and diverse talents. As a young woman she practised a number of arts and crafts and became a designer of stained glass windows. She also met a number of the Victorian great and good, including Ruskin and the pioneer housing reformer Octavia Hill, and through them was drawn into the management of accommodation and entertainment for London's poorer classes. Like many other reformers she became convinced that drink, rather than money, was the root of all evil and she opened teetotal clubs and 'Coffee Taverns' to combat its influence. When she took over a Lambeth music hall in 1880, what was later to become the Old Vic, it was to run it as a temperance entertainment centre but it became much more. Emma Cons managed the Old Vic full-time from 1894 to her death in 1912 when it passed to her niece Lilian Baylis. She was also a leading advocate of women's suffrage and one of the first three women members of the LCC.

## CONSTABLE, JOHN (1776–1837) *painter, lived here*
### 40 WELL WALK, NW3

## JOHN CONSTABLE, *painter*
### 2 LOWER TERRACE, NW3   HAMPSTEAD PLAQUE FUND

Constable was born in Suffolk and many of his best-known paintings, such as *The Haywain*, are views of that county, but he moved to London in 1795 and spent much of his life in the capital. Although now acknowledged as one of England's greatest artists, Constable was not a great success, either critically or financially, in his lifetime. He was not elected a full Royal Academician until 1829 and his financial security was only achieved a year earlier through an inheritance from his wife's father. The family moved to Hampstead in 1821 in the hope that the air would prove beneficial to the failing health of Constable's wife. Constable came to love the area, particularly the Heath and the changing quality of the sky and clouds, which he could observe on his frequent walks there. Constable was a prosaic and unpretentious man. When William Blake enthused about some of his work, crying, 'Why, this is not drawing, but inspiration!' Constable replied mildly, 'I never knew it before. I meant it for drawing.'

......................................................................................................................

## COOK, CAPTAIN JAMES (1728–1779) *circumnavigator and explorer, lived in a house on this site*

88 MILE END ROAD, E1

## CAPTAIN JAMES COOK, *explorer, lived here*
326, THE HIGHWAY, E1    **STEPNEY HISTORICAL TRUST**

The son of a farm labourer, Cook was born in Yorkshire and apprenticed to a firm of Whitby shipowners. In 1755 he transferred to the Royal Navy, becoming a Master four years later and demonstrating the talent for navigation and surveying that led to his appointment, in 1768, as commander of an expedition to Tahiti to observe the transit of Venus across the surface of the sun. From Tahiti Cook sailed on to New Zealand, circumnavigating and charting its islands, and then went on to the east coast of Australia, which he took possession of for Britain. It was to the house in Mile End Road, demolished earlier this century but described by the Victorian historian of London, Walter Besant, as 'a small and rather mean house', that Cook returned from this voyage in 1771. He was to make two other voyages of discovery. Between 1772 and 1775, in command of the *Resolution* and the *Adventure*, he sailed further south than almost any other navigator of the time and effectively disproved the theory that an enormous southern land mass, 'Terra Australis', existed. On his final voyage he was aiming to discover a passage round the north coast of America from the Pacific. However, this third voyage ended in tragedy. Landing at Karakakoa Bay in Hawaii with the intention of recovering a boat stolen by the natives, Cook and his men were attacked and Cook himself killed.

......................................................................................................................

## COPEMAN, SYDNEY MONCKTON (1862–1947) *immunologist and developer of smallpox vaccine, lived here*

57 REDCLIFFE GARDENS, SW10

Born in the cathedral close in Norwich, where his father was Canon and Rural Dean, Sydney Monckton Copeman won a scholarship to Corpus Christie College, Cambridge, and went on to undertake postgraduate medical research at St Thomas's Hospital in London. Much of his later career was to be spent in the public health service as a medical officer of the Local Government Board. In this role his interests were varied and wide-ranging but his principal claim to fame (and to the gratitude of later generations) lies in his work on smallpox vaccination. Although vaccination had been in existence since the eighteenth century, it was still a process dangerously open to bacterial infection. It was Copeman's achievements, through his experimental work, to transform vaccination against smallpox into a safe and sure operation. His methods of vaccine production continued to be used, largely unaltered, for eighty years until smallpox was officially declared a disease of the past in 1977.

......................................................................................................................

## COSTA, SIR MICHAEL (1808–1883) *conductor and orchestra reformer, lived here 1857–1883*

WILTON COURT, 59 ECCLESTON SQUARE, SW1

Sir Michael Costa was born in Naples as Michaele Andrea Agniello Costa and came to England as a young man. He decided to make the country his home and went on to become one of the leading figures in the musical life of London for nearly fifty years. As a composer, Costa was not especially talented. 'The good Costa has sent me an oratorio score and a Stilton cheese,' Rossini once wrote to a friend. 'The cheese was very good.' However, as a conductor and musical impresario, Costa played a major role in the musical life of Victorian England. One of the earliest conductors in the country to make use of the baton, he was director of music first at the King's Theatre (1830–1847) and then, after a dispute with the management, at the Royal Italian Opera (1847–1869), now the Royal Opera House. He was also conductor of the Philharmonic Society Orchestra, raising its standards until it could match the best in Europe, and directed a number of annual music festivals around the country from Birmingham to Leeds. The first person to be knighted for his services as a conductor, Sir Michael Costa was more responsible than anyone for what his biographer called 'the radical change which lifted English music between 1830 and 1880'.

---

COUNTY HALL, *the home of London government from 1922 to 1986; LCC 1889–1965, GLC 1965–1986*

MAIN ENTRANCE, COUNTY HALL, SE1

In 1905 the London County Council, tiring of the restrictions imposed by its offices in Spring Gardens, bought a site on the South Bank and held an open competition for architects to produce plans for a suitably impressive new headquarters for the city's government. A number of famous names, including Edwin Lutyens, submitted designs but the winner was a relatively unknown architect called Ralph Knott, whose monumental building was begun in 1909. Although the official opening was carried out by George V in 1922, Knott's vision was not finally realised until 1933. By 1965 the city had grown far beyond the jurisdiction of the LCC and a new body, still based in County Hall and known as the Greater London Council, was constituted. The GLC was abolished in 1986. Knott's imposing 'Edwardian Renaissance' County Hall is now home to the London aquarium and a luxury hotel.

---

COWARD, CHARLES (1905–1976) *rescuer of Jews from Auschwitz, lived here 1945–1976*

133 CHICHESTER ROAD, N9

When Charles Coward died, the head of the Department of the Righteous at Yad Vashem Holocaust Memorial in Jerusalem wrote to his family: 'We will long remember and pass on to our posterity Mr Coward's heroic and selfless actions, which he rendered in service to his fellow men.' Coward was a British soldier who was captured by the Germans near Calais in May 1940. As a POW, he was a persistent escapee and troublemaker and eventually, as a punishment, the Nazi authorities transferred him to a camp attached to a slave labour camp at Auschwitz. A fluent German speaker, Coward acted as liaison between guards and prisoners and, in that role, was able to witness the terrible crimes that were being committed against the Jewish slave labourers. He came up with an ingenious scheme to save lives. By bribing a sweet-toothed German guard with the chocolate that British prisoners received in Red Cross parcels, he took possession of the bodies and documents of non-Jewish prisoners who had died. A few at a time, Jewish prisoners were then given the identities of the dead and eventually smuggled out of the camps. In all, more than 400 Jewish slave labourers at Auschwitz were saved as a result of Coward's efforts. The 1962 film *The Password Is Courage*, starring Dirk Bogarde, is based on Coward's adventures earlier in the war as an escapee from POW camps.

---

COWARD, SIR NOEL (1899 –1973) *actor, playwright and songwriter, born here*

131, WALDEGRAVE ROAD, TEDDINGTON

SIR NOEL COWARD, *dramatist, songwriter and performer, lived here*

56, LENHAM ROAD, SUTTON   **BOROUGH OF SUTTON**

## SIR NOEL COWARD (1899–1973)
17 GERALD ROAD, SW1  **PRIVATE**

Although he became the epitome of metropolitan wit and sophistication, Noel Coward was born in the quiet, suburban surroundings of Teddington, the son of a piano salesman and a fiercely ambitious mother who devoted herself to furthering his early career on stage. As a teenager he appeared in a D.W. Griffith film but shot to fame in 1924 as the writer and star of *The Vortex*, a controversial drama about a tormented young drug addict and his difficult relationship with his mother. A succession of lighter, stylishly comic plays like *Hay Fever* and *Private Lives* kept him in the public eye throughout the 1920s and '30s and, when his type of drama became unfashionable after the war, he reinvented himself as a cabaret artist and masterly performer of his own songs. As somebody once said of Coward, 'he was his own greatest invention.' He himself attributed his perennial appeal and his talent to amuse to his capacity, often well disguised, for hard work. 'The only way to enjoy life,' he said, 'is to work. Work is much more fun than fun.'

## COX, DAVID (1783–1859) *artist, lived here*
34 FOXLEY ROAD, SW9

Born the son of a blacksmith near Birmingham, Cox worked at his father's forge and began his artistic career painting the lids of snuff boxes and providing scenery for travelling theatre companies. He took lessons from John Varley, a friend of Blake and a founder member of the Watercolour Society, and then earned his living as a drawing master in London and Hereford. He lived in Foxley Road from 1827 to 1841 but travelled and sketched throughout the country, particularly North Wales. He was a regular visitor to the small town of Betws-y-Coed and painted the inn sign for the Royal Oak there. In later life he began to paint in oils as well as watercolours but it is for his work in the latter medium that he remains best known. He died in Harborne near Birmingham where he had settled after leaving London in 1841.

## CRANE, WALTER (1845–1915) *artist, lived here*
13 HOLLAND STREET, W8

Born in Liverpool, where his father worked as a portrait painter, Walter Crane became well known as an illustrator, particularly of children's books, in the 1870s and, although he regularly exhibited paintings at the Royal Academy and the Grosvenor Galleries, it is for his illustrations that he is best remembered. Crane was a convinced socialist who was a member of Hyndman's Social Democratic Federation and, later, William Morris's Socialist League. Briefly Principal of the Royal College of Art in the 1890s, Crane also wrote books on the art of illustration and an influential work, *The Claims of Decorative Art*, which attempted to show that true art could only flourish in a society where wealth was more equitably distributed. When Crane died his old colleague Hyndman wrote of him that no one 'had a greater influence on the minds of doubters who feared that Socialism must be remote from and even destructive of the sense of beauty.'

## CREED, FREDERICK GEORGE (1871–1957) *electrical engineer, inventor of the teleprinter, lived and died here*

20 OUTRAM ROAD, ADDISCOMBE

Born in Nova Scotia, it was while he was working there for the Western Union Telegraph Company that Frederick Creed first formulated his belief that it ought to be possible to integrate a typewriter and a telegraphy system in order to transmit and receive information. He continued to work on his ideas when working in South America between 1888 and 1897 but it was only when he moved to Glasgow, where he established a workshop, that he was able to perfect his ideas and demonstrate their practical effectiveness. In 1898 his prototype teleprinter transmitted the *Glasgow Herald* newspaper to London at the rate of 60 words per minute. By the time the First World War broke out Creed's system was in use all over the world and the speed of his machines had risen to 200 words a minute. Creed, a restless innovator, continued to make improvements in his machines for much of the rest of his life.

## CRIBB, TOM (1781–1848) *bare-knuckle boxing champion, lived here*
### 36 PANTON STREET, SW1

Born near Bristol, Tom Cribb moved to London when he was in his teens and developed the muscles he required in his career as a bare-knuckle boxer, when he worked as a coal porter in the docks at Wapping. After a period in which he probably served briefly in the Navy, he turned to the prize ring to earn money and his first bout – seventy-six rounds against a veteran fighter named George Maddox – took place in 1805. Within a few years, Cribb was recognised as champion of England. His most famous fights took place in 1810 and 1811. He became a national hero when he twice defeated the black American boxer Tom Molyneaux, a former slave who had won his freedom through his prowess as a fighter. After his retirement from the ring Cribb, like many other boxers, became a landlord and he ran a pub in Panton Street for many years. When he died at the age of 67, he was buried in the churchyard of St Mary's, Woolwich where a large stone lion, paid for by public subscription, still stands guard over his grave.

## CRIPPS, SIR STAFFORD (1889–1952) *statesman, born here*
### 32 ELM PARK GARDENS, SW10

Born the son of a Conservative MP who later joined the Labour party and was in Ramsay MacDonald's two governments of 1924 and 1929–31, Cripps was also the nephew of the Fabian stalwart Beatrice Webb. He became a brilliantly successful lawyer and entered the same government in which his father was serving when he became Solicitor General in 1930. Like most of his colleagues he refused to join MacDonald's National Government and moved further to the left during the thirties. In 1939, in dispute with the Labour leadership over the best way for left-wing parties to oppose fascism, Cripps was expelled from the Labour party and obliged to sit as an independent MP throughout the war. Churchill recognised his ability and in 1942 he was given the vital role of minister in charge of aircraft production. Re-admitted to the Labour party after the war Cripps was Chancellor from 1947 to 1950 when ill health forced him to step down. He died two years later.

## CROMPTON, COLONEL R.E.B. (1845–1940) *electrical engineer, lived and worked here 1891–1939*
### 48 KENSINGTON COURT, KENSINGTON, W8

Born in Thirsk in Yorkshire, Crompton started his career in the army in India but he had always been interested in engineering since his schooldays and, by the time he was thirty, he had retired from military life and formed a company to manufacture electrical appliances of all kinds. Crompton went on to become one of the pioneers in the generation and distribution of electricity for lighting. (Crompton's earlier home in Porchester Gardens was the first in London to be lit effectively by electricity.) His generating station at Kensington Court, which supplied electricity to the surrounding neighbourhood, is no longer in use but can still be seen at the rear of the house. Crompton installed electric lighting at King's Cross station and at the Law Courts in London, among other places, and his talents were also in demand abroad – in the 1880s he provided electric lighting for the Vienna Opera House. Fittingly, in view of his earlier career, Crompton's inventiveness was also utilized by the army. In the Boer War he devised powerful searchlights for the troops to use and, in the First World War, he was one of the engineers who gave advice on the design of the revolutionary 'tank'. Crompton's long and productive life came to an end at his home in Ripon, Yorkshire, in 1940 at the age of ninety-five.

CROOKES, SIR WILLIAM (1832–1919) *scientist, lived here from 1880 until his death*
7 KENSINGTON PARK GARDENS, W11

Crookes was a significant contributor to many of the new fields of research in physics and chemistry that emerged in the nineteenth century. His discovery of the element thallium in 1861 led to his election as a Fellow of the Royal Society. He investigated the properties of vacuums, invented the radiometer in 1875 and his house in Kensington Park Gardens was, according to his biographer, the first in the country to be lit by electric light. At an age when most men have retired Crookes became interested in the newly discovered phenomenon of radioactivity and invented the spinthariscope, a device that detected alpha particles emitted from radioactive material by highlighting their impact on a fluorescent screen. Like many Victorian scientists he was also fascinated by psychical research and published the results of his own investigation into the medium Florence Cooke, proclaiming her materialization of spirits to be genuine.

CRUIKSHANK, GEORGE (1792–1878) *artist, lived here from 1850 to 1878*
263, HAMPSTEAD ROAD, NW1

GEORGE CRUIKSHANK
69–71 AMWELL STREET, EC1   **ISLINGTON BOROUGH COUNCIL**

Both Cruikshank's father, Isaac, and his older brother, Robert, were political caricaturists and George also began his working life as a satirist, helping to meet the huge demand in Regency England for prints that held up politicians and members of the royal family to ridicule. He moved on to book illustration, contributing images to an early English edition of *Grimm's Fairy Tales* and illustrating Dickens's *Oliver Twist* and several of Harrison Ainsworth's historical melodramas. Characteristically, Cruikshank claimed that all the credit for the success of these books belonged to his illustrations. In his later years Cruikshank, who had led a notably dissipated life as a young man, became a belligerent crusader for temperance. Works such as *The Bottle* of 1847 and *The Worship of Bacchus* of 1862 warn, with graphic immediacy, of the perils of over-indulgence.

CUBITT, THOMAS (1788–1855) *master builder, lived here*
3 LYALL STREET, SW1

As a speculative builder and developer Cubitt, who first moved to London in his early twenties, had more impact on the topography of the city than anyone else in the first half of the nineteenth century, with the possible exception of John Nash. Cubitt arrived as a master carpenter but by 1815 he had large workshops in the Gray's Inn Road and he became the first person to undertake all aspects of large-scale building schemes. Cubitt's building projects were widespread but his major achievements were on land that he leased from Lord Grosvenor, first in what became known as Belgravia and then in Pimlico. Towards the end of his life Cubitt was involved in the planning of the Great Exhibition and he was one of the people who, by guaranteeing a sum of money, ensured that the project, at one time in danger of coming to nothing, went ahead. His son, Lewis, carried on the family business and was the designer of King's Cross Station.

## CURTIS, WILLIAM (1746–1799) *botanist, lived in a house on this site*

51 GRACECHURCH STREET, EC3 **CITY OF LONDON**

William Curtis was born into a Quaker family in Hampshire and, as a boy of fourteen, he was apprenticed to his grandfather, an apothecary. He moved to London when he was twenty, soon becoming a partner in an apothecary's business, but he then sold his stake in it to pursue his interest in natural history. In 1772, he was appointed Praefectus Horti (or 'director') of the Chelsea Physic Garden, which was owned by the Society of Apothecaries, and later opened his own London Botanic Garden in Lambeth. Here, he grew medicinal and culinary plants, wild flowers, trees and shrubs, eventually cultivating upwards of 6,000 species in the garden. He also embarked on a career as a writer of richly illustrated books on botany and entomology. His magnum opus was *Flora Londinensis,* a multi-volume work, which documented the flowering plants to be found in London and its environs. *Flora Londinensis* is one of the most beautiful books on botany ever published in Britain, but it was a financial failure for Curtis. More successful commercially was *Curtis's Botanical Magazine* which, according to Curtis himself, brought him 'pudding' where the earlier work had brought only 'praise'.

## CURZON, GEORGE NATHANIEL, MARQUESS CURZON OF KEDLESTON (1859–1925) *statesman, Viceroy of India, lived here*

1 CARLTON HOUSE TERRACE, SW1

Born into the heart of the Victorian ruling élite, Curzon was a brilliant but arrogant man with a lordly disdain for those he saw as his intellectual or social inferiors. 'My name is George Nathaniel Curzon/I am a most superior person', a contemporary at Oxford wrote of him. Well travelled in Asia and an enthusiast for the architectural treasures of India, he was appointed Viceroy in 1898. His enthusiasm for India past was not matched by an enthusiasm for the political aspirations of many of its present inhabitants and, as a committed imperialist, he firmly opposed any erosion of the powers of the Raj. Resigning as Viceroy in 1905, Curzon went on to become Foreign Secretary in 1919. He was greatly disappointed not to become Prime Minister in 1923, particularly since he lost out to Stanley Baldwin, a man he considered to be 'of the utmost insignificance'. Soon afterwards Baldwin met Curzon in Downing Street and, he told a friend, 'got the sort of greeting a corpse would give an undertaker.'

## DADD, RICHARD (1817–1886) *painter, lived here*

15 SUFFOLK STREET, SW1

Many people have admired the intricate brushwork and vivid imagination of Richard Dadd's best-known painting *The Fairy Feller's Master-Stroke*, a strange vision of fantastic creatures at play amidst the grass and flowers of an English hedgerow, which can be seen in the Tate. Not so many people know the terrible details of Dadd's life. After a period at the Royal Academy, Dadd had begun a promising career as a professional painter and illustrator when, in 1842–3, he undertook a kind of Grand Tour of Europe and the Middle East. During these travels he suffered increasingly paranoid delusions, became violent towards his companion and secretly convinced that he was chosen by divine powers to fight the Devil in whatever form he took. On his return to England Dadd decided that one of these forms was that of his father, whom he killed in a frenzied attack with knife and razor. Apprehended, Dadd was declared insane and spent the rest of his life in Bedlam and Broadmoor, painting his strange and idiosyncratic visions.

## DALE, SIR HENRY (1875–1968) *physiologist, lived here*
MOUNT VERNON HOUSE, MOUNT VERNON, HAMPSTEAD, NW3

Henry Dale had a long and distinguished career in medical research. He was director of the National Institute of Medical Research, knighted in 1932 and was elected to the presidency of the Royal Society eight years later. His own most important work was into the chemical transmission of nervous impulses and he shared, with the German scientist Otto Loewi, the Nobel Prize for medicine in 1936. He lived at Mount Vernon House, an attractive late Georgian building which is now listed, from 1919 to 1942.

## DANCE, GEORGE, THE YOUNGER (1741–1825) *architect, lived and died here*
91 GOWER STREET, WC1

London owes two of its most interesting public buildings to the Dance family. George Dance the Elder was Clerk of the City Works in the 1730s and, in that capacity, was the architect of the Mansion House. His son, also George Dance, was a successful architect for fifty years. The Guildhall, although medieval in origin, was given much of its present-day appearance by alterations made by him in the 1780s. Dance, probably influenced by John Wood's development in Bath, designed the Crescent, the Circus and America Square which were all built in the 1770s. Sadly only the first of the three still retains any of the original houses. Dance designed the Newgate Prison, which was built between 1770 and 1778. No sooner was it completed than it was attacked by a mob during the Gordon Riots and reduced to a smouldering shell. Rebuilt, it survived until 1902 when it was finally demolished.

## DANIELL, THOMAS (1749–1840) *topographical artist, lived here*
14 EARLS TERRACE, W8

In the course of his long life Thomas Daniell worked as a topographical artist throughout this country and in Europe. However, his most characteristic work, and the work that brought him most renown, was that which originated in the great adventure of his life. In 1786, together with his nephew William, he set off for India and the pair travelled widely around the country, sketching and painting as they went. They returned in 1793, bringing with them unrivalled views of the scenery and architecture of what was, at the time, a largely hidden land. The Daniells' work was turned into the monumental *Oriental Scenery*, published in six parts between 1795 and 1807, and consisting of 144 aquatints created from the original drawings and watercolours.

## DANIELL, WILLIAM (1769–1837) *artist and engraver of Indian scenes, lived and died here*
135 ST PANCRAS WAY, NW1

When he was only a teenager William Daniell joined his uncle, Thomas Daniell (see above entry), on what became a ten-year journey around India, visiting and sketching many places that European artists had rarely, if ever, recorded before. Like his uncle, William drew on his Indian experiences for the rest of his working life but, again like his uncle, he became a well-known topographical artist, who exhibited a range of landscape and architectural paintings at the Royal Academy and elsewhere. In 1814 William set off again on another journey, this time around the coastline of his native land; eleven years later, *A Voyage Round Great Britain* was published in four volumes. This remarkable collection of more than 300 aquatint engravings had been described as a record of the 'last great artist's voyage before photography was invented'. William Daniell's other works included *Zoography*, a collection of detailed images of animals and plants in their natural habitat, and a painting of the Battle of Trafalgar which won the British Institution prize of £100 in 1826.

---

DANNREUTHER, EDWARD (1844–1905) *musician, lived here 1873–1894, host to Richard Wagner for 5 weeks in 1877*
12 ORME SQUARE   **WESTMINSTER**

Born in Strasbourg, Dannreuther went to the USA with his family as a young boy and then returned to Germany in his teens to study at the Leipzig Conservatory. He came to England in the 1860s and eventually settled permanently in London. Both as a performer and as a writer, he became a significant figure in the musical life of the capital. He introduced much new music from the continent to England and was a particular champion of the work of Richard Wagner, founding the Wagner Society in London in 1872. Dannreuther played host to the controversial German composer when Wagner, hoping to recoup financial losses he had sustained during his inaugural Bayreuth Festival, visited England in 1877 to conduct a series of concerts at the Royal Albert Hall. As well as being an early advocate of Wagner's music, Dannreuther was the soloist in the first performances in England of two of the most popular of all romantic piano concertos – Grieg's (in 1874) and Tchaikovsky's First (in 1876). The chamber concerts he held regularly at his home in Orme Square were important to London's musical life for many decades.

---

DARWIN, CHARLES (1809–1882) *naturalist, lived in a house on this site 1838–1842*
BIOLOGICAL SCIENCES BUILDING, UNIVERSITY COLLEGE, GOWER STREET, WC1

*Here Darwin thought and worked for 40 years and died in 1882.*
DOWN HOUSE, LUXTED ROAD, DOWNE   **BOROUGH OF BROMLEY**

Charles Darwin's father was the son of the eighteenth-century polymath Erasmus Darwin, whose writings contain some hints of the evolutionary theory his grandson was to elaborate, and his mother was the daughter of Josiah Wedgwood, founder of the famous pottery firm. He was born in Shrewsbury and educated there and at Edinburgh and Cambridge Universities. In 1831 he made the most significant decision of his life when he chose to embark as naturalist on the *Beagle*. In the course of the five-year voyage Darwin had the opportunity to study flora and fauna across the world and it was during these years that the seeds of his ideas about natural selection and the evolution of species were sown. It was not, however, until 1858 that he presented his ideas to the scientific world and he might never have done so had it not been for a paper sent to him by Alfred Russel Wallace, which made it clear that he was moving towards similar conclusions. The following year Darwin published *The Origin of Species* and the most wide-ranging of all nineteenth-century ideas burst on the wider public. Darwin, a quiet and retiring man, had spent the two previous decades in London and at Down House immersed in his research and he spent the rest of his life similarly engaged. He once wrote, 'When I am obliged to give up observation and experiment I shall die', and he was busy with his work until two days before his death.

---

DAVIES, EMILY (1830–1921) *founder of Girton College, Cambridge, lived here*
17 CUNNINGHAM PLACE, ST JOHN'S WOOD, NW8

Emily Davies was a curious mixture of radical and conservative. She was an advocate of women's suffrage, one of the organisers of the petition that was presented to Parliament in 1866, yet she believed that the suffrage should be restricted to unmarried women.

She believed passionately in the higher education for women, which she had been denied, yet she thought that female students should concentrate on the classics and mathematics rather than a more adventurous curriculum. Emily Davies's greatest achievement was the foundation of Girton, which began in 1869 with five students in a private house near Hitchin being schooled to take Cambridge examinations by private arrangement with sympathetic male examiners. The college moved to Cambridge itself in 1873 and became Girton College the following year. The university opened all its examinations to women ten years later but it was not until as late as 1948 that full degrees were awarded. Emily Davies survived to see the jubilee of the college she had begun with five students.

---

## DAY-LEWIS, C. (1904–1972) *Poet Laureate, lived here 1957–1972*

6 CROOMS HILL, SE10

'A poet,' C. Day-Lewis wrote, 'cannot choose his time or his subject-matter, any more than we can choose the parents who gave birth to us.' His own time was the thirties when, together with W.H. Auden and Stephen Spender, he represented a new force in English poetry and was associated with the causes of the Left. He was, for a time, a member of the Communist Party but left in 1939. After the war Day-Lewis became more and more the voice of the poetry establishment. He was Professor of Poetry at Oxford in the fifties and was appointed Poet Laureate after the death of John Masefield. As well as his poetry Day-Lewis published detective stories under the pseudonym of Nicholas Blake. One of his children is the actor Daniel Day-Lewis.

---

## DEFOE, DANIEL (1661–1731) *novelist, lived in a house on this site*

95 STOKE NEWINGTON CHURCH STREET, N16

Born into a nonconformist family called Foe (he did not add the extra letters to his name until he was in his forties) Daniel Defoe was educated at the dissenters' school, Stoke Newington Academy, where one of his fellow students was named Timothy Cruso. He led a remarkably various life. At one time or another in his career he was a hosiery merchant in Cornhill, a participant in the Monmouth Rebellion, the owner of a tile factory in Tilbury and an undercover agent for the government in the North and Scotland. He was also a pioneer journalist who produced hundreds of polemical pamphlets and newspaper articles, many of them published anonymously or pseudonymously. Such a life had its dangers in early eighteenth-century London and Defoe was both pilloried and imprisoned at different times. It was only when he was approaching sixty that he began work on the novels for which he is now remembered. The first part of *Robinson Crusoe* appeared in 1719, to be followed shortly by a sequel, and books like *Moll Flanders* and *Roxana* were published at intervals in the early 1720s. Defoe lived in Stoke Newington between 1709 and 1729 in two houses, both of which have been demolished. The house recalled by the Blue Plaque was in Church Street and had extensive grounds. Defoe Road now cuts through much of what was once the house and grounds.

---

## DE GAULLE, GENERAL CHARLES, *President of the French National Committee, set up the Headquarters of the Free French Forces here in 1940*

4 CARLTON GARDENS, SW1

## GENERAL DE GAULLE

99 FROGNAL, NW3   **HAMPSTEAD PLAQUE FUND**

It was De Gaulle's unshakeable belief in his own destiny and his unswerving loyalty to his idea of his country that made him so potent a leader for the Free French Forces after the fall of France in June 1940. 'De Gaulle,' he once said, characteristically referring to himself in the third person, 'is not left, De Gaulle is not right, De Gaulle is not in the centre. De Gaulle is above.'

This kind of self-dramatisation and self-belief was what was needed in his struggle against the Nazis and the collaborators of the Vichy regime. It did not make him an easy man for the Allies to accommodate. Churchill, who once described him as looking 'like a female llama surprised in her bath', found him a prickly and difficult man to have on the Allied side. After the war De Gaulle was, briefly, President of France in 1945 and then returned from retirement in 1958 to form the Fifth Republic, to award himself sweeping new powers and to attempt to solve the crisis in Algeria. He remained President for eleven years, until 1969, when he resigned after the French public had rejected his plans for further constitutional changes.

## DE HAVILLAND, SIR GEOFFREY (1882–1965) *aircraft designer, lived here 1909–1910*
### 32 BARON'S COURT ROAD, W14

The son of a clergyman, de Havilland was born in Surrey and, as a young man, exhibited the fascination with flight that was sustain his career. It was while he was living in Baron's Court Road that he built the first of his many planes, although he had not, at that time, ever seen an aeroplane in flight. It was not a success. On the machine's maiden flight in 1910, with de Havilland at the controls, it flew a distance of 100 feet and then crashed. Undeterred, he returned to the drawing board and one of his next designs, the BE-2, went on to become the standard British biplane in the First World War. After the war de Havilland set up the aircraft company that was to bear his name and the planes he designed, including the famous Moth, were renowned for their speed sand technological innovation. In the Second World War de Havilland's great contributions, for which he was knighted in 1944, was the creation of the Mosquito fighter-bomber, the fastest aircraft of its day. Although he became a very wealthy and influential man in the air industry, de Havilland never lost his simple enthusiasm for the idea of flight that inspired him while he was working on his first designs in Baron's Court Road – he was still flying for fun in his seventies. De Havilland was the uncle of two film stars – Olivia de Havilland and Joan Fontaine.

## DE LA MARE, WALTER (1873–1956) *poet, lived here 1940–1956*
### SOUTH END HOUSE, MONTPELIER ROW, TWICKENHAM

## WALTER DE LA MARE
### 195 MACKENZIE ROAD, BECKENHAM   **BOROUGH OF BROMLEY**

Many poets pursue relatively prosaic careers outside their writing. Walter De La Mare, while he was publishing the first of his volumes of delicate, lyrical poetry, was working for the Standard Oil Company. He worked for the company for nearly twenty years before he was able to devote himself to full-time writing. After leaving the oil industry, De La Mare published many further volumes of poetry for both adults and children, including *The Listeners*, *Peacock Pie* and *The Veil*, and edited several successful anthologies. He also wrote short stories and other, often idiosyncratic prose works such as *Memoirs of a Midget*, a bizarrely created 'autobiography' of the minute 'Miss M'. In later life, when living in Twickenham, De La Mare was awarded the CH and admitted to the Order of Merit.

## DELIUS, FREDERICK (1862–1934) *composer, lived here 1918–1919*
### 44 BELSIZE PARK GARDENS, NW3

Sir Thomas Beecham once described Delius as 'the last great apostle of romance, emotion and beauty in music'. He was born in Bradford, of German-Scandinavian descent, and, from 1890, lived almost entirely in France, returning only occasionally, as in the period at the end of the First World War which he spent in Belsize Park Gardens, to Britain. Among his best-known pieces are the opera *A Village Romeo and Juliet* and the orchestral pieces *Brigg Fair* and *On Hearing the First Cuckoo in Spring*. Delius lost his sight in the mid-1920s and it was only when he gained the devoted assistance of a young admirer of his work, Eric Fenby, that he was able to compose the works of his last years.

## DE MORGAN, WILLIAM (1839–1917) *ceramic artist and novelist, and his wife,* EVELYN DE MORGAN, *artist, lived and died here*

### 127 OLD CHURCH STREET, SW3

De Morgan's father was the first Professor of Mathematics at University College, London, and De Morgan himself studied there but he soon turned his attention to the decorative arts. He was for a time associated with the firm that William Morris and others established. De Morgan was a painter in the Pre-Raphaelite style and a designer of stained glass but he is best known for his work with glazed pottery, particularly for the tiles that he designed and created in the works he set up, first in his home in Chelsea and then at Merton and Fulham. At an age when most people are thinking of retiring De Morgan launched himself on a new career as a novelist and his first book *Joseph Vance*, a Dickensian tale of a builder's son who rises in the world, was a great success when published in 1906. De Morgan married Evelyn Pickering, a Pre-Raphaelite painter herself, in 1887 and she completed two novels that he left unfinished at his death.

## DE QUINCEY, THOMAS (1785–1859) *wrote 'Confessions of an English Opium Eater' in this house*

### 36 TAVISTOCK STREET, WC2

De Quincey arrived in London in 1802, a teenage runaway from home and Manchester Grammar School, and lived on the streets for a time, virtually destitute, a period he recalls in his most famous work *Confessions of an English Opium Eater*, first published in *The London Magazine* in 1821. Reconciled to his family, he went to Oxford but he frequently returned to London and it was on one of these trips that he first discovered the pleasures and perils of opium which he vividly describes in his book. De Quincey later wrote an account of his friendships with Coleridge and Wordsworth, the latter cut short by the poet's disapproval of his addiction, and, in order to earn money, of which he was chronically short, he became a prolific journalist. 'On Murder as One of the Fine Arts', an exercise in black humour in which De Quincey analyses a number of murders to reveal their varying aesthetic qualities, is his best-known essay. De Quincey died in Edinburgh where he had lived for many years, writing for *Blackwood's Magazine* there.

## DE VALOIS, DAME NINETTE (1898–2001) *OM, founder of the Royal Ballet, lived here 1962–1982*

### 14 THE TERRACE, BARNES, SW13

Her name may suggest she was French, but Ninette de Valois was born Edris Stannus in County Wicklow, Ireland. Passionately interested in dancing from her childhood, she became a ballerina in England and danced with Diaghilev's famous Ballets Russes, changing her name to the one by which she was known for the rest of her life, because successful dancers at the time were expected to be Continental rather than Irish. She never became the great prima ballerina that she dreamed of being but, after her retirement as a dancer, she went on to become the one person most responsible for the great achievements of British ballet in the twentieth century. In 1928, Lilian Baylis, the legendary manager of the Sadler's Wells and Old Vic theatres engaged Ninette de Valois as director of a ballet company at Sadler's Wells. Over the years de Valois turned it into one of the world's most famous companies and it eventually became the Royal Ballet. Under her direction, the company attracted the greatest dancers and choreographers of the day, from Margot Fonteyn and Sir Frederick Ashton to Antoinette Sibley and Kenneth MacMillan. She was also responsible for founding the establishment which became the Royal Ballet School. 'Classical ballet will never die,' Ninette de Valois said once and she did more than anyone to ensure that it thrived in Britain.

DEVANT, DAVID (1868–1941) *magician and first president of The Magic Circle, lived here 1915–1917*

1 ORNAN COURT, ORNAN ROAD, LONDON, NW3

Often described as Britain's greatest ever magician and illusionist, David Devant was born David Wighton in 1868 and became interested in magic trickery as a young boy. Sacked from one job for practicing conjuring tricks rather than attending to more pressing tasks, he eventually decided to earn his living from his magic. In his early twenties, he became the protégé of John Nevil Maskelyne, then Britain's most celebrated magician. Devant's fame soon outshone that of even Maskelyne and when The Magic Circle was formed in 1905, it was Devant who was invited to become its first president. He was particularly renowned for his illusions involving the apparent disappearance of human beings and also for a trademark trick, the 'Magic Kettle', a vessel from which he miraculously produced any liquid demanded by members of his audience. At the height of his career, Devant was struck down by illness and, sadly, this master illusionist was unable to perform for the last twenty years of his life.

DEVINE, GEORGE (1910–1966) *actor, artistic director of the Royal Court Theatre 1956–1965, lived here*

9 LOWER MALL, HAMMERSMITH, W6

George Devine presided over one of the most exciting periods in British drama during the twentieth century. Under his aegis as artistic director of the English Stage Company at its home at the Royal Court Theatre, plays such as John Osborne's *Look Back in Anger* and John Arden's *Serjeant Musgrave's Dance* revitalised an English theatre grown stale and complacent, and introduced the public to 'angry young men' and dramas of fire and social commitment. When he arrived at the Royal Court, Devine already had a track record as a theatrical innovator. Between 1936 and 1939 he had run the London Theatre Studio, which attempted to reform the training given to actors in Britain, and he had continued the work at the Old Vic Centre in the late 1940s. The George Devine Award, established after his early death in 1966, is given to encourage young theatre practitioners to continue the work to which Devine devoted his life.

DICKENS, CHARLES (1812–1870) *novelist, lived here*
48 DOUGHTY STREET, WC1

CHARLES DICKENS *lived in a house on this site when a boy in 1823*

141 BAYHAM STREET, NW1
**DICKENS FELLOWSHIP**

CHARLES DICKENS (1812–1870)
*author, stayed here in 1832*

92 NORTH ROAD, N6
**HARINGEY BOROUGH COUNCIL**

CHARLES DICKENS (1812–1870) *novelist, lived for a time in Furnivalls Inn close to this spot and there wrote Pickwick in the year 1836. This bust was modelled and presented by Percy Fitzgerald*

PRUDENTIAL BUILDING,
HIGH HOLBORN, WC1 **PRIVATE**

CHARLES DICKENS *While living in a house on this site wrote six of his principal works, characters from which appear in this sculptured panel*

15–17 MARYLEBONE ROAD, NW1   **DICKENS FELLOWSHIP**

CHARLES DICKENS, *novelist, lived in Tavistock House near this site, 1851–1860*

BMA HOUSE, TAVISTOCK SQUARE, WC1   **PRIVATE**

Although there are a number of plaques to London's greatest novelist in the city, only 48 Doughty Street survives as an original house in which he lived, and it is open to the public. By the time he moved into the house in 1837 he had survived the horrors of his childhood – a father imprisoned for debt in the Marshalsea Prison, his own misery and loneliness when sent to work in a blacking factory by Hungerford Stairs – to become, first a parliamentary reporter and then a best-selling novelist. *Pickwick Papers* had been a great success, he had married the previous year and he felt confident enough to take on what he called, 'a frightfully first-class Family Mansion, involving awful responsibilities'. During the time he was in Doughty Street, Dickens worked on *Oliver Twist* and *Nicholas Nickleby*. It was also during his time at Doughty Street that one of the great tragedies of his life occurred, the death of his wife's seventeen-year-old sister Mary Hogarth. Dickens was extraordinarily, some might say obsessively, attached to his sister-in-law and he was devastated by her death. 'From the day of our marriage,' he later wrote, 'the dear girl had been the grace and life of our home, our constant companion, and the sharer of all our little pleasures.' In 1839, his family growing, Dickens moved out of Doughty Street and into the property whose site is now marked on Marylebone Road. Twelve years later he moved into his last and grandest London home in Tavistock Square, staying there until he fulfilled his boyhood dream of buying Gad's Hill Place in Rochester.

........................................................................................................

DICKINSON, GOLDSWORTHY LOWES (1862–1932) *author and humanist*

11 EDWARDES SQUARE, W8

Educated at Charterhouse and King's College, Cambridge, Dickinson spent most of his life at the Cambridge college where he became a Fellow. No. 11 Edwardes Square was his London home from 1912 to 1920, which he shared with his sisters. Dickinson was a writer of books on classical philosophy and history but his largest impact on the world outside Cambridge was made during the First World War. As a pacifist he was appalled by the carnage of the trenches and he drafted a paper on a proposed League of Nations, almost certainly his idea for the name of the organisation, to be formed after the war was over. The League eventually came into being when politicians like Woodrow Wilson espoused the idea, but it was Dickinson who provided the crucial first steps towards its creation. The official biography of Goldsworthy Lowes Dickinson was written after his death by his friend, E.M. Forster.

........................................................................................................

DICK-READ, DR GRANTLY (1890–1959) *twentieth-century pioneer of natural childbirth, practised here 1935–1941*

25 HARLEY STREET, W1   **WESTMINSTER**

Dick-Read was one of the earliest doctors to advocate more natural childbirth. In his private clinic in Harley Street and in books like *Natural Childbirth*, published in 1933, he argued forcefully against the entrenched attitudes of obstetricians and gynaecologists of the time. A period spent in South Africa, between 1948 and 1953, in which he was able to observe traditional African birth methods, confirmed him in his pioneering opinions. Returning to England he was made the first President of the Natural Childbirth Association (now the National Childbirth Trust) when it was founded in 1956.

## DILKE, SIR CHARLES WENTWORTH (1843–1911) *statesman and author lived here*
76 SLOANE STREET, SW1

The son of a Liberal MP, Dilke entered Parliament himself in 1868 and throughout the 1870s and early 1880s was seen as the coming man on the radical wing of Gladstone's party. Indeed, many spoke of him as the natural successor to Gladstone. However, his career was disastrously derailed in 1886 when his involvement with a Mrs Crawford became public knowledge and he was cited in the ensuing divorce case. Although he returned to politics in 1892 and was long an active campaigner for causes such as women's suffrage and legislation to provide a minimum wage, he never again achieved government office. In the same year that he entered Parliament he published *Greater Britain*, an account of his travels in English-speaking countries, and he continued to write widely on imperial and European politics throughout his career.

## DISRAELI, BENJAMIN, EARL OF BEACONSFIELD (1804–1881) *statesman, born here*
22 THEOBALDS ROAD, WC1

## BENJAMIN DISRAELI *Prime Minister in 1868 and 1874–1880, worked in this building 1821–1824*
6 FREDERICK'S PLACE, OLD JEWRY, EC2 **CITY OF LONDON**

## BENJAMIN DISRAELI *lived here from 1839 to 1873*
93 PARK LANE, W1

## BENJAMIN DISRAELI *statesman, died here*
19 CURZON STREET, W1 **PRIVATE**

Disraeli's father, Isaac d'Israeli, was a literary historian, author of six volumes of *Curiosities of Literature*, and it was as a literary figure that his flamboyant son first came to public attention. Between 1826, when his first novel *Vivian Gray* appeared, and 1837, when he was elected to Parliament, Disraeli published several works of fiction and, even as politics began to take more and

more of his energies, the novels continued to appear, including *Coningsby* in 1844 and *Sybil* in 1845. He once told a friend, tongue only partially in cheek, 'When I want to read a novel, I write one.' As a politician Disraeli began as a leader of the small group of romantic Tory dissidents known as 'Young England' and then moved further and further towards the centres of power. Chancellor of the Exchequer on several occasions in the 1850s and 1860s, Disraeli briefly reached 'the top of the greasy pole' when he was Prime Minister for ten months in 1868, and again returned to power between 1874 and 1880. It was during his second administration that he developed his special relationship with Victoria, for whom he arranged the new title of Empress of India. However, during his final illness in 1881, he turned down the idea of a visit from the Queen. 'No, it is better not,' he said, 'she would only ask me to take a message to Albert.'

## DOBSON, FRANK (1886–1963) *sculptor, lived here*
14 HARLEY GARDENS, SW10

In the years immediately after the First World War Frank Dobson was Britain's leading avant-garde sculptor. The modernist critic and painter Roger Fry described his work as 'true sculpture and pure sculpture' and said that it was 'almost the first time that such a thing has been attempted in England'. Edith Sitwell invited him to design the backdrops for her 'entertainment' *Façade*, which also had music by William Walton. By the end of his career he had joined the establishment. He was professor of sculpture at the Royal College of Art from 1946 to 1953 and, in the latter year, he was elected a Royal Academician but the critical estimation of his work had gone down. Such sculptures as his large plaster group for the Festival of Britain, *London Pride*, were seen as old hat rather than avant-garde and even a major retrospective show of his output, which was staged three years after his death, did little to rescue his reputation. More recently a greater sense of his importance in twentieth-century British sculpture has begun to emerge.

## DOBSON, HENRY AUSTIN (1840–1921) *poet and essayist, lived here*
10 REDCLIFFE STREET, SW10

One of that long-extinct breed, the man of letters, Dobson was born in Plymouth and was educated in England and abroad before joining the Board of Trade as a clerk. He worked there for more than forty years while also publishing many volumes of undemanding verse, old-fashioned even at the time of publication, with quaint titles like *Vignettes in Rhyme* and *At the Sign of the Lyre*. Dobson was also an expert on eighteenth-century literature and wrote a series of biographies of writers such as Fielding, Horace Walpole and Goldsmith.

## DONAT, ROBERT (1905–1958) *actor, lived here*
8 MEADWAY, HAMPSTEAD GARDEN SUBURB, NW11

Born in Manchester, Donat overcame a childhood stutter to develop a remarkably resonant and beautiful voice which, together with his good looks, made him one of the most sought-after actors of his generation on both stage and screen. Sadly he suffered both from asthma, which contributed to his early death, and from insecurity and self-doubt, which prevented him from achieving as much as he might have done. However, despite turning down many roles and being obliged by ill health to withdraw from others, Donat gave some of the best-known and best-loved performances in the history of British cinema, including Richard Hannay in Hitchcock's *The Thirty Nine Steps* and the title role in *Goodbye, Mr Chips*. In his last role, in *The Inn of the Sixth Happiness*, Donat's last words on screen were the eerily prophetic, 'We shall not see each other again, I think. Farewell.' He died before the film was released.

## DONOVAN, TERENCE (1936–1996) *photographer*
30 BOURDON STREET, W1  **WESTMINSTER**

It was not only pop stars and models who became icons of the swinging sixties. So too did the men who photographed them. Terence Donovan was one of the best known celebrity photographers of that era. Born into a working-class family in Stepney, Donovan left school at a very young age to study at the London School of Engraving and Lithography and it was here that he first began to take photographs. After working as an assistant to the fashion photographer John French, he set up his own studio in 1959. In the 1960s Donovan and other well-known photographers, such as David Bailey and Brian Duffy, revolutionised fashion photography and helped define the 'look' of the era. Although most often associated with the 1960s, Donovan continued to work for *Vogue*, *Harper's Bazaar*, *Elle* and other high-profile magazines throughout his life. He was also a prolific director of commercials and rock-music videos, and directed one feature film, *Yellow Dog*, which focused on martial arts, one of his greatest passions. In 1996, suffering from illness and depression possibly exacerbated by medication use, Donovan took his own life.

## DOUGLAS, NORMAN (1868–1952) *writer, lived here*
### 63 ALBANY MANSIONS, ALBERT BRIDGE ROAD, SW11

Douglas, born in Austria of Scottish parents, was a cosmopolitan figure who lived much of his life in Europe and North Africa, particularly the island of Capri where his homosexuality was viewed with more tolerance than in Britain. He lived in Albany Mansions for a period during the First World War. Originally a diplomat in the Foreign Office, Douglas became famous for travel books like *Siren Land* and *Old Calabria*, packed with his own eccentric erudition, and notorious for his novel *South Wind*. This is set on the island of Nepenthe, a thinly disguised version of Capri, and tells the story of what happens when a bishop visits the island during the *sirocco*, the South Wind, which wreaks havoc with the islanders' sense of decency and morality. Considered almost unspeakably *risqué* at the time of its first publication, it now seems as eccentric as his travel books.

## DOWDING, LORD, AIR CHIEF MARSHALL (1882–1970) *leader of Fighter Command, lived here 1941–1951*

### 3 ST MARY'S ROAD, WIMBLEDON, SW19

Air Chief Marshal, Lord Hugh Dowding was almost singlehandedly responsible for Britain's victory in the Battle of Britain but one of his 'rewards' turned out to be the loss of his position as head of Fighter Command during the political infighting that took place in the RAF immediately after the victory. Born in Moffat in Scotland, Dowding began his career as an army artillery officer but learned to fly in 1913 and joined the Royal Flying Corps just before the outbreak of the First World War. By the 1930s he had risen to the rank of air marshal and, during that decade, did much to prepare the RAF for modern combat. Perhaps most significantly he encouraged the research and development of the radar system. In 1936 Dowding was appointed the first commander-in-chief of Fighter Command and, during the first difficult year of the Second World War, he was the most persistent advocate of the concentration of home defence against the threat of the Luftwaffe rather than risking men and aircraft in dangerous offensives. Despite pressure from both colleagues and politicians, including Churchill, Dowding got his way and the ultimate victory in the Battle of Britain proved the soundness of his strategy. None the less, at the end of 1940, he was ousted from his position as head of Fighter Command and retired from the RAF in 1942. Dowding, whose wife had died young, was interested in spiritualism and, after his retirement, published several books in which he claimed to have communicated through a clairvoyant with the spirits of airmen lost in the battle he so ably directed.

## DRYDEN, JOHN (1631–1700) *poet, lived here*
### 43 GERRARD STREET, W1

Dryden was educated at Westminster and Cambridge and began publishing poetry in his teens. Although most of his early writings were for the stage he also wrote, in successive years, stanzas mourning the death of Cromwell and a poem, *Astraea Redux*, to welcome Charles II back to his throne. This political flexibility was to prove useful to Dryden in the troubled years to come. He was made Poet Laureate in 1668 and the constitutional and religious conflicts of the time prompted him to write his great satire *Absalom and Achitophel* in which he found parallels in the Biblical story for the political ambitions and manoeuvrings around the succession to Charles. In later life Dryden became a Catholic, which lost him his court positions, and many of his later works were in the politically less compromising field of translation. His version of Vergil, published three years before his death, was described by Pope as 'the most noble and spirited translation I know in any language'. Almost certainly the plaque in Gerrard Street is on the wrong building and honours the house of Dryden's next-door neighbour rather than that of the poet himself.

---

## DRYSDALE, DR CHARLES VICKERY (1874–1961) *a founder of the Family Planning Association, opened his first birth control clinic here in 1921*

153A EAST STREET, WALWORTH, SE17

Drysdale combined a successful career as a research scientist with his role as one of the pioneers in dispensing family planning advice to the poorer citizens of London. An electrical engineer by training, Drysdale was the designer of a number of specialised electrical measuring instruments and worked as a scientist for the Admiralty, latterly as Director of Scientific Research there. He and his wife were early advocates of the need for proper family planning and they were long-term members of what had been called, in deference to those whose sensibilities might have been disturbed by anything other than euphemism, the Malthusian League, after the nineteenth-century theorist of population expansion, Thomas Malthus. Drysdale was the editor of the periodical *The Malthusian*. Also a member of the National Birth Control Council when it was founded, Drysdale opened the clinic in Walworth in 1921.

---

## DUKE-ELDER, SIR STEWART (1898–1978) *ophthalmologist, lived and worked here 1934–1976*

63 HARLEY STREET, W1

Born near Dundee, the son of a minister in the United Free Church, it was intended at first that Stewart Duke-Elder should follow his father into the ministry but he chose instead to study medicine at St Andrew's University and to specialise in diseases of the eye. He became a prolific writer of books on his subject, publishing seven volumes of his 'Textbook of Ophthalmology' between 1932 and 1954. Duke-Elder was also a distinguished practitioner, who was knighted when he was only in his thirties after performing a delicate eye operation on the Prime Minister of the day, Ramsay Macdonald. He went on to become Surgeon-Oculist to George VI and to the present Queen. In the Second World War, Duke-Elder was appointed ophthalmic consultant to the British Army with the rank of brigadier. During his service he devised an idiosyncratic but effective test for the night blindness from which many soldiers claimed to suffer in order to obtain a discharge from the forces. Duke-Elder asked a supposedly afflicted soldier to walk in the dark along a 12-inch plank across a latrine trench. If he fell in, he was a genuine sufferer from night blindness; if he didn't, he was a malingerer.

---

## DU MAURIER, GEORGE LOUIS PALMELLA BUSSON (1834–1896) *artist and writer, lived here 1874–1895*

NEW GROVE HOUSE, 28 HAMPSTEAD GROVE, NW3

## GEORGE LOUIS PALMELLA BUSSON DU MAURIER (1834–1896) *artist and writer, lived here 1863–1868*

91 GREAT RUSSELL STREET, WC1

Du Maurier became famous as a cartoonist on *Punch*, seen as a quintessentially English magazine, but, as his extravagantly lengthy name suggests, he was the grandson of French *emigrés* who had fled to England at the time of the French Revolution. Du Maurier was himself born in Paris, although his father had become a naturalised British citizen, and he returned to that city to study art in 1856. Despite the drawback of being almost blind in one eye, Du Maurier became one of the most admired black-and-white illustrators of Victorian England. In his final decade he launched himself on a new career as a bestselling novelist. *Trilby*, published in 1894, drew on his experiences of art student life in Paris and gave two new words to the language. The eponymous Trilby, an artist's model, wears a kind of hat that ever since has been given her name, and the sinister figure who guides her to fame as a singer is called Svengali.

....................................................................................................................................

## DU MAURIER, SIR GERALD (1873–1934) *actor manager, lived here from 1916 until his death*

CANNON HALL, 14 CANNON PLACE, NW3

The youngest son of the illustrator and novelist George Du Maurier, Gerald Du Maurier made his stage debut in 1894 and one of his earliest roles was a small part in an adaptation of his father's book *Trilby*. In 1904 he took the dual role of Captain Hook and Mr Darling in the first production of *Peter Pan* and two years later he scored a particular triumph as the gentleman thief Raffles in the stage version of the novel by E.W. Hornung. In 1910 he began a fifteen-year association with Wyndham's Theatre as actor-manager, a period that was probably the most successful of his career. He was knighted in 1922. Du Maurier was an advocate of a naturalistic style of acting, advising performers to behave as unselfconsciously as possible on stage. 'Do what you generally do any day of your life when you come into a room. Bite your nails, yawn, lie down on a sofa and read a book . . .'. One of his daughters was Daphne Du Maurier, the author of *Rebecca*.

....................................................................................................................................

## DYSON, SIR FRANK (1868–1939) *Astronomer Royal, lived here 1894–1906*

6 VANBRUGH HILL, BLACKHEATH, SE3

Astronomer Royal for more than twenty years, Dyson was particularly known for his work on the distribution of stars and was an expert on solar eclipses. The son of a Baptist minister, he was educated at Bradford Grammar School and Trinity College, Cambridge, before joining the Greenwich Observatory in 1894 and moving into the house in Blackheath. He progressed rapidly in his profession, was made a Fellow of the Royal Society in 1901 and became Astronomer Royal for Scotland four years later. He was transferred to the corresponding position in England in 1910 and held the post until 1933. He was knighted in 1915.

....................................................................................................................................

## EARNSHAW, THOMAS *site of the business premises of Thomas Earnshaw (1749–1829), noted watch and chronometer maker*

119 HIGH HOLBORN, WC1

Born in Ashton-under-Lyne, Earnshaw was apprenticed to a watch-maker there and moved to London to set up his own business. He worked from the premises in High Holborn for many years and has been described as 'the first to make chronometers so simple and so cheap as to be within the reach of private individuals'. In 1793 the commissioners of the Board of Longitude granted him the then sizeable sum of £3,000 as an award for the improvements he had made to the marine chronometer.

....................................................................................................................................

## EASTLAKE, CHARLES (1793–1865) *painter and first Director of the National Gallery, lived here*

7 FITZROY SQUARE, W1

Later in his life Eastlake became better known as an administrator and art historian than as an artist but his painting of *Napoleon on board the Bellerophon* had first made his name when he was in his early twenties. The artist had made sketches of the deposed French emperor on board the ship taking him to exile on St Helena when the *Bellerophon* had anchored briefly in Eastlake's home town of Plymouth. Eastlake went on to spend many years in Italy, only returning to England in 1830, and, during his years as President of the Royal Academy and first Director of the National Gallery, he continued to visit the country regularly, building up the collection of early Italian paintings. He died in Pisa, while undertaking another visit to purchase works for the gallery.

## EDDINGTON, SIR ARTHUR, OM (1882–1944) *mathematician and astrophysicist, lived here*

4 BENNETT PARK, BLACKHEATH, SE3

Eddington was the scientist to whom the opportunity fell to provide the first experimental confirmation of Einstein's General Theory of Relativity. The theory predicted that, because of the curvature of space, a ray of light passing close to the sun would bend inwards. Any such observation could only take place during a solar eclipse. One was expected in May 1919 and a Royal Society expedition to the west coast of Africa was despatched under Eddington's scientific leadership. Using the light from a star of precisely known position, a measurement was made and Einstein's prediction of the extent of displacement very closely matched. Eddington, who later described the moment of confirmation as the greatest of his life, was the most famous British astronomer of his time and a dedicated populariser of scientific ideas, author of such books as *The Nature of the Physical World* and *The Expanding Universe*.

## EDWARDS, EDWARD *pioneer of public libraries, lived as a boy in a house on this site 1825–c.1830*

11 IDOL LANE, EC3   **CITY OF LONDON**

Born in 1812, Edwards was one of the earliest advocates of a free library system and one of the pioneers of professional librarianship in Britain. He helped to reorganise the British Museum library in 1839, advised the MP William Ewart in his campaign to pass legislation for the provision of libraries and was for a number of years in the 1850s the first librarian at Manchester Free Library. Edwards wrote widely on bibliographical subjects and on library history. He died in 1886.

## EDWARDS, JOHN PASSMORE (1823–1911) *journalist, editor and builder of free public libraries, lived here*

51 NETHERHALL GARDENS, NW3

In the late Victorian and Edwardian periods two men made major financial contributions to the development of free public libraries in this country. One was the Scottish-born steel magnate Andrew Carnegie. The other was John Passmore Edwards. Edwards was born in Cornwall and made his fortune as a newspaper proprietor. He entered Parliament as a Liberal MP and then, in the 1890s, began to use his wealth to build libraries that ordinary men and women, unable to join subscription libraries, could use. Many of his libraries were built in his native Cornwall and in the deprived East End where examples can still be seen at Limehouse and Whitechapel. Passmore Edwards also contributed generously towards the establishment of the Whitechapel Art Gallery.

## ELDON, JOHN SCOTT, LORD (1751–1838) *Lord Chancellor, lived here*
6 BEDFORD SQUARE, WC1

In his poem *The Mask of Anarchy*, Shelley imagines a grim procession of vices marching through England and writes, in one stanza, that 'Next came Fraud and he had on/Like Eldon, an ermined gown'. John Scott, who ended his career as First Earl of Eldon, was a gifted lawyer who entered

Parliament in 1782 and became Lord Chancellor in 1801. He wore the ermined gown of the office almost uninterruptedly for the next twenty-six years and, from 1812, was a leading figure in one of the most hated of all British governments, the repressive regime of Lord Liverpool. Shelley's poem was a reaction to the Peterloo Massacre, in which government troops killed and wounded unarmed demonstrators at a meeting in Manchester. Eldon thought the meeting itself 'an overt act of treason' and approved the soldiers' actions. History has tended to agree with Shelley rather than Eldon.

## ELEN, GUS (1862–1940) *music hall comedian, lived here*
3 THURLEIGH AVENUE, BALHAM, SW12

Gus Elen was one of the stars of the music hall in its golden era and is remembered as one of the best of the performers whose songs and patter projected an image of the chirpy invincibility of the Cockney even amidst the squalor and hardship of the East End. Many of Elen's best-known songs were written for him by the talented team of Edgar Bateman (words) and George Le Brunn (music). These include 'She's Too Good to Live is Mrs Carter', 'It's a Great Big Shame' and, most famously, 'If It Wasn't for the 'Ouses In Between' with its celebration of the little East End backyard from which, 'Wiv a ladder and some glasses/ You can see to Hackney Marshes/ If it wasn't for the 'ouses in between'. Elen lived in Thurleigh Road for the last six years of his life.

## ELGAR, SIR EDWARD (1857–1934) *composer, lived here 1890–1891*
51 AVONMORE ROAD, W14

## SIR EDWARD ELGAR, (1857–1934) *composer, opened and recorded in these studios on 12 November 1931*
ABBEY STUDIOS, ABBEY ROAD, NW6  **WESTMINSTER**

## SIR EDWARD ELGAR, (1857–1934)
42 NETHERHALL GARDENS, NW3  **HEATH AND OLD HAMPSTEAD SOCIETY**

'Music is in the air,' Elgar is reputed to have once said, 'You simply take as much of it as you want.' Certainly Elgar was himself able to take music from the air but he had to work long and hard to establish himself as the pre-eminent English composer of his time. Born near Worcester, the son of an organist and music dealer, he worked as an orchestral violinist, as the conductor of small, local bands and, like his father, as an organist, all the while composing music that few wanted to hear, before he gradually found success in the 1890s. The decade culminated with *The Enigma Variations* and the oratorio *The Dream of Gerontius*, which firmly established his particular genius. By the time these appeared his brief sojourn in London was long over and he had returned to his spiritual and artistic home in Worcestershire. Knighted in 1904, Elgar continued to produce such masterpieces as his cello concerto and the symphonic study *Falstaff*, until the death of his wife in 1920 brought his creative life almost to an end. For the last ten years of his life he was Master of the King's Musick. The plaque in Abbey Road commemorates the opening of the studios by Elgar in 1931 and the recordings he made there with the London Symphony Orchestra and, the following year, with the young Yehudi Menuhin.

## 'ELIOT, GEORGE', MARY ANN CROSS (1819–1880) *novelist, lived here*
HOLLY LODGE, 31 WIMBLEDON PARK ROAD, SW18

## 'GEORGE ELIOT' (MARY ANN CROSS NÉE EVANS) (1819–1880) *novelist, died here*
4 CHEYNE WALK, SW3

Mary Ann (or Marian) Evans was born on a Warwickshire farm, where her father was a land agent, and received a much broader education than was usual for a woman of her time. She was familiar with several languages and was a translator before she was a novelist. Her translation of David Strauss's *Das Leben Jesu*, a German work that subjected the Gospels to stern textual criticism, appeared in 1846. Translating Strauss, she later admitted and, in particular, 'dissecting the beautiful story of the Crucifixion' had made her ill and was one of the reasons behind her ultimate loss of faith. The death of her father in 1849 enabled her to move to London where she worked as an assistant editor on *The Westminster Review* and began her long relationship with the already married George Henry Lewes. She braved Victorian morality by going to live with him in 1853 and their union lasted a quarter of a century until Lewes's death. In the year she herself died she married the much younger John Cross. George Eliot's first fiction was *Scenes of Clerical Life*, which appeared under her male pseudonym in *Blackwood's Magazine* in 1857. Dickens was one of the few people to recognise immediately that the tales were written by a woman. *Adam Bede* was published in 1859 to great acclaim and was followed by *The Mill on the Floss*, *Silas Marner* and, in 1871–2, her greatest novel, *Middlemarch*.

## ELIOT, T.S., OM (1888–1965) *poet, lived and died here*
3 KENSINGTON COURT GARDENS, W8

## T.S. ELIOT, *poet and publisher, worked here for Faber & Faber*
24 RUSSELL SQUARE, WC1   **CAMDEN BOROUGH COUNCIL**

Born in St Louis, Missouri, Eliot studied at Harvard and then spent time in Germany and at the Sorbonne before settling in England in his mid-twenties. His first collection of poems, *Prufrock and Other Observations*, was published in 1917 and five years later *The Waste Land* appeared, perhaps the single most analysed poem of the century. After *The Waste Land* his poetry became increasingly religious in tendency – he once described himself as 'classical in literature, royalist in politics and Anglo-Catholic in religion' – and culminated in the group of four long poems called *Four Quartets*. Eliot also made great efforts to revive poetic drama in plays such as *Murder in the Cathedral* and *The Cocktail Party* and was an exceptionally influential critic. As a director of the publishing firm Faber & Faber, he was largely responsible for building up a list of poets that represented the mainstream of the modern movement in Britain. In appearance Eliot could be as sombre and forbidding as some of his poetry. When Harold Nicolson met him he wrote in his diary, 'He is very yellow and glum'.

## ELLIS, HENRY HAVELOCK (1859–1939) *pioneer in the scientific study of sex, lived here*
### 14 DOVER MANSIONS, CANTERBURY CRESCENT, SW9

The son of a sea captain, Havelock Ellis was advised as a teenager to take a sea voyage to improve his health. Conveniently his father was in command of a ship bound for Australia and Ellis sailed there, where he settled for four years. Returning to Britain he qualified as a doctor but found more and more of his time consumed by his literary work (he edited volumes of Elizabethan and Jacobean plays) and by his wish to turn the light of science on sexual matters. His concern with making sense of sex must have been encouraged by the difficulties of his own marriage to Edith Lees, a woman more sexually interested in other women than in her husband, and by the complications of his own relationships with other 'new women' of the day. Ellis's *Studies in the Psychology of Sex*, scandalous and notorious in their day, appeared in six volumes between 1897 and 1910.

## ENGELS, FRIEDRICH (1820–1895) *political philosopher, lived here 1870–1894*
### 121 REGENT'S PARK ROAD, NW1

Engels was the son of a wealthy German factory owner and he was able to observe at first hand the effects of the Industrial Revolution on the urban poor when he came to Manchester to oversee his father's business interests there. The result was *The Condition of the Working Class in England*, published in 1845, the year after Engels had met Marx for the first time. In 1849 Marx, *persona non grata* with the authorities in Germany, arrived in London. Throughout the rest of Marx's life, Engels was an intellectual and financial support to him. At times it was only the allowance from the well-off Engels that enabled the impoverished Marx to keep himself and his family from destitution. Engels was Marx's closest collaborator, writing *The Communist Manifesto* with him and editing and completing the third volume of *Das Kapital* after Marx's death.

## EQUIANO, OLAUDAH (1745–1797) *writer*
### 73 RIDING HOUSE STREET, W1   **WESTMINSTER**

Born in a village in what was then the kingdom of Benin, Equiano was captured by slavers when he was ten or eleven years old and taken to the West Indies. After working as a slave there and in Virginia, he was bought by a British naval officer called Michael Pascal and, as Pascal's personal servant, was taught to read and write, visited London and witnessed a number of naval skirmishes in the Seven Years War. Pascal then sold Equiano to another ship's captain who took him to Montserrat. Working for an American Quaker merchant there, Equiano, although still a slave, was able to make money for himself and in 1766 he purchased his freedom. He moved back to London, making a precarious living as a hairdresser, but for financial reason was eventually obliged to go back to sea, although this time as a free man. He sailed on John Phipps's expedition in 1773 in search of a north-west passage to India, as did a young midshipman called Horatio Nelson. By the 1780s Equiano was a leading figure in the campaign to abolish the slave trade. In 1789, living at a house in what is now Riding House Street, he published his autobiography, *The Interesting Narrative of the Life of Olaudah Equiano or Gustavus Vassa, the African, Written by Himself*, which became a bestseller and, through its graphic descriptions of the cruelty of the slave trade, won many converts to the abolitionist cause. Equiano died in London in 1797, ten years before the Abolition of the Slave Trade Act was passed by the British parliament.

ESSEX STREET *was laid out in the grounds of Essex House by* NICHOLAS BARBON *in 1675. Among many famous lawyers who lived here were* SIR ORLANDO BRIDGEMAN *(c. 1606–1674),* LORD KEEPER; HENRY FIELDING (1707–1754), *novelist; and* BRASS CROSBY (1725–1793), *Lord Mayor of London.* JAMES SAVAGE (1779–1852), *architect had his office here.* PRINCE CHARLES EDWARD STUART *stayed at a house in the street in 1750.* REVEREND THEOPHILUS LINDSEY (1723–1808), *Unitarian minister, founded Essex Street Chapel here in 1774.* DR SAMUEL JOHNSON *established an evening club at the 'Essex Head' in 1783*

ESSEX HALL, ESSEX STREET, WC2

---

## EVANS, DAME EDITH (1888–1976) *actress, lived here*

109 EBURY STREET, SW1

'I may never have been very pretty,' Edith Evans once said, 'but I was jolly larky, and that's what counts in the theatre.' To sustain a career that lasted from a stage debut in 1912 to a last film appearance in 1976 she needed more than a gift for being 'jolly larky' and Edith Evans was, indeed, one of the great classical actresses of the century. She was particularly adept at comedy, playing everything from Shakespearean roles through Shaw and Wilde to modern parts. She was created a Dame of the British Empire in 1946, two years before her debut in sound films (she had appeared in two silent movies during the First World War) and six years before her most memorable film role as the formidable Lady Bracknell (a part she had already played on stage) in *The Importance of Being Earnest*. She went on to other notable performances in such movies as *Tom Jones* but theatre was always her first love and it is as a great stage actress that she will be remembered.

---

## EWART, WILLIAM (1798–1869) *reformer, lived here*

16 EATON PLACE, SW1

Educated at Eton and Christ Church, Oxford, Ewart became a barrister and entered Parliament in 1828. For the next forty years he was a consistent voice for liberal and humanitarian reform. In 1837 he succeeded in getting an act passed that reduced the large number of offences still punishable by hanging and in 1850 he sponsored a bill that led to the first establishment of free public libraries in the country. Ewart was also the first man to propose a scheme to mark the houses in London in which the famous had lived.

See also under entry for JOHN BEARD

---

## FABIAN SOCIETY *The site of 17 Osnaburgh Street where the Fabian Society was founded in 1884*

THE WHITE HOUSE, OSNABURGH STREET, NW1

The Fabian Society took its name from the Roman general Quintus Fabius Maximus, known as 'Cunctator' (the Delayer) because of his tactics in the war against Hannibal of avoiding a major battle and gradually wearing down the enemy by guerrilla tactics. The pioneering socialists of the Fabian Society believed in evolution rather than revolution, bringing in socialist measures gradually rather than through revolutionary confrontation with capitalist society. Among the founding members of the Fabian Society were Beatrice and Sidney Webb and George Bernard Shaw, who also wrote one of the first two Fabian tracts. The society, which has included in its membership writers and politicians from Ramsay MacDonald to H.G. Wells, Edith Nesbit to Keir Hardie, has often exerted an influence on left-wing British politics far greater than its numbers.

## FARADAY, MICHAEL (1791–1867)
*man of science, apprentice here*
48 BLANDFORD STREET, W1

## MICHAEL FARADAY (1791–1867)
WALWORTH ROAD, SE17
**BOROUGH OF SOUTHWARK**

Faraday is one of the great figures in the history of science. Indeed a leading authority has described him as 'possibly the greatest experimental genius the world has known'. Yet it was only through a series of coincidences and lucky opportunities that Faraday, who was born the son of a blacksmith and seemed destined to an undistinguished career, was able to make his genius known to the world. Apprenticed to a bookbinder in Blandford Street, Faraday was firstly lucky that his employer recognised his thirst for knowledge and allowed him freedom to acquire it. Secondly he was lucky that Sir Humphry Davy, to whom he introduced himself, was in need of a laboratory assistant at the time and was sufficiently impressed by Faraday to take him on. Faraday worked with Davy for a number of years and eventually succeeded him as Professor of Chemistry in the Royal Institution. However, Faraday's greatest discoveries were in the field of electricity. They included electromagnetic induction, the laws of electrolysis and the rotation of polarised light by magnetism. All these were among the greatest developments of nineteenth-century science and they were made by a man who might, had chance not intervened, have spent his life as a bookbinder.

---

## FAWCETT, DAME MILLICENT GARRETT (1847–1929) *pioneer of women's suffrage, lived and died here*
2 GOWER STREET, WC1

The younger sister of Elizabeth Garrett Anderson, the early advocate of the rights of women to become doctors, Millicent Garrett married Henry Fawcett when she was twenty and already a campaigner for extending the franchise to women. Fawcett had been blinded in a shooting accident soon after graduating from Cambridge but went on to become a prominent economist and politician, so particularly concerned with reform of the Raj that he was known as 'the honourable member for India'. Mrs Fawcett was involved in women's education – she was one of the founders of Newnham College, Cambridge – and organised pressure groups to campaign for votes for women. President of the National Union of Women's Suffrage Societies from 1897 to 1918, she had an ambivalent relationship with the more volatile suffragettes who supported the Pankhursts. Admiring of their bravery, she none the less deplored their militancy. She was created a Dame of the British Empire in 1925.

---

## FENTON, ROGER (1819–1869) *photographer, lived here*
2 ALBERT TERRACE, PRIMROSE HILL, NW1

The pioneer photographer Roger Fenton is best remembered for his images of the Crimean War, commissioned by a Manchester publisher, but he was also hired by the British Museum to photograph antiquities in its collection and was an early recorder of the architecture and landscape of mid-Victorian Britain. Born in Lancashire, the son of a successful industrialist and MP, Fenton studied painting in Paris before turning his attention to the new medium of photography. He was instrumental in establishing the organisation that later became the Royal Photographic Society and served as its secretary for three years. For largely unknown reasons Fenton gave up photography in 1861 and returned to the law, which he had also studied as a young man. He died at the age of forty-nine, probably from the long-term effects of bouts of cholera he had suffered in the Crimea.

........................................................................................................

## FENWICK, ETHEL GORDON (1857–1947) *nursing reformer, lived here 1887–1924*
### 20 UPPER WIMPOLE STREET, W1

Born in Morayshire in Scotland, Ethel Fenwick was the daughter of a doctor who died when she was still a small child. Her mother married again and Ethel was brought up in Nottinghamshire at the home of her stepfather, a local MP. At a time when nursing was still not considered an entirely proper career for a lady, she nevertheless chose to enter the profession and soon made her mark there. Matron at St Bartholomew's Hospital in Smithfield for several years in the 1880s, she became the leading light in campaigns to raise the status of nurses and was the first president of the British Nurses' Association when it was founded in 1887. She continued to lobby for reform in the nursing profession and, in the 1890s and early 1900s, advocated the state registration of nurses, a campaign that found her on the opposite side of the fence to the aging, invalid but still formidable Florence Nightingale. It was a campaign that did not see success until an act was passed in parliament in 1919. Ethel Fenwick subsequently became State Registered Nurse No. 1. A gifted journalist and writer, Ethel Fenwick was also editor of the *British Journal of Nursing* for more than half a century.

........................................................................................................

## FERRIER, KATHLEEN (1912–1953) *contralto, lived here*
### 97 FROGNAL, HAMPSTEAD, NW3

Kathleen Ferrier was one of the best-loved of British singers of the twentieth century and her early death from cancer was a great shock to her admirers throughout the world. Her active career as a singer had, indeed, been a short one because she started late. She began her working life as a telephone operator and it was only by chance that she was heard singing in a local choral competition in Lancashire by Malcolm Sargent. He advised her to study in London and, during the war years, she became much in demand as a concert artist. After the war she sang the title role in *The Rape of Lucrezia* by Benjamin Britten, who wrote other music especially for her, and was particularly acclaimed for her performances in works by Elgar, Mahler and Handel. According to her accompanist Gerald Moore, one of the last things Kathleen Ferrier said, shortly before her death, was, 'Now I'll have *eine kleine Pause*.'

*kathleen Ferrier*
*june 1950*

........................................................................................................

## FIELDING, HENRY (1707–1754) *novelist, lived here*
### MILBOURNE HOUSE, BARNES GREEN, SW13

Fielding was born in Somerset, educated at Eton and the University of Leyden and made his way to London in the late 1720s. There, for a number of years, he pursued a career as dramatist and satirist, lampooning the corruption and hypocrisies of Sir Robert Walpole's government. So successful was he in this that the government introduced the Licensing Act of 1737, which effectively banned his plays from the stage and brought his career as a dramatist to an end. He turned instead to the novel and, in 1748, when he was made justice of the peace for Westminster, to the law. As a novelist he wrote classics like *Tom Jones* and *Joseph Andrews*. As a lawyer he was famously incorruptible and struggled to impose some kind of honest dealing onto the chaotic world of eighteenth-century law enforcement. Among other innovations he formed the group of thief-takers who later became known as the Bow Street Runners. Fielding lived at Barnes between 1748 and 1752 and was there when *Tom Jones* was published. At the time not everyone was impressed by the book. 'I am shocked to hear you quote from so vicious a novel,' Dr Johnson said to a friend and there were some who attributed two earthquake shocks that hit London in 1749 to the malign influence of Fielding's work. Today it is considered one of the finest novels in the language.

........................

## FILDES, SIR SAMUEL LUKE (1844–1927) *artist, lived here 1878–1927*

### 31 MELBURY ROAD, W14

Born in Liverpool, Fildes began his career as a graphic artist and, as a young man in 1870, was chosen to illustrate Dickens's last, unfinished novel, *The Mystery of Edwin Drood*. He transformed one of his other early illustrations into a painting that was a success at the Royal Academy exhibition in 1874 and went on to produce a number of other, often sentimental canvases (*The Doctor*, of 1892, was the best known) that appealed to the tastes of the late Victorian middle classes. In later life Fildes was noted for his official portraiture of members of the royal family, including Edward VII and Queen Alexandra. His house in Melbury Road, surrounded by the homes of successful fellow-artists like Holman-Hunt and Sir Hamo Thornycroft, was designed by the well-known architect Norman Shaw.

........................

## FIRST, RUTH (1925–1982) AND SLOVO, JOE (1926–1995) *South African freedom fighters, lived here 1966–1978*

### 13 LYME STREET, CAMDEN, NW1

The plaque to Ruth First and Joe Slovo was unveiled by Nelson Mandela, some indication of the importance to the creation of the new South Africa of these two legendary fighters against apartheid. Ruth First was born in Johannesburg, daughter of two of the founder members of the South African Communist Party, and it was her lifelong communism that first led her into conflict with the authorities when she was a student. As a writer and polemicist for the communist party and for the ANC she had few equals and *117 Days*, her account of a period of imprisonment, remains a classic of prison literature. After returning to Africa, she was killed in Mozambique by a letter bomb, believed to have been sent by agents of the apartheid regime. Born in Lithuania, Joe Slovo came with his parents to South Africa when he was a child. He met and married Ruth First when they were both attending the University of Witwatersrand. Like her, he became a leading member of the communist party and the ANC and a bitter opponent of apartheid. Unlike her, he lived to see South Africa's first democratic elections and was Minister of Housing in the first post-apartheid government. He died of cancer in 1995. First and Slovo lived in Lyme Street for thirteen years while in exile from South Africa.

........................

## FISHER, ADMIRAL OF THE FLEET, LORD, OM (1841–1920) *lived here as First Sea Lord 1905–1910*

### 16 QUEEN ANNE'S GATE, SW1

The most charismatic naval officer of his time, 'Jacky' Fisher was born in what is now Sri Lanka and entered the Navy in 1854. A man of immense ambition and charm, he rose to be Commander of the Mediterranean Fleet between 1899 and 1902 and First Sea Lord from 1904 to 1910. In these positions he was able to ensure improvements to the Navy's ships and he was in power when the first of the Dreadnoughts was launched. In retirement at the start of the First World War, he was called back by Winston Churchill, who recognised a maverick after his own heart, and Fisher, although now an old man, still had the energy to undertake a massive ship-building programme. Large sums were invested in this expansion but, as Fisher told Churchill, 'The British Navy always travels first class.' Fisher resigned after the disaster of the Dardanelles campaign and spent much of his declining years penning vigorous letters to *The Times* on imperial and naval matters.

## FISHER, SIR RONALD AYLMER (1890–1962) *statistician and geneticist, lived here* 1896–1904

### INVERFORTH HOUSE, NORTH END WAY, NW3

Often considered the founder of modern statistics, Fisher began his career as a mathematician and astronomer, graduating from Gonville and Caius College, Cambridge, with a BA in Astronomy in 1912. While he was at Cambridge, Fisher was one of the founders of the Cambridge University Eugenics Society, and from 1933 became professor of eugenics at University College London for ten years. Today many of the ideas of eugenics are discredited but Fisher's interest reflected his fascination with the role that mathematical and statistical analysis could play in genetics as well as political and social beliefs that now appear outmoded. His 1930 book, *The Genetical Theory of Natural Selection*, has been described as completing 'the reconciliation of Darwinian ideas with Mendelian theory'. Fisher's work has also been of enormous importance in revolutionising the ways in which statistical analysis can be applied to the results of practical experiments in many different fields. His books *Statistical Methods for Research Workers* (1925) and *The Design of Experiments* (1935) remain standard textbooks, stressing the importance of quantitative analysis of data. 'To call in the statistician after the experiment is done,' Fisher once said, 'may be no more than asking him to perform a post-mortem examination: he may be able to say what the experiment died of.' Fisher ended his career as a professor of genetics at Cambridge and then chose to retire to Auckland, New Zealand, a city he had come to love as a visiting lecturer at the university, and it was there that he died in 1962.

## FITZROY, ADMIRAL ROBERT (1805–1865) *hydrographer and meteorologist, lived here*

### 38 ONSLOW SQUARE, SW7

Although a man of talent himself, Fitzroy is remembered today primarily because of his connection with one of the great figures of the nineteenth century. When Charles Darwin made the voyage as naturalist on the *Beagle,* during which he began the speculations that were to lead, finally, to his ideas on evolution, Fitzroy was the captain of the ship. After the *Beagle* voyage, Fitzroy's career was marked by both triumph and controversy. As a meteorologist he invented a 'Fitzroy Barometer' and instituted storm warnings, which were the forerunners of modern weather forecasts. However, his entry into Parliament in 1841 was marred by a disagreement with a former political colleague that ended in fisticuffs on the steps of the United Service Club, and his tenure as Governor of New Zealand was a troubled one. As he grew older Fitzroy's life became progressively more difficult. As the *Dictionary of National Biography* euphemistically puts it, he had 'a temperament naturally excitable' and pressure of overwork eventually drove him to suicide in 1865.

## FLANAGAN, BUD (1896–1968) *comedian and leader of the 'Crazy Gang', born here*

### 12 HANBURY STREET, E1

The Crazy Gang, which was enormously popular on stage and in low-budget British films from the 1930s until the early part of the '60s, was made up of three pairs of music hall comedians. Two of them were Jimmy Nervo and Teddy Knox, and Charlie Naughton and Jimmy Gold. The third and most famous pairing was Flanagan and Allen. Born Robert Winthrop in the East End, Bud Flanagan was teamed with Chesney Allen for the most successful part of his long showbiz career. Regulars of stage, screen and radio, Flanagan and Allen remained a partnership until ill health forced Chesney Allen into more or less permanent retirement in the late 1940s. Some of their amiable, sentimental songs, such as 'Underneath the Arches', remain familiar today.

## FLAXMAN, JOHN (1755–1826) *sculptor, lived and died here*
### 7 GREENWELL STREET, W1

Flaxman was born in York but, when he was still an infant, the family moved to London where his father, a plaster moulder, kept a workshop in Covent Garden. Flaxman, although delicate and sickly, showed precocious talent and was exhibiting models at the Royal Academy from 1770. His early ability must have been combined with an early arrogance because Thomas Wedgwood once said of him, 'It is but a few years since he was a most supreme coxcomb.' However, he also called him a 'true genius of sculpture' and the Wedgwood family provided Flaxman with much of his early work, designing for their pottery. Flaxman studied in Rome for seven years from 1787 and, when he returned to England, soon developed a reputation as the finest sculptor in the country, particularly noted for his funerary monuments. His illustrations for the works of Homer and Dante were also much admired. He became Professor of Sculpture at the Royal Academy in 1810 and was a long-time friend of William Blake, some of whose mystical religious views Flaxman shared.

## FLECKER, JAMES ELROY (1884–1915) *poet and dramatist, was born here*
### 9 GILMORE ROAD, SE13

Born in the unglamorous surroundings of Lewisham, Flecker was early drawn to the imagined mysteries of the East. He read Oriental languages at Oxford and joined the diplomatic service, gaining postings to both Constantinople and Beirut. He published several volumes of lushly romantic verse, including one entitled *The Golden Road to Samarkand*, and was an occasional contributor to the volumes of Georgian verse that were appearing regularly at the time. Flecker's best-known work, the verse drama *Hassan*, did not appear until several years after its author's premature death from tuberculosis.

## FLEISCHMANN, ARTHUR (1896–1990) *sculptor, lived and worked here*
### 92 CARLTON HILL, NW8 **WESTMINSTER**

Fleischmann was a much-travelled sculptor who arrived in London in 1948 and spent the rest of his life in the city, moving to Carlton Hill in 1958. He was born in Bratislava, studied in Vienna and spent ten years living and working in Australia before his arrival in England. Fleischmann was a Catholic and his many sitters, who ranged from the singer Kathleen Ferrier to the comic performer Barry Humphries, also included four of the century's popes. Always an innovative artist, he spent much time, from the sixties onwards, experimenting with the use of perspex in his art and using it in conjunction with water to produce elegant and original fountains and sculptures.

## FLEMING, SIR ALEXANDER (1881–1955) *discoverer of penicillin, lived here*
### 20A DANVERS STREET, SW3

One of the most important discoveries in modern medicine originated in a chance observation in 1928. The Scottish bacteriologist Alexander Fleming, returning to his laboratory at St Mary's

Hospital, Paddington after a holiday, noticed that a culture plate containing a particular bacteria had been exposed to contamination by a number of yeasts and moulds. More significantly, one of the moulds – *Penicillium notatum* – had killed the bacteria in the area of the plate it had affected. Further investigation revealed that the mould had remarkable antibiotic powers. Over the next twelve years Fleming, working with Oxford pathologists Howard Florey and Ernest Chain, strove to perfect a means of producing a drug that could be safely administered to patients. Success came in 1940 and all three shared the Nobel Prize for Chemistry five years later.

## FLEMING, SIR AMBROSE (1849–1945) *scientist and electrical engineer, lived here*
### 9 CLIFTON GARDENS, MAIDA VALE, W9

Born in Lancaster, Ambrose Fleming was Professor of Electrical Engineering at University College, London, for more than forty years, only finally retiring when he was in his late seventies. The inventor of the thermionic valve, a device for collecting and controlling the electrically charged particles emitted by an incandescent substance, Fleming combined his academic work with work as a consultant to the newly emerging electrical companies in the last decades of the nineteenth century and first decades of the twentieth century. At various times he was an advisor to Edison Bell, Swan, Marconi and the London Electricity Supply. The development of electricity as a means of supplying heat and light on a large scale owes much to Fleming.

## FLEMING, IAN (1908–1964) *creator of James Bond, lived here*
### 22 EBURY STREET, SW1

The writer of an obscure book on the birds of the West Indies gave his name to the most famous spy of the twentieth century. When Ian Fleming, an Eton and Sandhurst-educated journalist on the *Sunday Times*, was casting around for a suitable name for the amoral hero of his 1953 novel *Casino Royale*, he chanced upon the work of the blameless ornithologist and James Bond the British agent became. The book was an immediate success and Fleming went on to write a series of novels about Bond, including *Live and Let Die, Diamonds Are Forever* and *On Her Majesty's Secret Service*, which brought him fame and fortune. The films of the books, most of which have appeared since Fleming's death in 1964, have transformed Bond into a cultural icon, a character who has escaped the boundaries of the original novels into a wider world. The sardonic Fleming, and possibly the original James Bond, would be amused and perhaps amazed.

## FLINDERS, CAPTAIN MATTHEW, RN (1774–1814) *explorer and navigator, lived here*
### 56 FITZROY STREET, W1

One of the great European explorers of Australia, Flinders was born in Donington, Lincolnshire, the son of a doctor. He entered the Navy and in 1797, together with George Bass, he discovered the passage between Tasmania and Australia that is now called the Bass Strait. Commissioned by Sir Joseph Banks to explore the southern coast of Australia, Flinders was given command of a leaky and untrustworthy ship called the *Investigator*. 'Better an old tub than none at all,' Flinders is reported to have said and he proceeded to circumnavigate the continent in what one historian has called 'a vessel through which anyone could easily have poked a hole with a stick.' After this triumph came disaster. On his way home to England, Flinders was first shipwrecked and then forced to put into port at Mauritius where he was immediately interned by the French. He remained on the island for more than six years. He returned finally to England in 1810 but died four years later at the age of only forty.

## FLYING BOMB *The first Flying Bomb on London fell here, 13 June 1944*
### RAILWAY BRIDGE, GROVE ROAD, BOW, E3

The first V1, pilotless rockets, the so-called 'flying bombs', fell on London on the night and early morning of 12/13 June 1944. For a fortnight, attacks went on at a rate of about 100 V1s per day. Evelyn Waugh later wrote that, 'It was as impersonal as a plague, as though the city were infested with enormous, venomous insects.' On 18 June a V1 struck a direct hit on the Guards Chapel in Birdcage Walk, killing more than 100 people and injuring many more. However, after two months, air defences were stopping most of the V1s before they reached the capital and Londoners could heave a brief sigh of relief before the advent of Wernher von Braun's V2s.

## FONTANE, THEODOR (1819–1898) *German writer and novelist, lived here 1857–1858*
### 6 ST AUGUSTINE'S ROAD, NW1

Today Theodor Fontane is remembered as a novelist. His best-known book, *Effi Briest*, the story of the mismatch between a young wife and a much older husband and its tragic consequences, was published just a few years before his death. It has long been considered the greatest work of nineteenth-century German fiction and Thomas Mann once described it as 'one of the six most significant novels ever written'. However, Fontane did not begin writing fiction until he was well into his fifties. Before that, he was known as a poet and travel writer, and several of his travel books were about his experiences in England. In all, he spent a full four years in Britain, working as both a newspaper correspondent and as a press attaché at the German embassy. His most permanent home in the capital was the house in St Augustine's Road. Fontane was an unashamed Anglophile and he loved London. The city, he once wrote, 'has made an indelible impression on me, not just for its beauty, but for its magnificence, which amazes me. It is the model or quintessence of an entire world.'

## FORD, FORD MADOX (1873–1939) *novelist and critic, lived here*
### 80 CAMPDEN HILL ROAD, W8

Born Ford Hermann Hueffer, the son of Francis Hueffer, music critic for *The Times*, and the grandson of the painter Ford Madox Brown, Ford Madox Ford published many of his novels under the name Ford Madox Hueffer. He chose to exchange the Hueffer for another Ford in 1919, in the wake of post-war anti-German feelings. Brought up in what he termed 'the hothouse atmosphere of Pre-Raphaelism, where I was being trained for a genius', Ford published several volumes of verse, fairy tales and biography in the 1890s. He collaborated with Joseph Conrad on two novels in the early part of the century and published what is his finest achievement, the novel *The Good Soldier*, in 1915. Ford spent many of the post-war years in France and America and it was in Paris that he began writing *Parade's End*, which was published in four volumes between 1924 and 1928. As well as his fiction, Ford achieved much as an editor central to the modern movement. He founded and edited *The English Review* and *The Transatlantic Review*, in which he published work by D.H. Lawrence, Joyce, Ezra Pound, Gertrude Stein and many others.

## FORESTER, C.S. (1889–1966) *novelist, lived here*
### 58 UNDERHILL ROAD, DULWICH, SE22

Born in Cairo, C.S. Forester studied medicine before turning to writing the historical fiction for which he is remembered. Several of his books were filmed, most notably *The African Queen*, the story of a mismatched couple's dangerous journey down an African river, which John

Huston filmed with Humphrey Bogart and Katharine Hepburn. Most popular of all Forester's fiction, however, was the Hornblower series. This traces the career, from midshipman to admiral, of Horatio Hornblower, a naval hero of the Napoleonic wars, very loosely based on Nelson. Forester, early in his career, had written a biography of Nelson.

## FORSTER, E.M. (1879–1970) *novelist, lived here*
### ARLINGTON PARK MANSIONS, SUTTON LANE, TURNHAM GREEN, W4

'In no book,' E.M. Forster said once in an interview, 'have I got more down than the people I like, the person I think I am, and the people who irritate me. This puts me among the large body of authors who are not really novelists, and have to get on as best as they can with these three categories.' Despite this modest assessment of his work, Forster was one of the most admired English novelists of the twentieth century. Born in London, he was educated at King's College, Cambridge, and it was there that he became friends with a number of the people who were later to form what was known as the Bloomsbury Group. His first book, *Where Angels Fear to Tread*, was published in 1905 and his most famous novel, *A Passage to India*, which appeared in 1924, was also to be his last. In the last four and a half decades of his long life he published essays, criticism and collections of short stories but no novels. In 1945 he was elected an honorary fellow of King's and lived there for the rest of his life. *Maurice*, the story of a homosexual relationship, was written at the time of the First World War but only published after Forster's death.

## FORTUNE, ROBERT (1812–1880) *plant collector, lived here 1857–1880*
### 9 GILSTON ROAD, SW10

Born in Berwickshire, Fortune began a career that was to take him into the wilder regions of the Far East as a gardener's boy in the Edinburgh Botanic Gardens. It was when he was working for the Horticultural Society in London in 1843 that Fortune was chosen by the Society to lead an expedition to China, recently opened up to Westerners by the Treaty of Nanking, in search of exotic plants. That Fortune spoke not a word of any Chinese language and had absolutely no experience whatsoever of plant collecting seemed not to worry the Society. Their faith in him proved justified. Fortune proved his worth on the 1843 expedition and on further journeys through China, bringing back many plant specimens hitherto unknown in the West. In 1848, disguised as a Chinese peasant (and by this time familiar with the local language), Fortune smuggled tea plants out of China and into India, thus establishing what was to become one of the major industries of the sub-continent.

## FOSCOLO, UGO (1778–1827) *Italian poet and patriot, lived here 1817–1818*
### 19 EDWARDES SQUARE, W8

As a young man Foscolo saw Napoleon as Italy's potential liberator from the rule of the Austrian empire. He wrote poetry in praise of the Corsican general and fought for the French against the Austrian armies. As Napoleon's imperial ambitions became clearer, Foscolo's sense of betrayal was strong, although he continued to see France as the lesser of two evils. To this period of disillusionment belong his best works, the romantic novel *Last Letters of Jacopo Ortis* and the poem *Dei Sepolcri*. In 1814 the Austrians marched into Milan and Foscolo, who had had a love affair and a daughter with an English woman, went into exile, via Switzerland, in London. His years in London were years of suffering and poverty and he died in Turnham Green in 1827. Forty four years later, when the Italy for which he had fought had become a reality, his remains were taken from Chiswick and re-interred in Florence.

## FOX, CHARLES JAMES (1749–1806) *statesman, lived here*

46 CLARGES STREET, W1 · ORIGINALLY PUT UP IN 1912 ON 9 ARLINGTON STREET, NOW DEMOLISHED

One of the most colourful politicians of his time, Fox was distinguished by his talents and intelligence, his self-indulgence and recklessness, his prodigious exploits as gambler and *bon viveur*. As a child he had been comprehensively indulged by his father, the first Lord Holland. Once, when Charles had been promised the thrill of seeing a wall blown up with gunpowder but had, unfortunately, missed it, his father ordered the wall rebuilt so that his son could witness the second demolition. Fox entered Parliament at the early age of nineteen but most of his political career was spent in opposition, acting as the focus for the critics of Pitt the Younger's long reign as Prime Minister. The death of Pitt in 1806 finally opened the doors of office but Fox's period as Foreign Secretary in the so-called 'Ministry of All The Talents' was brief and he died in the same year as his great rival.

## FRAMPTON, GEORGE (1860–1928) *sculptor, lived and worked here*

32 QUEEN'S GROVE, ST JOHN'S WOOD, NW8

Probably the best-known sculpture by George Frampton is the statue of Peter Pan in Kensington Gardens, an uncharacteristic work by an artist who spent most of his career decorating the public buildings of Victorian and Edwardian England and celebrating the heroes of Empire. Frampton was born in London and studied under the artist W.P. Frith. He began to exhibit at the Royal Academy in the 1880s and became a Royal Academician in 1902. Six years later he was knighted. The Edith Cavell memorial, opposite the National Portrait Gallery, is Frampton's work and he produced statues of Queen Victoria that adorn public spaces in cities from Calcutta to Winnipeg.

## FRANKLIN, BENJAMIN (1706–1790) *American statesman and scientist, lived here*

36 CRAVEN STREET, WC2

Franklin made his first visit to London at the age of eighteen, working in a printing house there before returning to Philadelphia to continue his career as a printer and journalist. He was to spend many years in England and Europe including an almost uninterrupted stretch from 1757 to 1775. He lived in Craven Street for thirteen years. His earlier scientific experiments (including the one in which he used a kite to show that lightning was electrical in its nature) gave him an introduction to English intellectual circles and he became a friend of Burke, Hume and Adam Smith as well as receiving honorary degrees from three universities. In 1776, back in America, he fixed his signature to the Declaration of Independence, remarking as he did so, 'We must, indeed, all hang together or, most assuredly, we shall all hang separately.' Franklin's diplomatic skills and his knowledge of English society were largely instrumental in the signing of the Treaty of Paris seven years later, which ended the American War of Independence. He stayed on as the new republic's Minister in France until 1785 and then returned once more to America, where he was the President of the Pennsylvania Executive for three years before finally retiring from public life in 1788.

## FRANKLIN, ROSALIND (1920–1958) *pioneer of the study of molecular structures including DNA, lived here*

DONOVAN COURT, DRAYTON GARDENS, SW10

Many people have heard of James Watson and Francis Crick and the roles they played in uncovering the structure of DNA, which revolutionised the study of genetics. Because of her early death, fewer people know of the important contribution made by Rosalind Franklin. Franklin took a degree in chemistry at Cambridge and, after graduating in 1941, worked as a researcher both in London and Paris before she joined the new biophysical laboratory at King's College, London, and it was here that she undertook research into the crystallographic structure of DNA. Her results were to provide Crick and Watson with critically important data. Sadly, Franklin's death from cancer in 1958 robbed her of any opportunity to share the Nobel Prize that was awarded to Crick and Watson four years later.

........................................................................

## FREAKE, SIR CHARLES JAMES (1814–1884) *builder and patron of the arts, lived here*
### 21 CROMWELL ROAD, SW7

The house in which Freake himself lived from 1860 is in the heart of the area that he developed during the middle years of the nineteenth century. The son of a coal merchant, Freake was already a wealthy man when he began speculative building in Cromwell Road, Exhibition Road and their environs, but his projects there made him wealthier. A friend of the Prince of Wales, he was made a baronet in 1882. Freake was an enthusiast for music and the theatre and in the 1870s he had the National Training School for Music (now the Royal College of Organists) built, using his own money.

........................................................................

## FREUD, ANNA (1895–1982) *pioneer of child psychoanalysis, lived here 1938–1982*
### 20 MARESFIELD GARDENS, NW3

Anna, the youngest of Freud's six children, was the only one to follow him into the profession of psychoanalysis. As a teenager she read some of her father's work but it was only after the First World War that she began to train seriously as an analyst. Her father undertook her analysis in 1920 (something strictly against later psychoanalytic best practice, which bars close relations entering the analyst / analysand relationship) and she became a member of the Vienna Psychoanalytical Society in 1922. The following year she started her own psychoanalytic practice and was soon specialising in the analysis of children, the area in which she was to undertake most of her original work over the next half-century. Unmarried and devoted to her father, Anna became Freud's nurse during the succession of painful illnesses and operations that plagued the last decade and a half of his life. After his death she not only continued her own work in child psychology but also became the guardian of her father's memory and of Freudian orthodoxy. She died in 1982 and the house in Maresfield Gardens, Hampstead, where her father had spent the last year of this life and where she had lived for more than forty years, became the Freud Museum.

........................................................................

## FREUD, SIGMUND (1856–1939) *founder of psychoanalysis, lived here in 1938–1939*
### 20 MARESFIELD GARDENS, NW3

Freud was born in the small Moravian town of Freiburg and his family moved to Vienna when he was four years old. He lived there until he was an old man of eighty-two, through all the years in which he slowly elaborated the theories of psychoanalysis, the concept of the Oedipus Complex and the threefold division of the mind into id, ego and superego. To the Nazis, Freud's ideas were anathema. Not only were they the work of a Jewish thinker but they were representative of what the Nazis thought of as the sickness and decadence of the modern world. His books were burnt in Berlin. 'What progress we are making,' Freud wrote dryly to a colleague. 'In the Middle Ages they would have burned me. Now they are content with burning my books.' However, when the Nazis overran Austria, Freud's life as well as his writing was in danger and strenuous efforts were made to get him and his family out of Vienna. He came to London in 1938 and to 20 Maresfield Gardens (now the Freud Museum), where he spent the last year of his life writing *Moses and Monotheism*, his last significant work, and fighting against cancer of the jaw, which claimed his life on 23 September 1939.

---

## FRIESE-GREENE, WILLIAM (1855–1921) *pioneer of cinematography, lived here*
136 MAIDA VALE, W9

Born in Bristol, Friese-Greene was working as a photographer when he became interested in the possibilities of making images move. He moved to London in 1885, renting a studio in Piccadilly for his experiments. He lived in Maida Vale for the three years from 1888 to 1891, during which time he patented and demonstrated a camera of his own invention which, by shooting film at five frames a second, took what could have been a decisive step towards motion pictures. However, Friese-Greene was not a man blessed by luck. In 1891 he spent a brief period in jail when a company of which he was a director went bankrupt. His inventions were overtaken by those of other experimenters and, although he continued to patent various motion picture devices, including stereoscopic and colour systems, all proved either largely impractical or too visionary for his times. He died, an impoverished man, while giving a speech to a film industry convention.

---

## FRITH, W.P. (1819–1909) *painter, lived and died here*
114 CLIFTON HILL, NW8

With their meticulous detail and abundance of anecdotal incident, the crowded canvases of W.P. Frith were among the most popular of Victorian paintings. *Ramsgate Sands* (1853), *Derby Day* (1858) and *The Railway Station* (1862) are the best-known works of an artist whose paintings, when exhibited at the Royal Academy, occasionally had to be protected from their ardent admirers by specially constructed barriers. Frith, who was born the son of a Yorkshire innkeeper, studied at the Royal Academy schools and began as a painter of historical and literary subjects (his first major success was a study of Malvolio) but rapidly developed into the foremost depicter of contemporary Victorian life. He was a friend of Dickens and one of the best-known portraits of the novelist is his work.

---

## FROBISHER, MARTIN
See under entry for SIR HUGH WILLOUGHBY

---

## FROUDE, JAMES ANTHONY (1818–1894) *historian and man of letters, lived here*
5 ONSLOW GARDENS, SW7

Froude lost his faith amidst the turmoil of the Oxford Movement, the series of theological debates that culminated in John Henry Newman's conversion to Roman Catholicism. He lost his Oxford fellowship when the Sub-Rector of his college burnt a copy of his novel, *The Nemesis of Faith*, in front of the undergraduates in the college hall. Froude took the hint and resigned. For the next forty years he pursued his career as a historian outside the universities, publishing a twelve-volume *History of England from the Death of Cardinal Wolsey to the defeat of the Spanish Armada*, which became the foundation for future studies of the Tudor period. Froude was one of the first English historians to make extensive use of archival material, although fellow historians were not always complimentary about the results. 'He handles his authorities as a wilful baby uses her dolls,' wrote one, probably envious, contemporary. Froude was a friend of Carlyle and wrote a biography of the great man that Victorian readers thought to be outrageously frank. At the end of his life he returned to Oxford as Regius Professor of Modern History.

························································································································

## FRY, C.B. (1872–1956) *all-round sportsman, was born here*
144 ST JAMES'S ROAD, CROYDON

## C.B. FRY *scholar and sportsman, lived at*
NO. 8 MORELAND COURT, FINCHLEY ROAD, NW2   **HENDON CORPORATION**

Just listing the sporting achievements of C.B. Fry one gains some idea of why he is often considered the greatest all-round sportsman Britain has produced. As a cricketer, he captained both Sussex and England and is one of only three players ever to have scored six consecutive centuries in first-class matches. He held the world record for the long jump while he was still a student and won the 100 yards' sprint in the first international intercollegiate match between Oxford and Yale in 1894. He played football for England in one international match and was a good enough rugby player to represent Oxford in a varsity match and to turn out for the Barbarians. In an age when sportsmen are now specialists there will never be an all-rounder like him again. When advancing years prevented further athletic achievement, Fry became a writer and journalist. Through his friendship with the Indian prince and cricketer, Ranjitsinhji, he became an adviser to the Indian delegation at the League of Nations in Geneva in 1920. While he was in Geneva, Albanian diplomats approached him. They were looking for an English gentleman prepared to accept the throne of their country. Would Fry be interested in becoming King of Albania? The great all-rounder considered their offer carefully but eventually decided against it and returned to England to write about cricket matches instead.

························································································································

## FRY, MRS ELIZABETH (1780–1845) *prison reformer, lived here 1800–1809*
ENTRANCE TO ST MILDRED'S COURT, POULTRY, EC2   **CITY OF LONDON**

## ELIZABETH FRY
195 MARE STREET, HACKNEY, E8   **BOROUGH OF HACKNEY**

The daughter of a wealthy Quaker banker, Elizabeth Gurney married Joseph Fry in 1800 and lived in St Mildred's Court in the first years of her marriage. Her life was changed by a visit to Newgate in 1813, where she discovered hundreds of women and their children imprisoned in filthy and degrading conditions. She began to tour prisons in England and abroad, pushing for reforms and, in 1817, founded a society to provide aid to those suffering from the appalling conditions that prevailed in early nineteenth-century prisons. An American observer described the effects of her prison-visiting: 'I have seen Elizabeth Fry in Newgate and I have witnessed there the miraculous effect of true Christianity upon the most depraved of human beings.'

························································································································

## FUSELI, HENRY (1741–1825) *artist, lived here 1788–1803*
37 FOLEY STREET, W1

The son of a portrait painter, Fuseli was born in Zurich (his original name was Heinrich Füssli) and turned his back on a proposed career in the priesthood to follow in his father's footsteps. He came to England in the 1760s but left to spend eight years in Italy, studying the old masters and perfecting the technique he later applied to his paintings of grotesque visions (*The Nightmare* was exhibited at the Royal Academy in 1782) and of scenes from the great works of English literature, particularly the plays of Shakespeare. Returning to England, Fuseli became an important figure in the art world of his time and was elected Professor of Painting at the Royal Academy in 1799. He was a friend of William Blake, who wrote of him that he was, 'The only man that e'er I knew/Who did not make me almost spew.'

GABOR, DENNIS (1900–1979) *Physicist and inventor of holography, lived here*
79 QUEEN'S GATE, SW7

'The future cannot be predicted,' Dennis Gabor wrote in 1963, 'but futures can be invented.' Gabor had made his own significant contribution to the invention of the future sixteen years earlier when he had carried out the first experiments in what came to be called holography. Born in Budapest as Gábor Dénes, he studied and worked in Germany until 1933 when the Nazis came to power. As a Jew, his career and life were now in danger and he fled the country, settling in Britain. He went to work for the engineering company British Thomson-Houston in Rugby where he focused on the developing field of electron optics. Gabor conceived the idea of holography as early as 1947 and developed its basics using a conventional light source but it was only some years later, with the invention of the laser and its amplified light, that his technique became commercially viable. In the last few decades holography has proved its value in a wide range of fields from medicine and cartography to credit card security. Dennis Gabor won the 1971 Nobel Prize for Physics 'for his invention and development of the holographic method'.

GAGE, THOMAS (1721–1787) *commander of British forces in North America, lived here*
41 PORTLAND PLACE, W1

The son of the first Viscount Gage, Thomas Gage joined the Army in 1741 and, together with an American-born officer called George Washington, was among the few to distinguish himself in a disastrous expedition against the French and their Indian allies in America in 1755. Five years later the British government, recognising that Gage was becoming a specialist in American affairs, appointed him Military Governor of Montreal. By 1763 he was in charge of all British troops in North America. Appointed Governor of Massachusetts in 1774, Gage, despite his long experience in American affairs, showed a lack of diplomacy in his new post and a clash between his troops and the colonists at Lexington on 18 April 1775 was the first engagement of the War of Independence. After the Battle of Bunker Hill in June of the same year, Gage was once again given supreme military command in America, but he was by now a disillusioned and disappointed man. He resigned his post and returned to England.

GAINSBOROUGH, THOMAS (1727–1988) *artist, lived here*
82 PALL MALL, SW1 · *replaces plaque put up in 1881 by RSA at No. 80*

Although he became one of the great portrait painters of the day, Gainsborough did not move to London permanently until he was well into middle age. Born in Suffolk, he began his career in Ipswich. He moved in 1760 to Bath, where his sitters changed from county gentry and town merchants to the members of high society. Only in 1774, six years after becoming one of the founding members of the Royal Academy, did Gainsborough settle in the capital. Although it was his portraits that provided him with his substantial income, it may be that landscape painting was Gainsborough's great delight. Certainly many of his finest portraits place their sitters in meticulously rendered rural settings and he produced many landscapes during his London career, both in oils and in pencil chalk drawing. Gainsborough, an easy-going man, was not renowned for his promptness in delivering commissioned work, once writing that, 'painting and punctuality mix like oil and vinegar.'

GAITSKELL, HUGH (1906–1963) *statesman, lived here*
18 FROGNAL GARDENS, HAMPSTEAD, NW3

When Attlee retired as leader of the Labour party in 1955, the battle to succeed him and to lay claim to the soul of the party was between the left-wing Aneurin Bevan and the ex-Chancellor of the Exchequer Hugh Gaitskell, whom Bevan had once described as 'a desiccated calculating machine'. Victory went to Gaitskell but divisions between Bevanites and his own supporters were to bedevil Gaitskell's leadership over the next eight years. Gaitskell had been born into a well-to-do family, was educated at Winchester and Oxford and later claimed that it was his experiences in the General Strike of 1926 that made him a Socialist. He became an MP in 1945 and such was his ability that he was the choice to replace Stafford Cripps as Chancellor in October 1950. Under Gaitskell the Labour party lost a third successive election in 1959 and he faced serious problems within the party over defence policy, in particular. Gaitskell died suddenly and unexpectedly in January 1963.

......................................................................................................................................

## GALSWORTHY, JOHN (1867–1933) *novelist and playwright, lived here 1918–1933*

GROVE LODGE, ADMIRAL'S WALK, NW3

Galsworthy's work, even *The Forsyte Saga*, is little read today and is not held in very high critical esteem. Yet he was one of the few English writers to win the Nobel Prize for Literature (in 1932) and he was awarded the OM, having refused a knighthood. After Harrow and Oxford, Galsworthy became a barrister but practised little. With the encouragement of his wife-to-be and of Joseph Conrad, whom he had met by chance while travelling, he became a writer. His *annus mirabilis* as a writer came in 1906, when *The Man of Property*, the first Forsyte novel, was published and *The Silver Box*, the first of many successful plays on social themes, was staged. The Forsyte Saga continued to unroll until 1931, when a collection of stories called *On Forsyte Change* appeared, and Galsworthy also wrote several novels about the Charwells, cousins of the Forsytes.

See also under entry for ROBERT ADAM

......................................................................................................................................

## GALTON, SIR FRANCIS (1822–1911) *explorer, statistician and founder of eugenics, lived here for fifty years*

42 RUTLAND GATE, SW7

A cousin of Charles Darwin, Francis Galton was a versatile and gifted Victorian scientist whose work is overshadowed today by his advocacy of 'eugenics', selective breeding of the human race to produce, for example, greater intellectual and athletic skill. He himself saw it merely as building on the evolutionary ideas of his cousin but, after a century that has heard too much talk of a 'master race', eugenics seems a tainted idea. As a young man, Galton explored areas of southern Africa and published a *Narrative of an Explorer in Tropical South Africa* in 1855. Meteorology was an abiding interest and Galton, realising that air circulates in the opposite direction in high and low pressure areas, coined the word 'anti-cyclone' to describe the highs on the weather map. In a different field, he was the first person to suggest that fingerprints were so sufficiently individualised that they could be used by the police to identify criminals.

......................................................................................................................................

## GANDHI, MAHATMA (1869–1948) *philosopher and teacher, stayed here in 1931*

KINGSLEY HALL, POWIS ROAD, E3

## MAHATMA GANDHI (1869–1948) *lived here as a law student*

20 BARON'S COURT ROAD, W14

Gandhi's first experience of London was as a law student in the late 1880s. He returned in 1931 as a representative of the Congress Party at talks on Indian constitutional reform. Between these two dates he had spent two decades in South Africa, where he worked

as a lawyer for the often poor Indian community there, and, back in India, had established himself as the leading figure in the movement to force Britain out of the sub-continent by means of non-violent civil disobedience. After the relative failure of the 1931 conference he continued to campaign for British withdrawal from India and lived to see the British grant independence in 1947, what he described as 'the noblest act of the British nation'. Gandhi was a victim of the vicious conflict in the new India between Hindu and Moslem, assassinated on 30 January 1948 by a Hindu fanatic who believed that he had betrayed his co-religionists. The British politician Sir Stafford Cripps, in paying tribute to Gandhi, said that he knew of no other man 'who so convincingly demonstrated the power of the spirit over material things'.

## GANDY, JOSEPH MICHAEL (1771–1843) *architectural visionary, lived here 1833–1838*
### 58 GROVE PARK TERRACE, LONDON, W4

The son of a waiter at White's club, Joseph Gandy showed his talent for drawing at an early age and it won him a place as a student of architecture at the Royal Academy. After travel in Italy, where he was overwhelmed by the classical architecture he saw in Rome, he returned to London to attempt to make a career for himself. However, Gandy was a difficult and demanding man to employ as an architect since he found it almost impossible to compromise his own vision of what a building might be and listen instead to what his client wanted. Very few of his buildings were ever constructed. Most existed only on paper. The one successful partnership of his life was with fellow-architect Sir John Soane who used Gandy's exceptional skills as an architectural draughtsman to produce images of the buildings he was commissioned to build. Soane and Gandy shared a romantic taste for ruins and some of the latter's most striking and unusual watercolour images are of the more successful architect's buildings as they might look after they have fallen into decay. After Soane's death in 1837, Gandy's life went rapidly downhill. Two years later he was incarcerated in a lunatic asylum in Devon where he died in 1843.

## GARRETT ANDERSON, ELIZABETH (1836–1917) *the first woman to qualify as a doctor in Britain, lived here*

### 20 UPPER BERKELEY STREET, W1

## ELIZABETH GARRETT ANDERSON (1836–1917)
### LONDON GUILDHALL UNIVERSITY, COMMERCIAL ROAD, E1
**BOROUGH OF TOWER HAMLETS**

Elizabeth Garrett came from a family of high achievers (her younger sister became a prominent pioneer of women's suffrage) and decided at an early age that she wanted to make her career in medicine. It is difficult to credit the determination and persistence she required to pursue her ambition at a time when no woman was allowed to qualify as a doctor. She gained experience of dissections and operations as a nurse but was consistently refused admission to any medical school. By 1865 she had obtained the diploma of the Society of Apothecaries, which meant that she was listed on the medical register. The following year she opened the St Mary's Dispensary for Women, which was renamed the Elizabeth Garrett Anderson Hospital after her death, and eventually received her medical degree from the University of Paris in 1870. From 1873 to 1892 she was the only female member of the British Medical Association. When she was chosen mayor of Aldeburgh, the town in which she had grown up, in 1908, she achieved another, less publicised first for her sex – she was the first woman mayor in England.

## GARRICK, DAVID (1717–1779) *actor, lived here*
GARRICK'S VILLA, HAMPTON COURT ROAD

## GARRICK, DAVID *lived here 1750–1772*
27 SOUTHAMPTON STREET, WC2 **DUKE OF BEDFORD**

Garrick first came to London with Samuel Johnson, who had been his teacher at a school in Lichfield. Johnson embarked on a career as a hack writer; Garrick divided his time between the wine trade and amateur theatricals. In 1741 his first appearance on a public stage, as Richard III, in an out-of-the-way and unlicensed theatre in Whitechapel was a sensation, drawing audiences away from the officially approved theatres in Covent Garden and Drury Lane. Garrick decided he had found his vocation and he became and remained, until his retirement in 1776, the most acclaimed actor on the English stage. For thirty years, as manager of Drury Lane, he was also the most powerful figure in the London theatre. When someone once remarked to Dr Johnson that his old pupil had let his achievements go to his head, Johnson would have none of it. 'Here is a man who has advanced the dignity of his profession. Garrick has made a player a higher character. If all this had happened to me, I should have had a couple of fellows with long poles walking before me, to knock down everybody that stood in the way . . . Yet Garrick speaks to *us*.'

See also under entry for ADELPHI TERRACE

## GARTHWAITE, ANNA MARIA (1690–1763) *designer of Spitalfields Silks, lived and worked here*

2 PRINCELET STREET, E1

In the late seventeenth and eighteenth centuries Spitalfields became the centre for silk weaving in London, largely due to influx of Huguenot refugees from France, driven from their own country by the revocation of the Edict of Nantes, the document which guaranteed the toleration of their religious practices. Many of the finest silks to emerge from Spitalfields were the work of these exiled French weavers and designers. However, one of the greatest designers was the daughter of a Lincolnshire parson. The work of Anna Maria Garthwaite was clearly influenced by French design but, in the words of one historian of fashion, 'represented a very real and original contribution by England to the Rococo style'. Anna Maria Garthwaite's scrap-book of design ideas and several of her finished pieces are still in existence in the Victoria and Albert Museum.

---

## GARVEY, MARCUS (1887–1940) *Pan-Africanist leader, lived and died here*
53 TALGARTH ROAD, W14

'A people without the knowledge of their past history, origin and culture,' Marcus Garvey once wrote, 'is like a tree without roots' and he was committed to the idea that the black peoples of the world should not lose knowledge of their own roots. Born in Jamaica, Garvey worked as a printer as a young man before his involvement in strike action and industrial dispute put him out of work and sent him on travels which took him around the Caribbean and to London. In 1914, back on his native island, he founded the Universal Negro Improvement Association. He took its ideas to the USA two years later and rapidly became one of the most charismatic black leaders in the country, regularly attracting large crowds to his speeches and meetings. By 1920, the UNIA could claim a membership of 4 million people. Garvey's political activities attracted the unfavourable attentions of the authorities and, arrested for fraud in connection with the Black Star Line, a shipping company he had established to further his dream of black economic independence and the possibility of black emigration to Africa, he was tried, convicted and imprisoned. On his release, he was deported to Jamaica. Garvey returned to Britain in 1935 and died of a stroke there five years later.

---

## GASKELL, MRS ELIZABETH CLEGHORN (1810 –1865) *novelist, born here*
93 CHEYNE WALK, SW10

Although she was born in Chelsea, the daughter of a Unitarian minister, Elizabeth Stevenson was brought up, after her mother died, in the town of Knutsford, which she recreated as the Cranford of her fiction. In 1832 she married another Unitarian minister, William Gaskell, and settled with him in Manchester. She had a family of five children when she began her career as a novelist with the book *Mary Barton*, which drew upon her knowledge of the industrialised north and was subtitled *A Tale of Manchester Life*. Although Mrs Gaskell may appear to us the epitome of the staid and upright Victorian novelist, she was considered a daring moralist by her contemporaries. *Ruth* (1853) caused controversy because of its sympathetic portrait of an unmarried mother; *North and South* (1855) was thought unsparing in its depiction of industrial strife; and even her biography of her friend Charlotte Brontë received threats of legal action when it alluded too plainly to Branwell Brontë's relationship with a married woman. Mrs Gaskell died suddenly of heart failure at the age of fifty-five.

---

## GERTLER, MARK (1891–1939) *painter, lived here*
32 ELDER STREET, E1

## MARK GERTLER
1 WELL MOUNT STUDIOS, WELL MOUNT, NW3   **HAMPSTEAD PLAQUE FUND**

The son of Jewish immigrants, Gertler was born in Spitalfields and was inspired to become a painter as a teenager when he came across the autobiography of the Victorian artist William Powell Frith. He studied at the Slade School and found early success, gaining support and sales from members of the Bloomsbury Group and well-heeled patrons such as Edward Marsh and Lady Ottoline Morrell. Gertler was a Conscientious Objector during the First World War and his anti-war painting *The Merry-Go-Round*, which D.H. Lawrence described as 'great and true' but 'horrible and terrifying', provoked controversy in art circles. It is now recognised as one of the most potent images to emerge from the war years. Gertler was diagnosed with tuberculosis in 1920 and the rest of his life was a struggle against ill health, depression and increasing difficulty in selling his works. He committed suicide a few months before the start of the Second World War.

## GIBBON, EDWARD (1737–1792) *historian, lived in a house on this site 1772–1783*
7 BENTINCK STREET, W1

Born in Putney and educated at Westminster and Oxford, Gibbon converted to Roman Catholicism as an adolescent. His father was appalled and sent him to Lausanne where the earnest tuition of a Calvinist minister rapidly unconverted him. It was there that he made the one romantic attachment of his life, but his father was no more approving of his choice of wife than he was of his choice of religion. He told Gibbon to forget about her. 'I sighed as a lover, I obeyed as a son,' Gibbon sadly noted in his autobiography. The great work of Gibbon's life was, of course, the monumental *History of the Decline and Fall of the Roman Empire*, first published between 1776 and 1788. Although it was a great and immediate success, not everyone admired Gibbon's elegant prose style and expansive narrative. The Duke of Gloucester, introduced to the historian after publication of one of the volumes, remarked, 'Another damned, thick, square book! Always scribble, scribble, scribble! Eh, Mr Gibbon?'

## GIBSON, GUY, V.C. (1918–1944), *pilot, leader of the Dambusters Raid, lived here*
32 ABERDEEN PLACE, ST JOHN'S WOOD, NW8

Born in India in the days of the Raj, Guy Gibson joined the RAF in 1936 and, when the Second World War broke out three years later, he was already a bomber pilot. By 1943, he had been promoted to Wing Commander and was one of the most experienced and decorated pilots in the service. He was an obvious choice for the role of commanding officer of an important bombing mission to destroy German dams on the Ruhr. The mission was a triumphant success and Gibson became a hero, feted at the time and celebrated later in one of the most famous of all Second World War films. After the Dambusters Raid, he was awarded the Victoria Cross and he could easily have rested on his laurels but he was determined to return to active service. He pestered his superiors to allow him to do so and eventually they acceded to his demands. According to Barnes Wallis (the man who developed the bouncing bomb used in the Dambusters Raid), Guy Gibson was a 'man born for war... but born to fall in war.' Wallis was sadly proven right. In September 1944, Gibson was killed when the de Havilland Mosquito he was flying crashed near Steenbergen in the Netherlands.

## GILBERT, SIR W.S. (1836–1911) *dramatist, lived here*
39 HARRINGTON GARDENS, SW7

In 1871 William Schwenck Gilbert was known as the author of a collection of humorous verse, *Bab Ballads* (Gilbert was known as 'Bab' as a child), and as a moderately successful dramatist. In that year he collaborated for the first time with the composer Arthur Sullivan. *Thespis* was not a theatrical triumph but, three years later, Gilbert met the impresario Richard D'Oyly Carte and he staged the second Gilbert and Sullivan collaboration, *Trial by Jury*, in 1875. It was the start of a series of comic operas – others include *The Pirates of Penzance*, *H.M.S. Pinafore* and *The Mikado* – which were immensely popular at the time and are still regularly performed today. Relationships between Gilbert, Sullivan and D'Oyly Carte were not always amicable and Gilbert continued to write dramas outside the collaboration. However, it is his libretti for the Savoy operas (so called because it was at the Savoy Theatre that every work from *Iolanthe* in 1882 onwards was staged) that are remembered. Gilbert died in 1911 after heroically trying to save a young woman from drowning.

See also under entry for R. NORMAN SHAW

## GILLIES, SIR HAROLD (1882–1960) *pioneer plastic surgeon, lived here*
71 FROGNAL, NW3

Born in New Zealand, Gillies did his medical training at St Bartholomew's Hospital. During the First World War he came across men suffering from horrendously disfiguring injuries and it was to help some of these that he began to reconstruct both faces and lives. In 1920 he published *Plastic Surgery of the Face*, the founding text of his particular branch of medicine. During the Second World War Gillies's particular skills were once again of vital importance and he was made responsible for a series of plastic surgery units throughout the country, including a very large one at Basingstoke, which he ran personally. Outside his surgical work Gillies was a very talented amateur golfer who played the game for his adopted country.

## GISSING, GEORGE (1857–1903) *novelist, lived here 1882–1884*
33 OAKLEY GARDENS, SW3

A classical scholar whose academic career came to an abrupt end when he was imprisoned for theft, Gissing knew well the poverty and misery of late Victorian London which he evoked in his novels. Although he was a prolific novelist it was only towards the end of his life that he began to earn enough to release him from financial anxieties and from the necessity to supplement his income with poorly paid tutition work. It is entirely appropriate that his best-known novel, *New Grub Street*, is a bleak portrayal of the literary world in which the glib survive and those with integrity, like the hero Reardon, go to the wall. Gissing was twice married to women from the working class and both marriages were disasters. As Gissing's friend H.G. Wells explained, 'He felt that to make love to any woman he could regard as a social equal would be too elaborate . . . so he flung himself at a social inferior, whom he expected to be eager and grateful.' Unfortunate to the end, Gissing died just as his industry as a novelist was beginning to bring its rewards.

## GLADSTONE, WILLIAM EWART (1809–1898) *statesman, lived here*
11 CARLTON HOUSE TERRACE, SW1

W.E. GLADSTONE *delivered his last speech to his Greenwich constituents 30 November 1873 on the site of this plaque*

EGLINTON ROAD SCHOOL, PLUMSTEAD, SE18 **PRIVATE**

'Oh, William dear,' his wife once said to Gladstone, 'if you weren't such a great man you would be a terrible bore.' Luckily for their marriage he *was* a great man who, in a parliamentary career that lasted more than sixty years, became the Grand Old Man of British politics and the personification of Victorian Liberalism. Yet he started his career as a Conservative and, when elected as MP for Newark in 1832, it was as a youthful reactionary, opposed to almost all measures of reform. Under the influence of Robert Peel, in whose Cabinet he served in the 1840s, he moved further to the Left but he was still sitting as a

Tory when he was first made Chancellor of the Exchequer in 1852. It was not until 1859 that he crossed the floor of the House unequivocally and joined Palmerston's government, again as Chancellor. By 1868 he was Liberal Prime Minister and remained so for six years. It was during this period that his great rivalry with Disraeli developed. It may be apocryphal that Disraeli, when asked to define the difference between a calamity and a misfortune, said that, 'If Mr Gladstone fell into the Thames, that would be a misfortune. If someone were to pull him out, that would be a calamity.' Gladstone was Prime Minister on three subsequent occasions (1880–5, 1886 and 1892–4), although all of these ministries were bedevilled by disagreements within his party, particularly over Ireland.

See also under entry for SIR CHARLES LYELL

......................................................................................................................................

## GLAISHER, JAMES (1809–1903) *astronomer, meteorologist and pioneer of weather forecasting, lived here*

20 DARTMOUTH HILL, SE10

Glaisher was born in London and began his career at the Ordnance Survey. From 1838 until his retirement in 1874 he was the chief meteorologist at the Greenwich Observatory and it was in this capacity that he established the system for careful daily observation of meteorological phenomena which enabled scientific weather forecasting to take place. Many of the techniques that Glaisher pioneered are still used today. He was elected a Fellow of the Royal Society in 1849 and founded the Royal Meteorological Society in the following year. In pursuit of accurate information about weather formations Glaisher became an intrepid balloonist, making many ascents, and once climbed over seven miles from the ground in order to study atmospheric effects at that height.

......................................................................................................................................

## GODFREE, KATHLEEN ('KITTY') NÉE MCKANE (1896–1992) *lawn tennis champion lived here 1936–1992*

55 YORK AVENUE, EAST SHEEN, SW14

Unlike many of today's tennis players, barely into their teens before they are playing at the highest level, Kitty Godfree did not make her debut at Wimbledon until 1919, when she was twenty-three years old, but she soon established herself as one of the most talented of all British women players. She was twice winner of the women's singles title (in 1924 and 1926) and she also won five Olympic medals, including gold in the doubles at the Antwerp Games of 1920. With her husband Lesley Godfree she won the mixed doubles at Wimbledon in 1926. They are the only husband-and-wife partnership ever to do this. Kitty Godfree was also a fine badminton player and, during the 1920s, she won the women's singles four times at the All England Badminton Championship. She continued to play tennis until she was in her nineties. At the age of ninety, as the oldest surviving women's champion, she presented the trophy to Martina Navratilova at Wimbledon. In 1994, two years after her death, the Veterans Lawn Tennis Association of Great Britain established the Kitty Godfree Cup for women players aged sixty-five and over.

......................................................................................................................................

## GODLEY, JOHN ROBERT (1814–1861) *founder of Canterbury, New Zealand, lived and died here*

48 GLOUCESTER PLACE, W1

Educated at Harrow and Christ Church, Oxford, Godley was called to the Bar but rarely practised. He preferred to travel, visiting the United States in the early 1840s and publishing a well-received book, *Travels in America*, on the subject. He became interested in the possibilities of emigration and exchanged ideas with Edward Gibbon Wakefield, the theorist of colonisation. The colony in Canterbury was founded on plans elaborated by the two of them and Godley himself left England, troubled by ill health, to guide the fortunes of the fledgeling community. Godley's ideas about the relationship between colony and mother country were clear and forcibly expressed. 'I would rather,' he wrote, 'be governed by a Nero on the spot than by a board of angels in London because we could, if the worst came to the worst, cut off Nero's head, but we could not get at the board in London at all.' Godley stayed for three years in New Zealand and returned to England in 1852.

## GODWIN, GEORGE (1813–1888) *architect, journalist and social reformer, lived here*
24 ALEXANDER SQUARE, SW3

George Godwin was the son of an architect who entered his father's office as a young man and went on to run a thriving practice of his own, designing both churches and housing developments such as The Boltons, the palatial crescents off the Old Brompton Road. He was also a prolific writer on a wide variety of subjects. He wrote on architectural history (*Ancient Architectural Remains in Lower Normandy*) but was also the author of a farce, *The Last Day*, which was performed successfully on the London stage. In addition, he was one of the first to argue the need for a National Theatre. As editor of *The Builder* and in his architectural writings he was a consistent advocate of the importance of improving sanitary conditions in the dwellings of the urban poor. His unusual hobby was collecting the chairs of the famous. At his death he possessed chairs that had once belonged to, among others, Anne Boleyn, Alexander Pope, Lord Byron and (allegedly) Shakespeare.

## GOMME, SIR LAURENCE (1853–1916) *Clerk to the London County Council, folklorist and historian, lived here 1895–1909*

24 DORSET SQUARE, MARYLEBONE, NW1

When Laurence Gomme died in 1916, the obituary writer in *The Times* acknowledged that 'few men have had a more profound knowledge of the past and the present greatness of London, and few have done more to make London known to its people.' Gomme's knowledge of his native city was based on his service to it. From 1873 to his retirement in 1914, he worked first for the Metropolitan Board of Works and then for its successor, the London County Council, rising to the senior position of Clerk to the Council. Gomme, together with his wife, Alice, a pioneer in the study of children's games, was a founder member of the Folklore Society in 1878. 'I should like it to be settled once for all that folklore is a science,' he once wrote and, firm in this belief, he wrote and edited many scholarly books on the ancient traditions and folk-tales of Britain. It is fitting that Laurence Gomme should himself be honoured by a Blue Plaque because, during his career at the LCC, he was the major advocate of the Council taking over the running of the plaque scheme from the Royal Society of Arts.

## GOOSSENS *family of musicians, lived here 1912–1927*
70 EDITH ROAD, W14

The Goossens were a family, of Belgian extraction, who showed exceptional musical ability over three generations. Eugene Goossens, the son of a Belgian conductor, was born in France and studied at the Royal Academy of Music. He was Principal Conductor of the Carl Rosa Company for many years. Of his sons, Eugene worked as a conductor in America and Australia, wrote operas and symphonies and was knighted in 1955, and Leon was an oboist who played with many major orchestras around the world. Their sisters Sidonie and Marie were both instrumentalists of high standing.

## GORT, FIELD MARSHAL VISCOUNT, V.C. (1886–1946) *Commander-in-Chief at Dunkirk, lived here 1920–1926*

34 BELGRAVE SQUARE, SW1

John Standish Surtees Prendergast Vereker, 6th Viscount Gort was born into a family of Anglo-Irish aristocrats and soldiers. He was commissioned into the Grenadier Guards in 1905 and was already an experienced soldier when the First World War began nine years later. He served with great distinction on the Western Front throughout the war, winning a series of medals for bravery which culminated in the award of the Victoria Cross. When the Second World War broke out, Gort was given command of the British Expeditionary Force (BEF), which arrived in France at the end of September 1939. He was still in command when the BEF was separated from its French allies by the speed of the German attacks in the spring of 1940 and was forced to retreat northwards to the Channel in order to be rescued from the beaches at Dunkirk. Arguments then and now have raged over the question of whether Gort should be praised for his skill in rescuing the BEF from its parlous predicament or condemned for the role he played in placing it there. After Dunkirk, Gort left his position and, during the remaining years of the war, he served in a number of other roles including Governor of Gibraltar and Governor of Malta. He died in the year after the war ended.

## GOSSE, PHILIP HENRY (1810–1888) *zoologist, lived here; and* SIR EDMUND GOSSE (1849–1928), *writer and critic, born here*

56 MORTIMER ROAD, N1

Philip Gosse was a distinguished zoologist who refused to accept the views of his near-contemporary Darwin and clung tenaciously to the tenets of fundamentalist Christianity. He wrote a *Manual of Marine Zoology* and, in 1853, opened in London what was probably the first public aquarium in the world. His son Edmund wrote of his strange upbringing with his widowed father and his strict Plymouth Brethren beliefs in *Father and Son*, first published anonymously in 1907. Edmund Gosse escaped his father's world to become a librarian at the British Museum and, later, the House of Lords. He was a poet and critic who wrote widely on seventeeth-century literature and was ahead of his time in recognising the genius of Ibsen, two of whose plays he translated for an English audience.

## GOUNOD, CHARLES (1818–1893) *composer, stayed here in 1870*

15 MORDEN ROAD, BLACKHEATH, SE3

Gounod was born in Paris and studied at the Conservatoire there and in Rome. Although he wrote songs and much religious music, including masses, hymns and oratorios, it is as an operatic composer that he is best remembered. Like his fellow French composer Berlioz, he was fascinated by Shakespeare's works and, again like Berlioz, he wrote an opera based on the story of Romeo and Juliet. Gounod's best-known opera is a version of the story of Faust. Gounod came to England to escape the Franco-Prussian war and, although he was in London for four years in total, he spent only two months in Morden Road. During his time in England he made a number of settings of English poems by an array of writers including Byron and Shelley.

## GPO FILM UNIT LATER CROWN FILM UNIT, *pioneers of documentary film-making, had their studios here 1933–1943*

47 BENNETT PARK, BLACKHEATH, SE3

Formed in 1933, under the auspices of the General Post Office, the GPO Film Unit was at the heart of the British documentary movement, often considered this country's mist distinctive contribution to film-making in the 1930s. Led by John Grierson, a Scotsman who was evangelical about the educational potential of movies, the GPO Film Unit created some of the finest documentaries in film history. Grierson brought together a remarkable collection of talented individuals, including Humphrey Jennings (later to create some of the most familiar images of Britain in the Blitz), the Brazilian-born director Alberto Cavalcanti and the Canadian experimental film-maker Len Lye. The GPO Film Unit also attracted major talents from the other arts to work on these movies made in Blackheath. The 1936 film *Night Mail* is probably the most famous of all the unit's films, and has a poetic commentary by W.H. Auden with music by Benjamin Britten. Working on miniscule budgets (the unit's most expensive film cost £7,500 to produce), Grierson and his team created a sequence of notable documentary films. Grierson left the unit in 1937 and, although it continued to create some fine films, its short heyday was over. It became the Crown Film Unit in 1939 and, under this name, survived another thirteen years.

## GRACE, W.G. (1848–1915) *cricketer, lived here*
'FAIRMOUNT', MOTTINGHAM LANE, SE9

## W.G. GRACE
7 LAWRIE PARK ROAD, SE26 **LEWISHAM COUNCIL**

Statistics cannot fully convey the extent of W.G. Grace's dominance of cricket during the Victorian era. One of three cricketing brothers who all played in the first-class game, Grace was born near Bristol, first played for his county as a teenager and, by the end of a career that stretched well into the twentieth century, had amassed 54,896 first-class runs and scored 126 first-class centuries. More than that, he had become one of the emblematic figures of the Victorian Age, as familiar to the man in the street as the Prime Minister, and had presided over the years in which cricket was transformed into a national institution. Grace was well aware of his own importance to the game and was not averse to taking advantage of it. In one match, when he was bowled first ball in front of a large crowd, he refused to go, gesturing at the spectators and remarking to the successful bowler, 'They came to see me bat, not you bowl.'

## GRAHAME, KENNETH (1859–1932) *author of 'Wind in the Willows', lived here 1901–1908*
16 PHILLIMORE PLACE, W8

To outward appearances Kenneth Grahame was a conventional City man who worked for many years at the Bank of England. Yet he was also a contributor to the *Yellow Book*, house magazine of the more decadent artists of the 1890s, and author of two books, *The Golden Age* and *Dream Days*, which demonstrated a startling empathy with the hopes and interests of the young. *The Wind in the Willows* began as a series of stories Grahame told to his young son. When Grahame was persuaded to submit it to publishers (originally under the title of *The Wind in the Reeds*) it was rejected several times before Methuen agreed to publish it and the original reviews were not complimentary. In a few years, however, the story of Mole, Ratty and Toad came to be seen as a children's classic. Tragically the person for whom the tales had been written, Grahame's son Alastair, died in 1920 at the age of nineteen, almost certainly a suicide.

## GRAINGER, PERCY (1882–1961) *Australian composer, folklorist and pianist, lived here*

31 KING'S ROAD, CHELSEA, SW3

The composer and arranger of some of what is considered the most quintessentially 'English' music of the century (*Country Gardens, Handel in the Strand* and *Shepherd's Hey*) was born in Melbourne, Australia and spent much of his life in the USA. Percy Grainger came to Europe in 1895 and studied in Germany before moving to London in 1901, where he gained a reputation as a concert pianist and a composer with a particular interest in English folk song. He was one of the first people to use the Edison phonograph to make recordings of folk music, which he later transcribed and arranged. Grainger, who settled in the US in 1915, was an artist whose creativity was linked to a deep eccentricity. His diet consisted largely of rice, tinned peaches and stale bread and jam, he was an advocate of replacing words of Latin and French origin with Anglo-Saxon equivalents of his own devising – 'composer', for instance, was to become 'tone-wright' – and his personal and sexual life was a complicated mixture of obsession and sado-masochism. He once remarked in an interview that 'people like me ought to be burned at the stake', but he was one of the most original musical minds of his time.

## GRAVES, ROBERT (1895–1985) *writer, was born here*

1 LAURISTON ROAD, WIMBLEDON, SW19

Few poets have been as dedicated to the idea of being a poet as Robert Graves. 'To be a poet,' he once wrote in reply to a questionnaire sent out by a magazine, 'is a condition rather than a profession.' The son of the Irish-born songwriter and poet A.P. Graves, Robert Graves was educated at Charterhouse and joined the Royal Welsh Fusiliers at the outbreak of the First World War. He fought throughout the war and was severely injured, indeed reported dead in *The Times*, during the campaigns of 1916. After the war Graves went to Oxford and then, after a tempestuous relationship with the American poet Laura Riding, began what was to be a peripatetic life in search of the muse and poetic inspiration. Much of his later life was spent in Mallorca. Graves published poetry over a period of more than sixty years and was also a prolific writer of prose works, including the well-known versions of Roman imperial history, *I, Claudius* and *Claudius the God*. Poetry, however, remained Graves's obsession. 'Prose books,' he wrote, 'are the show dogs I breed and sell to support my cat.'

## GRAY, HENRY (1827–1861) *anatomist, lived here*

8 WILTON STREET, SW1

Gray contracted smallpox and died of the disease when he was only in his early thirties. He was a gifted anatomist who was elected a Fellow of the Royal Society when he was only twenty-five years old, but he would not be remembered today were it not for the publication that first appeared in 1853 and which has carried his name ever since. Gray's *Anatomy* has appeared in countless editions and imprints since its first publication and remains a standard medical textbook. Gray lived for much of his short life in the house in Wilton Street.

## THE GREAT EASTERN (LAUNCHED 1858) *largest steamship of the century was built here by I.K. Brunel and J. Scott Russell*

BURRELLS WHARF, 262 WEST FERRY ROAD, E14

Although it was Brunel's most ambitious project and remained the largest steamship constructed for fifty years after its launch, the *Great Eastern* was not one of the legendary engineer's most successful endeavours. Brunel intended the ship to carry passengers and mail to India non-stop (the enormous size was required to accommodate the coal needed to allow this) but design and construction were plagued by difficulties. The ship never achieved what Brunel, who died a year after its launch, had hoped and it was scrapped in 1888.

........................................................................................................................

## GREATHEAD, JAMES HENRY (1844–1896) *railway and tunnelling engineer, lived here 1885–1889*

3 ST MARY'S GROVE, BARNES, SW13

Born in South Africa, Greathead came to London as a young man and, at the age of twenty-four, was employed as an assistant to the engineer Peter Barlow in the construction of a subway under the Thames from Tower Hill to Pickleherring Street on the southern bank. Taking the basic idea of a tunnelling shield (to protect the workers as they dug and to avoid unnecessary disruption on the surface) from a much earlier design by Sir Marc Brunel, Greathead improved it significantly and the Tower Subway was built in less than a year. Greathead went on to work on a variety of other engineering and tunnelling projects as London's network of both overground and underground railways expanded. In the 1880s he was chief engineer on the City and South London Railway, again digging tunnels beneath the Thames. The 'Greathead Shield', incorporating the essentials of his original design, is still in use in the tunnelling industry today.

........................................................................................................................

## GREAVES, WALTER (1846–1930) *artist, lived here 1855–1897*

104 CHEYNE WALK, SW10

Walter Greaves's father was a Thames waterman and boat-builder who had guided Turner in boat journeys up and down the river. A generation later, Walter and his brother Henry did the same for Whistler and became studio assistants to the American-born painter. Walter Greaves was a talented, if untrained, painter himself and some of his views of Thames events such as the Boat Race and the Chelsea Regatta have a particular charm. In his lifetime he gained little recognition as an artist and, although an exhibition in 1911 brought him briefly out of obscurity, he ended his life as a Charterhouse pensioner.

........................................................................................................................

## GREEN, JOHN RICHARD (1837–1883) *historian of the English people, lived here*

4 BEAUMONT STREET, W1

## JOHN RICHARD GREEN (1837–1883) *historian of the English people, lived here 1866–1869*

ST PHILIP'S VICARAGE, NEWARK STREET, E1

One of the great successes of nineteenth-century history-writing was the work of a man who had left Oxford with a bare pass degree, who suffered for much of his adult life from bad health and who had to combine the composition of his *magnum opus* with an often urgent need to earn a living. Green's *Short History of the English People*, published in 1874, was one of the first attempts to write a concise yet complete history of England and also one of the first works of English historiography to pay much heed to social and cultural history. After his failure at Oxford, Green had been ordained and worked as a priest in some of the worst slums of Hoxton and Stepney throughout most of the 1860s, probably contracting tuberculosis in the process. The publication of his *Short History*, which was a huge commercial success, ensured financial stability, but he continued to be plagued by ill health and died in 1883, aged only forty-six.

........................................................................................................................

## GREENAWAY, KATE (1846–1901) *artist, lived and died here*

39 FROGNAL, NW3

## KATE GREENAWAY

147 UPPER STREET, N1   **ISLINGTON BOROUGH COUNCIL**

Kate Greenaway's first major success as a writer and illustrator of children's books was *Under the Window* in 1878 and she went on to publish many more and to attract the approving attention of Ruskin. 'No gasworks! no waterworks, no mowing machines, no sewing machines, no telegraph poles . . . ', he wrote in praise of her idyllic vision of demure and charming children playing in idealised landscapes. Harsher critics might claim that her illustrations were not so much charming as sickly sweet but her later works, including an illustrated version of Browning's *The Pied Piper of Hamelin*, were nearly all bestsellers. Indeed, attaching Greenaway's name to a book seemed a guarantee of substantial sales. From the 1880s she lived quietly with her parents and her brother at the house in Frognal.

---

## GREET, SIR PHILIP BEN (1857–1936) *actor-manager, lived here 1920–1936*

160 LAMBETH ROAD, SE1

One of the pioneers in the presentation of Shakespeare to as wide an audience as possible, Sir Ben Greet was named Philip at birth but was always known as Benjamin because, like the Biblical character, he was the youngest of a large family. Going on the stage in his early twenties he formed his own company in the 1880s and, in 1886, gave the first of what were to become his hallmark open-air productions of Shakespeare. He was the first to use Regent's Park as a regular venue for open-air theatre. From 1914 he was involved with the legendary Lilian Baylis in establishing the Old Vic and producing Shakespeare's works. Several generations of Londoners owed their first experience of Shakespeare to Ben Greet and he was knighted in 1929 for, as the citation said, his services 'to drama and education.'

---

## GRENFELL, JOYCE (1910–1979) *entertainer and writer, lived here in flat No.8 1957–1979*

34 ELM PARK GARDENS, SW10

Joyce Grenfell may have been half-American by birth (her mother was the daughter of a US railroad millionaire and she was the niece of Nancy, Lady Astor) but, both onstage and off, she was quintessentially English. Born in London, she attended RADA briefly but left when she married in 1929. It was not until 1938 when, at a dinner party, she gave an impromptu imitation of a Women's Institute speaker that she revealed her genius for comic monologue. One of the other guests at the dinner party had contacts in the theatre and, within a short time, Grenfell was on stage in a West End revue. She went on to work in theatre, radio, films and (eventually) television. In the mid-1950s, she even conquered the land of her mother's birth, appearing several times on the hugely popular Ed Sullivan show on TV, once with Elvis Presley whom she remembered, rather ungraciously, as 'a pasty-faced plump boy'. Whether playing the part of a harassed nursery teacher in her monologues, appearing as a lovelorn policewoman in the St Trinian's films or demonstrating her knowledge of classical music in the BBC quiz show *Face the Music*, Joyce Grenfell became an instantly recognisable and much-loved figure in the British media.

---

## *In a house on this site lived* SIR THOMAS GRESHAM (1519–1579)

GRESHAM HOUSE, 24 OLD BROAD STREET, EC2   **CITY OF LONDON**

Sir Thomas Gresham came from a wealthy London merchant family and became even wealthier through his own dealings as a financier both in England and abroad. He was ambassador in the Netherlands for three years after Elizabeth I had come to the throne and knew the city of Antwerp, with its great trading bourse, very well. Returned to England he pressed for a similar institution in London and devoted a portion of his huge wealth to the building of the first

Royal Exchange. The first brick was laid by Gresham himself in 1566 and on 23 January 1570 Elizabeth, having dined with Gresham, declared the building 'by an herald and trumpet to be called the Royal Exchange, and so to be called from henceforth and not otherwise'. Gresham House was the financier's lavish town house, built around 1560. After Gresham's death it passed to his widow. After her death, under the terms of Gresham's will, it became a college named after him and it was the first home of what later became the Royal Society. It was demolished in 1768.

---

## GRESLEY, SIR NIGEL (1876–1941) *locomotive engineer, had his office in this station*
WEST OFFICES, KING'S CROSS STATION (FACING GREAT NORTHERN HOTEL), PANCRAS ROAD/EUSTON ROAD, N1

Gresley was the leading figure in the last great age of steam in this country. Born in Edinburgh, he became the outstanding locomotive engineer of his day and was Chief Mechanical Engineer of the London and North Eastern Railway from 1923 until his death in 1941. As such he was responsible for the design of some of the most famous of all steam trains of the century including the legendary 'Flying Scotsman'. In 1938 another of his engines, the 'Mallard', reached a speed of 126 miles per hour, a world record for a steam-driven engine at the time and, now that the days of steam have almost come to an end, one that is unlikely ever to be surpassed.

---

## GREY, SIR EDWARD, VISCOUNT GREY OF FALLODEN (1862–1933)
*Foreign Secretary, lived here*

3 QUEEN ANNE'S GATE, SW1

Sir Edward Grey was Foreign Secretary for a longer consecutive period of time (1905–16) than any other holder of the office and held the post at the time Britain entered the First World War. On the eve of the war it was Grey who made the famous and mournfully prophetic remark, 'The lamps are going out over all Europe; we shall not see them lit again in our lifetime.' Grey had entered Parliament as its youngest MP when he was elected to represent Berwick-upon-Tweed in 1885 but he had had only a few years' experience of junior office when Campbell-Bannerman made him Foreign Secretary. After the war Grey was a leading advocate of the League of Nations and, as ambassador in Washington, strove unsuccessfully to bring the USA into the fledgeling organisation. When his book *The Charm of Birds* was published in 1925 he became, probably, the only politician to write a bestselling book on ornithology.

---

## GRIEG, EDVARD (1843–1907) *Norwegian composer, stayed here when performing in London*
47 CLAPHAM COMMON NORTH SIDE, SW4

The greatest of all Norwegian composers, Edvard Grieg was born in Bergen at a time when his country was not even an independent nation, but part of a union with Sweden under the rule of the Swedish king. Grieg's music, with its bold use of the folk tunes of his native country, was to play its part in the growth of national feeling in Norway during the second half of the nineteenth century and he lived to see Norwegian independence in 1905. Grieg wrote a great deal of music for solo piano and the German conductor Hans von Bülow went so far as to call him 'the Chopin of the North'. The works for which he is best known today are his piano concerto and the 'Peer Gynt' suite, which he wrote to accompany the first performance of the play by Ibsen. Love of Grieg's music was never restricted to Scandinavia. It was popular throughout Europe and much admired in England. He came to London six times in the years between 1888 and 1906 to conduct his own music. On these visits he stayed with his publisher George Augener, whose house overlooking Clapham Common is now the site for the Blue Plaque commemorating his famous guest.

## GRIMALDI, JOSEPH (1779–1837) *clown, lived here 1818–1828*
56 EXMOUTH MARKET, EC1

## JOSEPH GRIMALDI (1779–1837)
FINCHLEY MEMORIAL HOSPITAL, GRANVILLE ROAD, N12,
**BOROUGH OF BARNET**

One of a family of dancers and clowns, Grimaldi made his first appearance on stage when he was less than two years old and became the archetypal clown of the English pantomime. Perhaps his greatest success was in *Mother Goose*, in which he performed many times in the first decades of the nineteenth century. Grimaldi's memoirs were edited, after the clown's death, by an up-and-coming writer called Charles Dickens, but contemporary accounts of Grimaldi's stage presence are hard to come by. The *Dictionary of National Biography* in characteristic Victorian prose assures us that 'his grimace was inexpressibly mirth-moving; his singing of "Tippety Witchet", "Hot Codlins" and other similar ditties, roused the wildest enthusiasm', and this we must believe. Grimaldi was an obsessive performer and wore down his health to such an extent that he had to make his last appearance on stage in a chair, too weak to stand. In early February, at Holy Trinity Church in Dalston, there is a special Clowns' Service when a wreath is laid on the memorial to Grimaldi.

## GROOM, JOHN (1845–1919) *philanthropist who founded workshops for disabled girls nearby, lived here*

8 SEKFORDE STREET, EC1

John Groom was a pioneer in providing care for the disabled and in recognising that they need to contribute to their own support in order to lead as full a life as possible. Although not a wealthy man himself, Groom began his mission to the poor, and frequently disabled, flower girls of London when he was in his early twenties. His original Flower Girls' Mission was in Harp Alley near St Paul's and further shelters and workshops followed in later years. Through the charity work that Groom began (and which still continues today) many of the disabled whom he had seen in the streets, 'dying inch by inch of want and starvation', were provided with shelter and employment.

## GROSER, REVEREND ST JOHN (1890–1966) *priest and social reformer, lived here*
ROYAL FOUNDATION OF ST KATHERINE, 2 BUTCHER ROW, E14

Throughout the last two centuries the East End has attracted many dedicated priests and ministers who have been devoted to the needs and welfare of its poor. St John Groser, once described by an admirer as 'this majestic priest', was one of the best known and most loved of that number. In the 1920s and '30s he presided over the Stepney Tenants Defence League and in 1948 he became Master of the Royal Foundation of St Katherine. This had returned to the East End after a long exile near Regent's Park, begun in 1825 because of the expansion of the docks. St John Groser also tasted celluloid fame in 1951 when he played Becket in a film version of *Murder in the Cathedral*, which relied heavily on amateur talent.

## GROSSMITH, GEORGE, SENIOR (1847–1912) *actor and author, lived here*
### 28 DORSET SQUARE, NW1

Both George Grossmith and his younger brother Weedon were primarily interested in the stage. They grew up in a family that had theatrical connections with great names like Henry Irving and the Terrys, and they both embarked on careers as actors. George became a highly successful comic performer who took major roles in the original performances of many Gilbert and Sullivan operettas. Weedon also had some success as an actor and went on to manage Terry's Theatre in the Strand. However, the two brothers today are remembered solely because they wrote one of the classics of English humour, *The Diary of a Nobody*. This appeared originally in *Punch* in 1892, later in book form, and its portrayal of the minor trials and tribulations of Charles Pooter, the accident-prone, lower middle-class resident of Brickfield Terrace, Holloway, has ensured that the names of Weedon and George Grossmith have survived.

## GROSSMITH, GEORGE, JUNIOR (1874–1935) *actor-manager, lived here*
### 3 SPANISH PLACE, W1

Born into a theatrical and literary family, George Grossmith appeared first on the stage in a play written by his father, who also has a Blue Plaque to his name, and went on to be a regular performer at the legendary Gaiety Theatre in the Strand. His stock-in-trade was the impersonation of the foppish man-about-town or, in the slang of the day, the 'dude'. From 1914 he involved himself heavily in theatre management and wrote a series of musical comedies, rejoicing in titles like *The Bing Boys Are Here* and *Rogues and Vagabonds*; now wholly forgotten they were very popular in their day. In 1925 Grossmith appeared in the first production of *No, No, Nanette*, one of the few light musical comedies of the period that has survived and is still performed.

## GROTE, GEORGE (1794–1871) *historian, died here*
### 12 SAVILE ROW, W1

Much admired in his day, Grote is largely forgotten today but he was a man of many talents. His family had arrived in England from north Germany in the mid-eighteenth century and his grandfather founded the bank in Threadneedle Street where Grote spent more than thirty years of his life before retiring in 1843 to concentrate on his literary work. While working at the bank Grote devoted as much time as he could to literature and politics, being elected MP for the City of London in 1832. At Westminster he was a persistent but unsuccessful advocate of further parliamentary reform. After retiring from both banking and politics Grote was able to complete the *History of Greece*, on which he had been working intermittently since 1823, and it was published, in many volumes and to much critical acclaim, between 1846 and 1856.

## GUIZOT, FRANÇOIS (1787–1874) *French politician and historian, lived here 1848–1849*
### 21 PELHAM CRESCENT, SW7

Guizot was born into a Protestant bourgeois family in Nîmes just two years before the outbreak of the French Revolution. Initially a supporter of the Revolution, Guizot's father eventually became one of its victims and was guillotined in 1794. Guizot's mother took the family to Geneva where the boy grew up. Travelling to Paris as a young man, Guizot rapidly made a name for himself as a writer and scholar, and was made a professor of modern history at the Sorbonne in 1812. He entered politics as a supporter of moderate royalists disturbed by the reactionary tendencies of Charles X and, at the time of the 1830 Revolution, he was an opposition deputy committed to change. When Charles X abdicated and Louis-Phillippe replaced him as French king, Guizot was an enthusiastic advocate of this new constitutional monarchy. During Louis-Phillippe's rein he became one of France's most influential politicians, serving as Minister of Education and, later, as Prime Minister. As the monarchy drifted to the right, so too did Guizot. At the time of the 1848 Revolution against Louis-Phillippe's rule, he was so firmly linked to the discredited regime that he had to flee France. He arrived in London and lived at Pelham Crescent but he was soon able to return to his home country. The rest of his long life was spent immersed in the historical studies which had always been his chief interest.

---

## GUZMAN, JUAN PABLO VISCARDO Y (1748–1798) *Peruvian essayist and herald of South American independence, lived and died here*

### 185 BAKER STREET, W1 **WESTMINSTER**

Although he didn't live to see his vision translated into reality, Juan Pablo Viscardo y Guzman was one of the first writers to put forward the case for South American independence from Spain. Born in Peru's second largest city, Arequipa, Guzman spent the last years of his life far away from the Andean mountains of his homeland, in exile in Europe, where he was a tireless promoter of freedom for the Spanish colonies. From 1791 he lived in London and it was in this city that he wrote some of the political essays – 'Letter to Spanish Americans' and 'Peace and Prosperity in a New World' – for which he is best remembered. After staying at several addresses in the British capital, Guzman lodged in a house on the site of 185 Baker Street, that belonged to a Mr Allsop, and it was there that he died at the age of fifty. His writings went on to influence greatly the next generation of South American patriots.

---

## KING HAAKON VII (1872–1957) *led the Norwegian government-in-exile here 1940–1945*

### 10 PALACE GREEN, W8

One of the most admired and best-loved figures in Norwegian history was originally known as Prince Carl of Denmark and was born in a royal palace just outside Copenhagen. Both his father and then his older brother went on to become king of Denmark but Carl actually gained a throne before either of them. As Haakon VII, he was elected the first king of an independent Norway in 1905 and went on to rule that nation for more than fifty years. The great crisis of his reign was the Nazi invasion of his country in April 1940, and Haakon responded to it with courage and dignity. He refused to accept a German ultimatum to appoint Quisling as head of what would have been a puppet government and resolved to resist the invasion. In the face of overwhelming German military might, the resistance could not last long and, in June, the king and the legitimate Norwegian government were evacuated from the temporary capital that had been established at Tromsø and made their way to London. Even in exile Haakon became a potent symbol of the Norwegian resistance and his return to Norway at the end of the war was greeted with jubilation.

---

## HAGGARD, SIR HENRY RIDER (1856–1925) *novelist, lived here 1885–1888*

### 69 GUNTERSTONE ROAD, W14

When Haggard arrived at Gunterstone Road he was a not very successful lawyer who had just been called to the Bar. When he left, three years later, he was one of the most famous novelists in the country. The transformation was the result of publishing *King Solomon's Mines* in 1885 and *She* in 1887. Both books drew on the knowledge of Africa that he had built up during six years in the colonial service there, and on the wild and romantic imagination that lurked beneath his conventional exterior. *King Solomon's Mines* is an archetypal adventure story in which the three heroes (Sir Henry Curtis, Captain John Good and the narrator Allan Quartermain) venture into a mysterious African kingdom in search of the treasure of Solomon's mines; *She* also features a hidden kingdom in which She-Who-Must-Be-Obeyed, the beautiful queen Ayesha, guards the secret of eternal life. Haggard went on to write many more romances, although none has proved as popular as his two early books, and to live the life of a country squire on an estate in Norfolk.

## HALDANE, LORD (1856–1928) *statesman, lawyer and philosopher, lived here*

28 QUEEN ANNE'S GATE, SW1

Haldane entered Parliament in his early twenties as a Liberal and had his greatest influence on history in his time as Secretary of State for War in Asquith's administration. He undertook a wide-ranging programme of reforms, which sought to remedy the problems revealed in the Boer War. A properly constituted general staff was created, the foundations laid for what was to be the British Expeditionary Force of 1914 and, in 1907, the Territorial and Reserve Forces Act brought together all voluntary military forces under one umbrella, later named the Territorial Army. Haldane was a lawyer and was Lord Chancellor from 1912 to 1915. In the twenties, estranged from the Liberal party, he was in Ramsay MacDonald's first Labour government. Outside politics Haldane wrote a number of philosophical tracts.

## HALIFAX, EDWARD WOOD, 1ST EARL OF (1881–1959) *statesman, Viceroy of India and Foreign Secretary, lived here*

86 EATON SQUARE, SW1

Descended from a family that had been heavily involved in the politics of the nation since the time of the Civil War, Halifax was the one alternative to Churchill as Prime Minister when Neville Chamberlain resigned in May 1940. He stood aside, gave his support to Churchill and chose instead to serve as Ambassador to the US, where he played a vital role in fostering Anglo-American cooperation. Before the war Halifax had been Viceroy of India at the height of Gandhi's campaign of civil disobedience and had been appointed Foreign Secretary in Chamberlain's government in 1938. He was involved in the meetings with Hitler that led to the Munich agreement but, by the following year, he had recognised the limitations of appeasement and acknowledged the need to oppose the German dictator with force.

## HALL, HENRY (1898–1989) *dance band leader and broadcaster, lived here 1932–1959*

38 HARMAN DRIVE, CRICKLEWOOD, NW2

## HALL, HENRY ROBERT (1898–1989) *dance band leader and impresario, pioneer of BBC popular music 1924–1964, lived here 1957–1981*

8 RANDOLPH MEWS, W9 **WESTMINSTER**

Born in Peckham, Henry Hall worked for the Salvation Army, writing several marches for them before becoming resident band leader with the Midland Hotel in Manchester. This began his association with the London, Midland and Scottish Railway hotel chain and he was eventually in overall control of bands at thirty-two different hotels. While with the LMS he began to broadcast on radio, and in 1932 he took charge of the BBC Dance Orchestra. Soon he was a major radio personality and the public was familiar with his catchphrase, 'This is Henry Hall speaking, and tonight is my guest night', with his trumpet-playing and with his band's sign-off theme 'Here's to the Next Time'. His band was the first to appear on television and he continued to broadcast until the sixties but his name and sound will always be associated with the golden age of radio in the thirties and forties.

## HALL, KEITH CLIFFORD (1910–1964) *pioneer in the fitting of contact lenses, practised here 1945–1964*

140 PARK LANE, W1 **WESTMINSTER**

Keith Clifford Hall was one of the first opticians to recognise the importance and potential of the contact lens. With a colleague he wrote one of the first textbooks on the subject, *An Introduction to the Prescribing of Contact Lenses*, published in 1946, and he was a founder member of the Contact Lens Society. He acted as President of the society in 1947–8 and again in 1963–4.

## HALL, RADCLYFFE (1880–1943) *novelist and poet, lived here*
### 37 HOLLAND STREET, W8

Radclyffe Hall's *The Well of Loneliness* remains the best-known lesbian love story of the twentieth century. Published in 1928, the novel was immediately at the centre of controversy, the subject of an obscenity trial, and banned in this country for many years. 'I would rather put a phial of prussic acid into the hands of a healthy boy or girl,' ranted one newspaper editor at the time, 'than the book in question.' Born in Bournemouth and educated at King's College, London, Radclyffe Hall, who preferred to be known to her intimates as 'John', came into a large fortune in her twenties. She was able to devote the rest of her life to literature and to society. She published volumes of verse as well as the novels for which she was best known and, together with her lover and companion Una, Lady Troubridge, was a familiar figure in the often exotic world of upper-class lesbian society in both London and Paris.

## HALLAM, HENRY (1777–1859) *historian, lived here*
### 67 WIMPOLE STREET, W1

Hallam was the enormously erudite author of such books as *Europe During the Middle Ages, The Constitutional History of England from Henry VII to George II* and *Introduction to the Literature of Europe in the 15th, 16th and 17th Centuries*. All have suffered the common fate of the vast majority of historical works from the period and are unread save by a tiny number of specialist scholars. If Hallam is a name recognised at all today it is as the father of Tennyson's great friend and prospective brother-in-law Arthur Henry Hallam. The younger Hallam's death in 1833, at the tragically early age of twenty-two, moved Tennyson to begin the sequence of elegiac lyrics eventually published as *In Memoriam* in 1850. The older Hallam lived in Wimpole Street for many years and for a brief period of time would have been a close neighbour of Mr Barrett, father of the poet Elizabeth Barrett Browning.

## HAMMOND, J.L. AND BARBARA *social historians, lived here 1906–1913*
### 'HOLLYCOT', VALE OF HEALTH, HAMPSTEAD, NW3

Educated at Bradford Grammar School and Oxford, Hammond became a well-known Liberal journalist who edited *The Speaker* between 1899 and 1907 and was, for more than thirty years, a special correspondent of the *Manchester Guardian*. In 1901 he married Lucy Barbara Bradby and together they wrote many works of social history. These included a history of the Chartist Movement, a biography of the philanthropist Lord Shaftesbury and, most notably, a pioneering trilogy that examined the lives of the working classes – *The Village Labourer, The Town Labourer* and *The Skilled Labourer*.

## HANDEL, GEORGE FREDERICK (1685–1759) *musician, lived and died here*
### 25 BROOK STREET, W1

Handel was born in Halle, Germany, and arrived in London in 1712 after working as a musician and composer in his native land and in Italy. He had been court composer to the Elector of Hanover but had not pleased his master by taking long leaves of absence to try his fortune elsewhere. When the Elector became King George I of England, two years after Handel had settled in the country, relations between monarch and composer were not, at first, easy. *The Water Music*, composed for a regal procession along the Thames, is said to have been Handel's gesture towards reconciliation and, if so, it must have worked, since the composer worked his way back into George's favour. Handel remained in England for the rest of his life. His most remarkable achievements as a composer lie in his many oratorios, culminating in *The Messiah* of 1742. It is said that, after completing the part of the work that includes the famous 'Hallelujah Chorus', Handel was found by his servants with tears streaming down his face. 'I did think,' he said, 'I did see all heaven before me and the great God himself.'

---

## HANDLEY, TOMMY (1892–1949) *radio comedian, lived here*

34 CRAVEN ROAD, W2

During the Second World War the most popular radio comedy show, often gaining an audience of more than fifteen million listeners, was ITMA ('It's That Man Again'). Its characters (Mrs Mopp, Ali Oop, Funf the Spy) and its rich mix of puns, alliteration, catchphrases and sheer nonsense caught people's imaginations in a way that few radio programmes, before and since, have managed. 'That Man', presiding over the verbal chaos, was Tommy Handley. Born in Liverpool, Handley had served in the First World War and worked in variety before he started broadcasting for the BBC in 1925. ITMA ran throughout the war years and was in its twelfth series when Handley died suddenly of a cerebral haemorrhage on 9 January 1949.

---

## HANSOM, JOSEPH ALOYSIUS (1803–1882) *architect, founder editor of The Builder and inventor of the Hansom Cab, lived here*

27 SUMNER PLACE, SW7

Born in York, Hansom was an architect whose early success – when he was chosen to design Birmingham Town Hall in 1831 – turned to disaster. Complicated financial involvement with the contractors led to Hansom's bankruptcy and he was obliged to turn his inventiveness in other directions. He registered his idea of a 'Patent Safety Cab' in 1834 but, despite promises from the company established to exploit his idea, it was Hansom who was exploited and he only ever received a single payment of £300 for his invention. In 1842 he founded *The Builder* as a magazine for those in the profession and he continued to practise as an architect. Hansom was a Roman Catholic and much of his best work was done for the Church, including the Catholic cathedral in Plymouth and St Walburge's, Preston, with its huge, 306-foot high spire.

---

## HARDY, THOMAS (1840–1928)
*poet and novelist, lived here 1878–1881*

172 TRINITY ROAD, TOOTING, SW17

## THOMAS HARDY (1840–1928)
*poet and novelist, lived here*

16 WESTBOURNE PARK VILLAS, W2
**PRIVATE**

Although Hardy's name is, rightly, linked with the West Country, which appears, in disguised form, in his Wessex novels, he spent considerable periods of his life in London and clearly viewed the capital with an ambivalent mix of distaste and fascination. In his twenties he worked in an architect's office in the city and he and his long-suffering wife Emma lived for three years in Tooting between 1878 and 1881. Even after their move, in 1885, to Max Gate near Dorchester, which was to be Hardy's home until his death, the couple often spent three months of the year in London. Hardy's first novel, *Desperate Remedies*, was published in 1871 and he was soon earning far more as a writer than he ever had as an architect. Novels like *Under the Greenwood Tree*, *Far From the Madding Crowd* and *The Return of the Native* established his reputation but in the 1890s he gave up fiction, wearied by the criticism and accusations of immorality levelled against his later masterpieces *Tess of the D'Urbervilles* and *Jude the Obscure*. As a writer he returned to his first love, poetry, and published many volumes over the next thirty years. His first wife died in 1912 and Hardy, who had not been a noticeably sympathetic husband in her lifetime, began to write elegiac lyrics to her memory. He married for a second time in 1914 and died peacefully in January 1928. There is a macabre legend, somehow suited to Hardy, that his heart, which was to be buried separately from his other remains, was left unattended after removal and was eaten by a cat. A substitute had to be found.

See also under entry for ADELPHI TERRACE

---

## HARLEY, ROBERT
See also under entry for SAMUEL PEPYS

---

## HARMSWORTH, ALFRED, VISCOUNT NORTHCLIFFE (1865–1922)
*journalist and newspaper proprietor, lived here*

### 31 PANDORA ROAD, WEST HAMPSTEAD, NW6

Born in Dublin, Alfred Harmsworth was the eldest of five brothers who all distinguished themselves in the worlds of newspapers and politics. In partnership with his brother Harold he started the magazine *Answers to Correspondents* in 1888, while he was living in Pandora Road, and six years later the brothers bought the *Evening News*. Through eye-catching headlines and the use of illustrations to break up large areas of text, Harmsworth turned what had been a paper on the verge of bankruptcy into a success story. His status as Britain's first press baron was confirmed when he started the *Daily Mail* in 1896. Although snootily dismissed by the Marquess of Salisbury as 'by office boys for office boys', the *Daily Mail*, advertising itself under such slogans as 'the Busy Man's Daily Newspaper', was an immediate success. The *Daily Mirror*, originally intended as a newspaper aimed at women, was added to Harmsworth's empire in 1903 and in 1908 he marched firmly into the heart of the establishment when he bought *The Times*. Harmsworth's later career in politics was less successful. He suffered increasingly from ill health and nervous disorders and died in 1922.

---

## HARRISON, JOHN (1693–1776) *inventor of the marine chronometer, lived and died in a house on this site*

### SUMMIT HOUSE, RED LION SQUARE, WC1

In 1713 the government offered the then colossal sum of £20,000 as a prize to anyone who could discover a method of accurately determining longitude. Sixty years later the prize was awarded to John Harrison, a Yorkshire-born clockmaker who had spent his working life in painstaking efforts to build the most accurate chronometer known up to his time. In the early 1760s Harrison had devised a chronometer which, during a voyage to Jamaica, had determined the longitude within eighteen geographical miles. In 1765 the Board of Longitude's panel of experts came to Red Lion Square to examine Harrison's improved design and, on its recommendation, Harrison was granted half the prize. In 1773, aged eighty, he was finally acknowledged to have solved the problem and given the full amount. Harrison's house in Red Lion Square has been demolished and its site is occupied by an office block.

## HARTE, FRANCIS BRET (1836–1902) *American writer, lived and died here*
74 LANCASTER GATE, W2

Although born in New York State, Bret Harte is known as one of the earliest and best chroniclers of the American frontier, particularly the mining towns and camps of California. He travelled west in 1854 and, after working on various newspapers, became editor of *Overland Monthly* in 1868. In this periodical many of his most famous stories ('The Luck of Roaring Camp', 'The Outcasts of Poker Flat' and others) first appeared. In 1878 Harte travelled to Europe as a consular official and he never returned to the United States. It is curious that the writer who contributed so much to the creation of the archetypes of Western fiction – the gambler, the tart with a heart of gold, the stagecoach driver – should have spent his last years a stone's throw away from Hyde Park.

## HARTNELL, SIR NORMAN (1901–1979) *court dressmaker, lived and worked here 1935–1979*

26 BRUTON STREET, W1

'I thought of lilies, roses, marguerites and golden corn,' Hartnell wrote in his autobiography about the creation of one of his dresses. 'I thought of altar clothes and sacred vestments; I thought of the sky, the earth, the sun, the moon, the stars and everything heavenly that might be embroidered on a dress destined to be historic.' The dress was the one worn by the present queen on her Coronation Day in 1953 and it confirmed Hartnell as one of the most exclusive and original designers of the twentieth century. He was born in Streatham, the son of a pub landlord who later moved up the social ladder to become a wine merchant, and he went to Cambridge to study architecture. He set up as a society dressmaker soon after leaving university, finding his first customers among the Bright Young People of the 1920s. His first royal commission – to make the wedding dress for the marriage of the Duke of Gloucester and Lady Alice Montague Dougal Scott – came in the year he moved into the premises at 26 Bruton Street, which now carry the Blue Plaque and he was the royal dressmaker of choice for the rest of his life.

## HAWKINS, SIR ANTHONY HOPE (ANTHONY HOPE) (1863–1933) *novelist, lived here 1903–1917*

41 BEDFORD SQUARE, WC1

Published under the name of Anthony Hope, *The Prisoner of Zenda* is one of the best known of all tales of swash-and-buckle. The story of the English gentleman Rudolf Rassendyll and the adventures that result from his resemblance to the ruler of the Central European kingdom of Ruritania proved immensely popular when it was first published in 1894. It maintained this popularity throughout the following century and has been filmed several times, most notably in versions starring Ronald Colman and, later, Stewart Granger in the double role of Rassendyll and the king. Hawkins had trained as a barrister but became a full-time author after the success of *The Prisoner of Zenda*. He published a sequel, *Rupert of Hentzau*, and a number of other adventure stories and social comedies, but nothing matched his first success.

## HAWTHORNE, NATHANIEL (1804–1864) *American author, stayed here in 1856*
4 POND ROAD, BLACKHEATH, SE3

Born in Salem, scene of the witchcraft trials of the seventeenth century, Nathaniel Hawthorne was a descendant of one of the prosecuting magistrates at those trials. Although he began writing soon after graduating from Bowdoin College (and published a novel at his own expense in 1828), he was slow to earn much money from his work and spent long years as a hack writer and editor, occasionally obliged to take such positions as surveyor of the Boston Custom House, where he worked from 1839 to 1841, in order to make ends meet. Hawthorne finally gained critical acclaim with publication of *The Scarlet Letter* in 1850 and rapidly followed this novel of New England guilt and sin with his two other great works, *The House of the Seven Gables* and *The Blithedale Romance*. In 1853 his old college friend Franklin Pierce became US President and appointed Hawthorne US Consul in Liverpool. During his four years in Britain Hawthorne spent several months in London, staying at the house in Pond Road. He returned to America in 1860, after two years in Italy, and died in 1864, leaving several novels that he had begun but was unable to finish.

..................................................................................................................................

## HAY, WILL (1888–1949) *comic actor and astronomer, lived here 1927–1934*
### 45 THE CHASE, NORBURY, SW16

Will Hay was one of the best-known comedy stars in British film of the 1930s and 1940s, famous for his portrayal of pompous but slightly seedy characters in positions of minor authority – schoolmasters, a fire chief, a police sergeant. In the best of his films, *Oh, Mr Porter*, – still a classic British comedy – Hay plays an incompetent stationmaster despatched to Ireland to run a sleepy rural station. Hindered rather than helped by the station's two other employees, played by Hay's regular co-stars Moore Marriott and Graham Moffatt, the stationmaster organises an excursion trip which goes badly wrong when it is hijacked by gun-runners. By the time he first appeared in films, in the mid-1930s, Hay was already a seasoned performer in the music halls where he had worked for more than twenty years, including a period with Fred Karno's troupe, comic *alma mater* of Charlie Chaplin and Stan Laurel, among others. Offscreen, Hay was a scholarly and erudite man who spoke several European languages fluently and was a distinguished amateur astronomer. It was from his observatory at his house in Norbury that he discovered a strange 'spot' on the planet Saturn in 1933, and he was later recognised by the British Astronomical Association as the first to record it. In the mid-1940s, Hay was suffering from poor health, which forced his retirement from the screen, and he died in 1949 following a massive stroke.

..................................................................................................................................

## HAYDON, BENJAMIN ROBERT (1786–1846) *painter, and* ROSSI, JOHN CHARLES FELIX (1762–1839) *sculptor, lived here*
### 116 LISSON GROVE, NW1

Haydon was a flamboyant painter driven to produce huge canvases on Biblical and historical subjects (*The Raising of Lazarus*, *The Judgement of Solomon*) which, he was firmly convinced, would revolutionise what he saw as the effete British art of his day. Initially his epic paintings had some success but his increasingly florid and paranoid personality eventually alienated patrons and friends alike. Professional and financial problems mounted. The final indignity came when he exhibited his work at the Egyptian Hall in Piccadilly. The rival attraction was the American dwarf General Tom Thumb. Huge crowds flocked to see the dwarf; hardly anyone looked at Haydon's paintings. In 1846 Haydon killed himself. Ironically he may have misjudged his talents. He may have been a better writer than a painter. His diary, first published posthumously, is filled with anecdote and observation and provides a vivid portrait of London literary life, particularly in the teens and twenties of the new century when Haydon was a friend of Wordsworth and Keats, Hazlitt and Leigh Hunt.

CHARLES ROSSI, who had had the house in Lisson Grove built, was Haydon's landlord from 1817 to 1820. He was a largely undistinguished sculptor who was none the less commercially successful. He was employed by the Prince Regent to decorate Buckingham Palace, and the large caryatids still to be seen on the exterior of St Pancras New Church, opposite St Pancras station, were modelled by him.

## HAYGARTH, ARTHUR (1825–1903)

### 88 WARWICK WAY, SW1  WESTMINSTER

Our knowledge of the early years of cricket would be much poorer if Arthur Haygarth had not chosen to devote so much of his life to researching and recording the game. Haygarth was himself a useful cricketer and played in well over 100 first-class matches for MCC, Sussex and Middlesex between 1844 and 1861. As a right-hand batsman he scored more than 3,000 runs in his career, including a number of half-centuries, and he was considered a particularly difficult batsman for opposition bowlers to remove. 'His defence is really perfect,' a contemporary wrote, 'and he will play the best bowling with the greatest science and ease. He will take a long time to get an innings, and is of consequence of great annoyance to his opponents.' However, Haygarth's exploits on the field have been largely forgotten. It is as a cricket historian, compiler of 15 volumes of *Cricket Scores and Biographies*, covering the years from 1744 to his own time, that he is remembered. Published between 1862 and 1895, these volumes include more than 10,000 match scores and nearly 1,000 biographies of prominent cricketers.

## HAZLITT, WILLIAM (1778–1830) *essayist, died here*

### 6 FRITH STREET, W1

*In a house on this site lived* WILLIAM HAZLITT, 1829

### 6 BOUVERIE STREET, EC4  CITY OF LONDON

On his deathbed, Hazlitt's last recorded words were, 'Well, I've had a happy life.' Certainly he had an emotionally eventful one. Estranged from his first wife he became, in 1820, almost insanely enamoured of his landlord's daughter and his book *Liber Amoris* is a nakedly honest account of his three-year obsession, which ended only when the woman announced her love for another. The next year Hazlitt, now divorced, married a widow, Mrs Bridgewater, and they embarked on a continental tour. On the way back home the new Mrs Hazlitt left her husband and the marriage came to an abrupt end. Hazlitt had a prolific career as an essayist and critic. He wrote on both political and literary subjects but it is his essays and lectures on Shakespeare, on English comic writers and on the poets of his own time, that made and have sustained his reputation.

## HEARTFIELD, JOHN (1891–1968) *master of photomontage, lived here 1938–1943*

### 47 DOWNSHIRE HILL, HAMPSTEAD, NW3

Helmut Herzfeld's father and mother were radical writers and activists in Berlin, who were forced to flee the country to avoid imprisonment, leaving Helmut and his siblings to be brought up by relatives. He attended art college in Munich and was working as a commercial artist when the First World War broke out. During the war, Herzfeld feigned madness to escape service in the trenches and anglicised his name to John Heartfield as a deliberate protest against the bigoted nationalism he saw all around him in Germany. He was a member of the Berlin Dada movement in the years just after the war and began to use photography and photomontage as political and satirical weapons in the 1920s. When the Nazis came to power in 1933, Heartfield, who had mocked Hitler and his party mercilessly in his work, was in immediate danger of arrest and he went into exile in Czechoslovakia. There he continued to create his political photomontages and to work for the left-wing newspaper *AIZ*, which was published from Prague. Five years later, with Hitler threatening to occupy Czechoslovakia, Heartfield moved to England, where he was briefly interned as an enemy alien. He returned to Germany after the Second World War, settling in the communist East where he worked in the theatre and as an university lecturer.

## HEATH ROBINSON, W. (1872–1944) *illustrator and comic artist, lived here 1913–1918*
### 75 MOSS LANE, PINNER

Heath Robinson studied at Islington College of Art and the Royal Academy Schools and became a successful illustrator in the heyday of the illustrated book, the 1890s and the period before the First World War. Editions of works such as *Don Quixote, The Arabian Nights* and *The Water Babies* made Robinson's name and established his own distinctive style. Today the illustrator is best known for his comic drawings of elaborate, ramshackle machines – constructed from wheels, pulleys, gears, odd pieces of household equipment – which are designed to undertake simple tasks like raising one's hat or taking a biscuit out of a biscuit tin. His name has entered the language as an adjectival phrase and people describe any strange, rickety machinery as 'Heath Robinson'.

## HEINE, HEINRICH (1799–1856) *German poet and essayist, lived here 1827*
### 32 CRAVEN STREET, WC2

Heine was born of a Jewish family in Düsseldorf but converted to Protestantism in an unsuccessful attempt to gain entry into professions barred to Jews at the time. His early poetry caused a stir in German intellectual circles but his liberal views led him, in 1831, to move to Paris after he had despaired of significant radical change in the German states. He lived there for the rest of his life, originally in voluntary exile, but later unable to return permanently to his native land because his political and satirical writings had fallen foul of the censors. He spent four months in England in 1827 but he found London unsympathetic. 'Do not send a poet to London!' he wrote. 'The mere seriousness of everything, the colossal uniformity, the machine-like movement, the shrillness even of joy – this over-driven London oppresses fancy and rends the heart.'

## HENDERSON, ARTHUR (1863–1935) *statesman, lived here*
### 13 RODENHURST ROAD, CLAPHAM, SW4

Henderson left school at the age of twelve to work in an iron foundry. He went on to become one of the leading figures in the Labour party from its earliest incarnation as the Labour Representation Committee to its first taste of government under Ramsay MacDonald and its subsequent divisions in the thirties when he was, briefly, leader of the party. In 1903 Henderson was only the third LRC member to become an MP when he was elected in a by-election and, when he joined Asquith's all-party, wartime government in 1915, he was the first Labour party member to take a place in the Cabinet. In Ramsay MacDonald's first Labour government Henderson was Home Secretary and he was Foreign Secretary in the government of 1929–31. After the split in the Labour movement caused by Ramsay MacDonald's determination to stay on as Prime Minister of a 'National' government in 1931, Henderson spent much of the rest of his life working on behalf of the League of Nations and he was awarded the Nobel Peace Prize in 1934.

## HENDRIX, JIMI (1942–1970) *guitarist and songwriter, lived here 1968–1969*
### 23 BROOK STREET, W1

'I am what I feel', Jimi Hendrix once said, 'I play as I feel and I act as I feel. I can't express myself in any conversation. I can't explain myself like this or like that . . . But when I'm up on stage, it's all the world. It's my whole life.' Thirty years after his death Hendrix is as much a legend as he was in his own lifetime, and memories of him on stage and of his flamboyant methods of guitar-playing – behind his back, with his teeth – remain strong. Hendrix came to London in 1966 and formed the Jimi Hendrix Experience. The following year was their greatest year with three hits – 'Purple Haze', 'Hey Joe' and 'The Wind Cries Mary' – but he was still at the height of fame and notoriety three years later when he died of an accidental drugs overdose. His plaque is on a house next door to one on which there is also a plaque to a very different musician – George Frederick Handel.

## HENRY, SIR EDWARD (1850–1931) *Metropolitan Police Commissioner 1903–1918 and pioneer of fingerprint identification, lived here 1903–1920*

19 SHEFFIELD TERRACE, W8

Regarded as the most innovative and influential police commissioner London has ever had, Sir Edward Henry spent his early career in India. As Inspector General of the Bengal Police in the 1890s, Henry became interested in the possibility of identifying criminals through the use of fingerprints. Together with two Bengali colleagues, he devised a system of classifying and readily accessing fingerprints, which was taken up by police forces around the world and remains the basis for most classification systems used today. Returning to England in 1901 as Assistant Commissioner of Scotland Yard, Henry set up the first fingerprint bureau in the UK and was appointed Commissioner in 1903. He resigned from the post in 1918 in the aftermath of a damaging strike by London police officers. Knighted in 1906, Sir Edward Henry lived in Sheffield Terrace throughout his years as commissioner, and it was on the doorstep of the house that he was the victim of a shooting attack. Three shots were fired at him by a man aggrieved because he had been denied a cab licence. Henry was seriously wounded by one of the shots but later intervened on the would-be assassin's behalf, requesting a lenient sentence and even helping to fund the man's emigration to Canada after his release. After leaving the post of Commissioner, Henry moved to Ascot where he died in 1931.

## HENTY, G.A. (GEORGE ALFRED) (1832–1902) *author, lived here*

33 LAVENDER GARDENS, SW11

In the Victorian era thousands of books for boys advertised the glories of Empire in tales of plucky British adventurers engaged in manly combat with those unfortunate enough not to share their nationality. The most successful of these were written by G.A. Henty, whose earlier career as a war correspondent reporting on the many minor conflicts of the period had given him the ideal background to produce such fiction. After Cambridge, Henty had spent time in the Crimea and in Africa (he was acquainted with another larger-than-life newspaper correspondent, H.M. Stanley) and began to write his novels in 1868. For the next thirty years and more he produced books at the rate of several a year; titles like *Under Drake's Flag*, *With Clive in India* and *With the Allies in Pekin*, which combined narrative verve with an unquestioning jingoism that is hopelessly outmoded.

## HERBERT, SIR ALAN (A.P.H.) (1890–1971) *author, humorist and reformist MP, lived and died here*

12 HAMMERSMITH TERRACE, HAMMERSMITH, W6

Called to the Bar, Herbert never needed to practise as a barrister because he was soon earning a substantial income from his writing. He produced fiction, light verse and libretti for comic operas with equal facility and he was a very regular contributor to *Punch* at its time of greatest popularity. He did use his legal training for the creation of perhaps his best-known work, *Uncommon Law*, in which the cases of one Albert Haddock are used to genially reveal the absurdities of convoluted legal procedures. Herbert entered Parliament as an independent MP for Oxford University in 1935 and became known as an idiosyncratic campaigner for a variety of causes. He championed the idea of water-buses on the Thames and reform of notoriously illogical English spelling. His most lasting achievement in politics was the Matrimonial Causes Act of 1938, which he introduced originally as a private bill and which did much to reform divorce laws.

## HERFORD, ROBERT TRAVERS (1860–1950) *Unitarian minister, scholar, and interpreter of Judaism, lived and worked here*

DR WILLIAMS'S LIBRARY, 14 GORDON SQUARE, WC1

Dr Williams's Library came into being in 1716 on the death of Daniel Williams, a Presbyterian minister. He left much of his estate, including his library, to a charitable trust and a building in Redcross Street was erected to house the books. Long known as 'the Dissenters' Library', Dr Williams's collection, and the additions made to it over the years, had several further homes before coming to rest in Gordon Square as part of the University of London. It was then that it became the workplace and home of the Unitarian minister and scholar Robert Travers Herford. Herford was convinced of the importance of an understanding of Judaism to a true understanding of Christianity and over his long career wrote many books, with titles like *Christianity in Talmud and Midrash* and *Judaism in the New Testament Period*, intended to promote knowledge of the links between the two faiths.

## HERTZ, CHIEF RABBI DR JOSEPH (1872–1946) *Chief Rabbi of Great Britain and the Commonwealth, lived here 1937–1946*

103 HAMILTON TERRACE, NW8  **WESTMINSTER**

Born in Rebrin (then in Hungary, now in Slovakia), Hertz emigrated to the US with his family in 1884 and became a Rabbi ten years later. Appointed to a position in Johannesburg, Hertz found himself in the midst of the political struggle between the Boers and the British. His opposition to discrimination against non-Afrikaner groups and his pro-British attitude led Kruger to deport him during the Boer War but he returned to South Africa after the war. In 1913, after a brief period back in New York, Hertz became Chief Rabbi of the British Empire, a position he held for more than thirty years.

## HERZEN, ALEXANDER (1812–1870) *Russian political thinker, lived here 1860–1863*

1 ORSETT TERRACE, W2

Herzen was born into the Russian nobility but soon became known for his radical political views, suffering imprisonment in 1834 and eventually going into exile from Russia in 1847. He arrived in London in 1852 and stayed for more than a decade, establishing a Free Russian Press in Regent Square and publishing a periodical, *The Bell*, which was smuggled back into Russia and which, in its advocacy of reform and emancipation of the serfs, was highly influential. During his time in London he entertained a number of distinguished Russian visitors, including both Tolstoy and Dostoevsky. Despite the length of his stay in London he never became reconciled to the city. 'There is no town in the world,' he wrote, 'which is more adapted for training one away from people and training one into solitude than London.' Herzen died, still an exile, in Paris.

## HESS, DAME MYRA (1890–1965) *pianist, lived here*

48 WILDWOOD ROAD, NW11

Although she was a concert performer for fifty years, Myra Hess will always be remembered chiefly for the series of daily lunch-time concerts at the National Gallery that she organised during the Second World War. At a time when concert halls were closed and live performances of music few and far between, these concerts were enjoyed by many and were seen as embodying defiance of the war and the Blitz. Myra Hess was made a Dame of the British Empire in 1941 as a recognition of the role she was playing in maintaining the public's morale. Her war work was a culmination of a career that had begun in 1907 with a performance, conducted by Sir Thomas Beecham, of Beethoven's *Fourth Concerto* and which was to take her on major concert tours throughout Britain, Europe and the USA.

## HILL, GRAHAM (1929–1975) *World Champion Racing Driver lived here 1960–1972*
### 32 PARKSIDE, NW7

The so-called Triple Crown of Motorsport can be defined in two different ways but, whichever definition is chosen, only one driver has ever won it. Graham Hill is the only man to have won the Indianapolis 500, the Le Mans 24 hours race and the Monaco Grand Prix. Substitute the Formula One World Championship for the Monaco Grand Prix (as some people do) and Hill is still the only man to have won all three events. He began his Formula One career in 1958 and won his first world championship four years later. He won a second in 1968. Debonair and charming, Hill became the best-known figure in his sport and a popular personality on TV. In the early 1970s, he used the power of his name to attract sponsorship and set up his own Formula One team. Together with five other members of this Embassy Hill team, he was killed when the light plane he was piloting crashed in freezing fog on the Arkley golf course in north London. His son Damon Hill, fifteen at the time of his father's death, went on to win the Formula One World Championship, the only son of a former world champion ever to do so.

## HILL, OCTAVIA (1838–1912) *housing reformer, co-founder of the National Trust, began her work here*

### 2 GARBUTT PLACE, MARYLEBONE, W1

## OCTAVIA HILL *social reformer, established this garden, hall and cottages, and pioneered Army Cadets 1887–1890*

### RED CROSS GARDEN, REDCROSS WAY, SE1   **BOROUGH OF SOUTHWARK**

The daughter of a corn-merchant and banker, Octavia Hill was born in Wisbech and came to London in 1852 to work at a Christian Socialist-inspired Ladies' Guild run by her mother. There she met John Ruskin and it was Ruskin who, in 1864, supported her financially when she took on the leases of three houses in Marylebone with the intention of improving them as dwellings for the poor. This was the start of a lifelong career as a housing reformer and as a manager of homes and accommodation for London's less fortunate. Her principles were simple. 'Repairs promptly and efficiently attended to, references completely taken up, cleaning sedulously supervised, overcrowding put an end to, the blessing of ready-money payments enforced, accounts strictly kept, and, above all, tenants so sorted as to be helpful to one another.' She followed these principles for nearly fifty years of philanthropic work. A campaigner for the preservation of open spaces, Octavia Hill was also one of the founders of the National Trust in 1895.

## HILL, SIR ROWLAND (1795–1879) *postal reformer, lived here*
### 1 ORME SQUARE, W2

## SIR ROWLAND HILL, KCB (1795–1879) *originator of the Penny Post, lived here 1849–1879*

### ROYAL FREE HOSPITAL, POND STREET, HAMPSTEAD, NW3

Born in Kidderminster, Rowland Hill came from a family of teachers and was, until 1833, a teacher himself, who ran schools in the Midlands and London and was one of the founders of the Society for the Diffusion of Useful Knowledge. In the mid-1830s Hill became Secretary to the South Australian Commission and, in that capacity, learnt of the difficulties and cost of sending mail from England to the colonies. He extended his investigation into the postal system in general, and in an 1837 pamphlet *Post Office Reform: Its Importance and Practicability*, he advocated such measures as regular daily delivery and pre-paid postage by means of a 'stamp' or 'a bit of paper covered at the back with a glutinous wash'. After two years of campaigning

Hill's measures were accepted and a few months later the first British postage stamps – the Penny Black and the Twopenny Blue – went on sale on 6 May 1840. Hill was not a popular man with the Postmaster General, who accused him of being the initiator of 'wild and visionary schemes', but he was eventually given an important post within the Post Office where he could continue his reforms. He was knighted in 1860 and retired from the Post Office – which he had revolutionised – four years later.

---

## HILTON, JAMES (1900–1954) *novelist and scriptwriter, lived here*
42 OAKHILL GARDENS, WOODFORD GREEN

Hilton may not be an instantly familiar name today but two of his creations are well known and can, indeed, be said to have entered the language. Any elderly schoolmaster could be described as Mr Chips, after the character in Hilton's short novel *Goodbye Mr Chips*, and a place of earthly paradise (or a Chinese restaurant) can be described as Shangri-La, the Tibetan lamasery in his 1933 fantasy *Lost Horizon*, where death and ageing have been overcome. Born in Lancashire and educated at Cambridge, Hilton published his first novel when he was only twenty and went on to write a number of others. Many of his works were adapted for the screen and Hilton himself became a scriptwriter, moving to Hollywood, where he died in 1954.

---

## HITCH, PRIVATE FREDERICK, V.C. (1856–1913) *hero of Rorke's Drift, lived and died here*
62 CRANBROOK ROAD, CHISWICK, W4

The Battle of Rorke's Drift, in which a tiny force of British soldiers was besieged by an army of several thousand Zulus, is one of the best-known military engagements of the Victorian era, celebrated at the time for the heroism of the troops and immortalised for a later generation by the 1960s film *Zulu*. No fewer than eleven Victoria Crosses were awarded to the men who fought at Rorke's Drift and one of them went to Frederick Hitch. He was awarded his V.C. for the courage he and another soldier, Corporal William Allen, displayed when it became necessary to evacuate the small hospital at the former mission station which was at the heart of the fighting. According to the official medal citation, the two men 'were both severely wounded, but their determined conduct enabled the patients to be withdrawn from the hospital, and when incapacitated by their wounds from fighting, they continued, as soon as their wounds had been dressed, to serve out ammunition to their comrades during the night.' Hitch was so severely wounded that he had to be discharged from the army with a pension, aged only twenty-two. In later life he worked as a hotel commissionaire and, for many years, as a London cabbie. When he died, just before the outbreak of the First World War, his exploits had been largely forgotten but his heroism is now recorded on the Blue Plaque on the wall of the house in Chiswick, where he lived at the end of his life.

---

## HITCHCOCK, SIR ALFRED (1899–1980) *film director, lived here 1926–1939*
153 CROMWELL ROAD, SW5

## SIR ALFRED HITCHCOCK *famous film director was born near this site*
517 LEYTONSTONE HIGH ROAD, E11   **BOROUGH OF WALTHAM FOREST**

'I enjoy playing the audience like a piano', Hitchcock once said and, in a career as a film director that lasted more than fifty years, he showed enormous skill in manipulating audience reaction to the cinematic dramas he created. He also became one of the few directors who was a household name, and his portly, unmistakable figure – seen in uncredited cameo roles in most of his movies – was more familiar than the faces of some of his stars. The son of Catholic shopkeepers in London's East End, Hitchcock entered the silent film industry as a title-card illustrator and worked his way up the ladder to director. In the 1930s he was one of Britain's most successful directors, creating such classic movies as *The 39 Steps* and *The Lady Vanishes*. He moved to Hollywood in 1939 and his first film in America, *Rebecca*, won the Oscar for Best Picture the following year. Other successes (*Vertigo, Rear Window, North by Northwest*) followed, all noted for their visual inventiveness and their expert handling of suspense and tension. His 1960 movie *Psycho* may well have been the most shocking film its original audience members had ever seen, although, with characteristic mischievousness, Hitchcock claimed it was a comedy. Hitchcock made his last movie in 1976 and died at his home in Los Angeles four years later.

## HOBBS, JACK (1882–1963) *cricketer, lived here*
17 ENGLEWOOD ROAD, SW12

The first professional cricketer to be knighted, Sir Jack Hobbs was, arguably, the finest batsman England has produced and, in a first-class career lasting nearly thirty years, scored more than 61,000 runs and 197 centuries. He played in 61 Test matches and his Test average of 56.94 has been bettered by only a handful of players. In one of his earliest appearances he played against W.G. Grace; in one of his last Test matches he played against Don Bradman, thus linking two eras of cricketing history. After retiring from first-class cricket he seemed unconcerned that he had come so close to the remarkable achievement of two hundred first-class centuries. 'It doesn't worry me', he said, 'but it does seem to worry my friends.' The remark is typical of a sportsman who seems to have been a genuinely modest and gentle man.

## HODGKIN, THOMAS (1798–1866) *physician, reformer and philanthropist, lived here*
35 BEDFORD SQUARE, WC1

Today Hodgkin's name lives on in that of the glandular disease *lymphadenoma*, Hodgkin's disease, which he was the first to describe adequately. In his own time he was known for far more than an interest in one disease. Holder of various medical positions at Guy's Hospital, Hodgkin was also involved in campaigns to improve the treatment of prisoners and the mentally ill and was a man of wider scientific interests, from geography to ethnology and anthropology. He was a friend of the Jewish philanthropist Sir Moses Montefiore and accompanied him on six journeys through the Middle East and North Africa to investigate the plight of religious and ethnic minorities in these regions. On the last of these trips he caught dysentery and died in Jaffa (in modern Israel), where his grave can still be seen.

## HOFMANN, A.W. (1818–1892) *Professor of Chemistry, lived here*
9 FITZROY SQUARE, W1

Hofmann was born in Giessen, a university town near Frankfurt, and studied chemistry there under Justus von Liebig, among the greatest of all nineteenth-century chemists, who had made the Giessen laboratory into one of the most up-to-date in Europe. (Hofmann was later to write the official biography of Liebig.) Hofmann came to London in 1848 as Superintendent of the Royal College of Chemistry and stayed for fifteen years until the offer of a professorship in Berlin took him back to his native country. He stayed in Berlin for the rest of his life. Hofmann made contributions in many fields of chemistry but is perhaps best remembered for his discoveries of organic compounds, including formaldehyde and the aniline dye still known as Hofmann violet.

## HOGG, QUINTIN (1845–1903) *founder of the Polytechnic, Regent Street, lived here 1885–1898*

### 5 CAVENDISH SQUARE, W1

The Royal Polytechnic Institution first came into existence in the 1830s but, as the institution that pioneered the idea of polytechnic education in London, it was the brainchild of Quintin Hogg, merchant and philanthropist, who re-established it in premises at 309 Regent Street in 1882. Hogg had been interested in the education of the poor all his adult life. He later wrote of the very earliest beginnings of his life's work: 'My first effort was to get a couple of crossing sweepers whom I . . . offered to teach to read. With an empty beer bottle for a candlestick, and a tallow candle for illumination, two crossing sweepers for pupils, your humble servant as teacher, and a couple of Bibles as reading books, what grew into the Polytechnic (nearly twenty years later) was practically started.' In more recent years the Regent Street Polytechnic became part of the Polytechnic of Central London, itself now renamed the University of Westminster.

## HOLMAN HUNT, WILLIAM, OM (1827–1910) *painter, lived and died here*

### 18 MELBURY ROAD, W14

'No young man', Holman Hunt wrote in later life, 'has the faintest chance of developing his art into a living power, unless he investigates the dogmas of his elders with critical mind and dares to face the idea of revolt from their authority.' In his youth, as one of the founding members of the Pre-Raphaelite Brotherhood in 1848, Hunt had done exactly that and it was he who clung most steadfastly to the ideals of the Brotherhood as he grew older. His earlier paintings came under fierce attack from the critics and *The Times* in 1851 accused the Pre-Raphaelites of a 'strange disorder of the mind or eyes'. However, by the time Holman Hunt had moved into Melbury Road in the 1880s, all that was in the past. Paintings such as *The Light of the World* and *The Awakening Conscience* had become very popular with the Victorian audience, reproduced in prints in many a middle class home, and Holman Hunt was becoming a grand old man of British art. This status was confirmed in 1905 by the award of the Order of Merit.

## HOLST, GUSTAV (1874–1934) *composer, wrote The Planets and taught here*

### ST PAUL'S GIRLS' SCHOOL, BROOK GREEN, W8

Gustav Holst was born in Cheltenham into a musical family that originated in Sweden. His father was a piano teacher and choirmaster and his grandfather, who had moved to England from Latvia, was a harpist and composer. There seemed little doubt that Gustav would also make music his career and he attended the Royal College of Music in the 1890s where he began his lifelong friendship with Ralph Vaughan Williams. However, after leaving the RCM, he struggled for some years. 'Music-making as a means of getting money is hell,' he remarked and he was obliged to take a number of unappealing musical jobs, including playing the trombone in theatre orchestras, before the growing success of his own compositions and a career in teaching combined to provide him with some financial stability. St Paul's Girls School employed him as Director of Music in 1905 and, although he later took additional teaching posts, he held the job in Hammersmith for the rest of his life. Some of his best known works were inspired by, or refer to, this area of west London, including his 'St Paul's Suite', his 'Brook Green Suite' and his piece for military bands simply entitled 'Hammersmith'.

HOOD, THOMAS (1799–1845) *was born in a house on this site, 23 May 1799*

MIDLAND BANK, 31 POULTRY, EC2   **CITY OF LONDON**

THOMAS HOOD (1799–1845) *poet and humorist, lived in Rose Cottage on this site*

59 VICAR'S MOOR LANE, WINCHMORE HILL, N21   **BOROUGH OF ENFIELD**

THOMAS HOOD (1799–1845) *poet, died here*

DEVONSHIRE LODGE, 28 FINCHLEY ROAD, NW8   **PRIVATE**

Born the son of a London bookseller, Hood was haunted by ill health for most of his life but was a prolific writer of both comic and serious verse and a friend of most of the best-known literary figures of his day from Hazlitt and Charles Lamb to Charles Dickens. Hood's serious verse, such as *The Song of the Shirt* (first published in the Christmas 1843 issue of *Punch*), is marked by his social conscience ('Oh! God! that bread should be so dear/And flesh and blood so cheap'), his comic verse by a love of punning which, depending on one's viewpoint, is either remarkably ingenious or profoundly irritating. Hood, like many other nineteenth-century poets, is a figure whose reputation has faded almost completely but whose lines ('I remember, I remember/ The house where I was born') are often surprisingly familiar.

See also under entry for ROBERT ADAM

HOPKINS, GERARD MANLEY (1844–1889) *poet, lived and studied in Manresa House*

GATEPOST AT MANRESA HOUSE, HOLYBOURNE AVENUE, ROEHAMPTON, SW15

GERARD MANLEY HOPKINS

9 OAK HILL PARK, NW3   **HAMPSTEAD PLAQUE FUND**

At school and at Oxford Hopkins showed enormous academic and artistic promise, made many friends, including Robert Bridges (later to be Poet Laureate), and wrote much poetry. After his conversion to Roman Catholicism Hopkins renounced most of this life and resolved to join the Jesuit movement, studying as a novice at Manresa House and at Stonyhurst in Lancashire. As a Jesuit, Hopkins was directed to a varied number of posts, including exhausting spells in a number of industrial parishes, before being appointed Professor of Latin and Greek at University College, Dublin. He died of typhoid in Dublin in 1889. In 1875 Hopkins had taken up writing poetry again, producing 'The Wreck of the Deutschland', dedicated to the memory of five nuns who had died when a ship sank in the Thames estuary. It was submitted to a Jesuit monthly, which rejected it as too difficult for its readership. Hopkins continued to write poetry but chose not to publish it during his lifetime. Only when his friend Bridges produced an edition of his work, nearly thirty years after Hopkins's death, did his originality and genius begin to be appreciated.

HORE-BELISHA, LORD (1893–1957) *statesman, lived here*

16 STAFFORD PLACE, SW1

Hore-Belisha, who had first become an MP in 1923, was Secretary of State for War in the crucial years between 1937 and 1940. His attempts to institute wide-ranging and controversial reforms of the Army met with great resistance in some quarters and Hore-Belisha eventually resigned. His lasting achievements, however, were in the area of transport. In the mid-thirties, largely because of lack of regulation, deaths on British roads were running at an extraordinarily high rate, given the number of cars about at the time. Hore-Belisha as Minister of Transport introduced a Road Traffic Bill in 1934. 'If cars continue to be made at the same rate as now and with increasing cheapness,' he said in introducing the bill, 'there will soon be no pedestrians left.' The bill was passed and driving tests, speed limits and pedestrian crossings came into existence, the pedestrian crossings highlighted by what came to be known as 'Belisha' beacons.

## HORNIMAN, JOHN (1803–1893) AND FREDERICK JOHN HORNIMAN
### (1835–1906) *tea merchants, collectors and public benefactors, lived here*

COOMBE CLIFF CENTRE, COOMBE ROAD, CROYDON

John Horniman began in business as a tea merchant in the 1820s, trading from a warehouse in Shepherdess Walk. A Quaker, his commercial acumen and ingenuity (he was reputedly one of the first to have the idea of selling tea in packets) ensured that the business thrived. His son, Frederick John, was a similarly astute businessman and was also an inveterate traveller and collector who built up an enormous collection of curiosities, natural history specimens and artefacts from cultures throughout the world. This collection was first opened to the public in 1890 and eight years later the present Art Nouveau building was erected on the site of one of the Hornimans' properties in Forest Hill. In 1901 Horniman presented the museum and the grounds in which it stands to the London County Council as a gift to the people of the city. A Liberal MP for a Cornish seat during the last ten years of his life, he died at his town house in Hyde Park Terrace.

## THE HORNIMAN MUSEUM AND GARDENS *given to the people of London in 1901 by Frederick John Horniman, who lived near this site*

THE HORNIMAN MUSEUM, LONDON ROAD, SE23

## HOUSMAN, ALFRED EDWARD (1859–1936) *poet and scholar, wrote 'A Shropshire Lad' while living here*

17 NORTH ROAD, N6

First and foremost a classical scholar, Housman devoted much of his life to the production of a definitive edition of the obscure Latin poet, Manilius. However, he is remembered today for his own poetry and, particularly for the volume he wrote and self-published while living in this house. Housman was educated at Oxford, where he became chastely enamoured of Moses Jackson, a fellow student. Jackson's emigration to India in 1887 and subsequent marriage were the emotional triggers for much of the melancholic and nostalgic verse in 'A Shropshire Lad'. Mysteriously, Housman had failed spectacularly in his Oxford exams and left, without even a pass degree, to spend ten years as a clerk in the Patent Office. Nonetheless his classical achievements eventually earned him an appointment at London University in 1892 and in 1911 he became Professor of Latin at Cambridge where he spent the rest of his life. He published two further, slim volumes of his poetry in 1922 and in the year of his death.

## *Near this spot at 62 Fore Street on 29 January 1850 was born* SIR EBENEZER HOWARD (1850–1928) *founder of the Garden City Movement*

MOOR HOUSE, LONDON WALL, EC2   **CITY OF LONDON**

## EBENEZER HOWARD (1850–1928) *pioneer of the Garden City Movement, lived here*
50 DURLEY ROAD, N16

Born in London, Howard moved to America as a young man and worked as a stenographer in Chicago. Returning to his native city he took up the profession of parliamentary shorthand writer and he carried on this business through all the years that he was advocating and initiating the movement for garden cities. In 1898 he published his book *Tomorrow: A Peaceful Path to Real Reform*, in which he set out his ideas about creating communities that combined the best of both town and country, and the following year he formed the Garden City Association to promulgate these ideas. The first garden city was Letchworth in Hertfordshire, which was bought and developed in 1903, and this was followed, immediately after the First World War, by Welwyn Garden City. Howard was president of the International Garden Cities and Town Planning Association from 1909 until his death and was knighted in 1927.

## HOWARD, JOHN (1726?–1790) *prison reformer, lived here*
23 GREAT ORMOND STREET, WC1

## JOHN HOWARD
157-9 LOWER CLAPTON ROAD, E5 **BOROUGH OF HACKNEY**

Born in Hackney, Howard was the son of a wealthy upholsterer and first became aware of the horrors of contemporary prison life when he was himself, briefly, a prisoner of the French. His period as High Sheriff of Bedfordshire brought him face to face with the injustices and cruelties of the British prison system and he began a series of tours through the country to investigate prison conditions. What he saw was recorded in his book *The State of Prisons in England and Wales, with an account of some Foreign Prisons*, and Howard's determination to confront the authorities with the harsh reality, resulted in a number of acts of Parliament designed to alleviate prisoners' suffering. After publication of his major work in 1777 he continued to visit prisons in Britain and abroad and, in 1790, while visiting Kherson in the Ukraine, he caught a fever and died. The Howard League for Penal Reform perpetuates his name and continues the work that he began.

## HOWARD, LUKE (1772–1864) *'Namer of Clouds', lived and died here*
7 BRUCE GROVE, TOTTENHAM, N17

Some of the scientific terms applied to cloud formations – stratus, cirrus, cumulus – are so familiar that it takes quite a mental effort to acknowledge that somebody must one day have invented them. That somebody was Luke Howard and he did so just over two centuries ago. Howard was born in London in 1772, the son of a Quaker businessman. He never became a professional scientist – he spent his working life as a pharmacist – but he was fascinated by the skies and by meteorology from an early age. In December 1802 he presented a paper, 'On the Modification of Clouds', to the Askesian Society, a group of amateur enthusiasts for the natural sciences he had helped to found. The short paper essentially outlined the system for classifying clouds which is still in use today. This soon became widely known throughout Europe, and the German polymath Goethe was one of those to sing its praises, dedicating a short sequence of poems to Howard. Although he continued to work as a pharmacist, Howard went on to write other works on meteorology, including a pioneering book called *The Climate of London*, but it is for his method of naming clouds that he is remembered.

## HUDSON, W.H. (1841–1922) *W.H. Hudson's friends' Society of Quilmes, near Buenos Aires where the great writer was born on 4 August 1841, and where he spent his youth, has placed this bronze plaque at 40 St Luke's Road, London, the house in which Hudson lived his last years, and died on 18 August 1922*

40 ST LUKE'S ROAD, W11

Hudson was born in South America, and many of his best-known works celebrate the forests, pampas and wild life of that continent, yet he spent most of his adult life in London, often in poverty. He was a prolific writer, author of novels, memoirs of his youth and books on birds (including a standard work on Argentine ornithology) but it was not until the publication of *Green Mansions* in 1904 that Hudson reached anything other than a small readership. This strange fiction about a man venturing into the 'green mansions' of the South American jungle and finding love, tragically cut short, with Rima, a mysterious combination of beautiful girl and spirit of nature, proved extraordinarily successful. So too did the autobiographical *Far Away and Long Ago*, and Hudson ended his life a much revered and admired writer and naturalist. The memorial to Hudson in Hyde Park is a statue by Jacob Epstein, not of the man himself but of Rima, his best-loved creation.

....................................................................................................................

## HUGHES, ARTHUR (1832–1915) *Pre-Raphaelite painter, lived and died here*
EASTSIDE HOUSE, 22 KEW GREEN, RICHMOND

## ARTHUR HUGHES (1832–1915)
284 LONDON ROAD, WALLINGTON   **BOROUGH OF SUTTON**

Arthur Hughes was one of the leading figures in the second wave of Pre-Raphaelite painting, following eagerly in the footsteps of the founding members of the Brotherhood. Born in London, Hughes attended the Royal Academy Schools where he read with enthusiasm the Pre-Raphaelite journal *The Germ*. Eventually he met Millais, Rossetti and Holman Hunt, the three most significant founding members of the PRB, and, in 1857, was invited to join a Pre-Raphaelite exhibition in a gallery near Fitzroy Square. Soon after this he was one of a number of youthful admirers of Rossetti, including William Morris and Edward Burne-Jones, who worked on a series of murals at the Oxford Union. Another of the recruits to this project, Val Prinsep, recalled the work on the decoration as a time of great happiness. 'What fun we had!' he later wrote, 'What jokes! What roars of laughter!' Certainly the time with the Pre-Raphaelites was the most significant experience of Hughes's artistic life and he continued to work in the Pre-Raphaelite tradition for the rest of his long life.

....................................................................................................................

## HUGHES, DAVID EDWARD (1831–1900) *scientist and inventor of the microphone, lived and worked here*
94 GREAT PORTLAND STREET, W1

Hughes was born in London but went with his parents to America as a child and was brought up in Virginia. A man of varied talents, he was made a Professor of Music at a Kentucky college before he was out of his teens, but his first major achievement came in 1855 when he patented a printing telegraph. The companies that were established to exploit this patent eventually evolved into the giant Western Union Telegraph Company. Hughes returned to the land of his birth and continued to work on scientific and electronic problems. In 1878, in a communication to the Royal Society, he gave the world a practical means of electronically amplifying sound in the shape of the first microphone. Hughes died a wealthy man, enriched by his inventive genius, and he left much of his fortune to hospitals in London.

....................................................................................................................

## HUGHES, HUGH PRICE (1847–1902) *Methodist preacher, lived and died here*
8 TAVITON STREET, WC1

Hughes was the most prominent Methodist of the second half of the nineteenth century, the founder (and first editor) of *The Methodist Times* and of the West London Mission, which attracted large audiences to its services in the 1880s and 1890s. Born in Carmarthen, Hughes was originally intended for a legal career but chose instead to train as a Wesleyan minister, attending the Richmond Theological College and London University. After a period as a minister in Dover, Brighton and Oxford, Hughes's exceptional gifts as a preacher and platform orator were allowed to flourish at the West London Mission and in services held in St James's Hall, Piccadilly. He was made President of the Wesleyan Conference in 1898 but he was what would today be called a workaholic and he died only four years later, worn out by years of long hours and little rest.

## HUGHES, MARY (1860–1941) *friend of all in need, lived and worked here 1926–1941*
71 VALLANCE ROAD, E2

The daughter of Thomas Hughes, Christian Socialist and author of *Tom Brown's Schooldays*, Mary Hughes was brought up in a family where devotion to the needs of those less fortunate than oneself was both preached and practised. She was for many years a leading figure in the struggle to bring dignity to the lives of the East End poor. She bought a public house in Vallance Road in 1926 and converted it to a centre for education, trade unionism and Christian Socialism. While taking part in a march on behalf of the unemployed in the thirties, Mary Hughes was injured in a tram accident and spent her last years as an invalid.

## HUNT, LEIGH (1784–1859) *essayist and poet, lived here*
22 UPPER CHEYNE ROW, SW3

## LEIGH HUNT (1784–1859) *lived here*
16 ROWAN ROAD, W6    **PRIVATE**

Although Hunt was a poet – the poem 'Abou Ben Adhem and the Angel' with its famous opening lines 'Abou Ben Adhem (may his tribe increase!)/Awoke one night from a deep dream of peace' is his – he is now best remembered as an editor and journalist. Together with his brother John he founded and ran a weekly called *The Examiner*. Hunt acted as an editorial midwife to the second generation of romantic poets, publishing both Keats and Shelley in the pages of *The Examiner* and setting up a short-lived periodical with Shelley and another friend, Byron. He also used the pages of *The Examiner* as a vehicle for his political views and became a hero of radicalism in 1813 when he was imprisoned, together with his brother, for an article in which they had written of the Prince Regent that, 'This Adonis in loveliness was a corpulent man of fifty.' In later life he knew Dickens, and Hunt's effusiveness and charm were said to have contributed the pleasanter side to the character of the improvident Harold Skimpole in *Bleak House*.

## HUNTER, JOHN (1728–1793) *surgeon, lived here*
31 GOLDEN SQUARE, W1

Born in Scotland, Hunter followed his elder brother William to London to pursue a career in surgery. He became the most successful surgeon of his time and has often been hailed as the father of scientific surgery. Hunter's great concern was with an exact knowledge of anatomy. He ran a school of anatomy that attracted such pupils as Edward Jenner, the pioneer of vaccination, and he began the collection of anatomical specimens and curiosities that is now known as the Hunterian Museum and is housed in the building in Lincoln Inn's Fields occupied by the Royal College of Surgeons. Hunter's enthusiasm for experimentation was legendary but he was not always successful. In 1777, when the learned Dr Dodd was hanged at Tyburn for forgery, Hunter employed men to rush the body to a nearby house where he tried to resuscitate it in a bath of hot water. Dodd, however, remained beyond Hunter's powers of recall.

## *This was the home and museum of* DR WILLIAM HUNTER (1718–1783) *anatomist*
LYRIC THEATRE, GREAT WINDMILL STREET, W1

Born near Glasgow, the elder brother of John Hunter, William Hunter was originally intended for the Church but he studied medicine at Edinburgh University and arrived in

London in 1741 to practise as a physician. He rapidly became successful, particularly in the field of obstetrics, and was appointed physician-extraordinary to Queen Charlotte in 1764. His house in Great Windmill Street, already home to his varied collections of anatomical specimens, books, coins and works of art, became, in the 1770s, a centre for medical teaching with a lecture theatre and dissecting room attached. When Hunter died, his collections were bequeathed to Glasgow University where they formed the basis for the Hunterian Museum, opened in 1807 as the first public museum in Scotland.

## HUSKISSON, WILLIAM (1770–1830) *statesman, lived here*
28 ST JAMES'S PLACE, SW1

More often recalled for the manner of his death than for his political achievements, Huskisson was, allegedly, the first fatality of the Railway Age, being struck by an engine at the opening of the Liverpool and Manchester Railway in 1830. At the time of his death he was a much experienced politician, having first entered Parliament in 1796 as MP for Morpeth and a supporter of Pitt the Younger. He held junior office under Pitt and in the government of the elderly and ailing Duke of Portland between 1807 and 1809. His most substantial achievements came in the last decade of his life when he was President of the Board of Trade and, in 1827, Colonial Secretary. Huskisson was a leading pioneer of free trade and worked hard to modernise trading conditions between the colonies and the rest of the world. His statue, by the sculptor John Gibson, stands in Pimlico Gardens.

## HUTCHINSON, SIR JONATHAN (1828–1913) *surgeon, scientist and teacher, lived here*
15 CAVENDISH SQUARE, W1

Born in Selby in Yorkshire, Jonathan Hutchinson was a surgeon at the London Hospital for many years and was later Professor of Surgery. In his long career he gained most of the honours available to one of his profession, including Fellowship of the Royal Society, the presidency of the Royal College of Surgeons and, in 1908, a knighthood. Hutchinson was a gifted all-round scientist who made important contributions to fields as diverse as ophthalmology and neurology, natural history and pathology, but it was as a specialist in the field of venereal disease that his name is best remembered. He is said to have had the, perhaps, doubtful privilege of seeing more than a million cases of syphilis and the three primary symptoms of congenital syphilis, which he was the first to describe fully, are known as 'Hutchinson's Triad'.

## HUXLEY, LEONARD (1860–1933) HUXLEY, JULIAN (1887–1975) HUXLEY, ALDOUS (1894–1963) *men of science and letters, lived here*
16 BRACKNELL GARDENS, NW3

## SIR JULIAN HUXLEY FRS *lived here 1943–1975*
31 POND STREET, NW3  **PRIVATE**

The Huxleys were leading members of one of the great intellectual dynasties of the nineteenth and twentieth centuries. Leonard was the son of Darwin's defender T.H. Huxley and married a niece of the poet Matthew Arnold. He was connected with *The Cornhill Magazine* for more than thirty years, seventeen of them as editor. His son Julian won the Newdigate Prize for Poetry while he was at Oxford but made his career in science rather than literature, becoming Professor of Zoology at King's College, London, and Secretary to the Zoological Society of London. He published a number of books in which he explored the relations between science and society and was the first Director-General of UNESCO. Aldous Huxley, younger brother of Julian, became one of the most admired novelists of the 1920s with erudite and witty satires of contemporary society but is best remembered for his dystopian vision of a totalitarian future, *Brave New World*. In 1937 he moved to California where he spent most of the rest of his life, continuing to write fiction and to pursue his interests in mysticism and in altered states of consciousness. *The Doors of Perception* is his famous account of his own experiments in taking mind-expanding drugs and includes descriptions of his everyday surroundings as experienced after using mescaline. Even his trousers seemed extraordinary. 'Those folds in the trousers – what a labyrinth of endlessly significant complexity. And the texture of the grey flannel – how rich, how deeply, mysteriously sumptuous.'

## HUXLEY, THOMAS HENRY (1825–1895) *biologist, lived here*
### 38 MARLBOROUGH PLACE, NW8

'Darwin's Bulldog', as he once called himself, was born in Ealing and studied medicine at Charing Cross Hospital. Like the man whose work he was later to defend, Huxley went, as a young man, on a long voyage to some of the remotest parts of the world. Darwin's travels on the *Beagle* were matched by Huxley's on HMS *Rattlesnake* to New Guinea and the Australian coast. On his return he was elected a Fellow of the Royal Society but still found his future uncertain. 'Science in England,' he wrote, 'does everything – but pay. You may earn praise, but not pudding.' It was not until 1854 when he was appointed a Professor of Natural History at the Royal School of Mines that he gained some security. Huxley, unlike Darwin, was a combative and vigorous debater and won great renown as an eloquent champion of the ideas of evolution, most notably at a famous encounter with Bishop Wilberforce in Oxford in 1860. A biologist of distinction and achievement himself, Huxley was perhaps the first great populariser of science, writing books such as *Man's Place in Nature* and giving many scientific lectures to audiences of ordinary working men.

## HYNDMAN, HENRY MAYERS (1842–1921) *socialist leader, lived and died here*
### 13 WELL WALK, NW3

Hyndman came from a wealthy family, was educated at Cambridge and read for the Bar before deciding instead to launch a career as a journalist. Despite his background, Hyndman became one of the earliest advocates of the ideas of Karl Marx in Britain. He met Marx, who was living in exile in London, in the 1870s and read a French edition of the German's major work *Das Kapital* in the unlikely setting of Utah, where he was on a business trip. Returning from the land of Brigham Young and polygamy a convert to Marxian economics and a believer in imminent revolutionary upheaval, Hyndman established the Democratic Federation (later the Social Democratic Federation) in 1881 to propagate Marxist ideas and turned his journalistic skills to the same end. Marx was characterisically dismissive of Hyndman, calling him 'a weak vessel' who had only a superficial understanding of his ideas, but there is no doubt of Hyndman's flamboyant commitment to his own version of the cause.

## INNER LONDON EDUCATION AUTHORITY *the home of Inner London's Education Service from 1922; ILEA succeeding the London School Board (1870–1904) and the LCC (1904–1965)*
### MAIN ENTRANCE, COUNTY HALL, SE1

## INNES, JOHN (1829–1904)
### MANOR HOUSE, WATERY LANE, SW20

Innes was a wealthy London merchant and property developer who bought land in Merton in 1867 and spent the rest of his life turning it into his country estate. At his death he donated the greater part of his fortune to the development of horticultural research and experimentation. In 1910 Innes's bequest enabled the foundation of the John Innes Horticultural Institute at Manor House and it rapidly became the leading UK centre for research on plant breeding and genetics. Indeed its first director, William Bateson, actually coined the word 'genetics'. The Institute moved to Hertfordshire after the Second World War and, as the John Innes Centre, still exists at a site near Norwich.

## IRELAND, JOHN (1879–1962) *composer, lived here*
### 14 GUNTER GROVE, SW10

Like many of his contemporaries among English composers (including Ralph Vaughan Williams and Gustav Holst), John Ireland studied at the Royal College of Music under Sir Charles Stanford. His first great success as a composer was his *Second Violin Sonata* in 1917 and throughout his career he showed a greater fondness for chamber music, song and piano music than he did for larger scale orchestral or choral pieces. He wrote a piano concerto but chose not to produce either a symphony or an opera. Many of his best pieces are settings of words by a wide variety of English poets. In addition to his work as a composer, he taught at the Royal College and was organist and choirmaster at St Luke's in Chelsea.

## IRVING, EDWARD (1792–1834) *founder of the Catholic Apostolic Church, lived here*
### 4 CLAREMONT SQUARE, ISLINGTON, N1

Edward Irving was a charismatic nineteenth-century preacher whose views on the imminent second coming of the Lord frequently put him at odds with Church authorities. Born and brought up in Scotland, where he became friendly with the young Thomas Carlyle, he was ordained in the Church of Scotland and became pastor of the Caledonian Chapel in London in 1822. His powers as a preacher drew large audiences but his ideas about Christ's return worried many. 'The second coming of the Lord', he wrote in a letter, 'is the *point de vue*, the vantage ground ... from which, and from which alone, the whole purpose of God can be contemplated and understood.' In 1832 Irving was found guilty of deviating from the doctrine of the Church of Scotland and the doors of the Church closed against him. He promptly established his own congregation in which speaking in tongues and prophesying the closeness of millennial days were less of a problem. This developed, particularly after Irving's death in 1834, into the Catholic Apostolic Church.

## IRVING, SIR HENRY (1838–1905)
*actor, lived here 1872–1899*

### 15A GRAFTON STREET, W1

Born in Somerset as John Henry Brodribb, Irving became the greatest English actor of his time and was, in 1895, the first actor to be knighted. Making his first appearance on stage in 1856, Irving had to wait ten years before making his London debut. Perhaps, during his ten years in the provinces, Irving had not the hypnotic presence he had in his years of triumph. He himself said that he had once seen an old woman in tears at a performance of Hamlet and later, preening himself, had asked her if she had been moved. 'Indeed I was,' she said, 'I've a young son myself play-acting somewhere in the north, and it broke me up to think that he might be no better at it than you.' One of Irving's earliest successes was as the conscience-haunted murderer in *The Bells* and he went on to become actor-manager of the Lyceum for over twenty years. These were the years of his theatrical partnership with Ellen Terry, and they played most of the great Shakespearean roles together. The partnership ended in 1902 with a performance of *The Merchant of Venice*, and Irving died in Bradford three years later.

## IRVING, WASHINGTON (1783–1859) *American writer, lived here*
### 8 ARGYLL STREET, W1

In 1820 a work called *The Sketch Book* was published, purporting to be the work of 'Geoffrey Crayon, Gent.' and including that most American of folk tales, the story of Rip Van Winkle. The book was written by Washington Irving, already a popular author and journalist in the US. It also included brief essays on Westminster Abbey and other English subjects, which is not as surprising as it might appear as the author spent long periods of his life in London and in Europe and knew many of the English writers of the time, from Mary Shelley to Sir Walter Scott. Irving was the first American author to win an international reputation and audience. Later works by Irving include several inspired by his time as a diplomat in Spain during the late 1820s and a monumental five-volume biography of George Washington, published after his final return to his native country.

## ISAACS, RUFUS, 1ST MARQUESS OF READING (1860–1935) *lawyer and statesman, lived and died here*
### 32 CURZON STREET, W1

F.E. Smith once remarked that the story of Dick Whittington 'fades into pale ineffectiveness' when compared with the 'romance' of Rufus Isaacs's career. The son of a Jewish fruit merchant, Isaacs left school at fourteen to join the family firm. When he died in 1935 he had been Lord Chief Justice, Viceroy of India and, briefly, Foreign Secretary. The law provided Isaacs with the first rungs of the ladder of success and he became a leading advocate. He was MP for Reading from 1904 and a close friend of Lloyd George. Like 'the Welsh Wizard' he was implicated in the Marconi Scandal when it seemed that politicians had corruptly influenced the decision to award a lucrative contract to the Marconi Wireless Company and, like him again, escaped censure to rise to new heights. He was created Marquess of Reading after his return in 1926 from five years as the Viceroy of India.

## JACKSON, JOHN HUGHLINGS (1835–1911) *physician, lived here*
### 3 MANCHESTER SQUARE, W1

The son of a Yorkshire farmer, Jackson is considered to be the founding father of neurology in Britain. He studied medicine in London and, intrigued by the epilepsy suffered by his wife's cousin, he decided that he would concentrate his research on understanding the seizures that epileptics suffered. Through clinical observation and autopsies he came to the conclusion that patients' involuntary movements during seizures were the result of lesions in specific areas of the brain. Particular movements of the limbs, in both epileptics and non-epileptics, are associated, Jackson realised, with particular areas of the brain. Jackson, who worked for many years at the National Hospital for the Paralysed and Epileptics in Queen Square, by linking right-handedness with the left cerebral hemisphere, also demonstrated that the two cerebral hemispheres govern different sides of the body.

## JACOBS, W.W. (1863–1943) *author, lived here*
### 15 GLOUCESTER GATE, REGENT'S PARK, NW1

Jacobs was born in Wapping, where his father worked on the docks and wharves, and he started his working life as a clerk in the Post Office. He began to publish short stories in the 1890s in magazines such as *The Strand* and *The Idler* and was soon successful enough to resign from the Post Office to concentrate on his writing. He went on to publish a number of novels and many collections of stories, such as *Many Cargoes* (1896), *Light Freights* (1901) and *Night Watches* (1914). Many of these often humorous stories were set in the world of the dockers and sailors of the East End, which Jacobs knew from his childhood. Jacobs was also a gifted writer of the macabre, and one of his stories, 'The Monkey's Paw', remains a classic of the genre.

......................

## JAGGER, CHARLES SARGEANT (1885–1934) *sculptor, lived and died here*
67 ALBERT BRIDGE ROAD, BATTERSEA, SW11

Born in Yorkshire in 1885, Charles Jagger's life and career as a sculptor were shaped by the First World War. He studied art first in Sheffield and then in London and, at the outbreak of war in August 1914, he had just been awarded the prestigious Prix de Rome, which would have involved study in Europe. Jagger gave up the prize in order to enlist. He served both on the Western Front and at Gallipoli, was wounded several times, and received the Military Cross for 'distinguished and meritorious services in battle'. He is best known for his work on war memorials and one critic has described him as 'the only major artist to have made his reputation in this way'. Jagger's finest works are the Royal Artillery Memorial at Hyde Park Corner and the statue of a soldier reading a letter that stands on one of the platforms at Paddington Station and commemorates the 2,524 employees of the Great Western Railway company who died in the war.

......................

## JAMES, C.L.R. (1901–1989) *writer and political activist, lived and died here*
165 RAILTON ROAD, BRIXTON, SE24

'What do they know of cricket who only cricket know?' C.L.R. James once wrote, paraphrasing a line by Rudyard Kipling. Born in Trinidad, James was a fanatical devotee of cricket, earned his living from time to time as a cricket journalist and wrote *Beyond a Boundary*, now recognised as one of the classic books on the game. However, there was much more to James than his love of cricket. In a career that took him from the West Indies to Britain in the years of the Depression, and to the USA during the 1940s and 1950s, he became a highly respected thinker of the far left and an activist in a number of Trotskyist parties and organisations which had an influence far greater than their size and membership would suggest. As a writer, James was extraordinarily productive and wide-ranging. He wrote a novel, *Minty Alley*, which was said to be the first work of fiction by a black Caribbean author to be published in England; he helped the legendary cricketer Learie Constantine to write his autobiography; he published *The Black Jacobins*, a ground-breaking study of the Haitian Revolution of the 1790s; and he wrote a series of works of political theory. C.L.R. James spent his last years in Brixton and died there at the age of eighty-eight.

......................

## JAMES, HENRY (1843–1916) *writer, lived here 1886–1902*
34 DE VERE GARDENS, W8

Born in New York, Henry James studied briefly at Harvard Law School and began to write essays and reviews when he was in his early twenties. In 1869 he returned to Europe, which he had visited as a boy with his family, and after spending some time in Paris, he settled in London in 1876 (the year his first major novel, *Roderick Hudson*, was published) and lived in the city for the next twenty years. Even after moving to Rye he still spent much time in the capital and, having spent much of his adult life in England, he finally became a naturalised British citizen in 1915, the year before he died. Most of James's greatest works, such as *Portrait of a Lady*, *The Wings of the Dove* and *The Golden Bowl*, deal with interactions between the inhabitants of the centuries-old civilisations of Europe and the brasher, less sophisticated but more vital products of America. As he grew older his style, already elaborate, became yet more prolix and one critic alleged that there were three versions of the writer – James I, James II and The Old Pretender. An enthusiast, on the other hand, claimed that his idea of Heaven was 'eating *pâté foie de gras* and reading Henry James'.

........

## JEFFERIES, RICHARD (1848–1887) *naturalist and writer, lived here*
59 FOOTSCRAY ROAD, ELTHAM, SE29

## RICHARD JEFFERIES
20 SYDENHAM PARK ROAD, SE26 **LEWISHAM COUNCIL**

Born on a farm in a village near Swindon, Jefferies began his working life as a journalist on a local paper and came to the attention of a wider public in the early 1870s with natural history articles published in national magazines. For the rest of his life he produced a stream of books about the English countryside, often the Wiltshire countryside that he knew well, and the people who made a living from it. He also wrote fiction, including the once well-known children's book, *Bevis: The Story of a Boy*, and *After London*, a strange fable of the future in which the capital has become swampland and the central character traverses a landscape reverted to nature. Jefferies suffered from tuberculosis and died of the disease when still in his thirties.

........

## JELLICOE, ADMIRAL OF THE FLEET, OM (1859–1935) *lived here*
25 DRAYCOTT PLACE, SW3

Born in Southampton, Jellicoe had a distinguished naval career and was also commander of an international expedition overland to relieve legations trapped in Peking during the Boxer Rebellion of 1900. Aware of the need to modernise the Navy, Jellicoe became a gunnery expert and a protegé of the dynamic, reforming First Sea Lord, Sir John Fisher. At the outbreak of the First World War, he was given command of the Grand Fleet and in that role, he directed the British forces at the inconclusive Battle of Jutland in 1916. Churchill, angered by what he saw as a failure to act with sufficient boldness, is supposed to have remarked sourly that 'Jellicoe contrived to snatch defeat from the jaws of victory.' Jellicoe himself gave a fairer account of his caution during the engagement when he said, 'I had always to remember that I could have lost the war in an afternoon.'

........

## JENNINGS, HUMPHREY (1907–1950) *documentary film maker, lived here 1944–1950*
8 REGENT'S PARK TERRACE, NW1

'To the real poet,' Humphrey Jennings once wrote, 'the front of the Bank of England may be as excellent a site for the appearance of poetry as the depths of the sea.' Jennings himself found his most evocative poetry in images of Britain at war, becoming one of the great documentary film-makers of the Second World War. In his feature film *Fires Were Started* and in shorts such as *Listen to Britain*, he managed to encapsulate the kind of England and English values for which many believed they were fighting. The range of Jennings's artistic activities during his short life is remarkable. He helped to organise the International Surrealist Exhibition in London in 1936; he was one of the founders of Mass Observation, the pioneering exercise in social research which began in the late 1930s. Most of all, he made films. Interested in the medium from his schooldays, Jennings joined the GPO Film Unit in 1934. When this evolved into the Crown Film Unit in 1940, devoted to film-making for the war effort, he went on to become its most successful director. Only five years after the war ended, Jennings died on the Greek island of Poros, when he slipped and fell from a cliff face while scouting locations for a new film.

## JEROME, JEROME K. (1859–1927) *author, wrote 'Three Men in a Boat' while living here at Flat 104*

91–104 CHELSEA GARDENS, CHELSEA BRIDGE ROAD, SW1

Born in the Midlands but brought up in east London, Jerome K. Jerome, on leaving school, joined the great army of the city's lowly paid clerks. Escaping to become an actor and journalist, he made his name with the bestselling tale of a middle-class trio and their misadventures on a Thames boating expedition, *Three Men in a Boat*. Jerome went on to write much else, including successful plays and a less successful sequel to his bestseller called *Three Men on the Bummel*, but it is his story of the Thames trip that is remembered. In later years he reminisced nostalgically about the time in Chelsea Gardens when he was writing it. 'It was summer-time and London is so beautiful in summer. It lay beneath my window, a fairy city veiled in golden mist, for I worked in a room high above the chimney-pots; and at night the lights shone far beneath me, so that I looked down as into an Aladdin's cave of jewels.'

## JINNAH, MOHAMMED ALI (QUAID I AZAM) (1876–1948) *founder of Pakistan, stayed here in 1895*

35 RUSSELL ROAD, W14

It was when he was in London studying to become a lawyer that Jinnah, who had been born in Karachi in 1876, stayed for a time in Russell Road. After his return to India Jinnah became a successful lawyer and a member of the Indian National Congress. However, in 1913, he also joined the Indian Muslim League and, as its President, became increasingly disillusioned with both Gandhi's ideas on civil disobedience and Congress's domination by its Hindu majority. He resigned from the Congress party and, by 1940, he was demanding the creation of a separate Muslim state, Pakistan, once the sub-continent was freed from British rule. Against British unwillingness to partition the country, Jinnah could point to the fact that his party won virtually every seat in areas with a Muslim majority in the elections of 1946 and, when that failed to impress, many of his Muslim League followers took to using the more direct arguments of riots and violence. The British acquiesced in 1947 and Jinnah, Quaid-I-Azam or Great Leader, became first Governor-General of the newly created state. He died the following year.

## *This house was built for* AUGUSTUS JOHN (1878–1961), *painter*

28 MALLORD STREET, SW3

When Augustus John, as a leading portrait painter, was sent to paint Montgomery, the Field Marshal was not impressed. 'Who is this chap?' he asked. 'He drinks, he's dirty and I know there are women in the background.' Montgomery was right on all three scores. John prided himself on his bohemianism from the time he spent as a precociously talented draughtsman at the Slade School in the last years of the nineteenth century to his later years as a Grand Old Man of British art. Today, his reputation and his flamboyant painting have been overshadowed by the renewed critical appreciation of the much quieter and subtler work of his sister, Gwen. However, his paintings of gypsy life have an undeniable vitality and his portraits of writers as diverse as Thomas Hardy and Dylan Thomas are strikingly effective. The house in Mallord Street was built for John by the Dutch architect Robert Van t'Hoff and he lived there from 1914 until the mid-thirties.

## JOHNSON, AMY (1903–1941) *aviator, lived here*

VERNON COURT, HENDON WAY, NW2

'Amy, wonderful Amy', as the popular song of the thirties called her, was a Yorkshirewoman, born in Hull, who worked in a solicitors' office in London and seemed destined for an unexceptional life until she went to see the 1928 film *Wings*. So captivated was she by the image of the pilot presented by the movie that she decided to learn to fly herself in her spare time. Two years later she was one of the most famous women in the country, heroine of an epic solo flight from Britain to Australia. She married another air pioneer, Jim Mollison, in 1932 and together they undertook further publicity-grabbing flights, but the marriage ended in divorce in 1938. During the war Amy Johnson was commissioned as a pilot with the Air Transport Auxiliary and was killed when her plane, veering drastically off-course in bad weather, crashed into the Thames estuary.

## JOHNSON, DAME CELIA (1908–1982) *actress, was born here*
46, RICHMOND HILL, TW10

When she was asked once if she had any regrets about her career, the English actress Celia Johnson is said to have replied, 'Well, I'd have liked to have leant against walls in thrillers.' Unfortunately, no-one ever thought of casting her in a thriller. Instead, she was seen as a middle-class English everywoman and her most famous role will always be that of Laura Jesson, unexpectedly discovering love at a railway station in David Lean's *Brief Encounter*. Born in the house on Richmond Hill which now bears the Blue Plaque, Celia Johnson went on to study at RADA (because she 'thought it might be rather wicked', she later claimed) and was a familiar face on the London stage long before she became even better known on the screen. The first film role, which brought her any real attention, three years before *Brief Encounter*, was in the Noel Coward wartime film *In Which We Serve* and many of her earlier appearances were in adaptations of Coward plays. Throughout her career, she continued to be seen more on the stage than on the screen but she became one of Britain's most admired actresses and was created a Dame of the British Empire in 1981. She was married to the writer Peter Fleming, brother of the creator of James Bond.

## JOHNSON, DENIS (*c.* 1760–1833) *from his workshop on this site in 1819 made and sold Britain's first bicycle in its hobby-horse form*
69–75 LONG ACRE, WC2   WESTMINSTER

For many years Long Acre was the centre of London's coachmaking industry and Denis Johnson was a master coachmaker who worked at 75 Long Acre from 1818. During his period there he came across a wooden, two-wheel velocipede that a German nobleman had invented. Johnson used his skills as a coachmaker to improve the machine and patented the result under the name of the 'pedestrian curricle'. The wheeled machine was propelled by the rider's legs pushing against the ground and, under the nickname of 'the hobby-horse', was a passing craze on the streets of Regency London. Johnson continued as a coachmaker but he had patented what was undoubtedly Britain's first, if primitive, bicycle.

## JOHNSON, DR SAMUEL (1709–1784) *author, lived here. Born 1709. Died 1784.*
17 GOUGH SQUARE, EC4   CITY OF LONDON

*In a house on this site* DR SAMUEL JOHNSON *lived between 1765–1776*
JOHNSON'S COURT, FLEET STREET, EC4   CITY OF LONDON

DR SAMUEL JOHNSON *once occupied a room near the gatehouse*
ANCHOR BREWERY, SOUTHWARK BRIDGE ROAD, SE1   PRIVATE

It was Dr Johnson who famously said that when a man is tired of London he is tired of life. Yet Johnson himself was not a Londoner. Like so many of the city's most eminent citizens over the centuries, he became one. He arrived in London, accompanied by David Garrick, in 1737, in flight from failure as a schoolmaster and in pursuit of literary glory. He was slow to find it and came to know only too well the perils of hack writing. It was in Gough Square that he and his assistants worked for almost a decade on the work that was finally to rescue him from Grub Street, his *Dictionary of the English Language*, published in 1755. It made his reputation and, in 1762, a crown pension freed him of money worries. The following year he met Boswell and the process by which Johnson was transformed into the legendary figure of Boswell's biography was begun. The years in which Johnson and Boswell knew one another were the ones in which Johnson became indisputably the leading literary figure of his day and his gifts for brilliant conversation were shown to best effect. In 1773 Johnson and Boswell undertook a tour of Scotland and the Hebrides, which resulted in books by both of them, Johnson's *Journey to the Western Isles* and Boswell's *Tour of the Hebrides*. Yet, although Johnson was north of the border, he remained unrepentantly metropolitan, remarking to his companion at one point, 'By seeing London, I have seen as much of life as the world can show.' On his return to the city he continued to dominate London literary life for a further ten years and when he died, in 1784, he was buried in Westminster Abbey.

*In this house, occupied by* THOMAS DAVIES, *bookseller,* DR SAMUEL JOHNSON
*first met* JAMES BOSWELL *in 1763*

8 RUSSELL STREET, COVENT GARDEN, WC2

When Boswell arrived in London in 1762 he was a young man eager to meet the lions of the literary and social worlds. His particular desire was to be introduced to the great Samuel Johnson, and he tried on a number of occasions to engineer an encounter. When the first meeting came, however, it was by chance. Boswell knew Thomas Davies, an actor turned bookseller, and, on 16 May 1763, he was sitting with Davies and his wife in a small room behind the bookshop when Johnson entered. Boswell, knowing of Johnson's prejudice against the Scots, jokingly asked Davies not to say where he was from. Davies promptly introduced Boswell as a Scotsman. 'Mr Johnson,' Boswell said, 'I do indeed come from Scotland, but I cannot help it.' 'Sir,' replied Johnson, 'that, I find, is what a very great many of your countrymen cannot help.' From this unpromising beginning sprang a friendship that lasted more than twenty years, until Johnson's death, and occasioned the writing of what is generally taken to be the greatest biography in the language, Boswell's *Life of Johnson*.

......................................................................................................................

JOHNSTON, EDWARD (1872–1944) *master calligrapher, lived here 1905–1912*
3 HAMMERSMITH TERRACE, W6

Born in Uruguay of British parents, Johnston showed an early interest in lettering and he spent much time as a young man in the British Museum, studying the medieval illuminated manuscripts there. In 1899 W.R. Lethaby appointed him the first teacher of lettering at the Central School of Arts and Crafts and among his earliest pupils was the teenage Eric Gill. Johnston also taught at the Royal College of Art for many years. He produced superb calligraphic alphabets for private presses and wrote two notable books on his craft, but his most familar design is seen, in modified form, by millions of commuters and tourists each year. Johnston was responsible for the bull's eye symbol used by London Underground.

......................................................................................................................

JONES, DR ERNEST (1879–1958) *pioneer pyschoanalyst, lived here*
19 YORK TERRACE EAST, REGENT'S PARK, NW1

Not only did Ernest Jones, in effect, introduce psychoanalysis to Britain, but he was also Freud's official biographer. On Jones's fiftieth birthday, Freud wrote to him, 'I have always numbered you among my inmost family', and Jones remained committed to the Freudian cause throughout his life. Born near Glamorgan, Jones studied in Cardiff and London and research work in neurology brought him into contact with Freud's writings, then little known outside Austria and Germany. Jones was an immediate convert and he was soon a personal friend of the founder of psychoanalysis. In 1913 Jones founded the British Psychoanalytical Society and in 1920 the *International Journal of Psychoanalysis*, which he edited for thirteen years. His biography of Freud was published in the 1950s. Among Jones's other publications, mostly on psychoanalytical subjects, was a work on figure skating, a sport of which he was an enthusiastic exponent.

---

## JORDAN, MRS DOROTHY (NÉE BLAND) (1762–1816) *actress, lived here*
### 30 CADOGAN PLACE, SW1

## DOROTHY JORDAN (1762–1816)
### ASHBERRY COTTAGE, HONOR OAK ROAD, SE23    **PRIVATE**

Born in Ireland, Dorothy Bland made her first appearance on the stage in Dublin as a teenager and made her London debut at the Drury Lane Theatre in 1785. She was an instant success and remained one of the theatre's leading attractions for nearly thirty years, specialising in comedy roles and cross-dressing or 'breeches' parts. Hazlitt wrote of her that 'She was all gaiety, openness and good nature. She rioted in her fine animal spirits and gave more pleasure than any other actress, because she had the greatest spirit of enjoyment in herself.' It was not only on the stage that she gave great pleasure. She had a string of lovers and in 1790, the mother of five children already, she began her liaison with the Duke of Clarence, later William IV. Together they ushered ten little Fitzclarences into the world. William, under pressure to marry and produce an heir, ended the relationship in 1811 and, although Mrs Jordan continued to appear on stage in London, she fell into debt and escaped to France to evade her creditors. She died there in 1816.

---

## JOYCE, JAMES (1882–1941) *author, lived here in 1931*
### 28 CAMPDEN GROVE, W8

Born in Dublin, Joyce left Ireland for Paris in 1902 and, apart from a period following his mother's death the following year, he returned rarely and never for very long. He lived mostly in Trieste and Zurich for the rest of his life. His short stories were published as *Dubliners* in 1914 and his most famous work, *Ulysses*, was published in Paris on his fortieth birthday, 2 February 1922. The book deals with the events of one day (16 June 1904, the date on which Joyce had taken his first walk with Nora Barnacle, his lifelong partner) and the wanderings through Dublin of its two central characters, Stephen Dedalus and Leopold Bloom. Not every critic liked it – Virginia Woolf described it in enigmatic but unmistakably unflattering terms as 'merely the scratching of pimples on the body of the boot-boy at Claridges' – and it was not until 1936 that it was freely available in Britain. It is now seen as one of the central texts of modernism. For the rest of his life Joyce laboured over a work in progress that appeared finally in one volume as *Finnegans Wake* in 1939. During his stay in Campden Grove in 1931 Joyce chose to formalise his relationship with Nora Barnacle and the two were married on 4 June at Kensington Registry Office.

---

## KALVOS, ANDREAS (1792–1869) *Greek poet and patriot, lived here*
### 182 SUTHERLAND AVENUE, W9

Kalvos was born on the Greek island of Zakynthos and, after his father's death in 1812, travelled to Florence where he met the Italian poet Ugo Foscolo. He accompanied the older poet to Zurich and then to London, where Kalvos married an English woman. After her death he returned to Italy, involving himself in the activities of the Carbonari and publishing most of the poems by which he is best remembered. In the mid-1820s, disillusioned with both poetry and the politics of the Carbonari and the Greek Revolution, Kalvos retired to Corfu where he stayed for more than twenty years. From 1852, Kalvos lived once more in London, married again and died in the capital in 1869. In 1960 his remains were transferred to his home country.

......................................................................................................................

## KARLOFF, BORIS (WILLIAM HENRY PRATT) (1887–1969) *actor, was born here*
36 FOREST HILL ROAD, SE22

The silent film star Lon Chaney once advised William Henry Pratt, better known as Boris Karloff, that the route to success in the movies was to find something that other actors can't or won't do. Karloff was in his forties before he found the opportunity to make the most of Chaney's advice, but his appearance as Frankenstein's monster in the 1931 film, a role that Bela Lugosi had turned down, began his long and successful career as Hollywood's favourite horror actor. The son of a civil servant, Karloff was educated at an English public school and at London University and his family expected him to join the diplomatic service. However, he emigrated to Canada in 1909 and soon found himself work as an actor with a small touring company. This was the life he led, in Canada and the USA, for the next decade. For the decade after that he appeared in small roles in silent films before sound hit Hollywood and, a few years later, Karloff got his lucky break and made the big time. He continued to appear in horror movies, of varying degrees of quality, for the rest of his life.

......................................................................................................................

## KARSAVINA, TAMARA (1885–1978) *ballerina, lived here*
108 FROGNAL, NW3

Karsavina, born in St Petersburg, was the daughter of a well-known dancer and learnt her art at the Imperial Ballet School. However, her greatest successes as a ballerina came not with classical ballet but with the avant-garde company run by Diaghilev. She was the partner of the legendary Nijinsky and, between 1909 and 1913, the pair created most of the leading roles in new ballets choreographed by Michel Fokine, including the two famous and revolutionary works by Stravinsky, *The Firebird* and *Petrushka*. Karsavina married an English diplomat and moved to London after the First World War, becoming a Vice-President of the Royal Academy of Dancing and a much respected teacher who influenced younger generations of ballerinas, most notably Margot Fonteyn.

......................................................................................................................

## KEATS, JOHN *poet, lived in this house, b. 1795, d. 1821*
KEATS HOUSE (WENTWORTH PLACE), KEATS GROVE, HAMPSTEAD, NW3

*In a house on this site, The Swan and Hoop,* JOHN KEATS, *poet was born 1795*
MOORGATE PUBLIC HOUSE, 85 MOORGATE, EC2   **CITY OF LONDON**

Keats was born in London and went to school in Enfield. After leaving school he was apprenticed to an apothecary and he was himself licensed to practise in the profession, but chose to abandon it and concentrate on the writing of poetry. His first volume of verse was published in 1817 and attracted some favourable attention. It was also one of the targets of a vicious and snobbish critical assault by *Blackwood's Magazine* on the alleged literary and social pretensions of what the magazine termed the 'Cockney School' of poetry. Keats' younger brother Tom died of tuberculosis the following year and Keats, who had nursed him and was showing symptoms of the disease himself, moved into a house in Hampstead owned by a friend, the house now known as Keats House. It was at this time, despite ill health and the complications of his love for Fanny Brawne, who was living, with her family, next door, that Keats entered upon an extraordinary period of creativity, writing most of the poems, including 'Ode to a Nightingale' and 'Ode on a Grecian Urn', by which he is best remembered. However, he continued to grow sicker throughout the following two years and, after a last journey to Italy in search of a climate kinder to his tuberculosis, he died in Rome in 1821.

---

## KELLY, SIR GERALD (1879–1972) *portrait painter, lived here 1916–1972*
### 117 GLOUCESTER PLACE, W1

Gerald Kelly was a portrait painter to the establishment. Educated at Eton and Cambridge, he studied art in Paris and, uninterested in the experiments of the modernists, soon began to make his name in his chosen field. He was elected a Royal Academician in 1930 and became President of the Royal Academy for five years in the early 1950s. Among his best-known works are the state portraits he painted of George VI and his wife, the present Queen Mother, in 1945, the year Kelly himself was knighted.

---

## KELVIN, LORD (1824–1907) *physicist and inventor, lived here*
### 15 EATON PLACE, SW1

Born in Belfast, the son of a mathematics professor, William Thomson moved with his family to Glasgow in 1832. He attended university there and then studied at Cambridge before returning to Glasgow as professor of natural philosophy at the exceptionally early age of twenty-two. He remained in the post for more than half a century. Thomson was one of the most gifted exponents of both pure and applied science in the nineteenth century. He is remembered particularly as the man whose researches led to the first successful transatlantic telegraph cable in 1866 and for devising the 'absolute' scale of temperature that is named after him. Knighted for his work on the telegraph, Thomson was given the title of Lord Kelvin in 1892. The inscription on the memorial statue in his native Belfast sums up his career in science: 'He elucidated the laws of nature for the service of man.'

---

## KEMPE, CHARLES EAMER (1837–1907) *stained glass artist, lived and worked here*
### 37 NOTTINGHAM PLACE, W1

One of the most prolific artists in stained glass of the nineteenth century, Charles Eamer Kempe worked to revive the traditions of medieval craftsmanship and was associated with kindred spirits like William Morris in the creation of windows for both ecclesiastical and domestic buildings. Kempe's work can be seen all over the country but particularly fine examples are in St John's College, Oxford, in Durham Castle and in the parish church at Burford where a Jesse window shows his craftsmanship at its best.

---

## KENYATTA, JOMO (c. 1894–1978) *first President of the Republic of Kenya, lived here 1933–1937*
### 95 CAMBRIDGE STREET, SW1

Born in a village in what was then British East Africa, Kamau wa Ngengi (later to re-name himself Jomo Kenyatta) was educated at a mission school and worked as a clerk and a storekeeper before entering politics in the mid-1920s. In 1924, he joined the Kikuyu Central Association, founded to represent the interests of Kikuyu farmers in the colony, and rose rapidly in its ranks, becoming its general secretary three years later. He spent much of the 1930s and 1940s away from Africa, largely in London and other parts of the UK, but returned to Kenya immediately after the Second World War to become one of the leaders in the struggle for independence. Imprisoned for several years because of his assumed involvement with the Mau Mau Rebellion, he was released in time to become first prime minister and then president of the new Kenyan Republic. During his time in London, he worked briefly as a film extra and he can be seen playing a tribal chief in the Korda brothers' version of *Sanders of the River*, a novel by Edgar Wallace which is an uncritical celebration of the colonial rule in Africa which Kenyatta helped so much to sweep away.

---

## KEYNES, JOHN MAYNARD (1883–1946) *economist, lived here*
### 46 GORDON SQUARE, BLOOMSBURY, WC1

Born in Cambridge where his father (who outlived his famous son by three years) was a don, Keynes was educated at Eton and King's College. As an undergraduate and a young don he met many of the people who formed the nucleus of what became known as the Bloomsbury Group and he was to become a leading member of the group. During the First World War he was an adviser to the Treasury and he was present at the Versailles Peace Conference but resigned his position to protest against the punitive economic terms being imposed on Germany. *The Economic Consequences of the Peace*, published in 1919, was strikingly prescient about what those consequences might be. The depression in the thirties was the background for his enormously influential 1936 book *A General Theory of Employment, Interest and Money*. Appalled by the way a self-regulating market treated jobs and families as no more than 'a by-product of the activities of a casino', Keynes proposed a new and more interventionist role for governments in overseeing their economies. During the Second World War he was Britain's representative at the Bretton Woods Conference, from which the ideas of the IMF and the World Bank emerged. Keynes was, by this time, a sick man and he died in 1946.

---

## KHAN, SIR SYED AHMED (1817–1898) *Muslim reformer and scholar, lived here 1869–1870*
### 21 MECKLENBURGH SQUARE, WC1

Sir Syed Ahmed Khan was one of the great figures in the Muslim community in the British Raj and a man who strove to demonstrate that Muslims could be true to their Islamic identity and yet still flourish in a British-ruled India. Born in Delhi, Khan witnessed the tragic events of the Mutiny in 1857 and the consequences for Muslims. He realised that the future depended on the acquisition of Western knowledge and education and, to that end, he founded the Anglo-Oriental College at Aligarh. This was to educate entire generations of Indian Muslim leaders and to develop into the Aligarh Muslim University. Sir Syed Ahmed Khan's memory is revered in Pakistan and amongst the Muslims of India.

---

## KINGSLEY, CHARLES (1819–1875) *writer, lived here*
### 56 OLD CHURCH STREET, CHELSEA, SW3

Although probably little read today, Kingsley was one of the best known and influential of mid-Victorian writers. A clergyman, who became Professor of Modern History at Cambridge, he was drawn to the Christian Socialism advocated by F.D. Maurice and wrote *Alton Locke*, the story of a Chartist tailor, to highlight the suffering of those working in the sweated labour of the clothing trade. He wrote other fiction, including the historical novels *Hypatia* and *Westward Ho!*, but his best-known work today is *The Water-Babies*, a children's book in which the harshly treated chimney-sweep's boy Tom runs away from his master and is transformed into a water-baby. Not everybody appreciated Kingsley's brand of muscular Christianity. Gerard Manley Hopkins wrote that, 'he had a way of talking . . . with the air and spirit of a man bouncing up from the table with a mouth full of bread and cheese and saying that he meant to stand no blasted nonsense. There is a whole volume of Kingsley's essays which is all a munch and a not-standing-any-blasted-nonsense from cover to cover.'

## KINGSLEY, MARY (1862–1900) *traveller and ethnologist, lived here as a child*
### 22 SOUTHWOOD LANE, N6

Until her early thirties Mary Kingsley, the niece of the novelist Charles Kingsley, lived the life of a typical Victorian spinster, caring for her invalid parents. When they both died she was able to fulfil her long-standing wish to travel but, instead of a leisurely tour of the Continent, she chose to head for West Africa. In 1893 and 1894 she spent five months travelling and observing native customs around the Congo River. Her second journey started in December 1894 when she landed on the coast of Gabon and took a canoe up the Ogooué River. Her book *Travels in West Africa* was published in 1897. Three years later, during the Boer War, she went to South Africa as a nurse where she died of enteric fever.

## KIPLING, RUDYARD (1865–1936) *poet and story writer, lived here 1889–1891*
### 43 VILLIERS STREET, WC2 · REPLACES PLAQUE PUT UP IN 1940

Kipling's parents met at a picnic on the shore of Lake Rudyard in Staffordshire, which explains his unusual forename, but he was born in Bombay where his father was teaching at an art school. Sent to school in England, an experience he hated, Kipling returned to India in 1882 and worked as a journalist in Lahore. He was already writing poetry and short sketches and, when he ventured back to England in 1889, he was set to make his name in literary London. B*arrack Room Ballads* and several volumes of short stories were followed by *The Jungle Book*, written when, following marriage to an American, Kipling was living in Vermont. His best-known novel, *Kim*, was published in 1901 after his return from America. In 1907 he was the first English writer to be given the Nobel Prize for Literature. His stay in Villiers Street was at a time when, despite a burgeoning reputation, he was often short of cash. Luckily his rooms were above the premises of 'Harris the Sausage King' who, Kipling wrote, 'for tuppence gave as much sausage as would carry one from breakfast to dinner'.

## KITCHENER OF KHARTOUM, FIELD MARSHAL EARL, KG (1850–1916) *lived here 1914–1915*

### 2 CARLTON GARDENS, SW1

'If Kitchener was not a great man', Margot Asquith once remarked, 'he was, at least, a great poster.' His fiercely moustachioed countenance, staring out of the recruiting poster, and accusatory finger, pointing at the youth of Britain, together with the words 'Your Country Needs YOU' beneath, form one of the most familiar images of the First World War. Herbert Kitchener joined the army in 1870 and, after the usual campaigns in faraway places that were the lot of the Victorian professional soldier, won fame as the victor at the Battle of Omdurman in 1898, reconquering the Sudan and avenging the traumatic death of Gordon in Khartoum thirteen years previously. During the Boer War he became Commander-in-Chief and was largely responsible for the ruthless treatment of the Boers, which caused much controversy. Appointed War Minister at the beginning of the First World War, he foresaw a longer conflict than many of his contemporaries imagined possible and was the driving force behind the early recruitment campaigns. He drowned off the Orkneys in June 1916 when the ship he was on struck a mine.

---

## KLEIN, MELANIE (1882–1960) *psychoanalyst and pioneer of child analysis, lived here*

42 CLIFTON HILL, NW8

Born in Vienna into a solidly middle-class Jewish family, Melanie Klein was married at the age of twenty-one to a businessman whose work meant they had to travel widely, often far away from the intellectual stimulation she found in Vienna. In Budapest in 1910, already the mother of three children, she discovered the work of Sigmund Freud and, with it, her vocation. She underwent personal analysis with two of Freud's closest associates, Sandor Ferenczi and Karl Abraham, and her continuing interest in psychoanalysis led to her estrangement, and eventual divorce, from her husband. Qualified as a psychoanalyst she moved to England in 1926 where she lived, practised and wrote for the rest of her life. Klein's particular interest lay in the psychoanalysis of children, on which she wrote widely, and her views of the immense importance of fantasy in the first two years of life and the intense, ambiguous relationship between baby and mother were, and continue to be, controversial.

---

## KNEE, FRED (1868–1914) *London Labour party pioneer and housing reformer, lived here*

24 SUGDEN ROAD, SW11

Born in Frome, Somerset, Fred Knee left school to be apprenticed as a printer and later worked as a reporter for a local newspaper. Moving to London in 1890 he continued to work as both printer and journalist and became very involved with the nascent Labour movement of the period. He joined the Fabian Society and wrote frequently for the Labour journals and papers, but his most important work probably dates to his time as Secretary of the Workmen's National Housing Council, a pioneering attempt to form a pressure group demanding basic housing rights for the working classes. Knee lived at the address in Sugden Road between 1898 and 1901.

---

## KNIGHT, JOHN PEAKE (1828–1886) *inventor of the world's first traffic lights which were erected here 9 December 1868*

12 BRIDGE STREET, SW1  **WESTMINSTER**

Born in Nottingham, John Peake Knight left school at the age of twelve to work at Derby railway station and, over the next thirty years, worked his way up to a senior position on the London to Brighton line. In the mid-1860s fatalities on London's roads were very high and Knight, who also showed his ingenuity in many safety improvements on the railways, suggested introducing a signalling system similar to that used on the railways. The first traffic lights, all of 24 feet high, were installed in 1868 at the junction of Bridge Street, Parliament Street and Great George Street. Semaphore arms operated during the day, gas-lit coloured lights by night. Sadly, in the same year they were installed, a gas leak caused the lights to explode, injuring a passing policeman, and the experiment was abandoned.

---

## KNIGHT, DAME LAURA (1877–1970) AND HAROLD KNIGHT (1874–1961) *painters, lived here*

16 LANGFORD PLACE, ST JOHN'S WOOD, NW8

Laura Johnson was born in Derbyshire and attended Nottingham School of Art where she met the man who was to become her husband, fellow painter Harold Knight. Married in

1903, the Knights lived first in Staines on the Yorkshire coast and then in Cornwall where they stayed for more than a decade, part of a growing artistic colony there, and produced some of their most characteristic work. In later years Harold gained a reputation particularly as a portrait painter and Laura produced a long series of distinctive but idealised paintings of circus and gypsy life.

## KOKOSCHKA, OSKAR (1886–1980) *painter, lived here*
EYRE COURT, FINCHLEY ROAD, NW8

Born in Austria, Kokoschka began his career in the feverish Expressionist circles of pre-First World War Vienna. He was painter, draughtsman, author of controversial dramas and, for two years, the lover of the formidable Alma Mahler, widow of the composer. Badly wounded in the war, he taught in Dresden from 1919 to 1924 and then spent many years in travel, years that produced a series of intense views of great European cities. He was outspoken in his opposition to the Nazis and moved first to Prague and then, in 1938, to England. He became a naturalised British citizen in 1947, but from the 1950s lived and worked increasingly in Switzerland and his native Austria. In his longevity and in the range of his subject and style, Kokoschka was one of the major visual artists of the century.

## KORDA, SIR ALEXANDER (1893–1956) *film producer, worked here 1932–1936*
21/22 GROSVENOR STREET, W1

To the rest of the world in the 1930s, Alexander Korda *was* the British film industry. While other producers and directors were content to produce so-called 'quota quickies' for domestic consumption, it was Korda who had the ambition to try and beat Hollywood at its own game. With his company London Films and *The Private Life of Henry VIII* (1933), he succeeded. Starring Charles Laughton as the Tudor king the film was a worldwide blockbuster. When he arrived in Britain in 1931, Korda had already had a varied career in the movies. Born Sandor Kellner in a small village in Hungary, Korda had worked as a director and producer in Budapest, Paris, Berlin and Hollywood before deciding that London offered the best opportunities for a man of his talents and energies. After the success of *Henry VIII* he built Denham Studios outside London where he established his own roster of stars, including his second wife Merle Oberon. Other major movies – *Rembrandt, Things to Come, The Thief of Baghdad* – followed. During the Second World War, Korda spent much time in the USA, where he became a co-founder of the Society of Independent Motion Picture Producers and entered into a joint production deal with MGM. The venture ended in dispute and disagreement, however, and Korda re-launched his London Films company, which oversaw the making of further classic British movies, including *The Third Man* and Olivier's *Richard III*. Korda, the Eastern European who once jokingly remarked, 'It is not enough to be Hungarian; you must have talent too', became one of the greatest figures in British film history, and the BAFTA award for Best British Film is fittingly named after him.

## KOSSUTH, LOUIS (1802–1894) *Hungarian patriot, stayed here*
39 CHEPSTOW VILLAS, W11

Louis, or Lajos, Kossuth is remembered as one of the great national heroes of Hungary, the man who devoted his life to the struggle for independence from the Hapsburg Empire. Born into a noble family, he was briefly a lawyer and then edited a liberal and nationalist journal. In 1848, the year of Revolutions, he demanded independent government for Hungary and, at the head of a Committee of National Defence, set about organising the military means to achieve it. It was Kossuth who pressured the National Assembly in 1849 to declare that the Hapsburgs had forfeited their rights over the country and it was he who was, briefly, governor of the new Hungary. After the Hapsburgs defeated the Hungarian nationalists at the Battle of Temesvar in

August 1849, Kossuth went into an exile that lasted the rest of his long life. In the 1850s he lived mostly in London, where he was acclaimed as an exemplar of liberal values and beliefs, but his last decades were spent in Turin, writing memoirs of his own life and a history of the country to which he had devoted it.

---

## KROPOTKIN, PRINCE PETER (1842–1921) *theorist of anarchism, lived here*
6 CRESCENT ROAD, BROMLEY

A member of the old Russian nobility who served in the Imperial Army for five years, Kropotkin none the less became convinced of the importance of anarchism. Arrested and imprisoned in 1874 for spreading his anarchist ideas, Kropotkin escaped two years later and began his long years of exile, largely spent in London. It was not until the Russian Revolution in 1917 that he was able to return home, although he found the state that Lenin was forging unsympathetic. Kropotkin, who was also a geographer of international standing, published several classic works of anarchist thought, most notably *Mutual Aid* in 1902.

---

## LABOUCHERE, HENRY (1831–1912) *radical MP and journalist, lived here 1881–1903*
ST JAMES INDEPENDENT SCHOOL FOR BOYS, POPE'S VILLA, 19 CROSS DEEP, TWICKENHAM

During his lifetime, Henry Labouchere was renowned both as a campaigning journalist and as an unconventional, witty and flamboyant politician. As a journalist he was famous in his day for the despatches he sent from Paris when it was under siege in 1870 and 1871, and as the founder of the periodical *Truth* which, for many years, exposed social, political and financial scandals. As a politician he first sat in the House of Commons as a Liberal but his urbanely sardonic opinion of his leader (he once remarked that he did not 'object to Mr. Gladstone's always having the ace of trumps up his sleeve but only to his pretence that God had put it there') meant that he was never comfortable as a party yes-man. For the last twenty-six years of his career in the Commons, he sat as an unaffiliated and independent Radical. In an irony that he probably wouldn't have appreciated, this radical/liberal politician is now most often remembered in connection with a parliamentary intervention that resulted in the prosecution of gay men that lasted for eighty years. During a debate on the 1885 Criminal Law Amendment Bill, Labouchere proposed an amendment that extended criminal punishment to men taking part in 'any act of gross indecency', whether in private or in public. His amendment was carried and formed the legal basis for the prosecution of gay men up until the 1960s.

---

## THE LABOUR PARTY *was founded here, 27 February 1900*
CAROONE HOUSE, FARRINGDON STREET, EC4 ·
THE SITE OF THE CONGREGATIONAL MEMORIAL HALL

---

## LAMERIE, PAUL DE (1688–1751) *the King's silversmith, lived and worked 1738–1751*
40 GERRARD STREET, W1   **WESTMINSTER**

Born in the Netherlands, Paul de Lamerie came with his parents to join the Huguenot community in London when he was a small child. After an apprenticeship with another Huguenot craftsman, Pierre Platel, de Lamerie established his own business and, over the years, became one of the most important silversmiths of the eighteenth century, whose work was valued by royal and aristocratic families throughout Europe. An innovative designer and skilful entrepreneur, de Lamerie was also a friend of many of the leading artists and craftsmen in London at the time, including Hogarth. He moved his shop and living quarters to Gerrard Street, from their previous location in Great Windmill Street, in 1738.

## LAMB, CHARLES 'ELIA' (1775–1834) *lived here*
64 DUNCAN TERRACE, N1

CHARLES LAMB *was born in the chamber which formerly stood here 10 February 1775. 'Cheerful Crown Office Row (place of my kindly engendure) . . . a man would give something to have been born in such places.'*

2 CROWN OFFICE ROW, TEMPLE, EC4   **PRIVATE**

*This house was occupied by* CHARLES LAMB *September 1827 to October 1829*
CLARENDON COTTAGE, 85 CHASE SIDE, ENFIELD   **PRIVATE**

*This house was occupied by* CHARLES LAMB *October 1829 to May 1833*
WESTWOOD COTTAGE, CHASE SIDE, ENFIELD   **PRIVATE**

CHARLES LAMB *lived here*
WALDEN COTTAGE, EDMONTON   **PRIVATE**

CHARLES LAMB (1775–1834) *and* MARY LAMB (1764–1847), *writers, lived here*
LAMB'S COTTAGE, CHURCH STREET, EDMONTON, N9

Charles Lamb was born in the Temple, where his father was a lawyer's clerk, and went to school at Christ's Hospital. There he formed a lifelong friendship with Coleridge. From his twenties onwards Lamb wrote poetry, a number of not very successful dramas and books for children, often written in conjunction with his sister Mary, including the well-known *Tales from Shakespeare*. His most characteristic work is to be found in the essays he published under the pseudonym 'Elia'. Lamb's life was shaped by a family tragedy in the 1790s. His sister Mary, in a fit of insanity, fatally stabbed their mother and was committed to an asylum. She was released into the care of Charles, who spent the rest of his life looking after her. For many years Lamb worked at the East India House, but one anecdote suggests he was not an ideal employee. His superior rebuked him for bad time-keeping, saying 'You arrive late, Mr Lamb.' 'Yes, but see how early I leave,' Lamb replied.

## LAMBERT, CONSTANT (1905–1951) *composer, lived here 1947–1951*
197 ALBANY STREET, REGENT'S PARK, NW1

The son of a successful society portrait painter, Lambert was born in London and achieved his first triumph as a student at the Royal College of Music when Diaghilev commissioned him to write a ballet, *Romeo and Juliet*. Throughout the later twenties and thirties, Lambert was one of the leading young British composers and works such as *The Rio Grande*, heavily influenced by the jazz music that he much admired, continue to be regularly played. Later, in a career cut short by illness and an over-fondness for the pleasures of alcohol, Lambert was an innovatory and imaginative conductor of ballet, particularly for the Sadler's Wells company. A witty and erudite music critic, he also wrote one book, *Music Ho!* (1934), which remains worth the attention of any music-lover who likes strong opinions trenchantly expressed.

## LANG, ANDREW (1844–1912) *man of letters, lived here in 1876–1912*
1 MARLOES ROAD, W8

The man of letters is now an endangered, if not extinct, species. Andrew Lang was a prime example of the man of letters at the time, the late Victorian period, of his greatest influence.

Born in Selkirk, Lang became an Oxford don but arrived in London in 1875 intent on making his career as a writer and literary journalist. For the rest of his life he was both awesomely prolific and awesomely versatile and, although dismissed loftily by Henry James as cultivating 'the puerile imagination and the fourth-rate opinion', his work, particularly in the field of folklore and fairy tales, remains of interest. Lang also wrote poetry, fiction (including a novel in collaboration with his friend Rider Haggard), historical works on his native Scotland, translations of Homer and many volumes of essays and reviews.

......................................................................................................................................

## LANGTRY, LILLIE (1852–1929) *actress, lived here*
CADOGAN HOTEL, 21 PONT STREET, SW1


## LILLIE LANGTRY
8 WILTON PLACE, SW1 **PRIVATE**

Born on the Channel Islands, the daughter of the Dean of Jersey, Lillie Langtry (known as 'the Jersey Lily') is remembered as much for her beauty and her status as one of Edward VII's favourite mistresses as for her acting triumphs. However, despite the stigma attached to 'well-bred' ladies such as herself treading the boards, she appeared on stage for many years and several playwrights, including Oscar Wilde, wrote parts especially for her. In her early career she was also one of the first celebrities to earn money by appearing in magazine advertisements and endorsing particular products. 'Since using Pears' Soap for the hands and complexion,' she assured would-be purchasers of the toiletry in 1879, 'I have discarded all others.' The Jersey Lily was also a keen student of the Turf and became one of the foremost racehorse owners of her time.

......................................................................................................................................

## LASKI, HAROLD (1893–1950) *teacher and political philosopher, lived here 1926–1950*
5 ADDISON BRIDGE PLACE, W14

Laski was one of the leading intellectual figures of the Left during his lifetime and had a major influence on the ideology and legislative philosophy of the Labour party in the years immediately before and after the Second World War. Born in Manchester, the son of a Jewish merchant, Laski defied his father by marrying outside the Jewish community in 1911, the same year he began his undergraduate career at Oxford. A brilliant student, he went on from Oxford to teach in America before taking up a post at the LSE in 1920, becoming Professor of Political Science there six years later. Laski was to have a major impact on generations of students, many of whom went on to political careers. He was a member of the Labour party from the time of the First World War and was at the height of his political influence during his period on the party's National Executive, in the late thirties, and as its Chairman, in the first year of the Attlee government.

......................................................................................................................................

## LAUDER, SIR HARRY (1870–1950) *music hall artist, lived here 1903–1911*
46 LONGLEY ROAD, TOOTING, SW17

Lauder emerged from an impoverished childhood in Edinburgh and Arbroath, in which the death of his father had forced him to act as a breadwinner for the family at a very early age, to become one of the most popular and best-paid stars of the music hall. His kilted and tartan-clad figure presented an easily identifiable image of Scottishness and songs such as 'Roamin' in the Gloamin' and 'Just a Wee Deoch an' Doris', pitched midway between comedy and pathos, were successes not only in his native country but also with audiences in London and America. In 1919 Harry Lauder was knighted for his work in entertaining the troops at the Front in the First World War, a war in which he had lost his only son. He continued to perform and tour after the war (he toured the US twenty-two times in total) and, although he retired in the thirties, his final stage appearance came in 1947 at a small concert in the Gorbals in which the seventy-seven-year-old Lauder performed eight of his old songs, ending with the sentimental but affecting 'Keep Right On to the End of the Road'.

## LAUGHTON, CHARLES (1899–1962) *actor, lived here 1928–1931*
### 15 PERCY STREET, W1

Born in Scarborough, where his family ran a hotel, Laughton was drawn to the stage and was a star performer at RADA in the early 1920s. From there he moved on to West End success and marriage to a fellow actor, Elsa Lanchester, before launching what was to be a remarkable career as a film actor. His performance as Bluff King Hal in Alexander Korda's *The Private Life of Henry VIII* demonstrated his ability to project larger-than-life figures on to the screen and he went on to play such memorable roles as Quasimodo in *The Hunchback of Notre Dame* and Captain Bligh in *Mutiny on the Bounty*. These later films were made in Hollywood and Laughton spent much time in the US, eventually becoming an American citizen in 1950. He directed one movie, *The Night of the Hunter*, in 1955. With his great bulk and boisterous energy, Laughton might have been born to play Falstaff but he never did so, once refusing the part with the remark, 'I had to throw too many of his kind out of our hotel when I was sixteen.'

## LAVERY, SIR JOHN (1856–1941) *painter, lived here 1899–1940*
### 5 CROMWELL PLACE, SW7

Born in Belfast, Lavery was orphaned at an early age and sent to Scotland to be educated in Ayrshire. He studied at the Glasgow School of Art and later in London and Paris. Particularly successful as a portrait painter (his painting of the dancer Anna Pavlova is well known) he was knighted in 1918 and became a Royal Academician three years later. His second wife was Hazel Martyn, a beautiful young American artist thirty years his junior. In London in the early 1920s their salon became a common ground where English and Irish politicians involved in Treaty negotiations could meet and Lady Lavery's powerful friends included such disparate personalities as Michael Collins and Winston Churchill. Her face later appeared on the old Irish £1 note and she became one of the most easily recognised women in twentieth-century Ireland.

## LAWRENCE, DAVID HERBERT (1885–1930)
*novelist and poet, lived here in 1915*
### 1 BYRON VILLAS, VALE OF HEALTH, HAMPSTEAD, NW3

Born in Nottinghamshire, the son of a coalminer, Lawrence studied at the local university and taught as an elementary school teacher before publishing his first novel in 1911. Over the next two decades, until his early death from tuberculosis, Lawrence led a nomadic life with his German wife (she was distantly related to the First World War flying ace Baron von Richthofen) and moved from Cornwall to Australia, Italy to Mexico. Despite all the moves, Lawrence managed to produce an enormous body of work. He published poetry, short stories, novellas, essays and travel books as well as the great novels – *Sons and Lovers*, *The Rainbow*, *Women in Love* – on which his fame largely rests. Throughout his career Lawrence found himself in trouble for his frankness, particularly about sex, and, while he and Frieda were living in Byron Villas, *The Rainbow* was declared obscene by magistrates in London. His last novel, *Lady Chatterley's Lover*, which Lawrence himself thought was 'an honest, healthy book', was not published in an unexpurgated version in Britain until thirty years after his death.

## LAWRENCE, SUSAN (1871–1947) *social reformer, lived here*
### 44 WESTBOURNE TERRACE, W2

One of the first women to gain a leading position in the Labour party, Susan Lawrence trained as a mathematician at University College, London, and was elected to the LCC as an independent in 1910. Three years later she transferred her allegiance to the Labour party and served on London's governing body for another fifteen years. In the twenties she served two separate terms as Labour MP for East Ham North and she was Chairman of the Party in 1929/30.

## LAWRENCE, T.E. (1888–1935) *'Lawrence of Arabia', lived here*
### 14 BARTON STREET, SW1

Someone once described T.E. Lawrence as having 'a genius for backing into the limelight'. Before the First World War he worked as an archaeologist, helping to excavate the Hittite city of Carchemish. During the war he was appointed adviser to Prince Faisal, leader of the Arab revolt against the Turks, and, revealing an unexpected talent for guerrilla warfare, helped to mould the Arabs into an effective fighting force. The media seized on Lawrence's military success and his penchant for wearing Arab dress to create the image of the romantic hero that was to haunt him for the rest of his life. His years after the war were an ambivalent flight from fame. He changed his name twice and joined the RAF as an ordinary aircraftman. Yet he also wrote *The Seven Pillars of Wisdom*, which perpetuates the myth of the glamorous desert hero. In May 1935, retired from the RAF and living in Dorset, Lawrence was riding a motorcycle when he swerved to avoid a group of children. He was thrown off the bike and killed.

## LEAR, EDWARD (1812–1888) *artist and writer, lived here*
### 30 SEYMOUR STREET, W1

## EDWARD LEAR
### BOWMAN'S MEWS, SEVEN SISTERS ROAD, N1    BOROUGH OF ISLINGTON

Today Lear is best known for his nonsense rhymes, written for the amusement of his patron's grandchildren. Lear himself, almost certainly, would prefer to be remembered not as the creator of the 'Dong with the Luminous Nose', the 'Yonghy-Bonghy Bo' and 'the Pobble who has no toes', but as the skilled draughtsman and watercolourist that he was. He began his career drawing parrots in the Zoological Gardens and was engaged by the Earl of Derby to produce illustrations of the animals in his private menagerie. Later Lear was able to travel extensively, both around the Mediterranean and further afield in India, publishing illustrated books of his travels on his return. He lived for many years in Italy and died in San Remo in 1888. Lear, who never married, suffered from an unfortunate combination of epilepsy and depression, and the underlying melancholy of his nature can be seen beneath the surface of his nonsense verse.

## LECKY, W.E.H. (WILLIAM EDWARD HARTPOLE) (1838–1903) *historian and essayist, lived and died here*
### 38 ONSLOW GARDENS, SW7

The son of an Irish landowner, Lecky was educated at Trinity College, Dublin, and went on to become one of those prodigiously productive nineteenth-century historians whose collected works fill several bookshelves. His reputation was made by his *History of the Rise and Influence of the Spirit of Rationalism in Europe*, published in 1865, which showed a characteristically Victorian enthusiasm for the power of reason and an equally characteristic distrust of religious dogma. His greatest work was an eight-volume *History of England in the Eighteenth Century*, later extended to twelve, which appeared between 1878 and 1890. Lecky's emphasis in these volumes was on the later part of the century and, particularly, the relationship between England and his native Ireland. His chapters on Ireland were later published separately. Despite his commitment to Ireland, Lecky was a firm opponent of Home Rule and, as Unionist MP for Dublin University for the eight years before his death, argued consistently against its advocates in Parliament.

## LEIGH, VIVIEN (1913–1967) *actress, lived here*
54 EATON SQUARE, SW1

Born in Darjeeling, Vivian Mary Hartley (Leigh was a stage name taken from her first husband's forename) went to the Royal Academy of Dramatic Art as a teenager and was soon appearing in British films. She was signed to a five-year contract by the legendary producer Alexander Korda who, in 1937, cast her opposite Laurence Olivier in a film called *Fire Over England*. The two stars began a tempestuous relationship that spelled the end for both their marriages. Two years later she won the much publicised prize of the role of Scarlett O'Hara in *Gone With the Wind*. That an English actress should play a Southern belle was much commented on but George Cukor, originally scheduled to direct the film, said she got the part because 'there was an indescribable wildness about her' as if she was 'possessed of the devil'. She won an Oscar for her performance. Now married to Olivier, she continued a career on stage and screen and won a second Oscar, this time as a faded Southern belle, in *A Streetcar Named Desire*. In later life she suffered both personal problems – the marriage to Olivier broke up – and difficulties with her health, and she died of tuberculosis while still only in her fifties.

## LEIGHTON, FREDERICK LORD (1830–1896) *painter, lived and died here*
LEIGHTON HOUSE, 12 HOLLAND PARK ROAD, W14

Frederick, Lord Leighton was the embodiment of the Victorian art establishment. Born in Scarborough, the son of a physician, he showed great artistic talent at an early age and spent many years studying abroad, in Brussels, Paris and Rome. His first major painting, *The Procession of Cimabue's Madonna*, was the sensation of the 1855 Royal Academy exhibition and was bought by Queen Victoria. Leighton's subsequent career was one in which success seemed to follow effortlessly upon success. He was elected President of the Royal Academy in 1878, the year in which he was also knighted. He was made a baronet seven years later and raised to the peerage in the year of his death. Leighton House is one of the more extraordinary buildings to be distinguished by a Blue Plaque. Open to the public as a museum, it is a miniature monument to High Victorian taste. Its most striking feature is the Arab Hall, completed in 1879, whose walls are richly decorated with blue tiles collected by Leighton from the Middle East. Beneath a dome inlaid with coloured glass, also from the Middle East, is a small fountain.

## LENO, DAN (1860–1904) *music hall comedian, lived here 1898–1901*
56 AKERMAN ROAD, SW9

'London,' Dan Leno wrote of the city in which he lived, 'is a large village on the Thames where the principal industries carried on are music halls and the confidence trick.' At the height of the music hall's influence Dan Leno was one of its greatest stars. 'I came into the world a mere child,' he claimed and he was born in Agar Town, a slum area now covered by St Pancras Station, in 1860. By the time he died at an early age, worn out by endless appearances on stage, by alcoholism and bouts of insanity, he was a legendary figure, admired both by ordinary people who saw their lives reflected in his act and by many intellectuals who marvelled at his theatrical presence. Max Beerbohm wrote of him, 'I defy anyone not to have loved him at first sight, the moment he capered on the stage with that air of wild determination, squirming in every limb with some deep grievance that must be outpoured, bent but not broken, faint but pursuing, incarnate of the will to live in a world not at all worth living in.'

LETHABY, WILLIAM RICHARD (1857–1931) *architect, lived here 1880–1891*
20 CALTHORPE STREET, WC1

WILLIAM RICHARD LETHABY (1857–1931) *architect and first principal of this school 1896 to 1911*
CENTRAL ST MARTIN'S COLLEGE OF ART AND DESIGN,
SOUTHAMPTON ROW, WC1

Lethaby came to London in 1879 to work with the eminent architect Norman Shaw, and he remained with him until establishing his own firm in 1891. In 1896 Lethaby was chosen to be the founding principal of the Central School of Arts and Crafts (amalgamated in 1989 with St Martin's College of Art to form Central St Martin's College of Art and Design), and his ideas on art and design education, put into practice there, were to be influential as far afield as the Bauhaus in Germany. In 1900 Lethaby was also made Professor of Design at the Royal College of Art. Between 1906 and 1928 he was surveyor of Westminster Abbey and he published widely on architectural history, including volumes on the Abbey and on medieval art in Britain.

LEVER, WILLIAM HESKETH, 1ST VISCOUNT LEVERHULME (1851–1925)
*soap-maker and philanthropist, lived and died here*
INVERFORTH HOUSE, NORTH END WAY, NW3

The son of a Bolton grocer, William Lever made his immense fortune through a new method of manufacturing soap. Created from vegetable oils rather than the tallow traditionally used, Lever's 'Sunlight' soap was instantly popular with the public and, by the 1890s, his factory was producing 40,000 tons of it a year. Other household products – including Lifebuoy carbolic soap and Vim – followed, and Lever's fortune was assured. He entered politics as a Liberal MP in 1906, Lloyd George raised him to the peerage in 1917, and he became a Viscount three years before his death. Lever's philanthropy was on a scale to match his wealth. At Port Sunlight, his purpose-built factory on the Mersey, he created a model town for his workers, including hundreds of houses, two schools, a library, a museum and, later, an art gallery in memory of his wife. His most ambitious philanthropic project ended, however, in failure. At the end of the First World War, in an attempt to stimulate the economy of the Hebrides, Lever bought the islands of Lewis and Harris and planned a huge fishing and fish products industry there. The idea foundered in the face of persistent hostility from many of the locals. Lever died in 1925 and is buried at Port Sunlight. The company he founded in 1884 survives as the multinational conglomerate Unilever.

LEWIS, PERCY WYNDHAM (1882–1957) *painter, lived here*
61 PALACE GARDENS TERRACE, W8

Born on his father's yacht, off the coast of Nova Scotia, Wyndham Lewis lived in America as a small boy until his parents came to England in 1888. He studied at the Slade School of Art and then in Paris for several years, returning to England to become the dominant and noisiest figure in

Vorticism, the only genuinely home-grown modern movement in the visual arts in Britain. *Blast: The Review of the Great English Vortex* was a magazine edited by Lewis and Ezra Pound in 1914 and 1915, in which they scathingly criticised almost everybody in the arts apart from themselves and a select group of friends. As well as his work as a painter, Lewis expressed his ideas as a novelist in books like *Tarr* and *The Apes of God* but, as the twenties and thirties wore on, those ideas became increasingly fascist. Since his gift for making enemies was legendary, Lewis grew more and more isolated until he was fully deserving of Auden's description of him as 'that lonely old volcano of the Right'. After the Second World War, which Lewis spent in exile in Canada, he continued to write and a projected four-part fiction remained unfinished at his death.

## LEWIS, ROSA (1867–1952)
### CAVENDISH HOTEL, JERMYN STREET   **WESTMINSTER**

Born in the East End, Rosa Lewis owed her rise in society to her talents as a cook. In her twenties, these talents were employed by a succession of gourmet English aristocrats, including Lady Randolph Churchill, whose young son Winston was reputed to have once strayed into the kitchen, only to be chased out by Rosa with the cry of, 'Hop it, copper nob!' Edward VII, when Prince of Wales, was particularly delighted by her culinary skills and she was but one of the many women with whom he was alleged to have had an affair. Rosa Lewis bought the Cavendish Hotel in 1902 and ruled the roost there for the next fifty years. In later life, she was a London legend. She appears, very thinly disguised, as Lottie Crump in Evelyn Waugh's novel *Vile Bodies* and her eccentricity and cockney charm are celebrated in innumerable memoirs of the inter-war years. In the 1970s, the BBC drama T*he Duchess of Duke Street* owed much to Rosa's career at the Cavendish and Louisa Trotter, the character played by Gemma Jones, is very obviously based on her.

## LEWIS, TED 'KID' (1893–1970) *World Champion Boxer, lived and died here*
### NIGHTINGALE HOUSE, NIGHTINGALE LANE, SW12

Ted 'Kid' Lewis was one of the finest boxers Britain has ever produced and became welterweight world champion for the first time in 1915. He lost the title to the American Jack Britton the following year but won it again in 1917 and held on to it for two further years before Britton beat him once more. Born Gershon Mendeloff in the East End of London, Lewis assumed the name by which he is best known when he first stepped into the ring as a teenager and continued to use it for the rest of his life. Lewis's most controversial fight was with the French boxer Georges Carpentier and took place at London's Olympia in May 1922. Lewis had moved up a weight to fight at light-heavyweight but was still a stone and a half lighter than the Frenchman. None the less he was clearly winning the fight when Carpentier took what seemed to be unfair advantage of the referee's decision to stop proceedings to warn Lewis for holding and threw a punch the Londoner was not expecting. Lewis was knocked out and Carpentier was declared the victor amidst the booing of the London crowd. After his career as a boxer ended, Lewis worked briefly as a bodyguard for the politician Oswald Mosley in the days before Mosley's anti-Semitism became only too clear. According to Lewis's son, the day his father realised that Mosley was unashamedly anti-Semitic, he burst into the politician's office, punched him on the nose, handed in his resignation and left.

## LEYBOURNE, GEORGE (1842–1884) *music hall comedian 'Champagne Charlie', lived and died here*

### 136 ENGLEFIELD ROAD, N1

Some songs of the Victorian music hall linger on in the popular consciousness more than a hundred years after they were written. Two such songs were the work of George Leybourne. The 'daring young man on the flying trapeze', who 'flew through the air with the greatest of ease', was Leybourne's invention as was the persona of Champagne Charlie ('Champagne Charlie is my name/Champagne drinking is my game'), the monocled and bewhiskered indulger in 'fizz'. Sadly the character's habits reflected Leybourne's own and, after a period as one of the stars of the music hall, Leybourne was overcome by years of heavy drinking. He died in the house at Englefield Road, aged only forty-two.

## LILLY, WILLIAM (1602–1681) *master astrologer lived in a house on this site*
STRAND UNDERGROUND STATION, STRAND   **WESTMINSTER**

Famous in his own time, Lilly still has a high reputation among astrologers today and his book *Christian Astrology*, first published in 1647, remains in print in a number of different editions. He was born in Leicestershire and came to London as a young man to act as secretary to a gentleman named Gilbert Wright. When Wright died, Lilly married his widow and soon embarked on the occult and astrological studies that led to some calling him 'the English Merlin'. On at least one occasion, Lilly's supposed ability to look into the future put him in danger. In 1666, in the aftermath of the Great Fire of London, he was brought before a parliamentary committee and asked to explain predictions in a book *Monarchy or No Monarchy in England* which he had published fifteen years earlier. In the book, Lilly had included a number of woodcuts as illustrations of his visions, one of which showed a city by a river in flames. Suspecting his involvement in a plot to raze London to the ground, the committee members questioned him closely. Had he not been able to provide an explanation of the image, he might have well have faced dire consequences – even execution – but he was able to convince the MPs of his innocence.

## *In a house on this site lived* THOMAS LINACRE *physician (1460–1524)*
WALL AT REAR OF GPO (FARADAY BUILDING), KNIGHTRIDER STREET, EC4
**CITY OF LONDON**

Thomas Linacre was one of the earliest advocates in England of the new learning of the Renaissance. Born in Canterbury, he travelled in Italy where he encountered the enthusiasm for the rediscovery of texts from the ancient world and was taught Greek. He, in turn, passed on his knowledge of Greek to others, including Thomas More, on his return to England. In Italy he had also completed his medical studies and, later in life, he became one of Henry VIII's physicians and tutor to the young Princess Mary. As the king's physician he was largely instrumental in founding the Royal College of Physicians, the oldest medical society in England, in 1518.

## LIND, JENNY (MADAME GOLDSCHMIDT) (1820–87) *singer, lived here*
189 OLD BROMPTON ROAD, SW7

Jenny Lind, 'the Swedish Nightingale', was the Stockholm-born soprano who was a sensational success as a performer throughout Europe and America but was particularly triumphant on the London stage. By the time she arrived in England in May 1847 she had already been acclaimed in her native Sweden and in Berlin for roles in operas by, most notably, Bellini, Weber and Meyerbeer. For her appearance at Her Majesty's Theatre, Haymarket, in *Robert de Normandie* the audience included Queen Victoria and Prince Albert and an excited crowd of opera-lovers who had paid lavish prices and fought through immense crowds of onlookers in the Haymarket to take their seats. Jenny Lind's operatic career was relatively short but she went on to become a regular concert-singer and performer in oratorio. She married her accompanist Otto Goldschmidt in 1852 and, with him, she founded the London Bach Choir. She was appointed Professor of Singing at the Royal College of Music in 1883.

## LINDLEY, JOHN (1799–1865) *botanist and pioneer orchidologist, lived here from 1836 and died here*

BEDFORD HOUSE, THE AVENUE, W4

We owe the fact that we can all enjoy the beauties of Kew Gardens very largely to John Lindley. It was his investigation in 1838 into the conditions at the gardens that led him to recommend that they be turned over to the nation and used as the botanical headquarters for the country and his recommendations were acted upon. Born in Norwich, where his father owned a nursery garden, Lindley went on to become one of the leading botanists of the Victorian age. In addition to the part he played in the history of Kew, his list of achievements is remarkable. He was involved in the work of the Horticultural Society (later the Royal Horticultural Society) for many years; he lectured in botany at University College, London from the 1820s to the 1860s; he published many volumes on plants and their cultivation and was a founder editor of the magazine *The Gardeners' Chronicle*. He is also often described as the 'father of modern orchidology'. The middle of the nineteenth century was a period when more and more species of orchid were being discovered. It was Lindley who recognised that a systematic classification was required and it was he who provided one which has formed the basis for all such classification since his day.

## LINNELL, JOHN (1792–1882) *painter, lived here.* WILLIAM BLAKE (1757–1827), *poet and artist, stayed here as his guest*

'OLD WYLDES', NORTH END, HAMPSTEAD, NW3

In the course of his long life Linnell proved his originality and versatility as an artist many times. When he was only fourteen years old his draughtsmanship was brought to the attention of the landscape painter and art patron Sir George Beaumont, and he went on to study at the Royal Academy Schools. During a career of many decades he produced landscapes (mostly scenes from the Home Counties), watercolours, sculpture, engravings and portraits of many early Victorian worthies including Peel and Carlyle. However, he is best known for the insight and penetration which made him a friend and patron of Blake when that visionary genius had few supporters. Linnell assisted Blake in gaining financial help from the Royal Academy, he commissioned his engravings for *The Book of Job* and he became the nucleus of that group of younger artists, known (paradoxically) as 'the Ancients', who so revered and admired Blake in his last years. Although Blake enjoyed staying with Linnell at 'Old Wyldes', then part of an estate owned by Eton College, he was always possessed by a hypochondriac certainty that the area was exceptionally bad for his health.

## LISTER, JOSEPH LORD (1827–1912) *surgeon, lived here*

12 PARK CRESCENT, W1

In the mid-nineteenth century, despite advances in surgical and anaesthetic techniques, about half of those who underwent major surgery died as a result of their operations, succumbing to blood poisoning or gangrene. The man who did most to reduce that death rate was Joseph Lister. Lister attended University College, London, taking first an arts degree and then a medical degree, and it was while he was still at the college that he began to study the problem of septic poisoning. However, it was only when the French chemist Pasteur announced his theory of fermentation and putrefaction in 1862 that Lister was able to make the connection between invisible germs in the air and the post-operative deaths he saw every day. By this time Lister was Professor of Surgery at Glasgow University and Chief Surgeon at the Royal Infirmary there. He was able to put his theories into practice and his advocacy of cleanliness and antiseptics was soon seen, thanks to a dramatically reduced death rate, to work. In 1877 Lister was appointed to the chair of Clinical Surgery at King's College Hospital and moved into the house in Park

Crescent. He lived there until 1902, years in which his methods were adopted throughout the world and honours were heaped upon him. He was raised to the peerage in 1897, the first man to receive this reward for his services to medicine, and, five years later, was one of the original members of the Order of Merit.

## LLOYD GEORGE, DAVID, EARL LLOYD GEORGE OF DWYFOR (1863–1945)
*Prime Minister, lived here*

3 ROUTH ROAD, SW18

In a rather purple passage from his *Essays and Sketches in Biography*, Keynes described Lloyd George as 'This goat-footed bard, this half-human visitor to our age from the hag-ridden magic and enchanted woods of Celtic antiquity.' On another occasion Keynes is supposed to have said that when Lloyd George was alone in a room there was no one there. Both quotations reflect the paradoxical nature of one of the most successful and the most unfathomable of twentieth-century politicians. He entered Parliament in 1890 as MP for Caernarvon Burghs, the constituency he represented for more than half a century, and quickly demonstrated his oratorical powers and his political skills. As Chancellor of the Exchequer from 1908 to 1915 he introduced many radical reforms, including National Insurance and old age pensions. As Prime Minister from 1916, after Asquith had been deposed, to 1922 he was an effective war leader but his coalition with the Conservatives, continued after the war, destroyed his own Liberal party. By the end of the twenties he was presiding over a Liberal party that had only forty seats. Yet, even as late as 1940, Churchill wanted Lloyd George in his War Cabinet. Lloyd George excused himself on the grounds of age. He was made an earl in the year he died.

## LLOYD, MARIE (1870–1922) *music hall artiste, lived here*
55 GRAHAM ROAD, E8

The Queen of the music hall, Marie Lloyd was loved both by working-class audiences and by intellectual critics like T.S. Eliot and Max Beerbohm, who wrote of her that 'sheer joy of living was always her strongest point'. Born Matilda Wood, she made her debut on the stage as a teenager calling herself Bella Delmere but she soon changed her name to Marie Lloyd and, under this new identity, she rapidly became a star and remained one until her death. Her songs 'Don't Dilly Dally', 'The Boy I Love Sits Up in the Gallery', 'One of the Ruins That Cromwell Knocked About a Bit' ranged from the sentimental to the *risqué*, but all seemed somehow expressive of a particularly Cockney resilience in the face of life's difficulties. Marie Lloyd's own life had more than its share of difficulties. She was married three times, to largely feckless husbands, and was, towards the end of her life, increasingly dependent on drink. She was also often in conflict with music hall managers, because of her uncompromising defence of performers' rights, and was ostentatiously excluded from the first Royal Command Performance in 1912. She responded by adding a message to the posters outside the theatre where she was appearing: 'Every Performance by Marie Lloyd is a Command Performance by Order of the British Public.'

## LOCKYER, SIR NORMAN (1836–1920) *astronomer, physicist and founder of* Nature, *lived here 1876–1920*

16, PENYWERN ROAD, EARLS COURT, SW5

Norman Lockyer was one of the great and good of British science for more than half a century. Born in Rugby, the son of a schoolmaster, he began his career as a civil servant in the War Office, but his interest in astronomy and physics soon made him a well-known figure in the scientific world of Victorian Britain. He was elected to the Royal Society in 1862 and, in 1890, he was made the world's first professor of Astronomical Physics at the Royal College of Science in South Kensington. Lockyer's achievements over his long life were many and varied. He founded what became (and remains) one of the world's most prestigious scientific journals, *Nature*, and edited it for fifty-one years. He was the first to identify and name the element helium, recognising it as a new element from the spectroscopic observations of a solar eclipse. Lockyer also has a claim on being the founder of astro-archaeology. In his sixties he became fascinated with the idea that ancient sites, particularly Stonehenge, were built in alignment with the movement of heavenly bodies, and he published several books on the subject.

## LONDON AUXILIARY AMBULANCE SERVICE (1939–1945)
### STATION 39, WEYMOUTH MEWS  **WESTMINSTER**

The London Auxiliary Ambulance Service (LAAS) was formed in the summer of 1939 to assist the established emergency services in the treatment of those Londoners expected to be injured in the forthcoming war. At its height, the LAAS had more than 10,000 volunteer workers, most of them women, operating from 130 stations around the capital. During the devastating London raids of 1940–1941, and the renewed dangers of the V1 and V2 rocket attacks of the last two years of the war, the volunteers of the LAAS showed great courage and dedication in reaching and treating injured civilians. The plaque is on the wall of what was Station 39 in Weymouth Mews, Mayfair – one of the first stations to open in August 1939 and one of the last to close in July 1945.

## *Here lived* JOHN AND JANE LOUDON (1783–1843) AND (1807–1858). *Their horticultural work gave new beauty to London squares*
### 3 PORCHESTER TERRACE, W2

Born in Scotland, John Claudius Loudon was one of the most influential of nineteenth-century gardeners and he published widely on the subject including, most notably, an *Encyclopedia of Gardening* in 1822. He married his wife in 1830 and she too became a writer on matters horticultural, publishing in 1841 *The Ladies' Companion to the Flower Garden*. In the garden of their home in Porchester Terrace they created and tended a collection of nearly two thousand different species of plants. It was the Loudons who recommended the use of plane trees for the adornment of many London squares and Loudon himself, in his work on conservatories and glasshouses, invented a form of curving glass that Paxton was to find invaluable when he designed the Crystal Palace.

## LOVELACE, ADA, COUNTESS OF (1815–1852) *pioneer of computing, lived here*
### 12 ST JAMES'S SQUARE, SW1

One of the more exotic figures in the history of computing, Ada Lovelace was the daughter of Lord Byron through his brief and disastrous marriage to Annabella Milbanke. Brought up by her mother, herself a gifted mathematician, Ada showed a strong interest in mathematical studies which, in the context of the times, it was impossible for a woman to pursue in anything other than an amateur way. Introduced to Charles Babbage, who was working on the ideas for his calculating machines, Ada engaged in a long correspondence with him in which she was able at last to exercise her mathematical gifts. In many ways Ada saw the potential of Babbage's machine more clearly than its originator and, in a paper published in 1843, she predicted its use in the creation of graphics and complex music. The computing language ADA acknowledges her prescience and is named in Ada Lovelace's honour. Married to the Earl of Lovelace, Ada died aged only thirty-six, the same age at which her father had died.

## LOW, SIR DAVID (1891–1963) *cartoonist, lived here at No. 33*

MELBURY COURT, KENSINGTON HIGH STREET, W8

David Low was one of the most influential cartoonists of the century, a man of whom it was said, 'he draws as the fishes swim', and the inventor of Colonel Blimp, the walrus-moustached old soldier with politically incorrect opinions whose name has entered the language. Low was born in New Zealand and published his first cartoon in a Christchurch newspaper when he was only eleven years old. He moved to London in 1919, changed his signature from the colonial familiarity of 'Dave Low' to the British formality of 'Low' and began a career that, in the next forty years, saw him published by newspapers like the *Evening Standard* and the *Guardian* and weekly magazines like the *New Statesman* and *Punch*. Low, once described by Churchill as 'a green-eyed young Antipodean radical', was himself a man of the Left but, in his art, he ridiculed the pretensions of all parties. He was knighted in the year before his death.

## LUCAN, ARTHUR (ARTHUR TOWLE) (1887–1954) *entertainer and creator of Old Mother Riley, lived here*

11 FORTY LANE, WEMBLEY

Born in Ireland, Arthur Towle borrowed a stage name from the Lucan Dairy in Dublin and, together with his wife Kitty McShane, launched a successful career as variety performer and, from the thirties onwards, star of low-budget British comedy films. The duo appeared as Old Mother Riley and her daughter Kitty. Lucan developed his character over the years from a relatively standard example of stage Irishness into an inspired creation. Old Mother Riley became a manic bundle of energy, dressed in the garb of an Irish washerwoman, leaping madly about stage or film-set, alternatively wheedling or in a furious tantrum as she attempted to control the behaviour of her spirited and flirtatious daughter. Onstage turbulence was probably made more convincing because of an offstage relationship between Lucan and McShane that was notoriously tempestuous.

## LUGARD, LORD (1858–1945) *colonial administrator, lived here 1912–1919*

51 RUTLAND GATE, HYDE PARK, SW7

Frederick Lugard, as both soldier and administrator, was an exemplary servant of the Empire, particularly in Africa where he was influential in the creation of new territories for the British to rule. After making a name for himself as a soldier in the Sudan and in the annexation of Burma in 1886, Lugard showed his powers as a diplomat in negotiating treaties with local rulers in Uganda in 1890 and 1891. These enabled the British East Africa Company to open the country to British trade and, very shortly afterwards, a British protectorate. For two lengthy periods, divided by a spell as Governor of Hong Kong, Lugard represented the Empire in Nigeria and devised the so-called 'Lugard Rules' for creating a colonial administration on the foundations of pre-existing local institutions.

## LUTYENS, SIR EDWIN

See under entry for JOHN LOUGHBOROUGH PEARSON

*In a house on this site lived from 1854–1875* SIR CHARLES LYELL (1797–1875), *geologist and from 1876–1882* W.E. GLADSTONE (1809–1898), *statesman*

73 HARLEY STREET, W1

Charles Lyell was born in Scotland and educated at Oxford where his interest in geology was aroused. He qualified as a lawyer but spent more and more of his time in geological study, culminating in the four-volume *Principles of Geology* in 1830–33. Subtitled 'An attempt to explain the former changes in the earth's surface by reference to causes now in operation', the books were significant because of Lyell's insistence that the earth was formed not by dramatic, single-event catastrophes but by the long, slow effects of millions of years. In turning upside down the mental world of the nineteenth century, Lyell's ideas were matched and exceeded only by the work of his friend Darwin. It was also Lyell who was instrumental in persuading Darwin that his theories of evolution should be made public. Lyell died in the house in Harley Street in 1875 and the following year Gladstone, then leader of the opposition, moved in. He was living in the house when he returned as Prime Minister in the great Liberal landslide of 1880.

......................................................................................................

## MACAULAY, ROSE (1881–1958) *writer, lived and died here*
HINDE HOUSE, 11-14 HINDE STREET, W1

A travel writer who was reported to have said 'The great and recurrent question about abroad is, is it worth getting there?', and a prolific novelist who nevertheless gave up fiction for ten years, Rose Macaulay was one of the more idiosyncratic writers of the twentieth century. The daughter of a classics don, she studied at Oxford and published her first novel in 1906. She went on to publish many other novels, on both contemporary and historical subjects, but her two best-known works, *The World My Wilderness* and *The Towers of Trebizond*, were published in the last decade of her life after a fictional silence that had begun in 1940. *The Towers of Trebizond* begins with a sentence – ' "Take my camel, dear," said my aunt Dot, as she climbed down from this animal on her return from High Mass' – which must be one of the more arresting opening sentences in English fiction.

......................................................................................................

## MACAULAY, THOMAS BABINGTON, LORD (1800–1859) *historian and man of letters, lived here. This tablet was first erected by the London County Council in 1903 on Holly Lodge which stood on this site. It was re-erected here in 1969*
HOLLY LODGE (NOW ATKINS BUILDINGS, QUEEN ELIZABETH COLLEGE), CAMPDEN HILL, W8

## MACAULAY, ZACHARY (1768–1838) *philanthropist, and his son,* THOMAS BABINGTON MACAULAY, *afterwards* LORD MACAULAY (1800–1859) *historian and man of letters, lived here*
5 THE PAVEMENT, CLAPHAM COMMON, SW4

Zachary Macaulay was a London merchant who devoted much of his energy and capital to the fight against slavery. In his twenties he had witnessed the horrors of the slave trade at first hand and had even spent a period as governor of a colony of freed slaves in Africa. He was a leading member of the group of evangelical Christians known as 'the Clapham Sect' because it centred on Holy Trinity Church, Clapham. His son Thomas Macaulay was one of the leading intellectual figures of Victorian England and renowned in his lifetime as a poet, essayist, politician and historian. His *Lays of Ancient Rome*, poems dealing with episodes of Roman history, have lost their popularity today but were once familiar to generations of schoolchildren. His *History of England*, although it covers only a brief period of time, has great narrative and descriptive power and has been continuously in print since first publication. He was several times elected MP for Edinburgh, a member of the Cabinet before he was forty and raised to the peerage in 1857. Unlike poets such as Arnold and Tennyson, who expressed the doubts and anxieties of the Victorian intellectual, Macaulay – of whom Lord Melbourne once remarked, 'I wish I was as cocksure of anything as Tom Macaulay is of everything' – was the prime representative of the boundless self-confidence of the age.

## MACDONALD, GEORGE (1824–1905) *story teller, lived here 1860–1863*
20 ALBERT STREET, NW1

'I have never concealed the fact that I regarded him as my master,' C.S. Lewis wrote, referring to the Victorian novelist, poet and writer of Christian fantasy George MacDonald and the creator of Narnia is only one of many well-known authors, from G.K. Chesterton to W.H. Auden, who have expressed an admiration for MacDonald. He was born near Aberdeen, the son of a farmer, and was educated at the university there before he made his way south in the late 1840s. After unsuccessful spells as a religious minister in Sussex and in Manchester, he settled in London with the intention of forging a career as a writer. Over the next fifty years he published a wide range of works, from books of poetry to novels of Scottish country life, but it was children's books such as *The Princess and the Goblin* and *At the Back of the North Wind* that gained him his largest readership. MacDonald himself always denied that he was a children's author. 'I write, not for children,' he said, 'but for the child-like, whether they be of five, or fifty, or seventy-five.' More than a century after his death, his books still have the power to enthral both children and adults.

## MACDONALD, RAMSAY (1866–1937) *Prime Minister, lived here 1916–1925*
9 HOWITT ROAD, NW3

### RAMSAY MACDONALD

103 FROGNAL, NW3
**HAMPSTEAD PLAQUE FUND**

In Labour party history, Ramsay MacDonald is the great traitor, the man who abandoned his party to continue as Prime Minister in the National Government formed in 1931. 'Tomorrow,' he said on the eve of taking this step, 'every Duchess in London will be wanting to kiss me.' The thoughts of his own party, which was nearly destroyed at the ensuing elections, were better expressed by the left-wing MP James Maxton, who interrupted MacDonald's last speech as PM in 1935. 'Sit down, man,' Maxton shouted. 'You're a bloody tragedy.' MacDonald was the illegitimate son of a Scottish farm labourer who joined the Independent Labour Party in 1894 and was one of the twenty-nine Labour MPs returned in the 1906 elections. He was leader of the party from 1911–14 and again from 1922–31, during which time he was PM in two minority governments: the first Labour Prime Minister. Entirely dependent on Liberal support, neither government lasted long and, when a financial crisis made minority government unsustainable in 1931, he made the decision that consigned him to Labour's Rogues' Gallery. He continued as PM for four more years, with a largely Conservative Cabinet, and was replaced by Stanley Baldwin.

## McCORMACK, JOHN (1884–1945) *lyric tenor, lived here 1908–1913*
24 FERNCROFT AVE, NW3

More than sixty years after his death, the Irish tenor John McCormack retains much of the star status he possessed when he was alive and performing on stage and record. A John McCormack Society still exists to celebrate his life and his voice. Born in Athlone, where his parents worked in the woollen mills, McCormack first gained national attention for his singing when he took part as a teenager in the Feis Coil, the famous Irish festival of music and dance. Sponsors raised money to send him to Italy to be trained and his career was launched. He made his operatic debut in Italy and, by 1907, he was appearing at Covent Garden. Although he continued to take operatic roles until the 1920s, it was as a concert performer that McCormack really made his mark and he became increasingly popular in the USA. His first recordings were for phonograph cylinder in 1904 and he went on to make hundreds of recordings for the more familiar gramophone. Many of these survive, on which McCormack can be heard singing everything from Puccini arias to Irish nationalist songs like 'The Wearing of the Green', and they bear witness to a voice that still has power to move and charm audiences.

## MCGILL, DONALD (1875–1962) *postcard cartoonist, lived here*
5 BENNETT PARK, BLACKHEATH, SE3

Donald McGill used the very minor art form of the seaside postcard to create a world of his own. It was a world of large-busted, dominating wives, hen-pecked husbands, virago-like landladies and, of course, double entendres by the dozen. In one of his most famous cards a hugely fat man is unaware of the small boy sitting, hidden by his stomach, at his feet and, as the caption says, he 'can't see my little Willy'. This was but one of well over 10,000 designs created by McGill in a career that lasted nearly fifty years. The cartoonist was the subject of a famous essay by George Orwell, who was one of the first to recognise McGill's peculiar, and very English, comic skill.

## MCINDOE, SIR ARCHIBALD (1900–1960) *reconstructive surgeon, lived here in Flat 14*
AVENUE COURT, DRAYCOTT AVENUE, SW3

Archibald McIndoe was the plastic surgeon whose skills were concentrated on treating burned and disfigured airmen in the Second World War. Born in New Zealand in 1900, McIndoe arrived in Britain in 1930 after a period practising and studying surgery in America. His older cousin Harold Gillies was one of the pioneers of plastic surgery and it was on his advice that McIndoe turned from general to reconstructive surgery. In 1938 he was appointed consultant in plastic surgery to the RAF and, during the war, his hospital at East Grinstead helped to rehabilitate, both physically and psychologically, many hundreds of airmen badly disfigured by crashes and fires. Many of those treated by McIndoe formed what was known as the 'Guinea Pigs Club', which is still in existence today. After the war McIndoe was knighted and continued his work, helping to found the British Association of Plastic Surgeons and becoming its third president. McIndoe once described reconstructive surgery as 'the art of ordinary surgery raised to the nth degree of finesse'. When he died in 1960 there were very many who had reason to be grateful for his finesse as a surgeon.

## MACKENZIE, SIR MORELL (1837–1892) *throat surgeon, lived here*
32–33 GOLDEN SQUARE, W1   **WESTMINSTER**

Mackenzie had a distinguished career that was almost entirely eclipsed by one unfortunate misdiagnosis. Soon after qualifying as a surgeon he chose to specialise in diseases of the throat and in 1865, in Golden Square, he opened the first hospital specifically intended for patients suffering from such diseases. Twenty years later, as a recognised authority, he was called upon to examine the German Crown Prince, who had married Queen Victoria's eldest daughter. Mackenzie pronounced the Prince's throat condition to be non-malignant and the surgeon was knighted for his services. His diagnosis was wrong. The following year the Prince, by now the German Emperor Frederick III, died. Censured by the Royal College of Surgeons and his reputation in tatters, Mackenzie himself died in 1892.

## MACMILLAN, DOUGLAS (1884–1969) *founder of Macmillan Cancer Relief, lived here*

15 RANELAGH ROAD, SW1

Born in Somerset, Douglas Macmillan came to London as a young man and he worked as a civil servant there for more than forty years, first for the Board of Agriculture and then for the Ministry of Agriculture and Fisheries. However, it is not for his public service but for his charity work that he is remembered and honoured by the Blue Plaque. In 1912, Macmillan founded the Society for the Prevention and Relief of Cancer. The previous year he had watched his father die painfully of cancer and he was determined to create an organisation that would provide, in his own words, 'homes for cancer patients throughout the land, where attention will be provided freely or at low cost' and 'panels of voluntary nurses who can be detailed off to attend to necessitous patients in their own homes'. In the years since 1912, the charity he founded has changed its name several times – first to the National Society for Cancer Relief and, most recently, to Macmillan Cancer Relief – but the fundamental commitment to the relief of suffering has remained the same.

## THE RACHEL MCMILLAN COLLEGE (1930–1977); MARGARET MCMILLAN, CH (1860–1931) *pioneer of nursery education, lived here*

CREEK ROAD, DEPTFORD, SE8

The sisters Rachel and Margaret McMillan were born in the USA but their mother took them back to her native Scotland after the death of her husband, and they were brought up in Inverness. Both became Christian Socialists, Rachel writing optimistically to a friend in 1887 that 'I think when these teachings and ideas are better known, people generally will declare themselves socialists.' In Bradford, where they lived for a number of years, and in London, where they based themselves permanently in 1902, the sisters were pioneers of medical and educational reform. In 1908 they opened the first school clinic in Bow and six years later followed it with the first open-air nursery school in Peckham. Rachel, who had long suffered from ill health, died in 1917 and her sister gave her name to the college for training nursery-school teachers that opened in Deptford the year before Margaret herself died.

## MACNEICE, LOUIS (1907–1963) POET, LIVED HERE

52 CANONBURY PARK SOUTH, N1

In the thirties a critic imagined a horrible amalgam of all the Left-leaning poets of the day which he called MacSpaunday. The Spaunday came from Stephen Spender, W.H. Auden and C. Day-Lewis. The Mac came from Louis MacNeice. While it is true that MacNeice knew all the other poets from his time at Oxford and his sympathies were with the Left, even in a decade like the thirties his poetry was as much concerned with the personal as with the political. Born in Carrickfergus, the son of a Church of Ireland rector, MacNeice left Oxford with a first and published his first volume of poetry in 1929. Further volumes followed at intervals throughout his life as well as innovative radio plays and, in 1937, a collaboration with Auden, *Letters from Iceland*, which recorded their journey to that country. MacNeice joined the BBC in 1941 and remained until his death in 1963. He died from pneumonia contracted while recording a radio programme in a damp cave.

## *Site of Hindoostane Coffee House 1810 London's first Indian restaurant, owned by* MAHOMED, SAKE DEAN (1759–1851)

102 GEORGE STREET  **WESTMINSTER**

The Hindoostane Coffee House opened in George Street in 1810. Its owner was a remarkable man named Sake Dean Mahomed, who had been born in Bengal and served as a trainee surgeon in the army of the British East India Company. In the 1780s, he had made the momentous decision to accompany the officer he had served – an Anglo-Irishman named Godfrey Evan Baker – on his journey back to Cork and some years later he published *The Travels of Dean Mahomet*, usually reckoned to be the first book written by an Indian in English to be published. Mahomed arrived in London in 1808 and opened his restaurant two years later. It offered, in the words of one of its advertisements, 'Indian dishes in the highest perfection', but the public, it seemed, was not yet ready for them. The Hindoostane closed in 1812. Mahomed, undeterred, moved to Brighton with his Irish wife, Jane, and there they opened a private bathhouse, offering 'the Indian Medicated Vapour Bath, a cure to many diseases and giving full relief when every thing fails.' Indian baths proved very much more successful than an Indian restaurant and he even gained the patronage of royalty when he was appointed 'Shampooing Surgeon' to George IV, a regular visitor to Brighton. Sake Dean Mahomed died in his adopted town in 1851, at the age of ninety-one.

## MALLARMÉ STÉPHANE (1842–1898) *poet, stayed here in 1863*
6 BROMPTON SQUARE, SW3

Mallarmé spent the years 1862/3 in London, intent on improving his English, and for the rest of his life he taught English in various French lycées, mostly in Paris. While in London he married (at Kensington, now Brompton, Oratory) a German governess named Marie Gerhard. Mallarmé found London a congenial place, although perhaps for curious reasons. 'I love this perpetually grey sky,' he wrote. 'You don't need to think. The bright blue sky and the stars are really frightening things. You can feel at home here, and God cannot see you. His spy, the sun, does not care to come out of his shadows.' Mallarmé's earliest poetry was influenced by the Romantics and by Baudelaire. His later work uses elaborate symbols and metaphors, experiments with rhythm and syntax, and plays with the arrangement of words on the printed page. Cryptic and demanding, it has none the less had enormous influence on French poetry during the twentieth century.

## MALLON, DR JIMMY, CH (1874–1961) *warden of Toynbee Hall, champion of social reform, lived here*

TOYNBEE HALL, COMMERCIAL STREET, E1

For thirty-five years Jimmy Mallon was warden of Toynbee Hall, the original Universities' settlement in the East End, founded by Canon Samuel Barnett. Educated at Owens College, Manchester, Mallon was involved in social work in that city and had been secretary of the National League to Establish a Miminum Wage before becoming warden at Toynbee Hall in 1919. He was to remain there until he was nearly eighty years of age. Mallon also wrote on social affairs for a wide variety of magazines and newspapers and was twice a governor of the BBC. He was appointed a Companion of Honour in 1939.

## MALONE, EDMOND (1741–1812) *Shakespearean scholar, lived here 1779–1812*
40 LANGHAM STREET, W1

Born in Dublin and educated there at Trinity College, Edmond Malone was enabled by a large inheritance to settle in London in the 1770s and undertake a literary career. Among his friends were such luminaries as Dr Johnson, Sir Joshua Reynolds and Edmund Burke, who dedicated his *Reflections on the Revolution in France* to him. Malone was also instrumental in ensuring that Boswell's *Life of Dr Johnson* was published, cajoling and encouraging its often drunk and depressed author into completing it. However, the great work of Malone's life was his research into Shakespeare, culminating in the publication in 1790 of a multi-volume edition of the plays, which also included much information about Shakespeare's life and the theatrical world in Elizabethan and Jacobean England. Malone's stature as a Shakespearean scholar meant that he took a leading part in exposing the forgeries of William Henry Ireland who, in the 1790s, claimed to have discovered two hitherto unknown plays by Shakespeare.

## MANBY, CHARLES (1804–1884) *civil engineer, lived here*
### 60 WESTBOURNE TERRACE, W2

Manby worked with his father, who owned an ironworks in the Midlands, and, in the 1820s, was instrumental in the design of one of the earliest iron steamships. Moving to London in 1835 Manby became one of the leading engineers of the day. He was the first permanent full-time Secretary of the Institution of Civil Engineers but he was a restlessly inventive man who had his finger in many pies. He worked with the company established by Robert Stephenson, he patented a system of warming and ventilating buildings and he turned an amateur's interest in the stage into a serious involvement in the management of theatres like the Adelphi and the Haymarket. Manby was also what would today be called a consultant in a number of major engineering projects of the century, including the erection of the Crystal Palace and the construction of the Suez Canal.

## MANNING, CARDINAL HENRY EDWARD (1808–1892) *lived here*
### 22 CARLISLE PLACE, SW1

Henry Manning was, after John Henry Newman, the most significant figure in Roman Catholicism in nineteenth-century England. After taking first-class honours at Oxford he entered the Church of England, espousing High Church views, and he became Archdeacon of Chichester Cathedral and a notably eloquent preacher. In 1851 he converted to Catholicism and, in 1865, became Archbishop of Westminster. Ten years later he was appointed a Cardinal. Manning combined doctrinal orthodoxy in religious matters with a degree of radicalism in his social beliefs. He was a staunch advocate of papal infallability and yet was also a supporter of the rights of working men to form trade unions. He was also a prominent campaigner in the Temperance Movement.

## MANSBRIDGE, ALBERT (1876–1952) *founder of the Workers' Educational Association, lived here*
### 198 WINDSOR ROAD, ILFORD

Born in Gloucester, Mansbridge left school at fourteen to work as a clerk but he was an enthusiastic attender of evening classes who devoted much time to self-improvement and self-education. What he had attained himself, he wished others to attain and, in 1903, when he was working in the Co-operative movement, he and his wife founded an association intended to help working men gain access to higher education. The organisation, soon known as the Workers' Educational Association, rapidly expanded and Mansbridge worked as its national secretary. He refused to accept anything more than an average workman's wage in this post, which he held until 1916. In that year illness forced him to give up the secretaryship but he continued to be an influential and respected figure in the world of further and adult education.

## MANSFIELD, KATHERINE (1888–1923) *writer and her husband* JOHN MIDDLETON MURRY (1889–1957), *critic, lived here*
### 17 EAST HEATH ROAD, NW3

Born in New Zealand, Katherine Mansfield came to Britain in her teens and published her first short story in 1909, the same year that she left her first husband one day after they were married. She met

Middleton Murry two years later when she submitted some stories to a magazine he was editing and they became lovers, eventually marrying in 1918. By that time Mansfield had been diagnosed with tuberculosis and the couple travelled extensively through Europe in search of a climate that would be healthier for her. In 1922 she entered the institute near Paris run by the Russian philosopher Gurdjieff, half-guru, half-charlatan, where she died early the following year. In her literary career of less than fifteen years she published three volumes of short stories (*In a German Pension*, *Bliss* and *The Garden Party*) and won much acclaim as a subtle and original writer. Murry lived on for another thirty-four years, marrying three more times and writing widely on literary figures from Shakespeare to D.H. Lawrence, with whom he had had a turbulent and quarrelsome friendship.

..................................................................................................................................

## MANSON, SIR PATRICK (1844–1922) *father of modern tropical medicine, lived here*
### 50 WELBECK STREET, W1

Known as 'Mosquito Manson' because of the work he undertook with Ronald Ross into the transmission of malaria, Manson was born in Aberdeen and studied medicine there before moving, as a young man, to the Far East. There he was able to observe the more disfiguring symptoms of tropical diseases including elephantiasis, which causes huge swellings of the limbs. Manson traced the culprit to a species of nematode worm and also highlighted the role played by a type of gnat as intermediary between worm and human. Returning to London in 1889, Manson became the recognised authority in tropical medicine, was an adviser to the Colonial Office and established the School of Tropical Medicine in 1899.

..................................................................................................................................

## MARCONI, GUGLIELMO (1874–1937) *the pioneer of wireless communication, lived here in 1896–1897*

### 71 HEREFORD ROAD, W2

*From the roof of this building* GUGLIELMO MARCONI *made the first public transmission of wireless signals. Under the patronage of William Preece FRS, Engineering Chief, The General Post Office, 27 July 1896*

### THE POST OFFICE, ALDERSGATE STREET, EC1 **PRIVATE**

Born in Bologna, of an Italian father and an Irish mother, Marconi became interested in the possibilities of communication by radio waves as a young man when he read about the work of the German scientist Heinrich Hertz. Experimenting initially at the family estate, the Villa Grifone, he succeeded, by the end of 1895, in transmitting radio messages over a distance of more than a mile. Unable to gain funding for further work in Italy the bilingual Marconi came to Britain the following year and gained a useful patron in Sir William Preece, one of the directors of the GPO. In 1900 Marconi's Wireless Telegraph Company was registered and, the following year, the Italian transmitted the first wireless signals across the Atlantic from Cornwall to Newfoundland. Although it cannot be said that Marconi 'invented' radio he was undoubtedly the first to recognise its full commercial and communications potential. He went on to patent many more improvements in the field and to win the Nobel Prize for Physics in 1909.

## MARRYAT, CAPTAIN FREDERICK (1792–1848) *novelist, lived here*

### 3 SPANISH PLACE, W1

The son of an MP, Marryat went to sea at the age of fourteen and was in active service for many years, including a period in charge of a ship that cruised the waters around St Helena to ensure that no escape attempt was made by Napoleon. His experiences in the Navy were put to good use in the novels that he wrote, beginning with *The Naval Officer, or, Scenes and Adventures in the Life of Frank Mildmay*, published in 1829. The following year Marryat resigned from the service to concentrate on writing and produced, on average, a novel a year until his death, including *Peter Simple*, *Jacob Faithful* and *Mr Midshipman Easy*. His last great success was a children's book, *The Children of the New Forest*, in which he deserted the sea to tell a story of heroic Royalists and dastardly Roundheads during the English Civil War.

## MARSDEN, WILLIAM (1796–1867) *surgeon, founder of the Royal Free and Royal Marsden Hospitals, lived here*

### 65 LINCOLN'S INN FIELDS, WC2

In 1827 a young surgeon, William Marsden, found a desperately sick young woman on the steps of St Andrew's, Holborn. At that time all London hospitals demanded a letter of recommendation from a subscriber before they would admit a patient and Marsden was unable to find a hospital bed for the dying woman. Marsden vowed to do something to assist the sick poor and, the following year, he was instrumental in founding the Royal Free Hospital (from its inception it had royal patronage), the first hospital not to demand fees and recommendations. More than twenty years later Marsden's first wife died from cancer and he realised that, as he wrote in a letter at the time, 'we know absolutely nothing about the disease.' His response was to create the first hospital intended solely for patients suffering from cancer, which opened its doors in Canon Row, Westminster, in 1851. The hospital, now in Fulham Road, is today known by the name of its founder, one of the great (and often forgotten) figures of nineteenth-century health care.

## MARX, ELEANOR (1855–1898) *Socialist campaigner, lived and died here*

### 7 JEWS WALK, SE26

Eleanor was the youngest daughter of Karl Marx and was born in London, the city to which her father had travelled as an exile after his expulsion from first Germany and then France for his political activities. She grew up to be the child who was closest to Marx in his work, joining him at international socialist conferences when still only in her teens and acting as his secretary and amanuensis. In her twenties and thirties she became a prominent figure in English left-wing politics in her own right, helping to found the Socialist League with William Morris and others in 1884 and involving herself in many of the high-profile industrial disputes of the 1880s. Her love life was as unconventional as her politics but she made a terrible mistake when, in 1884, she fell for Edward Aveling, an unscrupulous womaniser who was a fellow member of the Socialist League. Fourteen years later, weary of Aveling's endless infidelities, Eleanor Marx committed suicide by drinking prussic acid. There is much evidence that the wretched Aveling was even more deeply involved in her death than first appeared. Certainly he signed the poison book, which authorised the chemist to sell prussic acid to Eleanor's maid and there has long been a strong suspicion that he persuaded poor Eleanor into a mutual suicide pact that he had no intention of carrying through himself.

MARX, KARL (1818–83) *lived here 1851–1856*
28 DEAN STREET, W1

### KARL MARX
101–8 MAITLAND PARK ROAD, NW3
**CAMDEN BOROUGH COUNCIL**

'In our time,' Marx once wrote, 'change is upon the world and cannot be stopped or channelled as we wish. The thing now is to understand it.' Marx devoted his life to understanding that change and to elaborating a vision of what future change might mean to human society. It was to prove the most potent and influential vision to emerge in the nineteenth century. Yet Marx's devotion to this work cost him (and his wife and family) dear in conventional, worldly terms. Born in Trier, from a prosperous, middle-class family, he entered radical politics in his early twenties and in 1848 wrote, in collaboration with his life-long friend and financial supporter Friedrich Engels, *The Communist Manifesto*. Revolution broke out throughout Europe in 1848; repression followed in 1849 and Marx was forced to flee Germany. He moved to London, where he spent the rest of his life, working in the British Museum on research for what was to become the three volumes of *Das Kapital*. His stay in Dean Street was a time of great hardship for Marx and his family. He was surviving almost solely on an allowance provided by Engels. Three of his six children died during the time in Soho and, in order to provide one of them with a proper burial, Marx was even obliged to borrow money for a tiny coffin.

MASEFIELD, JOHN, OM (1878–1967) *Poet Laureate, lived here 1907–1912*
30 MAIDA AVENUE, W2

Masefield wrote some of the most familiar lines in English poetry of the twentieth century. 'Sea Fever' with its opening line, 'I must go down to the seas again, to the lonely sea and the sky', and 'Cargoes', with its evocation of a 'Dirty British coaster with a salt-caked smoke-stack / butting through the channel in the mad March days', are both poems he published in his first collection which appeared in 1902. Masefield was born in Ledbury in Herefordshire and, orphaned at an early age, was sent by relatives to join the merchant navy when he was only thirteen. Ironically, for a writer renowned as 'the poet of the sea', life on board ship did not suit him. He suffered from terrible seasickness and, in 1895, deserted his ship when it docked in New York, spending a couple of years working at menial jobs around America. Returning to Britain in 1897, he began to publish verse and prose in newspapers and magazines and, after the appearance of his first book of poems, his career as a writer was assured. He went on to publish dozens of books, ranging from fiction and verse collections to an account of the Gallipoli campaign in the First World War. Masefield was appointed Poet Laureate in 1930 and held the position until his death in 1967 – only Tennyson was Poet Laureate for longer.

MATCHAM, FRANK (1854–1920) *theatre architect, lived here 1895–1904*
10 HASLEMERE ROAD, N8

Some of London's most famous theatres, from the Hackney Empire to the London Coliseum, were the work of the architect Frank Matcham. Born in Devon, Matcham came to the capital to join the architectural firm run by Jethro Robinson, who was consulting theatre architect to the Lord Chamberlain's office, the organisation then responsible for the licensing of theatres and plays in the city. Matcham married the boss's daughter and, when Robinson died, he found himself in charge of the business. He was still only in his mid-twenties and had had very little formal training as an architect. None the less, over the next few decades, Matcham became the country's leading theatre architect in an era when the number of theatres expanded enormously and he built dozens of them both in the capital and around the rest of Britain. The Grand Opera House in Belfast, the Buxton Opera House, His Majesty's Theatre in Aberdeen, the Grand Theatre, Blackpool and the Gaiety Theatre in Douglas on the Isle of Man are all theatres designed by Matcham which are still welcoming audiences today. Many of his other buildings have now gone, demolished before posterity learned to love them. By some calculations, five-sixths of his work has been destroyed in the ninety years since his death but the ones that survive show what a versatile and imaginative architect he was.

## MATTHAY, TOBIAS (1858–1945) *teacher and pianist, lived here*

21 ARKWRIGHT ROAD, NW3

Born in London to a family of German descent, Matthay was Professor of Pianoforte at the Royal College of Music from his early twenties to his mid-sixties. A gifted pianist himself, he is best known as a teacher who devised a system of piano playing that relied heavily on what he called, in the title of one of his books, *The Art of Touch*. In the first decade of the century he established his own school of piano, although he continued to teach at the Royal College until 1925, and included many musicians who later went on to concert careers amongst his pupils. He lived in Arkwright Road from 1902 to 1909.

## MATTHEWS, JESSIE (1907–1981) *musical comedy star of stage and films, was born in Berwick Street*

22 BERWICK STREET, W1  **WESTMINSTER**

Jessie Matthews was one of eleven children born to a poor family who lived in a flat behind a butcher's shop in Soho. As a child she took dancing lessons in a room above a local pub at 22 Berwick Street and it was her talents as a dancer and a singer that were first to lift her out of poverty. After appearing in the chorus lines of London shows she rose to stardom in the musical revues of the 1920s. Known as 'the Dancing Divinity', she turned to films in the 1930s and became one of the most popular stars of the decade on both sides of the Atlantic. In her later career she became a character actress and was, for many years, Mrs Dale in the popular BBC radio series *Mrs Dale's Diary*.

## MAUGHAM, WILLIAM SOMERSET (1874–1965) *novelist and playwright, lived here 1911–1919*

6 CHESTERFIELD STREET, W1

'I've always been interested in people,' Maugham once said, 'but I've never liked them.' In a writing career that spanned more than sixty years he turned his jaundiced eye on a wide variety of characters, from the slum dwellers of his first novel, *Liza of Lambeth*, to the expatriates of the Empire who people some of his most memorable short stories. Maugham trained as a doctor and it was a year's medical practice that gave him the material for his first novel. Spectacular success as a writer came in the Edwardian years. In 1908 he had four plays running simultaneously in the West End theatre and his name was made. His most famous novel, the autobiographical *Of Human Bondage*, was published in 1915 and was followed four years later by *The Moon and Sixpence*, the story of a man who deserts wife and business to lead an artist's life in Tahiti. Maugham himself married the daughter of Dr Barnardo in 1917, but the marriage was an unconventional one and his constant companion during his many travels was his secretary Gerald Haxton rather than his wife. In later years Maugham held court, as a Grand Old Man of literature, at his home at Cap Ferrat on the French Riviera.

## MAURICE, FREDERICK DENISON (1805–1872) *Christian philosopher and educationalist, lived here 1862–1866*

2 UPPER HARLEY STREET, NW1

Christian Socialism was one of the most influential moral and religious movements of Victorian England and its leader was F.D. Maurice who believed that 'a true socialism is the necessary result of a sound Christianity'. Maurice, was the son of a Unitarian minister and, although he studied at Cambridge, he was barred, as a dissenter, from taking a degree. However, he decided to join the Church of England in 1830, was ordained and became Professor of Theology at King's College, London, in 1846, having joined the college six years earlier as Professor of English Literature and History. In 1853 he published a collection of essays in which he questioned the doctrine of eternal punishment. The college promptly dismissed him from his post. Maurice was also a strong advocate of the social benefits of education and was instrumental in the founding of the Working Men's College in 1854, becoming its first principal.

## MAXIM, SIR HIRAM (1840–1916) *inventor and engineer, designed and manufactured the Maxim Gun in a workshop on these premises*

57D HATTON GARDEN, EC1

As Hilaire Belloc once pointed out, referring to the technological disadvantages suffered by so many of the colonised peoples of the Empire, 'Whatever happens, we have got/The Maxim Gun, and they have not.' The inventor of this embodiment of imperial power, the first fully automatic machine-gun, which allowed its operator to shoot 600 rounds a minute with devastating accuracy, was an American, born in the state of Maine. However, he perfected his most famous invention in Hatton Garden in 1883, became a naturalised British subject and was knighted in 1901. Maxim was also the inventor of other weaponry, including a pneumatic gun, and was interested in the problems of flight, patenting a flying machine in 1894.

## MAXWELL, JAMES CLERK (1831–1879) *physicist, lived here*

16 PALACE GARDENS TERRACE, W8

Einstein once remarked of the work of the Scots-born James Clerk Maxwell that it was 'the most fruitful that physics has experienced since the time of Newton'. Maxwell's great *Treatise on Electricity and Magnetism*, published in 1873, took Faraday's studies on electromagnetism, gave them a mathematical form and extended them into a complete theory. Maxwell's work led directly to the momentous discovery that light itself must be a form of electromagnetic radiation. Maxwell lived at Palace Gardens Terrace from 1860 to 1865 when he was a professor at King's College, London. Later he became the first Professor of Experimental Physics at Cambridge and supervised the construction and equipping of the world-famous Cavendish Laboratory there.

## MAY, PHIL (1864–1903) *artist, lived and worked here*

20 HOLLAND PARK ROAD, W14

According to the painter Whistler, black and white art could be summed up in two words: 'Phil May'. Born near Leeds, May struggled through years of poverty and a period spent in Australia to become the most successful cartoonist of his day. After returning from Australia in 1890 his work, particularly his bold and perceptive sketches of East End life, appeared regularly in *Punch* and his style became so well known that Phil May annuals were published. Yet despite this professional success and a settled family life, May was a compulsive drinker and he eventually died of cirrhosis of the liver, not yet aged forty and weighing only five stone at the time of his death.

## MAYER, SIR ROBERT (1879–1985) *philanthropist and patron of music, lived here in Flat no. 31*

2 MANSFIELD STREET, W1

At the end of his exceptionally long life Sir Robert Mayer could look back on an involvement with music which stretched from concerts in the 1980s back to encounters with Brahms in the 1890s. Born in Mannheim, Germany, the son of a merchant and brewer, Mayer was sent by his father to work in Britain in 1896. He became a naturalised citizen in 1902 and served in the British Army during the First World War. In 1923, successful in his businesses, he arranged the first of what were to become regular Robert Mayer Concerts for Children and in 1932 he was co-founder, with Thomas Beecham, of the London Philharmonic. He was knighted in 1939 for his services to music. By then he was long retired from business and could devote his time more wholeheartedly to his musical charities. He continued to do so throughout the post-war years and was still to be seen at concerts when he was a centenarian.

---

*On this site, until destroyed by bombing during the winter of 1940 stood an archway and* MAYFAIR'S OLDEST HOUSE, *'The Cottage 1618 AD', from where a shepherd tended his flock whilst Tyburn idled nearby*

STANHOPE ROW, W1 **WESTMINSTER**

In an air raid in the winter of 1940 there was a direct hit on Mayfair and a pub in Stanhope Row. Also destroyed in the blast was a cottage that, according to the inscription above its doorway, dated from 1618 and the reign of James I, thus making it the oldest dwelling place in the area. The unveiling of the plaque, part of the series of events to commemorate the 50th anniversary of the end of the Second World War, was attended by a number of older residents of Mayfair who remembered the cottage when it still stood.

---

## MAYHEW, HENRY (1812–1887) *founder of 'Punch' and author of 'London Labour and the London Poor', lived here*

55 ALBANY STREET, NW1

The son of a successful lawyer, Mayhew was sent to Westminster School from which he ran away to avoid a threatened flogging. After brief and inglorious employment in his father's office he drifted into journalism, edited the magazine *Figaro in London*, wrote a number of works for the stage and was one of the group that founded *Punch* in 1841. Mayhew was a friend of Dickens (he took part in Dickens's elaborate amateur theatricals) and wrote novels himself, but his fame rests on the work that originated in a series of articles for the *Morning Chronicle*, the multi-volume *London Labour and the London Poor*. In this extraordinary work of social investigation, Mayhew describes, often in their own words, the lives of those struggling to make a living on the streets of the capital. Water-carriers, nutmeg graters, dog finders, sellers of birds' nests, rag gatherers and street musicians are just a few of the often bizarre tradespeople Mayhew found and recorded.

---

## MAZZINI, GIUSEPPE (1805–1872) *Italian patriot, lived here*
183 GOWER STREET, NW1

*Dio e popolo. In this house* GIUSEPPE MAZZINI *the apostle of modern democracy inspired young Italy with the idea of unity, independence and regeneration of his country*

5 HATTON GARDEN, EC1 **PRIVATE**

*Dio Popolo Pensiero 1805–1872 In this country* GIUSEPPE MAZZINI *The apostle of modern democracy inspired young Italy with the ideal of the independence, unity and regeneration of his country*

10 LAYSTALL STREET, EC1    **PRIVATE**

GiUseppe Mazzini, the romantic prophet of Italian nationalism, was a great Anglophile and spent long years in exile in London. Even in 1849, when for a brief few months he held real political power in an abortive Roman republic, he could write to a friend that, 'I think very often under these radiant skies of the London fogs and always regretfully. Individually speaking I was evidently intended for an Englishman.' Mazzini was born in Genoa and, involved in radical politics from an early age, was expelled from his homeland in 1831. He arrived in London in 1837, lodging in Gower Street, and worked as a journalist. He also found time to organise a society for Italian workmen, which met in Laystall Street, and, in 1841, a school for Italian children in Hatton Garden. In 1844 Mazzini was victorious in a *cause célèbre* when he accused the British government of opening his mail and reporting its contents to the rulers of Italy. After the brief success of the Roman republic, Mazzini returned to London where he continued to hatch plans for democratic uprisings back in his native land. Opposed to the monarchical party which eventually brought a measure of self-government to Italy, a supporter of Garibaldi in his expedition against Sicily and Naples, Mazzini remained an idealist and a republican to the end of his life. He died in Pisa in 1872.

................................................................................................................

MEE, ARTHUR (1875–1943) *journalist, author and topographer, lived here*

27 LANERCOST ROAD, SW2

One of the great popularisers of knowledge this century, Mee was born near Nottingham and became a journalist in the 1890s. He was recruited by Alfred Harmsworth, who was impressed by the cross-indexed file of more than 250,000 press cuttings that the young Mee had amassed for his own use, and was given the opportunity to produce his own publications on subjects like history and natural history. In 1908 Mee began his *Children's Encyclopedia*, issuing it in fortnightly parts, and in 1919 he began a weekly *Children's Newspaper*, which ran for many years. The last years of Mee's life were given over to a series of topographical books, *The King's England*, in which he planned to describe many thousands of towns and villages throughout the country. Mee himself saw many of the volumes to press, each one devoted to a particular county, and the project was completed after his death.

................................................................................................................

MELBA, DAME NELLIE (1861–1931) *operatic soprano, resided here in 1906*

COOMBE HOUSE, DEVEY CLOSE (OFF BEVERLEY LANE),
KINGSTON UPON THAMES

Born Helen Porter Mitchell in a suburb of Melbourne, Australia, Nellie Melba did not begin the career that was to see her become the most famous female opera singer of her day until she was in her mid-twenties. Only when she accompanied her father on an extended business trip to Europe in 1886 did she get the opportunity to demonstrate the purity and power of her soprano voice on a larger stage than the concert halls of Melbourne. Taking the name of Melba from her native city, she made her operatic debut in 1887 in Verdi's *Rigoletto*, and was soon impressing audiences around the world. Her most favoured role was Mimi in Puccini's *La Bohème*, a part she continued to play long after her statuesque middle-aged figure could convincingly impersonate a young consumptive. Her voice, however, was still thrilling opera fans until the 1920s. Created a Dame of the British Empire for her services to the war effort in 1918, Melba was the epitome of the larger-than-life prima donna. She died in 1931 from an infection resulting from a facelift. Melba Toast and Peach Melba both owe their names to her.

## MELVILLE, HERMAN (1819–1891) *author of* Moby Dick, *lived here in 1849*
25 CRAVEN STREET, WC2

Herman Melville is now recognised as one of the greatest of all American writers but, for much of his life, he was a prophet without honour in his own country or, indeed, in any other country. His most famous novel, *Moby Dick*, the story of Captain Ahab's obsession with the great white whale of the title, never came close to selling out its first edition of 3,000 copies and earned its author the grand sum of $556.37. Six years after its publication Melville gave up fiction and retreated into a silence broken only by volumes of self-published verse. Melville's early life was filled with the adventurous travels that inspired his fiction and he sailed on board whaling ships to Polynesia and Hawaii in the early 1840s. He spent two months in London at the end of 1849, some time before the publication of *Moby Dick*, largely in order to sort out business with the English publisher Richard Bentley, who had agreed to produce editions of his earlier novels. It was during this period that Melville lodged in Craven Street, not far from where another famous American, Benjamin Franklin, has his residence in London commemorated by a Blue Plaque.

## MEREDITH, GEORGE, OM (1828–1909) *poet and novelist, lived here*
7 HOBURY STREET, SW10

One of the most revered literary figures of the late Victorian and Edwardian periods, Meredith was the author of such novels as *The Ordeal of Richard Feverel, The Egoist and Diana of the Crossways*. However, he thought of himself as a poet first and a novelist second and published volumes of his verse over a period of nearly sixty years. As a young man, in 1856, he posed for Henry Wallis's well-known painting *The Death of Chatterton*. Wallis repaid Meredith by running off with his wife. Out of the emotional turmoil of this domestic upheaval Meredith eventually produced the verse sequence *Modern Love*, an innovative work that explores the disillusionment and unhappiness of a doomed marriage. Meredith remarried in 1864. He moved into Hobury Street just after his first wife left him and stayed there from 1857 to 1859.

## METTERNICH, PRINCE (1773–1859) *Austrian statesman, lived here in 1848*
44 EATON SQUARE, SW1

Metternich, the son of a diplomat, was appointed Austrian Foreign Minister in 1809 and, in this role, was instrumental in arranging the marriage between Napoleon and the Austrian princess Marie-Louise. No friend to Napoleon, however, he committed the Austrians to the Grand Alliance against the French Emperor in 1813 and, after Napoleon's defeat, was one of the dominating figures at the Congress of Vienna. For the next thirty years Metternich represented reaction in Europe, the desire for a maintenance of the status quo that the ideas of the French Revolution and Bonaparte's ambitions had so severely shaken. 'Let us be conservative,' Metternich wrote, 'let us walk steadily and firmly on well-known paths; let us not deviate from these lines in word or deed . . .'. In 1848, the Year of Revolutions, uprisings occurred throughout Europe. Metternich and his family were forced to flee Austria and arrived in London, staying in Eaton Square from May to September.

## MEYNELL, ALICE (1847–1922) *poet and essayist, lived here*
47 PALACE COURT, W2

Alice Meynell came from an artistic family – her mother was a pianist and her younger sister was to become the well-known painter of Victorian battle scenes, Elizabeth Butler – and spent much of her childhood abroad, particularly in Italy. She converted to Catholicism in 1868 and much of her poetry, published in various volumes from 1875 to the time of her death, was imbued with her religious, often mystical, sense of life, death, God and the natural world.

Together with her husband, Wilfred Meynell, she was also responsible for rescuing the would-be priest and opium addict Francis Thompson from complete destitution and nursing his fragile talent as a religious poet. Much of the Meynells' income came from journalism and both edited a variety of periodicals. Alice in particular was a prolific essayist, anthologist and critic.

## MILL, JOHN STUART (1806–1873) *philosopher, lived here*
### 18 KENSINGTON SQUARE, W8

The son of the Utilitarian philosopher and historian James Mill, John Stuart Mill was educated for intellectual greatness from an early age. He began to study Greek at the age of three and was introduced to the higher ideas of maths and political economy when only eight. Unsurprisingly he was an unnervingly precocious child. When a female friend of the family asked the infant Mill how he was feeling after an attack of migraine, he replied, 'Thank you, madam, the agony has much abated.' As a young man he suffered the consequences of this hothouse education when he had a nervous breakdown but he recovered to become one of the great radical thinkers of the Victorian age. In such books as *Principles of Political Economy* and essays like *On Liberty* he advanced his views on the nature of the best relationship between the state and the individual and he was an enthusiastic champion of women's rights. In the latter he was influenced strongly by Harriet Taylor, who became his wife in 1851, two years after the death of her first husband and twenty years after Mill had first met her. She died in Avignon in 1858 and much of Mill's later life was spent there so that he could be close to her grave. He himself died in the French town in 1873.

## MILLAIS, SIR JOHN EVERETT, BT PRA (1829–1896) *painter, lived and died here*
### 2 PALACE GATE, W8

Millais, who came from an old Channel Islands family, was a prodigiously gifted artist who was exhibiting his paintings while still in his teens. In 1848–9, together with Rossetti and Holman Hunt, he launched the Pre-Raphaelite Brotherhood and his works were the first by which the fledgeling movement became known. Unfortunately this was because they were largely vilified by the critics. One of the few friendly critics was Ruskin. From 1853 his support was less likely since Millais had fallen in love with Ruskin's wife Effie and, after the marriage was annulled on the grounds of Ruskin's impotence, the two were wed in 1855. Millais now began his progress from *enfant terrible* to leading statesman of British art. He became one of the wealthiest of Victorian painters, more famous for his portraits of the great and good and for works of imperial celebration like *The Boyhood of Raleigh* than for the revolutionary vision of his youth. He was made President of the Royal Academy in the year he died.

## *Near this site stood* MILLBANK PRISON, *which was opened in 1816 and closed in 1890. This buttress stood at the head of the river steps from which, until 1867, prisoners sentenced to transportation embarked on their journey to Australia*
### MILLBANK, SW1

Occupying ground now covered by the Tate Gallery, Millbank Prison was originally the brainchild of the writer, reformer and philosopher Jeremy Bentham, who had outlined his plan for a revolutionary new form of prison (prisoners occupying the circumference of a circular building under perpetual surveillance by warders in the centre) in a 1791 work called *The Panopticon*. Bentham invested his own money in the project and lost most of it when the scheme foundered. The government took over and completed the building, but not to Bentham's original plans. The prison had several miles of labyrinthine passages and the story is told of a warder who spent seven years working there and still needed to mark his way with chalk on the walls for fear of getting lost. The prison closed in 1890 and the building was demolished thirteen years later.

## MILLER, LEE (1907–1977) *photographer and* PENROSE, ROLAND (1900–1984) *surrealist, lived here 1936–1947*

21 DOWNSHIRE HILL, HAMPSTEAD, NW3

During the 1920s and 1930s Roland Penrose worked as a painter in Paris, where he met many of the leading, avant-garde artists and writers of the day, including Picasso, whose biographer he was to later become. He also came to know many of the surrealists and, in 1936, the year that he moved into Downshire Hill, he organised the First International Surrealist Exhibition in London. Lee Miller was born in New York and began her career as a model, before moving behind the camera, first as an assistant to Man Ray in Paris and later as a fashion photographer in London and her native New York. She moved into Downshire Hill in 1939. Married in 1947, Miller and Penrose later lived at a Sussex farm, which was to be their home for the rest of their lives. Their careers continued to prosper. Miller's photojournalism, when she was the only female photographer to record many of the worst moments of the final years of the Second World War, is increasingly admired for its insight and its humanity. One of the founders of the ICA (the Institute of Contemporary Art), Penrose was an influential figure in the promotion of modern art, particularly surrealist art, in Britain and was knighted in 1966.

## MILNE, A.A. (1882–1956) *author, lived here*

13 MALLORD STREET, SW3

Like Lewis Carroll, the writer of another great children's classic, although at a much less elevated level, the author of *Winnie-the-Pooh* was a mathematician. After an education that began at the school his father ran (and where one of the teachers was, briefly, H.G. Wells), A.A. Milne won a maths scholarship to Cambridge but spent more time there editing the undergraduate magazine *Granta* than he did studying his subject. In 1906 Milne joined the staff of *Punch* as an assistant editor and, after service in the First World War, became well-known for his well-crafted, light-hearted plays, many of which were successes in the West End. (Ironically his one major flop was a play called *Success*.) World-wide fame followed publication of *When We Were Very Young*, children's verse he had written for his son Christopher Robin, and this was confirmed by the publication in 1926 of *Winnie-the-Pooh*. For the rest of his life Milne was renowned as the creator of Pooh, Piglet, Eeyore and the other inhabitants of the Hundred Acre Wood.

## MILNER, LORD ALFRED (1854–1925) *statesman, lived here*

14 MANCHESTER SQUARE, W1

One of the great advocates and exponents of British imperialism, Milner was actually born in Germany, one of an academic family that had settled there, and he was educated at a German university before commencing a brilliant career at Oxford. Milner served in the Civil Service with distinction and in 1897 was sent as High Commissioner to South Africa, his time there coinciding with Britain's most troublesome colonial conflict, the Boer War. From 1901 to 1905 he was Governor of the Transvaal and Orange River Colony, in charge of administering Boer territories. Returning to Britain, Milner, an eloquent supporter of enlightened imperial rule, became an influential figure in British politics, serving in Lloyd George's wartime Cabinet and as Colonial Secretary from 1919 to 1921. In this post he formulated many of the ideas that were to guide British colonial policy over the next decades as the colonies moved slowly but inevitably towards self-government.

## MIRANDA, FRANCISCO DE (1750?–1816) *precursor of Latin American independence, lived here 1802–1810*

58 GRAFTON WAY, W1

Born in Caracas, Miranda became a professional soldier in the Spanish army and fought as such in the American War of Independence. (Some Spanish troops fought against the British during the conflict.) Imbibing the revolutionary ideas that were in the air at the time, he fought for the French army after the Revolution but fled to England when the Terror was at its height. He was to remain in this country for many years, vainly petitioning Pitt and other politicians for help in liberating his native Venezuela from Spanish rule. Despite fiasco when he tried to foment a rising in 1806, Miranda persevered in his revolutionary plans and, in 1810, finally landed again in South America. He was, at first, successful in overthrowing the Spanish and declaring Venezuela independent but dissension arose on his own side and he was handed over to the Spanish. Imprisoned in Cadiz, he died five years later.

---

## MITFORD, NANCY (1904–1973) *writer, worked here 1942–1945*

HEYWOOD HILL BOOKSHOP, 10 CURZON STREET, W1

The Mitford sisters were the daughters of the eccentric aristocrat Lord Redesdale, and their lives also followed various and eccentric paths. Diana married Oswald Mosley, the leader of the British Union of Fascists; Unity, whose second name was Valkyrie, was so enamoured of Hitler and the Nazis that she moved to Germany and did not return until 1940; Jessica became a Communist and went to live in America. Nancy Mitford came to the public's attention as the chronicler of upper-class bohemia in novels like *Love in a Cold Climate* and *The Pursuit of Love*. Heywood Hill had opened his bookshop in Curzon Street in 1936 and, when he was called up during the war, he left the running of it to his wife. Nancy Mitford helped in the shop during the war years, leaving when the income from her writing became sufficient that she could live in France. She became and remained a partner in the booksellers for another twenty years.

---

## MONDRIAN, PIET CORNELIS (1872–1944) *painter, lived here*

60 PARKHILL ROAD, NW3

One of the major innovators of twentieth-century art, the Dutch painter Mondrian moved steadily in his career towards greater and greater abstraction, travelling beyond his involvement with the De Stijl Movement in architecture and painting until he achieved the style of rectilinear canvases painted in black, white and primary colours that are his most familiar and influential work. He was in Paris throughout the twenties and most of the thirties but moved to London in 1938, setting up his studio in Parkhill Road where he was surrounded by a small colony of younger, admiring artists such as Henry Moore, Barbara Hepworth and Ben Nicholson. Mondrian stayed in London until the summer of 1940 when, concerned about the increasing escalation of the war and the Blitz, he moved to New York.

---

## MONTEFIORE, SIR MOSES (1784–1885) *philanthropist and Jewish leader, lived here for sixty years*

99 PARK LANE, W1

In the course of his exceptionally long life Sir Moses Montefiore did much both to assist his fellow Jews in many lands and to improve the standing and reputation of Jews in Britain. Born in Leghorn, the son of a London merchant, Montefiore grew up to become so successful as a stockbroker in the City that he was able to retire from business at the age of forty and devote himself to philanthropy and public affairs. Over the next half-century Montefiore made many journeys, to the Middle East and to Eastern Europe, to plead the cause of oppressed Jewish communities and to use his money to establish Jewish businesses and settlements. In Britain he overcame prejudice to become Sheriff of London and a baronet. His hundredth birthday in 1884 was declared a public holiday in Jewish communities around the world and when he died the following year the then Lord Mayor described him as 'the most distinguished citizen of London'.

## MONTGOMERY, FIELD MARSHAL, VISCOUNT, OF ALAMEIN (1887–1976)
*was born here*

OVAL HOUSE, 52–54 KENNINGTON OVAL, SE11

'In defeat unbeatable; in victory unbearable,' as Churchill said of him, Bernard Montgomery was the most distinctive and, in many ways, the most successful British soldier of the century, loved and loathed in about equal measure. The son of an Anglican bishop, Montgomery joined the Army in 1908 and fought throughout the First World War, rising to command a battalion by the end of it. In the Second World War he distinguished himself during the retreat from Dunkirk and was singled out for high command by his superiors in the Army and by Churchill. Even so, it was chance (the death of another general in an air crash) that brought Montgomery charge of the Eighth Army and the opportunity to lead his men to the morale-boosting victory at El Alamein. In the Normandy invasion Montgomery was commander of the Allied land forces under Eisenhower and, despite the setback of defeat at Arnhem (the only substantial defeat of his career), it was Montgomery who accepted the German surrender at Lüneburg Heath. After the war Montgomery was Deputy Supreme Commander of NATO in Europe before retiring in 1958.

## MOODY, HAROLD (1882–1947) *campaigner for racial equality, lived and worked here*
164 QUEEN'S ROAD, PECKHAM, SE15

Born in Kingston, Jamaica, Moody came to London in 1904 to study medicine at King's College. A star student, he went on to triumph over the routine prejudice of the period and eventually established his own successful practice in Peckham. Involved throughout his career with philanthropic work and with providing assistance for his fellow black citizens, Moody, in 1931, set up The League of Coloured Peoples, its first meeting being held in the central YMCA in Tottenham Court Road. It was Moody who provided much of the energy behind the League and it was his desire to promote both the interests of black people and the cause of racial understanding that gave it strength during its brief existence. The League only survived the man who had given so much to it by four years and folded in 1951.

## MOORE, GEORGE (1852–1933) *author, lived and died here*
121 EBURY STREET, SW1

'To be aristocratic in art one must avoid polite society,' George Moore once remarked and, although he could not be said to have avoided it himself throughout his life, it was as a chronicler of far from polite society that he first made his name as a writer. Moore learnt, from his early years of bohemian life in Paris, the lessons of French realism and the novels he published when he returned to England, the most famous being *Esther Waters* in 1894, were highly influenced by the unflinching naturalism of Zola. Moore, who was an Irishman from County Mayo, removed himself from England to his native land in protest at the Boer War and became involved with Yeats and Lady Gregory in the revival of the Irish theatre. He returned to London in 1911 and moved into Ebury Street, staying there until his death. Gradually he became a Grand Old Man of literature, publishing many volumes of memoirs and essays and, in 1916, his last notable novel, *The Brook Kerith*, a fictionalised version of incidents from the life of Jesus.

## MOORE, HENRY OM (1898–1986) *sculptor, lived and worked here 1929–1940*
11A PARKHILL ROAD, HAMPSTEAD, NW3

'There are universal shapes,' Henry Moore once wrote, 'to which everyone is subconsciously conditioned and to which they can respond if their conscious control does not shut them off.' Throughout his long and creative career, Moore strove to embody those shapes in his work.

He was born in the Yorkshire mining town of Castleford at the end of the nineteenth century. After serving in the First World War as a teenager, he studied sculpture, first in Leeds and then at the Royal College of Art. His first one-man show took place in 1926. Moore moved into the house in Parkhill Road, Hampstead three years later, soon after he had received his first public commission (a relief sculpture on the walls of London Underground's HQ) and had married a Russian émigré named Irina Radetsky. He and Irina remained there until the Second World War. Over the next few decades, Moore became the most famous sculptor in Britain and his trademark reclining figures, often punctured by holes and spaces in their bodies, became familiar to a wide public. 'All art should have a certain mystery,' he once said, 'and should make demands on the spectator.' He continued to create his own mysterious art through a long and immensely productive life.

## MOORE, TOM (1779–1852) *Irish poet, lived here*
*This plaque was removed from 28 Bury Street, St James's in 1962*
85 GEORGE STREET, W1

During his lifetime Tom Moore was nearly as famous as his close friend Byron but today he is a name known to scholars rather than general readers. Yet some of his work remains very familiar indeed. From 1808 until 1834 Moore, who was born in Dublin and came to London in 1799, published collections of *Irish Melodies*, which used his own lyrics set to traditional Irish tunes. Among these are 'The Minstrel Boy', 'The Last Rose of Summer' and 'The Harp that Once Through Tara's Halls'. In his lifetime Moore's other great success was the series of oriental tales in verse he published as *Lalla Rookh*, although the aristocratic lady who told him, 'Mr Moore, I have not read your Larry O'Rourke; I don't like Irish stories', was clearly unaware that he could write of lands other than his own. In his will Byron entrusted Moore with his memoirs, but Moore was persuaded that publication of them would do his friend's memory no good and he destroyed them.

## MORGAN, CHARLES (1894–1958) *novelist and critic, lived and died here*
16 CAMPDEN HILL SQUARE, W8

As a novelist Morgan has been something of a prophet without honour in his own country. His fiction, which includes *The Fountain*, *Sparkenbroke* and *The River Line*, won greater acclaim on the Continent, particularly in France, than it did in Britain and he was elected a member of the Institut de France in the year before his death. Before his literary career began, Morgan was in the Navy and served in the First World War before being captured and interned in Holland. His first novel, *The Gunroom*, reflected his experiences as a midshipman. After the war he went to Oxford and then worked as journalist and drama critic for *The Times* during the twenties and thirties. His own plays, like his novels, remain unfamiliar to most British readers today, although he has developed something of a cult reputation among a small group of admirers.

## MORGAN, JUNIUS S. (1813–1890) *and* MORGAN, JOHN PIERPONT (1837–1913) *international bankers, lived here*
14 PRINCES GATE, SW1

The descendant of a Welsh farmer who had emigrated to America in the middle of the seventeenth century, Junius Spencer Morgan was already a successful businessman when, in 1854, he became a partner in the international banking firm of George Peabody and Company and moved to London. After Peabody's retirement ten years later, Junius took complete charge of the company and re-named it after himself. He died in Italy when a carriage in which he was riding was involved in an accident and he suffered severe head injuries. By that time his son, J.P. Morgan, had long been established as the man in effective charge of the banking business and it continued to go from strength to strength. In 1901, he was at the head of a coalition of investors and bankers who brought together a number of steel companies to form US Steel, the world's first billion dollar corporation. 'Of all forms of tyranny the least attractive and the most vulgar is the tyranny of mere wealth,' he is reported to have said but, in the first decade of the twentieth century, no plutocrat had more power than J.P. Morgan. Like his father, he died in Italy. When he did so he left behind the sort of wealth of which even his father could only have dreamed.

## MORRELL, LADY OTTOLINE (1873–1938) *literary hostess and patron of the arts, lived here*

10 GOWER STREET, WC1

Ottoline Cavendish-Bentinck married a Liberal MP, Philip Morrell, and, from about 1908, their London house and, especially, Garsington Manor, their country house near Oxford, became the gathering places for a whole generation of writers and artists. Everyone, from D.H. Lawrence to T.S. Eliot, Bertrand Russell to Aldous Huxley, enjoyed the patronage of the Morrells and, particularly, Lady Ottoline, who was an eccentric but generous hostess. Many of the writers repaid her hospitality by creating thinly disguised and cruelly satirical portraits of her in their works. In Lawrence's *Women in Love*, for example, it is not hard to find an original for Hermione Roddice, the literary hostess with whom Rupert Birkin has a deeply unsatisfactory affair. It was not hard for Lady Ottoline to see herself as the rather ridiculous Hermione and she was very hurt. By the late 1920s the Morrells were living more or less permanently in London and the salons and weekend parties had become a thing of the past.

## MORRISON, HERBERT, LORD MORRISON OF LAMBETH (1888–1965) *Cabinet minister and leader of the London County Council, lived here 1929–1960*

55 ARCHERY ROAD, ELTHAM, SE9

Herbert Morrison was one of the leading figures in Labour politics, in London politics and in national politics of the twentieth century. Secretary of the London Labour party in 1915, he was Mayor of Hackney four years later and was elected to the London County Council in 1922. He was to remain on the LCC until the end of the Second World War, becoming its leader in 1934. As Transport Minister in Ramsay MacDonald's second administration, he laid the basis for what became the integrated network of transport systems in the capital known as the London Passenger Transport Board. In Churchill's wartime coalition Cabinet he was Home Secretary and he played a central role in Attlee's post-war government as both Deputy Prime Minister and leader of the Commons. Twice defeated in the battle for the Labour leadership, in 1935 and 1955, Morrison was made a life peer in 1959.

## MORSE, SAMUEL (1791–1872) *American painter and inventor of the Morse Code, lived here 1812–1815*

141 CLEVELAND STREET, W1

Morse graduated from Yale in 1810 and arrived in London to study as a painter under his fellow-countrymen, Washington Allston and Benjamin West, both of whom were established in the artistic life of the city. Morse exhibited at the Royal Academy in 1813 but returned to America two years later where he worked as a portrait painter. Always interested in science as well as art, he experimented with the possibilities of using electricity as a means of communication and produced the earliest versions of the telegraph in the 1830s. After further experiment, Congress was persuaded to vote money for a line from Washington to Baltimore and the following year the first message was despatched from the capital. 'What hath God wrought?', it portentously asked. The Morse Code, for which Samuel Morse is now most famous, was originally devised for use with his telegraph.

## MOUNTBATTEN, EARL OF BURMA (1900–1979)

*and* COUNTESS OF BURMA (1901–1960)
*last Viceroy and Vicereine of India, lived here*

2 WILTON CRESCENT, SW1

One of the innumerable descendants of Queen Victoria who made up most of the royal and princely families of the early twentieth century, Lord Mountbatten was born Louis of Battenberg in Windsor in 1900. Because of the anti-German feeling prevalent at the time, his father changed the family name to Mountbatten during the First World War. Mountbatten was a career naval officer who served as a teenage midshipman in that war and as a captain, and later admiral, in the Second World War. Appointed head of South East Asia Command by Churchill, he collaborated with General Slim and others in directing the liberation of Burma and Singapore from the Japanese, and was given the unenviable job, as Viceroy, of overseeing the creation of the newly independent states of India and Pakistan in 1947. Mountbatten was Viceroy for five months before independence and stayed in India until June 1948. He went on to serve as First Sea Lord in the 1950s and as Chief of Defence Staff in the early 1960s. He was killed by an IRA bomb in 1979. Mountbatten had married Edwina Ashley, a goddaughter of Edward VII, in what was the society wedding of 1922, the Prince of Wales acting as best man. They became one of the most glamorous couples of the interwar years, although the marriage was a turbulent one and both had affairs. During the Second World War, Edwina Mountbatten worked tirelessly for the Red Cross and she was a high-profile Vicereine in India. Her relationship with the congress leader Nehru, widely rumoured to have been her lover, was a significant factor in the negotiations for independence. She predeceased her husband by nearly twenty years, dying in Borneo while visiting the country in connection with her charity work.

---

## MOZART, WOLFGANG AMADEUS (1756–1791) *composed his first symphony here in 1764*

180 EBURY STREET, SW1

## WOLFGANG AMADEUS MOZART (1756–1791)

20 FRITH STREET, W1 **ROYAL MUSICAL ASSOCIATION**

Mozart was brought to London as a child in 1764, together with his sister Nannerl, to impress English audiences with the same feats of musical precociousness that had already created a stir on the Continent. His father Leopold, court musician to the Archbishop of Salzburg, installed the family in lodgings, first in Cecil Court, then in Frith Street, and set about advertising the arrival of the prodigies. In a newspaper of March 1765, Leopold assured prospective visitors to the Mozarts that they 'may not only hear this young Music Master and his Sister perform in private; but likewise try his surprising Musical Capacity, by giving him anything to play at sight, or any Music without Bass, which he will write upon the Spot, without recurring to his Harpsichord.' London music-lovers, including the King and Queen, were suitably impressed. The Mozarts moved to Ebury Street, then on the very edge of town, for several weeks in the summer of

1764 after Leopold had fallen ill. Barred from playing any musical instruments during his father's recuperation, Wolfgang amused himself with composition. His first symphony was one of the results. The Mozarts left London in July 1765 and Wolfgang never returned.

## MUIRHEAD, ALEXANDER (1848–1920) *electrical engineer, lived here*
20 CHURCH ROAD, SHORTLANDS

Muirhead was a graduate of University College, London, who contributed greatly to the improvement of communications in the latter part of the nineteenth century. It was his invention, in 1875, of duplex cables that allowed telegraph companies to send messages in different directions simultaneously along the same cable. Muirhead also registered other electrical patents and, in the 1890s, established a factory at Elmers End to manufacture and distribute electrical instruments. He moved to the house in Bromley at the same time and lived there until his death.

## MUNRO, HECTOR HUGH, ALIAS 'SAKI' (1870–1916) *short story writer, lived here*
97 MORTIMER STREET, W1

Born in Burma, the son of a colonial policeman, Munro spent an unhappy childhood back in England, living with two maiden aunts in Devon. After a false start in Colonial service himself, he decided to become a writer. Taking his pen-name from that of the cup-bearer in the last stanza of 'The Rubaiyat of Omar Khayyam', Munro began to publish short satirical sketches in the late 1890s. In the first decade of the twentieth century he lived a peripatetic life as a foreign correspondent for the *Morning Post*, reporting from Russia and Eastern Europe, but, in addition to his despatches, he was sending home for publication the dark, witty short stories for which he is best remembered. Returning to London in 1908, he lived in Mortimer Street between 1911 and 1914. He continued to publish collections of his stories and also wrote two novels, one of them (*When William Came*) a bitter fantasy about an England under the rule of Germany. When the First World War broke out, Munro, although in his forties, enlisted and served as an ordinary soldier in the trenches. He was killed by a German sniper in 1916. His last words were 'Put that bloody cigarette out', addressed to a fellow soldier.

## MURROW, EDWARD R. (1908–1965) *American broadcaster, lived here in flat No. 5, 1938–1946*
WEYMOUTH HOUSE, 84–94 HALLAM STREET, W1

'Just because your voice reaches halfway around the world,' the legendary American broadcaster Ed Murrow once said, 'doesn't mean you are wiser than when it reached only to the end of the bar.' For a number of years during the Second World War, Murrow's voice did indeed reach halfway around the world. As a radio journalist for CBS, he brought home the realities of the war in Europe to the American people like no other reporter. Murrow joined CBS in 1935 and he was stationed in London when the war broke out in September 1939. He remained there, providing live radio broadcasts throughout the worst days of the Blitz. His sign-off farewell ('Good night, and good luck') became famous and was used in 2005 as the title of a film about Murrow directed by George Clooney. After the war, Murrow continued his radio career and also moved into television. His news show *See It Now* won awards for its journalism and is remembered particularly for its brave attacks on the scaremongering anti-Communism of Senator Joe McCarthy. President Kennedy appointed Murrow head of the United States Information Agency in 1961 but ill health dogged his final years and he died of cancer at the age of fifty-seven.

## MURRY, JOHN MIDDLETON
See under entry for KATHERINE MANSFIELD

## MYERS, GEORGE (1803–1875) *master builder, lived here 1842–1853*
### 131 ST GEORGE'S ROAD, SE1

Augustus Pugin is well known as the architect of some of the most striking Victorian Gothic buildings. However, although Pugin was the designer of such buildings as Southwark Roman Catholic Cathedral and St Mary's Cathedral, Newcastle, it was George Myers who supervised the actual building of them. Myers was born in Hull and first met Pugin when he was working at Beverley Minster, eight miles from his home town. Pugin was often slightly dismissive of Myers, referring to him in one letter as 'a rough diamond', but he was genuinely admiring of his practical, down-to-earth knowledge of medieval building techniques, and the two worked together on a large numbers of projects before the architect's tragic mental breakdown and early death in 1852. After the loss of his closet colleague, Myers continued to run his own firm of builders in Lambeth for another twenty years. It is probable that Myers carved the effigy of Pugin on the architect's tomb in St Augustine's Church, Ramsgate, a building on which they had collaborated in the 1840s.

## NAPOLEON III (1808–1873) *Emperor of the French, lived here 1848*
### 1C KING STREET, ST JAMES'S, SW1

Although he was the nephew of the man who was once England's greatest enemy, Napoleon III (as he was to become) spent several years in this country. As a young man he took refuge here in the aftermath of an unsuccessful attempt at a *coup d'état* in France and, later, settled in London after five years' imprisonment following an equally misjudged bid to win power. As an old man, following his country's defeat in the Franco-Prussian War, he went into exile at Chislehurst, Kent, where he died. In the intervening years he had taken the opportunity offered by the 1848 Revolution to return to France, win a convincing victory in presidential elections and consolidate his power so skilfully that he was able to throw off the constitutional mask and announce a Second Empire. He then ruled France for twenty years before meeting his nemesis in Bismarck's Prussians. His son, educated in England, was killed in a skirmish during the Zulu War. The Empress Eugenie, bereaved of both husband and son in a few years, lived on in England for more than forty years, dying in 1920.

## NASH, PAUL (1889–1946) *artist, lived in Flat 176, 1914–1936*
### QUEEN ALEXANDRA MANSIONS, BIDBOROUGH STREET, WC1

One critic wrote of Paul Nash that 'no artist has interpreted the beauty and rhythm of the English countryside as perfectly as he', yet he is often remembered chiefly for his work as a war artist. Nash trained at the Slade School of Art (he had originally intended to enter the Royal Navy but failed an entrance examination) and, at the outbreak of the First World War, he enlisted as a private. Later made an official war artist, Nash, in works like *Menin Road*, produced some of the most haunting images of the conflict. During the twenties and thirties he worked extensively as a landscape painter and created many distinctive book illustrations. He again became a war artist in 1939, working for the Air Ministry and the Ministry of Information.

## NEAGLE, DAME ANNA (1904–1986) *film and stage actress and her husband Herbert Wilcox CBE film producer and director, lived here 1950–1964*
### ALDFORD HOUSE, PARK LANE, W1 **WESTMINSTER**

Born Marjorie Robertson in Forest Gate, Anna Neagle started her career as a dancer while still in her teens and, during the thirties and forties, was one of the biggest stars of the British cinema. In films directed and produced by her husband, Herbert Wilcox, she played the great heroines of British history (Florence Nightingale, Edith Cavell, Queen Victoria twice) and later co-starred with Michael Wilding in a series of light comedies, often set in the drawing-rooms of Mayfair. During this time, she was, for seven consecutive years, the most popular British star at the box office. She also appeared in many stage plays and musicals. Anna Neagle was made a Dame of the British Empire in 1969. She and Herbert Wilcox lived in a top floor flat in Aldford House from 1950 to 1964.

## NEHRU, JAWAHARLAL (1889–1964) *first Prime Minister of India, lived here in 1910 and 1912*

### 60 ELGIN CRESCENT, W11

India's first Prime Minister was born into a family with a tradition of opposition to British rule – his father, Motilal Nehru, was a journalist, lawyer and leading nationalist – but he was educated at a British public school, Harrow, and at a British university, Cambridge. He lived in Elgin Crescent when he was reading for the Bar and a student at the Inner Temple. Returning to India, Nehru threw himself into nationalist politics. He joined the Congress party and was imprisoned by the British for the first time in 1921. He was to suffer many years of imprisonment over the next quarter of a century. Allied with Gandhi, but often representing more radical views than the Mahatma, Nehru was one of the leading figures in the Congress party throughout the thirties and the Second World War, and he was the obvious choice to become Prime Minister and Minister of External Affairs when India gained her independence in 1947. He remained in power until his death, pursuing a policy of industrialisation at home and neutrality abroad. His daughter, Indira Gandhi, and her sons continued his political dynasty.

## NELSON, LORD HORATIO (1758–1805) *lived here in 1797. Fell at Trafalgar 1805*

### 147 NEW BOND STREET (SITE), W1

## LORD HORATIO NELSON (1758–1805) *lived here in 1798*

### 103 NEW BOND STREET, W1

The son of a Norfolk clergyman, Nelson went to sea at the age of twelve and had already seen service around the world when the naval war against France broke out. During action in the Mediterranean he was blinded in his right eye, the eye to which he famously placed a telescope during the Battle of Copenhagen so that he could claim, quite correctly, that he could see no signal to withdraw. Nelson became a public hero in 1797 when he took a prominent role in the defeat of French and Spanish forces at Cape St Vincent. In the same year his right arm was shattered by grapeshot and had to be amputated but he was soon in action again, achieving one of the most stunningly comprehensive naval victories of the age of sail when he all but destroyed a French fleet at the Battle of the Nile. Returning as a conquering hero to Naples, he fell for the considerable charms of Emma Hamilton, the wife of the English ambassador there, and began a liaison which, despite the scandal attached to it, lasted until his death. Victory at Copenhagen followed in 1801, despite the timidity of his commanding officer, and Nelson reached his apotheosis at Trafalgar in 1805, dying aboard his flagship, the *Victory*, at the moment of his greatest triumph. Nelson was a naval genius but it would seem, on the evidence of a laconic memorandum issued before Trafalgar, that his preferred strategy was simplicity itself. 'In case signals can be neither seen nor perfectly understood,' he wrote, 'no captain can do very wrong if he places his ship alongside that of an enemy.'

## NEVILL, LADY DOROTHY (1826–1913) *horticulturalist, collector, writer and hostess, lived here 1873–1913*

### 45 CHARLES STREET, W1   **WESTMINSTER**

Born in Berkeley Square, the daughter of the Earl of Oxford, Lady Dorothy married Reginald Nevill in 1847 and came into possession of an estate in Sussex four years later, where she was able to indulge her love of plants and gardening. Her garden soon became a celebrated one. She was a regular correspondent of the Hookers, father and son, each of whom became director of the Royal Botanic Gardens at Kew, and she provided Darwin with rare plants for his studies. She was a renowned hostess, who numbered Disraeli among her many political friends, and wrote books on subjects as various as her family history and the cultivation of silk worms. Her three volumes of autobiography provide a fascinating portrait of upper-class life in the Victorian and Edwardian eras.

## NEWBOLT, SIR HENRY (1862–1938) *poet, lived here*
29 CAMPDEN HILL ROAD, W8

Even in his own lifetime the unswerving patriotism and unembarrassed celebration of imperial glory expressed by Newbolt's verse must have come to seem old-fashioned – Kipling without any of the ironies or subtleties. Today it seems antediluvian. We can no longer respond as Newbolt intended to poems like 'Drake's Drum' or share his belief that the Empire was built on virtues inculcated by the public schools ('Play up! Play up! and play the game!') but collections such as *Admirals All* (1897) were extremely popular at the time of first publication. Newbolt also wrote novels and short stories and was an authority on naval history, publishing a book on the naval encounters of the First World War. He was also active in public life, serving on many committees and writing a report that was to be very influential in the development of English literature as a university subject.

## *In a house near this spot* JOHN HENRY, CARDINAL NEWMAN *was born 21 February 1801*
17 SOUTHAMPTON PLACE, WC1   **CITY OF LONDON**

## *In this house* JOHN HENRY NEWMAN (1801–1890) *later Cardinal Newman, spent some of his early years*
GREY COURT, HAM STREET, HAM

Newman once wrote, 'God has created me to do him some definite service; He has committed some work to me which he has not committed to another.' The great drama of his life, and one of the great dramas of nineteenth-century religion in Britain, was the consequence of Newman's inability to find God's work within the Church of England. He began his career as a brilliant Anglican scholar and preacher and was one of the leading lights in the Oxford Movement, a High Church attempt to forge a path between Catholicism and the myriad voices of dissent and evangelicalism. By the early 1840s Newman was moving steadily towards a belief in Rome as the home of the true Church and he was received into the Roman Catholic Church in 1845. The apostasy of so prominent a figure in Victorian Anglicanism as Newman caused much controversy at the time. Newman himself, after ordination as a priest in 1846, devoted himself to the establishment of the Oratory of St Philip Neri near Birmingham and to the creation of a Catholic University in Ireland. He served as its rector in the 1850s and was appointed a Cardinal by Pope Leo XIII in 1879. Newman was a prolific and gifted writer whose *Apologia Pro Vita Sua*, written in response to fierce criticism of him by Charles Kingsley, is a classic account of a spiritual journey.

## NEWTON, SIR ISAAC (1642–1727) *natural philosopher, lived here*
87 JERMYN STREET, SW1

One of the greatest scientists of all time, Isaac Newton was born near Grantham in Lincolnshire, studied at Trinity College, Cambridge, and went on to make discoveries in the natural sciences and develop ideas in mathematics that mark a turning point in Western thought. Most famously, and possibly following a train of thought initiated by observing an apple fall to the earth, Newton discovered that all material objects on earth and space are affected by the force of gravity. As early as 1666 Newton had elaborated the form of mathematics known as calculus but did not publish his work, thus ensuring the quarrel with the German philosopher and mathematician Leibniz that Newton, a famously quarrelsome man, conducted after Leibniz, who arrived independently at the same mathematical method, *did* publish *his* work. Newton was also interested in optics and the theory of colours and, perhaps surprisingly, devoted a great deal of energy to researches into alchemy and mystical exegeses of the Bible. Particularly later in his life Newton was public figure as well as private scientist. He was elected as one of the MPs for Cambridge University in the aftermath of the Glorious Revolution, was made Master of the Royal Mint and was President of the Royal Society from 1703 until his death. Newton lived in Jermyn Street, first at 88 and then at 87, from the time he left the Warden's House at the Mint in 1696 until 1709.

---

## NICHOLSON, BEN, OM (1894–1982) *artist, lived and died here*
### 2B PILGRIMS LANE, NW3

Nicholson grew up in an artistic household – his father was one of the two poster artists known as the Beggarstaff Brothers and his mother was a painter – and he went to study at the Slade School of Art in 1910. He disliked the teaching style at the Slade, however, and later claimed that he spent most of his time in the nearby Gower Hotel, playing billiards with fellow artist-in-the-making Paul Nash. After leaving the Slade, Nicholson travelled widely in Europe and lived briefly in the USA. His first one-man exhibition was held in 1922 and, by the 1930s, influenced by his encounters with European artists like Picasso and Mondrian, he had become England's leading exponent and advocate of abstract art. In 1935 he organised the first British exhibition of abstract art, working with the short-lived Seven and Five Abstract Group. Nicholson's own work moved between pure abstraction and, especially after his move to Cornwall in 1939, still lifes and landscapes. After the Second World War, Nicholson, by then an internationally renowned artist, continued to work on small-scale paintings and the wood reliefs that he had first made in the 1930s, but he also created large murals for the 1951 Festival of Britain and for the Time-Life Building in London. He was Britain's representative at the Venice Biennale in 1954 and three years later was the first recipient of the newly created Guggenheim award. Nicholson's second wife was the sculptor Barbara Hepworth.

---

## NICOLSON, HAROLD (1886–1968) *and* VITA SACKVILLE-WEST *(1892–1962)* *writers and gardeners, lived here*
### 182 EBURY STREET, W1

One of the more unconventional marriages of the twentieth century, as described in the bestselling book *Portrait of a Marriage* by their son Nigel Nicolson, was that between Harold Nicolson and Vita Sackville-West. Both conducted separate lives; both pursued outside love affairs, most frequently with members of their own sex. Yet the unorthodox relationship lasted nearly half a century until Sackville-West's death. Nicolson was a diplomat and minor politician who also wrote some well-regarded biographies and some gossipy journals, published posthumously. Sackville-West was a poet, travel-writer and novelist whose intense relationship with Virginia Woolf inspired the latter's book *Orlando*. Today she is probably best known for the garden she and Nicolson created at their country home in Knole, Kent. She worked on it for many years, often doing the digging and planting herself. It may be that Cyril Connolly met her after she had been working on the garden. Certainly her dress appeared to him eccentric. 'She looked,' he told a friend, 'like Lady Chatterley above the waist and the gamekeeper below.'

NIGHTINGALE, FLORENCE (1820–1910) *lived and died in a house on this site*
10 SOUTH STREET, W1

## FLORENCE NIGHTINGALE
90 HARLEY STREET, W1   **PRIVATE**

Florence Nightingale took her Christian name from the town where she was born, the daughter of a wealthy Hampshire landowner. Convinced in her twenties of her vocation to nurse, she found it a difficult path for a woman of her class to follow at a time when nursing was not highly respected. She persuaded her family to allow her to visit hospitals and used her own allowance to establish an Institution for Sick Gentlewomen in London. When reports of the suffering of soldiers in the Crimean War reached England, Florence Nightingale managed to arrange for herself and thirty-eight nurses to be sent to the military hospital at Scutari. Her zeal and efficiency, and her recognition of the importance of hygiene, resulted in the death rate at the hospital dropping from 42 per cent to 2.2 per cent. Returning from the Crimea a national heroine in 1856, she spent the rest of her long life as a semi-invalid but campaigned tirelessly for improvements in the training of nursing and the standards of health care, cleverly manipulating the influence her reputation had brought her. She once boasted, probably correctly, that she had 'more political power than if I had been a borough returning two MPs'. In 1907 she became the first woman to be awarded the OM, allegedly receiving it with the words, 'Too kind, too kind.'

NKRUMAH, KWAME (1909–1972) *first President of Ghana, lived here 1945–1947*
60 BURGHLEY ROAD, CAMDEN, NW5

Kwame Nkrumah died in exile in Bucharest, where he had travelled for medical care, more than thirty-five years ago but his legend and his legacy live on. The leader of the first black African country to cast off the chains of colonial rule was voted Africa's man of the millennium in a BBC World Service poll that invited listeners across the continent to make their choice. Born in a small town in what was then the British colony known as the Gold Coast, Nkrumah went to school in Accra and became a teacher himself in his twenties. In 1935, he travelled to the USA to study at a university in Pennsylvania before arriving in London at the end of the Second World War with the intention of studying at the London School of Economics. Within a short time he was deeply involved in the anti-colonial movement of the time and he returned to his native country to organise political pressure for its independence from Britain. By 1949 he had created a new political party, the Convention People's Party, and, although Nkrumah was imprisoned several times over the next few years, his party triumphed in the elections that were held. Eventually, the British authorities accepted Nkrumah as head of an elected government and, within six years of his last release from prison, he was able to declare Ghana an independent nation.

## NOEL-BAKER, PHILIP (1889–1982) *Olympic sportsman, campaigner for peace and disarmament, lived here*

### 16 SOUTH EATON PLACE, SW1

Born Philip Baker (he added the Noel when he married Irene Noel in 1915), Noel-Baker had a brilliant career at Cambridge, both academically and athletically. In 1912 he was captain of the British Olympic team and, after the First World War, in which he served in the Ambulance Corps, he competed in further Olympics, winning a silver medal in the 1920 games. Noel-Baker attended the Versailles Peace Conference and served on the secretariat of the League of Nations in its early years. Elected to Parliament in 1929, he served in Attlee's government as Commonwealth Secretary between 1947 and 1950 and Minister of Fuel and Power in 1950–1. Noel-Baker's lifelong commitment to peace, and his unswerving opposition to nuclear weaponry, were recognised in 1959 when he was awarded the Nobel Peace Prize. Retiring from Parliament at the age of eighty, Noel-Baker reaffirmed his belief in disarmament, declaring that 'While I have the health and strength, I shall give all my time to the work of breaking the dogmatic sleep of those who allow the nuclear, chemical, biological and conventional arms race to go on.'

## NOLLEKENS, JOSEPH (1737–1823) *sculptor, lived and died in a house on this site*
### 44 MORTIMER STREET, W1

Nollekens was one of the great sculptors of the eighteenth century and in his studio in Mortimer Street, where he worked from 1771 until his death, he created portrait busts of all the great figures of his time from Dr Johnson to politicians like Fox and the younger Pitt. He was also a man notorious for his foul table manners – some of his aristocratic patrons insisted that he eat at a table on his own when he visited their country estates – and for his miserliness. Although he became a wealthy man, he was once seen pocketing nutmegs at a Royal Academy party and then pretending to search for the missing spices. His first biographer, J.T. Smith, who seems to have despised his subject, wrote that Nollekens 'will be long remembered as having held a conspicuous rank among contemporary artists . . . but as having, by assiduity rarely surpassed, and parsimony seldom equalled, amassed a princely fortune; from which, however, his avaricious spirit forbade him to derive any comfort or dignity . . .'.

## Headquarters of the NORWEGIAN GOVERNMENT IN EXILE *located here 1940–45*
### KINGSTON HOUSE NORTH, PRINCES GATE, SW7   WESTMINSTER

Following the invasion of their country by the Germans in the spring of 1940, the Norwegian government and parliament rejected an ultimatum to form a new administration, led by Vidkun Quisling, which would have been firmly under Nazi control. Instead King Haakon, Crown Prince Olav and many leading anti-Nazi politicians fled the country, most of them arriving eventually in London. For five years a Norwegian government in exile led the opposition to Nazi rule in Norway and it was focused on a new block of flats on the south side of Hyde Park. Leases on most of the flats at the recently built Kingston House North were taken out and it was there that a wide array of Norwegian offices and agencies from the Central Bank of Norway to the Norwegian Broadcasting Company were kept going, awaiting the time when they would be free to return home.

## NOVELLO, IVOR (1893–1951) *composer and actor manager, lived and died in a flat on the top floor of this building*

11 ALDWYCH, WC2

Ivor Novello was a man of many talents. His song 'Keep the Home Fires Burning' was one of the most popular of the First World War. He was one of the stars of the British silent cinema and crossed the Atlantic to make a movie with the legendary D.W. Griffith. On the stage he was the archetypal matinée idol, playing romantic leads in a succession of musical plays, often works that he had written and composed himself, such as *Glamorous Night* and *The Dancing Years*. Indeed he maintained that he was only successful in his own dramas. 'Although I make no claims that my plays are in any way better than anyone else's,' he wrote, 'they are apparently right for me. Whenever I have been in a play written by anyone else it has failed.'

---

## O'CASEY, SEAN (1880–1964)
*playwright, lived here at Flat No. 49*

OVERSTRAND MANSIONS, PRINCE OF WALES DRIVE, SW11

'All the world's a stage,' Sean O'Casey once wrote, 'and most of us are desperately unrehearsed.' His own particular drama began in Dublin where he was born into a poor Protestant family. After leaving school at the age of fourteen he worked in a variety of jobs and was drawn both to the left wing of Irish nationalism and to the stage. He had to wait until he was in his forties before his name was made as a dramatist when the Abbey Theatre staged *The Shadow of a Gunman* and *Juno and the Paycock* in successive years. In 1926 *The Plough and the Stars*, with what was seen as its insufficiently heroic portrait of people caught up in the Easter Rising, caused a riot at the Abbey. O'Casey was stung into leaving Dublin for London and he was never again to live in the city that had inspired his most famous plays. Although he continued to be a prolific playwright, and to write a sequence of highly praised but not entirely reliable autobiographies, he was never to gain the success of the 1920s. He died in England nearly forty years after leaving Ireland.

---

## O'HIGGINS, BERNARDO (1778–1842) *general, statesman and liberator of Chile, lived and studied here*

CLARENCE HOUSE, 2 THE VINEYARD, RICHMOND

The illegitimate son of an Irish adventurer who had risen from itinerant mule-trader to viceroy of Peru, O'Higgins was born in Chile and sent by his father to school in England. Returning to South America as a young man, his arrival coincided with the rise of the movement to free nations there from Spanish rule and O'Higgins became an enthusiastic nationalist. By 1813 he was Commander-in-Chief of Chilean forces, was effectively dictator of the country from 1817 and made the formal declaration of independence from Spain the following year. In the next five years he demonstrated his abilities as both soldier and administrator by driving Spanish troops from the new nation and organising its government. He resigned from power in 1823 and lived in exile in Lima until his death.

## OLDFIELD, ANN (1683–1730) *actress, first occupant of this house 1725–1730*

### 60 GROSVENOR STREET, W1

At the start of the eighteenth century the queen of
the London stage was Anne Bracegirdle, who owed
her fame to her appearances in the plays of Congreve
at the Drury Lane Theatre. Yet by 1707 she had
retired from the stage, her reputation eclipsed by that
of a new star. That star was Ann Oldfield, who had
made her debut in 1700 and soon shown her talents in
both comedy and tragedy. Unlike the plays of Congreve, in
which Mrs Bracegirdle won her renown, the plays in which
Ann Oldfield took her greatest roles, by lesser known dramatists,
are rarely revived. However, she continued to be the leading actress of her day until shortly before
her death. She was buried in Westminster Abbey, her body, at her own request, entirely wrapped in
a winding sheet because, 'One would not, sure, be frightful, when one's dead.'

## OLIVER, PERCY LANE (1878–1944) *founder of the first voluntary blood donor service, lived and worked here*

### 5 COLYTON ROAD, SE22

Born in St Ives, Cornwall, Percy Lane Oliver was working in London as a volunteer for the
Camberwell division of the British Red Cross Society in 1921 when he received an urgent call
from King's College Hospital. A blood donor was required and one of Oliver's colleagues, Sister
Linstead, became the first volunteer to donate blood. Oliver had the vision to realise that this
need not be a one-off response to an emergency but could be the start of a nationwide service.
He established a series of volunteer panels of donors around the country, the beginnings of what
was to become the National Blood Transfusion Service, and devoted the rest of his life to this
work. The plaque marks the house where Oliver lived and worked to administer his scheme.
One of the wards in King's is now named after him.

## ONSLOW, ARTHUR (1691–1768) *Speaker of the House of Commons from 1728 to 1761, lived in a house on this site*

### 20 SOHO SQUARE, W1

Onslow trained as a barrister and entered Parliament in 1720. Eight years later he was chosen
as Speaker and performed the duties of that office for the next thirty-three years, throughout
much of Walpole's premiership and well into the rule of Pitt the Elder. For the last eight years
of his time as Speaker, Onslow lived at Fauconberg House in Soho Square. The house was
demolished in the 1920s, having spent much of its later life as offices for Crosse & Blackwell.
Onslow's descendants are still represented in Parliament by the Tory MP Cranley Onslow.

## ORPEN, SIR WILLIAM (1878–1931) *painter, lived here*

### 8 SOUTH BOLTON GARDENS, SW5

Born in Dublin, Orpen studied there and at the Slade School of Art and began to exhibit
at the New English Art Club in the late 1890s. He rapidly gained a reputation as a brilliant
portraitist. During the First World War he was commissioned by the government to paint
pictures of battle scenes and of leading military personalities. The official painting of
the *Signing of the Peace Treaties at Versailles*, at the end of the war, was also Orpen's work.
He was knighted for his war work in 1918 and became a Royal Academician two years

later. Despite the success that came to him, he remained an unpretentious man. Writing a letter to a friend, he signed himself Sir William Orpen and appended a string of letters and honours to which he was entitled. Then he added, 'Otherwise known as Bloody Old Bill.'

......................................................................................................................

## ORWELL, GEORGE (1903–1950) *novelist and political essayist, lived here*
50 LAWFORD ROAD, NW5

## GEORGE ORWELL, *writer lived and worked in a bookshop on this site 1934–1935*
SOUTH END ROAD, NW3 **PRIVATE**

## GEORGE ORWELL, *novelist and essayist lived at 27B 1945*
27 CANONBURY SQUARE, N1 **BOROUGH OF ISLINGTON**

Eric Blair was an old Etonian who returned from serving in the Imperial Police in Burma, disgusted by colonialism, took the pen name of George Orwell (the latter name came, probably, from the Suffolk river) and began a precarious career as a freelance writer. Books in the thirties such as *Down and Out in Paris and London*, *The Road to Wigan Pier* and *Homage to Catalonia* gave him a reputation as a writer of bluntly honest prose but did not provide him with an adequate income. He took other jobs, including working at a Hampstead bookshop, and wrote quantities of journalism. During the war he worked for the *Observer* and at the BBC, which he memorably described as having an atmosphere 'something halfway between a girls' school and a lunatic asylum.' After the war his fortune was made by his two most famous novels, *Animal Farm* and *1984*, but Orwell was already a sick man and he died of tuberculosis in the year after the latter book's publication. Orwell was an unashamedly political writer and Cyril Connolly, who had been at school with him, once wrote that 'He would not blow his nose without moralising on conditions in the handkerchief industry.'

......................................................................................................................

## ÖSTERBERG, MARTINA BERGMAN (1849–1915) *pioneer of physical education for women, lived and worked here*

1 BROADHURST GARDENS, HAMPSTEAD, NW6

'Joy and brightness combined with strict discipline are essential to a good gymnastic lesson', wrote Martina Österberg in 1887, and her career was devoted to encouraging others to follow that precept. Born in Sweden, Österberg trained at the Royal Central Gymnastic Institute in Stockholm and moved to London in 1881. Working for the London School Board for the next five years, she passed on her experience of the Swedish gymnastic system to hundreds of teachers in the capital. Her work received much attention and, in 1883, a display of Swedish gymnastics by 100 girls from some of the poorest areas of London, organised by Österberg, was attended by the Prince and Princess of Wales and a host of other dignitaries. Österberg went on to found her own school of physical education at Hampstead. It transferred to Dartford in 1895 and is still in existence as Dartford College, part of the University of Greenwich. It was at Dartford that Österberg became one of the first people to introduce basketball to Britain, a game she had seen played during a visit to the USA. Under Österberg's guidance, the game metamorphosed into the game of netball, played by millions of schoolgirls in the decades since then.

......................................................................................................................

## 'OUIDA' (MARIA LOUISA DE LA RAMÉE) (1839–1908) *novelist, lived here*
11 RAVENSCOURT SQUARE, W11

Born in Bury St Edmunds of a French father and English mother, Maria Louisa de la Ramée took her pseudonym from a childish mispronunciation of one of her Christian names. She was an enormously popular writer of torrid romances in which impossibly handsome and dashing heroes, often guardsmen, performed miracles of derring-do and shone brightly in high society. The profits from such works as *Held in Bondage* (1863) and *Under Two Flags* (1867) enabled her to move to the Villa Farniola in Florence, where she lived a life of luxury and high emotional drama that could have come from one of her own novels. In her later years her popularity (and her profits) faded but she continued to live well beyond her means. Eventually evicted from the Villa Farniola, she became increasingly eccentric and increasingly impoverished, and she died in destitution in Viareggio.

## PAGE, SIR FREDERICK HANDLEY (1885–1962) *aircraft designer and manufacturer, lived here in flat 3*

18 GROSVENOR SQUARE, W1

Born in Cheltenham, Handley Page was one of the pioneers of the British aeronautical industry., founding the company that bore his name in 1909. The First World War brought the company much work from the Royal Flying Corps (RFC) and Handley Page, presented with by a senior figure in the RFC with the challenge of creating 'a bloody paralyser of an airplane', designed what was one of the world's earliest heavy bombers. In 1918 He built a four-engined bomber, which had the capacity to reach German cities and the industrial areas of the Ruhr, but the war ended before the aircraft, a portent of conflict to come, could be used. In the 1920s and 1930s Handley Page turned to civil aviation but, when the Second World War broke out, the company was once again directed towards the war effort. Many of the most famous (and effective) bombers of the war, such as the Halifax and the Hampden, were produced by Handley Page. In recognition of his contribution to the war effort, Handley Page was knighted in 1942. Handley Page Ltd, Britain's first publicly traded aircraft-manufacturing company, ceased trading under the name in 1970, eight years after its founder's death.

## PALGRAVE, FRANCIS TURNER (1824–1897) *compiler of 'The Golden Treasury', lived here 1862–1875*

5 YORK GATE, REGENT'S PARK, NW1

Palgrave's father changed his name from Cohen on his marriage and conversion to Christianity and was an eminent historian, particularly of the Middle Ages. His brother William became a Jesuit missionary in the Middle East and wrote an entertaining narrative of an expedition he undertook through Arabia, in disguise, at the behest of the French emperor Napoleon III. Francis Turner Palgrave, although he published a number of volumes of his own verse, is best remembered for *The Golden Treasury of best songs and Lyrical poems in the English language* (its full title), an anthology which has been almost continuously in print, in various editions, since first publication in 1861. Palgrave was advised in his choice of poems by Tennyson, who was a good friend.

## PALMER, SAMUEL (1805–1881) *artist, lived here 1851–1861*
6 DOURO PLACE, W8

## SAMUEL PALMER
42 SURREY SQUARE, SE17   **PRIVATE**

The highpoint of Palmer's life and career consisted of the years in which he became a disciple of the ageing William Blake and retired to the Kentish village of Shoreham to pursue his own artistic vision. When he was first introduced to Blake, the older artist asked him, 'Do you work with fear and trembling?' Palmer replied, 'Yes, indeed.' 'Then, you'll do,' Blake said. For the next ten years Palmer worked on his visionary landscapes in the isolated setting of Shoreham in the attempt to show that he would, indeed, do. Palmer's Shoreham work is now considered his best and, by the time he was living in Douro Place, the freshness of his youthful vision had faded. He was, and remained, relatively poor and was dependent on financial support from his father-in-law and fellow-painter John Linnell. Yet he was still working and continuing to produce both landscapes and illustrations to his own translation of Virgil. Palmer's work was rarely in sympathy with prevailing Victorian taste during his lifetime but has been much admired in recent years as that of a genuinely original English artist.

## PALMERSTON, HENRY JOHN TEMPLE, 3RD VISCOUNT (1784–1865)
*Prime Minister, born here*

20 QUEEN ANNE'S GATE, SW1

## 3RD VISCOUNT HENRY JOHN TEMPLE PALMERSTON, *statesman, lived here*

4 CARLTON GARDENS, SW1

## LORD PALMERSTON (1784–1865) *In this house formerly a Royal residence lived Lord Palmerston, Prime Minister and Foreign Secretary*

NAVAL AND MILITARY CLUB, 94 PICCADILLY, W1

Palmerston was in Parliament for nearly sixty years and he spent nearly fifty of those in office. Serving first as a Tory, he crossed the floor to join the Whigs because he supported parliamentary reform. He was rewarded with the Foreign Secretaryship, which he held throughout the 1830s and again from 1846 to 1851. In this role Palmerston was a pugnacious defender of British interests, even to the extent of initiating the ultimate in gunboat diplomacy when, in 1850, he threatened to bombard Athens because the government there had mistreated a Gibraltar-born merchant called David Pacifico, who could lay claim to British citizenship. Home Secretary between 1852 and 1855, Palmerston became Prime Minister when the difficulties of prosecuting the Crimean War brought down the government. Palmerston's belligerence was what the country required. Out of office briefly in the late 1850s, Palmerston became Prime Minister again in 1859 and died in office at the age of eighty-one. His last words were, reputedly, 'Die, my dear doctor, that is the last thing I shall do!' Palmerston, who was the last Prime Minister to ride to the House of Commons on horseback, lived at Carlton Gardens from 1846 to 1855 and at 94 Piccadilly, a house earlier occupied by George III's seventh son the Duke of Cambridge, from 1857 until his death.

## PANKHURST, EMMELINE (1858–1928) *and* PANKHURST, DAME CHRISTABEL (1880–1958) *campaigners for women's suffrage, lived here*

50 CLARENDON ROAD, HOLLAND PARK, W11

'The inferiority of women is a hideous lie which has been enforced by law and woven into the British Constitution,' Christabel Pankhurst wrote, 'and it is quite hopeless to expect reform of the relationship between the sexes until women are politically enfranchised.' She and her mother were, for many years, the leaders of the militant suffragette campaign to bring about that enfranchisement. Emmeline Pankhurst founded the Women's Social and Political Union in 1903 in her home town of Manchester after she grew disillusioned with what she saw as the timidity and ineffectiveness of existing organisations pressing for the vote for women. Her daughter Christabel was one of the first to use the new tactics they considered necessary to gain publicity for the WSPU when she heckled a government minister in a public meeting and was arrested for assaulting the police officers who attempted to evict her. Emmeline and Christabel remained leaders of the movement throughout its increasingly militant campaign and both suffered periods of imprisonment and, in Emmeline's case, forced feeding when she went on hunger strike. The WSPU's demands were suspended for the duration of the First World War and women over 30 were given the vote once the war ended. Equal voting rights with men were granted in 1928, the year Emmeline Pankhurst died. After the Great War, Christabel left Britain for the USA where, convinced of the imminence of the Second Coming of Christ, she became a leading evangelical speaker. She returned to Britain for a time in the 1930s but she was living in California when she died at the age of seventy-eight.

## PANKHURST, SYLVIA (1882–1960) *campaigner for women's rights, lived here*
### 120 CHEYNE WALK, SW10

Sylvia Pankhurst was, arguably, the most remarkable member of a very remarkable family of mother and three daughters. Emmeline Pankhurst was the founder and the charismatic leader of the Women's Social and Political Union in its struggle for women's suffrage. All three of her daughters, Christabel, Adela and Sylvia, campaigned vigorously for the WPSU. Sylvia Pankhurst had trained as an artist but, as a founder member of the WSPU, suffered the imprisonment and force-feeding that was imposed on its most militant campaigners. She broke with her mother because of her vehement opposition to the First World War. 'I could not give my name,' Sylvia wrote, 'to aid the slaughter in this war, fought on both sides for grossly material ends, which did not justify the sacrifice of a single mother's son.' After the war she visited Soviet Russia,
became a leading member of the British Communist Party but was expelled for refusing to accept party discipline and, in the thirties, campaigned against Italian occupation of Ethiopia. In her seventies she moved to Ethiopia and she died in Addis Ababa.

## PARRY, SIR CHARLES HUBERT (1848–1918) *musician, lived here*
### 17 KENSINGTON SQUARE, W8

Very nearly everyone knows one piece of music by Parry. It was he who, during the First World War, made the famous setting of Blake's poem 'Jerusalem', which is sung, with patriotic gusto, at the Last Night of the Proms. Sadly for Parry's posthumous reputation, that is just about the only piece by him that is regularly played. Yet in his Victorian and Edwardian heyday he was, with Stanford, one of the two composers who brought English music out of the doldrums and his many works, from symphonies and chamber music to oratorios like *Job* and *King Saul*, were widely praised and performed. As Director of the Royal College of Music from 1895 he was the English music establishment embodied and his influence on the next generation of composers was considerable.

## PATEL, SARDAR (1875–1950) *Indian statesman, lived here*
### 23 ALDRIDGE ROAD VILLAS, W11

One of a family that devoted itself to the cause of Indian independence (his elder brother was a leading supporter of Gandhi), Vallabhbhai Patel came to London before the First World War to qualify as a barrister. Returning to Indian he joined Gandhi's civil disobedience campaign in 1917 and was soon one of the Mahatma's most successful lieutenants, earning himself the honorary name of 'Sardar' or 'Leader'. President of Congress in 1931, he was imprisoned several times by the British in the 1930s and '40s but emerged from prison in 1945 to play an important part in negotiations for independence. After independence Patel played a crucial role in integrating the princely states into the new union and, in the three years before his death, wielded great power as Deputy Prime Minister to Nehru.

## PATER, WALTER (1839–1894) *aesthete and writer, lived and worked here 1885–1893*
### 12 EARLS TERRACE, W8

To a generation of cultured young men and women in late Victorian Britain who believed in 'art for art's sake', the writings of the Oxford don Walter Pater were of central importance. 'Art comes to you proposing frankly to give nothing but the highest quality to your moments as they pass,' Pater wrote in one of the essays collected in his book *Studies in the History of the Renaissance* and many people, including soon-to-be famous figures such as Oscar Wilde, took note of his words. The poet W.B. Yeats was another who was later able to say that, 'we looked consciously to Pater for our philosophy'. Pater was born in Stepney, the son of a doctor. His undergraduate career at Oxford was not a brilliant one but he became a don at Brasenose College and his writings soon began to attract attention. To some he seemed the representative of an unhealthy and effeminate aestheticism; to others he was an inspiration and his most famous work, the philosophical novel *Marius the Epicurean*, was a masterpiece. Pater spent much of his adult life in Oxford, looked after by his sisters, but he moved with them to the house in Earls Terrace in 1885, where, during the months outside academic terms, he lived for the next eight years.

## PATMORE, COVENTRY (1823–1896) *poet and essayist, lived here 1863–1864*
### 14 PERCY STREET, W1

Little read today, Coventry Patmore was one of the most popular of Victorian poets and his long sequence of poems in celebration of married love, *The Angel in the House*, one of the most widely quoted works of the time. Born into a literary family – his father was a journalist and friend of such writers as Lamb and Hazlitt – Patmore became involved with the Pre-Raphaelites and was an early contributor to *The Germ*, the Pre-Raphaelite house magazine. In 1847 he married Emily, the inspiration for *The Angel in the House*. She died in 1862. Two years later he married his second wife, Marianne, but he was also to outlive her and married for a third time in the 1880s. Patmore converted to Roman Catholicism in 1864, which may have had an effect on the popularity of his later work with the staunchly Church of England Victorian reading public. Certainly none of his later poetry had anything like the success of *The Angel in the House*.

## PEABODY, GEORGE (1795–1869) *philanthropist, lived here*
### 80 EATON SQUARE, SW1

Peabody was born in Massachussetts in a town then called South Danvers but now named after him. He moved to London in 1837 and established the merchant business that went through many incarnations to emerge, after Peabody's death, as Morgan Grenfell & Co. As a philanthropist, Peabody gave to many causes, encouraging education in America and even subsidising an expedition to the Arctic, but his chief legacies are the Peabody Buildings, the housing schemes for the poor that were established throughout London in the later part of the nineteenth century. These are not great works of architecture (Pevsner described one as 'familiar but none the less detestable') but they went some way towards fulfilling Peabody's ambition to 'ameliorate the condition of the poor and needy of this great metropolis'.

......................................................................................................................................

## PEAKE, MERVYN (1911–1968) *author and artist, lived here 1960–1968*

1 DRAYTON GARDENS, SW10

## MERVYN PEAKE (1911–1968)

SURREY COURT, 55 WOODCOTE ROAD, WALLINGTON    **BOROUGH OF SUTTON**

Born in China, the son of a missionary doctor and his wife, Mervyn Peake grew up to be one of the most versatile and least classifiable English writers and artists of the century. He studied art at the Croydon Art School and the Royal Academy Schools and published his first book, a children's story *Captain Slaughterboard Drops Anchor*, embellished by his own illustrations in 1939. During the war he worked as a war artist and visited Belsen soon after its liberation, an experience that was to haunt him for the rest of his life. The late forties were the most productive years of Peake's life. He created memorable illustrations for a number of classics of English literature, including 'The Rime of the Ancient Mariner' and *Alice in Wonderland*, and also produced three volumes (*Titus Groan, Gormenghast* and *Titus Alone*) of his own gothic fantasy about the life of Titus, 77th Earl of Groan and his crumbling, ritual-haunted castle of Gormenghast. By the late fifties Peake had begun to show signs of the Parkinson's disease that was to kill him and his last decade was troubled by an increasing inability to practise the drawing and illustration at which he excelled.

......................................................................................................................................

## PEARSON, JOHN LOUGHBOROUGH (1817–1897) *and later* SIR EDWIN LANDSEER LUTYENS (1869–1944), *architects, lived and died here*

13 MANSFIELD STREET, W1

Pearson was one of the most eminent and prolific of Victorian architects, particularly noted for his church architecture. Among a number of London churches that he built, St Peter's, Kennington Lane, and St Augustine's, Kilburn, one of the largest Victorian churches in the city, are particularly noteworthy. He was also a sensitive restorer and rebuilder of older churches, such as St Nicholas, Chiswick. Lutyens was described by one critic as 'the greatest English architect since Christopher Wren' and his work can be seen in smaller, private houses in the country, in ecclesiastical buildings like the Roman Catholic cathedral in Liverpool and in the great public buildings of Empire such as the Viceroy's House in New Delhi. Among his other gifts, Lutyens was a connoisseur of the pun. Once in a restaurant, on being given a helping of fish of poor quality, he told the waiter, 'This must be the piece of cod that passeth all understanding.'

......................................................................................................................................

## PEARSON, KARL (1857–1936) *pioneer statistician, lived here*

7 WELL ROAD, HAMPSTEAD, NW3

Pearson was a man of many intellectual abilities, who not only graduated from Cambridge as third wrangler (placed third in the mathematical tripos) but was also sufficiently erudite in German language and literature to be offered a Cambridge lectureship in the subject. He turned it down to study law but returned to mathematics in 1884 as a professor at University College, London. A fellow professor, Walter Weldon, turned to Pearson for assistance with statistical problems and Pearson devoted his intellectual energies to the subject, publishing over thirty important and pioneering papers on the subject between 1893 and 1901. Weldon also introduced Pearson to Francis Galton and, when Galton died in 1911 and left money for the creation of a Chair in the now controversial subject of eugenics, Pearson was its first holder. A lifelong socialist, Pearson refused all non-academic honours, including the knighthood that was offered to him in the year before his death.

PEEL, SIR ROBERT (1750–1830) *manufacturer and reformer, and his son* SIR ROBERT PEEL (1788–1850), *Prime Minister, founder of the Metropolitan Police, lived here*

16 UPPER GROSVENOR STREET, W1

Robert Peel the Elder was a wealthy northern cotton magnate who had entered Parliament in 1790 and was knighted ten years later. His son, also Robert, was educated at Harrow and Christ Church, Oxford, and became an MP the year after he graduated. In the course of a political career that lasted over forty years, the younger Peel was twice Home Secretary, twice Prime Minister and twice he split his party over a matter of principle. In 1829 he brought forward a measure to remove most of the remaining penal laws against Roman Catholics and, although it passed into law, it broke the Tory party in two. Nearly twenty years later, this time as Prime Minister, Peel's insistence on free trade and the repeal of the Corn Laws had a similar effect. Peel's most famous act as Home Secretary was to introduce the Metropolitan Police. When policemen are called 'bobbies' this is a reminder that they were created by 'Bobby' Peel. In June 1850 Peel was thrown from his horse and a few days later died of the injuries he had received.

PELHAM, HENRY (*c.*1695–1754) *Prime Minister, lived here*

22 ARLINGTON STREET, SW1

Although he held the office for more than a decade, Henry Pelham is one of the least remembered of prime ministers. However, Gladstone, in the following century, admired him and claimed that he was one of the only eighteenth-century politicians to show any signs of financial competence. Pelham spent his early years in Parliament as a supporter of Walpole and he came to power shortly after Walpole's departure from politics. Using his own talent for political survival, and that of his brother the Duke of Newcastle, he remained Prime Minister until his death, despite crises like Bonnie Prince Charlie's rebellion that took place during his time in office. He was succeeded by his brother. The plaque to Pelham is on the rear of the building and overlooks Queen's Walk, Green Park.

*In a house on this site* PEPYS, SAMUEL *diarist, was born (1633–1703)*

WESTMINSTER BANK, SALISBURY COURT, EC4   **CITY OF LONDON**

*Site of the Navy Office where* SAMUEL PEPYS *lived and worked. Destroyed by fire 1673*

SEETHING LANE, EC3   **CITY OF LONDON**

SAMUEL PEPYS. (1633–1703) *diarist and Secretary of the Admiralty, lived here 1679–1688*

12 BUCKINGHAM STREET. WC2

Pepys was born in 1633 in a house in Salisbury Court, off Fleet Street, the son of a tailor, and was educated at school near St Paul's Cathedral and at Magdalene College, Cambridge. When his famous diary was begun, on 1 January 1660, he was married and working in London as a lowly and poorly paid civil servant. The years in which he kept his diary were also the years in which his professional life flourished as he became a more and more significant and prosperous naval administrator. He ceased keeping his diary in May 1669, largely because he believed, wrongly, that he was going blind. After the period covered by the diary Pepys, despite setbacks that included a brief stay in the Tower at the time of the Popish Plot, continued his successful career in public life. At the time of the Glorious Revolution, he retired to a substantial property at Clapham. His *Diary*, in shorthand, was kept with his other papers at his old college and a selection was finally deciphered and published in 1825. The diary owes its popularity to its combination of the domestic and the public. Pepys records graphically two of the great events in London's history – the Fire and the Plague – but he also tells us, for example, in an entry of 4 April 1666, that he went 'home, and being wash-day, dined upon cold meat'.

*In a house formerly standing on this site lived* SAMUEL PEPYS (1633–1703), *diarist and* ROBERT HARLEY. EARL OF OXFORD (1661–1724), *statesman; and in this house lived* WILLIAM ETTY (1787–1849), *painter, and* CLARKSON STANFIELD (1793–1867), *painter*

14 BUCKINGHAM STREET. WC2

Pepys moved into his house in Buckingham Street in 1688 but was soon obliged to move out to Clapham when the Glorious Revolution put him out of political favour. Harley, who moved into the house in 1700, was a Whig politician. He became Speaker in the House of Commons the year after he moved into Buckingham Street and was Chancellor of the Exchequer and, effectively, head of the government in 1710. After his retirement from politics he was able to spend more time amassing his large collection of books and manuscripts, which now forms a valuable part of the British Library. William Etty was born in York and became the leading painter of nudes and figure studies of his time. He lived in the house now on the site of Pepys's mansion for many years and, between 1826 and 1831, his fellow painter Clarkson Stanfield lodged with him. Stanfield was a marine painter who, unusually, had gained first-hand experience of his subject by serving in the Navy before turning to art.

PERCEVAL. SPENCER (1762–1812) *Prime Minister, lived here*

59-60 LINCOLN INN'S FIELDS. WC1

Remembered more for the manner of his death than for any political achievements, Perceval entered Parliament in 1796 as MP for Northampton and was a strong supporter of Pitt the Younger. Chancellor of the Exchequer from 1807, he became Prime Minister in 1809. On 11 May 1812, as he was walking through the lobby of the House of Commons, he was shot and fatally wounded by John Bellingham, a deranged and bankrupt Liverpool broker who blamed the government for his financial setbacks. Perceval remains the only British Prime Minister to have been assassinated. His government was not popular and nor was Perceval himself. One witness in a Midlands town records hearing the news when a man ran down the street in a state of great excitement, shouting 'Perceval is shot, hurrah!', and it was not thought appropriate to give the dead Prime Minister a public funeral for fear of the disturbances that might attend it.

## PETRIE, SIR WILLIAM MATTHEW FLINDERS (1853–1942) *Egyptologist, lived here*

### 5 CANNON PLACE, NW3

Grandson of the explorer Matthew Flinders, Petrie devoted his life to archaeology and published nearly a hundred scientific works, including a massive three-volume *History of Egypt*. His first archaeological research was done in England and he published a book on Stonehenge, but ancient Egypt had been his consuming interest since childhood and his major excavations were all designed to increase our knowledge of that civilization. For close on fifty years, and well into his old age, he returned again and again to dig in Egypt and his excavations yielded much new information about such monuments as the pyramids and temples at Giza. Petrie was also Professor of Egyptology at University College, London, for many years and he left his extraordinary personal collection of ancient Egyptian artefacts to the college where they can still be seen.

## PETTY, WILLIAM, EARL OF SHELBURNE, 1ST MARQUESS OF LANSDOWNE (1737–1805) *Prime Minister, supporter of American Independence, lived here*

### THE LANSDOWNE CLUB, 9 FITZMAURICE PLACE, BERKELEY SQUARE, W1

Between the ministry of William Pitt the Elder and that of his son, William Pitt the Younger, Britain was governed by a series of aristocratic prime ministers, most of whose names have been forgotten by the general public. One of these was William Petty, the Earl of Shelburne, who held the highest office in government for a brief but crucial period in Anglo-American relations from July 1782 to April 1783. Shelburne was born in Dublin and his peerage was an Irish one but he studied at Christ Church, Oxford and then bought a commission in the 20th Regiment of Footguards. He fought in the Seven Years' War and was still serving in the army when he first entered politics. An early supporter of the rights of American colonists and an opponent of attempts to tax them unfairly, Shelburne was given a post in government while still in his twenties but his stance on American issues soon led to his dismissal. He returned to government some years later as Home Secretary and was chosen as Prime Minister following the death of the previous incumbent, the Marquess of Rockingham. Rockingham's ministry had already acknowledged the independence of the American states; it was left to Shelburne's ministry to sign the peace treaty with them that ended the American War of Independence.

## PEVSNER, SIR NIKOLAUS (1902–1983) *architectural historian, lived here from 1936 until his death*

### 2, WILDWOOD TERRACE, NW3

'All art, so long as it is sound and healthy, serves building,' Nikolaus Pevsner wrote in the 1930s, stating his belief that architecture was the queen of all the arts. His profound love of architecture found its greatest expression in his monumental creation, *The Buildings of England*, a forty-six volume series of county-by-county guidebooks to the notable buildings of the British Isles, which were published between 1951 and 1975 and continue to appear in revised editions today. No other country has such a remarkable record of its architecture and it was the work of a man who, as his name suggests, was not himself British. Nikolaus Pevsner was born in Leipzig, studied art history at a number of universities in Germany and was working as an academic when Hitler came to power. As a Jew, Pevsner lost his job and he moved to London, eventually becoming a member of the teaching staff at Birkbeck College. After the war, he remained in Britain and embarked on the series of long journeys around the country, which gave him the raw material for his *magnum opus*. It was a vast and exhausting task he had set himself but the dedication to his volume on Bedfordshire suggests one way in which he sustained himself while undertaking it. It reads: 'To the inventor of the ice lolly'.

## PHELPS, SAMUEL (1804–1878) *tragedian, lived here*
8 CANONBURY SQUARE, N1

Born in Devonport, Phelps decided early in his life that he wanted a career in the theatre but it was not until 1837 that he made his debut on the London stage – he played Shylock at the Haymarket – and it was not until he took over the management of Sadler's Wells in 1844 that he was able to achieve his greatest success. At the time the omens were not favourable. As Phelps himself wrote, 'I took an obscure theatre in the north of London . . . and nearly the whole of my brethren in the profession and many out of it, said it could not last a fortnight.' Much to Phelps's satisfaction his management lasted eighteen years and his greatest triumphs were in Shakespearean roles. Phelps lived with his wife in Canonbury Square from the time he took on Sadler's Wells until the death of his wife in 1867.

## PICK, FRANK (1878–1941) *pioneer of good design for London Transport, lived here*
15 WILDWOOD ROAD, NW11

For much of the first half of the twentieth century London Underground had a deserved reputation for the quality of the design work to be seen on its stations and in its advertising. The man most responsible for this was Frank Pick, who joined the Underground in 1906 and eventually rose to the position of Vice-Chairman of the London Passenger Transport Board when it was created in 1933. Pick was one of the founders of the Design and Industries Association in 1915 and was, throughout his career, committed to the widespread use of strong and distinctive design in industry. At the Underground he commissioned high quality posters from artists such as McKnight Kauffer, Graham Sutherland, Frank Brangwyn and Frank Newbould and it was Pick who was responsible for inviting the calligrapher and designer Edward Johnston to create the particular font used on the Tube and the bull's eye symbol that, in modified form, still exists today.

## PINERO, SIR ARTHUR (1855–1934) *playwright, lived here 1909–1934*
115A HARLEY STREET, W1

The 1890s was a remarkable decade for English theatre. The plays of Oscar Wilde were staged for the first time; Bernard Shaw's first plays were written, although he had difficulties getting them performed. And a number of other playwrights wrote dramas that are still popular today. One of these dramatists was Arthur Pinero, who deserted a career in his father's law office to become an actor and then turned to writing both farces and 'social problem' plays. *The Second Mrs Tanqueray*, first staged in 1893, tells an ultimately tragic tale of a woman with a past. *Trelawny of the 'Wells'*, from 1898, is a nostalgic comedy in which Rose Trelawny, star of the Bagnigge Wells Theatre, has to choose between the stage and married life. During the years Pinero lived in Harley Street his popularity declined dramatically, but his plays are still revived today.

## PISSARRO, LUCIEN (1863–1944) *painter, printer, wood engraver, lived here*
27 STAMFORD BROOK ROAD, CHISWICK, W6

The French impressionist painter Camille Pissarro made several visits to London and some of his most distinctive paintings are of English suburban landscapes. His son Lucien, who exhibited with his father in the last Impressionist group exhibition in Paris in 1886, came to England in 1890 and it became his home. He even became a founding member in 1911, together with artists like Sickert and Augustus John, of the quintessentially English Camden Town Group. Lucien Pissarro was a versatile artist, equally at home as a painter, as a wood engraver and, perhaps most originally, as a printer. His Eragny Press, which he founded in 1894 and for which he designed type-fonts, produced some of the most interesting work to emerge from the private presses of the period. He lived at Stamford Brook Road for the last thirty-four years of his life.

---

## PITT, WILLIAM, EARL OF CHATHAM (1708–1778) *Here lived three Prime Ministers: WILLIAM PITT, EARL OF CHATHAM; EDWARD GEOFFREY STANLEY, EARL OF DERBY (1799–1869); WILLIAM EWART GLADSTONE (1809–1898)*

### 10 ST JAMES'S SQUARE, SW1

The elder Pitt, son of an MP, entered parliament in 1735 and was one of its leading figures for the next forty years. A powerful orator and skilful political intriguer, he was effectively Prime Minister during one of the most formative periods in British imperial history, the first years of the Seven Years' War, when the country won control of large areas of India and of the Americas. Despite the victories of the time, Pitt was compelled to resign and, apart from a brief return to power in the late 1760s, he remained a brooding presence in opposition for the rest of his active life. He spoke out against policies in the American colonies, declaring that, 'If I were an American, as I am an Englishman, while a foreign troop was landed in my country, I would never lay down my arms.' His last speech in the House of Lords, when he was already a dying man, was a plea to his countrymen to seek an honourable exit from the American Revolution. He lived in St James's Square during his period in power. The Earl of Derby, who lived in the house in the Square for nearly twenty years, has been largely forgotten save by historians but he was three times Prime Minister, in 1852/3, 1858/9 and 1866–8. Gladstone, in contrast, remains the most famous of Victorian politicians. He lived at 10 St James's Square briefly in the early 1890s.

---

## PITT, WILLIAM, THE YOUNGER (1759–1806) *Prime Minister, lived here 1803–1804*

### 120 BAKER STREET, W1

Few men have devoted their lives so exclusively to politics as William Pitt. The son of a Prime Minister, he entered Parliament in 1781 and was only twenty-four when he became the youngest man in British history to hold that same office. He was in power for the next seventeen years. Many of these years were years of warfare as Britain fought against, first, the armies of revolutionary France and, second, those of Napoleon. Pitt felt obliged to enact repressive measures to counteract potential radicalism at home and also introduced income tax in 1798 as a means of paying for the struggle against the French. His government also passed the Act that brought the Irish and British parliaments together in 1800. He resigned the following year when the King vetoed the Catholic Emancipation, which Pitt thought a necessary accompaniment to the union. Brought back in 1804 he was already an ill man, worn out by years of overwork and too keen a devotion to port wine, and he died in January 1806. According to taste, one can believe that his last words were, 'I think I could eat one of Bellamy's veal pies,' or the more noble, 'Oh, my country! How I leave my country!' Both versions are probably apocryphal.

---

## PITT-RIVERS, LIEUTENANT GENERAL AUGUSTUS HENRY LANE FOX (1827–1900) *anthropologist and archaeologist, lived here*

### 4 GROSVENOR GARDENS, SW1

Born in Yorkshire, a member of the Lane Fox family, Pitt-Rivers inherited a new name, together with large estates in the West Country, from his great-uncle in 1880. For many years he was a professional soldier and eventually rose to the rank of Lieutenant-General.

Alongside his Army career he had also maintained his own interest in collecting objects from human cultures all over the world and, in 1883, he presented these collections to Oxford University where they formed the nucleus of the Pitt-Rivers Museum. As he grew older, and particularly after his inheritance, Pitt-Rivers was able to devote more of his time to his investigations into the past and and his excavations of Romano-British and Saxon sites on his own lands were, for their time, models of archaeological field work. Pitt-Rivers was the first person to hold the post of Inspector of Ancient Monuments.

## PLAATJE, SOL (1876–1932) *black South African writer, lived here*
### 25 CARNARVON ROAD, E10

Solomon Tshekisho Plaatje was one of the leading South Africans of his time, a writer and editor who published *Mhudi*, often considered the first novel written by a black South African, and a politician who became the first General Secretary of the African National Congress on its formation in 1912. As a young man, Plaatje was a court interpreter during the siege of Mafeking and, after the war, edited two newspapers that were among the first to address a black audience. In 1916 he published *Native Life in South Africa*, his best-known book and a powerful denunciation of the effects of government legislation in 1913 on black South Africans. Its opening sentence ('Awaking on Friday morning, June 20th 1913, the South African native found himself, if not actually a slave, a pariah in the land of his birth.') continued to resonate through many more decades of South African history. Plaatje lodged briefly in London while on a delegation to British government officials.

## PLACE, FRANCIS (1771–1854) *political reformer, lived here 1833–1851*
### 21 BROMPTON SQUARE, SW3

Although he never held political office, Place was at the heart of radical politics from the time of the British Jacobins in the 1790s to the time of the Chartists in the 1840s. As a youth he was apprenticed to a breeches-maker and his first involvement with political activity was when, in 1793, he helped organise a strike by the Breeches-makers Benefit Society. The strike was unsuccessful and Place was marked as a trouble-maker. Unable to find work, he and his wife, as he later recalled, 'suffered every kind of privation consequent on want of employment and food and fire'. Place was, however, a man of resource and, despite setbacks, he had, by 1801, established a tailor's shop and his career as 'the radical tailor of Charing Cross' was underway. As the business prospered Place devoted more and more time to politics. He campaigned to elect a Radical MP for Westminster, was instrumental in repealing the anti-trade union Combination Laws and, in the agitation for parliamentary reform in the early 1830s, he was a leading figure. In 1838 he helped draft the petition that became the People's Charter. He was also an early advocate of birth-control.

## PLATH, SYLVIA (1932–1963) *poet, lived here 1960–1961*
### 3 CHALCOT SQUARE, PRIMROSE HILL, NW1

Sylvia Plath has been described as 'one of the most powerful and lavishly gifted poets of her time', but she is now remembered as much for the tragedy of her self-inflicted death as she is for her work. Born in Boston in the USA, she was a star student at Smith College but was haunted by the death of her father when she was eight and attempted suicide during her time there, an experience fictionalised in her novel *The Bell Jar*. Despite her emotional and mental traumas, she graduated from Smith *summa cum laude* and won a scholarship to travel to England and study at Cambridge. There she met the poet Ted Hughes and they were married in 1956. After a period of time spent living in America, Plath became pregnant and the couple moved to London where her first child was born in the flat in Chalcot Square. Hughes and Plath separated in the autumn of 1962 and she moved into another flat, also in Primrose Hill, which had once been the home of W.B. Yeats. On the morning of 11 February 1963, during one of the coldest English winters on record, Sylvia Plath killed herself by placing her head in a gas oven, having first ensured that there was no possibility the gas could seep through to where her children were sleeping. It was only after her suicide that Plath, who wrote in one of her poems, 'Dying / Is an art, like everything else. / I do it exceptionally well', was fully recognised as a poet of major significance.

## PLAYFAIR, SIR NIGEL (1874–1934) *actor-manager, lived here*
### 26 PELHAM CRESCENT, SW7

Originally trained as a barrister, Playfair did not make his professional stage debut until 1902 but he quickly showed that he was capable of a range of parts from Shakespeare to Shaw. For nearly twenty years he was happy to pursue his career as a character actor but, after the First World War, he took on the management of the Lyric Theatre, Hammersmith, often known as 'The Blood and Flea Pit' because of its less than uplifting decor and repertoire. Playfair transformed the theatre and raised its status and reputation immeasurably. A revival of *The Beggar's Opera* received nearly fifteen hundred performances, the legendary Ellen Terry made her last stage appearance there, and contemporary playwrights like A.A. Milne and A.P. Herbert, who lived nearby in Hammersmith, premiered their works there. Playfair made the theatre his own and when he left, the year before his death, its fortunes declined.

## POLIDORI, JOHN (1795–1821) *poet and novelist, author of 'The Vampyre' born and died here*
### 38 GREAT PULTENEY STREET, W1   **WESTMINSTER**

In the summer of 1816 the poets Shelley and Byron, together with Shelley's wife Mary, were staying in Switzerland. Conversation turned frequently to the supernatural and all three began to write stories on the subject. Only one was finished and that was *Frankenstein* by Mary Shelley. Also staying in the house was Byron's friend and physician John Polidori, and he also wrote a supernatural tale, *The Vampyre*, one of the earliest of all stories of the undead. Published as if by Byron himself, in order to increase sales, the book none the less failed to make Polidori any money, but its portrait of the vampire as a suave, decadent aristocrat established a pattern that has been repeated in countless novels and films since. Polidori followed romantic tradition by dying young in 1821. His sister later became the mother of the poets Dante Gabriel and Christina Rossetti.

## *In a house in this court* ALEXANDER POPE, *poet, was born 1688*
### 32 LOMBARD STREET, EC3   **CITY OF LONDON**

## ALEXANDER POPE (1688–1744) *poet, lived in this row, Mawson's Buildings 1716–1719*
### MAWSON ARMS PUBLIC HOUSE, 110 CHISWICK LANE SOUTH, W4

'If Pope be not a poet, where is poetry to be found?' Dr Johnson asked in his *Lives of the English Poets*, and Pope continues to be seen as the finest poet of the first half of the eighteenth century. He was born in London, the son of a Roman Catholic linen-draper, and was largely self-educated. In 1700, the year the family moved out of London, Pope suffered a debilitating and permanently damaging illness. He was never to grow above 4 feet 6 inches in height, was afflicted with a hunchback and, throughout his life, needed to wear bodices and jackets designed to support his weakened spine. His first poetry was published in 1709 (although Pope claimed to have written much of it as a precocious teenager) and his name was made by the mock-epic *The Rape of the Lock*, which appeared three years later. Translations of Homer followed and Pope continued to publish poetry throughout his life, most notably the *Moral Essays* and the several books of *The Dunciad*, a withering assault on the pretensions and foolishness of contemporary culture. As a Roman Catholic, Pope found it increasingly difficult to live in London in the aftermath of the 1715 Jacobite rebellion and it was then that he moved out to Mawson's Buildings in Chiswick. He stayed there until 1719 when he moved to Twickenham where he spent the rest of his life.

## POPPER, KARL (1902–1994) *philosopher, lived here 1946–1950*

16 BURLINGTON RISE, EN4

Born and educated in Vienna, Karl Popper had already published the first of his ground-breaking works of philosophy (*The Logic of Scientific Discovery*) when the rise of Nazism persuaded him to leave his native country. He went to New Zealand where he spent the war years before arriving in Britain in 1946. He became a professor at the London School of Economics and published a series of books, including *The Open Society and Its Enemies* and *Conjectures and Refutations*, which established his reputation as one of the greatest political theorists and philosophers of science of the twentieth century. It was while living in the house in Burlington Rise that Popper had a famous argument with Wittgenstein. Visiting rooms in Cambridge to address a meeting at which his fellow Austrian thinker was present, Popper fell into a heated debate with him about the nature of philosophical inquiry. Wittgenstein picked up a poker from the fireplace and brandished it to emphasise the points he was making. He challenged Popper to come up with an example of a moral rule. 'Not to threaten visiting lecturers with pokers,' Popper said whereupon an enraged Wittgenstein stormed out of the room.

## PORTUGUESE EMBASSY *These two houses were the Portuguese Embassy (1724–47). The* MARQUESS OF POMBAL, *ambassador 1739–1744, lived here*

23-24 GOLDEN SQUARE, W1

Pombal, born near Coimbra, was the greatest Portuguese statesman of the eighteenth century. He came to London as ambassador relatively early in his career and moved into the embassy in Golden Square, which was at the time one of the great centres of the capital's diplomatic life. The legations of Bavaria, Genoa and Russia, among others, were also in the square. After nearly five years in England, Pombal moved on to Vienna. Returning to his own country, he was made foreign secretary in 1750 and, in 1756, Prime Minister. He held office in Portugal for the next twenty years, introducing major reforms in an attempt to remodel his country into the kind of commercial power England knew well had become. He fought hard to combat the obscurantism of the Church and to encourage education, improvements in agriculture and a revitalisation of Portugal's colonies. Perhaps his most lasting achievement was to oversee the rebuilding of Lisbon after the disastrous earthquake of 1755.

## POUND, EZRA (1885–1972) *poet, lived here 1909–1914*

10 KENSINGTON CHURCH WALK, W8

'Literature is news that stays news,' Ezra Pound once wrote and his long and turbulent career in the arts regularly made headlines, if not always for the right reasons. Pound was born in a small town in Idaho at a time when the territory had not even been officially admitted to the Union as the 43rd state of the USA. He came to London when he was in his early twenties and rapidly established himself as one of the most flamboyant spokesmen for literary modernism. He was a central figure in both Imagism and Vorticism, two movements which embodied the avant-garde in England in the years before and during the First World War. He was a friend of T.S. Eliot and acted as editor and artistic midwife to his poem *The Waste Land*. He was a tireless propagandist for other writers he admired and all the time he was writing and publishing his own verse. *The Cantos* were begun in 1915 and he worked upon them for the rest of his life. Pound moved to Italy in the 1930s and his later life was blighted by his active support for Fascism. He was condemned as a traitor, put on trial and incarcerated in a mental asylum after the Second World War but nothing can diminish his stature as one of the greatest poets of the twentieth century.

---

*In this house* THE PRE-RAPHAELITE BROTHERHOOD *was founded in 1848*

7 GOWER STREET, WC1

For a few short years the Pre-Raphaelite Brotherhood was the most daring and revolutionary art movement nineteenth-century England produced, dismissive of most post-Renaissance art and nearly all Royal Academicians, reserving its praise for the Italian painters of the quattrocento who had preceded Raphael. The PRB was largely the result of the meeting of three young painters – John Millais, William Holman Hunt and Dante Gabriel Rossetti. To take membership up to the mystic number of seven, the painters James Collinson and Frederick Stephens, the sculptor Thomas Woolner and Rossetti's brother William, a budding art critic, were invited to join. Holman Hunt wrote that, 'when we agreed to use the letters PRB as our insignia, we made each member solemnly promise to keep its meaning strictly secret.' Although that secrecy did not last long and the youthful idealism of the Brotherhood lasted only a little longer, the foundation in Gower Street of the movement was one of the most significant moments ever in British art.

---

PRIESTLEY, J.B. (1894–1984) *novelist, playwright and essayist, lived here*

3 THE GROVE, HIGHGATE, N6

Priestley was born in Bradford, educated at Cambridge and came to London to embark on a career as a critic and journalist. The publication of *The Good Companions* in 1929, a picaresque tale of a concert party's travels round the country, made him a bestselling novelist. Many other novels followed and so too did plays, most famously those such as *Time and the Conways*, which drew on the eccentric notions of J.W. Dunne about the nature of time, and a large array of miscellaneous works. During the Second World War, Priestley, representative of English common sense and Yorkshire bluntness, was a notably successful broadcaster whose talks were second in popularity only to those of Churchill. Priestley's long and varied literary career made him a lot of money. Once a group of people in his club were discussing what they would do if they had the then enormous sum of £100,000, when Priestley walked in. 'Jack,' one asked, 'what would you do if you got £100,000?' 'I've got £100,000,' he replied. 'But,' his questioner persisted, 'what would you do if you got another £100,000?' 'I've got another £100,000.'

---

PRIESTLEY, JOSEPH (1733–1804) *scientist, philosopher and theologian, was Minister to the Gravel Pit Meeting here in 1793–1794*

RAM PLACE, E9

PRIESTLEY, JOSEPH, *theologian, scientist and discoverer of oxygen, lived in a house on this site 1792–94*

113, LOWER CLAPTON ROAD, E5    **BOROUGH OF HACKNEY**

One of the great polymaths of eighteenth-century England, Priestley was a pioneer chemist who was one of the discoverers of oxygen, a radical religious thinker who attacked doctrines such as the Virgin birth and a political philosopher who was an early supporter of the French Revolution. The American President Thomas Jefferson described Priestley's as 'one of the few lives precious to mankind'. Despite unorthodox religious views Priestley was a minister for most of his adult life. He moved to Birmingham in 1780 and the decade that followed was, in many ways, the most productive of his life. In 1791, however, a mob used his sympathies for the French Revolution as an excuse to burn down his house and laboratory and Priestley settled in Hackney where he succeeded another famous nonconformist thinker, Richard Price, as preacher at the Gravel Pit Meeting. Priestley spent the last ten years of his life in America and died in Northumberland, Pennsylvania. He is buried in the Quaker burial ground there.

....................................................................................................................

## PRIORY OF ST JOHN THE BAPTIST, HOLYWELL *The site of this building forms part of what was once the precinct of the Priory. Within a few yards stood from 1577 to 1598 the first London building specially devoted to the performance of plays and known as 'The Theatre'.*

86–88 CURTAIN ROAD, EC2

....................................................................................................................

## PURDEY, JAMES, THE YOUNGER (1828–1909) *gunmaker, built these premises in 1880 to house his new showrooms and workshops*

57–58 SOUTH AUDLEY STREET, W1   **WESTMINSTER**

James Purdey the Elder founded the most famous gunshop in the world in 1814 when, at the age of thirty, he set up on his own near Leicester Square after working for another great gunsmith, Joseph Manton, in Oxford Street. His son, James Purdey the Younger, who inherited the business on his father's death in 1863, was the man who made the Purdey name famous throughout the world. He invented and patented a number of improvements in the design of the guns he sold and, in 1881, made the move to South Audley Street, where the company still has its headquarters. Since 1814 many and varied celebrities, from royalty to Soviet leaders, from Charles Darwin to Bing Crosby, have ordered their guns from Purdey's.

....................................................................................................................

## THE QUEEN'S HALL

HENRY WOOD HOUSE, LANGHAM PLACE   **WESTMINSTER**

The Queen's Hall was opened in 1893 and its inaugural concert given in November of that year in the presence of the Prince of Wales. Its exterior was modelled on the Pantheon in Rome and its interior decorated in florid high-Victorian style. Its architect, the eccentric T.E. Knightley, involved himself in every detail of the décor and once hung up a string of dead mice in the painters' workshop to illustrate the exact shade of grey – the same as a mouse's belly – that he wanted. In 1895 the young Henry Wood presided over the first series of Promenade Concerts in the new Queen's Hall, which had already gained a reputation for the high quality of its acoustics, and the proms were held there every year until 1941. In May of that year a fire bomb fell on the hall and the building was gutted. After the war, various schemes were proposed for rebuilding the hall but funds to do so were never forthcoming. The site is now a hotel.

....................................................................................................................

## RACKHAM, ARTHUR (1867–1939) *illustrator, lived here*

16 CHALCOT GARDENS, NW3

The Edwardian era was a golden age for English illustration and Arthur Rackham was one of the most distinctive and successful illustrators of the period. Born in London, Rackham studied at Lambeth School of Art and began his career working for one of the many illustrated magazines of the time. His great success, however, came with his illustrations to classic stories, often fairy tales. An edition of *Grimm's Fairy Tales* published in 1900 showed the fantastic, almost surreal quality of his imagination, and many other volumes followed over the next forty years, including notable editions of *Alice's Adventures in Wonderland*, *Gulliver's Travels* and *A Christmas Carol*. Rackham lived in Chalcot Gardens from 1903 to 1920.

## RACZYŃSKI, COUNT EDWARD (1891–1993) *Polish statesman, lived here 1967–1993*
### 8 LENNOX GARDENS, SW1

Born into a distinguished and aristocratic Polish family, Raczyński was destined to spend more than fifty years of his long life in exile from his native land. He entered the diplomatic service immediately after the First World War and he was Polish ambassador in London during the build up to the Second World War. Indeed, it was Raczyński who, on behalf of his country, signed the Anglo-Polish Treaty in August 1939, which formalised the earlier British guarantee that it would come to the aid of Poland in the event of hostilities and which ultimately led to Britain declaring war on Germany a month later. It was impossible for him to return home while the Nazis were in power and he remained in Britain as a prominent member of the Polish government in exile. When the war was over, the advent of communism meant his exile was extended and he continued to live in London. In 1979, aged eighty-eight, he was chosen as the fourth President of the Republic of Poland in exile and went on to serve a seven-year term in office. Not long before his death, still active in politics and aged more than a hundred, he married his third wife.

## RAGLAN, LORD FITZROY SOMERSET, 1ST BARON, (1788–1855) *commander during the Crimean War, lived here*

### 5 STANHOPE GATE, W1

'Someone had blundered', Tennyson wrote in his poem about the Charge of the Light Brigade. That someone was Lord Raglan who, although he evaded official censure, bore much responsibility, as Commander-in-Chief, for the sequence of miscommunications that sent the Light Brigade charging suicidally into the Valley of Death. Raglan had entered the Army fifty years before the Crimean War and had fought at Waterloo, losing an arm in the battle. He had not seen active service again until he was promoted to Field Marshal and sent to head the disastrously ill-prepared expedition against the Russians in 1854. His efficacy as commander was not improved by his frequent inability to remember that the French were no longer the enemies but the allies of the British forces. He died on 28 June 1855 and proved a convenient scapegoat for setbacks and sufferings over which he had much less control than the charge of the six hundred.

## RAMBERT, DAME MARIE (1888–1982) *founder of Ballet Rambert, lived here*
### 19 CAMPDEN HILL GARDENS, W8

Born in Warsaw, Marie Rambert first became entranced by the possibilities of dance when she was living in Paris before the First World War. After working with Nijinsky and others on *The Rite of Spring*, she joined Diaghilev's Ballet Russe for several seasons before arriving in London in 1917. The following year she married the playwright and theatre manager Ashley Dukes and became a British subject. For the rest of her life she was to be an inspirational figure in British ballet, founder of the company that still bears her name and the driving force behind the Ballet Club, which fostered the talents of dancers like Alicia Markova and choreographers like Frederick Ashton. Marie Rambert was made a Dame of the British Empire in 1962 and retained her vitality and *joie de vivre* into old age, still prepared, in her seventies and at unexpected moments, to demonstrate her ability to turn cartwheels across the floor.

## RATHBONE, ELEANOR (1872–1946) *pioneer of family allowances, lived here*
TUFTON COURT, TUFTON STREET, SW1

Born in Liverpool, where her father was a Liberal MP, Eleanor Rathbone grew up in a large Quaker family in which the value and importance of public service was taken for granted. From the time she left Oxford until her death she was involved in many of the great causes of the day from women's suffrage to housing issues to the Spanish Civil War. However, her most important work was her research and analysis of family economics, which began before the First World War in her native Liverpool. In books such as *The Disinherited Family* in 1924 and *The Case for Family Allowances* (1940), she argued the case for a radical reassessment of the state's relation to the family. Her work was a major influence on the legislation introduced by Attlee's government in 1945.

## RATTIGAN, SIR TERENCE (1911–1977) *playwright, was born here*
100 CORNWALL GARDENS, SW7

'A playwright must be his own audience,' Terence Rattigan once wrote, 'A novelist may lose his readers for a few pages; a playwright never dares lose his audience for a minute.' For much of his career there was little danger that Rattigan would lose his audience. He was one of the most popular English dramatists of the twentieth century and plays like *The Browning Version*, *The Winslow Boy* and *The Deep Blue Sea* were all major West End hits. From the late 1930s to the late 1950s, Rattigan's name on a new play more or less guaranteed critical and commercial success. It was only with the advent of so-called 'kitchen sink' drama that his style of well-made theatre about the upper middle classes came to seem outmoded. Rattigan attempted to broaden his range with a piece, *Variation on a Theme,* that openly addressed the issue of homosexuality (he was gay himself) but its comparative failure persuaded him that he was out of touch with contemporary culture. He moved to the West Indies and rarely returned to Britain in the last fifteen years of his life. He died of bone cancer in his sixties but survived long enough to see a revival in his reputation as a dramatist of substance and to be knighted for his achievements in the theatre.

## RAVILIOUS, ERIC (1903–1942) *artist, lived here*
48 UPPER MALL, HAMMERSMITH, W6

One of the most gifted and versatile artists of his generation, Eric Ravilious went on a scholarship from Eastbourne College of Art to the Royal College where he numbered such people as the painter John Piper and the illustrator Edward Bawden as his friends and contemporaries. Ravilious worked in many different media. He painted watercolour landscapes and large-scale murals; he was active in the design of glass, furniture and pottery for the Wedgwood firm. However, he was, and remains, best known for his work as an illustrator and, particularly, as a wood engraver. During the Second World War, he served as an official war artist attached to the Royal Marines and he was killed when the ship he was sailing on went down off the coast of Iceland.

## RAY-JONES, TONY (1941–1972) *photographer, lived and worked here*
102 GLOUCESTER PLACE, W1 **WESTMINSTER**

Tony Ray-Jones was a gifted and innovative British photographer who died tragically young. Born in Wells, Somerset, he moved to the USA to work on magazines and for advertising and he was heavily influenced by the creative work produced by American photographers. Returning to Britain in 1965, he set out to document photographically the British at leisure, spending the next few years visiting seaside towns, country festivals and society events to record what he saw there. The Institute of Contemporary Arts organised a one-man touring exhibition of his work called 'The English Seen'. Tony Ray-Jones died of leukemia in 1972, aged only thirty.

RED HOUSE *built in 1859–1860 by* PHILIP WEBB, *architect, for* WILLIAM MORRIS, *poet and artist who lived here 1860–1865*

RED HOUSE LANE, BEXLEYHEATH

Called the Red House because of the red brick used by the architect instead of the more traditional fieldstone, William Morris's dream home for himself and his new wife Jane was built in a meadow in what was then rural Bexleyheath. Webb, a close friend of Morris and later to become, like him, a founding member of the Society for the Protection of Ancient Buildings, adapted a traditional cottage form cleverly into an appropriate living and working space for an artist. Sadly, although the Morrises spent five largely happy years in the Red House and entertained their fellow Pre-Raphaelites there, they were obliged finally to return to central London. Morris suffered from rheumatism in the damp and cold of the country, the plans for Burne-Jones and his wife to join the Morrises in a small artistic community there foundered and Morris's private income was no longer sufficient to his needs. The Red House continues in use as a private house.

REES, SIR MILSOM (1866–1952) *surgeon, lived here*

18 UPPER WIMPOLE STREET, W1 **WESTMINSTER**

Sir Milsom Rees was a larger-than-life Welshman who rose to the top of his profession, acting as consultant laryngologist to the royal family for more than twenty years, while enjoying a range of sporting interests that ran from golf and boxing to big game hunting. Rees was also consultant laryngologist to the Royal Opera House and treated many of the opera stars and divas of the day. He invented a throat spray intended to relieve the stresses that singers placed on their vocal apparatus which he named the 'Melba Spray' after Dame Nellie Melba.

REID DICK, SIR WILLIAM (1878–1961) *sculptor, worked here in Studio 3, 1910–1914*

CLIFTON HILL STUDIOS, 95A CLIFTON HILL, NW8

Born in Glasgow, Reid Dick was apprenticed to a stonemason for five years before attending the art college in his native city. Moving south to London, he rapidly established himself as one of the most versatile and reliable creators of public monuments in the country. His statues stand in cities throughout the country (his Lady Godiva was erected in Coventry in 1949) but his finest and most characteristic work can be seen in London. George V near the Houses of Parliament and F.D. Roosevelt in Grosvenor Square are both sculpted by Reid Dick. His work can also be seen further afield than London and other British cities. Like most sculptors of his generation, Reid Dick worked on war memorials and the lion on the Menin Gate at Ypres is by him. Perhaps the Reid Dick sculpture that has the most striking site of all is his statue of David Livingstone, which looks out over the Victoria Falls in Zimbabwe. Reid Dick held the post of King's (later Queen's) Sculptor in Ordinary for Scotland for more than twenty years until his death, when he was in his eighties, in 1961.

REITH, LORD (1889–1971) *first director-general of the BBC, lived here 1924–1930*

6 BARTON STREET, SW1

As the BBC's first Director-General, appointed in 1922 after a career spent in radio communication, the dour and high-minded Scot John Reith set the tone for what rapidly became a British institution. As he wrote in his autobiography, 'It was . . . the combination of public service motive, sense of moral obligation, assured finance and the brute force of monopoly which enabled the BBC to make of broadcasting what no other country has made of it.' After finishing at the BBC in 1938, he worked as Chairman of the British Overseas Airways Corporation and, during the Second World War, served in the Cabinet for two years before falling out with Churchill. The power of Reith's impact on broadcasting in this country can be measured by the fact that his influence, however residually, is still felt at the BBC more than sixty years after he left it.

---

## RELPH, HARRY (1851–1928) *'Little Tich', music hall comedian, lived and died here*
93 SHIREHALL PARK, HENDON, NW4

## HARRY RELPH (1867–1928) *site of birthplace of Harry Relph, 'Little Tich', music hall comedian*
BLACKSMITHS' ARMS, CUDHAM LANE, CUDHAM    **BOROUGH OF BROMLEY**

Whenever someone short is called 'Tich' Harry Relph is indirectly remembered, for it was his stage name that gave rise to the usage. Relph, in turn, took his stage name from a Victorian *cause célèbre* in which a Wapping butcher's son, Arthur Orton, claimed to be the long-lost heir to the ancient Hampshire family of Tichborne. The Tichborne Claimant was a man of 25 stone and provided an ideal contrast to Relph, who was 4 feet 6 inches in height with even more disproportionately dwarfish legs. (He also had five fingers and a thumb on each hand and six toes on each foot.) On the music hall stage Relph, in the guise of Little Tich, turned his disadvantages into a very successful comic act. The centrepiece of his act was an extraordinary 'Big Boot Dance', which the artist Paul Nash saw and described. 'His strangest and most compelling asset,' Nash wrote, 'were his feet . . . (they) were habitually inserted into the most monstrous boots, long, narrow and flat, so long that he could bow from the boots and lean over at almost an acute angle from his heels.'

---

## RESCHID, MUSTAPHA PASHA (1800–1858) *Turkish statesman and reformer, lived here as an ambassador in 1839*

1 BRYANSTON SQUARE, W1

In the nineteenth century the battle within the Ottoman Empire, 'the sick man of Europe', was one between the forces of reaction and the forces of reform. Mustapha Pasha Reschid was firmly in the camp of the reformers. As an enthusiast for all things Western and a firm opponent of Russian ambitions in the Black Sea, Reschid was an ideal choice as ambassador to both France and Britain, roles that he undertook in years of increasing tension between the great powers. Back in Turkey, Reschid became Minister of Foreign Affairs and eventually Grand Vizier. In this role he strove vigorously to implement reform, modernisation, and re-organisation of the army despite the entrenched resistance of conservatism.

---

## REYNOLDS, SIR JOSHUA (1723–1792) *portrait painter, lived and died in a house on this site*
FANUM HOUSE (SITE OF 47), LEICESTER SQUARE, WC2

## SIR JOSHUA REYNOLDS (1723–1792)
9 GERRARD STREET, W1    **PRIVATE**

To William Blake, Reynolds represented everything he hated. 'This man was hired to depress art,' Blake wrote on the title page of his copy of Reynolds's writings. To almost every other contemporary, Reynolds embodied art. Born near Plymouth, Reynolds studied painting in London and Rome and established himself as a portrait painter in the 1750s. Soon he was the most successful portrait painter in London and in 1760 moved into his house in Leicester Square (or Fields as it then was), which was equipped with a large and magnificent studio. In

1768 Reynolds was elected the first President of the newly formed Royal Academy and he was knighted the following year. His *Discourses on Art*, the lectures he gave to the students at the Royal Academy, express his own sense of the importance of tradition and the study of the Old Masters. Reynolds knew all the great and good of his day, including Dr Johnson, whose portrait he painted several times, and it was at his suggestion that Johnson's famous literary club was inaugurated at the Turk's Head, Gerrard Street. Reynolds was forced to give up painting three years before his death because he was losing his sight.

## RICARDO, SIR HARRY (1885–1974) *mechanical engineer, was born here*
13 BEDFORD SQUARE, WC1

'The advent of the motor-car, then a fascinating but wayward mechanical toy thrilled me,' Harry Ricardo once wrote, remembering his teenage years when his grandfather had been one of the very few people in Britain to own a car. By the time he wrote those words, he had become one of the country's leading experts on the internal combustion engine and a man who had done more than most to develop it. Ricardo was born into a wealthy and intellectually gifted family and he went up to Cambridge to study Mechanical Sciences. Whilst he was there, he began to take a special interest in internal combustion engines and he was still only an undergraduate when he made his first major contributions to their improvement. During the First World War, Ricardo's engineering brilliance was essential to the development of tanks which were useful battlefield weapons rather than just newfangled and noisy contraptions of little real value. After the war, Ricardo continued his researches and the company he founded in 1927 to support and exploit them is still in business today and still bears his name. The house in Bedford Square, which now bears the Blue Plaque, was his childhood home and, at the age of twenty-one, he filed his first patent from this address.

## RICHMOND, GEORGE (1809–1896) *painter, lived here*
20 YORK STREET, W1

Born in London, Richmond studied at the Royal Academy Schools under Fuseli and, as a very young man, was one of the group of painters, including John Linnell and Samuel Palmer, who formed an admiring circle around the ageing William Blake. He later named one of his sons, also to become a painter of some renown, William Blake Richmond. As he grew older Richmond became less and less the revolutionary who had responded to Blake's vision and more and more the conventional academic painter. He was made an Associate of the Royal Academy in 1857 and a full Royal Academician ten years later. By that time he was best known as a portrait painter of the great and good of the day, particularly churchmen, and his intense little landscapes of the 1820s (and the youthful indiscretion of a Gretna Green marriage in 1831) had been long forgotten.

## *In these studios lived and worked the artists* CHARLES RICKETTS (1866–1931), CHARLES SHANNON (1863–1937), GLYN PHILPOT (1863–1937), VIVIAN FORBES (1891–1937), JAMES PRYDE (1866–1941), F. CAYLEY ROBINSON (1862–1927)

LANSDOWNE HOUSE, 80 LANSDOWNE ROAD, W11

## RIE, DAME LUCIE (1902–1995) *potter, lived and worked here, from 1939 until her death*
18 ALBION MEWS, W2

Born in Vienna, the daughter of a medical consultant, whose friends included Sigmund Freud, Lucie Rie grew up in the city, studied at art school there and was already a well-known studio potter when the Nazi seizure of power in Austria forced her to leave the country in 1938. She moved to London and remained there for the rest of her long life. In 1946, she was joined in her work by a young German potter named Hans Coper and they remained close colleagues until Coper's death in 1981. Between them, Rie and Coper, with their very different styles and methods of creating ceramics, had a major influence on generations of British potters. Despite her stature as one of the greatest potters of the twentieth century, she was remarkably modest and would deny that she was an artist. 'I make pots,' she said simply, 'Put flowers in them, use them. They are for use.' The interior of Rie's house and studio in Albion Mews was redesigned for her by Sigmund Freud's architect son Ernst, like her another refugee from Nazi Germany whose artistic talents flourished in a new country.

## RIPON, GEORGE FREDERICK SAMUEL ROBINSON, MARQUESS OF
(1827–1909) *statesman and Viceroy of India, lived here*

### 9 CHELSEA EMBANKMENT, SW3

George Frederick Robinson was born into the heart of the British political establishment and, in the course of a career that spanned six decades, he held many of the major offices of state. His father was the Tory Chancellor of the Exchequer known as 'Prosperity Robinson' and George Frederick was actually born during his father's brief five-month tenure of the Prime Ministership. Inheriting the title of Earl of Ripon in 1859 and the political responsibilities that went with it, he was successively Secretary for War, Secretary for India, Lord President of the Council and, between 1880 and 1884, Victoria's representative in India. As Viceroy, Ripon was a largely liberal figure who made some efforts to involve Indians in his administration. After returning from India he was Colonial Secretary in Gladstone's last government. Ripon was also, at one point in his life, the Grand Master of the Freemasons in England but was obliged to resign when he converted to Catholicism in 1874.

## RIZAL, DR JOSE (1861–1896) *writer and national hero of the Philippines, lived here*

### 37 CHALCOT CRESCENT, NW1

The son of a Filipino father and a Chinese mother, Rizal attended the University of Saint Thomas in Manila and travelled to Spain to do postgraduate work in Madrid in 1882. He was in Europe for the next five years and in 1886 he wrote his novel *Noli Me Tangere*, which was extremely critical of the Catholic Church in the Philippines and of Spanish colonialism in general. This brought him the unwanted attentions of the authorities and he continued to spend most of his time outside his native country. He visited London briefly in late 1888 and it was then that he lived in Chalcot Crescent. He returned to Manila in 1892 to found a political organisation called the Liga Filipina, which campaigned for peaceful change in the islands. The authorities almost immediately exiled him to Mindanao, where he spent four years. When revolution broke out in the Philippines in 1896 Rizal, despite his advocacy of non-violence, was arrested, tried for sedition and executed by firing squad.

## ROBERTS, EARL FREDERICK SLEIGH (1832–1914) *Field-Marshal, lived here*

### 47 PORTLAND PLACE, W1

If one had to pick a single soldier to exemplify the British Army in its imperial heyday, it would probably be Roberts. Born at Cawnpore, he was educated at Eton and Sandhurst and then returned to India. During the Indian Mutiny he arrived at the siege of Delhi to find the city still swarming with mutinous sepoys. This he greeted with a characteristic eagerness for action. 'I could hardly believe my good luck,' he wrote. 'I was actually at Delhi and the city was still in possession of the mutineers!' Later in the Mutiny, Roberts won the Victoria Cross. His most famous exploits came in Afghanistan where the natives proved exceedingly restless and provokingly unprepared to accept British interests as their own. During the Second Afghan War (1878–80), Roberts quelled rebellious tribesmen in Kabul and made a forced march to relieve British forces in Kandahar – the stuff of which legends are made. Later honours followed. Roberts was Commander-in-Chief in India for seven years and was in the field in the Boer War when he was nearly seventy. He died during the early months of the First World War when he caught a chill while visiting soldiers in the trenches and it developed into pneumonia.

## ROBERTS, WILLIAM (1895–1980) *artist, lived, worked and died here 1946–1980*
### 14 ST MARK'S CRESCENT, PRIMROSE HILL, NW1

The son of a carpenter, William Roberts was born in Hackney and grew up to be one of the most distinctive and idiosyncratic English painters of the twentieth century. He left school at the age of fourteen but won a scholarship to the Slade School of Art a year later which allowed him to continue his education. As a young man, he worked briefly at the famous Omega Workshop in Bloomsbury and he was a contributor to the very first issue of *Blast*, house magazine for Vorticism, the only significant avant-garde movement in the arts of the time to have its origins in Britain. Roberts was a war artist in both world wars. In the First World War, he served as a gunner in the Royal Artillery before being recruited to work as an artist attached to the Canadian War Records Office; during the Second World War he moved out of London to work in Oxford, but he was also appointed an official war artist by the Ministry of Information and travelled once more to France to paint what he saw. He moved to the house in St Mark's Crescent, which bears the Blue Plaque, immediately after the war and remained there for the rest of his life.

## ROBESON, PAUL (1898–1976) *singer and actor, lived here 1929–1930*
### 1-2 BRANCH HILL, HAMPSTEAD, NW3

'I shall take my voice wherever there are those who want to hear the melody of freedom', Paul Robeson once said and in his long and courageous career as a performer, he sang in front of audiences from Moscow to the Hebrides, from his native America to the valleys of South Wales. Born the son of a runaway slave who became a preacher, Robeson was an academic and sporting star at Rutgers University and initially intended to become a lawyer. He left the law profession in 1923 when a secretary in the firm, he had joined refused to take dictation from a Negro. Robeson had already appeared on the professional stage and he now chose to make his way as an actor and singer. By 1928, when he sang 'Ol' Man River' for the first time in the musical *Showboat*, he was a star. During the time he was living in Hampstead, Robeson appeared in a landmark production of *Othello*, Peggy Ashcroft co-starring as Desdemona. He was a regular visitor to London and was often far more popular in Europe than he was in America, where his outspoken defence of his political and social beliefs cost him dear. A supporter of the Soviet Union in the 1930s and a committed anti-fascist, Robeson was accused of being a communist in the McCarthy era, and his passport was revoked for eight years in the 1950s. Although his later life was dogged by controversy and ill-health, he continued to give his support to the nascent civil rights movement in America and to progressive causes around the world. One of the greatest and most gifted Afro-Americans, Robeson died in Philadelphia at the age of seventy-seven.

## ROBINSON, JAMES (1813–1862) *pioneer of anaesthesia and dentistry, lived and worked here*
### 14 GOWER STREET, WC1

The son of a naval captain, Robinson trained at London University and Guy's Hospital and, in his twenties, became surgeon dentist at the Royal Free Hospital, which William Marsden had founded in 1828. In the 1840s Robinson pioneered the use of anaesthesia in dentistry and, in 1848, reached the peak of his profession when he was appointed one of the dentists to the Royal Family. In 1862, the same year in which he founded the National Dental Hospital, Robinson's life was brought to an abrupt and tragic end. While pruning a tree in his garden, his hand slipped and he stabbed himself in the thigh with the knife he was using. Unable to summon help, he eventually died from loss of blood.

---

*Under these arches* ALLIOTT VERDON ROE *assembled his AVRO No.1 triplane. In July 1909 he made the first all-British powered flight from Walthamstow Marshes*

RAILWAY ARCHES AT WALTHAMSTOW MARSH RAILWAY VIADUCT, WALTHAMSTOW MARSHES, E17

Pioneer British aeronaut Alliott Verdon Roe was born in 1877 and began to develop his ideas on powered flight by creating scale models of the planes he went on to build. His first successful full-scale aircraft (although it had a wing span of only 20 feet and weighed only 200 lb) was the Roe Triplane and it was this that made the historic flight of approximately 300 metres over the Marshes. Roe went on to build combat aircraft in the First World War and to create Avro, one of the world's greatest aircraft-manufacturing companies. He was knighted in 1929 for his services to aviation.

---

ROGERS, DR JOSEPH (1821–1889) *health care reformer, lived here*

33 DEAN STREET, W1

The older brother of the political economist and economic historian James Rogers, Joseph Rogers was a medical practitioner who was one of the leading campaigners for reforms of the nineteenth-century Poor Laws. As medical officer at the Strand workhouse and later at the Westminster Infirmary, he saw the results of these laws at first hand and devoted much of his life to improving the lot of those they affected. He was founder and sometime president of the Poor Law Medical Officers' Association and his views regularly brought him into conflict with the powers that be. He was several times suspended from his duties at both the Strand and Westminster, but each time his supporters obliged the authorities to reinstate him.

---

ROHMER, SAX (1883–1959) *creator of Dr Fu Manchu, lived here*

51 HERNE HILL, SE24

Under his pseudonym Sax Rohmer, the English journalist and novelist Arthur Henry Ward wrote a series of stories about the inscrutable and sinister Chinese criminal genius Fu Manchu. Titles such as *The Yellow Claw, Moon of Madness* and *Emperor Fu Manchu* appeared over a period of nearly fifty years. The character also appeared in dozens of movies, radio programmes and TV episodes. Fu Manchu embodies, with almost laughable obviousness, Western fears of Asian power and influence, of an encroaching 'yellow peril'. Rohmer, in his unselfconscious narratives, assuages any such fears by ensuring that Fu Manchu, despite his almost superhuman intelligence, is consistently thwarted by his arch-enemy Nayland Smith.

---

*In a house on this site lived* DE ROKESLEY, GREGORY *eight times Mayor of London 1274–1281 and 1285*

72 LOMBARD STREET, EC3   **CITY OF LONDON**

---

*Here lived* SAMUEL ROMILLY *law reformer. Born 1757. Died 1818.*

21 RUSSELL SQUARE, WC1

## SIR SAMUEL ROMILLY

6 GRAY'S INN SQUARE, WC1 **PRIVATE**

Born the son of a watch-maker of Huguenot descent, Romilly became both a successful lawyer and an effective advocate of radical reform of the law. He read widely in the works of European philosophers like Rousseau and the Encyclopedists, acclaimed the early events of the French Revolution and was convinced that the severity of the British penal code was self-defeating. Made Solicitor-General in 1806, he secured the abolition of the death penalty for a number of classes of petty theft and was a voice in Parliament against slavery and for the freedoms of the individual. In 1818 his wife died and, overwhelmed and distraught, Romilly committed suicide three days later in his house in Russell Square.

## ROMNEY, GEORGE (1734–1802) *painter, lived here*

HOLLY BUSH HILL, NW3

Born in Lancashire, Romney had, by 1762, established himself as a portrait painter in the north of England and was married with a young family. In that year he made the decision to move to London. He left his wife and children behind in Lancashire, supposedly on the advice of Sir Joshua Reynolds who had told him that art and marriage don't mix. Over the next thirty years and more, Romney became one of the most successful portrait painters of the day. In 1781 he began a series of portraits of Emma Hamilton, later Nelson's mistress, some of which are among his best-known works. Romney's later years were clouded by illness and insanity. He returned to the Lake District where his long-suffering wife, who can have seen little of him over the decades, nursed him for the last three years of his life.

## ROSEBERY, 5TH EARL (1847–1929) *Prime Minister and first Chairman of the London County Council, was born here*

20 CHARLES STREET, W1

Rosebery succeeded Gladstone as Prime Minister in 1894 and held the office for fifteen difficult months in which both the Liberal party and the Cabinet itself were riven by faction and strife. Rosebery's consolation was horseracing. His horses won the Derby both times the race was run during his premiership. To win had been a long-held ambition. As an undergraduate at Oxford he had been faced with the choice between continuing his studies and continuing his ownership of a horse. He chose the horse, writing to his mother, 'I have left Oxford. I have secured a house in Berkeley Square and I have bought a horse to win the Derby.' His confidence was misplaced. The horse came last. In 1889 Rosebery, who had already served as Foreign Secretary and was to do so again, was elected to the newly formed LCC and became its first Chairman. In this capacity he was the first person to suggest that the LCC should commemorate the houses of the famous.

## ROSENBERG, ISAAC (1890-1918)
*lived in the East End and studied here*

WHITECHAPEL LIBRARY, 77 HIGH
STREET, E1

Rosenberg was born in Bristol, the son of Jewish emigrés from Russia, and brought up in the East End where his father was a market trader. He showed talent first as a painter rather than a poet and, although obliged to leave school at the age of fourteen to work as an apprentice engraver, he eventually found patrons in a wealthy Jewish family. They paid for him to study at the Slade School of Art. By now, Rosenberg was also writing poetry. He travelled to South Africa, for health reasons and to pursue a career as a portrait painter, in the same year the First World War broke out. Rosenberg returned to England and enlisted in the Army in 1915. Although he had published some of his poems before the start of the war, he was almost unknown at the time of his death in action in 1918. Posthumous publication of his poetry has established his reputation as a war poet worthy to rank with Owen and Sassoon.

## ROSS, SIR JAMES CLARK (1800-1862) *polar explorer, lived here*

2 ELIOT PLACE, BLACKHEATH, SE3

Nephew of the explorer John Ross, James Ross accompanied his uncle on several voyages to the Arctic, including one sponsored by the gin distiller Felix Booth. On one of these, in 1831, he made his great discovery of the north magnetic pole. Between 1839 and 1843 Ross, together with Captain Crozier, sailed into the Antarctic and they were the first men to venture into its pack-ice. Their discoveries included the 12,000 foot volcano Mount Erebus (named after one of their ships) and an island, a sea and a great ice shelf, all of which were named after Ross. On his return to England, Ross was knighted. In 1848 he was the government's choice as commander of the official expedition in search of Sir John Franklin who had disappeared, together with 129 men and officers, while attempting to navigate the North West Passage. Ross failed to locate Franklin or his men, who included his old companion Crozier.

## ROSS, SIR RONALD (1857-1932) *Nobel Laureate, discoverer of the mosquito transmission of malaria, lived here*

18 CAVENDISH SQUARE, W1

Ross owes his fame to his recognition that there was a link between the disease malaria and the bite of the mosquito. Born in India, Ross studied at St Bartholomew's Hospital in London and then returned to the country of his birth where he was employed by the Indian Medical Service for nearly two decades. It was during those years that he undertook the work on malaria for which he was awarded the Nobel Prize for Medicine in 1902. Ross's later career was spent in Britain where he was a professor of Tropical Medicine at Liverpool University and at King's College Hospital, London. In the last years of his life he was involved with the Institute for Tropical Diseases to which he gave his name. As well as his medical interests, Ross was a published poet and novelist.

## ROSSETTI, CHRISTINA GEORGINA (1830–1894)
*poetess, lived and died here. Bronze plaque erected by the Duke of Bedford, taken over by the GLC in 1975.*

### 30 TORRINGTON SQUARE, WC1

Christina Rossetti came from a highly talented family that was notable for both its artistic and religious sensibility. Of her brothers, Dante Gabriel was a renowned poet and Pre-Raphaelite painter and William Michael was an art critic and man of letters, one of the early advocates in Britain of Walt Whitman's poetry. Her older sister Maria became an Anglican nun. Christina was herself deeply religious and her engagement to James Collinson, one of the founder members of the Pre-Raphaelite Brotherhood, was broken off, in all likelihood, because, when he became a Roman Catholic, he could not share her High Anglican beliefs. Some of her earlier verse was published in the Pre-Raphaelite magazine *The Germ* and she went on to publish a number of collections in her lifetime. The strange, cryptic fairy-tale 'Goblin Market' is probably her best-known work and she also wrote the words for one of the most famous of Christmas carols, 'In the Bleak Mid Winter'.

## ROSSETTI, DANTE GABRIEL (1828–1882) *poet and painter, born here*
### 110 HALLAM STREET, W1

*In this house lived* DANTE GABRIEL ROSSETTI *in 1851 and from 1856 to 1859.* WILLIAM MORRIS (1834–1896), *poet and artist, and* SIR EDWARD BURNE-JONES (1833–1898), *painter*

### 17 RED LION SQUARE, WC1

DANTE GABRIEL ROSSETTI, *poet and painter, and* ALGERNON CHARLES SWINBURNE (1837–1909), *poet, lived here*

### 16 CHEYNE WALK, SW3

The son of the first Professor of Italian at King's College, London, Rossetti was a poet and painter who was, together with his friends Millais and Holman Hunt, one of the founder members of the Pre-Raphaelite Brotherhood. During the 1850s his muse and chief model was the ex-milliner's assistant Elizabeth Siddall, whom he finally married in 1860. Unfortunately, Lizzie, or 'Guggums' as Rossetti called her, was possibly consumptive, certainly melancholic and increasingly addicted to laudanum. Rossetti did not help their difficult relationship by continuing to see other women and in 1862 Elizabeth Siddall committed suicide. Rossetti, consumed by guilt and grief, buried the manuscript copy of his poetry with her. Several years later, in a bizarre episode, he exhumed the body in order to recover the poems. Rossetti lived in Cheyne Walk from 1862 to 1882, increasingly dependent on drugs and alcohol to deal with depression and insomnia. The household was a strange one. In addition to its exotic human members (Rossetti himself and, for a time, Swinburne), it included a small menagerie of unusual animals. Rossetti was particularly fond of his wombats and drew a caricature of himself mourning the death of one of them.

## ROTHENSTEIN, SIR WILLIAM (1872–1945) *painter and writer lived here 1899–1902*
### 1 PEMBROKE COTTAGES, EDWARDES SQUARE, KENSINGTON, W8

Born in Bradford, the son of a German wool merchant who had settled in England, Rothenstein attended the Slade School of Art and then studied in Paris. A friend of many of the famous figures of *fin-de-siècle* artistic London, including Aubrey Beardsley and Max Beerbohm, Rothenstein soon became well known for his portraits and was a leading member of the New English Art Club from the mid-1890s. During the First World War, Rothenstein, like many Britons with German names, was keen to prove his patriotism and volunteered to work as an official war artist. He travelled several times to the Front, and a number of his war paintings are among his most successful and memorable works. After the war he became one of the leading lights of the British art establishment, serving as principle of the Royal College of Art for fifteen years. When the Second World War broke out, Rothenstein was in his sixties but he once again became an official war artist. His 1942 book *Men of the RAF* is his account of his travels around RAF stations in England, illustrated by forty portraits of officers and men. Two of his sons also achieved prominence in the art world, Michael as a painter and John as a critic and director of the Tate Gallery.

---

## ROWLANDSON, THOMAS (1757–1827) *artist and caricaturist, lived in a house on this site*

16 JOHN ADAM STREET, ADELPHI, WC2

One of the great caricaturists and satirists of his age, Rowlandson indulged himself in many of the vices he castigated in others. He was an enthusiastic boozer who numbered among his friends the legendarily dissolute George Morland, a painter who suggested as his own epitaph the words, 'Here lies a drunken dog.' He was a reckless gambler who squandered a £7,000 inheritance in a matter of months and spent the rest of his life turning his hand to anything that might bring in some cash. Yet Rowlandson also produced some of the most vigorous, technically skilful and imaginative satirical prints ever made. During the Napoleonic Wars, his persistent belittling of the pretensions of the French Emperor was evident in hundreds of prints. Born in London, Rowlandson lived most of his life in the capital and was a resident of John Adam Street in the early years of the nineteenth century.

---

## ROY, RAM MOHUN (1774–1833) *Indian scholar and reformer, lived here*

49 BEDFORD SQUARE, WC1

One of the first people to attempt a synthesis between the religious ideas of India and those of the West, Roy published an English version of the Hindu *Upanishads* and wrote a book, *The Precepts of Jesus*, in which, although unconvinced by the claims to deity, he acknowledged Jesus as a valuable moral teacher. In 1828 he founded the Brahmo Samaj to further his ideas of rationalist Hinduism and was an early campaigner against the practice of suttee, in which a wife burned herself on the pyre of her late husband. Roy came to England in 1830 and died in Bristol in 1833. His ornate tomb can still be seen in the city's Arnos Vale cemetery.

---

## ROY, MAJOR GENERAL WILLIAM (1726–1790) *founder of the Ordnance Survey, lived here*

10 ARGYLL STREET, W1

Although the Ordnance Survey did not officially come into being until the year after William Roy's death, it was on the firm foundations of his work that the national survey was established. Roy was born in Lanarkshire and first displayed his skills as a surveyor and cartographer in the aftermath of the defeat of Bonnie Prince Charlie at the Battle of Culloden. For nearly a decade Roy worked on mapping the whole of Scotland, thus opening up and domesticating the wilder landscapes for incoming English troops. He joined the Army and continued his surveying both south of the border and abroad. Elected a Fellow of the Royal Society in 1767, Roy was also fascinated by the remains the Romans had left of their incursions into the north and a book, *Military Antiquities of the Romans in Britain*, was published after his death.

## RSPCA (1824–)

### 77–78 ST MARTIN'S LANE  **WESTMINSTER**

The first national society devoted to animal rights was launched in London in 1824 as the Society for the Prevention of Cruelty to Animals (SPCA). At a time when cruelty to animals was commonplace, and the idea that they deserved compassionate treatment was far from being the norm, the Society struggled to make in impact in its early years. However, by 1840, its work was beginning to be acknowledged and when, in that year, Queen Victoria gave her permission for the SPCA to add the word Royal to its name, it marked a genuine change in public attitudes towards the treatment of animals. The plaque is on a building which marks the site of Old Slaughter's Coffee House (demolished in 1843) and it was in a room at the coffee house that the inaugural meeting of the SPCA was held on 16 June 1824. Amongst those attending were the MPs William Wilberforce, famous for his campaigns against slavery, and Richard Martin, an Irishman known as 'Humanity Dick' because of his concern for the rights of animals. From this small beginning the RSPCA has grown to become the hugely successful and respected organisation it is today.

## RUSKIN, JOHN (1819–1900) *man of letters, lived in a house on this site*

### 26 HERNE HILL, SE24

'I takes and paints/Hears no complaints/And sells before I'm dry/Till savage Ruskin/ He sticks his tusk in/Then nobody will buy.' These doggerel lines by Shirley Brooks, adopting the persona of a Royal Academician, reflect the power Ruskin had, at the height of his career, as art critic and cultural authority. A champion of Turner and later of the Pre-Raphaelites, Ruskin was also greatly influential as an interpreter of the achievements of the anonymous craftsmen who created the Gothic cathedrals of Europe. As a social critic he grew more radical with age and his awareness of the squalor and suffering of the times ('I simply cannot paint or read,' he wrote, 'because of the misery I know of') affected him profoundly. His own personal life was disastrous. His marriage to Effie Gray was annulled because of non-consummation (allegedly Ruskin, used to the sight of the smooth marble of statuary, was appalled by his wife's pubic hair) and, in later life, he became obsessed by the much younger Rose La Touche. She died, insane, in 1875, and memories of her haunted Ruskin as he passed into a period of his life in which he suffered frequent breakdowns. In the last decade of his life the great critic of Victorian art and morality lived with a cousin and her family in the Lake District, never writing and rarely even speaking.

## RUSSELL, BERTRAND (1872–1970) *philosopher and campaigner for peace, lived here in flat No. 34, 1911–1916*

### 34 RUSSELL CHAMBERS, BURY PLACE, WC1

'Three passions, simple but overwhelmingly strong, have governed my life,' Bertrand Russell wrote in his autobiography, 'the longing for love, the search for knowledge, and unbearable pity for the suffering of mankind.' These three passions governed a long life that was, by any standards, a remarkable one. Born into a family which had provided political leaders since the fifteenth century – his grandfather was the Whig prime minister Lord John Russell – Bertrand Russell became a pacifist and radical who was still a thorn in the side of the establishment when he was in his nineties. Beginning his career as a mathematician, he was a Fellow of Trinity College, Cambridge, but was deprived of his fellowship and eventually imprisoned during the First World War for his open opposition to the conflict and his allegedly seditious writings. He took the opportunity of a stay in Brixton prison to write *An Introduction to Mathematical Philosophy*, published the year after the war ended. It was for his works of popular philosophy, culminating in *The History of Western Philosophy*, that he became best known, and he was awarded the 1950 Nobel Prize for Literature. Russell's continued abhorrence of warfare and violence led to his support for the Campaign for Nuclear Disarmament , of which he was the first president. In 1961, aged eighty-nine, he was again imprisoned briefly after a peace demonstration in London. He died in 1970, two years short of becoming a centenarian. Russell was once asked what he would say to God if, after death, he found himself before Him. 'I would reproach him for not giving us enough evidence of his existence', he replied.

---

## RUSSELL, LORD JOHN, 1ST EARL (1792–1878) *twice Prime Minister, lived here*
### 37 CHESHAM PLACE, SW1

Russell was a force in British politics for more than half a century, first gaining a seat in the Commons in 1813. He was one of the advocates of parliamentary reform in 1830 and he was the man who, in 1832, rose to propose the great Reform Bill of that year. He was Prime Minister from 1846 to 1852, Foreign Secretary under both Aberdeen and Palmerston and was again, briefly, installed in Downing Street after Palmerston's death in 1865. Russell was a frail and relatively short man, a fact which seemed to surprise some of the Devonshire voters when he was campaigning there in 1831 amidst the agitation for parliamentary reform. Sydney Smith, campaigning with him, was swift to supply the reason for Russell's smallness of stature. 'My dear friends,' he said, 'before this Reform agitation commenced Lord John was over six feet in height. But, engaged in looking after your interests, fighting the peers, the landlords, and the rest of your natural enemies, he has been so constantly kept in hot water that he is boiled down to the proportions in which you now behold him.'

---

## RUTHERFORD, DAME MARGARET (1892–1972) *actress, lived here 1895–1920*
### 4 BERKELEY PLACE, WIMBLEDON SW19

One of the great character actresses of the English stage and films, Margaret Rutherford was a latecomer to fame and stardom. She was in her thirties before she made her professional debut on the stage and in her mid-forties when she appeared in her first film. Most often playing eccentric, slightly dotty characters, she became one of the most unlikely but best-loved British movie stars of her day, while continuing to appear regularly on the stage. Her most famous roles included the bicycle-riding psychic Madame Arcati in Coward's *Blithe Spirit*, Miss Prism in the 1952 version of Wilde's *The Importance of Being Earnest*, the formidable headmistress Miss Whitchurch in *The Happiest Days of Your Life* and the Duchess of Brighton in *The VIPs*, for which she won an Oscar as Best Supporting Actress. She was also memorable as Agatha Christie's spinster detective, Miss Marple, in four films. The house in Wimbledon was where Rutherford was brought up by an aunt after the death of her mother. Tragedy had already visited the family before this death. In

1883 her father, suffering from mental illness, had killed her grandfather and attempted suicide. Incarcerated in an asylum, he was released after nine years into the care of his wife and his brother, the London politician John Benn (grandfather of Tony Benn), and it was during this period that Margaret Rutherford was born. Her father had to be hospitalised once again soon after her birth and Rutherford was to be haunted throughout her life by the idea that she herself might suffer from inherited insanity. Triumphantly, she overcame her inner doubts and demons to become a British institution, and was created a Dame of the British Empire in 1967.

## SALISBURY, ROBERT GASCOYNE CECIL, 3RD MARQUESS OF *(1830–1903)*
*Prime Minister, lived here*

21 FITZROY SQUARE, W1

'English policy is to float lazily downstream,' the Marquess of Salisbury once wrote, 'occasionally putting out a diplomatic boathook to avoid collisions.' As both Foreign Secretary and Prime Minister on three occasions between 1885 and his death, he was in the strongest of positions to put into practice the policy he advocated. The last man to serve as Prime Minister while still retaining his place in the House of Lords, Salisbury was born into a family that had been involved in the government of the nation since the reign of Elizabeth I. After a brief diversion from the career expected of him, when, as a young man just out of Oxford, he visited the goldfields of Australia, Robert Cecil entered the family business when he was elected an MP in 1853. Foreign Secretary in the 1870s, the Marquess of Salisbury, as he was after the deaths of his father and his elder brother, became leader of the Tory Party when Disraeli died in 1881. He became Prime Minister for the first time four years later and was eventually to hold the post for a total of thirteen years. He retired from public life in 1902 because of continuing ill health and died the following year.

## SALMOND, SIR JOHN MAITLAND (1881–1968) *Marshal of the Royal Air Force, RAF Commander, lived here 1928–1936*

27 CHESTER TERRACE, NW1

Born into an army family – his father was a major-general in the Royal Engineers – Salmond attended Sandhurst and then served as an infantry officer in Africa before deciding to learn to fly in 1912. He was one of the first, and most successful pupils of the Central Flying School. Having joined the RFC, the forerunner of the RAF, Salmond's rise was swift and, by 1917, he was director-general of military aeronautics at the War Office and the youngest member of the Army Council. At the end of the First World War he commanded the RFC in France and, in 1930, took over from Sir Hugh Trenchard as the second Chief of Air Staff. One historian of the service has noted that, 'if Trenchard laid the foundations of the RAF, Salmond started erecting its superstructure upon them'. In 1933 Salmond retired from the post, to be replaced by his elder brother Geoffrey. His brother died suddenly within a month of taking office and Salmond returned

briefly as acting chief. During the Second World War, he was director of armament production at the Ministry of Aircraft Production but he resigned in 1941 after falling out with his notoriously difficult ministerial boss, Lord Beaverbrook. Other war work was given to him but ill health finally forced his retirement in 1943. He died twenty-five years later, a legendary figure in the history of the RAF.

## SALVIN, ANTHONY (1799–1881) *architect, lived here*
### 11 HANOVER TERRACE, NW1

Described by the architectural historian Nikolaus Pevsner as 'the most successful restorer and purveyor of castles in the second half of the nineteenth century', Salvin began his career as a pupil of the Regency architect John Nash. Setting up his own practice in the 1820s, he went on to restore many old houses and to build his own Victorian interpretations of medieval and Elizabethan country mansions. Windsor Castle received much attention from Salvin and he was also the original architect of the aviary in the Regent's Park Zoo.

## SAN MARTIN, JOSE DE (1778–1850) *Argentine soldier and statesman, stayed here*
### 23 PARK ROAD, NW8

Together with Simon Bolivar, with whom he later came into conflict, San Martin was one of the great liberators of South American nations from Spanish imperialism. Born in Yapeyu in Argentina, he became a national hero when he led an army to victory against the Spanish at the Battle of San Lorenzo in 1813. Four years later, in January 1817, his army crossed the Andes into Chile to inflict another defeat on the Spanish and he entered Peru as the saviour of the people, becoming *de facto* ruler there in 1821. However, disputes with Bolivar further north, and with others, led him to resign the following year and sail to exile in Europe. While in London, he lived for a few months in Park Road in 1824 and, after a long period in France, he eventually died in Boulogne in 1850.

## SANTLEY, SIR CHARLES (1834–1922) *singer, lived and died here*
### 13 BLENHEIM ROAD, NW8

The nineteenth-century music critic Henry Chorley wrote of Charles Santley that he was 'the best baritone and bass singer that has been in England since the memory of man'. Born in Liverpool, Santley spent time studying in Italy and made his concert debut in a performance of Haydn's *Creation* in 1857. He was still performing half a century later and recordings exist that allow modern music-lovers to compare their assessment of his voice with that of Chorley. Although, as a young man, Santley was particularly noted for his roles in Italian opera, he returned in his later career to concert and oratorio performance. He was knighted in 1907.

## SARGENT, SIR MALCOLM (1895–1967) *conductor, lived and died in a flat in this building*
### ALBERT HALL MANSIONS, KENSINGTON GORE, SW7

Although he is now remembered solely as a conductor, Malcolm Sargent began his career as an organist, training at the Royal College of Organists and working as a cathedral organist. He made his debut as a conductor in 1921 when one of his own compositions, *Rhapsody on a Windy Day*, was performed at a Promenade concert. Sargent rapidly became one of the most popular and versatile of English conductors, particularly at home with choral music. He worked with Diaghilev's Ballet Russe in the late 1920s, was made conductor of the Royal Choral Society in 1928 and was in Liverpool with the Philharmonic Orchestra there in the 1940s. From 1950 he was the chief conductor of the BBC Symphony Orchestra and, until his death, he was the public face of the Proms concerts.

## SARTORIUS, JOHN F. (*c.* 1775–*c.*1830) *sporting painter, lived here 1807–1812*
### 155 OLD CHURCH STREET, SW3

The Sartorius family originally came from Nuremberg but moved to England in the early eighteenth century and soon established themselves in the artistic life of London. John F. Sartorius was the last of four generations of the family who made their careers as painters of sporting subjects, particularly horses and hunting. It is often difficult to distinguish the work of one generation of the Sartorius family from the next but it is undoubtedly true that John F. first exhibited at the Royal Academy in 1802. One of his best-known paintings is known as *Coursing in Hatfield Park*, which depicts the Marchioness of Salisbury, a Regency aristocrat who was renowned for taking daily exercise in the park until well into her ninth decade.

## SASSOON, SIEGFRIED (1886–1967) *writer, lived here 1925–1932*
### 23 CAMPDEN HILL SQUARE, W8

### SIEGFRIED SASSOON (1886–1967)
### 54 TUFTON STREET, SW1  **WESTMINSTER**

Born in Kent to a Jewish father and a Catholic mother, Sassoon came from a comfortable upper-middle-class background and was educated at Marlborough and Clare College, Cambridge. Enlisting at the very outbreak of hostilities, Sassoon served in Flanders throughout much of the First World War. Before the conflict, he had a very minor reputation as a poet, but the poems he wrote about the conflict, filled with compassion for his fellow soldiers and an angry contempt for the generals and for patriotic cant, made his name. His first collection was published in 1917, the same year he threw away the Military Cross he had been awarded for conspicuous bravery and launched a one-man protest against the war. 'I have seen and endured the sufferings of troops,' he wrote in a defiant letter to his colonel, 'and I can no longer be a party to prolong these sufferings for ends which I believe to be evil and unjust.' Sassoon had influential friends and, instead of being court-martialled, was conveniently diagnosed with shell shock and sent to Craiglockhart Hospital. There he met Wilfred Owen and gave much encouragement to the younger man's interest and talent in writing poetry. Sassoon continued to write and publish poetry after the war, much of it concerned with his religious and spiritual development that led him eventually to the Catholic church. He also published a series of autobiographical and semi-autobiographical works.

## SAUNDERS, SIR EDWIN (1814–1901) *dentist to Queen Victoria, lived and died here*
### FAIRLAWNS, 89 WIMBLEDON PARKSIDE, SW19

Saunders was a dental surgeon and a lecturer in dental surgery who became dentist to the Royal Family in 1846. Knighted in 1883, Saunders won all the honours that his profession offered. He was president of the British Dental Association and founder and twice president of the Odontological Society. The plaque to Saunders is to be found on the gate pier rather than on the house itself.

## SAVARKAR, VINAYAK DAMODAR (1883–1966) *Indian patriot and philosopher, lived here*
### 65 CROMWELL AVENUE, HIGHGATE, N6

Vinayak Damodar Savarkar is one of the heroic figures in the struggle to free India from British rule. As a student at Fergusson College in Poona, he led protests against the Raj and was denied his degree. However, he won a scholarship that took him, in 1906, to London to study law. In London he was a forceful presence among Indian students living in the city and in 1910, following the murder of a British official back in India, Savarkar was arrested on suspicion of being implicated in the crime. Despite a daring attempt in Marseille to escape the ship that was taking him back to India for trial, he was tried and sentenced to fifty years' imprisonment. Released after fourteen years' confinement, Savarkar found himself a hero of the freedom movement and became a prominent figure in many campaigns for political and social reform. After independence in 1947 and the assassination of Gandhi the following year, Savarkar, in a bizarre twist of fate, found himself accused of conspiring with the assassin Godse (a member of the political party Savarkar had founded) to murder the Mahatma. He was acquitted and outlived nearly all the other founding fathers of the new India to die in 1966 at the age of eighty-three.

---

*Opened in 1881* THE SAVOY THEATRE *was the first public building in the world to be lit throughout by electricity*

SAVOY THEATRE, STRAND, WC2   **WESTMINSTER**

Built in 1881 by the impresario Richard D'Oyly Carte, the Savoy was intended for the production of the highly successful operas by Gilbert and Sullivan, and the first to be staged was *Patience* in that year. Other favourites followed in the 1880s including *The Mikado* and *The Gondoliers*. The partnership of Gilbert and Sullivan and their profitable arrangement with D'Oyly Carte came to an end partly because Gilbert felt that £500 spent on new carpets at the Savoy was too extravagant. Sullivan sided with D'Oyly Carte and the threesome never again achieved the success it had previously enjoyed. The innovative lighting system was installed by Siemens and Co. and the power for it was generated by steam engines on an adjoining site.

---

SAYERS, DOROTHY L. (1893–1957) *writer of detective stories, lived here 1921–1929*
24 GREAT JAMES STREET, WC1

Best known as the creator of the insouciant, upper-crust detective Lord Peter Wimsey, Dorothy L. Sayers had many other achievements to her name, ranging from translating Dante to inventing the long-lasting advertising slogan, 'Guinness is Good for You'. Born in Oxford but brought up in East Anglia, where her father was a vicar, she was a brilliant student who returned to the city of her birth with a scholarship to Somerville College and graduated with first-class honours in modern languages. Her first novel, *Whose Body?*, was published in 1923 and introduced the character of Lord Peter Wimsey. Sayers went on to write a dozen more novels and volumes of short stories featuring Wimsey and, in the later books, his intellectual sparring partner and future wife, Harriet Vane. President of the Detection Club for the last eight years of her life, Sayers had, by this time, abandoned the detective story and turned her attention elsewhere. In the war years she had written a sequence of radio plays about the life of Christ – she was a committed Christian throughout her life – and her last years were spent in translation work. Her version of Dante's *Divine Comedy* was unfinished at the time of her death.

---

SAYERS, TOM (1826–1865)
27 CAMDEN HIGH STREET, NW1

Only the third sportsman to be honoured with a Blue Plaque, Tom Sayers came to prominence in the sport of prizefighting, which, at the time he fought, was strictly speaking illegal. None the less, huge crowds turned out to attend his greatest fight – against the American John Heenan – in Farnborough, Hampshire, in April 1860. Heenan outweighed Sayers by several stones and was 6 inches taller. In the sixth round he broke Sayers's arm with a punch but the fight went on for another thirty-six bloody rounds until, amid scenes of chaos and confusion as the ring ropes broke and the crowd surged forward, the contest was declared a draw. Sayers was born in Brighton and began his prizefighting career in the 1840s. He routinely fought men much larger than himself and, although today he would be classed as a middleweight, he won the British heavyweight championship in 1857 and defended it successfully several times. He retired after the Heenan fight and died of tuberculosis a few years later. Sayers is buried in Highgate Cemetery, and more than 100,000 people are said to have lined the route of his funeral procession.

## SCAWEN-BLUNT, WILFRID (1840–1922) *diplomat, poet and traveller, founder of Crabbet Park Arabian Stud, lived here*

15 BUCKINGHAM GATE, SW1

A flamboyant romantic, born into a world of Victorian propriety that he despised, Wilfrid Scawen-Blunt was a poet (although not a very good one), an explorer and admirer of Arabic lands, an outspoken opponent of imperialism and a breeder of Arabic horses. Appropriately he married a granddaughter of Byron, although he was the lover of many more women, including William Morris's wife Jane. He campaigned against British rule in Egypt and Ireland, serving a brief period in an Irish prison for his troubles, and lived on to become a grandly inspiring, semi-legendary figure to poets and writers such as Yeats and Pound. After settling on family estates at Petworth in Sussex, he founded the Crabbet Park Arabian Stud.

## SCHOPENHAUER, ARTHUR (1788–1860) *philosopher lived and studied here in 1803*

EAGLE HOUSE, HIGH STREET, WIMBLEDON, SW19

One of the greatest of nineteenth-century philosophers, Arthur Schopenhauer was born in Danzig (Gdansk) and spent most of his life in Germany but he lived briefly in London when he was in his teens. His parents, both great Anglophiles, journeyed around Britain in 1803 and, while they toured the country, they placed the fifteen-year-old Schopenhauer in the care of the Reverend James Lancaster. Lancaster ran a school in what is now Eagle House, a Jacobean building first constructed for one of the original members of the East India Company. Schopenhauer hated his time there and disliked much of what he experienced of English life. In truth, when he grew up, he discovered that he disliked much of what he experienced in general. 'Life is so short, questionable and evanescent,' he wrote, 'that it is not worth the trouble of major effort.' As a philosopher he was famous for his gloom and his pessimism but his greatest book, *The World as Will and Representation*, although a failure when first published, went on to become one of the most influential works of philosophy of the century. In the 150 years since his death, many people have been inspired by what one admirer called the 'fierceness with which he reveals the deepest recesses of the human heart'.

## SCHREINER, OLIVE (1855–1920) *author, lived here*

16 PORTSEA PLACE, W2

Like many other women writers of the nineteenth century, Olive Schreiner was obliged to publish her work originally under a male pseudonym, since its subject matter was deemed too shocking for a woman to examine. *The Story of an African Farm* was published in 1883 under the name Ralph Iron. Set in South Africa, it tells the story of a free-thinking young woman, Lyndall, who rebels against her fiercely religious background. Schreiner herself was the daughter of a German missionary who appalled her family by adopting free-thinking and feminist beliefs. After *The Story of an African Farm* she published little further fiction. She married a South African lawyer and politician and together they campaigned for women's rights and other progressive causes. During the Boer War they supported the Boers and were both interned by the British. She lived in Portsea Place for only a few months in the late 1880s.

---

## SCHWITTERS, KURT (1887–1948) *artist, lived here*
39 WESTMORELAND ROAD, BARNES, SW13

Schwitters was born in Hanover and it was in his home city that he created his own one-man art movement, a variant of Dadaism that he called 'Merz'. The name came from letters within the word Commerzbank, which he tore from a newspaper and used in one of his collages. The collages also made use of labels, bus tickets, broken bits of wood and other pieces of rubbish that took Schwitters's fancy. In 1923, discontent with the small scale of paintings and collages, Schwitters began to turn his entire house into one fantastic, rubbish-filled construction, the so-called 'Merzbau'. When the Nazis came to power Merz was seen as a prime example of 'degenerate' art and Schwitters fled first to Norway and then to London. In 1945 he moved to the Lake District and three years later he died in Kendal, leaving behind another Merzbau under construction in a large barn.

---

## SCOTLAND YARD, *first headquarters of the Metropolitan Police 1829–1890*
MINISTRY OF AGRICULTURE BUILDING, WHITEHALL PLACE, SW1

---

## SCOTT, SIR GEORGE GILBERT (1811–1878) *architect, lived here*
ADMIRAL'S HOUSE, ADMIRAL'S WALK, HAMPSTEAD, NW3

Scott was the pre-eminent architect of Victorian England, entrusted with many major public buildings, and one of the leading practitioners of the Gothic Revival style. In the 1830s Scott and his partner designed workhouses established under the new Poor Laws, but he soon graduated to grander buildings and his career culminated in such immediately identifiable London landmarks as the Albert Memorial and St Pancras Station. All the honours of his profession came to him. He was President of the Royal Institute for British Architects, Professor of Architecture at the Royal Academy and was given a knighthood in 1872. Indirectly Scott was responsible for the foundation of the Society for Protection of Ancient Buildings in 1877. William Morris was so incensed by what he saw as Scott's insensitive restoration of the Minster at Tewkesbury that he wrote a furious letter of protest to a magazine. Other readers responded and the SPAB, one of the first-ever societies for the preservation of a nation's heritage, was formed.

---

## SCOTT, SIR GILES GILBERT (1880–1960) *architect, designed this house and lived here 1926–1960*

CHESTER HOUSE, CLARENDON PLACE, W2

The grandson of George Gilbert Scott, Giles Gilbert Scott, like his grandfather, was a prolific architect who received high honours in his lifetime. He was knighted in 1924 and received the OM in 1944. His most notable works may well be the Anglican Cathedral in Liverpool and the University Library in Cambridge but his designs and constructions can be seen in London as well. These include Battersea Power Station and Waterloo Bridge but his most significant work in the capital was a reconstruction. On 10 May 1941 the House of Commons was bombed and became 'an impenetrable inferno of flames'. After the war Scott was commissioned to rebuild the House of Commons in the tradition of the original design by Barry and Pugin.

## SCOTT, CAPTAIN, ROBERT FALCON (1868–1912) *Antarctic explorer, lived here*
### 56 OAKLEY STREET, SW3

Scott was one of the heroic failures of imperial Britain, the man who led his men to the South Pole only to find that a Norwegian expedition had beaten them to the prize. On the way back he and the four men with him all died in the snows of Antarctica. Before he succumbed to cold and starvation Scott wrote in his journal, 'Had we lived, I should have had a tale to tell of the hardihood, endurance and courage of my companions which would have stirred the heart of every Englishman. These rough notes and our dead bodies must tell the tale.' It is the kind of rhetoric which, though still moving, is now hopelessly outmoded. Shackleton, the Antarctic explorer who never lost a man on his expeditions, seems a more contemporary hero. Yet, at the time, Scott, a naval officer who had led a previous expedition to the Antarctic in the first years of the century, was hailed as a great explorer and posthumously knighted. His statue, sculpted by his widow Kathleen, stands in Waterloo Place.

---

## SEACOLE, MARY (1805–1881) *Jamaican nurse, heroine of the Crimean War, lived here*
### 14, SOHO SQUARE, W1

## MARY SEACOLE, *Jamaican nurse, heroine of the Crimean War, lived in a house on this site*
### 147, GEORGE STREET, W1  **WESTMINSTER**

Everyone has heard of Florence Nightingale and her achievements. Not enough people have heard of Mary Seacole, who played an equally heroic role in nursing British soldiers during the Crimean War, often tending their wounds while under fire herself. Born in Jamaica, the daughter of a free black woman and a Scottish army officer, she had already shown her abilities in the field of medicine before the Crimean War broke out. Yet, when she offered her services to the British government she was turned away, doubtless because of her colour. Undaunted, she financed her own journey to the Crimea and there established the British Hotel near Balaclava. At the end of the war she was bankrupt but was rescued by public subscription when her work was given publicity by a number of newspapers. Her autobiography, *The Wonderful Adventures of Mrs Seacole in Many Lands*, was published in 1857 and reappeared in a modern edition in the 1980s.

---

## SEFERIS, GEORGE (1900–1971) *Greek ambassador, poet and Nobel Laureate, lived here 1957–1962*
### 51 UPPER BROOK STREET, W1

As a child Giorgios Stylianou Seferiades witnessed the last days of the Ottoman Empire. He was born in Smyrna, now Izmir in Turkey, in 1900 and grew up in the large Greek community there. Educated in Paris, he joined the Greek diplomatic service in the 1920s, beginning a highly successful career that ended with his years as Greek Ambassador to the UK, when he lived in Upper Brook Street. Throughout his time as a diplomat, he also wrote poetry published under the name George Seferis. 'I am fully conscious,' he once wrote, 'that we do not live in a time when the poet can believe that fame awaits him, but in a time of oblivion.' None the less, Seferis's poetry, which he began to publish in the 1930s, was soon recognised as a remarkable attempt to re-imagine Greece's literary heritage and to re-cast it in a modern idiom. *Mythistorema*, a collection of short poems published in 1935, is a re-fashioning of Homeric myth, and much of Seferis's other work is imbued with his own sense of the continuing presence of Greece's classical past. In 1963 he was awarded the Nobel Prize for Literature for 'his eminent lyrical writing, inspired by a deep feeling for the Hellenic world of culture'. Seferis died in Athens in 1971.

## SELFRIDGE, HARRY GORDON (1858–1947) *Department Store Magnate lived here 1921–1929*

THE LANSDOWNE CLUB, 9 FITZMAURICE PLACE, W1

Born in Wisconsin and brought up in Michigan, Gordon Selfridge joined the Chicago department store Marshall Field as a young man. Over twenty-five years service, he worked his way from a lowly position to a partnership in the company, married a rich wife and amassed a sizeable fortune of his own. In 1906, Selfridge and his wife did what wealthy American couples did in the Edwardian era. They crossed the Atlantic and visited London. Unimpressed by the quality of British retailing, Selfridge decided to invest some of his money in a superstore in Oxford Street that would show Londoners how Americans shopped. It opened in 1909 and, thanks to Selfridge's innovations in marketing and advertising, it was a huge success. Allegedly, it was Selfridge who first came up with the adage that, 'The customer is always right'. Unfortunately, the owner of the most famous store in town was an extravagant man with a fondness for high living and gambling. The 1930s Depression and unwise investments combined to destroy much of his fortune. He died in Putney in relative poverty in 1947.

## SHACKLETON, SIR ERNEST HENRY (1874–1922) *Antarctic explorer, lived here*

12 WESTWOOD HILL, SE26

Although he has been overshadowed in the English popular imagination by Captain Scott, Shackleton was one of the greatest of Antarctic explorers. After school at Dulwich (he would have walked to school from the house in Westwood Hill), the Irish-born Shackleton entered the Merchant Marine and, in 1901, joined Scott's first Antarctic expedition. In 1907 he was put in command of a further British Antarctic expedition which reached the south magnetic pole for the first time and came within 97 miles of the South Pole itself. Desire to reach the Pole and the determination to preserve the safety of his men, which was one of Shackleton's main virtues as an explorer, came into conflict and Shackleton turned back. On the eve of the First World War he set out with the Imperial Trans-Antarctic Expedition, intending to trek right across the Antarctic plateau by way of the Pole. Unfortunately, his ship *Endurance* became trapped in the ice of the Weddell Sea and broke up. Shackleton and five men made an epic 800-mile journey in the ship's life-boat to South Georgia and then, together with two companions, he crossed the island's 7,000-foot mountain range to reach a whaling station and raise the alarm. All his men were rescued. Shackleton died of heart failure in 1922 while on his way south in yet another expedition.

## SHARP, CECIL (1859–1924) *collector of English folk songs and dances, lived here*

4 MARESFIELD GARDENS, NW3

English music in this century, from Vaughan Williams and Delius to Benjamin Britten, has owed much to the folk music that diligent collectors rescued from potential oblivion in the late nineteenth and early twentieth centuries. The most successful of all these collectors of the previously unrecorded music of the countryside was Cecil Sharp. He began his career in the law and spent some time in Australia as a lawyer in his twenties but returned to Britain in 1889 to pursue his true interests in music. From 1896 to 1905 he was Principal of the Hampstead Conservatoire of Music. He also began his journeys into English country villages, where he talked to the oldest inhabitants, listened to them sing the songs they remembered from their childhood, and used the newly invented phonograph to record them. Later Sharp travelled to the east coast of America where he found that even older forms of English folk music had often been preserved in the isolated communities descended from the original settlers. Cecil Sharp died in 1924 but his work is carried on by the English Folk Song and Dance Society, with their headquarters at Cecil Sharp House near Regent's Park.

## SHAW, SIR EYRE MASSEY (1830–1908) *First Chief Officer of the Metropolitan Fire Brigade, lived here 1878–1891*

WINCHESTER HOUSE, 94 SOUTHWARK BRIDGE ROAD, SE1

An Irish army officer, who had briefly been head of the police and fire services in Belfast, Captain Eyre Massey Shaw became head of the Metropolitan Fire Brigade in 1861 after the death of its previous commander, James Braidwood, in a vast conflagration of warehouses in Tooley Street. He remained in charge for the next thirty years and presided over the transformation of the capital's firefighting forces into one of the most up-to-date and effective in the world. A friend of the Prince of Wales, later Edward VII, who was a great devotee of fires and fire-fighting and a regular visitor to the scenes of major conflagrations in the capital, Shaw became a Victorian celebrity. He was even honoured by Gilbert and Sullivan who included his name in one of their operettas. In *Iolanthe*, the Fairy Queen sings of Captain Shaw and wonders, 'Could thy Brigade/ With cold cascade/ Quench my great love'. The man himself was in the theatre on the first night in 1882 and the actress playing the Fairy Queen addressed her song directly to him, much to the amusement of those in the audience who knew that the Captain had quite a reputation as a ladies' man.

## SHAW, GEORGE BERNARD *lived in this house from 1887–1898. 'From the coffers of his genius he enriched the world.'*

29 FITZROY SQUARE, W1

'I am a typical Irishman,' Shaw once said, 'my family came from Yorkshire.' Whatever his family's origins, Shaw was born in Dublin and moved to London as a young man. He joined his mother who, involved in a bizarre and indefinable relationship with a charismatic music teacher called Vandeleur Lee, was already in lodgings there. For the next ten years he endeavoured to earn a living as a writer, producing a sequence of unsuccessful novels and a mass of poorly paid (or unpaid) journalism. His family continued to support him. 'I did not throw myself into the struggle for life,' he later wrote, 'I threw my mother into it.' Gradually, however, he was gaining a reputation as a socialist speaker and organiser and as one of the most brilliant journalists in London, a witty and opinionated music critic (under the pseudonym Corno di Bassetto) and an avant-garde drama critic, enthused by the new theatre of writers like Ibsen. In the 1890s he began to write plays himself and, although he found initially that their 'difficult' themes made it impossible to stage them, he had set off on the path that led him to world-wide fame. In 1898 he married Charlotte Payne Townshend, 'my green-eyed millionairess', but financial escape from literary bohemia did not lessen his output. Old plays from the nineties began to gain an audience and he continued to pour forth new ones, including such famous works as *Man and Superman*, *Major Barbara*, *Pygmalion* and *St Joan*. In the twentieth century the persona of 'GBS' that Shaw had created in the socialist and literary worlds of 1880s London became famous throughout the world. He won the Nobel Prize for Literature in 1925. He lived in Fitzroy Square for eleven years before his marriage. His later years were spent in the Hertfordshire village of Ayot St Lawrence.

## *This house, designed by* R. NORMAN SHAW, *architect, for* FREDERICK GOODALL, *painter, was later the home of* W.S. GILBERT, *writer and librettist*

GRIMS DYKE, OLD REDDING, HARROW WEALD

Shaw was born in Edinburgh in 1831 and became one of the most versatile of British architects of the second half of the nineteenth century. His work ranged from public buildings like New Scotland Yard to private houses like the Old Swan House in Chelsea and the Tudor-style building he created for Goodall in Harrow Weald. He also provided the layout of the Bedford

Park suburban development at Turnham Green and designed its church, pub and many of the houses. He continued to be a force in British architecture into the twentieth century. He died in 1912. Frederick Goodall (1822–1904) was a historical painter who became a Royal Academician in 1863, seven years before Shaw built the house for him. W.S. Gilbert moved into the house in 1890 and lived there until his accidental death in 1911.

## SHE, LAO (1899–1966) *Chinese writer, lived here 1925–1928*
### 31 ST JAMES GARDENS, NOTTING HILL, W11

Born in Beijing, the son of a palace guard who was killed in the Boxer Rebellion, Lao She became one of the most important figures in twentieth-century Chinese literature. His novel about a Beijing rickshaw puller, which first appeared in China in the 1930s and was translated into English as *Rickshaw Boy* in the 1940s, is still considered to be a modern classic. He followed it with a series of other novels and plays, which brought him fame and popularity. Despite his great reputation, Lao She did not escape the persecutions of writers and intellectuals that were part of Mao's Cultural Revolution in the 1960s. He was accused of counter-revolutionary tendencies and beaten in public by members of the Red Guard. The humiliation was too much for him and he committed suicide by throwing himself into a Beijing lake. Lao She lived in London for a number of years as a young man, working as a lecturer in Chinese in what was then the School of Oriental Studies (now the School of Oriental and African Studies) at the University of London. For much of that time he stayed in the house in Notting Hill on which his Blue Plaque now stands.

## SHELLEY, MARY (1797–1851) *author of* Frankenstein *lived here 1846–1851*
### 24 CHESTER SQUARE, SW1

The daughter of the novelist and political philosopher William Godwin and his wife, the feminist thinker Mary Wollstonecraft, the woman who was to create one of the most famous of all fictional monsters was only seventeen when she began a romantic relationship with Percy Bysshe Shelley. She fled the country with the poet and, in the summer of 1816, the two of them were staying near Geneva, close to a villa rented by Lord Byron. One evening Byron challenged the others to write a horror story. This challenge was the catalyst that eventually produced *Frankenstein*. Mary Shelley's famous character allegedly came to her in a dream. 'I saw the pale student of unhallowed arts kneeling beside the thing he had put together,' she wrote in the introduction to an edition of the novel published fifteen years later. 'I saw the hideous phantasm of a man stretched out, and then, on the working of some powerful engine, show signs of life, and stir with an uneasy, half vital motion.' After Shelley's death, Mary continued with her own literary career and published several more novels but none had the astonishing success of *Frankenstein*. Thirty years after the death of her famous husband, she herself died of a brain tumour in the house in Chester Square which now carries her Blue Plaque.

## SHELLEY, PERCY BYSSHE (1792–1822) *poet, lived here*
### 15 POLAND STREET, W1

## PERCY BYSSHE SHELLEY
### APPLEGARTH HOUSE, NELSON SQUARE, SE1   **BOROUGH OF SOUTHWARK**

From his teenage years Shelley, although from an impeccably ruling-class background, was an extreme radical in politics and religion. Expelled from Oxford after circulating a pamphlet he had written called *The Necessity of Atheism*, he arrived in London and found lodgings in Poland

Street. Quarrelling violently with his MP father, he then eloped to Scotland with his sixteen-year-old mistress. Together they spent a nomadic three years during which Shelley distributed his own pamphlets inveighing against his particular dislikes – royalty, meat-eating and religion were among them – and attempted to establish communes of like-minded individuals. He also began to publish his poetry. Shelley's domestic arrangements, always complicated, became yet more so when he eloped again with Mary Godwin, soon to be the author of *Frankenstein*, and her teenage stepsister. His discarded wife later committed suicide in the Serpentine. Shelley's new entourage finally settled in Italy for the last four years of his life, where he produced his finest poetry. He died in a boating accident in the Bay of Spezia, aged not yet thirty, and was cremated on an Italian beach.

..................................................................................................................

SHEPARD, E.H. (1879–1976) *painter and illustrator, lived here*

10 KENT TERRACE, REGENT'S PARK, NW1

Although he was a prolific illustrator for much of his long life, Shepard will always be remembered for his work in drawing the famous inhabitants of the Hundred Acre Wood. Shepard entered the Royal Academy Schools in 1897 and began working for *Punch* in 1907. After service in the First World War, he was appointed to *Punch's* regular staff and, when another *Punch* contributor, A.A. Milne, wanted someone to illustrate some children's verse for the magazine, Shepard was recommended. Milne was at first reluctant to believe that Shepard was the man for the job but he was finally persuaded and the process by which Pooh, Piglet, Christopher Robin and the others were transformed into some of the best-loved figures in children's literature was underway. Shepard continued to work for *Punch* and other illustrated magazines until the 1950s and provided illustrations for many other books, including a much-loved edition of *The Wind in the Willows*, but it was the work with Milne that gave him fame and, thanks to a generous royalty agreement, fortune.

..................................................................................................................

SHEPHERD, THOMAS HOSMER (1793–1864) *artist who portrayed London, lived here*

26 BATCHELOR STREET, N1

The best known of a large family of topographical artists, Thomas Hosmer Shepherd made his name with the publication of *Metropolitan Improvements*, which appeared in forty-one parts between 1827 and 1831. 'Behind the book,' wrote the architectural historian Sir John Summerson, 'is the apprehension that London, within a matter of fifteen or twenty years, had taken on a new character', and Shepherd's work was popular precisely because it did record the changes in the capital during the Regency period. Shepherd moved to Batchelor Street in 1818, when it was on the edge of the built-up area of north London, and remained there until 1841.

..................................................................................................................

SHERATON, THOMAS (1751–1806) *furniture designer, lived here*

163 WARDOUR STREET, W1

Sheraton, who was born in Stockton-on-Tees and did not settle in London until he was nearly forty, was the most original furniture designer in the generation after Chippendale. Despite his originality and gifts he was never a successful businessman and he remained poor, eking out his living by teaching drawing. As well as the volumes of his own designs (*The Cabinet-Maker and Upholsterer's Drawing Book* of 1791 and *The Cabinet Dictionary* of 1803) Sheraton, who was a devout Baptist, also published a number of religious tracts. He died in Golden Square, Soho, where he had moved with his family in 1795.

..................................................................................................................

SHERIDAN, RICHARD BRINSLEY (1751–1816) *dramatist, lived here*

14 SAVILE ROW, W1

## RICHARD SHERIDAN *dramatist and statesman, lived here 1795–1802*
### 10 HERFORD STREET, W1

Sheridan, a man of wide-ranging talents, pursued careers in both politics and the theatre. As a politician he entered Parliament in 1780 and became the confidant of Charles James Fox and the Prince Regent, and a speaker renowned for his wit and eloquence. He remained an MP for more than thirty years. Before entering Parliament he had made his name as a dramatist. *The Rivals*, first performed at Covent Garden in 1775, was a first-night failure but Sheridan rewrote parts of it and it played a successful second night eleven days later. It includes the character Mrs Malaprop, whose gift for mangling and misapplying words ('He is the very pineapple of politeness') added 'malapropism' to the language. *The School for Scandal*, written in a tremendous hurry and first staged at Drury Lane in 1777, is nevertheless considered one of the great comedies of the English theatre. After *The Critic*, in 1779, Sheridan wrote little for the theatre but he continued to be a major shareholder in the Drury Lane Theatre until it burned to the ground in 1809. A friend expressed surprise to find him watching the theatre burn, with a glass of wine in his hand. 'A man may surely be allowed,' Sheridan said, 'to take a glass of wine by his own fireside.'

## SHORT, SIR FRANK (1857–1945) *engraver and painter, lived here*
### 56 BROOK GREEN, W6

For more than half a century 56 Brook Green, Hammersmith, was the home of Frank Short who began his career as an engineer and ended it as President of the Royal Society of Painter Etchers and Treasurer of the Royal Academy. Short once declared that 'An artist must be a workman – and an artist afterwards, if it please God,' and his own early training as an engineer probably influenced the careful craftsmanship he displayed when he turned, as a young man, to the fine arts. He was a particularly skilled etcher and engraver who made his own tools and even invented new ones to suit the new techniques he devised. Short was the first engraver to be admitted to full membership of the Royal Academy and he was knighted in 1911.

## SIBELIUS, JEAN (1865–1957) *composer, lived here in 1909*
### 15 GLOUCESTER WALK, W8

'My symphonies,' Sibelius once wrote, 'are music, conceived and elaborated as an expression of music, without any literary basis. A symphony should be music first and last.' He dedicated his long life to the primacy of music and became the greatest of all Scandinavian composers. Born in Finland, the son of a surgeon, he was originally destined for the law but studied instead at Helsinki Conservatory. His symphonic poems based on incidents in Finnish mythology launched his career and he went on to write seven symphonies, a violin concerto and further symphonic poems. Sibelius's music proved particularly popular in Britain and he visited the country on a number of occasions to conduct concerts of his work. Sibelius wrote little in the last thirty years of his life and, after the completion of 'Tapiola' in 1926, published little except for a few works for piano. He died of a stroke in September 1957 and was laid to rest at his family home Ainola in the countryside north of Helsinki.

## SICKERT, WALTER (1860–1942) *painter and etcher, lived and worked here*
### 6 MORNINGTON CRESCENT, NW1

## W.R. SICKERT *had his school of painting and engraving here 1927–1934*
### 1 HIGHBURY PLACE, N1   **BOROUGH OF ISLINGTON**

Born in Munich, Sickert began his working life as an actor and his work as a painter continued to reflect his interest in the stage. He studied at the Slade but, in 1882, abandoned his training there to become Whistler's pupil and studio assistant, later developing into the most influential and successful of Whistler's British followers. In the catalogue notes to an early exhibition, Sickert called upon his fellow artists to 'render the magic and the poetry which they daily see around them' and he strove to do that in his own work, from the time of the New English Art Club of the 1880s through to the Camden Town Group, which he was instrumental in establishing in 1910, and beyond. His paintings of music halls and urban, working-class life, influenced by Degas and French Impressionism as well as Whistler, made him the leading figure in his generation of English painters. The house in Highbury Place was the last of several private and informal ateliers that Sickert organised during the years he lived in London.

---

SIEBE, AUGUSTUS (1788–1872) *pioneer of the diving helmet, lived and worked here*
5 DENMARK STREET, WC2

The 'closed' diving helmet revolutionised diving by allowing the diver to remain underwater for longer and to dive deeper. Many of the great engineering projects of the Victorian era could not have been carried out without the work of divers, and they could not have done their work without the 'closed' helmet. It was invented by the German Augustus Siebe who lived and worked in Denmark Street for nearly half a century. Siebe was born in Germany and had fought for the Prussian army against Napoleon before moving to London the year after Waterloo. After living first in High Holborn, Siebe moved to Denmark Street in 1828 and it was there, twelve years later, that he designed his revolutionary 'closed' helmet. A man of great ingenuity and inventiveness, he created many other machines at his workshop there, including a weighing machine and an ice-making machine. At the Great Exhibition of 1851, Siebe won several medals for his inventions. The company he invented, Siebe Gorman, survived until the 1990s.

---

THE SILVER STUDIO, *established here in 1880.* ARTHUR SILVER (1853–1886), REX SILVER (1879–1965), HARRY SILVER (1881–1971), *designers, lived here*

84 BROOK GREEN ROAD, W6

For more than eighty years the Silver Studio in Brook Green supplied designs for fabrics, textiles and wallpapers to most of the leading stores of London including Liberty's and Sanderson's. Founded by Arthur Silver in his twenties, at a time when William Morris and the Arts and Crafts movement dominated the avant-garde of design in Britain, the studio was at its height during the Art Nouveau period of the 1890s and the Edwardian years. However, under the control of Arthur Silver's two long-lived sons Rex and Harry, the studio survived until 1963. Its contents were left to the Hornsey School of Art and a plaque erected to mark the Silvers' workplace in 1981.

---

SIM, ALASTAIR (1900–1976) *actor, lived here 1953–1975*
8 FROGNAL GARDENS, NW3

One of the most admired and best-loved comic actors of his generation, Alastair Sim was born in Edinburgh and began his career as a teacher of elocution in his native city. It was not until he was in his late twenties that he moved to London and made his professional debut as an actor and, even once he had done so, he was slow to become a star. He appeared in his first film in 1935 and, over the next decade and a half, he gradually became a familiar face in all kinds of British films. By 1950 he was finally getting top billing in major feature films. Whether playing Dickens's Ebenezer Scrooge in *A Christmas Carol* or donning drag to play the headmistress in

*The Belles of St Trinian's*, Sim was a master of his art. Between 1948 and 1951, he was also the elected Rector of the University of Edinburgh. In his rectorial address, he recalled a theatrical disaster from his early career, an incident which revealed 'with conclusive certainty that I was a fool and that I had always been a fool and was likely to remain a fool.' Since then, he went on, 'I have been as happy as any man has a right to be'.

......................................................................................................

## SIMON, SIR JOHN (1816–1904) *pioneer of public health, lived here*
### 40 KENSINGTON SQUARE, W8

Simon trained at St Thomas's Hospital, where he later became a surgeon and a lecturer in pathology, and showed his talents as a medical man while still in his twenties. He was elected to the Royal Society in 1845 after delivering a markedly original paper on the thyroid gland. Simon's interest in medical research was, however, primarily practical and he had already turned his attention to the questions of sanitary reform that were to occupy him for the rest of his life. In 1848 he was appointed the first Medical Officer for Health in London and began extensive research into the state of public health in the capital. The results were published in several weighty volumes in the 1850s and over the decades to come Simon was to see many of his recommendations adopted both in England and abroad. He lived in Kensington Square from 1868 until his death.

......................................................................................................

## SINGH, MAHARAJAH DULEEP (1838–1893) *last ruler of Lahore, lived here 1881–1886*
### 53 HOLLAND PARK, W11

At the age of five, Duleep Singh was the nominal ruler of the Sikh empire his father Ranjit Singh, the so-called 'Lion of the Punjab', had created. At the age of eleven, he was deposed by the British in the aftermath of the Second Anglo-Sikh War. At the age of fifteen he was sent into exile in England. Apart from two short visits to India in the 1860s, he was never to live in his native land again. In 1886, he made an abortive attempt to thwart the ruling of the India Office that he should not return home and sailed for the Punjab without the blessing of the British. He claimed he was intending to lead the Sikhs in a holy war against the Raj but he was intercepted at Aden and sent back to Europe. For most of his days, the Maharajah was obliged to lead the life of an idle but wealthy English aristocrat, shooting in Scotland (where he became known as 'the Black Prince of Perthshire'), touring the pleasure spots of Europe and improving the estate he had bought in East Anglia. Throughout his long exile in England he was a favourite of Queen Victoria who was godmother to his eldest son. Perhaps her fondness for him owed something to the fact that he had, as a young boy, presented her with the Koh-i-Noor diamond, now part of the crown jewels.

......................................................................................................

## SITWELL, DAME EDITH (1887–1964) *poet, lived here*
### FLAT 42 GREENHILL, HAMPSTEAD HIGH STREET, NW3

One wit unkindly described the Sitwells (Edith and her brothers Osbert and Sacheverell) as 'two wiseacres and a cow' and the literary critic F.R. Leavis was of the opinion that they belonged 'to the history of publicity rather than poetry'. Yet, for some years in the twenties, the Sitwells were the public face of modernism in the arts and Edith's own verse then, and the poetry she wrote during the Second World War, were highly acclaimed. Born into an eccentric upper-class family, Edith Sitwell escaped a miserable childhood through poetry and music and *Façade*, which remains her best-known work, combines her verse with the music of William Walton. It received a stormy reception at its first public performance in 1923 and established her in the public mind as representative of the most avant-garde in the arts. She also wrote a novel based on the life of Swift and a study of a subject she knew well, *English Eccentrics*. She herself became a noticeably eccentric and theatrical figure in later life.

## SLOANE, SIR HANS (1660–1753) *physician and benefactor of the British Museum, lived here 1695–1742*

4 BLOOMSBURY PLACE, WC1

*The ground to the west of this building was given to the parish of Chelsea in 1733 by* SIR HANS SLOANE, *President of the Royal Society. Born 1660. Died 1753*

KINGS MEAD, KING'S ROAD, SW3

Born in County Down in Ireland, Sloane studied medicine in London and in France before travelling, in 1787, to Jamaica as personal physician to the newly appointed governor, the Duke of Albemarle. After the death of the Duke, Sloane returned to England, bringing with him hundreds of plant and animal specimens he had collected. Back in England, Sloane's professional life flourished, his practice in Bloomsbury was patronised by the rich and the famous and he rose to become physician to the royal family. Success brought wealth and Sloane used his money to expand his collection. No longer primarily natural history specimens, this came to include what Sloane described in his will as 'my library of books, drawings, manuscripts, prints, medals and coins; ancient and modern antiquities, seals and cameos, intaglios and precious stones; agates and jaspen, vessels of agate, jasper and crystal; mathematical instruments, drawings and pictures, and all other things.' Other things included such oddities as the 9-foot-wide horns of an extinct Irish Giant Elk. Sloane bought the property in Chelsea in 1712 to house his collection. On his death the objects accumulated by the man known to contemporaries as 'The Great Collector' were sold to the nation and formed the basis of the British Museum.

*Impresario* DON ARDEN *and mod band* SMALL FACES *worked here 1965–1967*

52–55 CARNABY STREET   **WESTMINSTER**

Small Faces, one of the most influential bands of the 1960s, consisted of Steve Marriott (1947–1991), Ronnie Lane (1946–1997), Kenney Jones (b.1948) and Jimmy Winston (b.1945), who was replaced by Ian McLagan (b.1945) after the band's first couple of singles. Beginning as a mod group, by 1967 they had evolved into one of Britain's first psychedelic bands and hits like 'Here Come the Nice' and 'Itchycoo Park' were peppered with drug references only the cognoscenti were supposed to recognise. Unfortunately those in 'Itchycoo Park' were also noted by someone in authority at the BBC which briefly banned the record until the band came up with a cover story that the song was about nothing more subversive than Steve Marriott's memories of an East London park near his childhood home. Don Arden (1926–2007), a mercurial and controversial band manager and music agent, signed up the Small Faces within half an hour of first hearing them in 1965. He piloted them towards their first chart successes but sold his contract with them to Andrew Oldham, former manager of the Rolling Stones, two years later. Today, Arden is best known as the father of Sharon Osbourne.

## SMILES, SAMUEL (1812–1904) *author of 'Self Help', lived here*

11 GRANVILLE PARK, SE13

One of the virtues seen as most quintessentially Victorian was best encapsulated by Samuel Smiles in his 1859 book, *Self Help*. 'The spirit of self-help,' he wrote, 'is the root of all genuine growth in the individual; and, exhibited in the lives of many, it constitutes the true source of national vigour and strength.' Smiles was born in Scotland and, before the publication of his most famous work, had involved himself in the newly developing railways and written a biography of the railway pioneer George Stephenson. *Self Help* sold throughout the world and its influence was felt in some unlikely places. In Japan his ideas were welcomed. The Khedive of

Egypt had texts from the book placed on the walls of his palace and the professor of philosophy who taught Mao-Tse-Tung was another enthusiast. The titles of later books by Smiles indicate the stern simplicity of his ideas. *Character* in 1871 was followed four years later by *Thrift*, and *Duty* appeared in 1880.

......................................................................................................................

## SMIRKE, SIR ROBERT (1781–1867) *architect, lived here*
### 81 CHARLOTTE STREET, W1

Sir Robert Smirke was the most successful of a family of architects – both his father and his brother shared his profession – and many of his buildings can still be seen in London. Smirke studied at the Royal Academy Schools, was articled to Sir John Soane and travelled extensively in Italy and Greece before being appointed architect to the Board of Trade. Success came early to him and he was elected a Royal Academician at the age of thirty. Both the former premises of the Royal Mint and the central part of the riverside Custom House are the work of Smirke, but his best-known building is the British Museum. Completed in 1847, the Museum, in its frontage to Great Russell Street, is based on Greek architecture, which Smirke had so admired on his travels. The great circular Reading Room was the work of his younger brother, Sidney.

......................................................................................................................

## SMITH, F.E., EARL OF BIRKENHEAD (1872–1930) *lawyer and statesman, lived here*
### 32 GROSVENOR GARDENS, SW1

From his days at Oxford, where he was president of the Union, F.E. Smith had a reputation for flamboyance and brilliance. After some years as a university lecturer, during which time he was also called to the Bar, Smith entered Parliament as Conservative MP for Walton in Liverpool in 1906 and joined the coalition government in the First World War. He was Lord Chancellor from 1919 to 1922 and Secretary of State for India for four years under Stanley Baldwin's premiership. In his courtroom appearances, Smith was renowned for the elegant tartness of his wit, often dangerously exercised at the expense of the judge in the case. When one judge, exasperated by what he saw as Smith's interference in his legal domain, said to him, 'What do you suppose I am on the bench for, Mr Smith?', Smith witheringly replied, 'My Lord, it is not for me to attempt to fathom the inscrutable workings of Providence.'

......................................................................................................................

## SMITH, SIR FRANCIS PETTIT (1808–1874) *pioneer of the screw propeller, lived here* 1864–1870
### 17 SYDENHAM HILL, SE26

The son of a Kentish postmaster, Francis Pettit Smith was working as a farmer near Hendon in Middlesex when he chanced upon the discovery that was to change his life. Since boyhood he had been interested in model boats and, experimenting with methods of propulsion, he came up with a boat that was sent hurtling across the large pond on his land by means of a wooden screw driven by a spring rather than by a paddle wheel. Convinced his new method was superior to the old, he abandoned farming and took out a patent. A large prototype vessel he demonstrated on the Thames had an accident, in which the screw, revolving beneath the water at its stern, hit an obstacle and broke in half. The accident, however, was a happy one, since the half-broken propeller worked better than it had when undamaged. Like many an innovator before him, Smith had immense difficulties persuading the powers that be that his invention was worth backing but eventually the Admiralty was convinced that screw-propelled steamships were the ships of the future. Despite this, he received little money from his invention and was, at one point, forced to return to life as a farmer. Only in the last decades of his life did he get his due. He was appointed curator of the Patent Office Museum in South Kensington, received a monetary testimonial of several thousand pounds and was knighted three years before he died.

## SMITH, STEVIE (1902–1971) *poet, lived here 1906–1971*
1 AVONDALE ROAD, N13

Stevie Smith was one of the most unusual and individual English poets of the twentieth century and a poem like 'Not Waving but Drowning' is as familiar as any by much more widely known writers. Born in Hull, she was christened Florence Margaret Smith and was known as Peggy by her family but her nickname of 'Stevie', originally given her because a friend spotted a supposed resemblance to a jockey named Steve Donoghue, was the name that stuck. When she was a toddler she moved with her mother from Hull to Palmers Green in North London in order to live with her aunt and she stayed there for the rest of her life. Her mother died when she was teenager and her formidable aunt, referred to as 'the Lion aunt' in her fiction, became the most important person in her life. She never married. For thirty years she worked as private secretary to Sir Neville Pearson, a magazine publisher, and she began to publish her idiosyncratic and offbeat verse in the 1930s. *Novel on Yellow Paper*, her first novel, appeared in 1936. She went on to publish two more novels and more than a dozen volumes of her poetry.

## SMITH, SYDNEY (1771–1845) *author and wit, lived here*
14 DOUGHTY STREET, WC1

Today Sydney Smith is remembered, if at all, as the wit who said of Lord Macaulay that 'He has occasional flashes of silence that make his conversation perfectly delightful,' and who once remarked, on meeting an acquaintance, 'I am just going to pray for you at St Paul's, but with no very lively hope of success.' In his day Smith was known as a brilliant talker, 'the Smith of Smiths', but also as a journalist (one of the founders of the *Edinburgh Review*) and a writer whose book *The Letters of Peter Plymley* was a civilised and amusing plea for religious tolerance. He was, for some years, at the heart of the Whig political and intellectual establishment but, as a relatively poor clergyman, he was obliged, in 1809, to accept the living of Foston, a small village in Yorkshire. For a man who once wrote, 'in the country I always fear that creation will expire before tea-time,' this was a harsh exile but he stayed there twenty years, writing witty letters to his grand friends and occasionally escaping 'the healthy grave' of the countryside to his old haunts in the city.

## SMITH, W.H. (1825–1891) *bookseller and statesman, lived here*
12 HYDE PARK STREET, W2

So familiar a part of British life has W.H. Smith & Son become that it takes an effort of imagination to remember that there was once an original W.H. Smith and an original Son. The Son was the man who is commemorated by the plaque in Hyde Park Street. He joined his father's newspaper business in 1846 and three years later the first of Smith's railway bookstalls opened. Son soon took over from Father in expanding the business and securing a monopoly of the station bookstalls on the London & North West Railway. Because of his determination to sell only the most respectable of literature, Smith was dubbed by contemporary wits the 'North-Western Missionary'. Smith began a distinguished parliamentary career when he was elected Conservative member for Westminster in 1868. He served in the Cabinet under both Disraeli and the Marquess of Salisbury and, from 1886 until his death, was leader of the Tories in the House of Commons.

## SMITH, WILLIAM, MP (1756–1835) *pioneer of religious liberty, lived here*
16 QUEEN ANNE'S GATE, SW1

Smith was an MP for most of the years between his first election for the borough of Sudbury, Suffolk, in 1784 until his final retirement from politics in 1830. Throughout this career, which he began as a supporter of Charles James Fox, Smith was a liberal who campaigned for the lifting of religious and political restrictions on Roman Catholics and dissenters, and worked, with Wilberforce and others, for the abolition of slavery. A familiar figure in the political life of his time, Smith was renowned for the length of his speeches and for his willingness to attend late sittings of the House when many others had disappeared for dinner. As one satirical verse put it, 'At length when the candles burn low in their sockets/Up gets William Smith with his hands in his pockets.'

---

## SMITHSON, JAMES (1764–1829) *scientist, founder of the Smithsonian Institution, lived here*
9 BENTINCK STREET, W1

'Every man is a valuable member of society,' James Smithson once wrote, 'who by his observations, researches, and experiments procures knowledge for men.' By his own definition, then, Smithson was a valuable member of society. The illegitimate son of an English duke, he spent his life wandering Europe, conducting scientific experiments and corresponding with like-minded savants across the continent. Elected to the Royal Society when he was still in his early twenties, he became an eager experimenter in mineralogy. He coined the word 'silicate' and his work on zinc carbonates was so admired that a French scientist named a mineral ore of zinc 'Smithsonite' in his honour. Smithson published twenty-seven scientific papers in his lifetime, including ones on the chemical content of a lady's teardrop and an improved method of making coffee. However, when he died in Genoa in 1829, he was largely unknown outside the small circle of his fellow scientists and he would have remained so had it not been for the instructions in his will. He left the bulk of his considerable fortune to found an institute of learning in the USA, a country he had never visited. His name lives on in the world-famous Smithsonian Institution.

---

## SOPWITH, SIR THOMAS (1888–1989) *aviator and aircraft manufacturer, lived here 1934–1940*
46 GREEN STREET, MAYFAIR, W1

In the course of his long life Sopwith witnessed the development of the aircraft industry from the days of the earliest flying machines to supersonic flight and he made his own major contribution to that development. He won a prize for a flight across the English Channel in 1910, the year after Blériot had made his pioneering flight, and two years later founded his own aviation company. Many of the planes used by the Royal Flying Corps in the First World War came from Sopwith's factory at Kingston-upon-Thames. As the aircraft companies grew larger, Sopwith remained an important figure and, as chairman of the Hawker Siddeley Group for many years, he oversaw production of many of the planes, including the Hurricane, used in the Second World War as well. He was also an enthusiastic yachtsman who competed in the America's Cup in the thirties.

---

## SOSEKI, NATSUME (1867–1916) *Japanese novelist, lived here 1901–1902*
81 THE CHASE, CLAPHAM, SW4

Soseki, one of Japan's greatest novelists, was also a scholar of English Literature and it was to pursue his academic interests that he was sent by the Japanese Education Ministry to London in 1900. Soseki's stay in London was not a happy one. Living on limited funds, he was isolated, lonely and distressed by the casual prejudice he encountered in the city. After he returned to Japan, Soseki taught English Literature at Tokyo University but gave up teaching in 1907 to concentrate on his writing. In a relatively short career as a writer, Soseki was remarkably prolific. Like much Japanese fiction at the time his work was published first as serialisations in newspapers. His best-known novels include *Wagahai wa neko de aru* (I Am A Cat), *Botchan*, the story of a young rebel that one critic has described as 'the Japanese equivalent of Huckleberry

Finn', and *Kokoro*, an account of the relationship between a young man and his spiritual and moral teacher, that is generally accepted as his masterpiece. Soseki, who had been plagued by poor health for most of his adult life, died of a gastric ulcer at the age of only forty-nine.

## SPILSBURY, SIR BERNARD (1877–1947) *forensic pathologist, lived here 1912–1940*
### 31 MARLBOROUGH HILL, NW8

Spilsbury first came to public notice when he gave evidence in the 1910 trial of Dr Crippen for the murder of his wife and, from then until his death, he was an expert witness in dozens of notorious cases. No murder trial in the 1920s and 1930s was considered quite complete until Spilsbury had taken the witness stand and provided the kind of scientific evidence which could either exonerate the accused or condemn them to the gallows. From the Brides in the Bath Murders to the Brighton Trunk Murders, his cases were the stuff of which front page headlines were made and Spilsbury himself became more famous than the killers he helped to convict. During the Second World War, he played a critical role in Operation Mincemeat, an elaborate deception involving secret plans found on a corpse, which was intended to fool the Germans into thinking that Greece and Sardinia, rather than Sicily, were the target for Allied invasion in 1943. In his later years Spilsbury suffered a series of personal losses. Two of his three sons died, one during the London Blitz, and he himself was increasingly subject to bouts of ill health. In December 1947, he gassed himself in his laboratory at University College, London.

## SPURGEON, CHARLES HADDON (1834–1892) *preacher, lived here*
### 99 NIGHTINGALE LANE, SW12

In these less religious times it is hard to credit the impact made by preachers in the Victorian age. One of the most successful of the century was Charles Spurgeon who, in 1855, addressed a sermon in the open air of a Hackney field to an audience estimated at between 12,000 and 14,000. The Metropolitan Tabernacle, near the Elephant and Castle, was built especially to accommodate his congregation in 1859–61 and, seating 6,000, was filled to capacity week after week. A contemporary wrote, 'Half an hour before time the aisles were solid blocks and many stood throughout the service, wedged in by their fellows and prevented from escaping by the crowd outside who . . . stood in throngs as far as the sound could reach.' Spurgeon died in 1892 and is buried in Norwood Cemetery.

## STANFORD, SIR CHARLES (1852–1924) *musician, lived here 1894–1916*
### 56 HORNTON STREET, W8

Born in Dublin and educated as a choral scholar at Queen's College, Cambridge, Stanford went on to become one of the pillars of the musical establishment. He became Professor at the Royal College of Music in 1882, Professor of Music at his old university five years later and was knighted in 1901. During his lifetime his oratorios and operas like *Much Ado About Nothing*, *Shamus O'Brien* and *The Veiled Prophet of Khorassan* were acclaimed by critics and audiences alike. Today they are largely forgotten, although some of his choral and church music continues to be performed. Perhaps Stanford's greatest service to English music was as a teacher. Over a period of forty years at the Royal College of Music he taught very nearly every significant English composer of the first half of the twentieth century including Vaughan Williams, Gustav Holst and Sir Arthur Bliss.

## STANHOPE, CHARLES, 3RD EARL (1753–1816) *reformer and inventor, lived here*
### 20 MANSFIELD STREET, W1

Stanhope was a maverick English aristocrat who, although he was married to the sister of Pitt the Younger, was a firm opponent of the war against France that the government of his brother-in-law waged in the 1790s. He greeted the outbreak of the French Revolution with enthusiasm and even after the bloody events of the Terror he defied public opinion by advocating non-interference in French affairs. The public responded in the shape of a mob, which attacked his house in Mansfield Street in 1794 as a protest against Citizen Stanhope's revolutionary sympathies. Stanhope was also an inventor who created a type of lens that is named after him and several improvements to contemporary printing processes. He was the father of eccentric traveller Lady Hester Stanhope, who settled in a remote convent in the Lebanon and ended her days in the Middle East, proclaiming her powers as a prophet and recipient of occult knowledge.

## STANLEY, SIR HENRY MORTON (1841–1904) *explorer and writer, lived and died here*
2 RICHMOND TERRACE, WHITEHALL, SW1

'There are hundreds of people around me – I might say thousands without exaggeration . . . There is a group of the most respectable Arabs; and as I come nearer I see the white face of an old man among them . . . We raise our hats and I say: "Dr. Livingstone, I presume?" And he says: "Yes."' So Stanley recorded the most famous encounter in the history of exploration. Stanley, product of a Welsh workhouse, had run away to America in 1859, fought on both sides in the American Civil War and ended up as a newspaperman. His paper, the *New York Herald*, had sent him in search of the missing Livingstone in 1869 and he tracked him down two years later. Together they explored the northern reaches of Lake Tanganyika and, after Livingstone's death, Stanley made a further expedition in which he circumnavigated Lake Victoria and traced the Congo River to the sea. Stanley was a tough and ruthless man and both this expedition and his later journey to rescue Emin Pasha were marked by brutal treatment of native Africans and considerable loss of life.

## STANLEY, W.F.R. (1829–1909) *inventor, manufacturer and philanthropist founded and designed these halls and technical school*

STANLEY HALLS, 12 SOUTH NORWOOD HILL, SE25

Stanley was a man of many talents who was an accomplished musician, an artist and photographer, and an architect. However, his greatest gift was as an inventor and deviser of scientific instruments. He founded a firm to manufacture mathematical drawing instruments in London in 1854 and the following year patented his first major invention – the 'Panoptic Stereoscope'. Many more followed in the course of a long, creative life and his work in improving the theodolite and other surveying instruments proved particularly valuable. Towards the end of his life he put some of the money he had made from his inventions into the foundation of the public hall (1903) and the technical school (1907) in South Norwood.

## STANSFIELD, CLARKSON
See under entry for SAMUEL PEPYS

## STAUNTON, HOWARD (1810–1874) *British World Chess Champion, lived here 1871–1874*
117 LANSDOWNE ROAD, W11

The only Englishman ever to have been acknowledged as the World Chess Champion, Staunton gained his title by beating the French player Saint-Amant in 1843 and held it throughout the rest of the 1840s. Rumoured to be the illegitimate son of an earl, Staunton was born in Westmorland and grew up to be a man of wide-ranging interests and achievements, producing a large, annotated edition of Shakespeare and writing extensively on the theatre and educational theory as well as on chess. However, it is as Victorian England's greatest advocate of chess that he is remembered. Staunton wrote a chess column in the *Illustrated London News* for nearly thirty years, published several books on the subject, and gave his name to a design of chess pieces that became standard. Defeated by the German player Adolf Anderssen in an international chess tournament he himself had organised in London in 1851, Staunton relinquished the title (never entirely official, anyway) of World Champion but continued to play, and beat, many of the finest players of the time. He died in his London home in 1874 and is buried in Kensal Green Cemetery, where his grave is now marked by a memorial stone decorated with the image of a large chess piece.

........................................................................................................................................................

STEAD, W.T. (1849–1912) *journalist and reformer of great renown lived here 1904–1912*
5 SMITH SQUARE  **WESTMINSTER**

William Thomas Stead was one of the most colourful and controversial journalists of the Victorian age. He became editor of the *Pall Mall Gazette* in 1883 and two years later he launched the paper on a crusade against child prostitution. Stead went to prison after arranging for the purchase of an underage girl in order to prove to himself, and to his readers, how easy it was to procure the young for sexual purposes. He spent three months inside Holloway Prison but, as a result of the publicity the case had attracted, the age of consent was raised from thirteen to sixteen. After his release, he continued to campaign for a wide range of causes, from spiritualism and pacifism to women's rights and the need for a universal language. Stead's death was as dramatic as much of his life had been. He was one of those who lost their lives when the Titanic sank on its maiden voyage across the Atlantic in 1912. One of the many legends that have attached themselves to the true history of the Titanic is that Stead the spiritualist had long foreseen his death by drowning and that, as the ship went down, he sat calmly smoking a cigar, awaiting the inevitable end. There is no convincing evidence that this particular legend is true and, given Stead's energetic personality, it seems unlikely that he would have resigned himself so readily to his fate.

........................................................................................................................................................

STEER, PHILIP WILSON (1860–1942) *painter, lived and died here*
109 CHEYNE WALK, SW10

Born in Birkenhead, Steer studied art in Paris and was among the first English painters to introduce the works and the techniques of the French impressionists to this country. With Sickert and others, he was, in 1886, one of the founding members of the New English Art Club, which was established to exhibit the French-influenced *plein air* painters who found the Royal Academy an uncongenial, if not impossible, place to show their work. Steer taught for many years at the Slade School of Art where he was a major influence on the next generation of English painters. A bachelor, Steer lived an ordered and regular life at Cheyne Walk for more than forty years. His friend William Rothenstein wrote, 'He was extremely matter of fact; in life, for him, there was little romance. Without a brush in his hands, he was indifferent to most things save dry feet and freedom from draughts.'

........................................................................................................................................................

STEPHEN, SIR LESLIE (1832–1904) *scholar and writer, lived here*
22 HYDE PARK GATE, SW7

Stephen was a leading member of one of the great intellectual dynasties of the nineteenth century. His father was Professor of Modern History at Cambridge. His brother was a high court judge and legal historian. His nephew, J.K. Stephen, wrote light verse, became insane, died young and has had the posthumous misfortune to be proposed as a candidate for the role of Jack the Ripper. Leslie Stephen's most remarkable achievement was the *Dictionary of National Biography*, of which he was founding editor and for which he wrote many articles. Among the children from his second marriage – he had first been married to one of Thackeray's daughters – were the novelist Virginia Woolf and the painter Vanessa Bell.

## STEPHEN, VIRGINIA (VIRGINIA WOOLF) *novelist and critic, lived here 1907–1911*
29 FITZROY SQUARE, W1

The daughter of the eminent Victorian critic and scholar Sir Leslie Stephen, Virginia Stephen moved out of the family home in Hyde Park Gate on her father's death in 1904, together with her sister Vanessa and her brothers Thoby and Adrian. They lived first in Gordon Square, Bloomsbury, and then, after the tragedy of Thoby's unexpected death in 1906, Adrian and Virginia moved to Fitzroy Square. The house there became, just as had the house in Gordon Square, a meeting-place for the friends (Lytton Strachey, Leonard Woolf, Clive Bell) who formed the nucleus of what has since become known as the Bloomsbury Group. It was at Fitzroy Square that Virginia Stephen, who married Leonard Woolf in 1912, began her first novel *The Voyage Out*.

## STEPHENSON, ROBERT (1803–1859) *engineer, lived here*
35 GLOUCESTER SQUARE, W2

The son of George Stephenson, the locomotive engineer, Robert Stephenson assisted his father on the pioneering Stockton & Darlington Railway and on the *Rocket*, the fastest engine of its time. In 1833 he was appointed Chief Engineer of the London and Birmingham Railway, the first line to run into the capital and, after this opened successfully, was in much demand as railway construction began to spread throughout the world. He also built bridges in Britain and abroad, including one across the St Lawrence in Montreal which was, for a number of years, the longest in the world. Robert Stephenson entered Parliament in 1847 and served as MP for Whitby until shortly before his death.

## STEVENS, ALFRED (1817–1875) *artist, lived here*
9 ETON VILLAS, NW3

One of the more interesting and neglected English painters and sculptors of the nineteenth century, Stevens was born in Blandford Forum and his precocious talent was fostered by a local clergyman. This proved a mixed blessing. His patron was determined that Stevens should gain proper training but, in the absence of a suitable teacher in this country, shipped his protegé off to Italy. The sixteen-year-old Stevens, unable at first to speak any Italian and short of funds, led a hand-to-mouth existence in Naples and Florence for several years, copying works for none-too-scrupulous dealers. In Rome in 1840 he met the Danish sculptor Thorwaldsen and worked in his studio before returning to England two years later. His greatest work is the Wellington monument in St Paul's, which was commissioned in 1856. Bad luck, which seemed to haunt Stevens's life, haunted this project and the equestrian statue of the Iron Duke was not finally erected until forty-five years after the artist's death.

## STILL, SIR GEORGE FREDERIC (1868–1941) *paediatrician, lived here*
28 QUEEN ANNE STREET, W1

Educated at Caius College, Cambridge, where he took a first in Classics, Still trained at Guy's Hospital and began his career at the Great Ormond Street Hospital. In 1897 he published a paper called 'On a Form of Chronic Joint Disease in Children', which identified for the first time a chronic rheumatoid arthritis peculiar to children, now often known as Still's disease. Still spent most of his working life at King's College Hospital, which he joined in 1899 and where he was the first Professor of the Diseases of Children from 1906 to 1935. In the last years before his retirement Still was also physician to Princess Elizabeth (now the Queen) and Princess Margaret.

## STOKER, BRAM (1847–1912) *author of 'Dracula' lived here*

18 ST LEONARD'S TERRACE, SW3

The title of Stoker's first publication, *The Duties of Clerks of Petty Session in Ireland*, gave little hint of the literary career ahead of him. Born and educated in Dublin, Stoker was a civil servant who wrote drama reviews in his spare time until he came to the attention of the legendary actor Sir Henry Irving. Irving persuaded him to London to act as his manager, a job Stoker held for twenty-seven years. *Dracula*, his tale of Transylvanian vampirism, was published in 1897. Perhaps the vampiric Count owed something to his charismatic patron, of whom Stoker wrote, 'So great was the magnetism of his genius, so profound was the sense of his dominancy that I sat spellbound.' Perhaps the story was no more than the product, as Stoker's son later claimed, of 'a nightmarish dream after eating too much dressed crab'. Whatever its origins, *Dracula* has proved extraordinarily successful and Stoker's Count, through the movies, is familiar to millions who have never read the novel.

## STONE, MARCUS (1840–1921) *artist, lived here*

8 MELBURY ROAD, W14

The son of a Royal Academician, Marcus Stone showed his first picture at the Academy when he was only eighteen and went on to become one of the leading genre painters and illustrators of the second half of the nineteenth century. During the 1860s he attracted attention both as the illustrator of a number of novels by Trollope and as a painter of canvases on historical and literary subjects. His later works, for which he is now best remembered, are most frequently sentimental scenes in which attractive but bashful maidens pose decoratively before their suitors. Such titles as *A Stolen Kiss*, *A First Love Letter*, *A Sailor's Sweetheart* and *Two's Company, Three's None* accurately reflect both the charm and the limitations of Stone's work. In his lifetime Stone found himself hopelessly outmoded as a painter but, as appreciation of Victorian culture has risen over the past thirty years, so has appreciation of his undemanding but skilful art.

## STOTHARD, THOMAS (1755–1834) *painter and illustrator, lived here*

28 NEWMAN STREET, W1

Born in London, Stothard was apprenticed to a pattern-drawer and later was able to study at the Royal Academy Schools. His work as a painter in oils consists of scenes from classical mythology, such as *Ajax Defending the Body of Patroclus*, and scenes from the classic works of English literature, particularly Shakespeare. Stothard was one of the artists invited by the engraver and entrepreneur John Boydell to contribute to his ambitious plan to produce a Shakespeare Gallery of original works that could then be reproduced and sold. However, it was as an illustrator that Stothard showed particular originality and his designs for editions of books such as *The Pilgrim's Progress* and *Gulliver's Travels* retain their freshness in a way that his paintings do not. In all Stothard, who became Librarian at the Royal Academy in 1812, produced more than 3,000 illustrations.

## STRACHEY, LYTTON (1880–1932) *critic and biographer, lived here*

51 GORDON SQUARE, WC1

A leading member of the Bloomsbury Group, which also included Leonard and Virginia Woolf and Clive and Vanessa Bell, Strachey revolutionised the art of biography in iconoclastic works such as *Eminent Victorians* (1918), *Queen Victoria* (1921) and *Elizabeth and Essex* (1928). Witty and irreverent, Strachey rescued biography from the stifling and deadening hand of the 'official life'. For many years he lived in a *ménage à trois* with the painter Dora Carrington and her husband. He died in 1932, exiting with the characteristic remark, 'If this is dying, I don't think much of it.' Carrington was so devastated by his death that she committed suicide in the same year.

................................................................

## STRANG, WILLIAM (1859–1921) *painter and etcher, lived here 1900–1921*
### 20 HAMILTON TERRACE, NW8

William Strang was born in Dumbarton but came to London to study at the Slade School of Art under the French painter, long resident in England, Alphonse Legros. Strang was to stay in the capital throughout his career as painter, etcher and illustrator. As a painter Strang was a fine colourist who often worked in the tradition first established by the French Impressionists. As an etcher and an illustrator, who produced illustrations for editions of 'The Rime of the Ancient Mariner', 'Don Quixote' and Kipling's short stories, he combined realism with the fantastic in what is his best and most original work. The house in Hamilton Terrace where Strang lived for the last twenty years of his life had, in the 1880s, been the residence of the composer Sir George McFarren.

................................................................

## STREET, GEORGE EDMUND (1824–1881) *architect, lived here*
### 14 CAVENDISH PLACE, W1

Street was among the many English architects who were massively influenced by the writings of the passionate, half-French enthusiast for all things Gothic, Augustus Pugin, and his belief that Gothic architecture was 'not a style but a principle'. Born in Essex, Street worked in the office of Sir George Gilbert Scott and became a recognised authority on medieval architecture with the publication in 1855 of *Brick and Marble in the Middle Ages*, his notes on an architectural tour of the north of Italy. Street's was a productive career but his best-known building is one he undertook towards the end of it. Indeed his difficulties with the immensely complex task of designing and building the Law Courts in the Strand were said to have shortened his life. Certainly the Courts were not completed until after Street's death in 1881.

................................................................

## STRYPE STREET
*Formerly Strype's Yard, derives its name from the fact that the house of* JOHN STRYPE, *silk merchant, was situated there. At that house was born in 1643 his son* JOHN STRYPE, *historian and biographer, who died in 1737*
### 10 LEYDEN STREET, E1

The elder John Strype, who died when his son was five years old, established his silk business in the street that took his name at a time when that area in the east of the city was a centre of that particular trade. His son entered the Church and was rector of Leyton for nearly seventy years. He wrote widely on church history, amassing a huge array of historical documents and manuscripts and publishing biographies of ecclesiastical figures such as Cranmer. He also produced new editions of the *Survey of London*, originally produced by John Stow in 1598, enlarging and indeed rewriting much of it.

................................................................

## STUART, JOHN MCDOUALL (1815–1866) *first explorer to cross Australia, lived and died here*
### 9 CAMPDEN HILL SQUARE, W8

Stuart, who was born in Scotland, went on to become one of the greatest of Australian explorers. He emigrated to the new colony of South Australia in 1838 and arrived in Adelaide, which had been founded only two years earlier and was still little more than a rough settlement of wooden huts and tents. Stuart worked for a number of years as a surveyor but it was not until 1858 that he was able to make the first of his six expeditions. On his sixth expedition he left Adelaide on 25 October 1861 and nine months later was able to record in his journals, 'I advanced a few yards on to the beach, and was gratified and delighted to behold the water of the Indian Ocean in Van Diemen's Gulf.' Stuart underwent severe privations while crossing the continent and, in 1864, he returned to England in failing health. He died in Campden Hill Square two years later.

........................................................................................................

## SVEVO, ITALO, ALIAS FOR SCHMITZ, ETTORE (1861–1928) *writer, lived here 1903–1913*

### 67 CHARLTON CHURCH LANE, CHARLTON, SE7

Born in Trieste into a cosmopolitan family of Austro-Italian Jews, Ettore Schmitz showed an early interest in literature, but family difficulties forced him to abandon his studies as a teenager and take a job as a clerk in a bank. He worked there for nearly twenty years. In the 1890s, under the pseudonym Italo Svevo, Schmitz published two novels at his own expense, *A Life* and *As I Grow Older*, but they received little attention and most of the few readers they had were puzzled by his oblique, ironic style. 'This incomprehension baffles me,' Svevo wrote plaintively, 'it demonstrates that they just don't follow me.' He published nothing for a quarter of a century, although he continued to write. Married in 1898, he worked for his father-in-law's paint business and it was while establishing a branch of the firm in London that he lived, intermittently, in Charlton. In 1907 he made what was to be the most significant friendship of his life when he met the young James Joyce, who was working as an English teacher in Trieste. Joyce admired Svevo's two earlier novels and his encouragement was a powerful stimulus for the older writer at a time when few others recognised his gifts. In 1923 Svevo, again at his own expense, published *The Confessions of Zeno*, a strange but compelling account of an ordinary man grappling with his own neuroses and his addiction to tobacco. Svevo was involved in a car crash in September 1928 and died a few days later.

........................................................................................................

## SWINBURNE, ALGERNON CHARLES (1837–1909) *poet, and his friend,* THEODORE WATTS-DUNTON (1832–1914), *poet, novelist, critic, lived and died here*

### 11 PUTNEY HILL, SW15

The son of an admiral, Swinburne was educated at Eton and Oxford where he became interested in Pre-Raphaelitism and got to know Rossetti. He gained early celebrity with the poetic drama *Atalanta in Calydon*, which Ruskin described as 'the grandest thing ever done by a youth, though he is a demonic youth'. By publishing *Poems and Ballads* in 1866, a collection characterised by themes of moral and spiritual rebellion and by a flirtation with the sadistic and the sexually ambiguous, Swinburne outraged many of the arbiters of Victorian taste. One critic described him as 'the libidinous laureate of a pack of satyrs'. Meanwhile Swinburne was making a descent into alcoholism from which he was rescued by the minor poet and critic Theodore Watts-Dunton, who carried him off to the more sedate suburban pleasures of Putney. Together the two friends lived and worked at The Pines, Putney Hill, from 1879 to Swinburne's death thirty years later.

See also under entry for D.G. ROSSETTI

........................................................................................................

## SZABO, VIOLETTE, GC (1921–1945) *secret agent, lived here. She gave her life for the French Resistance*

### 18 BURNLEY ROAD, STOCKWELL, SW9

Violette Bushell's father was English and her mother French, and she was brought up in south London. In 1940 she met a captain in the Free French Forces, Etienne Szabo, and they were married in August 1940. Two years later he was killed in action in North Africa. Violette Szabo's fluency in French made her an ideal candidate for SOE work in occupied France and in April 1944 she made a dangerous journey from Paris to Rouen, contacting scattered members of a resistance unit as she went. Shortly after D-Day she was again dropped into France but this time she and her French guide were ambushed by a German patrol and Violette Szabo was captured. After interrogation, during which she revealed nothing, she was sent to the concentration camp at Ravensbrück and there, some time in late January or early February, she was shot. Posthumously she was awarded both the George Cross and the French Croix de Guerre and her short but courageous life was celebrated in the book and film *Carve Her Name with Pride*.

## TAGLIONI, MARIE (1804–1884) *ballet dancer, lived here in 1875–1876*
### 14 CONNAUGHT SQUARE, W2

A twentieth-century ballet critic wrote, 'All that romantic poetry, painting and music could express, Taglioni could express in her dancing', and romantic writers like Théophile Gautier and Victor Hugo were rapturous in their responses to her Paris performances. She was the daughter of an Italian choreographer and it was in works arranged by her father, most notably *La Sylphide*, that she scored her greatest triumphs not only in Paris but also in London and St Petersburg. In Russia she was especially idolised and it was there that, at one farewell banquet, a pair of her ballet shoes was served as one of the courses, 'cooked . . . with a special sauce'. Later in life she was a teacher of dance and she ran a school in London at the time she was living in Connaught Square.

## TAGORE, RABINDRANATH (1861–1941) *Indian poet, stayed here in 1912*
### 3 VILLAS ON THE HEATH, VALE OF HEALTH, HAMPSTEAD, NW3

Tagore was a man of wide talents and wrote novels and short stories as well as poetry in his native Bengali. He was also a painter and composer, setting many of his poems to music. He won the Nobel Prize for Literature in 1913, the first Asian writer to do so. His best-known work is probably *Gitanjali*, a collection first published in India, which Tagore himself then translated into English prose poems. Tagore visited England a number of times. His first impressions of London in 1912 were not good. 'I reached London and stayed in a hotel,' he wrote. 'Everyone seemed like phantoms. The hotel used to empty after breakfast and I watched the crowded streets. I was in despair. It was not possible to know this humanity or enter into the heart of another place.' He found lodgings in Hampstead through his friend and admirer, the artist William Rothenstein.

## TAIT, THOMAS SMITH (1882–1954) *architect, lived here*
### GATES HOUSE, WYLDES CLOSE, NW11

The name of Thomas Smith Tait may not be familiar to most readers but many of his buildings will be. A highly influential architect in the 1920s and 1930s, Tait was responsible for some of London's most iconic buildings of that era including Selfridges in Oxford Street, the Daily Telegraph Building in Fleet Street and Unilever House at Blackfriars. Born in Paisley in Scotland, the son of a stonemason, he went on to study at the Glasgow School of Art and moved to London to work for an architectural firm that was designing new galleries for the British Museum. Over the next fifty years, Tait established himself as one of Britain's leading architects and the firm, eventually known as Burnet, Tait & Lorne, received some of the largest and most prestigious commissions both at home and abroad. Sydney Harbour Bridge could not have been built as it stands without Tait because the design for its pylons was his. In the late 1920s, he also turned his attention to domestic architecture, designing private houses in the village of Silver End in Essex which were amongst the first flat-roofed, modernist houses in Britain. Some of these modernist ideas were reflected in changes Tait made to his own residence, Gates House in Hampstead, which now also carries a Blue Plaque commemorating him.

........................................................................................................................

## TALLEYRAND, PRINCE (1754–1838) *French statesman and diplomatist, lived here*
21 HANOVER SQUARE, W1

Talleyrand was one of the great survivors in the turbulent politics of the France of his time. Born into an aristocratic family, he entered the Church as one of the most worldly of priests, even in an age when piety and belief were not necessarily requisites for ordination. In 1789 when the Revolution began, he was Bishop of Autun, yet in the Assembly of the Estates General, he was the one who proposed that the landed property of the Church be confiscated. During the worst excesses of the Revolution, Talleyrand was an emigré in England and America but he returned to France in 1796 and was Foreign Minister under the Directorate and under Napoleon. When the Napoleonic cause seemed lost, Talleyrand intrigued elegantly against his former Emperor and was, briefly, Prime Minister under the restored Bourbons. He lived in Hanover Square from 1830 to 1834 as French ambassador under Louis Philippe. Perhaps the key to Talleyrand's success was his imperturbability. On one occasion Napoleon, suspecting treachery, screamed abuse at him for half an hour in front of a horrified court. Talleyrand remained totally impassive, merely remarking to a friend later, 'What a pity so great a man should be so ill-bred.'

........................................................................................................................

## TALLIS, JOHN (1816–1876) *publisher of 'London Street Views', lived here*
233 NEW CROSS ROAD, SE14

John Tallis inherited the family bookselling and publishing business on the death of his father in 1842 and, under his guidance, the firm flourished. It became one of the leading cartographic publishers of the Victorian period and established offices in Edinburgh, Dublin and even New York. The *London Street Views*, directories that included maps and line drawings of the streets of the city, 'the whole forming a complete Stranger's Guide through London', were first published in the 1840s. Tallis's ambitions eventually outstripped his finances. His attempts to create a rival to the *Illustrated London News* in his *Illustrated News of the World* ended in failure and he went bankrupt in 1861. His maps and directories remain, however, highly collectable.

........................................................................................................................

## TATE, HARRY (RONALD MACDONALD HUTCHINSON) (1872–1940) *music hall comedian, lived here*
72 LONGLEY ROAD, SW17

## HARRY TATE (1872–1940)
27 CAMDEN ROAD, SUTTON **BOROUGH OF SUTTON**

Tate, whose real name was Ronald MacDonald Hutchinson, began his career in music hall as an impressionist, imitating the better-known stars of the business like George Robey, but in the first decade of the century he began to top the bill himself as the performer of short comic sketches. These sketches, such as 'Motoring' in which a chauffeur and his son display comprehensive ignorance of the workings of the internal combustion engine, were very popular. Catchphrases from Tate's sketches, like the question 'How's your father?', which he used in many routines as a means of deflecting the attention of his fellow performer from Tate's own inability to answer a question, became common property and were used in very different contexts. Tate died in 1940 from injuries he received during an air raid.

........................................................................................................

## TAUBER, RICHARD (1891–1948) *lyric tenor, lived here in Flat 297, 1947–1948*
PARK WEST, EDGWARE ROAD, W2

Although he has been dead for more than half a century, Richard Tauber left hundreds of recordings and his extraordinary voice lives on. Born in Linz in Austria, Tauber made his stage debut in 1913, singing one of the Mozartian roles (Tamino in *The Magic Flute*) for which he was soon to become famous. He went on to perform for many years at the Dresden Opera and the Vienna State Opera, where he formed his productive collaboration with Franz Lehar, whose popular operettas soon included at least one 'Tauber' song written with the tenor's particular vocal gifts in mind. Tauber's range, from opera to the lightest of popular songs, was remarkable and he became, by far, the best-known singer in Germany and Austria. However, when the Nazis came to power, Tauber, whose father was half-Jewish, was made unwelcome in both countries and he came to Britain where he stayed for the rest of his life, becoming a naturalised British citizen. He made his last stage appearance at Covent Garden in 1947, already ravaged by the lung cancer that was to kill him the following year.

........................................................................................................

## TAWNEY, RICHARD HENRY (1880–1962) *historian, teacher and political writer, lived here*
21 MECKLENBURGH SQUARE, WC1

Professor of Economic History at the LSE in the thirties and forties, involved with the Workers' Educational Association for more than forty years, Tawney was one of the leading intellectual lights of the Left in the first half of the twentieth century. His best-known book is *Religion and the Rise of Capitalism*, published in 1926, an often impassioned account of the interactions between religious beliefs and the social, political and economic developments that led to capitalism. Tawney himself came from an upper-middle-class background but turned his back resolutely on the class into which he had been born. On one occasion someone tried to persuade him to admit middle-class students into his WEA tutorials, arguing that they too were God's handiwork. 'Are you sure?' Tawney asked. In later years Tawney became the archetypal absent-minded professor, setting fire to his clothing with his pipe or emptying it thoughtlessly into his turn-ups, and wearing outfits that one observer said made him look like 'a street musician caught up in gunfire'.

........................................................................................................

*The world's first regular high definition* TELEVISION SERVICE *was inaugurated here by the BBC 2 November 1936*
ALEXANDRA PALACE, WOOD GREEN, N22

In 1936 the BBC acquired part of Alexandra Palace, constructed the world's first television transmitter and prepared to broadcast the world's first regular television service. A trial transmission of a variety show called *Here's Looking at You* was made on 26 August in that year and then, on 2 November, a regular service was begun. This was suspended during the war years and did not fully resume until 1946.

........................................................................................................

## TEMPEST, DAME MARIE (1864–1942) *actress, lived here 1899–1902*
24 PARK CRESCENT, W1

Born Mary Susan Etherington, Marie Tempest made her debut on the London stage in her early twenties as a singer but soon turned to acting and won considerable acclaim for her performance as Becky Sharp in an adaptation of Thackeray's *Vanity Fair*. She appeared in many of the most successful drawing-room comedies of the Edwardian era and, as the years passed, she made a graceful transition from leading lady to character roles. As an older actress she was the first interpreter of roles in plays by writers like Somerset Maugham and Noel Coward. Coward wrote *Hay Fever* with Marie Tempest in mind.

---

## TENNYSON, ALFRED, LORD (1809–1892) *poet, lived here in 1880 and 1881*
9 UPPER BELGRAVE STREET, SW1

## ALFRED LORD TENNYSON
15 MONTPELIER ROW, TWICKENHAM  **PRIVATE**

The third surviving son of a Lincolnshire rector, Tennyson was one of a large, talented and highly neurotic family, a family haunted by violence, epilepsy and alcoholism. He went on to become Poet Laureate for forty years and an embodiment of Victorian values. He left Cambridge without a degree but it was there that he met A.H. Hallam, the friend whose early death in 1833 moved Tennyson to write *In Memoriam*. *In Memoriam* was finally published in 1850, which was Tennyson's *annus mirabilis*. He was also married to Emily Sellwood, to whom he had been engaged for many years, and was confirmed in the position of Poet Laureate. Unlike many laureates, Tennyson continued to publish poetry of high quality after his appointment, including, most notably, *Idylls of the King*, his version of the Arthurian legends. He was given a seat in the House of Lords in 1883. In private gatherings Tennyson was an enthusiastic reader of his own verse. The diarist William Allingham records an occasion after dinner in June 1865 when Tennyson asked him, 'Allingham, would it disgust you if I read *Maud*? Would you expire?' Reassured that Allingham wouldn't expire, Tennyson proceeded to recite the whole poem, occasionally making brief comments such as 'That's wonderfully fine' and 'That was very hard to read.'

---

## TERRISS, WILLIAM (1847–1897) *hero of the Adelphi melodramas met his untimely end outside this theatre 16 December 1897*

STAGE DOOR, ADELPHI THEATRE, MAIDEN LANE, WC2  **WESTMINSTER**

Terriss was a leading Victorian actor, now remembered for his unfortunate death as much as for any of his performances. The son of a barrister, he had been in the Navy and had worked as a tea-planter and an engineer before he found success as an actor, working with the legendary Henry Irving at the Lyceum Theatre. He moved on to the Adelphi where he played the hero's role in many of the melodramas for which the theatre was famous. At seven o'clock on the evening of 16 December 1897, approaching the stage door to appear in the lead role that evening, Terriss was fatally stabbed by another actor in the company, Richard Prince, who was sure that he, not Terriss, should be receiving the audience's adulation. At his trial Prince was declared insane and sent to Broadmoor, where he died forty years later. Thousands of mourners turned out to watch Terriss's funeral procession pass through the streets of the capital.

---

## TERRY, DAME ELLEN (1847–1928) *actress, lived here*
22 BARKSTON GARDENS, SW5

## ELLEN TERRY *the great actress, lived here from 1904 to 1920*
215 KING'S ROAD, SW3  **PRIVATE**

One of a large theatrical family, Ellen Terry appeared on stage from childhood and, in her teens, was renowned for her beauty. At the age of seventeen she married the middle-aged painter G.F.

Watts, a disastrous union of which no good came save some luminous paintings Watts made of his wife. Divorced from Watts and remarried, Terry entered on the most successful partnership of her career when she became leading lady to Sir Henry Irving in his elaborate productions of Shakespeare at the Lyceum Theatre. She worked with Irving for twenty-five years and appeared in all the principal Shakespearean female roles, from Ophelia to Lady Macbeth. After leaving the Lyceum she was less frequently seen on the stage but Shaw wrote the role of Lady Cicely Wayneflete in *Captain Brassbound's Conversion* specially for her after she had complained that there were few decent parts for the more mature woman.

---

## THACKERAY, WILLIAM MAKEPEACE (1811–1863) *novelist lived here*
2 PALACE GREEN. W8

## WILLIAM MAKEPEACE THACKERAY. *novelist, lived here*
16 YOUNG STREET. W8

## WILLIAM MAKEPEACE THACKERAY, *novelist, lived here 1854–1862*
36 ONSLOW SQUARE. SW7

## WILLIAM MAKEPEACE THACKERAY
16 ALBION STREET. W2   **PRIVATE**

Thackeray was born of Anglo-Indian parents in Calcutta and went to school at Charterhouse, then in its original home in the centre of London. After time at Cambridge (he left without a degree) and as an art student in London and Paris, Thackeray began to have some success as a journalist and to publish collections of satirical sketches and parodies. He had married in 1836 but this provided him with the central tragedy of his life. His wife showed early signs of mental instability and, after the birth of their third daughter in 1840, had to be confined. Thackeray turned to longer fiction, beginning with *Catherine*, his own parody of the 'Newgate' fiction popular at the time, and culminating in the achievement of *Vanity Fair*, published in monthly parts in 1847 and 1848. Thackeray himself recognised what he had done in this novel. Years later, passing down Young Street, where he had lived from 1847 to 1854, he joked with a friend. 'Down on your knees, you rogue, for here *Vanity Fair* was penned, and I will go down with you, for I have a high opinion of that little production myself.' From the publication of *Vanity Fair* onwards, Thackeray was seen as Dickens's only rival as a major novelist and further books such as *Pendennis* and *The History of Henry Esmond* confirmed his standing. As the 1850s went on, like Dickens, he undertook lecture tours in Britain and America and embarked on more fiction but he suffered recurrent bouts of ill health and died on Christmas Eve 1863, aged only fifty-two.

---

## THEATRE ROYAL, MARYLEBONE (1832–1959)
71 CHURCH STREET. MARYLEBONE   **WESTMINSTER**

During a century of use as a theatre, the now-demolished building in Church Street went under a number of different names and managements. Sometimes known as the Portman Theatre, sometimes as the Royal Alfred, it had its longest incarnation as the Theatre Royal, Marylebone, and was best known as the venue for cheap and bloodthirsty melodramas. Managers of this theatre, which had the biggest stage of any in London, occasionally tried to move it upmarket; in the late 1840s an actress called Mrs Warner moved from Sadler's Wells to run the Marylebone theatre, and her ambitious programme included Shakespeare, Sheridan and Beaumont and Fletcher. The venture was not a success and the theatre reverted to its previous, less-demanding dramatic fare. It attracted its greatest audiences in the late 1850s and early 1860s under the management of Joseph Cave, but it was still staging barnstorming melodrama in 1904 when a young Charlie Chaplin appeared there in a Sherlock Holmes play. The theatre became a cinema in 1932, suffered bomb damage in the Second World War, and was eventually demolished to make way for a parade of shops in 1959.

......................................................................................................................

## THOMAS, DYLAN (1914–1953) *poet, lived here*
### 54 DELANCEY STREET, NW1

Thomas was born in Swansea but he seems to have had little fondness for his home town or for Wales. 'The land of my fathers,' he once remarked. 'My fathers can have it.' He began to write poetry as a schoolboy and his first volume was published in 1934. In that year he moved to London and embarked on a precarious career as a freelance writer and broadcaster. He rapidly established a reputation for flamboyant behaviour and heavy drinking. His popularity as a poet grew after the war, leading to invitations to lecture tours of the United States, on one of which he succumbed, still in his thirties, to a lethal combination of drink and drugs taken to combat exhaustion. His most popular work today is probably *Under Milk Wood*, a radio play first broadcast the year after his death and set in a small fishing town in South Wales called Llareggub ('Bugger all' backwards).

......................................................................................................................

## THOMAS, EDWARD (1878–1917) *essayist and poet, lived here*
### 61 SHELGATE ROAD, SW11

Born in Lambeth, Thomas went to Oxford and married Helen Noble in 1899. He had already published his first book, *The Woodland Life*, when he was only nineteen and, to support his wife and the family that they started, he continued to produce books in great numbers to meet publishers' deadlines and to make money. In one period between 1910 and 1912 he wrote twelve works and drove himself to a nervous breakdown and the verge of suicide. He met the American poet Robert Frost in 1913 and it was Frost who persuaded him to begin writing the poetry for which he is now remembered. Thomas wrote to another friend, 'I may as well write poetry. Did anyone ever begin at thirty-six in the shade?' In 1915 Thomas enlisted in the Army and was killed at the Battle of Arras two years later. Of his poems, only a few had appeared in print under a pseudonym, Edward Eastaway.

......................................................................................................................

## THOMPSON, SIR BENJAMIN, COUNT RUMFORD (1753–1814) *inventor and adventurer, lived here*
### 168 BROMPTON ROAD, KNIGHTSBRIDGE, SW3

Thought by some to be a genius and by others to be a charlatan, Benjamin Thompson was, quite possibly, both. Certainly he was one of the more remarkable men of his day. Born in Massachusetts, Thompson's early career as a schoolmaster was interrupted by suspicions that he was spying for the British in the War of Independence and he fled to London, deserting his wife and young child. In London he gained recognition for his scientific work and was elected to the Royal Society at the age of only twenty-six. Five years later, for rather mysterious reasons, he was knighted by George III. While travelling in Europe, Thompson had met Prince Maximilian of Bavaria and, in 1784, he accepted, the Prince's invitation to work as an advisor and civil servant in Munich. He proved an able and imaginative administrator who instigated a series of military and social reforms. His most lasting legacy in Germany is the English Garden in the city. In 1791 Thompson was made a Count of the Holy Roman Empire and took the name of Rumford, the New England town from which he had to flee ignominiously fifteen years earlier. As a scientist Thompson is best remembered for his experiments investigating the nature of heat, and for his role in the founding of the Royal Institution 'for diffusing the knowledge and facilitating the general introduction of useful mechanical inventions and improvements'. Rumford's own useful inventions included a smokeless chimney, a revolutionary design of kitchen stove and an early version of thermal underwear. Soon after the foundation of the Royal Institution, Rumford, a notoriously quarrelsome man, fell out with his associates there and left London for Paris where he died in 1814.

........................................................................................................

## THOMSON, JAMES (1700–1748) *poet, author of Rule Britannia, lived and died here*
### THE ROYAL HOSPITAL, KEW FOOT ROAD, RICHMOND

Throughout much of the eighteenth century and well into the nineteenth, a poem called *The Seasons*, which celebrated the delights of the natural world, was one of the most popular in the English language. More than a hundred and thirty editions of it appeared in the century after its initial publication in 1730. Its author was a Scotsman, James Thomson, who was born in Roxburghshire, the son of a clergyman. 'I know no subject more elevating, more amazing, more ready to the poetical enthusiasm, the philosophical reflection, and the moral sentiment than the works of nature,' Thomson once wrote and his multitude of readers clearly agreed with him. The other work for which Thomson remains famous is *Rule Britannia*, a song for which he wrote the words and Thomas Arne provided the music. It first appeared in a masque about King Alfred performed at a fete given by the Prince of Wales in the grounds of Cliveden House in Buckinghamshire. Thomson, a London resident since the 1720s, moved to Richmond in 1736. Twelve years later, he met his end after taking a boat trip on the Thames from Hammersmith back to his home. Although it was August, the day was unseasonably cold and Thomson caught a fatal chill.

........................................................................................................

## THORNDIKE, DAME SYBIL (1882–1976) *actress, lived here 1921–1932*
### 6 CARLYLE SQUARE, SW3

The daughter of a canon of Rochester Cathedral, Sybil Thorndike had originally intended to pursue a career as a concert pianist. After breaking her wrist this became an impossibility and she turned to the stage, making her debut in 1904. In her long career she played an immense range of characters, from the tragic heroines of Greek drama, through Shakespearean roles, female and occasionally male, to the leading parts in modern plays. George Bernard Shaw wrote the role of St Joan in his play of that name with her in mind. She played the part in the original production of 1924 and it remained one of her most famous characters. Created a Dame of the British Empire in 1931, she continued to appear on stage and screen until the 1960s. She was married to fellow actor Lewis Casson for more than sixty years. Once asked whether she had ever contemplated divorce during the marriage, she replied, 'Divorce? Never. But murder, often.'

........................................................................................................

## THORNE, WILL (1857–1946) *trade union leader and Labour MP, lived here*
### 1 LAWRENCE ROAD, WEST HAM, E13

Will Thorne was one of the great veterans of the Labour movement, who was born into mid-Victorian Britain and lived to see the Attlee government come into power. He was a member of West Ham town council from 1891 until the year of his death, was General Secretary of the union he had founded, the National Union of Gasworkers and General Labourers (later the National Union of General and Municipal Workers), for forty-five years and a Labour MP for West Ham from 1906 until 1945. These were the achievements of a man who had first been sent out to work at the age of six and who had moved to London originally to work as a labourer at the Beckton gasworks.

........................................................................................................

## THORNYCROFT, SIR HAMO (1850–1925) *sculptor, lived here*
### 2A MELBURY ROAD, W14

In becoming one of Britain's leading sculptors of the nineteenth and early twentieth centuries, Sir Hamo Thornycroft was following a family tradition. His grandfather, father and mother were all sculptors. Thornycroft worked in his parents' studio and entered the Royal Academy Schools in 1869, becoming ARA in 1881 and a full Royal Academician seven years later. Many of his works still stand in public places in London. His monument to General Gordon is in Victoria Embankment Gardens and a statue of Cromwell stands in front of the Houses of Parliament. There are also works by him in Kew Gardens. Thornycroft was knighted in 1917, fifteen years after his older brother John, a naval architect and engineer, had received the same honour.

........................................................................................

## TILAK, LOKAMANYA (1856–1920) *Indian patriot and philosopher, lived here 1918–1919*
10 HOWLEY PLACE, W2

Bal Gangadhar Tilak, often known by the honorary title of Lokamanya, was a Brahmin who became a lawyer and journalist and one of the most effective advocates of India's independence from Britain in the decades preceding the First World War. Unlike nationalists such as Gandhi, Tilak was no enthusiast for passive resistance, believing, as he once wrote, that 'There is no empire lost by a free grant of concession by the rulers to the ruled', and in 1908 he was arrested for allegedly inciting his followers to violence against the British. The trial that ensued became an important focus for nationalist feelings and, when Tilak was sentenced to six years' transportation, those feelings ran high. Tilak himself spent his time in prison quietly engaged in scholarly study of Hindu texts. He stayed in Howley Place at a time when he was visiting London to pursue a legal action for defamation against the British journalist Sir Valentine Chirol.

........................................................................................

## *On this site lived the famous clockmakers* THOMAS TOMPION FRS *the Father of English clockmaking (1638–1713) and* GEORGE GRAHAM FRS (1673–1751). *Both buried in Westminster Abbey.*

67 FLEET STREET, EC4   **CITY OF LONDON**

........................................................................................

## TOSTI, FRANCESCO PAOLO (1846–1916) *composer and singer, lived in a house on this site*
12 MANDEVILLE PLACE, W1   **WESTMINSTER**

Tosti studied at Naples under the Italian composer Mercadante and became singing master to the Princess of Savoy, later to be Queen of Italy. He made his first visit to London in 1875, returning each year before deciding to settle permanently in the city in 1880. Very rapidly Tosti became an important figure in London's musical establishment, singing master to the royal family and a teacher at both the Royal College of Music and the Royal Academy of Music. His songs, written in both Italian and English, included popular favourites such as 'Forever', 'Lamento d'Amore' and 'At Vespers', and he gained many imitators who strove to write ballads 'alla Tosti'. He was knighted in 1908 and died in Mandeville Place, where he had lived for twenty years, in 1916.

........................................................................................

## TOWNLEY, CHARLES (1737–1805) *antiquary and collector, lived here*
14 QUEEN ANNE'S GATE, SW1

Born into a wealthy Catholic family in Lancashire, Charles Townley inherited his father's estates at the age of five and developed his love of classical antiquity when he visited Italy as a young man. He began his collection of Roman and Greek statuary and works of art in 1768 and his wealth enabled him to build up one of the finest such collections in Europe. Despite his knowledge of the classical world, he published nothing beyond a dissertation on an ancient helmet found at Ribchester. After his death most of his collection was bought by the British Museum.

## TOYNBEE, JOSEPH (1815–1866) *aural surgeon, and his son* TOYNBEE, ARNOLD (1852–1883) *social philosopher, lived here 1854–1866*

BEECH HOLME, 49 WIMBLEDON PARKSIDE, SW19

The son of a Lincolnshire farmer, Joseph Toynbee studied medicine in London and went on to become a pioneer in the scientific study of diseases of the ear. In 1855, he established the first ear, nose and throat unit in Britain at St Mary's Hospital, Paddington and he wrote books on his area of specialist interest which were standard works for decades after his accidental death at the age of only fifty-one. A long-time sufferer from tinnitus, Toynbee had become convinced that a cure for his condition could be found through inhaling vapours of chloroform and prussic acid. He was mistaken. Far from being a cure, the inhalation proved fatal and Toynbee died a martyr to the cause of otology. Toynbee's son Arnold was an Oxford-educated economic historian who was a leading light in late nineteenth-century campaigns to provide the poor of London's East End with social and educational opportunities that they might otherwise be denied. He died of tuberculosis at the age of only thirty. Toynbee Hall, a social centre in Whitechapel which still plays an important role in the local community, is named after him.

## TREE, SIR HERBERT BEERBOHM (1853–1917) *actor-manager, lived here*

31 ROSARY GARDENS, SW7

## SIR HERBERT TREE, *actor-manager, lived on this site*

76 SLOANE STREET, SW1 **PRIVATE**

Tree was the older half-brother of Sir Max Beerbohm, who once claimed that the actor had added 'Tree' to the family name because he was unable to imagine enthusiastic audiences calling out 'Beerbohm! Beerbohm!' After working briefly in the offices of his father, a grain merchant, Tree was persuaded to try for a career on the stage after a succession of triumphs in amateur dramatics. From 1887 he ran the Haymarket Theatre, where he first produced two of Oscar Wilde's comedies and scored a great personal triumph as the mesmeric Svengali in an adaptation of Du Maurier's novel *Trilby*. With the profits from *Trilby*, Tree went on to build Her Majesty's Theatre, also in the Haymarket, where he both staged lavish productions of Shakespeare and introduced audiences to new plays, including, in 1914, Shaw's *Pygmalion*. Eccentric, generous and vain, Tree was once reported (by his half-brother) to have remarked, 'I can stand any amount of flattery as long as it's fulsome enough.'

## TREVES, SIR FREDERICK (1853–1923) *surgeon, lived here 1886–1907*

6 WIMPOLE STREET, W1

One of the leading figures in the late Victorian and Edwardian medical world, Treves is now best remembered for his association with one patient, Joseph Merrick – the so-called 'Elephant Man'. Born in Dorchester, the son of a furniture upholsterer, Treves studied medicine in London and then joined the London Hospital, the institution with which he was associated for the rest of his professional life. He was a specialist in abdominal surgery and a pioneer in appendectomy, an operation he carried out on Edward VII a few days before the king's planned coronation; Treves was instrumental in having the coronation postponed. He retired from medicine a short time later and devoted the rest of his life to writing. Treves died in the south of France in December 1923 and Thomas Hardy, a close friend, wrote a memorial poem that appeared in *The Times*. Treves's connection with Joseph Merrick dates from 1884 when he first came across the horribly deformed 'Elephant Man' in a London freakshow. Two years later Sir Frederick arranged for Merrick, who was by this time homeless, to live in rooms belonging to the London Hospital. Merrick spent the four happiest days of his otherwise wretched life in the rooms Treves provided and died there in 1890. Eighty years after his own death, Treves is far more famous for the compassion he showed to a destitute 'freak' than he is for his successes as a royal surgeon.

## TROLLOPE, ANTHONY (1815–1882) *novelist, lived here*
### 39 MONTAGUE SQUARE, W1

'Three hours a day will produce as much as a man ought to write,' Trollope wrote in his *Autobiography*. If we assume that he followed his own rule, Trollope made exceptionally good use of his three hours a day, for he produced forty-seven novels together with volumes of short stories, travel-writing and even a biography of Cicero. Born in London, the son of the author of the best-selling *Domestic Manners of the Americans*, Mrs Frances Trollope, Trollope was educated at Harrow and Winchester and began his career inauspiciously as a lowly clerk in the Post Office. Being despatched to Ireland in the early 1840s proved the making of him. Work prospered, he met his future wife and he wrote his first novel, *The Macdermots of Ballycloran*, which is set in Ireland. Of the forty-six novels that followed, the best known are the Barsetshire books, set in his invented rural county in the West of England, and the Palliser series, which depicts the world of Victorian politics and high society. Trollope moved to Montague Square in 1873 and it was there that he wrote *The Way We Live Now*, a satirical panorama of Victorian life that is probably his best-known work outside the Barset and Palliser chronicles.

## TURING, ALAN (1912–1954) *code-breaker and pioneer of computer science, was born here*
### 2 WARRINGTON CRESCENT, MAIDA VALE, W9

Alan Turing was educated at Sherborne and King's College, Cambridge, where he gained an outstanding degree and was accepted as a Fellow of the college in 1935. In that year he turned his formidable mind to the problem posed by the German mathematician David Hilbert about the potential 'decidability' of all mathematical questions. In addressing this problem Turing formulated the concept of the 'Turing Machine', which has become the foundation of the modern theory of computation and computability. During the Second World War, Turing worked at the code-breaking headquarters at Bletchley Park, where he was the leading figure behind the cracking of the German Enigma codes. After the war he moved to the newly established computing laboratory at Manchester University, where he continued to explore the ideas that had fascinated him since his undergraduate days. Harrassed because of his homosexuality, still implicated in the cloak-and-dagger world of GCHQ (the post-war successor to Bletchley Park), Turing grew increasingly unhappy and isolated and eventually committed suicide by cyanide poisoning in June 1954.

## *Here in the former* TURK'S HEAD TAVERN, JOSHUA REYNOLDS *and* DR SAMUEL JOHNSON *founded* THE CLUB *in 1764*
### 9 GERRARD STREET, W1   **WESTMINSTER**

Built on the site of a previous tavern in 1758, the Turk's Head Tavern was run by a man named Christopher Winch who had previously been landlord in another pub of the same name in Greek Street. The tavern's chief claim to fame is that it was in rooms on its first floor that the informal group known as The Club, founded by Dr Johnson and Joshua Reynolds, had its first meeting in 1764. Among its original nine members were Burke and Goldsmith and later additions to the membership included the actor David Garrick and Johnson's biographer Boswell. From 1825 to 1957 the building was the Westminster General Dispensary. It is now a Chinese supermarket but many of the original interior fittings are still in existence, hidden behind modern partitions.

## TURNER, CHARLES (1774?–1857) *engraver, lived here*
### 56 WARREN STREET, W1

Many of the well-known painters of the late eighteenth and early nineteenth centuries, men like Sir Thomas Lawrence, Sir Henry Raeburn and J.M.W. Turner, owed at least some of their fame to the work of Charles Turner who made engravings from their paintings which were seen by many more people than the originals. Turner was born in Woodstock and studied at the Royal Academy Schools. Although he practised aquatint and stipple it was with the mezzotint method of engraving that he achieved his greatest success. Turner lived at 56 Warren Street for just under four years before, in April 1803, moving his expanding family and business a short distance to number 50. He stayed there for the rest of his life.

## TURNER, JOSEPH MALLORD WILLIAM (1775–1851) *artist and Royal Academician was born in a house on this site*
21 MAIDEN LANE, WC2  **WESTMINSTER**

## J.M.W. TURNER, RA (1775–1851) *painter, designed and lived in this house*
40 SANDYCOMBE ROAD, TWICKENHAM

## J.M.W. TURNER, RA *lived here*
23, QUEEN ANNE STREET, W1  **PORTMAN ESTATE**

## J.M.W. TURNER *landscape painter, lived and worked in this house*
119 CHEYNE WALK, SW3  **TURNER HOUSE COMMITTEE**

## J.M.W. TURNER, *RA landscape painter, often painted sunsets near this tree*
NORTH SIDE, CAMPDEN HILL SQUARE GARDENS, W8  **PRIVATE**

Often regarded as England's greatest painter, Turner was born in Maiden Lane where his father was a barber and wig-maker who was later forced out of business by the decline in the habit of wearing wigs. Although his schooling was limited, Turner showed his gifts as an artist at an early age when he entered the Royal Academy Schools when he was only fourteen, exhibiting his first watercolour at the Academy show the following year. It was as a watercolourist that Turner first came to the public's attention, often working with his friend Thomas Girtin on landscape and architectural subjects. Girtin died young in 1802 and Turner is said to have remarked, 'If Tom Girtin had lived, I should have starved.' Elected RA in the same year as Girtin died, Turner was moving from watercolour to oils and to larger and larger canvases. His career went from strength to strength and travels abroad inspired work like *Hannibal Crossing the Alps* and *The Field of Waterloo*. By the 1830s and '40s, the decades from which his most famous works (*The Fighting Temeraire*, *Rain, Steam and Speed*) date, Turner had developed an extraordinary and unique style. Constable described the later works as 'painted in tinted steam'. Turner himself, when asked once about art, was content to reply, 'It's a rummy business', and leave it at that.

## TUSSAUD, MADAME MARIE (1761–1850) *artist in wax, lived here 1838–1839*
24 WELLINGTON ROAD, ST JOHN'S WOOD, NW8

The woman who gave her name to the most famous waxworks exhibition in the world was born Marie Gresholtz in Switzerland. At an early age she began work for the wax modeller J.C. Curtius, her uncle according to some accounts, and, while still in her teens, created wax figures of several of the most famous men and women of her day, including Benjamin Franklin and Voltaire. For a short period she was attached to the French court of Louis XVI and Marie Antoinette but, after the Revolution, she was imprisoned by the authorities and forced to create death masks of the unfortunates sent to the guillotine. In several cases, including that of Marie Antoinette, she was obliged to model in death those she had earlier modelled in life. In 1794 she inherited Curtius's wax museum and, after a brief marriage to a soldier named Tussaud, left France for England in 1802. For more than thirty years Madame Tussaud's exhibition toured Britain before finding a more permanent home, not far from its present site, in Baker Street. It was at this time that the famous Chamber of Horrors, originally known as the 'Separate Room', was created. Madame Tussaud continued to take an active role in her museum until she was well into her eighties. Several of the figures still on display at Madame Tussaud's are her work.

## TWAIN, MARK (SAMUEL LANGHORNE CLEMENS) (1835–1910) *American writer, lived here in 1896–1897*

23 TEDWORTH SQUARE, SW3

Samuel Langhorne Clemens took as his *nom de plume* a cry heard on the Mississippi from men measuring the depth of the river. 'Mark Twain' meant the water was two fathoms deep. His reputation as a writer and humourist was made by *The Innocents Abroad* in 1869, an account of travels in Europe and further afield, and his two best-known books, *Tom Sawyer* and *Huckleberry Finn*, followed in 1876 and 1884. Other notable works include *The Prince and the Pauper* from 1882 and *A Connecticut Yankee at King Arthur's Court* from 1889. In the 1880s Twain's investments in a publishing firm and a typesetting invention went disastrously wrong and he was forced into bankruptcy. In his time in Tedworth Square, Twain was still trying to remake his fortune through lecture tours, to pay off the last of his creditors and, more personally still, to overcome his grief at the death of one of his daughters. His last decade, back in America, was equally filled with tragedy. His wife died in 1904 and five years later so too did his second daughter. The amiable humorist and wit of the 1860s ended his life an embittered and savagely satirical pessimist.

## TWEED, JOHN (1863–1933) *sculptor, lived here*

108 CHEYNE WALK, SW10

Born in Glasgow, Tweed studied art in that city, in London and in Paris where he became friends with Rodin. He made his reputation as a portrait and memorial sculptor. Among Tweed's best-known works are the statue to Clive in Whitehall, of Kitchener in Horseguards' Parade and the Peers' War Memorial at the House of Lords. He also oversaw the final completion of Alfred Stevens's ill-fated memorial to the Duke of Wellington in St Paul's, which had actually been begun several years before Tweed's birth.

*105 Catholic Martyrs lost their lives at the* TYBURN GALLOWS *near this site 1535–1681*

8 HYDE PARK PLACE, W2 **WESTMINSTER**

## TYBURN TREE, *site of*

TRAFFIC ISLAND AT THE JUNCTION OF EDGWARE ROAD AND BAYSWATER ROAD, W2

Tyburn may have been used as a place of execution as early as the twelfth century and certainly by the end of the fourteenth century it had become the principal place where London criminals met their end. It was to remain so until 1783 when public executions were transferred to a gallows outside Newgate Prison. Among the famous names to die at Tyburn were the pretender to Henry VII's throne, Perkin Warbeck, the eighteenth-century criminal mastermind Jonathan Wild, and the legendary prison escapologist Jack Sheppard. Some reports claim that as many as 200,000 people witnessed Sheppard's death. The problem with Tyburn as a deterrent was highlighted by the novelist and magistrate Henry Fielding. 'The day appointed by law for the thief's shame,' he wrote, 'is the day of glory in his own opinion. His procession to Tyburn and his last moments there are all triumphant; attended with the compassion of the weak and tender-hearted, and with the applause, admiration and envy of all the bold and hardened.'

The Westminster plaque specifically commemorates those who lost their lives at Tyburn for their Catholic faith, from the Carthusian and Bridgettine monks who refused to submit to the demands of Henry VIII in 1535 to the martyred (and later canonised) Archbishop of Armagh, Oliver Plunket. Hyde Park Place has been, in the twentieth century, the site of a Catholic religious foundation. The Benedictine Tyburn Convent was established in 1903, only a hundred yards from the probable site of the gallows, and, although destroyed in the Second World War, it was refounded in a new building further down Hyde Park Place in the 1950s.

........................................................................................................................

## UNDERHILL, EVELYN (1875–1941) *Christian philosopher and teacher, lived here*
50 CAMPDEN HILL SQUARE, W8

The daughter of a barrister, Evelyn Underhill studied philosophy and social science at King's College, London, and entered a period of spiritual confusion in which she questioned the liberal agnosticism in which she had been brought up. From this she emerged a committed Christian with a particular interest in the English mystical tradition exemplified by works like *The Cloud of Unknowing* and Walter Hilton's *Scala Perfectionis*. She later produced editions of both these works. In 1911 she published a book, *Mysticism*, which was read and admired by the Catholic theologian Friedrich von Hügel, who became a friend and spiritual mentor. She went on to write a number of other works on mysticism and to become an Oxford lecturer on the philosophy of religion. She lived in Campden Hill Square from the time of her marriage in 1907 to the lawyer Hubert Stuart Moore.

........................................................................................................................

## UNITED STATES EMBASSY (1863–1866)

### HENRY BROOKS ADAMS (1838–1918) *US historian, lived here*
98 PORTLAND PLACE, W1

Adams came from one of the most distinguished of American families. Both his grandfather and his great-grandfather became President and his father was a politician and diplomat who was ambassador to England during the American Civil War. It was during this period that the embassy was in Portland Place and that Henry Brooks Adams lived there, acting as his father's secretary. In later life he became a novelist, biographer and historian whose *magnum opus* was a nine-volume history of the United States under its third and fourth presidents, Jefferson and Madison. He also wrote what is possibly the best known of American autobiographies, *The Education of Henry Adams*. Adams's comfortable and privileged life was tragically blighted by the suicide of his wife in 1885 and, after her death, he spent many years in travel, both in Europe and in the Pacific islands.

........................................................................................................................

## UNWIN, SIR STANLEY (1884–1968) *publisher, was born here*
13 HANDEN ROAD, SE12

'Much is written,' Stanley Unwin once said, 'of the power of the press, a power which may last but a day; by comparison little is heard of the power of books, which may endure for generations.' Unwin himself devoted his life to the power of books and, as chairman of the publishing firm of Allen & Unwin for many years, was responsible for bringing the works of authors as diverse as Bertrand Russell and J.R.R. Tolkien before the public. President of the Publishers' Association in

England for two years in the thirties, Unwin was also a respected figure abroad and served two terms, between 1936 and 1938 and 1946 and 1954, as president of the International Publishers' Association. He wrote several books on publishing and on the book trade.

----

## VAN BUREN, MARTIN (1782–1862) *eighth US President, lived here*
7 STRATFORD PLACE, W1

The first US President to be born under the US flag, Van Buren was the son of a tavernkeeper and farmer in New York State and began his career as a lawyer. Elected to the Senate as a Democrat in 1821 he was Governor of New York in 1828 and became a solid supporter of Andrew Jackson for President. Jackson rewarded him with the position of Secretary of State and, in his second term of office, that of Vice-President. Van Buren followed Jackson as President, narrowly winning the election of 1836. His period in office was dominated by financial crises that Van Buren's policies did little to alleviate and he lost heavily to the Whig opposition in 1840. Despite a further attempt to regain the presidency in 1848, Van Buren never again returned to high office.

----

## VANE, SIR HARRY, THE YOUNGER (1612–1662) *statesman, lived here. Beheaded 1662*
GATEPOST OF VANE HOUSE, ROSSLYN HILL, NW3

Vane was one of the most significant figures on the Parliamentary side in the struggle against Charles I. Born the son of a politician who had, at one time, served as one of Charles's chief counsellors, Vane was an early convert to the Puritan view of religion and to republicanism. In 1635 he sailed for Massachusetts where he spent a troubled two years as Governor before returning to England and entering Parliament. He was soon at the heart of the parliamentary opposition to Charles and, after the death of Pym in 1643, he was, effectively, its leader. One contemporary wrote that, for the next ten years, Vane was 'that in the state which Cromwell was in the field'. None the less, he took no part in the proceedings against the King and, growing disillusioned with the increasing power of Cromwell, he retired from politics in 1653. Despite this he was arrested at the Restoration, sent to the Tower and eventually beheaded. All that remains of his home, Vane House, is a gatepost to which the plaque is attached.

----

## VAN GOGH, VINCENT (1853–1890) *painter, lived here 1873–1874*
87 HACKFORD ROAD, SW9

## VINCENT VAN GOGH, *famous painter lived here in 1876*
160 TWICKENHAM ROAD, ISLEWORTH   **PRIVATE**

Van Gogh's famously tormented life came to an end in July 1890, two days after a self-inflicted gun wound. Two years earlier, in an eerily prescient comment, he wrote, 'A lot of money is paid for a painter's work once he's dead.' This has proved to be dramatically so in the case of Van Gogh himself and works such as *The Potato Eaters*, *Sunflowers* and *Cornfield with Flight of Birds*, which found no buyers in his lifetime, would now change hands for millions, if not tens of millions, of pounds. Before the tragic journey that took him through self-mutilation and incarceration in an asylum and eventual suicide, Van Gogh had, as a young man, spent some time in London. He arrived first in June 1873 and stayed for more than a year, working as an assistant at the international art dealers Goupil and Co. It was during this period that he lodged in Hackford Road with a Mrs Loyer. Van Gogh, emotionally volatile as always, fell in love with his landlady's daughter and was much hurt by her rejection. After a period with Goupil's in Paris, Van Gogh returned to England in Spring 1876 and, after teaching in Ramsgate, lived and worked in Isleworth where a local clergyman, impressed by the young Dutchman's intense religious feelings, employed him as an occasional teacher and preacher. Van Gogh returned to Holland in January 1877.

## VAUGHAN WILLIAMS, RALPH (1872–1958) *composer, lived here from 1953 until his death*
### 10 HANOVER TERRACE, REGENT'S PARK, NW1

The leading composer of the renaissance in English music in the first half of the twentieth century, Vaughan Williams was born in Gloucestershire. Although he trained not only with Stanford at  the Royal College of Music but with Bruch in Berlin and Ravel in Paris, Vaughan Williams's interest in Tudor and Elizabethan music, in the work of Purcell and in folk-song, combined to produce compositions that were unmistakably English in character and influence. From his first published work (a setting of a poem by the dialect writer William Barnes) to late works like his Christmas cantata *Hodie*, Vaughan Williams was a prolific composer in many musical forms. He wrote nine symphonies, operas such as *Hugh the Drover* and *Sir John in Love* (a version of *The Merry Wives of Windsor*), and perennially popular works like the *Fantasia on a Theme by Thomas Tallis*. Despite all the honours he won, culminating in the OM in 1935, he remained remarkably modest about his musical achievements. Of his *London Symphony* he once commented to a friend, 'I realise now it is not as boring as I thought it was.'

## VENTRIS, MICHAEL (1922–1956) *architect and decipherer of Linear B, lived here*
### 19 NORTH END, HAMPSTEAD, NW3

One of the great achievements of archaeological decipherment was the work of a man who was, in the best sense, an amateur. Michael Ventris was by profession an architect but, from his teenage years, he was fascinated by the undeciphered Minoan scripts that Sir Arthur Evans had found on tablets unearthed in Crete. The second of these, Linear B, was found by Evans only at the Minoan site of Knossos and the tablets were assumed to be the records and inventories of the palace there. For many decades after Evans's original discovery, scholars had laboured to interpret the texts with little success. Ventris's great insight was that Linear B did not represent some mysterious Cretan language but was actually an early form of Greek. Ventris's theory, with its implication of Greek control of Minoan civilization, was controversial. It was just beginning to be generally accepted when, tragically, Ventris was killed in a car accident.

## VIVEKANANDA, SWAMI (1863–1902) *Hindu philosopher, lived here in 1896*
### 63 ST GEORGE'S DRIVE, SW1

A disciple of the legendary mystic Ramakrishna, Swami Vivekananda was one of the central figures in the transmission of Hindu philosophy and mysticism to the West. He was born Narendranath Dutta into an upper-class family in Calcutta and first met Ramakrishna as a student in 1881. It was the pivotal moment in his life. Adopting the name of Vivekananda during his wanderings through India following the death of his guru five years later, he became the greatest advocate of the Hindu spirituality Ramakrishna had embodied. Vivekananda's eloquence, intelligence and integrity made him one of the leading figures at the Parliament of World Religions, held in Chicago in 1893 and often described as the first attempt to create a worldwide conversation between different faiths. Staying on in the USA to lecture, he and his ideas attracted the admiring interest of many people from intellectuals, like the Harvard philosopher and psychologist William James to ordinary Americans in search of spiritual enlightenment. The Swami made several trips to London, during the second of which, in the autumn of 1896, he lodged in the house in St George's Drive, Westminster. He died in India in 1902, fulfilling his own prophecy that he would not live to see forty.

VOLTAIRE (1694–1778) *French philosopher, playwright and satirist, lodged in a house on this site 1727–1728*

10 MAIDEN LANE, WC2  **WESTMINSTER**

Voltaire was a noted admirer of the English and of English society and lived in exile in London, mostly lodging in Maiden Lane, from 1726 to 1729. On one occasion he was recognised in the streets, not only as a foreigner but as that worst of all foreigners, a Frenchman, and was pursued through the streets by an angry mob. He saved himself by mounting a pedestal and crying, 'Brave Englishmen, am I not already unhappy enough in not having been born among you?' If the story is to be believed, his words turned the mob's mood from anger to delight and he was carried triumphantly home on the shoulders of two of the brave Englishmen. On his return to France he published his *Lettres Philosophiques*, in which he uses his knowledge of English society as a means of attacking the abuses of the French *ancien régime*. In his day Voltaire was the embodiment of the philosophical beliefs of the Enlightenment and one of the most famous men in Europe. Today he is best known for novellas like *Zadig* and, especially, *Candide*, which describes the adventures and misadventures of a naive innocent and his relentlessly optimistic tutor, Dr Pangloss.

VON HÜGEL, BARON FRIEDRICH (1852–1925) *theologian, lived here 1882–1903*

4 HOLFORD ROAD, NW3

Von Hügel was born in Florence, where his father was the Austrian consul, but he settled in London in 1871 and lived in England for most of his life. He wrote on religion and philosophy and was particularly interested in mysticism and in the problems that nineteenth-century Biblical criticism had highlighted in the relationship between the accepted Christian version of history and that being revealed by archaeology and linguistic study. He was a close friend of two of the leaders of what came to be known as the Catholic Modernist Movement, Loisy and Tyrrell, both of whom were excommunicated by the church for venturing beyond the intellectually orthodox. Von Hügel was committed to the idea of different faiths learning from one another and was a founder member of a London group that brought together Jewish and Christian scholars.

VOYSEY, C.F.A. (1857–1941) *architect and designer, lived here*

6 CARLTON HILL, NW8

The son of a distinguished, if controversial, Victorian theologian, Voysey became an architect and the most original designer in the Arts and Crafts Movement in the generation after William Morris and Burne-Jones. Voysey's great aim in his work on country houses, such as Broadleys near Lake Windermere, was to integrate all the objects in the house, fabrics and furnishings, with the plan of the house itself and then to place that house in an appropriate relationship with its natural surroundings. In pursuit of this ambitious aim, he became an innovative designer of wallpaper, textiles, furniture and metalwork as well as an architect. Voysey built no more houses after 1910 but his influence was immense and his designs widely imitated.

WAINWRIGHT, LINCOLN STANHOPE (1847–1929) *Vicar of St Peter's, London Docks, lived here 1884–1929*

CLERGY HOUSE, WAPPING LANE, E1

In the late nineteenth and early twentieth centuries the often wretched conditions of life in the East End were alleviated by the selfless work of many churchmen. One of those most devoted to the welfare of the poor was Lincoln Stanhope Wainwright who was the vicar of St Peter's, London Docks, for fifty-five years. During those years he helped to provide his parishioners with schools and clubs, with better medical facilities and with a variety of opportunities to improve their lot. On the fiftieth anniversary of his arrival at St Peter's, the Bishop of London presented Wainwright with a cheque for £1,000, expressing the hope that, for once, he might spend the money on himself rather than his parishioners.

........................................................................................................................................

## WAKLEY, THOMAS (1795–1862) *reformer and founder of 'The Lancet', lived here*
### 35 BEDFORD SQUARE, WC1

Far from being the pillar of the medical establishment that it is today *The Lancet* began life as a campaigning journal, critical of the Royal College of Surgeons and a voice for medical reform. Its founder was Thomas Wakley, a Devon-born surgeon, who had trained at Guy's Hospital and began to publish *The Lancet* in 1823 as a response to what he saw as abuses and lack of standard practices in the medical profession. Wakley was also a political radical who became MP for Finsbury in 1835 and made a maiden speech in which he denounced the conviction and transportation of the Tolpuddle Martyrs. He left Parliament in 1852 but continued to lobby for reform, particularly for legislation against the adulteration of food and drink. The Food and Drink Act of 1860 was his final legacy.

........................................................................................................................................

## WALEY, ARTHUR (1889–1966) *poet, translator and orientalist, lived and died here*
### 50 SOUTHWOOD LANE, HIGHGATE VILLAGE, N6

Although he never visited the Far East, Waley became an authority on Chinese and Japanese literature and, in translations such as *One Hundred and Seventy Chinese Poems* (1918) and his version of *The Pillow Book of Sei Shonagon* (1928), he was the leading interpreter of Eastern culture for generations of British readers. Born Arthur David Schloss, he was educated at Rugby and King's College, Cambridge, and changed his Germanic surname at the start of the First World War, taking his mother's maiden name. He worked for a number of years in the Print Room of the British Museum and had close ties to many members of the Bloomsbury Group.

........................................................................................................................................

## WALKER, SIR EMERY (1851–1933) *typographer and antiquary, lived here 1903–1933*
### 7 HAMMERSMITH TERRACE, W6

Walker was a master printer, typographic designer and historian of printing who, in addition to founding the Doves Press with Cobden-Sanderson, was instrumental in the establishment of William Morris's famous Kelmscott Press. Morris knew Walker because they were neighbours in Hammersmith and it may well have been a lecture given by Walker at an Arts and Crafts exhibition in 1888 that acted as the catalyst for Morris's thoughts about the design and printing of books. Certainly when the Kelmscott Press was begun it was Walker on whom Morris relied for his technical expertise, and one contemporary described him as 'the quiet, unassuming yet infinitely knowledgeable adviser'. After Morris's death, Walker continued, for nearly forty years, to produce fine books on private presses and to invent new types and new methods of engraving and reproduction.

........................................................................................................................................

## WALLACE, ALFRED RUSSEL (1823–1913) *naturalist, lived here*
### 44 ST PETER'S ROAD, CROYDON

In June 1858 a communication arrived at Charles Darwin's home from a naturalist working in the Malay archipelago. That naturalist was Alfred Russel Wallace who, independently, had come up with the idea of natural selection. Darwin had formulated his theory of the origin of the species some years before but had not published it beyond the circle of his scientific friends. Now he was persuaded that his work ought to be made public. The first step was a joint paper by Darwin and

Wallace given to the Linnaean Society in 1858. Wallace, in 1858, already had many years experience in collecting and classifying species. In his twenties he had undertaken a daring trip to the Amazon basin in search of exotic flora and fauna (all his specimens were lost in a shipwreck) and he had spent some years in Malaysia. He went on to live to the age of ninety and gain a respect as a naturalist that was only slightly tarnished by his excursions, later in life, into spiritualism.

## WALLACE, EDGAR (1875–1932) *writer, lived here*
6 TRESSILLIAN CRESCENT, SE4

EDGAR WALLACE, *reporter. Born London 1875 Died Hollywood 1932. Founder member of the Company of Newspaper Makers. 'He knew wealth and poverty yet had walked with kings and kept his bearing. Of his talents he gave lavishly to authorship but to Fleet Street he gave his heart.'*

CORNER OF FLEET STREET AND LUDGATE CIRCUS, EC4  **PRIVATE**

The illegitimate son of an actress, Wallace was adopted by a Billingsgate fish-porter and grew up in the poorer streets of London. He found his *métier* as a journalist and worked as a correspondent for Reuters and the *Daily Mail* during the Boer War. His great scoop was the news of the 1901 Peace Treaty, which the Mail headlined before the government was officially informed of it. Kitchener immediately banned Wallace from every war front. As a thriller writer Wallace was enormously prolific, producing more than a hundred and fifty novels and volumes of short stories, including such titles as *The Four Just Men*, *Sanders of the River* and *The Mind of Mr J.G. Reeder*. He also harboured political ambitions and stood as a parliamentary candidate, remarking, 'A writer of crook stories ought never to stop seeking new material.' He died in Hollywood where he was working on the script of *King Kong*.

## WALPOLE, SIR ROBERT (1676–1745) *Prime Minister, and his son* HORACE WALPOLE (1717–1797) *connoisseur and man of letters, lived here*
5 ARLINGTON STREET, SW1

The title 'Prime Minister' was originally intended to be a term of abuse, indicating someone who had more power in government than was good for the nation, and it had been applied to other politicians before Robert Walpole. However, Walpole was the politician to whom the title most aptly applied and it is as the first Prime Minister that he is remembered. Entering Parliament in 1701, he was Secretary-at-War as early as 1708, spent a brief period in the Tower in 1712 on charges of corruption and then ran the nation's government from 1721 to 1742, his effectiveness almost entirely based on a system of bribes, sinecures and corruption of the kind for which he had been imprisoned. His youngest son, Horace, was given lucrative government offices by his father even before he had graduated from Cambridge, and he entered Parliament himself in 1741. However, he took little active interest in politics and retired, without regret, from the House of Commons in 1767, describing it as 'that splendid theatre of pitiful passion'. Inheriting money and estates from his father, Horace Walpole was not inconvenienced by the need to work and he devoted his life to writing and to the gradual transformation of a small property at Twickenham into the elaborately 'Gothic' castle known as Strawberry Hill. His vivid and witty letters and his book *The Castle of Otranto*, the first 'Gothic' novel, remain worth reading.

## WALTER, JOHN (1739–1812) *founder of 'The Times', lived here*
113 CLAPHAM COMMON NORTH SIDE, SW4

The son of a London coal merchant, John Walter entered the family business in 1755 and also became a successful underwriter at Lloyd's. At the height of his prosperity he bought the house on Clapham Common but a combination of shipping losses and a decline in the coal trade bankrupted him and he was obliged to leave the house in 1784, ten years after entering into possession of it. Unbowed by his bankruptcy, Walter raised money to establish a printing business in Printing House Square and, on the first day of 1785, he launched *The Daily Universal Register*. Three years later the name was changed to *The Times* and a British institution was born. John Walter died in Teddington in 1812 but his newspaper lived on and several generations of his family, nearly all also called John Walter, followed in his footsteps at *The Times*.

## WARLOCK, PETER (PHILIP ARNOLD HESELTINE) (1894–1930) *composer, lived here*

### 30 TITE STREET, SW3

One of the more interesting British composers of the twentieth century, Peter Warlock was born Philip Heseltine in the Savoy Hotel, son of a well-to-do upper-middle-class family. His interest in music was encouraged by Delius, whom he met in 1911 when he was an Eton schoolboy, and he dropped out of university education to become, briefly, music critic for the *Daily Mail*. For the rest of his life he struggled to make a freelance living as editor, writer and composer of original songs. His best-known piece is probably the *Capriol Suite* from 1926. He adopted the pseudonym of Peter Warlock early in his career and it may reflect his interest in the occult and black magic. While Warlock was living in his flat in Chelsea in 1930 he was suffering from long periods of depression and he was found there on the morning of 17 December, dead from gas-poisoning.

## WATERHOUSE, ALFRED (1830–1905) *architect, lived here*

### 61 NEW CAVENDISH STREET, W1

In the high Victorian period the prevailing architectural style was the Gothic and not only religious buildings but also secular ones were designed to echo the great cathedrals and churches of the medieval era. One of the great exponents of Victorian Gothic architecture was Alfred Waterhouse. From a Liverpool Quaker family, Waterhouse studied in Manchester and, after travelling abroad, began to practise in that city, designing the town hall. In 1865 he moved to London. He was a prolific and inventive architect and two of the greatest Victorian buildings in the city are his work. The Natural History Museum, built between 1873 and 1881, is more Romanesque than Gothic in its architectural forms but works superbly as a cathedral to nineteenth-century science and culture. The Prudential Assurance Buildings, whose red-brick splendour dominates one side of Holborn, are, however, aggressively Gothic and were begun by Waterhouse in the late 1870s.

## WATERHOUSE, JOHN WILLIAM (1849–1917) *painter, lived here 1900–1917*

### 10 HALL ROAD, NW8

Many of the best-known paintings of the Victorian era, familiar from myriad posters, postcards and calendars, are the work of J. W. Waterhouse. Particularly fond of subjects from classical mythology, from Shakespeare and from the works of the Romantic poets, Waterhouse created *The Lady of Shalott*, *Hylas and the Nymphs*, *Echo and Narcissus*, *La Belle Dame Sans Merci*, *Ophelia* and more than 200 other paintings in a successful career spanning almost fifty years. He was born in Rome in 1849, the son of two painters who had moved to Italy in search of artistic inspiration. The family returned to England in the late 1850s and the young Waterhouse entered the Royal Academy Schools in 1870. Returning to Italy several times in the 1870s and 1880s, he painted genre scenes of Italian life but was already producing the works on classical and mythological subjects that were to make his name. Several of his works from the 1880s, including *The Lady of Shalott*, probably his single most famous painting, were bought by the wealthy collector Sir Henry Tate and remain on view in the gallery on Millbank created by him. Waterhouse moved to Hall Road at a time when many other artists lived in St John's Wood. The St John's Wood Art Club, which he joined, also had members such as Sir Lawrence Alma-Tadema and George Clausen. When he died in 1917, Waterhouse's work looked outmoded but, such is the whirligig of public taste, he is now more popular than he has ever been.

## WAUGH, BENJAMIN (1839–1908) *founder of the National Society for the Prevention of Cruelty to Children, lived here*

26 CROOM'S HILL, SE10

Born in Yorkshire and educated at a nonconformist college in Bradford, Waugh became a Congregational minister and moved south to Newbury and, later, Greenwich to follow his vocation. He also took up religious journalism and was, for more than twenty years, the editor of a periodical called *The Sunday Magazine*. He met Sarah Smith who, under the pseudonym Hesba Stretton, was a popular writer of the day and together they founded the London Society for the Prevention of Cruelty to Children in 1884. Waugh went on to establish the society at a national level and, for the rest of his life, was an influential figure in the field of child welfare, giving his stamp of approval to a number of important parliamentary campaigns to improve the lot of children.

## WAUGH, EVELYN (1903–1966) *writer, lived here*

145 NORTH END ROAD, GOLDERS GREEN, NW11

During an audience with the Pope, Randolph Churchill introduced Evelyn Waugh with the words, 'I expect you know my friend Evelyn Waugh, who, like you, Your Holiness, is a Roman Catholic.' Waugh had become a Catholic in 1930 and his best-known novel, *Brideshead Revisited*, describes the emotional entanglement of the artist Charles Ryder with a family of Catholic aristocrats out of sympathy with the demands of the modern world. So too was Waugh, whether it was the febrile world of upper-class hedonists satirised in his earlier novels, published in the late twenties and thirties, or the post-war world of welfare and Labour government which he hated. After his marriage in 1937 to his second wife and service in the war (he decided that warfare was 'like German opera, too long and too loud') he increasingly withdrew to his country house in Combe Florey in Somerset, where he maintained his privacy by attaching a notice to the house gates that read, 'No admittance on business.'

## WEBB, PHILIP
See under entry for RED HOUSE

## WEBB, SIDNEY (1859–1947) *and* BEATRICE WEBB (1858–1943), *social scientists and political reformers, lived here*

10 NETHERHALL GARDENS, NW3

## SIDNEY WEBB, *social researcher and reformer, founder of the LSE, was born in a house on this site 13 July 1859*

38–44 CRANBOURN STREET, WC2   **WESTMINSTER**

Sidney Webb was born in Cranbourn Street, where his mother had a millinery and hairdressing shop, and he grew up to be a civil servant and an early member of the Fabian Society. He was elected to the LCC in 1892, the same year he married Beatrice Potter, a member of a wealthy family who had helped Charles Booth in compiling some of the information for his huge survey, *Life and Labour of the London Poor*. Together the Webbs became the leading social investigators and theorists of the Left in Britain for the next fifty years. They published widely on trade unionism, local government and social history and founded both the London School of Economics in 1895 (it had its first home in the Adelphi) and the political weekly the *New Statesman* in 1913. Sidney entered Parliament, becoming a member of Ramsay MacDonald's first Labour government. Both of the Webbs had great intellectual influence on the development of the Labour party. In *The New Machiavelli*, the novel by their friend H.G. Wells, they appear thinly disguised as the Baileys, 'two active self-centred people, excessively devoted to the public service.'

...................................................................................................................

## WEISZ, VICTOR ('VICKY') (1913–1966) *cartoonist, lived in a flat in this building*

WELBECK MANSIONS, 35 WELBECK STREET, W1

Born in Berlin, of a Hungarian-Jewish family, Victor Weisz moved to Britain from Nazi Germany in 1935 and, under the pseudonym of 'Vicky', became the leading cartoonist of the Left in the 1950s and early 1960s. He worked for several major newspapers, including the *Daily Mirror* and the *Evening Standard*, and published a number of collections of his work. His most abiding image was that of the then Prime Minister, Harold Macmillan, as 'Supermac', a kind of caped conservative flying into action against his political foes. Ironically, although perhaps inevitably, Macmillan was delighted rather than distressed by Vicky's image of him as a moustachioed super-hero.

...................................................................................................................

## WEIZMANN, CHAIM (1874–1952) *scientist and statesman, first President of the state of Israel, lived here*

67 ADDISON ROAD, W14

Born in Russia and educated in Germany, Weizmann first came to England to teach biochemistry at Manchester University. He became a naturalised British citizen in 1910 and moved to London during the First World War as director of the Admiralty Laboratories. Nearer to the centres of power, Weizmann was able to lobby influential figures on behalf of his Zionist views and in 1917, the year he moved into Addison Road, the then Foreign Secretary, Arthur Balfour, publicly declared Britain's support for the idea of a Jewish 'national home' in Palestine. In 1920, the year he left Addison Road, Weizmann became president of the Zionist Organisation and when, after years of diplomacy and discussion and the horrors of the Second World War and the Holocaust, the state of Israel came into being, the ageing Weizmann was its first President.

...................................................................................................................

## WELLCOME, SIR HENRY (1853–1936) *pharmacist, founder of the Wellcome Trust and Foundation, lived here*

6 GLOUCESTER GATE, NW1

Henry Wellcome's career as a purveyor of medicines took him from Garden City, Minnesota, where he grew up, to a knighthood and riches in London. After graduating from a College of Pharmacy in Philadelphia, Wellcome first became a travelling salesman, touting his wares through the often hostile territories in the West, which he knew from his youth. In 1880 he sailed for England and established, with a college friend, the firm of Burroughs, Wellcome & Co. At first an agency for importing American drugs, it soon began to manufacture its own products and it was Wellcome who had the brilliant idea of compressing medicines, then mostly taken in liquid or powder form, into small solids that he called 'tabloids'. The word, now more familiar in the context of the newspaper industry, was originally a brand name of Burroughs, Wellcome. Wellcome's idea brought him great wealth and he was able to devote the rest of his life to charity, collecting and archaeology. His name lives on, in his adopted country, in the institutions that his benefactions created.

## WELLS, H.G. (1866–1946) *writer, lived and died here*

13 HANOVER TERRACE, NW1

*The site of the birthplace of* H.G. WELLS, *born 21 September 1866*

ALDERS DEPARTMENT STORE, BROMLEY HIGH STREET, BROMLEY,
**BROMLEY BOROUGH COUNCIL**

Wells was born in Bromley, the son of a cricketer turned
unsuccessful tradesman. After an unhappy period apprenticed to
a draper and as a student teacher at a grammar school, he won
a scholarship to the Normal School of Science in Kensington
(now Imperial College) where one of his teachers was T.H.
Huxley, who made a deep impression. After graduating, Wells
continued to teach but also embarked on a journalistic and
literary career. His early successes, like *The Time Machine* and *The
War of the Worlds*, were 'scientific romances' but he later displayed
an equal talent for novels, like *Kipps*, which drew on his
knowledge of the lives and dreams of the lower middle classes.
Wells was a lifelong socialist (although an idiosyncratic one) and
became for much of the first half of the twentieth century, an
example, like Shaw, of the writer as public figure. In a letter to
Henry James he once defined his own belief in the social importance of writing. 'To you,' he wrote
to James, 'literature like painting is an end; to me literature like architecture is a means, it has a use.'

---

## WESLEY, CHARLES (1707–1788) *divine and hymn writer, lived and died in a house on
this site, and his sons* CHARLES (1757–1834) *and* SAMUEL (1766–1837) *also lived here*

1 WHEATLEY STREET, W1

CHARLES WESLEY *Adjoining this site stood the house of* JOHN BRAY, *scene of Charles
Wesley's evangelical conversion 21 May 1738*

13 LITTLE BRITAIN, EC1   **CITY OF LONDON**

The younger brother of John Wesley, Charles Wesley studied at Oxford where he formed a like-
minded group of religious enthusiasts, the Oxford Methodists. John joined the group, became its
leading figure and later took over the name for his followers in the great evangelical movement.
Charles accompanied his brother on his misconceived, and near-disastrous, trip to evangelise the
American colonies. On their return to England, Charles experienced his conversion to 'the saving
faith' at the house of John Bray and John underwent a similar religious experience a few days later.
Charles composed thousands of hymns in his life, including such well-known ones as 'Hark, the
Herald Angels Sing' and 'Love divine, all loves excelling'. His sons both pursued careers as musicians.
Charles was a well-known organist and his brother Samuel, who appalled the family by converting to
Catholicism, was a child prodigy who went on to become both organist and composer.

---

## WESLEY, JOHN (1703–1791) *evangelist and founder of Methodism, lived here*

47 CITY ROAD, EC1

'I look upon all the world as my parish,' John Wesley once wrote in his journal and his career
embodies this belief. From Oxford, where he had studied, been ordained and become a
fellow of Lincoln College, he set off in 1735, accompanied by his brother Charles and George
Whitefield, to take God's word to the Indians of the American colonies. The Indians proved
uninterested in God's word and some of the colonists were actively hostile to the trio's
missionary zeal. Wesley returned to England in 1738 and, encouraged by a profound spiritual

experience in which he felt the assurance of God's love and his own salvation, he embarked on his extraordinary journeys around the country, in which he preached to vast crowds of ordinary men and women. It is said that in his lifetime Wesley travelled 250,000 miles and preached 40,000 sermons. The first Methodist chapel was founded at Bristol and in 1744 Wesley held a conference of preachers that was the forerunner of the annual Methodist Conference. Wesley wished his movement to remain within the Church of England but by the time of his death Methodism had effectively burst the bounds of orthodoxy and Methodist chapels were officially designated Dissenting Meeting Houses.

## WESTMACOTT, SIR RICHARD (1775–1856) *sculptor, lived and died here*
14 SOUTH AUDLEY STREET, W1

The son of a sculptor, Westmacott studied under his father and then in Italy, where he was the pupil of Canova. Returning to England in 1797 he established a successful studio in London. The statue of the Duke of York of the nursery rhyme, which stands on a column facing the Mall, is Westmacott's work. According to the wits of the time, the statue was placed on a 124-foot column so that the Duke could be well out of reach of his creditors. Westmacott's best-known work is the gigantic *Achilles*, which stands in Hyde Park. This metal statue of the naked warrior, cast from cannon captured from the French, was financed by money raised by 'the women of England' to honour the Duke of Wellington. Some of the women of England, unaccustomed to sculptural nudity, were highly embarrassed by Westmacott's work and it was not a success.

## WHALL, CHRISTOPHER WHITWORTH (1849–1924) *stained glass artist, lived here*
19 RAVENSCOURT ROAD, W6

Like William Morris, Christopher Whitworth Whall opposed the trend in mid-nineteenth-century Britain towards mass production and away from the skill and dedication of the individual craftsman. He became the leading designer of stained glass in the Arts and Crafts Movement and his work can be seen in many parts of the country, most notably, perhaps, in the Lady Chapel at Gloucester Cathedral. With two others, Whall established the Glass House in Fulham as a centre for the training of future stained glass artists and his influence was also felt through the classes he took at the Central School of Art and, later, at the Royal College of Art.

## WHEATSTONE, SIR CHARLES (1802–1875) *scientist and inventor, lived here*
19 PARK CRESCENT, W1

Although he had no formal scientific training, Wheatstone, the son of a Gloucester music seller, became Professor of Experimental Physics at King's College, London, in 1834, a position he held until his death. He was responsible for a variety of inventions, from the concertina to the first recorded patent for an electric telegraph. He was also the first person to introduce the word 'microphone', to describe a sound magnifier he had devised. Among physicists his name is known chiefly for the 'Wheatstone Bridge' circuit for measuring electrical resistance. Ironically he was not the actual inventor of this but was responsible for popularising it. Wheatstone lived in Park Crescent for the last ten years of his life.

## WHEELER, SIR MORTIMER (1890–1976) *archaeologist, lived here*
27 WHITCOMB STREET, WC2

Born in Glasgow, Mortimer Wheeler became one of the great figures of British archaeology during the twentieth century and a powerful populariser of the subject on radio and television. In the 1920s and '30s Wheeler carried out revealing excavations at St Albans, the Roman Verulamium and at

Maiden Castle, the greatest Iron Age hillfort in Britain, where he unearthed bodies that he believed were those of some of the last defenders of their culture against the Roman invaders of AD 43. Immediately after the Second World War, Wheeler was Director-General of archaeology, working on the very ancient Indus valley cities of Mohenjo-Daro and Harappa, before returning to London to take up a post at the newly founded Institute of Archaeology in India. Wheeler was a great believer in his own gifts as an archaeologist and once published an article in which he showed contrasting photos of two digs. One, apparently haphazard and the work of a rival archaeologist, was captioned 'Chaos'. The other, ordered, organised and his own, was captioned 'Discipline'.

---

## WHISTLER, JAMES ABBOT MCNEILL(1834–1903) *painter and etcher, lived here*
### 96 CHEYNE WALK, SW10

Born in Lowell, Massachussetts, the son of a military engineer, Whistler was sent to West Point. In 1855, deciding on an artistic rather than a military career, he left America, first for Paris and then for London. Over the years he established a reputation as a painter and wit whose provocative remarks were as well known as his views of the Thames and his portrait of his mother. Not everyone was impressed by Whistler's work. In 1877 Ruskin noted of one painting exhibited at the Grosvenor Gallery that 'I never expected to hear a coxcomb ask two hundred guineas for flinging a pot of paint in the public's face.' Outraged, Whistler sued for libel and, after a lengthy *cause celébre*, won and was awarded a farthing's damages. Although forced into bankruptcy soon afterwards, Whistler retained his self-assurance and bowed to no one in admiration of his own talents. When a gushing female enthusiast for his work said, 'I only know of two painters in the world, yourself and Velasquez,' Whistler's response was prompt. 'Why drag in Velasquez?' he asked.

---

## WHITAKER, JOSEPH (1820–1895) *publisher, founder of Whitaker's Almanack, lived and died here*

### WHITE LODGE, SILVER STREET, ENFIELD

Born in London, the son of a silversmith, Whitaker was apprenticed to a bookseller at the age of fourteen and went on to become one of the most successful publishers and booksellers of the nineteenth century, whose influence continues to be felt strongly in the very different book trade of today. *The Bookseller*, still the leading trade journal, was founded by Whitaker in 1858. In 1868 Whitaker published the first edition of what has almost become a British institution, *Whitaker's Almanack*, which is still published in a new edition each year. Throughout his career, Whitaker was active in bookselling charities. Perhaps his most unusual charity work was raising £2,000 to send to Parisian booksellers, trapped in the city during the siege of 1870–71. As a consequence of this Whitaker was one of the first Britons into Paris after its relief.

---

## WHITE, WILLIAM HALE (MARK RUTHERFORD) (1831–1913) *novelist, lived here*
### 19 PARK HILL, CARSHALTON

One of the great subjects of Victorian literature was loss of faith and the anguish that attended it. By thinly fictionalising his own spriritual journey, William Hale White treated that subject from the perspective of a nonconformist. Born in Bedford, White went as a young man to train as an independent minister but found his vocation seriously compromised by an increasing inability to keep quiet about his religious doubts. He was eventually expelled from his training college and turned instead to the Civil Service and to the worlds of journalism and literature to earn his living. *The Autobiography of Mark Rutherford*, published in 1881, purported to be the life-story of a dissenting minister who, like White, had travelled from faith to lack of faith, and was a great success. A number of other novels appeared under the pseudonym of Mark Rutherford while White continued to publish other work, including a study of John Bunyan, under his own name.

*The house of* RICHARD WHITTINGTON *Mayor of London stood on this site 1423*

20 COLLEGE HILL, EC4   **CITY OF LONDON**

RICHARD WHITTINGTON, *four times Mayor of London founded and was buried in this church 1422*

ST MICHAEL ROYAL, COLLEGE HILL, EC4   **CITY OF LONDON**

Dick Whittington, the character of legend and pantomime, had his origins in a real individual. Richard Whittington was a wealthy merchant who was four times mayor of London (in 1397, 1398/9, 1406/7 and 1419/20) and, in his will, left money for the improvement of the city. Newgate Prison was rebuilt and almshouses and a hospital established, using Whittington's legacies. The story of Dick Whittington and his cat, now familiar from pantomime, first appeared in print in the early seventeenth century, although it must have been circulating orally before then. Some scholars have suggested linguistic confusion between 'cat' and the French word 'achat' meaning trade as the reason for the cat's appearance in the story.

WILBERFORCE, WILLIAM (1759–1833) *and the Clapham Sect worshipped in this church. Their campaigning resulted in the abolition of slavery in the British Dominions 1833*

HOLY TRINITY CHURCH, CLAPHAM COMMON, SW4

WILLIAM WILBERFORCE, *opponent of slavery, died here*

44 CADOGAN PLACE, SW1

*On the site behind this house stood until 1904 Broomwood House (formerly Broomfield) where* WILLIAM WILBERFORCE *resided during the campaign against slavery which he successfully conducted in Parliament*

111 BROOMWOOD ROAD, SW11

The son of a wealthy merchant, Wilberforce was born in Hull and was educated at Cambridge where he met the younger Pitt, already in training for the world of politics. Through Pitt, Wilberforce himself became an MP but the direction of his parliamentary career was changed by his conversion to an evangelical form of Christianity. For nineteen years he campaigned for the abolition of the slave trade, a campaign which culminated in a parliamentary ban on the trade in 1807. Wilberforce turned his attention to the whole institution of slavery in Britain's overseas possessions. The Emancipation Act was finally passed in the year of Wilberforce's death. Many of Wilberforce's closest allies, including Zachary Macaulay and Virginia Woolf's great-grandfather, the lawyer and politician James Stephen, attended Holy Trinity Church and the group became known as the 'Clapham Sect' or, half-derisively, 'the Saints'. One of Wilberforce's sons was the Bishop involved in the famous debate with Thomas Huxley on Darwin's theories.

WILDE, LADY JANE FRANCESCA 'SPERANZA' (1821–1896) *poet and essayist, lived here 1887–1896*

87 OAKLEY STREET, CHELSEA, SW3

Most often remembered as the mother of Oscar Wilde, Lady Jane Francesca Wilde published Irish nationalist verse under the pseudonym of 'Speranza' (one book bears the dedication, 'To Ireland'), and several volumes on Irish and Celtic folklore under her own name. Calling herself 'Speranza' (the Italian word for 'hope'), because the *nom de plume* reflected both her aspirations for Ireland and her belief that she was descended from medieval Italian aristocrats, she was an ardent nationalist from her youth. In a newspaper article she penned in 1848, she claimed that 'the long-pending war with England has already commenced' but, despite her outspokenness, she managed to avoid the legal prosecution that sent several of her colleagues in the nationalist movement to convict settlements in Australia. After marrying the surgeon William Wilde, she presided over an influential literary and political salon in Dublin for more than thirty years, although she had to suffer the humiliation of her husband's frequent and quite open infidelities. After his death she moved to London and continued to hold court in Oakley Street to a dwindling band of literary and political acolytes. She died in 1896 while her famous son was imprisoned in a Reading gaol.

........................................................

## WILDE, OSCAR (1854–1900) *wit and dramatist, lived here*
### 34 TITE STREET, SW3

*The first performances of 'A Woman of No Importance' 19 April 1893 and 'An ideal Husband' 3 January 1895 by* OSCAR WILDE *were presented at this theatre*

### THEATRE ROYAL, HAYMARKET, SW1 **WESTMINSTER**

'Somehow or other I'll be famous,' Oscar Wilde is reported to have said when asked what he would do after leaving Oxford, 'and if not famous, I'll be notorious.' If the story is true (and it seems too good to be so) he possessed the ability to look into the future as well as all his other gifts of wit, intelligence and literary skill. Oscar Wilde's spectacular fall from grace, his journey from fame to notoriety, is one of the best-known and most tragic stories in the history of literature. Early in 1895 he was the fêted author of epigrammatic comedies like *Lady Windermere's Fan* and *The Importance of Being Earnest* and a man lionised by London society. The Marquess of Queensberry, disapproving of Wilde's friendship with his son Lord Alfred Douglas, sent a note addressed to Wilde 'posing as a Somdomite'. Unwisely, Wilde decided to sue for libel and set in motion a sequence of events that ended with Wilde, by the close of 1895, prosecuted and imprisoned for homosexuality. After his release from prison Wilde was a broken man and he died in exile in Paris. Stories, mostly apocryphal, of his last words emphasise that he retained his wit to the end. While staying in a Paris hotel room he certainly did say, 'This wall-paper will be the death of me – one of us will have to go,' although it was not on his deathbed.

........................................................

## WILLAN, DR ROBERT (1757–1812) *dermatologist, lived here*
### 10 BLOOMSBURY SQUARE, WC1

A Yorkshireman, born near Sedbergh, Robert Willan came from a Quaker family and studied medicine at Edinburgh University. In 1783 he was given the job of physician to a public dispensary in Carey Street, London, and it was there that he began to undertake the work into diseases of the skin which made his name. In 1798 he began to publish his findings in a work of classification called *The Description and Treatment of Cutaneous Diseases* and he continued to add to this magnum opus over the next ten years. Willan died of heart failure while on a visit to Madeira.

## WILLIAMS, HENRY SYLVESTER (1867–1911), *Anti-slavery and civil rights campaigner, first black councillor in Westminster*

### 38 CHURCH STREET, W2  **WESTMINSTER**

'The time has come,' Henry Sylvester Williams once said, 'when the voice of black men should be heard independently in their own affairs.' As the founder of the African Association (later the Pan-African Association) and as the organiser of the very first Pan-African Conference, which was held in Westminster Town Hall in July 1900, he was a pioneer in campaigns to ensure that black voices were heard. Born in a small town in Trinidad, Williams went as a young man to Canada to study law and arrived in London in 1896 to study for the Bar but was soon drawn into political life, campaigning and lecturing on issues ranging from temperance to anti-imperialism. Williams later spent time practising as a barrister in South Africa before returning to London where he was elected to the Marylebone Borough Council in 1906. Representing the Labour Party in the Church Street ward, he was the first black councillor in Westminster and only the second in the entire country.

## WILLIS, 'FATHER' HENRY (1821–1901) *organ builder, lived here*

### 9 ROCHESTER TERRACE, NW1

The greatest organ builder of the Victorian era, Henry Willis was the founder of a firm which continues to this day the tradition he established. Born into a musical, but far from wealthy, family, he played the organ from an early age and his first major commission, to rebuild the organ at Gloucester Cathedral, came in 1847. At the Great Exhibition four years later Willis achieved a major triumph when an organ, equipped with a number of improvements he had devised himself, was chosen to give a recital for Queen Victoria and Prince Albert. For the rest of the century he and his firm built or rebuilt thousands of organs around the Empire, from Calcutta Cathedral to the Royal Albert Hall. In recognition of his pre-eminence in his field he was unofficially but widely known as 'Father' Willis.

## WILLOUGHBY, SIR HUGH

*This plaque is in memory of* SIR HUGH WILLOUGHBY (D.1554), STEPHEN BOROUGH (1525–1585), WILLIAM BOROUGH (1536–1599), SIR MARTIN FROBISHER (1535?–1594) *and other navigators who in the latter half of the sixteenth century set sail from this reach of the River Thames near Ratcliff Cross to explore the Northern Seas*

### KING EDWARD MEMORIAL PARK, SHADWELL, E1

In England of the 1550s the race was on to find a quicker route to the wealth of the East. In 1553 merchants in London equipped three ships 'for the discovery of regions, dominions, islands and places unknown' and placed Sir Hugh Willoughby in charge. He chose to aim for a supposed 'North-East Passage' to these new places and to the Indies. He got as far as Russian Lapland where he perished, together with his companions from two of his ships. The other ship, commanded by Richard Chancellor and Stephen Borough, became separated from Willoughby and sailed successfully into the White Sea. Chancellor made an epic journey to the Russian court at Moscow; Borough survived to become chief pilot of the Muscovy Company, founded later to trade with the Russians. Stephen Borough's younger brother, William, was also on Chancellor's ship as a teenager and went on to become an expert navigator who drew up charts of the northern waters he first saw on that 1553 expedition. Frobisher was a Yorkshireman, who decided that a North-West Passage to India and China existed and thought he had found it in what is now known as Frobisher Bay in present-day Canada. He sailed three times across the Atlantic but found only suffering and hardship rather than a route to the silks and spices of the East. He was knighted for his services against the Armada.

## WILSON, EDWARD ADRIAN (1872–1912) *Antarctic explorer and naturalist, lived here*

BATTERSEA VICARAGE, 42 VICARAGE CRESCENT, SW11

Wilson, who was a doctor trained at St George's Hospital, Paddington, was also an enthusiastic amateur naturalist, with a particular interest in ornithology, and a skilled watercolour painter whose work was used to illustrate a number of natural history books. He accompanied Scott on both of his Antarctic expeditions and became a particular friend. Scott wrote that Wilson was 'the life and soul of the party, the organiser of all amusements, the always good-tempered and cheerful one, the ingenious person who could get round all difficulties.' On the second expedition Wilson participated in what fellow-explorer Cherry-Garrard described as 'the worst journey in the world', a mid-winter search for penguin eggs, and in the final journey to the South Pole. He was one of the five to reach the Pole and discover that Amundsen had been there first, and he died with his companions on the return journey.

## WINANT, JOHN GILBERT (1889–1947) *United States Ambassador 1941–1946, lived here*

7 ALDFORD STREET, W1

Before entering politics Winant was a schoolteacher and had fought with the American Expeditionary Force in the First World War. He first won high office as Governor of New Hampshire in 1925 and he went on to serve two more two-year terms as Governor of the state in the difficult depression-ridden years of the early thirties. Although a Republican, Winant was a great admirer of the Democrat President Franklin D. Roosevelt and in 1941 Roosevelt rewarded this admiration by offering Winant the position of Ambassador to the Court of St James, replacing Joseph Kennedy. Winant was Ambassador throughout the difficult war years and also served on the commission which defined the zones of Allied forces' occupation of post-war Germany. He retired in 1946 to write his memoirs. The following year Winant, who had been prone to bouts of depression as a young man, committed suicide.

## WINGFIELD, MAJOR WALTER CLOPTON (1833–1912) *father of lawn tennis, lived here*

33 ST GEORGE'S SQUARE, SW1

A bust of Major Wingfield stands at the entrance to the museum at Wimbledon to confirm his status as the father of lawn tennis. During the nineteenth century a number of attempts were made to popularise up-dated versions of the real tennis that had been played since the time of Henry VIII. In 1873 the Major published a *Book of Games*, in which he outlined his own version, and he took out a patent on his 'New and Improved Court for Playing the Ancient Game of Tennis'. Wingfield's version of tennis, largely the same that is played today, proved instantly popular. In 1875 the All England Croquet Club set aside one of its grounds specifically for the new game and two years later the club became officially known as the All England Croquet and Lawn Tennis Club and supervised the first Wimbledon singles championship. Modern tennis was underway.

## WODEHOUSE, P.G. (1881–1975) *writer, lived here*

17 DUNRAVEN STREET, W1

Sean O'Casey described P.G. Wodehouse as 'English literature's performing flea'. Wodehouse, characteristically, took it as a compliment, calling one of his autobiographical works *Performing Flea* and remarking: 'all the performing fleas I have met impressed me with their sterling artistry and that indefinable something which makes the good trouper.' After school at Dulwich, Wodehouse began to work as a bank clerk but was soon earning enough from his stories to concentrate on his writing. Over seventy years he created a rich array of comic characters, most famously Bertie Wooster and his omnicompetent valet Jeeves, who appeared first in 1917 in *The Man With Two Left Feet* and subsequently in many further books. During the Second World War, Wodehouse, who had been living in France and was captured by the Germans, made some injudicious broadcasts from Berlin for which he received much criticism. After the war he moved to America, taking American citizenship in 1955. A few weeks before his death, a knighthood indicated that the British establishment had finally forgiven his wartime foolishness.

## WOLFE, GENERAL JAMES (1727–1759) *victor of Quebec, lived here*
MACARTNEY HOUSE, GREENWICH PARK, SE10

As a young soldier, Wolfe had taken part in battles against Bonnie Prince Charlie but it was only when he arrived in America that he began to distinguish himself and to rise swiftly up the ladder of promotion. In 1759 he was made Major-General and put in charge of 9,000 men who were sent up the St Lawrence River to oppose the French in Quebec. After some months of stalemate Wolfe devised a plan of attack that involved a feigned assault below the city and a perilous ascent by his own troops of a narrow path to the Heights of Abraham above Quebec. In the ensuing battle both Wolfe and the French Commander, Montcalm, were killed but the British forces eventually prevailed and Quebec surrendered. It was Wolfe whom George II famously defended after hearing one of his courtiers describe the soldier as mad. 'Mad, is he?', the king said. 'Then I hope he will *bite* some of my other generals.'

## WOOD, SIR HENRY (1869–1944) *musician, lived here*
4 ELSWORTHY ROAD, NW3

Sir Henry Wood was a composer who wrote operettas and an oratorio, but his fame rests squarely on his work as a conductor and, particularly, on his introducing the season of concerts that has now become a national institution, the Proms. In 1895 Wood was appointed conductor of the newly formed Queen's Hall Orchestra and began the Promenade concerts in October of that year. The concerts rapidly became popular and the opportunity to promenade soon disappeared but Wood continued to conduct a series of such concerts for the rest of his life. The Queen's Hall was destroyed in the Blitz and, despite Wood's wish to rebuild it, the Proms transferred to the Albert Hall. Wood had conservative musical tastes but did allow for the performance of pieces with which he was unsympathetic. In 1912 he began rehearsals for Schoenberg's *Five Pieces for Orchestra* by telling his players, 'Stick to it, gentlemen. This is nothing to what you'll have to play in twenty-five years' time!'

## WOOLF, LEONARD AND VIRGINIA *lived in this house 1915–1924 and founded the Hogarth Press in 1917*
HOGARTH HOUSE, PARADISE ROAD, RICHMOND

## VIRGINIA WOOLF
50 GORDON SQUARE, WC1   **CAMDEN BOROUGH COUNCIL**

The Woolfs moved to Richmond three years after their marriage and the Hogarth Press was begun partly to assist Virginia through one of the periodic bouts of mental distress from which she suffered. Among the Press's earliest publications were works by Katherine Mansfield and T.S. Eliot and stories by both of the Woolfs themselves. During the period at Richmond, before moving back into the heart of Bloomsbury in 1924, Virginia Woolf published *Night and Day*, her second novel, and *Jacob's Room*, the first of her novels to appear under the Hogarth Press imprint.

See also under entry for VIRGINIA STEPHEN

## WREN, SIR CHRISTOPHER (1632–1723) *architect, lived here*
THE OLD COURT HOUSE, HAMPTON COURT GREEN, EAST MOLESEY

'Since the time of Archimedes,' a contemporary wrote of Wren, 'there scarce ever has met in one man, in so great perfection, such a mechanical hand and so philosophical a mind.' The churches that Wren built in the aftermath of the Great Fire, and especially St. Paul's Cathedral, bear witness to the truth of this and yet his first interests were science and mathematics. Born in Wiltshire, the son of a clergyman, Wren studied at Oxford and became Professor of Astronomy at Gresham College, London, in 1657, returning to Oxford four years later as Savilian Professor of the same subject. It was not until 1665 that he had an opportunity to design his first building – a chapel at Pembroke College, Cambridge. The devastation inflicted on London by the Great Fire the following year was enormous and Wren was one among several who submitted plans for the rebuilding of the city. Although his more elaborate plans – which envisaged broad new thoroughfares surrounded by large public spaces, including a vast piazza on the site of Fleet Street – proved impractical, he had found his life's work. Over the next forty years Wren designed, and supervised the building of, more than fifty churches to replace the ones lost in the fire. His greatest triumph was the construction of the new St Paul's, which opened in 1697, although the dome was not completed until thirteen years later. Wren, who had worked closely on the cathedral until its completion, died in 1723, aged ninety-one.

## WYATT, THOMAS HENRY (1807–1880) *architect, lived and died here*
77 GREAT RUSSELL STREET, W1

The son of a London police magistrate, Wyatt was one of a family that, over several generations, produced a large number of architects and sculptors. In some ways his younger brother, Matthew Digby Wyatt, who was involved in the organisation of the Great Exhibition and later knighted, was a better-known figure but Thomas Henry was a prolific designer of both ecclesiastical and secular buildings. Some of Wyatt's most prestigious work, like the Park Lane mansion, Brook House, has since been demolished but other buildings, such as the houses at Nos 18–19 Kensington Palace Gardens, survive.

## WYATVILLE, SIR JEFFRY (1766–1840) *architect, lived and died here*
39 BROOK STREET, MAYFAIR, W1

Born as Jeffry Wyatt into a family that produced many well-known architects, Wyatville took his extended name as a supposed honour at the time he was working at Windsor Castle. George IV, king at the time, was graciously pleased to allow the augmentation as a means of distinguishing him from other members of the family. The reconstruction and remodelling of Windsor Castle was the high point of a career that began when he joined his uncle, Samuel Wyatt, in his practice in the Strand. He went on to become, perhaps, the leading country house architect of the Regency period, designer of many neo-Gothic and neo-Tudor mansions and restorer of palaces like Chatsworth House in Derbyshire.

## WYNDHAM, SIR CHARLES (1837–1919) *actor-manager, lived and died here*
20 YORK TERRACE EAST, NW1

Although he became one of the most popular actors of his time and, in 1902, was only the third member of his profession to be knighted, Charles Wyndham (born Charles Culverwell) had to struggle against family disapproval and early lack of success to make his name. His father insisted that he study medicine and, in his twenties, he spent time as a general practitioner (he failed to attract any patients) and as a surgeon in the Federal Army during the American Civil War. Only when he was in his thirties did his acting career take off and he then went on to a twenty-year period as actor-manager of the Criterion and founded two new theatres in London, Wyndham's (he had taken this as his stage name in his early days as an aspiring actor) and the New in St Martin's Lane. One of Wyndham's most consistently successful roles, and the only one he played on film, was as the eighteenth-century actor David Garrick in a play of that name.

## YEARSLEY, DR JAMES (1805–1869) *The Father of English Otology, founded the Metropolitan Ear Institution here in 1841*

32 SACKVILLE STREET, W1  **WESTMINSTER**

Born in the West Country, Yearsley studied at St Bartholomew's Hospital and then practised in Cheltenham and Ross-on-Wye before returning to London in 1838. In that year he established the Metropolitan Ear and Throat Hospital in Fitzroy Square which moved to Sackville Street three years later. Yearsley, together with two colleagues, also founded *The London Medical Directory*, a practical guide-book to medical facilities in the capital. As a specialist in deafness, Yearsley's greatest insight was to realise that diseases of the nose and throat, as well as diseases of the ear, can lead to loss of hearing. His stature as a pioneer of otology is recognised by the annual Yearsley Memorial Lecture at the Ear, Nose and Throat Hospital.

## YEATS, WILLIAM BUTLER (1865–1939) *Irish poet and dramatist, lived here*

23 FITZROY ROAD, NW1

## WILLIAM BUTLER YEATS, *lodged here for twenty-four years*

5 WOBURN WALK, WC1  **ST PANCRAS BOROUGH COUNCIL**

Born in Dublin, the son of the artist John Butler Yeats, Yeats's childhood was divided between Ireland and London. The family stayed in Fitzroy Road from 1867 to 1873. Yeats's first book of poems was published in 1889 and many were to follow. His early verse shows the heavy influence of his interest in mysticism and the occult – he was a member of many of the esoteric societies that flourished in the 1890s – and of his long, largely unrequited love for the actress and Irish nationalist Maud Gonne. Through her he was led to his involvement, both as playwright and co-director of the Abbey Theatre, with the Irish stage. The Easter Rising and the tumult of the ensuing years affected Yeats deeply and he became an increasingly public figure. He was a Senator in the Irish Free State for six years in the 1920s. His private life was shaped by his late marriage and by the mediumistic powers his wife appeared to possess. Her automatic writing was instrumental in the creation of Yeats's philosophical credo *A Vision*, published in 1925, and, indirectly, the flowering of his later poetry. Yeats, indisputably the greatest Irish poet of the twentieth century, was awarded the Nobel Prize for Literature in 1923 and died in France in 1939.

## YOUNG, THOMAS (1773–1829) *man of science, lived here*

48 WELBECK STREET, W1

Known to his contemporaries as 'Phenomenon' Young, Thomas Young was a polymath of whom Sir Humphry Davy wrote, 'He knew so much that it was difficult to say what he did not know.' The sheer range of Young's interests perhaps worked against him in a world that was gradually moving towards the specialisation of the present. He read half a dozen ancient languages and he took the first steps towards the decipherment of the Rosetta Stone. He was a practising physician and published medical treatises. He was Professor of Natural Philosophy at the Royal Institution and his 1807 lectures set out the basis of the wave theory of light. At the time of his death he was working on a dictionary of ancient Egyptian hieroglyphics.

## ZANGWILL, ISRAEL (1864–1926) *writer and philanthropist, lived here*

288 OLD FORD ROAD, BETHNAL GREEN, E2

Born in the East End to immigrant parents, Zangwill grew up to be a well-known playwright and novelist and a leading spokesman for Jewish and Zionist causes. Many of his books contain vignettes of Jewish life in the Victorian and Edwardian city but he is best remembered for his 1892 novel *Children of the Ghetto*, in which he drew on his own childhood memories to produce a vivid portrait of the immigrant Jews of Whitechapel and their daily struggles. Zangwill was also the founder and first President of the International Jewish Territorial Organisation.

## ZOFFANY, JOHANN (1733–1810) *painter, lived here 1790–1810*

65 STRAND-ON-THE-GREEN, CHISWICK, W4

Born in Frankfurt-am-Main as Johannes Zauffaly, Zoffany had already gained experience as a painter both in his native Germany and in Rome when he arrived in England about 1760. At first, without the necessary contacts and with poor English, Zoffany found it hard to make a living, but his breakthrough came when he was commissioned by David Garrick to produce both family portraits and paintings of the actor in his theatrical roles. Through these he came to the attention of the court and he had the patronage of the King and Queen for the next few years. It was George III who nominated him for membership of the Royal Academy in 1768, the year after it was founded. In the 1770s Zoffany worked in Italy again and in the 1780s he went even further afield, living and working in Calcutta. Returning to England he moved to Strand-on-the-Green, where he died in 1810. He is buried nearby in Kew Churchyard.

## ZOLA, EMILE (1840–1902) *French novelist, lived here 1898–1899*

QUEEN'S HOTEL, 122 CHURCH ROAD, UPPER NORWOOD, SE19

The son of an Italian engineer, Zola was born in Paris and started his career working for a publisher and practising journalism. As a novelist he became the leading figure in French naturalism and his Rougon-Macquart novels form an epic, twenty-volume survey of the late nineteenth century, seen through the respective fortunes of two families. Zola's time in Upper Norwood was a time of exile. The Dreyfus Case, in which a Jewish army officer was (wrongly) accused of treason and imprisoned on Devil's Island, split France into Dreyfusards and anti-Dreyfusards. Zola was one of the most impassioned and eloquent of Dreyfus's supporters and published a letter in a newspaper attacking the military authorities. He escaped to England for eleven months to avoid imprisonment himself for libel. Zola died in 1902 in a bizarre and unfortunate accident, suffocated by charcoal fumes.

## ZYGIELBOJM, SZMUL 'ARTUR' (1895–1943) *Jewish Worker's Bund leader, Representative to the Polish Parliament in exile who took his life in protest at the world's indifference to Nazi extermination of the Jews, lived here 1942–1943*

PORCHESTER SQUARE, W2 **WESTMINSTER**

Szmul Zygielbojm was born in Borowica, Poland, and began his working life in a factory at the age of ten. Self-educated, he became a leading figure in the Jewish Socialist Party and was elected to Warsaw Town Council in 1927. When war broke out he helped organise the city's defences but when the Nazis took control he was forced to flee, first to Brussels and then to London where he became a member of the Polish Parliament in Exile. In May 1943, three weeks after the start of the Warsaw uprising, Zygielbojm committed suicide as a protest against Allied indifference to the fate of the Jews in Europe. The plaque was sponsored by the Szmul Zygielbojm Memorial Committee.

# BIBLIOGRAPHY

During the writing of this book, I have unashamedly plundered other reference works in search of material. This book could not have been written without the *Dictionary of National Biography*, which shares with the *Oxford English Dictionary* the distinction of being the finest work of reference in English. Because of its openness to anecdote and individuality, the DNB is also one of the most pleasurable of reference works through which to browse. Other books that have proved valuable to me were:

Bullock, A., and Woodings, R.B. (eds), *The Fontana Dictionary of Modern Thinkers*, Fontana, 1983

*Chambers' Biographical Dictionary*, Chambers, 1997

Cohen, M.J. (ed.), *The Penguin Dictionary of Twentieth Century Quotations*, Penguin, 1995

Dakers, Caroline, *The Blue Plaque Guide to London*, Macmillan, 1981

Drabble, M. (ed.), *The Oxford Companion to English Literature*, OUP, 1998

Gardiner, J., and Wenborn, N., *The History Today Companion to British History*, Collins and Brown, 1995

Hibbert, B., and Weinreb, C. (eds), *The London Encyclopedia*, Papermac, 1993

Hartnoll, P. (ed.), *The Oxford Companion to the Theatre*, OUP, 1993

Katz, E. (ed.), *The Macmillan International Film Encyclopedia*, Macmillan, 1998

Marsh, Jan, *The Pre-Raphaelites: Their Lives in Letters and Diaries*, Collins and Brown, 1997

Porter, Roy, *The Greatest Benefit to Mankind: A Medical History of Humanity*, Fontana, 1999

Rees, Nigel, *Cassell Companion to Quotations*, Cassell, 1999

Schmidt, Michael, *Lives of the Poets*, Phoenix, 1999

Uglow, J. (ed.), *The Macmillan Dictionary of Women's Biography*, Papermac, 1999

Welch, R. (ed.), *The Oxford Companion to Irish Literature*, OUP, 1996

# LIST OF NAMES BY PROFESSION

ACTORS AND ACTRESSES
*(see also Dramatists and
Playwrights and Music Hall
Artistes and Comedians)*

Aldridge
Coward
Donat
Du Maurier, Gerald
Garrick
Greet
Grenfell
Grossmith
Irving, H.
Johnson, C.
Jordan, D.
Karloff
Langtry
Laughton
Leigh
Matthews
Oldfield
Playfair
Sim
Tempest
Terris
Terry
Thorndike
Tree
Wyndham

ARCHAEOLOGISTS AND
COLLECTORS

Carter
Horniman
Petrie
Pitt-Rivers
Sloane
Townley
Ventris
Wheeler

ARCHITECTS AND
BUILDERS

Adam
Barry
Basevi

Bentley
Bodley
Butterfield
Campbell
Cockerell
Cubitt
Dance
Freake
Gandy
Godwin
Hansom
Howard, E.
Lethaby
Lutyens
Matcham
Pearson, J.L.
Pevsner
Salvin
Scott, George G.
Scott, Giles G.
Shaw, R.
Smirke
Street
Tait
Voysey
Waterhouse
Webb
Wren
Wyatt
Wyatville

ARTS PATRON

Morrell

ARTISTS

Alma-Tadema
Bomberg
Brangwyn
Brown, Ford Madox
Burne-Jones
Canaletto
Constable
Cox
Crane
Dadd
Daniell
Eastlake

Etty
Fildes
Forbes
Frith
Fuseli
Gainsborough
Gertler
Goodall
Greaves
Haydon
Holman Hunt
Hughes
John
Kelly
Knight, H.
Knight, L.
Kokoschka
Lavery
Lear
Leighton
Lewis
Linnell
Millais
Mondrian
Morris
Nash
Orpen
Palmer
Pissarro
Pre-Raphaelite Brotherhood
Pryde
Ravilious
Reynolds
Richmond
Ricketts
Roberts, W.
Robinson, F. Cayley
Romney
Rossetti, D.G.
Sartorius
Schwitters
Shannon
Short
Sickert
Stanfield
Steer
Stevens

Stone
Stothard
Strang
Turner, J.M.W.
Van Gogh
Whistler
Zoffany

AVIATORS

Cayley
Cobham
Gibson
Johnson, A.
Roe
Sopwith

BALLET DANCERS

Astafieva
De Valois
Karsavina
Rambert
Taglioni

CARTOONISTS AND
ILLUSTRATORS

Ardizzone
Bairnsfather
Bateman
Beardsley
Beerbohm
Bestall
Caldecott
Cruikshank
Du Maurier
Heath Robinson
Greenaway
Low
McGill
May
Peake
Rackham
Rowlandson
Shepard
Shepherd
Weisz ('Vicky')

COMPOSERS,
CONDUCTORS AND
MUSICIANS

Ambrose
Arne

Balfe
Bartok
Bax
Beard
Beecham
Benedict
Bennett, W.S.
Berlioz
Bliss
Boult
Brain
Bridge
Britten
Butt
Costa
Chopin
Clementi
Coleridge-Taylor
Colyer
Dannreuther
Delius
Elgar
Ferrier
Goossens
Gounod
Grainger
Grieg
Hall, H.
Handel
Hendrix
Hess
Holst
Ireland
Lambert
Lind
Matthay
McCormack
Mozart
Novello
Parry
Pears
Santley
Sargent
Sharp
Sibelius
Stanford
Tauber
Tosti
Vaughan Williams
Warlock
Wood

CRAFTSMEN AND WOMEN

Chippendale
Clarkson
De Morgan
Garthwaite
Hartnell
Johnson
Johnston
Kempe
Lamerie
Lethaby
Purdey
Rie
Sheraton
Silver Studio
Tompion
Turner, C.
Walker
Whall

DOCTORS, SURGEONS
AND MEDICAL
PRACTITIONERS

Blackie
Bright
Cavell
Clover
Copeman
Dale
Dick-Read
Drysdale
Duke-Elder
Fleming
Freud
Garrett Anderson
Gillies
Gray
Hall, K.
Hodgkin
Hunter, J.
Hunter, W.
Hutchinson
Jackson
Jones
Klein
Linacre
Lister
Mckenzie
Manson
Marsden
Moody

Nightingale
Oliver
Rees
Robinson, J.
Rogers
Ross, R.
Saunders
Seacole
Simon
Spilsbury
Still
Toynbee, J.
Wakley
Wellcome
Willan
Yearsley

## DRAMATISTS AND PLAYWRIGHTS

(see also Actors and Actresses
and Music Hall Artistes and
Comedians)
Gilbert
Phelps
Pinero
Rattigan
Sheridan

## EDUCATIONALISTS

Davies, E.
Hogg
McMillan
Mansbridge
Mayer

## ENGINEERS

Barlow
Bazalgette
Brunel
Gresley
Manby
Ricardo
Smith, F. P.
Stephenson

## EXPLORERS AND TRAVELLERS

Beaufort
Bligh
Borough, S.
Borough, W.

Chichester
Cook
Flinders
Frobisher
Kingsley, M.
Oates
Ross
Scott, R.F.
Shackleton
Stanley, H.M.
Stuart
Willoughby
Wilson

## GARDENERS AND BOTANISTS

Banks
Bridgeman
Brown, R.
Curtis
Don
Fortune
Innes
Lindley
Loudon
Nevill
Sackville-West

## HISTORIANS

Besant, W.
Carlyle
Froude
Gibbon
Gomme
Green
Grote
Hallam
Hammond
Lecky
Macaulay, T.
Petrie
Pitt-Rivers
Strype
Tawney

## HISTORIC BUILDINGS AND SITES

Adelphi Terrace
Alexandra Palace
Aubrey House
Bow Street

Cato Street
Chelsea China
Congregational Memorial Hall
(Labour Party)
County Hall
Essex Street
Fabian Society
Flying Bomb
Horniman Museum
Innner London Educational
Authority
Mayfair's oldest house
Millbank Prison
Portuguese Embassy
Priory of St. John the Baptist
Red House
Savoy Theatre
Scotland Yard
Silver Studio
Strype Street
Tyburn
United States Embassy

## INVENTORS AND INDUSTRIALISTS

Arkwright
Baird
Blumlein
Caslon
Creed
Earnshaw
Hansom
Harrison
Hughes, D.
Johnson, D.
Knight, J.
Marconi
Maxim
Morgan, J.
Morse
Muirhead
Selfridge
Stanhope
Turing
Wheatstone
Willis

## JOURNALISTS AND PUBLISHERS

Arnold, E.
Edwards, J.P.

Harmsworth
Huxley, L.
Mayhew
Mee
Murrow
Smiles
Stead
Stephen, L.
Tallis
Unwin
Walter
Whitaker

## LAWYERS

Bridgeman, O.
Eldon
Fielding, J.
Haldane
Isaacs
Romilly

## MUSIC HALL ARTISTES
## AND COMEDIANS
(see also Actors and Actresses
and Dramatists and Playwrights)

Chevalier
Collins Music Hall
Elen
Flanagan
Grimaldi
Handley
Lauder
Leno
Leybourne
Lloyd
Lucan
Relph
Tate

## NOVELISTS

Allingham
Austen
Bagnold
Ballantyne
Bennett
Benson
Blyton
Burnett
Burney
Chesterton
Collins, W.

Compton-Burnett
Conan Doyle
Conrad
Defoe
Dickens
Eliot, G.
Fielding
Fleming, I.
Ford
Forester
Forster
Galsworthy
Gaskell
Gissing
Grahame
Haggard
Hall, R.
Hardy
Harte
Hawkins
Hawthorne
Henty
Hilton
Holtby
Hope
Huxley, A.
James
Jerome
Joyce
Kingsley, C.
Kipling
Lawrence, D.H.
Macaulay, R.
Marryat
Maugham
Melville
Meredith
Milne
Mitford
Moore, G.
Morgan
Orwell
'Ouida'
Priestley, J.B.
Rohmer
Schreiner
Shelley, M.
Smollett
Stoker
Thackeray
Trollope
Twain

Wallace, E.
Waugh, E.
Wells
White
Wodehouse
Woolf, V.
Zangwill
Zola

## OVERSEAS VISITORS

Adams
Bello
Benes
Ben-Gurion
Berlioz
Canaletto
Cetshwayo
Chopin
Clementi
De Gaulle
Engels
Foscolo
Franklin, B
Gandhi
Gounod
Haakon VII
Hawthorne
Heine
Herzen
Irving, W.
Jinnah
Kalvos
Khan
Kossuth
Kropotkin
Mahomed
Mallarmè
Marx
Mazzini
Metternich
Mondrian
Mozart
Napoleon III
Nehru
Nkrumah
O'Higgins
Patel
Plaatje
Pombal
Reschid
Rizal

Roy, R.M.
San Martin
Savarkar
Seacole
Singh
Tagore
Talleyrand
Tilak
Twain
Van Buren
Van Gogh
Voltaire
Weizmann
Winant
Zola
Zygielbojm

## PHILANTHROPISTS AND REFORMERS

Barnardo
Barnett
Besant, A.
Bonn
Booth
Bradlaugh
Buxton
Chadwick
Chisholm
Clayton, E.
Cons
Coward
Edwards, E.
Ewart
Fawcett
Fry
Gresham
Groom
Hill, O.
Hill, R.
Howard, J.
Hughes, M.
Knee
Macaulay, Z.
Macmillan, D.
Mallon
Mayer
Montefiore
Noel-Baker
Peabody
Place
Rathbone

Rogers
Smith, W.
Stanley, W.
Toynbee, A.
Waugh, B.
Webb, S. and B.
Wellcome
Wilberforce

## PHILOSOPHERS AND POLITICAL THEORISTS

Ayer
Bagehot
Burke
Engels
Haldane
Keynes
Kropotkin
Laski
Marx, E.
Marx, K.
Mill
Popper
Tawney
Vivekananda
Voltaire
Webb, S. and B.

## PHOTOGRAPHERS

Fenton
Heartfield
Jennings
Ray-Jones

## POETS

Arnold, M.
Baillie
Betjeman
Blake
Bloomfield
Browning, Elizabeth Barrett
Browning, R.
Chatterton
Coleridge
Day-Lewis
De La Mare
Dobson
Dryden
Eliot, T.S.
Flecker
Graves

Heine
Hood
Hopkins
Housman
Hunt
Keats
Kipling
Macneice
Mallarme
Meynell
Moore, T.
Newbolt
Patmore
Pope
Pound
Rosenberg
Rossetti, C.G.
Rossetti, D.G.
Sassoon
Shelley
Sitwell
Smith, S.
Swinburne
Tennyson
Thomas, D.
Thomas, E.
Thomson
Yeats

## POLITICIANS AND ADMINISTRATORS

Ashfield
Astor
Avebury
Baring
Bonham-Carter
Brailsford
Brooke
Burns
Castlereagh
Cecil
Chamberlain, J.
Churchill, R.
Cobden
Cole
Cripps
Curzon
Dilke
Eldon
Fox
Gaitskell

Garvey

Godley

Grey

Haldane

Halifax

Henderson

Hill

Hore-Belisha

Huskisson

Hyndman

Kenyatta

Knee

Lawrence, S.

Lugard

Milner

Morrison

Onslow

Pankhurst, E. and C.

Pankhurst, S.

Place

Pick

Raczynski

Rathbone

Reith

Ripon

Shaw, E. M.

Smith, F.E.

Smith, W.H.

Thorne

Vane

Williams, H. S.

## PRIME MINISTERS

Asquith

Attlee

Baldwin

Bonar Law

Campbell-Bannerman

Canning

Chamberlain, N.

Churchill, W.

Derby

Disraeli

Gladstone

Lloyd George

MacDonald

Palmerston

Peel

Pelham

Perceval

Petty

Pitt the Elder

Pitt the Younger

Rosebery

Russell

Salisbury

Walpole

## RELIGIOUS FIGURES

Annesley

Aurobindo

Becket

Barnett

Carlile

Groser

Herford

Hertz

Hughes, H.

Irving, E.

Manning

Maurice

Newman

Priestley, J.

Spurgeon

Tyburn Martyrs

Underhill

Von Hu[um]gel

Wainwright

Waugh, B.

Wesley, C.

Wesley, J.

## SCIENTISTS AND MATHEMATICIANS

Ayrton

Babbage

Banks

Beaufort

Cavendish

Cayley

Chain

Crookes

Darwin

Dyson

Eddington

Faraday

Fitzroy

Fleming

Franklin

Freud

Gabor

Galton

Glaisher

Gosse, P.

Hofmann

Huxley, J.

Huxley, T.

Jones, E.

Kelvin

Lovelace

Maxwell

Newton

Pearson, K.

Smithson

Turing

Wallace, A.R.

Young

Lyell

## SCULPTORS

Adams-Acton

Bayes

Dobson, F.

Flaxman

Fleischmann

Frampton

Gaudier-Brzeska

Moore

Nollekens

Rossi

Stevens, A.

Thornycroft

Tweed

Westmacott

## SOLDIERS AND SAILORS

Allenby

Baden-Powell

Beatty

Bligh

Burgoyne

Chichester

Clive

Cochrane

De Gaulle

Fisher

Fitzroy

Gage

Gort

Hitch

Jellicoe

Kitchener

Lawrence, T.E.

Miranda

Montgomery
Nelson
Raglan
Roberts
Roy, W.
Szabo
Wolfe
Wolseley

SPORTSMEN AND
SPORTSWOMEN

Abrahams
Beresford
Chambers
Chapman
Cribb
Fry
Godfree
Grace
Haygarth
Hill
Hobbs
Lewis, T.
Wingfield

WRITERS (see also
Novelists and Poets)

Beerbohm
Barrie
Belloc
Borrow

Boswell
Brittain
Burney
Carlyle
Chesterfield
Chesterton
De Quincey
Dickinson
Dobson, A.
Douglas
Ellis
Fontane
Gosse
Grossmith
Harte
Hazlitt
Herbert
Herzen
Hudson
Irving, W.
Jacobs
James
Jefferies
Jerome
Johnson, S.
Lamb
Lang
Lewis
Lilly
MacDonald, G.
Malone

Mansfield
Mayhew
Mee
Meynell
Milne
Morrell
Murry
Nevill
Nicolson
O'Casey
Palgrave
Pater
Peake
Pepys
Plaatje
Polidori
Ruskin
Scawen-Blunt
Schreiner
Shaw, G.B.
She
Smiles
Smith, S.
Stephen, L.
Voltaire
Waley
Watts-Dunton
Wilde
Zangwill

# LIST OF NAMES BY POSTAL CODE

**E1**

Annesley
Barnardo
Borough, S.
Borough, W.
Bradlaugh
Buxton
Cavell
Cook
Flanagan
Frobisher
Garthwaite
Gertler
Green
Mallon
Rosenberg
Strype
Wainwright
Willoughby

**E2**

Hughes, M.
Zangwill

**E3**

Barnardo
Flying Bomb
Gandhi

**E5**

Howard, John
Priestley

**E8**

Fry, E.
Lloyd

**E9**

Priestley, J.

**E10**

Plaatje

**E13**

Thorne

**E14**

Great Eastern
Groser

**E17**

Roe

**EC1**

Betjeman
Caslon
Chatterton
Cruikshank
Grimaldi
Groom
Marconi
Maxim
Mazzini
Wesley, C.
Wesley, J.

**EC2**

Becket
Bloomfield
Disraeli
Fry
Gresham
Hood
Howard, E.
Keats
Newman
Priory Of St John
   The Baptist

**EC3**

Clayton
Curtis
De Rokesley
Edwards, E.
Pepys
Pope

**EC4**

Cleary
Congregational
   Memorial Hall
Hazlitt

Johnson, S.
Lamb
Linacre
Pepys
Tompion
Wallace, E.
Whittington

**EN4**

Popper

**KT5**

Bestall

**N1**

Britten
Chisholm
Collins Music Hall
Gosse
Greenaway
Gresley
Irving, E.
Lamb
Lear
Leybourne
Macneice
Orwell
Phelps
Shepherd
Sickert

**N5**

Chamberlain, J.
Sickert

**N6**

Betjeman
Coleridge
Dickens
Housman
Kingsley, M.
Priestley, J.B.
Savarkar
Waley

**N8**

Matcham

**N9**

Coward

**N13**

Smith, S.

**N16**

Defoe

**N21**

Hood

**N22**

Television

**NW1**

Beatty
Cochrane
Cockerell
Cruikshank
Dickens
Engels
Fabian Society
Fenton
Fontane
Gomme
Grossmith Senior
Haydon
Jacobs
Jennings
Jones
Lambert
Macdonald, G.
Maurice
Mayhew
Mazzini
Palgrave
Rizal
Roberts
Rossi
Salvin
Shepard
Sickert
Thomas, D.
Vaughan Williams
Wellcome

Wells
Willis
Wyndham
Yeats

## NW2

Bomberg
Fry
Hall
Johnson, A.

## NW3

Asquith
Baillie
Barnett
Besant, W.
Bliss
Brailsford
Brain
Butt
Cole
Constable
Dale
De Gaulle
Delius
Du Maurier, George
Du Maurier, Gerald
Edwards, J.P.
Ferrier
Freud
Gaitskell
Galsworthy
Gertler
Gillies
Greenaway
Hammond
Heartfield
Hill, R.
Hopkins
Huxley, A.
Huxley, J.
Huxley, L.
Hyndman
Karsavina
Keats
Lawrence, D.H.
Linnell
Macdonald
Mansfield
Marx
Matthay
Mccormack

Mondrian
Moore
Murry
Orwell
Pearson, K.
Petrie
Pevsner
Pitt The Elder
Rackham
Romney
Salisbury
Scott, George G.
Sharp
Sim
Sitwell, E.
Stevens
Tagore
Tree
Vane
Ventris
Von Hu[Um]Gel
Webb, S.
Wood

## NW4

Chapman
Relph

## NW5

Brown, Ford Madox
Nkrumah
Orwell

## NW6

Bayes
Boult
Elgar
Harmsworth

## NW7

Hill, G.

## NW8

Adams-Acton
Alma-Tadema
Bazalgette
Beecham
Britten
Davies
Fleischmann
Frampton
Frith
Gibson

Hertz
Hood
Huxley, T.H.
Klein
Knight, L. And H.
Kokoschka
San Martin
Santley
Spilsbury
Strang
Voysey

## NW11

Abrahams
Donat
Hess
Pick
Tait
Waugh, E.

## SE1

Bligh
County Hall
Greet
Hill, O.
Hill, R.
Ilea
Shaw
Shelley

## SE3

Dyson
Eddington
Gounod
Hawthorne
Mcgill
Ross, J.

## SE4

Wallace, E.

## SE5

Chamberlain, J.

## SE7

Barlow

## SE8

Mcmillan

## SE9

Grace

Morrison

## SE10

Chesterfield
Day-Lewis
Glaisher
Waugh, B.
Wolfe
Wolseley

## SE11

Montgomery

## SE12

Unwin

## SE13

Flecker
Smiles

## SE14

Tallis

## SE15

Cobham
Moody

## SE17

Babbage
Drysdale
Palmer

## SE19

Aldridge
Besant, A.
Zola

## SE22

Blyton
Forester
Karloff
Oliver

## SE23

Gounod
Horniman

## SE24

James, C.L.R.
Rohmer
Ruskin

**SE25**

Coleridge-Taylor
Conan Doyle
Stanley, W.

**SE26**

Baird
Grace
Jefferies
Marx, E.
Shackleton
Smith, Sir F.P.

**SE29**

Jefferies

**SW1**

Alexander
Arnold, M.
Ashley
Astor
Austen
Avebury
Bagehot
Balcon
Baldwin
Beardsley
Bennett
Bentham
Campbell-
    Bannerman
Cecil
Chamberlain, N.
Chichester
Chopin
Churchill, W.S.
Cobden
Conrad
Costa
Cribb
Cubitt
Curzon
Dadd
De Gaulle
Dilke
Evans
Ewart
Fisher
Fleming, I.
Gainsborough
Gladstone
Gort
Gray

Grey
Haldane
Halifax
Haygarth
Hore-Belisha
Huskisson
Jerome
Jordan
Kelvin
Kenyatta
Kitchener
Knight, J.
Langtry
Lawrence, T.E.
Leigh
Lovelace
Macmillan
Macmillan, D.
Manning
Metternich
Millbank Prison
Moore, G.
Morgan
Mozart
Napoleon Iii
Newton
Nicolson
Palmerston
Peabody
Pelham
Pitt The Elder
Pitt-Rivers
Raczyński
Rathbone
Reith
Russell
Sackville-West
Scawen-Blunt
Scotland Yard
Shelley
Smith, F.E.
Smith, W.
Stanley, H.M.
Tennyson
Townley
Tree
Vivekananda
Walpole
Wilberforce
Wilde
Wingfield

**SW2**

Mee

**SW3**

Astafieva
Benson
Chelsea China
De Morgan
Eliot, G.
Fleming
Godwin
Granger
Hunt
Jellicoe
John
Kingsley, C.
Mallarmè
Milne
Place
Ripon
Rossetti, D.G.
Sartorius
Sloane
Scott, R.F.
Smollett
Stoker
Swinburne
Terry
Thackeray
Thorndike
Turner
Twain
Warlock
Wilde

**SW4**

Barry
Bentley
Burns
Grieg
Henderson
Macaulay, Z.
Macaulay, T.
Walter
Wilberforce

**SW5**

Allenby
Arnold, E.
Carter
Orpen
Terry

**SW7**

Baden-Powell
Bagnold

Bairnsfather
Bartûk
Blackie
Bonar Law
Booth, C.
Borrow
Churchill, W.S.
Cole
Compton-Burnett
Fitzroy
Freake
Froude
Gabor
Galton
Gilbert
Hansom
Lavery
Lecky
Lind
Lugard
Playfair
Rattigan
Sargent
Stephen, L.
Thackeray
Tree

**SW9**

Baylis
Cox
Ellis
Leno
Szabo
Van Gogh

**SW10**

Belloc
Brunel
Copeman
Cripps
Dobson, A.
Dobson, F.
Fortune
Franklin, R.
Gaskell
Greaves
Grenfell
Ireland
Meredith
Pankhurst
Peake
Steer
Tweed
Whistler

**SW11**

Douglas
Henty
Knee
O'casey
Thomas, E.
Wilberforce
Wilson

**SW12**

Bateman
Elen
Hobbs
Lewis, T.
Spurgeon

**SW13**

De Valois
Fielding
Schwitters

**SW14**

Godfree

**SW15**

Benes
Hopkins
Swinburne
Watts-Dunton

**SW16**

Bax

**SW17**

Hardy
Lauder
Tate

**SW18**

Eliot, G.
Lloyd George

**SW19**

Chain
Graves
Saunders
Schopenhauer
Toynbee

**SW20**

Innes

**TW10**

Johnson, C.

**W1**

Ambrose
Ashfield
Asquith
Ayer
Babbage
Baird
Balfe
Banks
Baring
Basevi
Beaufort
Bello
Benedict
Berlioz
Bodley
Bonn
Boswell
Bridgeman
Bright
Browning, E.B.
Brummell
Burgoyne
Burke
Burnett
Burney
Campbell
Canaletto
Canning
Cato Street Conspiracy
Cayley
Clarkson
Clive
Clover
Collins
Conan Doyle
Cons
Dick-Read
Disraeli
Dryden
Duke-Elder
Eastlake
Faraday
Flaxman
Flinders
Fox
Fuseli
Gage
Garrett Anderson
Gibbon

Gladstone
Godley
Green
Grossmith Junior
Grote
Hall, K.C.
Hallam
Handel
Hartnell
Hazlitt
Hendrix
Hill, O.
Hofmann
Hogg
Hughes, D.
Hunter, J.
Hunter, W.
Hutchinson
Irving, H.
Irving, W.
Isaacs
Jackson
Johnson, S.
Kelly
Kempe
Lamerie
Laughton
Lear
Lister
Lutyens
Lyell
Macaulay, R.
Mackenzie
Malone
Manson
Marryat
Marx
Matthews
Maugham
Mayer
Mayfair's Oldest House
Milner
Miranda
Mitford
Montefiore
Moore, T.
Morse
Murrow
Neagle
Nelson
Nevill
Nicolson
Nightingale
Nollekens

Oldfield
Onslow
Palmerston
Patmore
Pearson, J.L.
Peel
Pinero
Pitt The Younger
Polidori
Portuguese Embassy
Purdey
Raglan
Ray-Jones
Rees
Reschid
Reynolds
Richmond
Roberts
Rogers
Rosebery
Ross, Ronald
Rossetti, D.G.
Roy, W.
Salisbury
Seacole
Selfridge
Shaw, G.B.
Shelley
Sheraton
Sheridan
Smirke
Smithson
Sopwith
Stanhope
Still
Stothard
Street
Talleyrand
Tempest
Tosti
Trollope
Turk's Head
Turner
Us Embassy
Van Buren
Waterhouse
Veisz
Wesley, C. And S.
Westmacott
Wheatstone
Winant
Wodehouse
Woolf
Wyatt

Wyatville
Yearsley
Young

W2

Ayrton
Barrie
Bennett
Bonham-Carter
Brooke
Browning, R.
Churchill, R.
Churchill, W.S.
Dickens
Handley
Hardy
Harte
Herzen
Hill, R.
Lawrence, S.
Loudon
Manby
Marconi
Meynell
Rie
Schreiner
Scott, Giles G.
Smith, W.H.
Stephenson
Taglioni
Tauber
Thackeray
Tilak
Tyburn
Zygielbojm

W4

Beresford
Forster
Gandy
Hitch
Lindley
Pope
Zoffany

W5

Balcon
Blumlein
Chambers

W6

Brangwyn
Cobden-Sanderson

Devine
Herbert
Hunt
Johnston
Pissarro
Ravilious
Short
Silver Studio
Walker
Whall

W8

Aubrey House
Beerbohm
Bridge
Burne-Jones
Carlile
Chesterton
Clementi
Crane
Daniell
Dickinson
Eliot, T.S.
Ford
Foscolo
Grahame
King Haakon Vii
Hall, Radclyffe
Holst
James
Joyce
Lang
Lewis
Low
Macaulay, T.
Maxwell
Mill
Millais
Morgan
Newbolt
Palmer
Parry
Pater
Petty
Pound
Rambert
Sassoon
Sibelius
Simon
Stanford
Stuart
Thackeray
Turner, J.M.W.
Underhill

W9

Ardizzone
Ben-Gurion
Brittain
Fleming, A.
Friese-Greene
Hall, H.
Kalvos
Turing

W11

Chevalier
Crookes
Forbes Hudson
Kossuth
Nehru
'Ouida'
Pankhurst, E. And C.
Patel
Pryde
Rickets
Shannon
She
Singh

W12

Aurobindo

W14

Burne-Jones
Cetshwayo
Chesterton
Coleridge
Elgar
Fildes
Gandhi
Garvey
Goossens
Haggard
Holman Hunt
Jinnah
Laski
Leighton
May
Stone
Thornycroft
Weizmann

WC1

Brittain
Burne-Jones
Butterfield
Carlyle

Cavendish
Chesterfield
Dance
Darwin
Dickens
Disraeli
Du Maurier, George
Earnshaw
Eldon
Eliot, T.S.
Fawcett
Harrison
Hawkins
Herford
Hodgkin
Howard, J.
Hughes, H.
Keynes
Khan
Lethaby
Morrell
Nash
Newman
Novello
Perceval
Pre-Raphaelite
  Brotherhood
Ricardo
Robinson
Romilly
Rossetti, C.G.
Rossetti, D.G.
Roy, R.M.
Sloane
Smith, S.
Strachey
Tawney
Wakley
Willan
Woolf
Wyatt
Yeats

WC2

Adam
Adelphi Terrace
Arkwright
Arne
Austen
Baird
Boswell
Bow Street
Caldecott
Chippendale

Colyer
De Quincey
Dickens
Essex Street
Etty
Franklin, B.
Garrick
Heine
Johnson, D.
Johnson, S.
Kipling
Marsden
Melville
Novello
Pepys
Perceval
Reynolds
Rowlandson
Savvoy Theatre
Stanfield
Terriss
Turner, J.M.W.
Voltaire
Webb, S. And B.
Wheeler

## BECKENHAM

De La Mare

## BEXLEYHEATH

Red House

## BROMLEY

Blyton
Kropotkin
Wells

## CARSHALTON

White

## CROYDON

Creed
Horniman
Wallace, Alfred R.

## EDMONTON

Keats
Lamb

## ENFIELD

Lamb
Whitaker

## HAM

Newman

## HAMPTON

Beard
Ewart
Garrick
Wren

## HARROW

Ballantyne
Gilbert
Goodall

## ILFORD

Mansbridge

## NORTH CRAY

Castlereagh

## PINNER

Heath Robinson

## RICHMOND

Chadwick
Hughes,
    Arthur
O'higgins
Thomson
Woolf, V.
    And L.

## SHORTLANDS

Muirhead

## TEDDINGTON

Coward

## TWICKENHAM

De La Mare
Tennyson
Turner,
    J.M.W.
Van Gogh

## WEMBLEY

Lucan

## WESTMINSTER

Allingham
Dannreuther
Lewis, R.
Lilly
Mahomed
Headquarters Of
    The Norwegian
    Government In
    Exile
Small Faces
Stead
Williams, H.S.

## WOODFORD

Attlee
Hilton
Minibh ex elenim
dolessecte core core
dunt pratueros